Infancy and Early Childhood

Edited by

YVONNE BRACKBILL

INFANCY

AND

EARLY

CHILDHOOD

A Handbook and Guide to Human Development

THE FREE PRESS, *New York*

COLLIER-MACMILLAN LIMITED, *London*

First Printing

Introduction

M any people think that the scientific study of infant behavior originated quite recently. In fact, the average American psychologist would probably cite the last ten years as an era of unprecedented interest in studies of early childhood development. Actually, however, research in infancy and early childhood has an impressively long history. Figure A shows, for five-year intervals since 1890, the average number of research publications in the area of infant behavior issuing from the four countries that have produced the most such research.

The most salient aspect of Figure A is the discrepancy between the amount of infant research done in the United States and the amount done in other countries—five-and-one-half times as much, in fact, as the research output of Germany, Britain, and the USSR combined. (Notice that the apparent size of the discrepancy is reduced since Figure A is drawn to a logarithmic scale.) Several points deserve consideration in such a comparison. First, foreign studies are underrepresented to an unknown extent in relation to American studies simply because it is more difficult to locate foreign language articles than English language articles in United States libraries.

A second point to remember in evaluating the relative volume of infant research in various countries is that the United States has—and has had for some time—a much larger number of people whose training makes it possible for them to carry out behavioral research. At present there are over 22,000 members of the American Psychological Association. Membership in all European psychological associations combined is but a fraction of APA membership. The number of Soviet behavioral scientists currently investigating infancy and early childhood is difficult to estimate; only since 1960 have Soviet psychologists been allowed to use infants and young children as subjects of investigation. (This was previously the exclusive domain of physicians and physiologists.)

A third consideration in assessing national contributions to infant research is the emigration of European scientists to Britain and the United States during the 1930s. Again, no one can estimate accurately the extent to which the westward movement of displaced scientific persons has influenced the volume of infant research, chiefly because the indirect effects of this emigration have been more telling than the direct effects. For example, Kurt Lewin was but one *émigré*, yet his forceful personality attracted many students who, prior to meeting him, had been headed in other professional directions than developmental psychology.

Another salient aspect of Figure A is the extravagant increase in the amount of infant research during the late 1920s that was reflected in the publication rate shortly thereafter. This increase, subsequently stopped short by the depression and the Second World War, can be attributed to the sudden availability of financial support for infant research from private philanthropic sources, principally the Laura Spelman Rockefeller Foundation. Because of these funds and because of the enthusiasm for longitudinal research of Dr. Lawrence K. Frank,

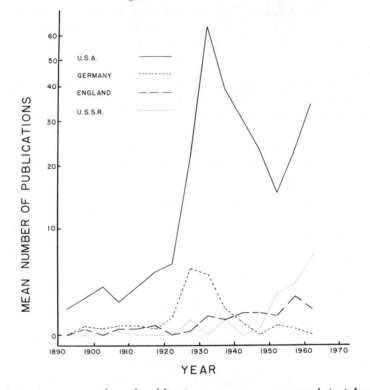

YEAR

Figure A. *Average number of publications per year on research in infant behavior for the four most research productive countries during the last 73 years.*

(The last entry is based on a 3-year interval, 1960–1962.) The entries on which this figure is based come from data, part of which is published in Y. Brackbill (Ed.), *Research in infancy and early childhood: A cross-indexed bibliography.* Baltimore: Williams & Wilkins, 1964.

then Director of the Laura Spelman Rockefeller Foundation, an impressive amount of programmatic research took root and blossomed between 1925 and 1930. This research included longitudinal programs at the University of Minnesota, the University of California at Berkeley, the Child Research Council of Denver, the Harvard School of Public Health, Yale University, the Merrill-Palmer Institute in Detroit, and the Fels Institute in Yellow Springs, Ohio. (The University of Iowa, whose infant research publication output was unparalleled during the same era, was best known then, as now, for its short-term, cross-sectional studies.)

One thing that Figure A does not reveal is the changing content of infant research from 1890 to the present day. In 1890 the emphasis was on global reports of infant development, to a large degree "baby biographies"—diary-like accounts of the general development of a single child. At the present time, the typical investigation focuses on the development of a particular process in children as a whole, e.g., on sensory function and its development, on the attainment of concepts, on language acquisition. This more contemporary view of infancy and early childhood is represented in this book as a review of growth and development in all its aspects during the first three years of life. (The chapter on language development also covers the fourth year of life.)

This book is dedicated to the understanding of infancy and early childhood and to its corollary, the prediction and understanding of human development and adult behavior. It is meant to combine the comprehensiveness of a handbook with the comparative brevity of a textbook, to be understandable to undergraduate students, yet full enough in text and bibliographic content to be useful to advanced students and research workers.

The preparation of this volume was supported in part by USPHS grant 1-K3-MH-5925 and by grant GB 4784 from the National Science Foundation. The book's preparation also owes a great deal to the competence, perseverance, and sheer courage of Mrs. Gail Adams and Mrs. Dale Weese.

Contributors

ALFRED STEINSCHNEIDER
University of New York, Upstate Medical Center

WILLIAM C. SPEARS
Skidmore College

RAYMOND H. HOHLE
University of Iowa

DAVID H. CROWELL
University of Hawaii

YVONNE BRACKBILL
University of Denver

M. M. KOLTSOVA
Pavlov Institute of Physiology, Leningrad

FREDA REBELSKY
Boston University

RAYMOND H. STARR, JR.
University of Cincinnati

ZELLA LURIA
Tufts University

DAVID ELKIND
University of Rochester

DARRELL K. ADAMS
University of Denver

CHARLOTTE B. LORING
University of Denver

DANIEL G. FREEDMAN
University of Chicago

ROBERT M. MARTIN
University of Colorado Medical Center

Contents

Infancy and Early Childhood

Chapter 1

Developmental

Psychophysiology

ALFRED STEINSCHNEIDER

This work was supported in part by a grant from the National Institutes of Health, MH-04605. The author wishes to express his gratitude to Dr. J. B. Richmond and Dr. S. D. Garrard for their extremely helpful comments and constructive criticisms of the manuscript; to Dr. P. Boschan, Dr. L. Eckhardt, and Mrs. J. Steivang, R.N., for their assistance in obtaining bibliographic material; and to Mrs. J. Ciabotti, Mrs. B. Bart, and Miss S. L. Swann for the preparation and proofreading of the manuscript.

$\mathbb{I}$t is extremely relevant in a book dealing with infancy that recognition be given to the importance of psychophysiologic activity. The interactional process between the infant and his environment, and more specifically, infant and parent is limited by virtue of the infant's inability to communicate verbally. Consequently, this interaction can probably best be conceptualized at a physiologic or biochemical level. As suggested by Richmond and Lipton (1959), "The communication to the infant, in terms of how he is fed, clothed, fondled, and diapered, is physiologic" (p. 79). One can add to this that the communication *by* the infant is also physiologic. Furthermore, it is on this physiologic base that one sees the subsequent development of more complex cognitive and social processes.

Anticipating the discussions to follow, it is reasonable to assume that each neonate brings to the interactional scene his own unique pattern of physiological reactions and, as a result, is not a passive recipient of environmental influences. Discussing the potential significance of the observation that some neonates are hypersecretors of gastric acid, Mirsky (1953) speculated:

> The infant with gastric hypersecretion has a stomach which is behaving constantly as that of the hungry normosecreting infant. Therefore, it is questionable whether such a hypersecreting infant can respond to feeding with the same degree of relaxation as does the normosecretor. It may be that in such instances, even the mother with an excellent integrative capacity will be only partially successful in her efforts to provide that satiation which permits the infant to pass successfully through the biological and into the psychological phases of dependency. As a result, infantile dependent needs will persist. The degree with which the infantile dependent wishes persist will depend upon the quantitative aspects of the mother's integrative capacity as well as upon the rate of gastric secretion (pp. 172–173).

The major significance of this hypothesis rests not with the question of validity but with its implications for a conceptual schema in which to consider an infant's transactions at a given moment of time and the development of such complex psychological processes as emotions, personality, and learning. In addition, the study of psychophysiology in infancy and early life should lead to a greater understanding of psycho-physiological disorders and the potential importance of organ predisposition in the development of such disorders. Lipton, Steinschneider, and Richmond (1967) have reviewed a number of psychosomatic disorders in children, including asthma, infantile eczema, anorexia nervosa, and peptic ulcers, and have discussed the value of the concept of multiple etiologies; foremost among these are psychophysiologic factors and individual differences in psychophysiologic responsivity.

It is basic in a chapter such as this that an attempt be made to deal with the problem of definition; what is meant when we speak of psychophysiology?; what particular body of knowledge, techniques, and intents does this term subsume? The resolution of this kind of a problem is by no means simple. This is so because definitions are by their very nature arbitrary and, to a certain extent, disruptive of the very unity inherent in a living organism engaging in a multiplicity of actions and interactions. Furthermore, the very same activities can be conceptualized at any one of a number of different levels; from ultra-ultra structure and function to ones dealing with the "total" organismic structure (i.e., body) and function. Definitions are, however, of extreme value when they serve the purposes of facilitating understanding and communication. This can best be done if we do not too rigidly attempt to define the limits of this term and recognize at the outset that to do so would probably lead to nonproductive polemics.

In the first issue of the journal entitled *Psychophysiology* three separate authors attempted to define the subject matter of this area. Ax (1964) suggested that "psychophysiology is best defined by its goals and methods as they are described in the reports published by its research workers" (p. 8). Such a definition is circular in that it hinges on the activities of persons considered to be psychophysiologists. Stern (1964) also takes issue with this definition recommending instead "that any research in which the dependent variable is a physiological measure and the independent variable a 'behavioral' one should be considered psycho-physiological research" (p. 90). By intent such a definition would exclude those situations in which the dependent variable is behavioral and the independent variable, physiological.

Still a third definition, and one that we prefer, was suggested by Darrow (1964a).". . . psychophysiology is the science which concerns those physiological activities which underlie or relate to psychic functions" (p. 4). Such a statement has the characteristics of being relatively straightforward and of sufficient breadth necessary in a definition of this kind.

The study of psychophysiology has concerned itself primarily with the adult organism. This can be understood, in part, by the more ready cooperation offered by adults to such investigations. Recently, there has been a surge of research efforts dealing with the neonate. Probably the one group of children studied least is between one and five years of age.

In considering this a chapter on developmental psychophysiology we are attempting to recognize that marked changes take place during the first few years of life. These changes could affect not only the magnitude of the relation between psychic and physiological events, but the direction as well. There is no implication that we are dealing solely with a maturational development as opposed to one dependent upon environmental influences. In all likelihood this represents an interactional system wherein both types of processes assume a crucial role.

This chapter will attempt to review much of the data dealing with psychophysiology in the child. Because of the author's limitations those studies concerned primarily with hormonal or biochemical changes will not be included. However, it should be recognized that many of the psychophysiologic processes to be discussed are mediated by biochemical reactions. Emphasis throughout will be on those investigations concerned with infancy and the first few years of life. In certain instances, especially when considering methodological issues, it will be necessary to refer to studies employing either older children or adults.

At the outset we will consider issues of primary methodologic significance. This is necessitated by the recognition that data can best be understood within the logic of the research design and analytic techniques employed in its collection and evaluation. This will be followed by a review of those physiological changes occurring in conjunction with various psychological processes. For the most part the different end organ responses will be discussed individually. To a large extent this does not do justice to the interaction between the various response systems. This approach, however, is selected in the interest of clarity.

Response Measures

Students of psychophysiology not only must concern themselves with the intricacies of complex instrumentation but also the means of extracting some measure or measures of the physiological response. To a large extent these latter problems stem from the fact that the physiological activity being recorded is a continuous one. In essence, we are dealing with an ongoing process and attempting to correlate a change in some physiological process with a definable change in some psychological process. This difficulty is further compounded in those situations where the psychological process in question has no clearly specifiable onset. When comparing and evaluating response measures one should keep in mind that the choice is often based on the primary intent of the specific study. Furthermore, there is no necessarily best measure for all purposes.

In the following discussion, we will consider a number of different techniques employed by a variety of authors. For the purpose of simplicity we will focus on those experimental situations in which the investigator has control over the onset of stimulation (i.e., auditory or visual stimuli). However, it should be evident from the following that even in such relatively straightforward experimental situations investigators differ widely in their choice of response measures.

CARDIAC AND RESPIRATORY RESPONSES

The normal electrocardiogram of a single cardiac cycle is a representation of a complex set of electrochemical events initiated in the sinoatrial node of the heart. Psychophysiologists, for the most part, have not been concerned with changes within a single cardiac cycle. Rather they have dealt with the changing relationship of one cardiac cycle to

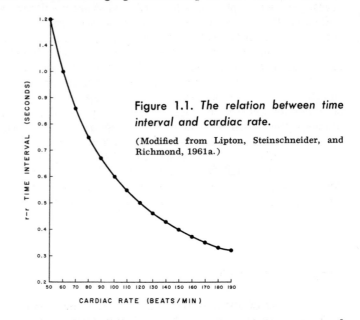

Figure 1.1. *The relation between time interval and cardiac rate.*

(Modified from Lipton, Steinschneider, and Richmond, 1961a.)

another. Thus the basic cardiac response unit has been the time interval between two clearly definable aspects of the cardiac cycle or some mathematical transformation of this time interval. The latter has taken the form of describing cardiac activity in terms of cardiac rate or the number of cardiac cycles per minute.

The conversion to rate of the time interval between the r-waves of two successive cardiac cycles is accomplished by means of the following formula:

$$\frac{60}{r\text{-}r \text{ interval (sec)}} = \text{rate (cycles/min)}$$

Unfortunately, the transformation from time interval to rate is nonlinear. Figure 1.1 demonstrates this relation between rate and time interval. It can be seen from this figure that a constant decrease in the r-r interval results in an unequal increase in cardiac rate. A decrease from an initially "long" *r-r* interval results in a smaller increase in heart rate when contrasted to an identical decrease from an initially "small" interval. Thus at the very outset the investigator is required to make certain fundamental assumptions about cardiac physiology: that is, which is more "meaningful," equality of cardiac rate or time interval? Authors have differed in their choice of the basic unit of measurement. In some instances the discrepancies noted between studies may relate to this choice.

In addition to differences in the unit of measurement, investigators vary in the way in which they analyze or determine the occurrence or properties of the response. One approach has been to obtain the average cardiac rate during the entire period of stimulation as well as for a comparable time period before and after stimulation (Bridger & Reiser, 1959). Lacey (1956) attempted to obtain a measure of "maximal sympathetic-like activity" from each stimulus trial by deriving the average of the six fastest heart rate cycles during both the stimulus and prestimulus periods. Still another technique has been to obtain the average heart rate of the five cardiac cycles preceding and following the onset of stimulation (Bartoshuk, 1962a, 1962b).

Several other approaches have been recommended, each of which attempts to take into account the observation that the cardiac response to discrete stimuli is patterned. In the neonate, shortly following the onset of stimulation, the cardiac rate progressively increases until it reaches a maximum after which it progressively decreases and levels off at near prestimulation levels. More accurately, the initial phase of the response assumes the shape of an ogive whereas the return phase resembles a backward "S" (Fig. 1.2).

Keen, Chase, and Graham (1965) used an approach which is basically an extension of the one employed by Bartoshuk (1962a, 1962b). These authors obtained an average response curve by determining the mean of successive blocks of three heart beats.

In an early report, Lipton, Steinschneider, and Richmond (1960) extracted from each stimulus-response trial the single instantaneous heart rate at each second during stimulation, the five seconds prior to stimulation, and the ten seconds following the end of stimulation. However, in a following methodologic report these same authors (Lipton, Steinschneider, & Richmond, 1961a) were critical of the use of this technique for their purposes and detailed still another approach. These authors were primarily interested in developing a procedure which would allow for the identification of individual differences in responsivity. They reasoned that subjects would probably differ not only in the magnitude and temporal aspects of the response curve but also in their variabilities. A consequence of the variability of the temporal aspects of the response would be to underestimate the average magnitude responses when employing their originally described technique. Furthermore, the greater the variability of the timing of the various phases of the response, the greater would be this understimulation. The implications of this for the purpose of defining individual differences can be understood from the following hypothetical example. Let us assume that we are interested in comparing two subjects, both of whom show the same magnitude response characteristics and prestimulation heart rates. They do, however, differ in the variability of the temporal aspects of the response curve. Let us then obtain for each subject their average response curve by determining the mean heart rate at each of several fixed time periods following the onset of stimulation. The results from such a procedure would be to conclude that these subjects differ in the heart rate change to stimulation. Furthermore, the subject with the least temporal variability would appear to demonstrate the greatest heart rate response.

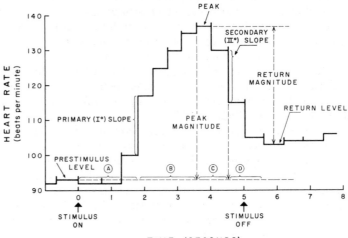

TIME (SECONDS)

Figure 1.2. *Schematic illustration of the cardiac rate response to a discrete stimulus demonstrating both the magnitude and time parameters extracted from each stimulus trial.*

The circled capital letters indicate the time segments: (A) primary slope time, (B) peak minus primary slope time, (C) secondary slope time, (D) return minus secondary slope time. (Modified from Lipton, Steinschneider, and Richmond, 1966.)

In order to avoid this difficulty Lipton, Steinschneider, and Richmond (1961a) obtain from each stimulus-response trial several response measures that, when recombined, fairly adequately describe the original response curve (see Fig. 1.2). These response measures are of two types: magnitude and time. Among the magnitude measures are heart rate at the peak and at the end of the response. In addition, they extract from each trial the largest change in cardiac rate prior to reaching the peak and a comparable value between the peak and return heart rates. The timing of these magnitude measures is also recorded. These various response measures subsequently are analyzed separately for the purpose of obtaining individual response characteristics.

Essentially the same problems (unit of measurement and response measure) have to be considered when respiratory responses are evaluated. Furthermore, the approaches employed are basically no different from those already discussed for the cardiac response. In addition, several authors have further subdivided the respiratory cycle into the inspiratory and expiratory phase and considered these from the point of view of its association with psychological events.

ELECTRODERMAL RESPONSES

A variety of techniques have been employed to measure the electrical response characteristics of the skin (Landis & Forbes, 1933; Rothman, 1954). However, two measurement procedures have been employed most commonly: the apparent resistance offered by the skin to an externally generated potential (exosomatic) and the potential difference between two skin sites (endosomatic). Even in the application of these two techniques investigators differ markedly. For example, in a recent study Tursky and O'Connell (1966) surveyed, by means of a questionnaire, two hundred thirty members of the Psychophysiological Society. Of the questionnaires mailed, forty-one replies were obtained. Only three members indicated that they employed endosomatic procedures. Following an analysis of the techniques used for exosomatic recording these authors concluded, ". . . that there is considerable variability in recording procedures even before the signal reaches the recording apparatus" (p. 239).

Generally, discrete sensory stimulation results in a uniphasic skin resistance response reflecting a decrease in the apparent skin resistance (Fig. 1.3). The data from a number of different types of investigations would suggest that the change in resistance is the resultant of at least two different electrophysiological processes (Darrow, 1964b; Edelberg & Wright, 1964; Wilcott, 1964). Darrow (1964b) hypothesized that sweat gland activity plays a dominant role when the basal level reflects low apparent resistance (high level of excitation). At low excitation levels and high apparent skin resistance, a change in skin resistance is due to modifications primarily in the relatively nonconducting layers of the skin. These mechanisms overlap when the excitation level is between the two extremes.

A number of different measurement units have been employed in evaluating the exosomatic response. The simplest and least quantitative is to determine the frequency (or percentage) of a response to a given experimental situation. More quantitative measures include the absolute change in resistance (measured in ohms), ratio of change in resistance to prestimulation resistance level, ratio of resistance change to the maximum resistance change noted for the subject, the reciprocal of resistance change (conductance), log conductance, conductance change (peak conductance minus prestimulation conductance), and the log resistance plus a constant divided by the prestimulus level (Haggard, 1945). This list is by no means a complete one. Some of these measurements were employed for theoretical reasons, others in an attempt to correct statistically for the response distribution, and still others in the hope of correcting for the observation that the magnitude of the response is related to the prestimulation level.

In view of this large list of different measurement approaches, several studies were conducted in the hope of determining the most appropriate units to employ. Hunt and Hunt (1935) intercorrelated five such measures (percentage occurrence, resistance change, ratio of resistance change to initial resistance, ratio of resistance change to maximum

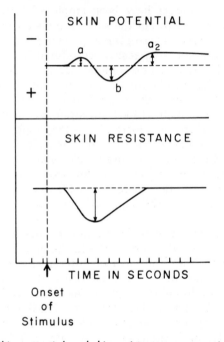

Figure 1.3. *Skin potential and skin resistance response to stimulation.*

(Modified from Burstein *et al.*, 1965.)

change, and conductance change). High rank order correlation coefficients (in normal subjects ranging from .83 to .99) were obtained for all comparisons. On the basis of these results and the desire for simplicity, Hunt and Hunt recommended the use of resistance change and percentage frequency of occurrence.

Lacey (1947) and Lacey and Siegel (1949) used a somewhat different approach in comparing measurement units. These authors evaluated each of several measures in terms of the normality of the frequency distribution and their independence from initial level. Conductance was the only measure studied that adequately fulfilled these criteria. Problems associated with the observation that the response is often related to the prestimulation level will be discussed more fully in a subsequent section.

Interested readers are referred to the recently published article by

Montagu and Coles (1966) for a comprehensive review on the measurement of skin resistance responses.

The skin potential response to stimulation differs from that obtained when recording skin resistance. Generally the potential response curve is multiphasic (see Fig. 1.3). Forbes (1936) and Forbes and Bolles (1936) have demonstrated that following stimulation there is usually a negative potential (a) followed by a positive potential (b). However, uniphasic wave forms consisting of either a pure negative or positive potential were also obtained (Wilcott, Darrow, & Siegel, 1957; Wilcott, 1958). Burstein, Fenz, Bergeron, and Epstein (1965) have recently identified a second negative (a_2) deflection (from the prestimulation base line) following the b potential.

Forbes (1936) has argued that the a and b potentials result from two different mechanisms. Support for this conclusion stems from his observation that the a potential occurs to relatively innocuous stimuli whereas the b potential usually results when stimulation is "exciting." Furthermore, the magnitude of the b and not the a potential diminishes with stimulus repetition. Forbes further hypothesized that the b wave is probably due to sympathetic stimulation (and related to sweating) and the a potential to nonsympathetic activity. Recent support for the hypothesis of a dual mechanism comes from Darrow (1964b) who notes pure monophasic negative potential changes when the subject is at a low level of excitement and there is no perspiration. However, at high excitement levels purely monophasic positive potentials were obtained. A diphasic wave form was obtained between the extreme excitement levels.

Comparisons have been made between the exosomatic and endosomatic responses by a number of authors. Jeffress (1928) determined the correlation coefficient between the deflection magnitude of the skin resistance and skin potential responses and found this value to be about .95. In a comparable study, Grings (1953) obtained an eta correlation coefficient of .47. The eta coefficient was employed because the scatterplot between these two measures was nonlinear. Wilcott (1958) subdivided his subjects into three groups on the basis of the predominant skin potential wave form type (uniphasic negative, uniphasic positive, and diphasic) and analyzed only that wave form. An examination of the response latencies revealed no difference between potential and resistance responses when considering the uniphasic negative or diphasic group. However, the latency of the uniphasic positive potential response was consistently longer than the resistance response. The average correlation coefficients for the magnitude characteristics between these two electrodermal responses were .90 for the uniphasic negative group, .88 for the uniphasic positive group, and .62 for the group having predominantly diphasic skin potential responses. The amplitude of the diphasic response was the sum of the a and b deflections. In this same study a significant positive correlation (.72–.76) was obtained between base level and skin resistance response magnitude. A comparable analysis for the skin potential responses failed to result in a significant coefficient.

Burstein *et al.* (1965) more recently intercorrelated, for each of twenty subjects, the magnitude of each of the waves comprising the endosomatic response ($a-$, $b-$, a_2 potential) and the sum of these three in addition to the maximum deflection of the exosomatic response. The most significant and highest correlations were obtained for the b potential vs. total skin potential (.74), a_2 potential vs. total skin potential (.65), b potential vs. skin resistance (.50), and total skin potential vs. skin resistance (.66). For this latter comparison all subjects yielded a positive correlation. Furthermore, fifteen of these were statistically significant.

It would seem from this review that both the endosomatic and exosomatic procedures fundamentally measure the same basic physiological processes. However, for certain purposes one technique is more appropriate than the other. Forbes (1964) has presented a discussion of some of the considerations to be made in arriving at a choice.

There has been some concern over the presence of electrodermal phenomena in infants. Jones (1930a), employing a variety of different types of stimuli, identified exosomatic responses, though of decreased magnitude, in children over three months of age. He also noted that mild electric shock was the most effective type of stimulus in producing such responses. Skin resistance changes were not found to occur in response to visual stimuli or "pleasant" stimulation. Crowell, Davis, Chun, and Spellacy (1965), studying newborns and employing a number of different stimuli, obtained resistance change 18 per cent of the time. The specific stimulus and percentage of responses are as follows: 40 and 75 watt light, 4 per cent; 50 db pure tones, 19 per cent; 80 db modulated pure tones, 26 per cent; nitrogen puff to the abdomen, 11 per cent; auditory clicks, 19 per cent; and an olfactory stimulus consisting of glacial acetic acid, 19 per cent. These results contrast with those obtained by Stechler, Bradford, and Levy (1966) who also studied newborns by means of a puff of nitrogen to the abdomen. They, however, recorded skin potential changes. An endosomatic response was obtained in 63 per cent of the stimulus trials. Of further significance, newborns showed four types of wave forms: solely negative, solely positive, and, less frequently, a biphasic response. The initial potential in the biphasic response was sometimes positive and at other times negative.

ELECTROENCEPHALOGRAM (EEG)

The EEG is characterized by an ongoing flow of wave forms differing seemingly at random from moment to moment in their shape, frequency, and amplitude. This constantly changing pattern can be modified by such factors as central nervous system maturation, motor activity, state of consciousness and pattern, as well as type of stimulation. The changes in EEG activity will also vary with lead placement.

Analysis of the EEG requires a separation of the "signal" (related to the input or psychological process being evaluated) from the "background noise" (related to preceding and ongoing processes). The procedures employed in effecting this differentiation have varied from careful and prolonged visual examination of EEG records to the use of complex computer systems.

Probably the simplest approach to an analysis of these responses is that suggested by Withrow and Goldstein (1958) in their study of audition. They compared the EEG trace during stimulation with the tracing for a comparable period prior to the onset of the stimulus and counted the number of times a change was noted. Each change was equally weighted in the final tally.

Derbyshire, Fraser, McDermott, and Bridge (1956) introduced an additional element of quantification into their scoring system. These authors, also employing auditory stimuli, were able to identify visually a number of different changes. These were classified both in relation to the timing ("on effect," "continued response," "off effect," and "delayed reaction") as well as the nature of the change. The latter consisted of a decrease or increase in wave-form voltage, the appearance of the K-complex, a gradual increase of the various waves, the formation of 12 to 13 per sec waves or high voltage 5 to 7 per sec waves. Each stimulus trial was rated on a scale from 1 to 5 depending upon the number of components present and the degree of confidence in the identification of a response. This scoring system was subsequently modified by Derbyshire and Farley (1959) into a 7 point scale based on the timing and character of the response change.

Still another class of techniques has employed the concept of superimposition (Ellingson, 1960; Goodman, Appleby, Scott, & Ireland, 1964; Barnet & Goodwin, 1965). Basically, the EEG traces resulting from a number of identical stimulus trials are superimposed photographically or electronically on one another. Essentially this technique calls for

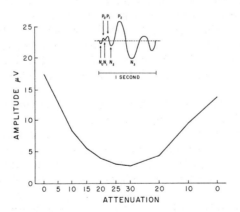

Figure 1.4. *Average amplitude of the EEG evoked response* ($P_2 - N_3$) *as a function of auditory intensity.*

A typical averaged evoked response is presented in inset. (Modified from Barnet and Goodwin, 1965.)

obtaining an average of the various stimulus trials at fixed time periods. Figure 1.4 contains the characteristic response pattern obtained by Barnet and Goodwin (1965) in their study on newborns. From these average curves, the investigator can obtain measures of amplitude and latency.

A slight departure from this approach has been suggested recently by Palmer, Derbyshire, and Lee (1966). On the basis of their experiences as well as the reports of others, they have selected a specific wave form (or template) as the most characteristic response to auditory stimuli. This template takes "the form of a damped oscillation with a negative peak at 100 msec, a positive at 300, and a second negative at 500 msec" (p. 204). The actual EEG response to a signal stimulus is multiplied by the template and the second integral of this product obtained. The result of this operation represents the degree to which the template response is present in the obtained response.

Prestimulation Level

Long-term recording of various physiological processes reveals a continuum of functioning levels. Some of these alterations have been noted to occur in conjunction with changes from sleep to wakefulness or variation in muscle tension. For example, as behavioral activity decreases (sleep) in the newborn, heart rate decreases (Bridger, Birns, & Blank, 1965), respiration becomes more regular, skin resistance increases (Wenger & Irwin, 1936), skin potential decreases (Stechler et al., 1966), systolic and diastolic blood pressure decreases (Moss, Duffie, & Emmanouilides, 1963; Gupta & Scopes, 1965), gastric secretory rate decreases (Engel, Reichsman, & Segal, 1956) and the EEG assumes a characteristic pattern (Scheibel & Scheibel, 1964). In addition, baseline (or unstimulated) activity has been observed to vary with the age of the subject (Moss & Adams, 1962; Contis & Lind, 1963; Kaye, 1964; Scheibel & Scheibel, 1964; Lipton, Steinschneider, & Richmond, 1966).

When considering psychophysiological responses it is almost impossible to avoid a discussion, both theoretical and statistical, of the significance of organ function prior to stimulation. Wilder (1957, 1958) has written on the importance of this variable as a determiner and modifier of the subsequent response for a large number of biological systems. In his considerations, Wilder was impressed with what appeared to be a generalizable relation between the prestimulus level and the response. This relation has come to be known as the "Law of Initial Value" and is formulated as follows:

> The change of any function of an organism due to a stimulus depends, to a large degree, on the prestimulus level of that function. That applies not only to the intensity (i.e., extent and duration) of

response, but also to its direction. The higher this prestimulus level (the initial value), the smaller the tendency to rise on function-raising stimuli, the greater the tendency to drop on function-inhibiting stimuli. With more extreme high or low levels, there is a progressive tendency to "no response" or to "paradoxic reactions," i.e., to a reversal of the type of response: rise instead of fall, and vice versa (Wilder, 1958, pp. 200–201).

The report by Lacey (1956) did much to alert psychophysiologists to the potential significance of the prestimulation level.

These articles were followed by a number of discussions which attempted to resolve some of the mathematical and theoretical issues inherent in the proposed relation. It was evident that failure to take into account the effect of prestimulation function (where relevant) might lead to the development of erroneous conclusions concerning an evaluation of relative responsivity. One group of subjects, when contrasted to a second group, may be "more responsive" in a given experimental situation either because of greater responsivity or solely because they were operating (for one reason or another) at a lower prestimulation level. The same can be said when comparing individuals. Thus one of the problems facing the investigator is to choose a research design which would equate the prestimulus levels in all subjects regardless of the experimental situation. One such design is to test all subjects only when at a "basal state" or at comparable behavioral states. However, all too often the very nature of the experiment precludes this approach. Consequently an alternative has been to attempt a statistical solution.

The applicability of the Law of Initial Values to a given set of experimental data has frequently been demonstrated by means of the correlation coefficient. A statistically significant negative coefficient between change score and prestimulation level supports the existence of this relationship. Block and Bridger (1962) have been critical of this measure and argue, ". . . the correlation coefficient in itself conveys no information concerning the magnitude of the functional relation between the variables concerned" (p. 1229). Instead, they suggest, as a more appropriate measure, the slope of the regression of response change on initial level. However, Steinschneider and Lipton (1965) have indicated that these two statistical measures, correlation coefficient and slope of the regression, evaluate different aspects of the same relation. Whereas the slope is a measure of the change in response per unit change in the initial level, the correlation coefficient (squared) is a measure of the increased precision in estimating the response by virtue of knowing the prestimulation level. Consequently, these latter authors have suggested that both measures be employed in evaluating the effect of initial level on the response.

The Law of Initial Values has been found to apply to group data. However, it is argued that the LIV is fundamentally an intrasubject phenomenon and the observation of a similar relation for group data stems from a failure to test all subjects at comparable prestimulation levels. In support of this hypothesis, Oken and Heath (1963) were unable to find significant correlations between response change and prestimulus level for group data when prestimulation excitation level across subjects was held constant. This was accomplished by obtaining from each neonate (tested repetitively) either the mean response (and its prestimulus level) or an estimate of maximal reactivity.

Both cardiac and respiratory rate magnitude responses in neonates and young children change in accord with the Law of Initial Values (Bridger & Reiser, 1959; Lipton, Steinschneider, Bergman, & Richmond, 1965; Lipton, Steinschneider, & Richmond, 1961a, 1961b, 1965a). In these studies the stimulus was such as to cause an increase in rate. Oken and Heath (1963) have also demonstrated that this phenomenon applies to heart rate responses when techniques of pacification are employed. Prior to "stimulation" the infants in their study were all crying. Stimulation consisted of one of three pacification techniques: feeding, offering a pacifier, and sitting the subject upright. For every infant tested, the pacification resulted in greater heart rate drops when the prestimulation heart rate was greatest.

Questions have been raised concerning the generality of the Law of Initial Values. For example, Hord, Johnson, and Lubin (1964) did not find this phenomenon applicable to skin temperature or GSR responses when measured in conductance units. Greater skin conductance changes tended to occur when the prestimulus skin conductance was high. This is the converse of the expected relation. These authors do point out the significance of the choice of response units. Were the GSR expressed in resistance units, the Law of Initial Values would have been demonstrated.

Wilder's formulation also mentions that the initial level would have an effect on the temporal aspects of the response. It is, however, difficult to know what the specific relationship should be in order for it to be consistent with this generalization. Lipton and his associates (Lipton et al., 1961a, 1965b) have examined the temporal characteristics of the cardiac and respiratory rate response to discrete stimuli in newborns and older children. Their results consistently failed to demonstrate any significance to the initial level as a predictor of the subsequent temporal responses.

It would appear from this brief review that the prestimulation function of a response system is a potential determiner of the subsequent response. This does not suggest that the initial level is a significant variable for all response measures within a given response system. Nor does it imply that all end organs will be responsive in the same direction to changes in the initial level. Rather, it does reveal that efforts should be directed toward a determination of the possible significance of this variable in influencing the results obtained from a given study.

Once having demonstrated the applicability of either the Law of Initial Values or, more generally, the significance of the prestimulation level, one is still left with the problem of incorporating this observation into a procedure for comparing individuals or groups.

Probably the simplest approach is that suggested by Block and

Bridger (1962), Lacey and Lacey (1962) and used by Bridger and Birns (1962) and Bridger *et al.* (1965). Block and Bridger state

> . . . an alternate expression of the LIV is that with optimal operation of the LIV there exists little or no relation between prestimulus and stimulus levels; that is, stimulus value is relatively constant and independent of prestimulus values. The stimulus produces a consistent stimulus level of organ activity regardless of the prestimulus level of activity. If prestimulus level is not much below stimulus level, a small change in level or organ activity occurs upon stimulation, whereas if prestimulus level is far below stimulus level, a large delta must occur for the level of organ activity to reach the stimulus level (pp. 1230–1231.)

Thus one can avoid the problem of the initial level by analyzing response level (stimulus level) rather than response change. Consistent with this approach Bridger and Birns (1962) obtained the mean cardiac rate response level without considering initial level in their newborn study of "soothing stimuli." Steinschneider and Lipton (1965) have discussed the concept of response level constancy and do not find much experimental support for it. Rather they find in their review that the response level itself can also be influenced by the prestimulus level.

The use of percentage change has been considered by Lacey (1956), Churchill (1962), and Benjamin (1963) and found to be inadequate.

Lacey (1956) proposed the response level as the basic measure to be used in conjunction with a regression model, the latter allowing for an evaluation of the Law of Initial Values. In his arguments in favor of the response level, Lacey was also critical of the change score. These criticisms have been responded to by a number of authors (Bridger & Reiser, 1959; Benjamin, 1963; Steinschneider & Lipton, 1965) who in turn have pointed out the fundamental similarity between the two response measures providing one takes into account the initial level.

Lacey has also developed a mathematical procedure for obtaining a response score free of the effect of the initial value. This is defined as:

$$\text{Autonomic Lability Score} = 50 + 10\ [y_z - x_z r_{xy}/(1 - r^2_{xy})^{1/2}]$$

where x_z is the initial level expressed in standard deviation units; y_z, the response level expressed in standard deviation; r_{xy}, the correlation between initial and response levels. By means of this technique each response is expressed as a deviation score from the response expected at a given prestimulation level. Several authors have been critical of the autonomic lability score (Bridger & Reiser, 1959; Block & Bridger, 1962; Steinschneider & Lipton, 1965).

Steinschneider and Lipton (1965) have employed a somewhat different approach and obtain several measures derived from the individual regression line (change vs. initial level). These include the slope and variability around the regression line, the discriminability ratio (slope/variability) and a score representing maximal and mean responsivity. Another comparative measure employed by Bridger and Reiser (1959) is the crossover point. This is the prestimulus level at which no response tends to occur.

In this section we have attempted to deal with a number of issues resulting from the observation that responsiveness can be influenced by the prestimulation levels. These issues as well as others not considered here (i.e., the mechanisms by which prestimulus level effects responsivity) will require many more controlled observations before they can be adequately resolved. It is, therefore, essential that particular attention be given to the experimental design and the reporting of sufficient detail to allow for effective evaluations and comparisons with other published studies.

Sensation and Perception

AUDITORY STIMULI

The studies to be considered in this section have been concerned either with determining the physiological concomitants of audition or the evaluation of hearing by employing physiological response measures. The latter stems from a need to develop objective procedures for the determination of possible hearing loss in infancy and early childhood. A number of different auditory stimuli have been employed ranging from brief and repetitive clicks to single frequencies and broad frequency spectrum sounds (white noise). Possibly because of the relative ease in generating this type of stimulus, audition has probably been explored more than any other type of sensory modality.

Butterfield (1962) studied three mentally retarded children ranging in age from seven years to fourteen years and ten months by employing a 1024 cps tone at two intensity levels; one about 40 db above threshold and the other at 5 db below threshold. No differences in the cardiac response to these two stimuli were obtained. Reporting on a single newborn subject, Beadle and Crowell (1962) were also unable to demonstrate any consistent effect of stimulus intensity on cardiac rate. Barnet and Goodwin (1965) delivered repetitive clicks at the rate of 1/sec to a group of normal newborn infants. They did not find a significant relation between change in heart rate and stimulus intensity.

These results are at variance with those obtained by Bartoshuk (1964) and Steinschneider, Lipton, and Richmond (1966). The data obtained by Bartoshuk were derived from thirty newborn subjects repetitively stimulated by a one-second duration 1000 cps tone at four different intensities. Increasing stimulus intensity was clearly associated with an increase in the magnitude of the cardiac rate response (Fig. 1.5). Furthermore, the relation between the logarithm of the heart rate response and stimulus intensity in decibels was approximately linear.

By comparing these responses to unstimulated control trials it would also appear from these data that the absolute threshold in the neonate for cardiac rate responses was between 48.5 and 58 db (the background noise level in this study was 10.5 db).

Steinschneider *et al.* (1966) also found a positive correlation between stimulus intensity and the magnitude of the cardiac rate response in their study of the neonate ($N = 9$). They, however, employed a white noise stimulus. In addition to demonstrating a magnitude effect, increasing auditory intensity resulted in a decreased latency and an increased duration of the cardiac rate response. Similar results have been obtained in a study of children ranging in age from one and one half to four years (Lipton *et al.*, 1965).

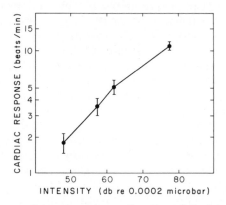

Figure 1.5. *Average cardiac response as a function of the intensity of a 1000 cps tone.*

(Modified from Bartoshuk, 1964.)

Suzuki, Kamijo, and Kiuchi (1964) studied changes in respirations to a 500 cps tone of varying intensities. A total of forty-five normal newborns took part in this investigation. Three types of respiratory changes were evaluated: (1) change in respiratory rate or depth; (2) decrease in regularity; and (3) the occurrence of a sudden deep inspiration. Only the latter was related to stimulus intensity. As the intensity increased so did the per cent occurrence of a deep inspiration. In contrast, Stubbs (1934) did find that increasing intensity resulted in an increase in the frequency of respiratory responses. This effect was most clearly demonstrable when considering those responses representing an increase in rate and a decrease in amplitude.

Electroencephalographic responses to changing auditory intensities were recorded by Derbyshire *et al.* (1956) in twenty-two patients, fifteen of whom were from a school for the deaf. These authors concluded that intensity had no apparent effect on the form of the response. However, the amplitude and the complexity of the response increased in association with increased intensity near threshold levels. Goldstein, Kendall, and Arick (1963) were unable to find any consistent relationship between EEG change and intensity in their investigation of 34 children suspected of having a hearing deficit. These authors employed the Derbyshire-Farley procedure in evaluating the EEG responses. However, Ortiz-Estrada, Deutsch, and Hernandez-Orozco (1963), studying normal children, did observe a positive relation between intensity and the frequency of EEG changes. Barnet and Goodwin (1965), studying apparently normal newborn infants, did demonstrate that the evoked EEG response was modified by change in stimulus intensity. Although the earliest components of the evoked response ($P_0 - N_1$ and $P_1 - N_2$, Fig. 1.4) were not affected by intensity, the amplitude of the largest component ($P_2 - N_3$) was positively correlated with the intensity of stimulation. In addition, for the central-temporal leads, the latency of this large component increased as the stimulus intensity was increased.

Sound stimuli consisting of single frequencies are capable of producing physiological responses (Derbyshire et al., 1956; Suzuki et al., 1964; Crowell et al., 1965). Stubbs (1934), studying newborns, obtained respiratory responses to four different sound frequencies: 128, 256, 1024, and 4096 cps. In general, a greater percentage of respiratory responses occurred to the higher frequencies. This was most evident when the baby was asleep.

A single reported study is available which demonstrates, in the newborn, that the cardiac response is influenced by the duration of stimulation (Keen et al., 1965). Increasing the duration from two to ten seconds resulted in both a prolongation and an increase in the magnitude of the initial acceleration phase. Stimulus duration was not found to affect the respiratory rate response. Stubbs (1934), in an earlier study on the neonate, did, however, find that increasing the duration of stimulation from one to fifteen seconds was associated with a progressive increase in the frequency of respiratory responses. The respiratory change noted with the greatest frequency was an increase in rate and a decrease in amplitude.

A number of authors have observed that with repetitive presentation of the same stimulus there is a decrease in physiological responsiveness. Two studies dealing with newborns have demonstrated the significance of stimulus duration on the development of this phenomenon. Bridger (1961, 1962), employing pure tones, found that increasing the duration of stimulation resulted in a decrease in the number of stimulus trials prior to the cessation of cardiac responses. Keen et al. (1965) were unable to demonstrate habituation to a two-second duration buzzer but noted an effect within a few trials to a ten-second duration stimulus. Furthermore, the habituation persisted for at least twenty-four hours. These same authors did not find habituation of the respiratory rate response.

Intertrial interval is another variable of significance in the development of habituation. Bridger (1961, 1962) noted that decreasing the interval between trials facilitated habituation for cardiac rate. Similar results were obtained by Derbyshire et al. (1956) for the EEG response. Bartoshuk (1962b) did not find a differential effect on the rate of cardiac rate habituation when the intertrial interval was varied from fifteen to sixty seconds. In another study by the same author (Bartoshuk, 1962a), a five-second intertrial interval was found to produce greater habituation when contrasted with a sixty-second interval.

Several other interesting aspects concerning habituation should be mentioned. The habituation process appears to be relatively specific to the characteristics of the stimulus employed. Habituation of a sound at a given frequency or intensity does not appreciably affect the subsequent response to a stimulus of a different frequency or intensity (Bridger, 1961, 1962; Bartoshuk, 1962a, 1962b). There is also the suggestion from the experiment by Keen *et al.* (1965) that experience with a two-second duration stimulus will influence the cardiac response, twenty-four hours later, to a ten-second stimulus.

The simultaneous occurrence of a motor response to stimulation appears to be related to certain aspects of the physiological response. The amplitude of the EEG evoked response was not correlated with behavioral activity. However, longer response latencies were associated with less behavioral responses (Barnet & Goodwin, 1965). These same authors found that the greatest changes in cardiac rate occurred in conjunction with either a startle or general body movements.

VISUAL STIMULI

Few studies have been performed on the effect of visual stimuli on autonomic nervous system response measures. One such investigation was reported by Smith (1936). Infants less than ten days of age were exposed to a five-minute duration light of three different hues: blue, green, and red. Prior to each stimulus presentation the infant was maintained in the dark for five minutes. In addition to recording the amount of bodily activity and crying, measures of respiratory rate were also obtained. The mean respiratory rate was essentially the same for each of the three hues.

Eichorn (1951) obtained respiratory responses to a flashing white light in subjects less than three months of age. These changes consisted of either prolonged inspiration or expiration and deepened respirations. However, these responses were rarely present after the first few stimulus presentations. Similar rapid adaptation of the cardiac rate response was also noted. Generally the cardiac rate response, when it occurred, consisted of an increase. Cardiac rate acceleration was also found by Lipton and Steinschneider (1964) to a blinking light.

A skin conductance change was obtained in only 4 per cent of the trials in which a three-second duration continuous white light was presented (Crowell *et al.*, 1965). Intensity of stimulation did not affect these results. In the study by Eichorn (1951), galvanic skin responses were obtained in only two out of thirty-eight infants and these only to the initial presentations of the flashing light. Thus visual stimuli have not been found effective in eliciting a change in either skin resistance or conductance.

Additional studies employing visual stimuli and autonomic response changes will be discussed in a subsequent section dealing with attention.

Electroencephalographic responses to visual stimuli have been the subject of a number of investigations. Ellingson (1958) was able to show that about 75 per cent of full term newborns have EEG responses in the occipital area to a brief light flash. Several differences were noted between the responses obtained in newborns and adults. The newborn had a more variable wave form and amplitude with greater "fatigability" and a longer latency.

Repetitive light flashes at a rate greater than two per second resulted in EEG changes occurring at the onset of stimulation (on response) and again at the end of the series of flashes (off response) (Ellingson, 1958; Engel, 1961).

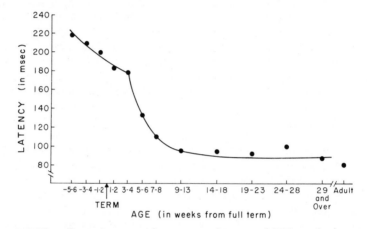

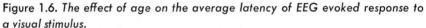

Figure 1.6. *The effect of age on the average latency of EEG evoked response to a visual stimulus.*

(From Ellingson, 1960.)

The full term, normal newborn EEG evoked response generally consists of an initial positive wave followed by a longer duration negative wave (Ellingson, 1960). Newborns varied in the nature of this response wave form. In some subjects the negative wave was followed by a second positive wave. A small percentage of full term newborns (2.3 per cent) had an initial negative wave in response to the visual stimulus. This latter type of response was more evident in premature infants.

Both the latency and the amplitude of the EEG response have been found to vary with age. Ellingson (1960) measured the time interval between the onset of a single light flash and the peak of the positive wave. Figure 1.6 contains the average response latencies at different ages. Examination of this figure reveals that the latency (a) tends to decrease with age and (b) asymptotes at two different age levels. Ellingson suggests that the first portion of the overall latency curve might be associated with scotopic vision whereas the second portion is due to the photopic system. Engel and Butler (1963) also found a decrease in response latency with age. They did not find a curve with a dual asymptote. These authors, however, used a somewhat different measure of latency, recording the time interval from the onset of stimulation to the first identifiable response.

A study of the change in EEG response amplitude as related to age was conducted by Dustman and Beck (1966). Subjects ranging in age from one month to eighty-one years were stimulated with one hundred flashes of light, each flash two to three seconds from the previous one. The average EEG response (recorded from occiput) was obtained by means of computer and plotted. The response magnitude was determined by measuring the perimeter of the curve over a fixed time period. These results revealed that the magnitude of the EEG response increased with age, reaching a peak at about five to six years of age. Subsequently, except for one age period, the magnitude progressively decreased and leveled off at about age sixteen years. There was a temporary increase in magnitude at ages thirteen to fourteen years. Unfortunately, these investigators do not report data on the newborn. Ellingson (1960), however, did find responses of greater magnitude in the newborn when compared to adults.

Repetitive visual stimulation will produce "driving" of the electrical activity recorded from the occipital cortex. That is, the rhythm of the electroencephalogram simulates that of the visual stimulus. This can take the form of an immediate appearance in the EEG of a wave frequency matched to the frequency of the visual input. Still another pattern that has been identified is at first an increase in the amplitude of the EEG wave followed by the gradual assumption of the input frequency (Mirzoyants, 1961).

Investigators agree that photic driving or following occurs in the newborn period, though they disagree on the frequency of its occurrence (Eichorn, 1951; Ellingson, 1958, 1960; Mirzoyants, 1961; Glaser & Levy, 1965). By way of example, Ellingson (1958) obtained photic driving in only two newborns out of seventy-nine studied (2.5 per cent). This contrasts with approximately 50 per cent reported by Glaser and Levy (1965).

There is the suggestion that the incidence of photic driving increases with age. Furthermore, the frequency of photic stimulation resulting in the greatest amount of "driving" corresponds to the predominant EEG frequency occurring naturally.

Electrical impulses originating from the retina can be obtained by fixing an electrode to the cornea and a reference electrode to an indifferent area such as the forehead or hand (Riggs, 1958). The result has been referred to as the electroretinogram (ERG). Stimulating a dark-adapted adult eye with a white light results in a complex wave form characterized by an initial negative wave (*a* wave) and a subsequent positive potential (*b* wave). Experimental work with excised eyes as well as theoretical considerations would suggest that the *a* wave originates from the receptor cells whereas the *b* wave is generated by the bipolar cells (Riggs, 1958).

Zetterström (1951) studied a group of children from the newborn period up to one year of age by means of single light flashes. Generally an ERG was noted during the first two to three days of life. However, when a potential was identified at this age it consisted only of a slight rise in the base line. With development, the *b* wave became apparent. Comparisons with the adult wave revealed this potential (in the neonate) to be less in magnitude and to have a longer latency and duration. By one year of age the magnitude had increased and its duration and latency had decreased to the point at which it was comparable to the adult *b* wave. Except in three out of thirteen subjects, the *a* potential was not discernible by one year of age. In a subsequent study on prematures by the same author (Zetterström, 1952) it was determined that the greater the prematurity, the longer the time interval from birth to the appearance of the ERG.

The results obtained by Horsten and Winkelman (1960) are at variance with those of Zetterström. Employing a high intensity light stimulus and adequate dark adaptation, these investigators found both *b* and *a* potentials in all of the full term and premature infants studied.

In another study on the effect of age on the ERG, Zeidler (1959) tested subjects between the ages of five and eighty years. This author attempted to relate the amplitude of the *b* potential with age and sex. In general, the *b* potential had a greater amplitude in females. Furthermore, both males and females demonstrated an increase in the magnitude of this potential between ages five to ten and eleven to twenty years. In males the average potential progressively decreased with age beyond this latter period. Females, however, do not show a decrease with age until after fifty years.

Zetterström (1955) obtained the flicker fusion frequency in three groups of infants varying in age from newborn to eight weeks as a function of intensity of stimulation. She defined the fusion frequency as the lowest flash frequency at which ERG responses failed to occur with each light flash. According to her results the flicker ERG was absent in newborns less than twenty-four hours of age even with extremely intense stimulation. However, by age two to three days a flicker response was obtained in all babies studied. With increasing age, flicker could be obtained with decreasing intensities of stimulation. In addition, the maximum fusion frequency increased. By one week of age a transition from a purely scotopic to a photopic response could be identified when employing very bright flashes. The flicker fusion response at six to eight weeks was no different from that seen in adults.

In a recent article by Barnet, Lodge, and Armington (1965), the ERG was obtained in the neonate to a number of different stimulating conditions. The ERGs to each experimental situation ($N = 250$) were analyzed by a Mnemotron computer of average transients and an average response curve obtained. To an intense flickering orange light the ERG consisted of an *a* and *b* as well as an *x* potential. The latter is a positive wave occurring between the other two potentials and apparently is a more direct result of the photopic function. Decreasing the intensity of the orange light flash resulted in a decrease in the amplitude of the *x* potential, a decrease in the amplitude of the b wave, and an increase in the latency of the b wave. The latency of the x wave was not influenced by the intensity of the orange light. As the intensity of a white light was decreased there was a loss of the a potential, an increase in the latency of the b wave, and a decrease in the amplitude of the b wave. These results are taken as support that both the scotopic and photopic systems are functional in the newborn.

TACTILE STIMULI

For the most part, studies employing tactile stimulation have been concerned primarily with evaluating autonomic responsivity. In general two methods of delivering such stimuli have been used: an air stream and digital stroking. Neither of these procedures represents pure touch stimuli. For example, the air stream not only applies a pressure change to the appropriate skin area but also is associated with a slight change in skin temperature and sound level. Stroking an area with a finger could also deliver a slight temperature stimulus in conjunction with its tactile component. Three autonomic response measures have been obtained to these stimuli: cardiac rate, respiratory rate, and skin temperature changes.

Data have been obtained by Brossman and Greenberg (1957) and Richmond and Lipton (1959) on the effect of tactile stimuli when applied to different skin sites. Richmond and Lipton (1959), studying newborns, obtained greater increases in cardiac rate when an air stream or stroking was applied for one minute to the abdomen as opposed to similar stimulation of the anus. Interestingly, stroking the anus often resulted in a slowing of cardiac rate. In another study from this same laboratory, stimulation of the mucous membranes of the lips resulted in greater cardiac responses than comparable stimulation of the abdomen (Lipton, Richmond, Weinberger, & Hersher, 1958).

Grossman and Greenberg (1957) also studied newborn infants employing similar stimuli to the cheeks, lips, abdomen, genitalia, and anus while recording cardiac rate and skin temperature from the forehead, abdomen, and toe. The greatest skin temperature changes were noted when recordings were taken from the toe and abdomen. Furthermore, the largest average toe temperature rise occurred when the genitals were stimulated whereas the abdominal temperature showed the greatest change when the stimulus was applied to the abdomen. When analyzing the cardiac data, these authors also considered the possible significance of the degree of motor response to stimulation. Keeping the degree of motor response constant, the skin area stimulated did not differentially influence the cardiac response. There was, however, a tendency for the heart rate increase to be greater following abdominal as compared to anal stimulation. This latter trend is consistent with the observations by Richmond and Lipton (1959).

The duration of tactile stimulation was investigated in a study by Steinschneider, Lipton, and Richmond (1965). An air stream, just sufficient to indent the skin, was delivered to an area just above the umbilicus and varied in duration between one and five seconds. In general, increasing the duration of stimulation resulted in an increase in the duration and magnitude of the initial phase as well as the "latency" of the return phase of the heart rate response.

The influence of degree of hunger on cardiac responsivity to tactile stimulation was explored by Lipton and colleagues (1958). These investigators found that hunger increased cardiac rate responsivity to stimulation in the neonate.

A number of investigators have noted a decreased cardiac response when the stimulus produced little or no simultaneous change in motor activity (Grossman & Greenberg, 1957; Bridger & Reiser, 1959; Richmond & Lipton, 1959). These observations would appear to be at variance with those obtained in two studies on the effect of motor restraint (Lipton et al., 1960, 1965b). In these latter studies an air stream was delivered above the umbilicus to newborns while under varying degrees of motor restraint (completely free to move, completely restrained by means of a swaddling technique, motor restraint limited to the lower extremities). Motor restraint resulted in fewer motor responses to stimulation. However, the cardiac and respiratory responses were, for the most part, not significantly modified by restraining the baby. It should, however, be emphasized that this conclusion applies to those trials in which a change in motor activity occurred. Thus, these authors concluded that ". . . the newborn infants retained the *capacity* to respond viscerally to the air stream in a remarkably similar manner when restrained" (Lipton et al., 1965b, p. 563).

In a recent report cardiac rate responses to an abdominal air stream stimulus were studied in a group of infants during the first five months of life (Lipton et al., 1966). Only those trials were analyzed in which a motor response occurred. Contrasted with the newborn period, by two and one-half months of age the cardiac rate response curve was characterized by a slight decrease in rate preceding an attenuated increase in rate and a tendency for the heart rate to return to below prestimulation levels. In addition, the response reaction time and the duration of the initial acceleration phase had decreased.

Soothing or Pacification

Emphasis throughout this discussion has thus far been on those experimental situations and processes that are "exciting." Several studies, however, have been concerned with an evaluation of procedures for reducing or decreasing the level of excitement and the effectiveness of stimulation during these latter efforts.

Brackbill, Adams, Crowell, and Gray (1966) exposed twenty-four full term neonates to four fifteen-minute, sequentially presented experimental conditions: paired heartbeats (78 bpm), metronome (72 bpm), unfamiliar lullabies, and no sound. During each of these periods behavioral measures were obtained in addition to heart rate, variability of heart rate, and respiration. Continuous sound stimulation, regardless of type, resulted in a decrease in heart rate and an increase in the regularity of both cardiac rate and respiration. These were statistically significant when compared to the "no sound" condition. It should also be pointed out that crying and general motor activity concomitantly decreased during the sound conditions.

Varying degrees of motor restraint have been studied as a means of quieting normal newborns. In their original study, Lipton *et al.* (1960) obtained cardiac and respiratory rate measures while infants were either completely swaddled or free to move. Swaddling resulted not only in more sleeping but also in a decreased cardiac and respiratory rate. Responses to an air stream stimulus when under these experimental conditions were not consistently modified across subjects. Whereas some subjects were more responsive, others were less so when swaddled. These observations were confirmed in a more extensive study in which three degrees of motor restraint were employed (Lipton *et al.*, 1965b). Thus, although motor restraint produced quieting or pacification, it did not affect the capacity to respond.

In still another study, Bridger and Birns (1962) determined the cardiac rate and behavioral response to immersing an infant's foot in ice water either while the baby was sucking on a pacifier or his head was being gently rocked. Considering only those infants on whom behavioral evidence of soothing was obtained, the average cardiac rate level reached secondary to stimulation was lower when compared to a "no soothing" condition. Neither of the two soothing techniques proved to be more effective than the other.

These last results concerning responsivity during pacification would seem to contradict those obtained by Lipton *et al.* (1960, 1965b). Whereas these latter authors found no significant effect of soothing on responsivity, Bridger and Birns obtained a decrease in responsivity. This discrepancy could relate to differences in methodology. Lipton, Steinschneider, and Richmond evaluated only those trials during which a motor response occurred to stimulation. Bridger and Birns derived their conclusions from those subjects in whom the behavioral response was indicative of effective soothing. However, when all subjects were grouped together, soothing did not significantly affect the cardiac response to stimulation.

Attention

Attention has been defined as the "selective awareness of certain sensory messages with the simultaneous suppression of others" (Hernández-Peón, Scherrer, & Jouvet, 1956, p. 331). This definition is consistent with the one suggested by Woodworth and Schlossberg (1954) and Gibson and Olum (1960). Fundamental to this conceptualization is both a selective facilitation of certain sensory inputs and an "inhibition" or diminished effectiveness of all others.

Sokolov (1963) has discussed in detail several presumably different response systems which affect sensory sensitivity and probably relate to the attention process. Of major significance for this discussion are the orientation, defense, and adaptation reflexes. Each of these refers to a complex set of unconditioned motor and autonomic reactions. The orientation reflex occurs to any change in stimulation (both onset and offset) and results in an increased sensitivity to stimulation. This pattern of responses is independent of stimulus quality although generally elicited to stimuli of low to moderate intensity. Another interesting feature of this reaction pattern is the tendency for it to diminish in intensity with repetition of stimulation. In contrast, the "effect" of the defense reflex is ". . . the breaking away from, or limitation of the activity of the stimulus" (p. 14). These, too, represent generalized reactions and are independent of the stimulus quality, although elicited primarily by intense stimulation. The adaptation reflexes are, however, responsive to the quality of stimulation and result in an increase in sensitivity to specific stimuli. Pupillary changes to light and dark are examples of adaptation reflexes. Neither the adaptation nor the defense reflexes diminish with stimulus repetition. The orientation reflex is associated with peripheral vasoconstriction and cephalic vasodilatation, whereas both cephalic and peripheral vasoconstriction are associated with the defense reflex.

Lacey (1959) and Lacey, Kagan, Lacey, and Moss (1963) have presented data as well as neurophysiological arguments to support their hypothesis that cardiac rate deceleration is associated with efforts to increase "environmental intake." This contrasts with cardiac rate acceleration which occurs with "rejection of the environment" and a decrease in sensory sensitivity. In a recent review, Graham and Clifton (1966) have attempted to reconcile this and the previously discussed approaches by suggesting that cardiac rate deceleration is a component of the orientation reflex and cardiac rate acceleration a component of the defense reflex.

In view of the original definition, it is questionable whether any of the experiments to be related and purported to investigate attention can, in fact, be said to be studying this phenomenon. None of these experiments has presented data necessary to satisfy the fundamental requirements inherent in the above definition.

In a most interesting study, Stechler et al. (1966) recorded behavioral motility and skin potential responses to an air stream stimulus in a group of fifteen infants less than one week of age. Prior to stimulation by the air stream, each infant was presented either a visual stimulus consisting of nonintersecting black lines (experimental condition) or no visual stimulus (control). The air-stream stimulus was delivered only after the infant had "fixated" the visual stimulus for at least ten seconds. Apparently the infant was attending to the visual stimulus during the experimental condition and at the moment of air-stream stimulation.

The effect of visual fixation was to decrease motor activity, although no change in skin potential level was observed. However, the skin potential response to the air stream was influenced by visual fixation. In this latter condition the latency of the skin potential response was shorter and its magnitude greater.

> It is clear that electrodermal reactivity is enhanced during the state of target fixation, which fact indicates that the relative motor quiescence during this state is not simply an indication of overall inhibition. This state corresponds perhaps best to one of vigilance in more mature individuals, when spontaneous activity by the organism is held in check while receptivity to new stimuli is enhanced (p. 1248).

A different approach to the study of attention in early life was taken by Kagan and associates. These investigations derived, to some extent, from earlier observations on adults which demonstrated that cardiac rate deceleration occurred during attention to visual or auditory stimuli (Lacey, 1959; Lacey *et al.*, 1963). A group of fifty-five first and second grade boys were presented with a battery of experimental situations, some requiring that they attend to visual or auditory stimuli and others in which they were asked to free associate or make up a story (Kagan & Rosman, 1964). During these various situations both cardiac and respiratory activity were recorded. Those tests requiring attention to external stimulation resulted in an increase in respiratory rate and a decrease in both cardiac rate and respiratory rate variability. Regular respiration has also been noted to occur when newborns either fixated or pursued a visual target (Brazelton, Scholl, & Robey, 1966).

In a later report, Kagan and Lewis (1965) reviewed their results obtained on a group of infants initially tested at six months of age and then again at thirteen months. (The data obtained during this latter age had not been fully analyzed.) At age six months, thirty-two infants (sixteen boys and sixteen girls) were each presented with three different groups of stimuli. One group consisted of pictures of faces and geometric designs (male face, female face, black-white bull's eye, black-white checkerboard, nursing bottle, panda bear) each presented for twelve seconds. A second group of stimuli represented thirty-second duration patterns of blinking lights (single blinking light, a blinking light moving horizontally, a blinking light moving in the form of a square helix). Thirty-second duration auditory stimuli were also presented (intermittent tone, modern jazz music, human voices reading an English paragraph—female, male and mother). Each stimulus was presented four to five times. Cardiac rate was recorded prior to and during each stimulus presentation. In addition, fixation time and the amount of arm movement and vocalization were measured. An assessment of cardiac deceleration was made by dividing the stimulus presentation into periods and obtaining, for each, the mean of the five lowest beats. These were subtracted from a comparable measure derived for the prestimulus period.

A number of interesting results were obtained in this study. For the visual stimuli there was a significant tendency for the amount of deceleration to decrease with repeated presentation of the same stimulus; that is, for habituation to occur. Sex was not found to be significant. The row and helix pattern of blinking lights resulted in more sustained cardiac deceleration when compared to the single blinking light.

Correlation coefficients were obtained as a means of evaluating the relation between fixation time and degree of cardiac deceleration. This was done separately for each group of visual stimuli and sex. Of the four coefficients determined, only one proved to be statistically significant (*rho* = .43; male, light matrix). Subjects were also divided into two equal groups; those with the longest total fixation times were considered a high-attention group and the remaining a low-attention group. The cardiac rate decelerations for these two groups were then compared for those stimulus trials in which fixation time was nine seconds or more. The results revealed a greater deceleration for the high-attention subjects.

The auditory stimuli failed to produce a significant habituation effect. Sex and the specific nature of the auditory stimulus did prove significant variables. Whereas females showed the greatest deceleration to the music, males tended to decelerate more to the tones.

Although we have emphasized in this review those results dealing with physiological change, Kagan and Lewis (1965) conclude after evaluating both the cardiac and behavioral data, "It does not seem imprudent to suggest that assessment of fixation time alone is not as faithful an index of the construct 'intensity of attention,' as is the combination of fixation time and cardiac change" (p. 127).

In view of the suggestion that cardiac deceleration in response to stimulation is a measure of attention, the observations made by Lipton *et al.* (1966) would seem to be relevant to this discussion. These authors have reported that, in the newborn, the initial phase of the cardiac rate response to an air stream stimulus is solely one of acceleration. However, when infants are tested at two and one-half months with the same stimulus, the immediate response is a slight deceleration followed by an attenuated acceleration phase. This deceleration is even more pronounced at five months of age. It would be interesting to speculate on the possibility that this progressively increasing deceleration is a reflection of the development of attention in infancy.

Learning

A number of studies have been conducted in infancy and early childhood which demonstrate that various physiological responses can be conditioned to either previously noneffective stimuli or stimuli whose physiological responses have been adapted (or habituated) out. Change in skin resistance has been the most common physiological response used in this regard. Jones (1928) briefly presented his observations on three infants studied over a four-month period. Changes in skin resistance were obtained to previously indifferent stimuli (cutaneous, auditory, visual) following less than fourteen trials paired with electric shock. In a subsequent, more detailed report, Jones (1930b) presented data on a single infant studied intensively during the seventh to ninth month of life. Employing an electrotactual stimulus and the subsequent skin resistance change as the unconditioned stimulus (US) and response (UR) respectively, Jones was able to demonstrate conditioning to two stimuli previously ineffective in eliciting a skin resistance response: a sound produced by the tapping of a small armature against an induction coil and a flashing light.

A major impetus for the study of skin-resistance conditioning stemmed from the need to develop an objective technique for the evaluation of auditory function. Hardy and Bordley were early proponents of this approach (Bordley & Hardy, 1949; Hardy & Bordley, 1951–1952). At the start of the test procedure an auditory stimulus of presumably greater than threshold intensity was presented in conjunction with an electric shock. "The shock is of sufficient intensity to cause the patient some anxiety in anticipating the stimuli to follow" (Bordley & Hardy, 1949, p. 754). The reflex response to this latter stimulus was a consistent decrease in skin resistance. Generally the intense auditory stimulus was presented first and after a brief time overlapped with the shock stimulus. This was continued until the subject responded consistently to the sound with a decrease in skin resistance. The sound intensity was then progressively decreased until a threshold was obtained and the intensity subsequently increased. Throughout this procedure the shock was administered following each skin resistance response to the auditory stimulus. Conditioning to the initial intense sound usually required from two to twelve trials. Although children varied a good deal, the average interval between the onset of the conditioned stimulus (CS) and the conditioned response (CR) was on the order of one and one-half seconds. This technique had been employed with children as young as seven months. "It has been found, however, in working with children under eighteen months of age, that in some instances satisfactory skin-resistance changes have not been registered. The precise cause of this condition has not been determined. . . ." (Hardy & Bordley, 1951–1952, p. 353). This conditioning technique or some modification of it has been used successfully by other investigators (Barr, 1953; Shimizu, Sugano, Segawa, & Nakamura, 1957; Withrow & Goldstein, 1958).

Goldstein, Ludwig, and Naunton (1954) directed their efforts toward an attempt to identify possible variables associated with either failure or difficulty to condition. The criteria for defining difficulty included the need for more than three trials to obtain initial conditioning and the need for frequent reinforcement after conditioning had occurred. A total of forty children were studied, eighteen of whom were considered to be aphasic whereas twenty-two were regarded as purely deaf. This categorization was made independently of the results from the conditioning experience. The results clearly demonstrated that, in general, children with aphasia had difficulty with conditioning. Except for two, the children who were solely deaf were readily conditioned. This study was repeated with a group of sixteen children ranging in age from eleven months to thirteen years, and similar results were obtained.

Grings, Lowell, and Rushford (1959) critically reviewed the assumption that skin resistance audiometry with children represented an example of classical conditioning. They questioned the adequacy of the learning criteria and the general failure to control for possible pseudo-conditioning. Grings, Lowell, and Honnard (1961) subsequently compared the conditioning process in a group of severely deaf children (ages two to six years) when the CS was in the same sensory modality as the deficiency as opposed to a stimulus related to an intact sensory system. The US was electric shock and the UR a change in skin conductance. In the first session and for half the subjects, the CS was a 100 db 500 cps sound. Light was used as the CS in the second session. The reverse sequence was employed for the remaining subjects. During each session eight nonreinforced acquisition test trials (light or sound alone) were interspersed between twenty reinforced trials. This was followed by five extinction trials. The results clearly demonstrated an increase in both the frequency and magnitude of the conditioned responses toward the end of the conditioning trials for the light stimulus. However, the comparable measures progressively *decreased* when the sound was employed, suggesting adaptation or habituation. Thus conditioning seemed to have occurred to the light but not the sound.

Employing the vascular response to a cold stimulus as the UR and US respectively, Tonkova-Yampol'skaya (1961) studied the conditioning process in two-year-old children. The CS consisted of either a bell or a white light. A bell of another tone was used as a differential conditioned stimulus. At the outset the US clearly produced vasoconstriction. However, following experience with the CS, the UR progressively changed until this response either did not occur or was actually in the reverse direction (vasodilatation). Conditioned responses were generally formed within four to ten trials. The latency between the CS and CR was two to three seconds. In 50 per cent of the children studied, stable discrimination could not be established. These same subjects occasionally demonstrated vasodilatation to the differential CS, loss of the CR to the CS, and more often showed either no response or a vasodilatation to the US once the conditioning procedure was instituted.

Krachkovskaia (1959) conducted a study during the neonatal period on the relation between the peripheral blood leukocyte count and food intake. Blood for study was obtained at fifteen minutes and one hour prior to feeding as well as thirty minutes, one hour, and two hours following feedings. Up to the fifth day of life there was no consistent change in the leukocyte count in relation to food intake. By the sixth day of life most neonates demonstrated an increase in leukocytes an hour after feedings. An increase was also noted prior to feeding in the majority of subjects eight days old. This latter occurrence was hypothesized to represent a conditioned response. Additional studies were subsequently conducted to explore this hypothesis. Three children, one month old, were investigated prior to and following a change in the feeding schedule (from every three to every four hours). During the first day of the changed schedule the leukocyte count continued to rise at the same time as previously. However, by the eighth feeding on the new schedule the rise no longer occurred two hours following the last feeding but was present one hour prior to the next feeding period. Thus the previous CR appears to have been extinguished and a new one established. Changing the method of feeding was also found to influence the appearance of the prefeeding leukocytosis.

In a most interesting and provocative study, Polikanina (1961) followed the changing relation between autonomic and somatic responses during the course of a conditioning procedure in infants one to three months premature. The US was ammonia vapors and the CS a tone of 500 cps. In the smaller prematures the UR generally consisted of a decrease in respiratory rate (at times, breathholding), an increase in cardiac rate, facial flushing, grimacing, blinking, swallowing, and sucking movements. With development, there was added to this response complex active defense reactions including motor restlessness, squinting, and head movements from side to side and away from the location of the stimulus source. Polikanina divides the development of the CR into three stages. In infants one to one and a half months premature, respiratory CRs were first noted in less than six trials (ages twelve to twenty-one days). Several trials later the motor and cardiac CR began to appear. These responses, however, were irregular in occurrence. The second stage started by age three to four weeks and consisted first of stabilization of the motor CR, taking the form of an active defense reaction. The cardiac rate CR stabilized last. In the third stage the motor CR began to assume a more prominent role, appearing in a greater percentage of trials and becoming more frequent when compared to the autonomic responses. Furthermore, in some babies the autonomic responses failed to develop following the presentation of the CS. Polikanina concluded that:

> The difference in time of formation of temporary connections to autonomic and motor functions apparently indicates that these two types of connections are formed at different levels of the central nervous system. The earlier appearance of the autonomic components of the defense CR in premature infants, and the dissociation observed in this case in the appearance of respiratory and cardiac reactions, show that during the early stages of ontogeny in man there still is not the necessary coordination between the autonomic and somatic components (p. 57).

On the basis of the earlier discussion dealing with physiological changes to sensory stimulation it would seem that a number of reflex changes occur in response not only to the US but also to the CS. The nature of these unconditioned responses to the CS, both qualitatively as well as quantitatively, could play a very significant role in the subsequent development of conditioned responses whether physiological or motor. This proposition would also apply to those experimental situations in which the initial responses to the CS are first adapted or habituated out. The very process of habituation could be an active one and therefore in some way modify the subsequent learning process. It would thus seem necessary that the investigator be aware of the character of these responses and their possible relevance and implications for the interpretation of any obtained learning results. For example, it is conceivable that some of the differences in learning or conditionability noted between individuals of the same age as well as longitudinally could relate not to differences in the fundamental learning process but in the qualitatively and quantitatively different unconditioned physiological responses to the unconditioned and conditioned stimulus.

Emotions and Personality Characteristics

To some extent the studies reviewed in this section could readily be expanded to include many of those concerned primarily with the effect of discrete sensory stimulation. For example, those stimulus trials in which a startle response is elicited can be considered "unpleasant." In addition, those procedures pacifying an irritable infant can be said to be "pleasant." However, only those studies will be discussed at this point wherein the primary intent is the investigation of emotional responses or personality characteristics. This approach is admittedly arbitrary though followed in the interest of decreasing repetition.

Engel *et al.* (1956) had the opportunity of studying intensively a child fifteen months of age with a gastric fistula. Frequent behavioral observations were made in conjunction with determinations of gastric acid secretory rate. Based on behavioral observations six affects were identified: contentment, joy, depression, depression-displeasure, irritation, and rage. Depression was associated with statistically the lowest and rage the highest secretory rate. The remaining four affects were not significantly different from one another. These results were not confirmed in a subsequent study of a four-year-old girl also with a gastric fistula (Reichsman, Samuelson, & Engel, 1965).

Sternbach (1962) attempted to generate a variety of affects in eight-year-old children by means of the motion picture "Bambi." During the presentation of the film continuous recordings were obtained of skin resistance, gastric motility, respiration, cardiac and eyeblink rate, and finger pulse volume. Few statistically significant results were obtained. The "saddest" scene resulted in an increase in skin resistance and a decrease in eyeblinks. The stomach period significantly increased during the "nicest-happiest" scene. No significant changes were observed for the "scariest" or "funniest" scenes.

As a means of producing frustration Jost (1941) required normal children to learn an extremely difficult series of numbers by the anticipation method. This situation resulted in a decrease in skin resistance and an increase in heart rate. Emotionally disturbed children tested in the same situation showed the same direction of change but of greater magnitude.

In a study of children over eight years of age, Darling (1940) related personality characteristics to autonomic nervous system measures. Intercorrelating a number of autonomic response measures obtained on the same group of children, galvanic reactivity was found to correlate positively with conductance level. Furthermore, systolic blood pressure, diastolic blood pressure, and pulse pressure were positively correlated with one another. In addition, these two groups of measures were negatively intercorrelated. When these autonomic measures were compared with the personality variables it was noted that children with low blood pressure level and high skin resistance reactivity were bold, cooperative, attentive, alert, hyperactive and tended to be in an unrestrained, manic, or excited state. In contrast, children with high blood pressure and low skin resistance reactivity were timid, uncooperative, destructive, somnolent, sluggish, and inhibited, blocked, or in a withdrawn state.

Jones (1950, 1960) presented a battery of emotion-provoking situations to a group of nursery-school children and simultaneously recorded skin resistance reactivity and overt reactions. Correlations (within a child) between these two reaction types were generally low. ". . . We can recognize patterns of at least three sorts, as represented by the 'externalizer,' who displays a somewhat infantile pattern of marked overt but reduced or infrequent galvanic responses; the 'internalizer,' who reverses this relationship; and the 'generalizer,' who tends to respond with a total discharge, both overt and internal" (Jones, 1950, p. 163). Children between the ages of twelve to eighteen found to have high GSR reactivity were noted to be less talkative, less animated, more restrained in their social behavior, more calm, more deliberative, more good-natured, more cooperative, and more responsible than children with low GSR reactivity.

Although outside the age group intended for this review, it is important to consider the follow-up of the above subjects studied again at ages thirty-three to thirty-seven years. On the basis of interview data these subjects were classified into three groups: "symptom-free," "psychosomatic," or "psychiatric." The subjects in each category were evaluated in terms of their earlier designation as high or low reactor. In general, more of the high reactors tended to be in the "symptom-free" category.

Helper, Garfield, and Wilcott (1963) tested emotionally disturbed children (six to thirteen years) by rating behavior and recording skin conductance during a somewhat threatening interview. On the basis of the conductance changes, subjects were classified as either high or low reactors. In general, the high reactors showed less motor activity and less appropriate affect.

Employing a somewhat different procedure, Doerr and Hokanson

(1965) subdivided a group of normal children (ages seven to eleven years) into three categories depending upon their resting heart rate. Half of these subjects were exposed to a frustrating experience which was preceded and followed by a scored performance problem. The other half did not receive the frustrating experience. Several interesting results were obtained. In general, (a) frustration resulted in an increase in cardiac rate, (b) there was no difference in the prefrustration performance score for the three heart rate groups, and (c) there was a negative relation between the improvement noted in the postfrustration performance and the basal heart rate. The last observation, though not the second, was found to be consistent with the inverted-U hypothesis proposed by Malmo (1958) and relating activation level to performance.

Individual Differences

The majority of studies dealing with psychophysiological relations have been most concerned with identifying group trends. However, a number of investigators have designed their experiments with the hope of being able to define those factors unique to the individual. For the most part these investigations have not attempted to determine whether the differences noted between subjects are due to genetic or experiential factors. Impetus for the study of individual differences in the field of psychophysiology stems from an attempt to better understand the development of emotion, personality, and psychophysiological pathology.

A number of such studies have been reported recently dealing specifically with the newborn period. All of these have demonstrated, by one means or another, and for a variety of end organ systems, that neonates respond differently to stimulation. Richmond and Lustman (1955) tested one group of newborns by obtaining the change in skin temperature following the immersion of a limb in 45°C water. A second group was presented a sound stimulus and the pupillary response was recorded. In both situations, marked individual response differences were noted.

Bridger and Reiser (1959) obtained cardiac rate responses to repetitive presentations of an air stream stimulus in a group of fifteen normal newborns on two successive days. The data from each session were analyzed by fitting a regression line between cardiac rate change and prestimulus heart rate and obtaining for each subject the crossover point, average stimulus value, slope, and variability of the regression line. Correlation coefficients obtained between the two sessions were statistically significant for each of these measures except the standard error of estimate. Also employing the heart rate response of newborns to an air stream stimulus, though a different method of data extraction, Steinschneider, Lipton, and Richmond (1964) present data to support the conclusion that significant individual differences occur both for the slopes of regression and the variability around the regression line. Additional measures found to reveal significant subject variation include maximal reactivity (average change in heart rate at the lowest prestimulus level), discriminability, the temporal aspects of the response curve (both within subject mean and variability) and various measures of homeostatic capacity (Lipton *et al.*, 1961b; Richmond, Lipton, & Steinschneider, 1962).

In a series of newborn studies on the effect of a variety of experimental conditions on cardiac rate response to stimulation, data were obtained that add to the growing evidence on individual differences. The technique in each of these studies was to test the same subject under each of several experimental conditions. Correlation coefficients were obtained for each response measure to determine if the individual neonate maintained his position relative to the group in spite of changes in the variable under consideration. These studies dealt with the effect of varying degrees of motor restraint (Lipton *et al.*, 1965b), intensity of white noise (Steinschneider *et al.*, 1966), and stimulus duration (Steinschneider *et al.*, 1965). In each study a number of statistically significant and high correlations between conditions were obtained. This applies to both the magnitude and temporal characteristics of the cardiac-response curve.

These studies demonstrate not only that neonates differ from one another but also that they maintain their relative degree of responsiveness in the face of stimulus variation within the same sensory modality. A question of significance concerns the stability of single end organ responsivity over time. Lipton *et al.* (1966) studied cardiac rate responsivity in fourteen subjects as newborns and again at two and one-half and five months. Very few of the correlations between the newborn period and the subsequent ages proved to be statistically significant. However, a number of significant positive coefficients were obtained between the two older age periods. These authors suggest the possibility that basic maturational changes in cardiac control take place during the first months of life, resulting in the failure to predict responsivity from the newborn period. Employing a much older group of subjects (74 to 209 months) and autonomic response changes to a cold-pressor test, Lacey and Lacey (1962) obtained high correlations with a repeat test obtained on the same subjects four years later.

The fundamental approach in the above studies has been to consider each end organ response individually. Another problem of great interest concerns the predictability of responsivity across different end organ systems. For example, does the child with the greatest cardiac rate responsivity also demonstrate the greatest degree of skin conductance change? A number of studies would point to a negative answer.

Lacey and Van Lehn (1952) employed a cold-pressor test on a group of subjects ranging in age from six to eighteen years. The response measures included systolic and diastolic blood pressure, heart rate and heart rate variability, palmar conductance, and pulse pressure. There seems to be little question that these response systems do not act in concordance with one another. A subject who is a hyperreactor in one response system might be hypo-, hyper-, or normo-reactive in another. Rather, each subject has a patterned set of responses to stimulation. Furthermore, this pattern of responses tends to be reproducible on retest. Similar conclusions were reached by Lacey and Lacey (1962) in their four-year follow-up study on the responses to a cold-pressor test. Failure to find significant correlations for different response systems or for different properties of the same response system has also been observed in the neonate (Grossman & Greenberg, 1957; Lipton *et al.*, 1961b; Steinschneider *et al.*, 1964).

Wenger has taken a somewhat different approach in his investigation of individual differences (Wenger, 1941, 1942, 1943; Wenger & Ellington, 1943). This approach derives from the hypothesis that the autonomic nervous system is composed of two antagonistic branches: the adrenergic and the cholinergic. Furthermore, one branch may predominate over the other. The fundamental approach was to obtain a single measure indicative of the amount and direction of this predominance or imbalance.

A battery of response measures was obtained from a group of normal children ranging in age from six to eleven years. These measures were intercorrelated and factor analyzed and an autonomic factor (Nu) identified. To obtain a measure of the amount of autonomic imbalance expressed by a given child, seven of the more appropriate response measures were chosen and a multiple regression equation based on standard scores was derived. The measures employed in this equation consisted of persistence of red dermographia, salivary output, heart period, standing palmar skin conductance, volar skin conductance, respiration period, and pulse pressure. Repeated study on the same subject as well as on different groups of individuals pointed to stability of the multiple regression equation and the resulting measure of autonomic imbalance.

Jost and Sontag (1944), using the seven end organ responses suggested by Wenger, correlated the results for twins, siblings, and unrelated children. In addition to performing these correlations on the individual end organ response, the measure of autonomic balance was derived and similarly intercorrelated. This study was performed three consecutive years on different children ranging in age from six to twelve years. Whether considering the response measures separately or the composite score representing autonomic balance, there was a consistent tendency for twins to be more alike than siblings who in turn were more alike than unrelated paired children.

This approach would seem to be at variance with those results previously discussed which demonstrated that individuals differ in their patterning of responses. A further criticism of the search for a single measure of autonomic imbalance derives from the recent review on the autonomic nervous system in early life by Lipton *et al.* (1965a) in which the authors conclude, "It seems misleading and inappropriate, with the knowledge currently available, to view the autonomic nervous system of the young child *simply* * in terms of predominant parasympathetic or sympathetic function" (p. 207). However, these two approaches are not necessarily incompatible. For the most part, the study of autonomic balance deals with unstimulated end organ functioning whereas the patterning approach is concerned with responses to stimulation. Furthermore, the former technique or theoretical approach emphasizes the communality (albeit small) between response measures whereas the other focuses on the discrepancies. Thus it is not unreasonable to presume that the search for and the implications of individual differences in autonomic imbalance would actually complement a similar evaluation of individual differences in response patterning and vice versa.

Concluding Remarks

Although a good deal of research effort has been expended, the study of psychophysiology of infancy and early childhood is still in the toddler stage. Much has been done to improve the necessary instrumentation and to allow for obtaining, in many instances, relatively movement-free tracings. A good deal of progress has been made in understanding many of the analytic and methodological problems involved. Sufficient data have been obtained to appreciate the importance of variation in discrete sensory input. However, a number of significant and major problem areas are still left virtually untouched.

The bulk of studies dealing with this age period have been performed on neonates. This probably derives from the fact that, to a large extent, newborns are readily available. Many longitudinal studies are needed extending not only through the first year of life but beyond as well. The data presently available in the fields of developmental psychology, developmental physiology, and developmental psychophysiology, clearly point to the large number of changes taking place during the first years of life; not only quantitative but qualitative changes as well. Studies of this type would allow for a large increase in available psychophysiological knowledge. The data from some of the studies reviewed would strongly suggest that satisfactory predictions can be made from one age group to another. This type of predictability, however, should not be anticipated for all response measures and across all age groups. In fact such extreme stability would be most surprising indeed. This conclusion stems primarily from two additional considerations. It is reasonable to expect that individuals would differ in the rate at which physiological maturation takes place as well as the ultimate level reached. Differential experiences would be another potential factor acting to diminish evidence of stability.

Although those studies employing single measures of physiological activity are certainly productive of greater understanding, there is a

* Italics added.

need for investigations during which multiple end organ responses are recorded. Multiple response studies of this type in conjunction with the presentation of a number of different environmental conditions should serve to broaden our appreciation of the significance of response patterning. A resolution of the importance of response-stereotopy and stimulus- or situational-stereotopy can best be accomplished in this fashion. It should also allow for greater insights into the importance of an individual's unique pattern(s) of responsivity in the development of complex psychological processes, maternal-child interaction, and psychosomatic disorders.

The studies dealing with soothing and pacification procedures suggest a most fruitful area for investigation. A number of different techniques are presently being employed by parents to placate an irritable infant and as a means of expressing love and affection. The effectiveness of these efforts could play a major role in the evolution of an appropriate symbiotic relation. The observation that certain infants become even more disturbed physiologically with the application of a specific method of communicating warmth would partially explain the failure of some parent-child diads to effect a meaningful and positive relationship. For example, some babies might actually become more irritable, as evidenced by increased motor activity and heart rate, when motor restraint is imposed during the process of "cuddling." This could be interpreted by the mother as a rejection of her love with the effect that she, in turn, could become less demonstrative and stimulating or actually openly hostile toward the baby.

The great majority of psychophysiological studies in early life have dealt primarily with the process of sensation or perception. It is essential that more complex psychological processes receive physiological elaboration. One of the difficulties in realizing this goal is inherent in the ability to identify, in nonverbal organisms, the appropriate psychological process. The requirement, at least in the early stages of this exploration, is for defining criteria independent of the physiological responses. Only after sufficient psychophysiological data have been obtained under a variety of comparable conceptual situations can we hope to modify these criteria by incorporating physiological changes. This strategy, to some extent, has been employed by Kagan and Lewis (1965) in their studies on attention.

The psychophysiology of the learning process is another area of extreme significance and requires a great deal of further exploration. There seems to be little question that physiological processes can be modified by experiential factors. Greater understanding of the factors facilitating the development and persistence of learned physiological responses should greatly add to our knowledge of the role of learning in the production or modification of psychosomatic disorders. Simultaneous measurement of physiological activity during the learning of a behavioral response might suggest hypotheses to account for at least some of the variance obtained.

Still another study area incorporating the learning paradigm is the elaboration of secondary motives and drives. Explorations of this type are of especial relevance for the investigator of infancy and early childhood, for it is during this age period that this development is at least initiated. Fundamental to an understanding of this process are more basic data concerning not only the learning process but also the psychophysiology of emotion and primary drives. In this context, Ax (1964) has introduced the concept of the Physiological Learning Aptitude. "Whereas much maladjustment and neurosis may be due to the learning of the wrong motives or an incompatible combination, there also may be many people who simply learn secondary motives slowly, require much reinforcement, or retain motives poorly with the result that their behavior does not coordinate well with that of their associates" (p. 12).

In his presidential address before the American Psychosomatic Society, Engel (1954) commented:

> . . . the inescapable fact is that there is as yet no physiology of the mother-infant symbiotic unit, or of object relationship. Nothing is known of the physiology of separation, grief, and depression; other than embryology, there is no real comparative physiology of growth and development; the physiology of moods and affects is incomplete; there is no physiology of love, and only meager knowledge of sexual processes, erotic phenomena, and sexuality. Yet much evidence suggests that such processes are concerned in intimate but obscure ways with the development of a wide variety of somatic changes, including pathological changes (p. 370).

Unfortunately, this summary statement is still applicable today.

The student of developmental psychophysiology should not want for lack of "mountains to climb" or "continents to explore." Rather the need is for imaginative conceptualizations evaluated within the framework of compulsiveness over research design, technique, data collection, and data analysis.

References

Ax, A. F. Goals and methods of psychophysiology. *Psychophysiology,* 1964, 1, 8–25.

Barnet, A. B., & Goodwin, R. S. Averaged evoked electroencephalographic responses to clicks in the human newborn. *Electroenceph. clin. Neurophys.,* 1965, 18, 441–450.

Barnet, A. B., Lodge, A., & Armington, J. C. Electroretinogram in newborn human infants. *Science,* 1965, 148, 651–654.

Barr, B. Pure tone audiometry for pre-school children: a preliminary report. *Acta Otolaryng.,* 1953, Supp. 110, 89–101.

Bartoshuk, A. K. Human neonatal cardiac acceleration to sound: habituation and dishabituation. *Percept. motor Skills,* 1962, 15, 15–27. (a)

———. Response decrement with repeated elicitation of human neonatal cardiac acceleration to sound. *J. comp. physiol. Psychol.*, 1962, 55, 9–13. (b)

——. Human neonatal cardiac responses to sound: a power function. *Psychon. Sci.*, 1964, 1, 151–152.

Beadle, K. R., & Crowell, D. H. Neonatal electrocardiographic responses to sound: methodology. *J. speech hearing Res.*, 1962, 5, 112–123.

Benjamin, L. S. Statistical treatment of the law of initial values (LIV) in autonomic research: a review and recommendation. *Psychosom. Med.*, 1963, 25, 556–566.

Block, J. D., & Bridger, W. H. The law of initial value in psychophysiology: a reformulation in terms of experimental and theoretical considerations. *Ann. N.Y. Acad. Sci.*, 1962, 98, 1229–1241.

Bordley, J. E., & Hardy, W. G. A study in objective audiometry with the use of a psychogalvanometric response. *Ann. Oto., Rhino. and Laryng.*, 1949, 58, 751–759.

Brackbill, Y., Adams, G., Crowell, D. H., & Gray, M. L. Arousal level in neonates and preschool children under continuous auditory stimulation. *J. exp. child Psychol.*, 1966, 4, 178–188.

Brazelton, T. B., Scholl, M. L., & Robey, J. S. Visual responses in the newborn. *Pediatrics*, 1966, 37, 284–290.

Bridger, W. H. Sensory habituation and discrimination in the human neonate. *Amer. J. Psychiat.*, 1961, 117, 991–996.

——. Sensory discrimination and autonomic function in the newborn. *J. Amer. Acad. Child Psychiat.*, 1962, 1, 67–82.

Bridger, W. H., & Birns, B. M. Neonates' behavioral and autonomic responses to stress during soothing. *Rec. Adv. Biol. Psychiat.*, 1962, 5, 1–6.

Bridger, W. H., Birns, B. M., & Blank, M. A comparison of behavioral ratings and heart rate measurements in human neonates. *Psychosom. Med.*, 1965, 27, 123–134.

Bridger, W. H., & Reiser, M. F. Psychophysiologic studies of the neonate: an approach toward the methodological and theoretical problems involved. *Psychosom. Med.*, 1959, 21, 265–276.

Burstein, K. R., Fenz, W. D., Bergeron, J., & Epstein, S. A comparison of skin potential and skin resistance responses as measures of emotional responsivity. *Psychophysiology*, 1965, 2, 14–24.

Butterfield, G. A note on the use of cardiac rate in the audiometric appraisal of retarded children. *J. speech hearing Dis.*, 1962, 27, 378–379.

Churchill, E. Appendix. *Ann. N.Y. Acad. Sci.*, 1962, 98, 1322–1326.

Contis, G., & Lind, J. Study of systolic blood pressure, heart rate, body temperature of normal newborn infants through the first week of life. *Acta Paediatrica Suppl.*, 1963, 146, 41–47.

Crowell, D. H., Davis, C. M., Chun, B. J., & Spellacy, F. J. Galvanic skin reflex in newborn humans. *Science*, 1965, 148, 1108–1111.

Darling, R. P. Autonomic action in relation to personality traits of children. *J. abn. soc. Psychol.*, 1940, 35, 246–260.

Darrow, C. W. Psychophysiology, yesterday, today, and tomorrow. *Psychophysiology*, 1964, 1, 4–7. (a)

——. The rationale for treating the change in galvanic skin response as change in conductance. *Psychophysiology*, 1964, 1, 31–38. (b)

Derbyshire, A. J., & Farley, J. C. Sampling auditory responses at the cortical level: a routine for EER-audiometric testing. *Ann. Otol., Rhinol., Laryng.*, 1959, 68, 675–697.

Derbyshire, A. J., Fraser, A. A., McDermott, M., & Bridge, A. Audiometric measurements by electroencephalography. *Electroenceph. clin. Neurophysiol.*, 1956, 8, 467–478.

Doerr, H. O., & Hokanson, J. E. A relation between heart rate and performance in children. *J. person. soc. Psychol.*, 1965, 2, 70–76.

Dustman, R. E., & Beck, E. C. Visually evoked potentials: amplitude changes with age. *Science*, 1966, 151, 1013–1015.

Edelberg, R., & Wright, D. J. Two galvanic skin response effector organs and their stimulus specificity. *Psychophysiology,* 1964, 1, 39–47.

Eichorn, D. Electrocortical and autonomic response in infants to visual and auditory stimuli. Unpublished doctor's dissertation, Northwestern University, 1951.

Ellingson, R. J. Electroencephalograms of normal, full-term newborns immediately after birth with observations on arousal and visual evoked responses. *Electroenceph. clin. Neurophysiol.,* 1958, 10, 31–50.

————. Cortical electrical responses to visual stimulation in the human infant. *Electroenceph. clin. Neurophysiol.,* 1960, 12, 663–677. Reprinted in Y. Brackbill & G. G. Thompson (Eds.), *Behavior in infancy and early childhood: A book of readings.* New York: Free Press, 1967.

Engel, G. L. Selection of clinical material in psychosomatic medicine: the need for a new physiology. *Psychosom. Med.,* 1954, 16, 368–373.

Engel, G. L., Reichsman, F. Segal, H. L. A study of an infant with a gastric fistula: I. Behavior and the rate of total hydrochloric acid secretion. *Psychosom. Med.,* 1956, 18, 374–398. Reprinted in Y. Brackbill & G. G. Thompson (Eds.), *Behavior in infancy and early childhood: A book of readings.* New York: Free Press, 1967.

Engel, R. Evaluation of electroencephalographic tracings of newborns. *J. Lancet,* 1961, 81, 523–532.

Engel, R., & Butler, B. V. Appraisal of conceptual age of newborn infants by electroencephalographic methods. *J. Pediatr.,* 1963, 386–393.

Forbes, T. W. Skin potential and impedance responses with recurring shock stimulation. *Amer. J. Physiol.,* 1936, 117, 189–199.

————. Problems in measurement of electrodermal phenomena—choice of method and phenomena—potential, impedance, resistance. *Psychophysiology,* 1964, 1, 26–30.

Forbes, T. W., & Bolles, M. M. Correlation of the response potentials of the skin with "exciting" and non- "exciting" stimuli. *J. Psychol.,* 1936, 2, 273–285.

Gibson, E. J., & Olum, V. Experimental methods of studying perception in children. In P. H. Mussen (Ed.), *Handbook of research methods in child development.* New York: John Wiley & Sons, Inc., 1960, Pp. 311–373.

Glaser, G. H., & Levy, L. L. Photic following in the EEG of the newborn. *Amer. J. Disord. Child.,* 1965, 109, 333–337.

Goldstein, R., Kendall, D. C., & Arick, B. E. Electroencephalic audiometry in young children. *J. speech hearing Disord.,* 1963, 28, 331–354.

Goldstein, R., Ludwig, H., & Naunton, R. F. Difficulty in conditioning galvanic skin responses: its possible significance in clinical audiometry. *Acta Otolaryng.,* 1954, 44, 67–77.

Goodman, W. S., Appleby, S. V., Scott, J. W., & Ireland, P. E. Audiometry in newborn children by electroencephalography. *Laryngoscope,* 1964, 74, 1316–1328.

Graham, F. K., & Clifton, R. K. Heart-rate change as a component of the orienting response. *Psychol. Bull.,* 1966, 65, 305–320.

Grings, W. W. Methodological considerations underlying electrodermal measurements. *J. Psychol.,* 1953, 35, 271–282.

Grings, W. W., Lowell, E. L., & Honnard, R. R. GSR conditioning with preschool-age deaf children. *J. comp. physiol. Psychol.,* 1961, 54, 143–148.

Grings, W. W., Lowell, E. L., & Rushford, G. M. Role of conditioning in GSR audiometry with children. *J. speech hearing Disord,* 1959, 24, 380–390.

Grossman, H. J., & Greenberg, N. H. Psychosomatic differentiation in infancy. I. Autonomic activity in the newborn. *Psychosom. Med.,* 1957, 19, 293–306.

Gupta, J. M., & Scopes, J. W. Observations on blood pressure in newborn infants. *Arch. Dis. Childh.,* 1965, 40, 637–644.

Haggard, E. A. Experimental studies in affective processes: II. On the quantification and evaluation of "measured" changes in skin resistance. *J. exp. Psychol.,* 1945, 35, 46–56.

Hardy, W. G., & Bordley, J. E. Evaluation of hearing in young children. *Acta Otolaryng.*, 1951–1952, 40, 346–360.

Helper, M. M., Garfield, S. L., & Wilcott, R. C. Electrodermal reactivity and rated behavior in emotionally disturbed children. *J. abn. soc. Psychol.*, 1963, 66, 600–603.

Hernández-Peón, R., Scherrer, H., & Jouvet, M. Modification of electric activity in cochlear nucleus during "attention" in unanesthetized cats. *Science*, 1956, 123, 331–332.

Hord, D. J., Johnson, L. C., & Lubin, A. Differential effect of the law of initial value (LIV) on autonomic variables. *Psychophysiology*, 1964, 1, 79–87.

Horsten, G. P. M., & Winkelman, J. E. Development of the ERG in relation to histological differentiation of the retina in man and animals. *Arch. Ophth.*, 1960, 63, 232–242.

Hunt, W. A., & Hunt, E. B. A comparison of five methods of scoring the galvanic skin response. *J. exp. Psychol.*, 1935, 18, 383–387.

Jeffress, L. A. Galvanic phenomena of the skin. *J. exp. Psychol.*, 1928, 11, 130–144.

Jones, H. E. Conditioned psychogalvanic responses in infants. *Psychol. Bull.*, 1928, 25, 183–184.

——. The galvanic skin reflex in infancy. *Child Develop.*, 1930, 1, 106–110. (a)

——. The retention of conditioned emotional reactions in infancy. *J. genet. Psychol.*, 1930, 37, 485–498. (b)

——. The study of patterns of emotional expression. In M. L. Reymert (Ed.), *Feelings and emotions*. New York: McGraw-Hill, 1950, Pp. 161–168.

——. The longitudinal method in the study of personality. In I. Iscoe and H. W. Stevenson (Eds.), *Personality development in children*. Austin: Univer. Texas Pr., 1960, Pp. 3–27.

Jost, H. Some physiological changes during frustration. *Child Developm.*, 1941, 12, 9–15.

Jost, H., & Sontag, L. W. The genetic factor in autonomic nervous system function. *Psychosom. Med.*, 1944, 6, 308–310.

Kagan, J., & Lewis, M. Studies of attention in the human infant. *Merrill-Palmer Quart. Behav. Developm.*, 1965, 11, 95–127.

Kagan, J., & Rosman, B. L. Cardiac and respiratory correlates of attention and an analytic attitude. *J. exp. Child Psychol.*, 1964, 1, 50–63.

Kaye, H. Skin conductance in the human neonate. *Child Developm.*, 1964, 35, 1297–1305.

Keen, R. E., Chase, H. H., & Graham, F. K. Twenty-four hour retention by neonates of an habituated heart rate response. *Psychon. Sci.*, 1965, 2, 265–266.

Krachkovskaia, M. V. Reflex changes in the leucocyte count of newborn infants in relation to food intake. *Pavlov J. high. nerv. Sys. Act.*, 1959, 9, 193–199. Reprinted in Y. Brackbill & G. G. Thompson, (Eds.), *Behavior in infancy and early childhood: A book of readings*. New York: Free Press, 1967.

Lacey, J. I. The evaluation of autonomic responses: toward a general solution. *Ann. N.Y. Acad. Sci.*, 1956, 67, 123–164.

——. Psychophysiological approaches to the evaluation of psychotherapeutic process and outcome. In E. A. Rubinstein and M. B. Parloff (Eds.), *Research in psychotherapy*. Washington, D.C.: Amer. Psychol. Ass., 1959, Pp. 160–208.

Lacey, J. I., Kagan, J., Lacey, B. C., & Moss, H. A. The visceral level: situational determinants and behavioral correlates of autonomic response patterns. In P. H. Knapp (Ed.), *Expression of the emotions in man*. New York: Int. Univer. Pr., 1963. Pp. 161–196.

Lacey, J. I., & Lacey, B. C. The law of initial value in the longitudinal study of autonomic constitution: reproducibility of autonomic responses and response patterns over a four-year interval. *Ann. N.Y. Acad. Sci.*, 1962, 98, 1257–1290.

Lacey, J. I., & Van Lehn, R. Differential emphasis in somatic responsivity to stress: an experimental study. *Psychosom. Med.,* 1952, 14, 71–81.

Lacey, O. L. An analysis of the appropriate unit for use in the measurement of level of galvanic skin resistance. *J. exp. Psychol.,* 1947, 37, 449–457.

Lacey, O. L., & Siegel, P. S. An analysis of the unit of measurement of the galvanic skin response. *J. exp. Psychol.,* 1949, 39, 122–127.

Landis, C., & Forbes, T. W. An investigation of methods of measurement of the electrical phenomena of the skin. *Psychiat. Quart.,* 1933, 7, 107–114.

Lipton, E. L., Richmond, J. B., Weinberger, H., & Hersher, L. An approach to the evaluation of neonate autonomic responses. Paper presented at the annual meeting of the American Psychosomatic Society, Cincinnati, March 31, 1958.

Lipton, E. L., & Steinschneider, A. Studies on the psychophysiology of infancy. *Merrill-Palmer Quart. Behav. Developm.,* 1964, 10, 103–117.

Lipton, E. L., Steinschneider, A., Bergman, A. B., & Richmond, J. B. Children's sensitivity to varying sound intensities. Presented at the American Psychosomatic Society annual meeting, April 30–May 2, 1965.

Lipton, E. L., Steinschneider, A., & Richmond, J. B. Autonomic function in the neonate: II. Physiologic effects on motor restraint. *Psychosom. Med.,* 1960, 22, 57–65.

———. Autonomic function in the neonate: III. Methodological considerations. *Psychosom. Med.,* 1961, 23, 461–471. (a)

———. Autonomic function in the neonate: IV. Individual differences in cardiac reactivity. *Psychosom. Med.,* 1961, 23, 472–484. (b)

———. The autonomic nervous system in early life. *New Eng. J. Med.,* 1965., 273, 147–153, 201–208. (a)

———. Swaddling, a child care practice: historical, cultural and experimental observations. *Pediatr. Suppl.,* 1965, 35, 521–567. (b)

———. Autonomic function in the neonate: VII. Maturational changes in cardiac control. *Child Developm.,* 1966, 37, 1–16.

———. Psychophysiologic disorders in children. In M. L. and L. Hoffman (Eds.), *Review of child development research,* Vol. 2. New York: Russell Sage Foundation, 1967 (in press).

Malmo, R. B. Measurement of drive: an unsolved problem in psychology. In M. R. Jones, (Ed.), *Nebraska symposium on motivation.* Lincoln: Univer. Nebraska Pr., 1958. Pp. 229–265.

Mirsky, I. A. Psychoanalysis and the biological sciences. In F. Alexander and H. Ross (Eds.), *20 years of psychoanalysis.* New York: W. W. Norton & Company, Inc., 1953, Pp. 155–176.

Mirzoyants, N. S. Changes in electrical activity of the brain in early childhood in response to a flicker stimulus. *Pavlov J. high. nerv. Sys. Act.,* 1961, 11, 31–36.

Montagu, J. D., & Coles, E. M. Mechanism and measurement of the galvanic skin response. *Psychol. Bull.,* 1966, 65, 261–279.

Moss, A. J., & Adams, F. H. *Problems of blood pressure in childhood.* Springfield: Charles C. Thomas, 1962.

Moss, A. J., Duffie, E. R., Jr., & Emmanouilides, G. Blood pressure and vasomotor reflexes in the newborn infant. *Pediatrics,* 1963, 32, 175–179.

Oken, D., & Heath, H. A. The law of initial values: some further considerations. *Psychosom. Med.,* 1963, 25, 3–12.

Ortiz-Estrada, P., Deutsch, E., & Hernandez-Orozco, F. An electroencephalographic method for evaluation of hearing in children. *Ann. Otol. Rhinol. Laryngol.,* 1963, 72, 135–148.

Palmer, C. W., Derbyshire, A. J., & Lee, A. W. A method of analyzing individual cortical responses to auditory stimuli. *Electroenceph. clin. Neurophysiol.,* 1966, 20, 204–206.

Polikanina, R. I. The relation between autonomic and somatic components in the development of the conditioned defense reflex in premature infants. *Pavlov J. high. nerv. Sys. Act.,* 1961, 11, 51–58.

Reichsman, F., Samuelson, D., & Engel, G. Behavior and gastric secretion: II.

A study of a four-year-old girl with gastric fistula. Presented at the annual meeting, American Psychosomatic Society, April 30–May 2, 1965.

Richmond, J. B., & Lipton, E. L. Some aspects of the neurophysiology of the newborn and their implications for child development. In L. Jessner and E. Pavenstedt (Eds.), *Dynamic psychopathology in childhood.* New York: Grune & Stratton, Inc., 1959. Pp. 78–105.

Richmond, J. B., Lipton, E. L., & Steinschneider, A. Autonomic function in the neonate: V. Individual homeostatic capacity in cardiac response. *Psychosom. Med.*, 1962, 24, 66–74.

Richmond, J. B., & Lustman, S. L. Autonomic function in the neonate: I. Implications for psychosomatic theory. *Psychosom. Med.*, 1955, 17, 269–275.

Riggs, L. A. The human electroretinogram. *Arch. Ophthal.*, 1958, 60, 739–749.

Rothman, S. *Physiology and biochemistry of the skin.* Chicago: Univer. Chicago Pr., 1954.

Scheibel, M. E., & Scheibel, A. B. Some neural substrates of postnatal development. In M. L. and L. W. Hoffman (Eds.), *Review of child development research*, Vol. 1. New York: Russell Sage Foundation, 1964. Pp. 481–519.

Shimizu, H., Sugano, T., Segawa, Y., & Nakamura, F. A study in psychogalvanic skin resistance audiometry. *Arch. Otolaryng.*, 1957, 65, 499–508.

Smith, J. M. The relative brightness values of three hues for newborn infants. *Univer. Iowa Stud. Child Welf.*, 1936, 12, 91–140.

Sokolov, Ye. N. *Perception and the conditioned reflex.* New York: Pergamon Pr., 1963.

Stechler, G., Bradford, S., & Levy, H. Attention in the newborn: effect on motility and skin potential. *Science*, 1966, 151, 1246–1248.

Steinschneider, A., & Lipton, E. L. Individual differences in autonomic responsivity: problems of measurement. *Psychosom. Med.*, 1965, 27, 446–456.

Steinschneider, A., Lipton, E. L., & Richmond, J. B. Autonomic function in the neonate: VI. Discriminability, consistency and slope as measures of an individual's cardiac responsivity. *J. genet. Psychol.*, 1964, 105, 295–310.

———. Stimulus duration and cardiac responsivity in the neonate. Paper presented at the biennial meeting of the Society for Research in Child Development. March 24–27, 1965.

———. Auditory sensitivity in the infant: effect of intensity on cardiac and motor responsivity. *Child Developm.*, 1966, 37, 233–252.

Stern, J. A. Toward a definition of psychophysiology. *Psychophysiology*, 1964, 1, 90–91.

Sternbach, R. A. Assessing differential autonomic patterns in emotions. *J. Psychosom. Res.*, 1962, 6, 87–91.

Stubbs, E. M. The effect of the factors of duration, intensity and pitch of sound stimuli on the responses of newborn infants. *Univer. Iowa Stud. Child Welf.*, 1934, 9, 75–135.

Suzuki, T., Kamijo, Y., & Kiuchi, S. Auditory test of newborn infants. *Ann. Otology, Rhinol., and Laryngol.*, 1964, 73, 914–923.

Tonkova-Yampol'skaya, R. V. Characteristics of vascular conditioned reflexes in two-year-old children. *Pavlov J. high. nerv. Sys. Act.*, 1961, 11, 63–65.

Tursky, B., & O'Connell, D. N. Survey of practice in electrodermal measurement. *Psychophysiology*, 1966, 2, 237–240.

Wenger, M. A. The measurement of individual differences in autonomic balance. *Psychosom. Med.*, 1941, 3, 427–434.

———. The stability of measurement of autonomic balance. *Psychosom. Med.*, 1942, 4, 94–95.

———. A further note on the measurement of autonomic balance. *Psychosom. Med.*, 1943, 5, 148–151.

Wenger, M. A., & Ellington, M. The measurement of autonomic balance in children: method and normative data. *Psychosom. Med.*, 1943, 5, 241–253.

Wenger, M. A., & Irwin, O. C. Fluctuations in skin resistance of infants and adults and their relation to muscular processes. *Univer. Iowa Stud. Child Welf.*, 1936, 12, 143–179.

Wilcott, R. C. Correlation of skin resistance and potential. *J. comp. physiol. Psychol.*, 1958, 51, 691–696.

———. The partial independence of skin potential and skin resistance from sweating. *Psychophysiology*, 1964, 1, 55–66.

Wilcott, R. C., Darrow, C. W., & Siegel, A. Uniphasic and diphasic wave forms of the skin potential response. *J. comp. physiol. Psychol.*, 1957, 50, 217–219.

Wilder, J. The law of initial value in neurology and psychiatry: facts and problems. *J. nerv. ment. Dis.*, 1957, 125, 73–86.

———. Modern psychophysiology and the law of initial value. *Amer. J. Psychotherapy*, 1958, 12, 199–221.

Withrow, F. B., Jr., & Goldstein, R. An electrophysiologic procedure for determination of auditory threshold in children. *Laryngoscope*, 1958, 68, 1674–1699.

Woodworth, R. S., & Schlosberg, H. *Experimental psychology.* New York: Henry Holt & Co., 1954.

Zeidler, I. The clinical electroretinogram: IX. The normal electroretinogram. Value of the b-potential in different age groups and its differences in men and women. *Acta Ophth.*, 1959, 37, 294–301.

Zetterström, B. The clinical electroretinogram: IV. The electroretinogram in children during the first year of life. *Acta. Ophth.*, 1951, 29, 295–304.

———. The electroretinogram in prematurely born children. *Acta Ophth.*, 1952, 30, 405–408.

———. Flicker electroretinography in newborn infants. *Acta Ophth.*, 1955, 33, 157–166.

Chapter 2

Sensory and Perceptual Processes in Infants

WILLIAM C. SPEARS

RAYMOND H. HOHLE

The section on vision was written by W. C. Spears, Skidmore College, Saratoga Springs, N.Y.; the sections concerned with audition, chemical senses, somesthesis, and vestibular functions were written by R. H. Hohle, University of Iowa, Iowa City, Ia.

The capacity to respond to stimulation is an essential property of living organisms. Specialized sense receptor cells are activated by various forms of energy changes in the environment, and these receptor excitations are encoded and transmitted as nerve impulses. Nerve impulses seem to be qualitatively the same throughout the nervous system, however, suggesting that differential sensory qualities are correlated primarily with activation of particular sensory channels, i.e., activation of particular cortical loci by impulses from specific receptors, selectively sensitive to particular kinds of stimulus energies.

This chapter is concerned with the development of sensory and perceptual processes in infants. In keeping with a view of specific sensory channel sensitivity, the several sense modalities are treated separately; the discussion of each includes a definition of the primary or adequate stimulus, identification of relevant anatomical and physiological aspects of the system, and a review of behavioral data bearing on functions of the system.

Since the behavioral studies to be reviewed are concerned with observations of very young subjects, special problems of observational methods are involved. Standard psychophysical methods can be used, but certain modifications in their application are necessary. Verbal reports, for example, cannot be obtained from infants; instead, reflexes, spontaneous behavior, and learned responses must be used as indicators. In general, as Gibson and Olum (1960) have pointed out, any method used with young children should require actions of the child for which he is spontaneously motivated and should be as nearly independent as possible of language skills. If instructions are necessary they should be given by demonstration or training. Details of methods and procedures that have been used, and descriptions of the kinds of responses that have been observed will be considered more fully in discussions of specific studies.

Vision

THE STIMULUS FOR VISION

The adequate stimulus for vision is electromagnetic energy which, when absorbed by the pigment substances of specialized receptor cells of the eye, is transformed into the basic nerve excitations responsible for the sensations associated with vision. The visible spectrum of electromagnetic radiation consists of wavelengths from approximately 400 mμ to 760 mμ, a band comprising about $\frac{1}{70}$th of the measurable electromagnetic spectrum. Wavelengths within this band, in interaction with the visual system, produce the sensation of *light*. Exposure to radiation beyond these limits can injure tissue. Thus, ultraviolet radiation can damage the anterior portion of the eye, including the cornea (snow-blindness), while infrared radiation may injure the retina (eclipse-blindness) (Adler, 1959).

While the *physical* energy of a quantum of radiation is inversely proportional to the wavelength, the *physiological* effectiveness of various portions of the visible spectrum is such, for both scotopic (rod) vision and photopic (cone) vision, as to produce bell-shaped curves of luminous efficiency, with maximal sensitivity in the middle portion of the curves at about 507 mμ and 555 mμ respectively. Although it is possible, therefore, to specify light in terms of absolute units (ergs or watts per second), it is generally necessary to express it in terms of radiant energy as adjusted by luminosity factors, that is, in terms of photometric units ultimately based on brightness matches made by the human eye under light- and dark-adapted conditions.

The two physical characteristics of light which are significant for vision are *wavelength* and *intensity*. These correspond principally to the subjective experiences of *hue* and *brightness*, the psychophysical correlates being dominant wavelength and luminance. *Saturation*, a third dimension of experience, is a matter of wavelength composition; its psychophysical correlate is colorimetric purity. Burnham, Hanes, and Bartleson point out that, with a given color stimulus, "The *hue*, *saturation*, and *brightness* of a color response all depend to some extent on variations *in all three* psychophysical attributes. . . ." (1963, p. 22). The complicated interaction of hue, saturation, and brightness can be quickly indicated. The absolute threshold for any visible wavelength, except those over 650 mμ, is an essentially colorless experience of "light"; then, further increases in intensity produce at first only changes in brightness and, finally, "color." This range is called the *photochromatic interval*, and it represents the luminance difference between absolute light threshold and specific color thresholds. With a further increase in intensity, saturation at first increases and then decreases; finally only brightness remains. With the exception of colors associated with 473 mμ, 513 mμ, 577 mμ, and the complement of 495 mμ, hues also tend to shift with variations in intensity. This is known as the Bezold-Brücke phenomenon. The perception of color must, in any event, involve all three attributes. White, gray, and black, which lack hue and saturation, are termed *achromatic* colors: white is an achromatic color of maximal brightness, and black, of minimal brightness.

There are many types of units used to measure radiant and luminous energy or flux. *Luminous flux* or *light flux* is defined as "the amount of light . . . radiated, measured relative to the light radiated from a standard source and under conditions which take account of the sensitivity of the eye to light of different wavelengths. . . ." (Wright, 1949, p. 14). Its basic unit, the *lumen*, is the flux emitted by a point source of one standard *candle* [1] within a unit solid angle, such a source producing 4π lumens.

Luminance, or photometric brightness, the luminous flux radiated in a given direction by a unit area of a surface normal to that direction, can be expressed in lumens/cm^2 (lamberts), or if per foot-square or meter-square, as one foot-lambert or meter-lambert. *Illumination*, the lumens falling on a given unit area of a similarly normal surface, and varying inversely as distance from the source, is expressed as foot-candles (ft-c) or meter-candles (lux). A meter-candle is the intensity of illumination at one meter from a point source of one candlepower. If a surface is perfectly diffusing, and the illumination 10^4 lux, the luminance is one lambert. Both luminance and illumination can be measured directly by various photoelectric and photovoltaic cells. This is not true of *retinal illuminance*, which is expressed in *trolands*, the latter defined as equal to "the luminance of 1 candle per square meter when the area of the entrance pupil of the eye is 1 square millimeter" (Burnham *et al.*, 1963, p. 111).

THE HUMAN VISUAL SYSTEM

The Adult Visual System. The visual system consists of the eyes, which contain the optical and photoreceptor elements (rods and cones of the retina) as well as the first neural transmission elements of the system, and the pathways which lead, via the lateral geniculate bodies, to the visual projection area (Brodmann area 17). This is the path for ". . . those optic impulses which reach consciousness" (Brodal, 1959, p. 122). To this we must add a muscular system for adjustments, motions, and positioning of the eyes; the pretectal regions (and probably the superior colliculi) involved in certain of the adjustments and movements; a portion of the frontal cortex (area 8 especially) necessary in man for voluntary conjugate movements; and cortical association areas for interpretation of sense data, sensory integration, and memory (areas 18 and 19). In man the visual cortex has become the center for primary

[1]. An area 1 cm^2 of the surface of a full radiator at the temperature at which platinum solidifies has a luminous intensity of 60 candles in the direction normal to the surface.

visual reactions—fixation, reflex direction of eyes to light, accommodation, and so on. The anatomy and function of the human visual system are too complex to be summarized easily and clearly, and the reader is referred to the many individual and collaborative works now available and well represented by Davson's book on the physiology of the eye

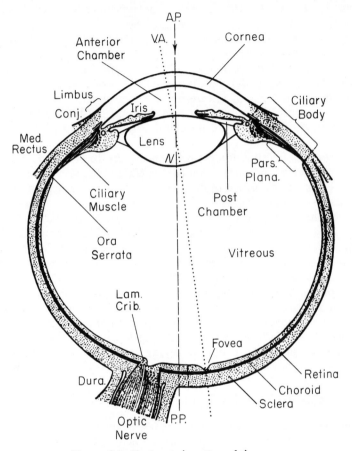

Figure 2.1. *Horizontal section of the eye.*

(P. P.) posterior pole; (A. P.) anterior pole; (V. A.) visual axis. (From Davson, *Physiology of the Eye,* 1963.)

(1963) in addition to the four-volume series edited by Davson (1962). We will note only a few points and terms which have special relevance for the studies to be reviewed.

The globe of the adult eye is about 24 mm in diameter. The innermost lining, the retina, contains an outer layer of pigmented epithelium and, inwardly, layers of photoreceptor cells, connecting nerve cells, and ganglion cells (see Fig. 2.1). The axons of the latter converge to a point in the nasal portion of the retina, their departure at the optic nerve being marked by a pale circular area known as the optic disc or "blind spot." Lateral to this disc and the optic axis of the eye is the fovea, about .3 to .4 mm in diameter and essentially rod free. Stimulation of this site provides the clearest daylight or photopic vision.

The optical mechanism of the eye, concerned with focusing images on the retina, consists of the cornea, the aqueous humor, the lens, and the vitreous body. The image is inverted relative to the external object; nevertheless, the object is normally perceived as upright and of "correct" size. Changes in the distance of observed objects require changes in focus; these are accomplished by increases or decreases in lens curvature (accommodation). *Near focus*, or accommodation for near objects, originates in contraction of the ciliary muscles which permits relaxation of suspensory ligaments and "bulging" of the lens. There is a decrease with age in the range of accommodation, the linear distance between near and far points of clear focus. In terms of diopters—the diopter being defined as the reciprocal of focal length in meters—the child has a range of 16 D and the older adult, 1 D. Accommodation for near objects is generally accompanied by convergence of the eyes and constriction of the pupils, the combined reaction being known as the *near response*. The pupillary change improves depth of focus and reduces the effects of chromatic and spherical aberrations on acuity.

The amount of illumination to which the eye is exposed affects pupil size, and pupil size, in turn, affects the amount of light entering the eye. The diameter of the pupil can vary from about 2 to 8 mm, hence pupil size changes can effect a sixteen-fold change in amount of light reaching the retina. The *light reflex*, the constriction of the pupil upon reception of light by the rods and cones, is subcortical in origin, and consensual as well as direct, i.e., stimulation of one eye produces constriction in both pupils. Pupillary constriction as well as the other components of the near response can also be elicited by electrical stimulation of the cortical occipital eye field. Dilatation results from decreased illumination or, as the *psychosensory reflex*, in response to a variety of sensory and "psychic" stimuli from the central and autonomic nervous systems.

Figure 2.2 (from Polyak, 1941) conveys some idea of the structural and functional complexity of the retina. About 110,000,000 rods and 6,500,000 cones converge on 1,000,000 optic nerve fibers which in turn connect with 500,000 cells in the lateral geniculate. Functionally, the rods and cones lie between the optical apparatus and optic nerves, the foveal cones being generally held to have single connections to ganglion cells in contrast to the multiple connections of the rods and extrafoveal cones. Convergence is more marked in the predominantly "rod" areas (beyond 1.5° from the foveal center). Maximal cone representation is at the foveal center and maximal rod density at about 15° to 20° from that center.

Generally, observed physiological differences will parallel the distribution and neural organization as well as the structural and absorption characteristics of rods and cones. *Spatial induction* (the influence of one part of the retina upon another) and *temporal induction* (the effect of prior upon succeeding stimuli) lead to simultaneous and successive contrast which, along with *adaptation* (a change of state resulting from prolonged stimulation), are affected by the above factors. Photopic acuity and color discrimination are best in the fovea, while light sensitivity and scotopic acuity are maximal at about 15° to 20°. Maximal visual acuity, defined by Brindley (1960, p. 174) as "the angular resolving power of vision, or the least angular difference between two

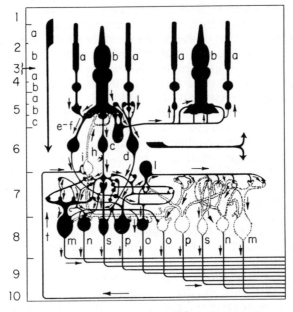

Figure 2.2. *General scheme of the primate retina.*

(a, b) Rods and cones, or the photoreceptors where the nervous impulses are generated by physical "light" (in the scheme only the left group of the photoreceptors is assumed to be stimulated by light); (c) horizontal cells by means of which the impulses are transmitted to the surrounding rods and cones; (d, e, f, h) centripetal bipolar cells of the mop, brush, flat, and midget varieties, which "transmit" the impulses from the photoreceptors to the ganglion cells, the bipolars serving as "analysers"; (i) centrifugal bipolar cell, a variety of the "amacrine cells," which probably receives the impulses from the centripetal bipolars, from the ganglion cells, and also from the brain by way of the centrifugal or efferent fibers (t) and transmits them back upon the photoreceptors (a, b); (1) an "amacrine cell" which possibly intercepts a part of the bipolar impulses and spreads them over the surrounding territory; (m, n, o, p, s) ganglion cells which receive impulses from the centripetal bipolars and transmit them to the brain along their axons called "optic nerve fibers." (From Polyak, *The Retina*, 1941.)

contours that can be distinguished from each other visually," the *minimum separable*, is limited in the fovea by cone size and spacing. Perimetric studies of color sensitivity and discrimination have indicated that the periphery is essentially "colorless" and the fovea the center for color discrimination. Both acuity and color discrimination, however, are probably at least partially determined by processes in more central neurons of the visual system.

The "duplicity theory of vision," proposed by Max Schultze, is consistent with many of the facts of vision. Schultze concluded, according to Pirenne (1962, p. 25) that ". . . in the human retina, the cones work at high intensities only and give sharp, colored vision, whereas the rods function in dim light and mediate colorless, blurred vision." The existence of two systems is also suggested by the Purkinje effect—the shift in brightness values of colors with changes in illumination level, blues becoming relatively brighter than reds as illumination decreases. The mesopic or Purkinje section of the range of visual sensitivity (1 to 10^{10} log units) involves both rods and cones, and the curves of differential sensitivity to wavelength produced in this section lie between the luminosity curves obtained at the scotopic (10^{-6} to 10^{-3} cd/m^2) and photopic (10 to 10^4 cd/m^2) portions of the range. Correspondingly, the spectral absorption curves for rhodopsin (the known rod pigment), particularly, and iodopsin (a proposed cone pigment) are similar to the scotopic and photopic luminosity curves, and times for pigment regeneration are comparable to times required for cone and rod adaptation under conditions of dark adaptation (about 7 and 30 minutes, respectively). Other evidence for two systems is offered by the typical two-stage curves describing increases in acuity and critical flicker frequency with increasing luminance and the changes in threshold sensitivity obtained with dark adaptation, the stages reflecting the relative activity and sensitivities of the cones and rods (and their pigments).

The optic tract from the optic chiasma to the geniculate is made up of optic nerve fibers from the nasal half of the contralateral retina (these having crossed at the chiasma) and the uncrossed fibers from the temporal half of the homolateral retina. This arrangement, along with the 120° overlap of the two monocular fields, channels impulses from corresponding points of the retinae (points in the nasal portion of one retina overlapping those in the temporal portion of the other) to adjacent areas of the same visual cortex. Here the two "representations" are fused into a single visual percept. The retina appears to have point-to-point representation in the lateral geniculate as well as the visual cortex. In the latter, the more central portions are represented at the occipital tip while the periphery is represented more anteriorly and proportionately less.

The muscular apparatus of the eye consists of both smooth, intrinsic and striated, extrinsic muscles. Intrinsic muscles control adjustments of the lens and pupil while six extrinsic muscles control various movements (rotations) of each eyeball. Both extrinsic and intrinsic muscles are involved in eyelid opening and closure which serves, in conjunction with the lacrimal glands, to protect the cornea and conjunctiva (McEwen, 1962). The normal result of the adjustments and movements is that the eye is directed toward the object of regard and focused so that the clearest possible image falls on the fovea. Steady fixation, under normal conditions, is brief, and rapid saccadic "flicks" serve to recover fixation of fixed or moving objects. The *fixation reflex*, which, according to Davson, is both response to peripheral stimulation and maintenance of fixation, is representative of "psycho-optical reflexes (opticokinetic nystagmus, visual righting reflexes, corrective fusion movements) in which light patterns are the primary stimulus.

Eye movements and reflexes do not in themselves provide a physiological basis for the *projection of the retina into space*. A number of experimental and clinical observations, in fact, suggest that the stability of objects is dependent upon innervation to the muscles rather than feedback from them. The question of the essential cue for the apparent direction of objects is an important one for space perception, and the reader is referred to Davson's detailed discussion.

The Infant Visual System. Visual response in the infant is limited although, with the exception of the fovea, all parts of the eye necessary for sight are completely formed at birth (Peiper, 1963). The infant eye is characterized by an incompletely developed fovea, a relatively "short" eyeball (from 16 to 19 mm in diameter), a relatively large and spherical lens, and incomplete myelination of the optic nerve fibers, the optic disc consequently appearing gray rather than white in color. Foveal immaturity in infants, together with difficulties in accommodation and ocular muscle imbalance, result in poor fixation, focusing, and coordination of eye movements. Consensual pupillary reactions are present at birth, but both constriction and dilation (especially the latter) are sluggish. Available evidence suggests that adult latencies of .2 to .3 second for constriction, and .3 to .5 second for dilation, are not attained until the twelfth year.

The shortness of the eyeball in infants, together with a relatively high refractive index of the cornea, results in a tendency toward hyperopia or farsightedness. This condition is found in about 75 per cent of newborn infants, and about 30 per cent show astigmatism (Cook & Glasscock, 1951). Mann (1964) states that hyperopia is generally between +3 and +6 diopters (in terms of the necessary correcting lens). According to Brown (1961), hypermetropia tends to increase up to the age of six or seven years. A myopic (nearsighted) tendency is then produced by the lengthening of the eyeball (about 5 to 6 mm) being offset by decreases in refracting power of the lens. Early changes in ability to accommodate are probably related to the postnatal growth of the circular fibers of the ciliary muscles. According to the data of Haynes, White, and Held (1965), these changes are apparently sufficient to enable the four-month-old infant to approximate an adult level of performance. These investigators used "dynamic retinoscopy," a sharply focused streak of light projected through the pupillary opening, with modifications in the reflected image as the index of the refractive state of the eye. They found that while the "alert, newborn infant" can focus his eye only on targets at a particular distance (19 cm on the average), the four-month infant can accommodate rapidly to changes in target distance and about as accurately as can the normal adult.

The retina is not fully differentiated at birth. Mann (1964) writes that the period from the eighth month of intrauterine existence to the fourth postnatal month is the period within which the cone nuclei increase in number, and the cones themselves become highly specialized. Myelination of optic fibers is not complete, and the fact that acceleration of the process is observed in both premature and full term infants after birth suggests that light may facilitate development (Zubek & Solberg, 1954). While the relation of myelination to function is not entirely clear, it apparently is necessary for an adult level of functioning.

Little can be said about the level of maturation of the rest of the visual system at birth. Studies of EEG activity, alpha waves in particular, indicate that although the occipital cortex first shows activity by the fourth month at three to four cycles per second, the adult alpha rate of ten cycles per second is not observed until the age of twelve. Heck and Zetterström (1958), in an analysis of "on- and off-response" activity in the visual cortex of subjects from twelve hours to twenty-one years of age, found that of forty subjects less than one year of age, none responded to single, one-second stimuli at 700 to 1000 lux and only a few subjects to flicker stimuli. They suggest that the relaying of light stimuli from the retina might be hampered by incomplete myelination of the nerve fibers.

According to Mann (1964), the six extraocular muscles can be recognized at about one to one and one-half fetal months; the third, fourth, and sixth cranial nerves that supply these muscles arise about the same time. The ophthalmic and lacrimal branches of the fifth nerve are also visible then. In the newborn, stimulation of the areas served by the fifth nerve, (including the cornea, conjunctiva, and lid) results in the *corneal* or *sensory blink reflex*. The *optical blink reflex*, caused by bright light or an approaching object, apparently has the optic nerve as its afferent link. The eyes often function independently at birth although conjugate movements and opticokinetic nystagmus can be observed (Alpern, 1962). Brown (1961) states that coordination of the muscles is learned gradually from the age of six weeks onward, and that lapses from the straight position become less frequent as binocular vision improves. During the first six weeks fixation is probably monocular and essentially reflex: in the first few days of life fixation is limited to a light or a distinct, large object within a distance of two feet. Binocular fixation develops with foveal maturity subsequent to the period in which fixation is monocular and alternating. From about four months of age, visual acuity, voluntary convergence, and binocular vision show rapid improvement.

Neither the blinking nor the lacrimal apparatus is well developed in the newborn. The sensory blink is present but the optical blink reflex is probably absent until the fourth or fifth postnatal month. McEwen (1962) states that there is generally only a low rate of blinking. With respect to tear production, he comments that the necessary neural equipment is not complete until one to seven weeks after birth, so that the infant is able to cry but can neither "tear" nor weep.

Response and Method. The measurable responses of the young infant and child that have been used in studies of sensory development can be classified as general motor activity and as specific reactions such as physiological changes (EEG, ERG, respiration, pulse), reflexes (pupillary, blinking, eye-on-the-neck), and voluntary responses (fixation, pursuit, reaching, grasping, naming, matching to standard). The particular measure employed is determined by the subject's age level and capacity as well as by the experimental design, apparatus, and procedure.

In general, the measurement of color discrimination, brightness discrimination, and acuity should be made with some control for the various capacities of the visual apparatus. For example, as Riesen comments, with reference to use of opticokinetic nystagmus as an indicator of acuity, the sensitivity of the peripheral retina to motion *per se* could be a confounding factor (1960).

BASIC VISUAL CAPACITIES

Sherman and Sherman (1925) used a small flashlight as a stimulus in a dimly lit room to obtain constriction in 96 full term infants ranging in age from one hour to twelve days. The pupillary reflex was very sluggish up to twelve hours and sluggish or good in infants from twelve to thirty-four hours of age. Sherman *et al.* (1936) varied the intensity of light and concluded, from data obtained with 273 infants, that the pupillary reflex becomes more adequate with age and that it varies with stimulus intensity, although the relation of pupil size to intensity is not entirely consistent. Guernsey (1929) obtained similar results for 25 infants who were eight hours to six months of age. The average pupil size varied from about 1 mm in diameter at birth to 1.3 mm at six months. These values are somewhat less than those cited as typical by Peiper (1963). The findings reviewed by Peiper also indicate that pupillary "unrest," the consensual alternation of constriction and dilation of the adult pupil under diffuse light, develops slowly over the first four or five months. Such "unrest" is generally considered to be centrally determined.

A number of studies have demonstrated differential effects on general motor activity and certain specific responses that can be related to length of dark adaptation and to variations in stimulus intensity. Stabilimeter-polygraphic records of activity changes, in terms of oscillations per time unit or number of active seconds per minute, as well as observational records of crying and activity generally indicate that inhibition of activity increases with stimulus intensity, and that sensitivity to light increases with length of dark adaptation. Irwin and Weiss (1934), with 67 infants less than ten days of age, found that following 30 minutes of dark adaptation activity increased under a *minimal* light condition (approximately .002 ft-c) but not under a *dim* (.02 ft-c) or *moderate* (3.9 ft-c) light condition. Activity in the dark adaptation period was not necessarily maximum, as had been suggested by Weiss' earlier findings. Weiss (1934) had used the same light stimulus values as well as two levels of a 420 cps tone (50 and 75 db) to study the separate and combined effects of light and sound stimulation. Both polygraphic and observational records were kept of activity during five minutes of dim light (the control period) and six minutes of minimal or moderate light. It was found that, relative to the control period, moderate light decreased activity and minimal light increased it. Weiss found that sound stimulation also inhibited activity and that a combination of moderate light and a 75 db tone was most inhibiting.

Redfield (1937) used a different method to confirm Weiss' finding that general activity in neonates is inversely related to light intensity. She first exposed her subjects, age seven to nine days, to one of four periods of dark adaptation—either one, five, ten, or twenty minutes. Immediately thereafter, the illumination was raised 1.5 ft-c for all infants for a five-minute test period. Redfield reasoned that increased sensitivity to light resulting from longer periods of dark adaptation should enhance the quieting effect of subsequent illumination. Her prediction was confirmed: the longer the preceding dark-adaptation period had been, the less the infant cried and the lower his general activity. In a subsequent study (1939), Redfield again found that light had a generally inhibiting effect and that sensitivity increased with dark adaptation.

Irwin (1941) studied the activity of more than 300 infants under ten days of age as a function of three intensities of light (5, 25, and 50 ft-c) following dark adaptation. He found that activity decreased inversely with light intensity. Conversely, activity increased when a preliminary light-adaptation period was followed by a dark-adaptation period. Bronshtein *et al.* (1958), using suppression of the sucking response as a measure, found similar relations to stimulus intensity for both light and sound.

These studies indicate that there is appreciable sensitivity to light in the early days of life but give little information as to thresholds. Two studies primarily concerned with the relation of vitamin A intake to sensitivity are more informative although the subjects are beyond the neonatal period. Friderischsen and Edmund (1937) tested 106 infants, 88 of whom were between one and ten months of age and the remainder, between twelve and twenty-four months. The basic responses observed were *mimic* (squeezing eyelids together, raising of eyebrows, "frowns") and *oculomotor* (eyes moving rapidly and together towards light). Head turns and grasping were observed in older subjects. Each infant was first dark adapted for thirty minutes. A lamp was positioned while unlit at 10 cm from the eyes of the infant with the filters for weakest transmission in place, a Tscherning glass No. 6.50. The lamp then flashed for one or two seconds on about a dozen trials, at various spatial positions. Filters were changed as necessary to obtain the minimum reflexible point of response. Data presented for two "very young" subjects that were obtained over a ninety-minute dark-adaptation period indicate changes in sensitivity of about two log units, that is from a 4.00 or 4.25 glass at two minutes to about 6.00 or 6.25 at ten and ninety minutes. This drop may represent cone changes primarily. Lewis and Haig (1939) used head movement as a response. This was observed in a darkened room by means of the extent of movement of a vial of radium paint fastened to subject's forehead. The subjects, from about one to ten months of age, were dark adapted for thirty minutes. A light of variable intensity was then presented at 10 cm and moved back and forth over an arc of 180°. Filters were used to control intensity, and the lowest intensity that evoked a response was taken as threshold. The mean value for the 26 infants was 2.9 log units, with a range of 2.4 to 3.3. For a large control group of adults and older children tested in a similar fashion, the mean value was 2.1 log units, with a range of 1.6 to 2.5. Threshold and age were not systematically related over the ages tested. Neither study found a consistent relation between vitamin A intake and sensitivity, although in cases of actual deficiency administration was helpful.

By the end of the first year of life the absolute threshold seems quite comparable to that of the adult human. While the ERG studies of Zetterström (1951, 1952) and the EEG study by Heck and Zetterström (1958) suggest some limitations with respect to light reception and transmission at the periphery and possibly in the pathways to the visual cortex, there appears little question of the infant's capacity to respond to light energy *per se*. There is also evidence, stemming from studies by Peiper (1926) and Trincker and Trincker (1955) that differential sensitivity to hue can be demonstrated in the first few days of life.

A number of studies have dealt with the development of monocular and binocular fixation, pursuit movements, and eye coordination. Sherman and Sherman (1925) observed movements made in a darkened room in response to a lighted flashlight moved through a limited arc 15 inches distant from the subject. Uncoordinated movements predominated at first, although all subjects showed good coordination by thirty-four hours of age. Overall, 20 of the 96 subjects could fixate but not coordinate well up to thirty-four hours.

Ling (1942) studied the development of sustained visual fixation and eye movements as well as postural responses and other phenomena associated with fixation, e.g., diverted regards, blinking, and size of palpebral fissure. Her subjects were twenty-five infants from seven minutes to twenty-four weeks of age at the start of the experiment. The study lasted ten weeks. The results were briefly as follows. Sustained visual fixation was absent at birth; it appeared in rudimentary form a few hours later and peaked at four to five weeks. Eye postures and movements of fixation developed in four stages—monocular fixation, monocular dominance, alternation of dominance, and binocular fixation. Binocular fixation appeared at about seven weeks and was characterized by convergence which, although initially jerky, became smooth and continuous with time and practice. Conjugate deviations, important for fixation, were functional at birth but the coordinate compensatory movements needed for stable fixation with head movement were not effective until four to five weeks. Both frequency of blinking and size of palpebral fissure were affected by intensity of illumination and by growth. With age, blinking decreased in frequency, while the palpebral fissure increased in size, although individual differences were marked and consistent. The general developmental picture presented by Ling's data is supported by a study by Kistiakovskaya (1959) on infants from ten days to three months of age.

Ling makes two statements on the development of fixation that are particularly worth noting. The first is simply that the disagreement among various investigators as to age of first fixation is probably a matter of difference in experimental situations and procedures. The second is that the early "fixations" reported by some observers are probably peripheral rather than central ocular responses. They are, that is, essentially passive and slow and lack the characteristic body and head immobilization typical of active fixation. Ling considers them as more representative of diffuse sensitivity to light and darkness than of specific isolation and localization of an object.

In a recent study of fixation, Dayton *et al.* (1964b), used stimulus presentation apparatus similar to McGinnis' in combination with electrooculographic recording (the recording of changes in corneal-retinal potential occasioned by eye movement). The targets, black dots four inches in diameter on a white field, moved over the inner surface of the semispherical experimental chamber at 16° per second. Illumination was kept constant at 25 ft-c. The investigators found that of the 45 infants tested, who ranged in age from eight hours to ten days, 17 demonstrated fixation reflexes, and that the tracings appeared similar for both eyes. They also reported that saccadic movements were relatively coarse, indicating an underdeveloped feedback mechanism. Some differences were noted between infants as to "quality" of following (type of saccadic movements and maintenance of fixation). The size of the target and lack of precise fixation point, as well as the observed "coarseness" of saccades, would seem to raise some question as to the basis for fixation.

Guernsey (1929) reported than 60 per cent of the eye movements of subjects under two weeks of age were uncoordinated as compared with only 30 per cent over six weeks. About 80 per cent gave blinking reflexes but only to actual contact or intense light stimuli. Fixation was still absent during the second month. McGinnis (1930) obtained clear evidence for optokinetic nystagmus in the first few hours after birth. The number of responses was influenced by the number and speeed of the stripes making up the moving visual field as well as by the subject's age. Pursuit, the smooth tracking of an object with few opposed movements had a slower development; it was observable only at five to six weeks. Beasley (1933) studied vertical, horizontal, and circular pursuit movements in 251 infants, from two and one-half hours to twelve days of life, using three different types of stimuli: a diffuse spot of light presented in a darkened field, the experimenter's hand, and a dark blue cylinder in a dimly lighted field. The order of appearance of the types of pursuit was similar to that obtained in older subjects by Jones (1926) and Morgan and Morgan (1944).

M. C. Jones (1926) observed the response of 365 infants to movements of a small flashlight presented at a distance of one foot in a lighted room. Horizontal, vertical, and rotary pursuit movements were first noted at fifteen, thirty-five, and sixty-five days, respectively. All infants followed horizontally by 105 days and in the other directions, by 125 days. Although blinking to facial contact was present at birth, "defensive" blinking was first noted at forty-five days, and in all subjects, by one hundred and twenty-five days. Jones comments that while the eyes appear well-coordinated at birth and turn slowly towards the light, neither true fixation nor following is present at that time. Morgan and Morgan (1944) followed eighteen infants over the first ninety days of life with respect to both pursuit and response to social stimulation. The pursuit stimulus was a red, white, and blue pinwheel, six inches in diameter, presented at a distance of fourteen inches. In 75 per cent of the infants, fixation was present at 5 to 10 days, brief horizontal pursuit at 11 to 15 days, and continuous pursuit at 46 to 50 days. A moving person evoked brief pursuit at 36 to 46 days and continuous pursuit at 61 to 65 days.

Schneidemann and Robinette (1932) were unable to obtain data on eye dominance in subjects less than two years old by using a simple "pin-hole" test. Updegraff (1932) could not obtain reliable data below the age of three with a V-scope, a truncated cone that restricted viewing of an object to the use of one eye or the other. Updegraff concluded that either the test was not reliable at that age or that eye dominance was not established before three years.

In summary, there is ample evidence of light sensitivity in the young infant. There are also some data suggesting that at the age of one month the infant has an absolute threshold possibly two log units higher than the adult's as well as photopic and scotopic luminosity curves similar to those of the adult. While fixation of light appears soon after birth, it is generally held that fixation of objects at that time is neither sustained nor accurate enough to permit smooth pursuit movements and binocular fixation. Foveal immaturity, together with deficiencies in accommodation due to incomplete development of the ciliary muscles and to the proportions of the eyeball, may result in lack of clarity of retinal image. Even though optokinetic nystagmus can be demonstrated shortly after birth, convergence and coordinating movements of the eyes are passive and slow (and more reflexive) than is true later. The pupillary response, blinking, and the palpebral response show a similar gradual development.

VISUAL ACUITY

Visual acuity, or resolving capacity of the eye, is typically assessed in terms of either minimum detectable separation of two contours (minimum separable acuity), or minimum detectable width of a line against a uniform background (minimum visible acuity). The usual index of acuity is defined as the reciprocal of the angle (in minutes) subtended by the minimum detectable distance separating two contours.

Often, however, acuity is described in Snellen notation, which relates an observer's resolving capacity to some standard in terms of relative viewing distance: a Snellen notation of 20/30, for example, would indicate that the observer's performance at twenty feet is equivalent to that of "standard" observer at thirty feet. The standard is usually taken to be a visual acuity of 1.0, which is approximately the average minimum separable acuity for adults with normal vision. Using this standard, then, if an observer is able to discern a space between two contours separated by an angular distance of one minute, he is said to have acuity of D/D, where D is the distance at which the test is conducted.

One of the earliest studies of acuity in young children was reported by Peckham (1933). Pictures of familiar objects of various sizes were presented at a distance of ten feet, and on each presentation the subject was told to select from a tray of block replicas of the pictures, that block matching the picture. The range of sizes of pictures was such that the smallest, with an overall width of one-quarter inch, had elements subtending one minute of arc at ten feet, and the elements of the largest subtended an angle of one minute at one hundred feet. Acuity for each subject was determined in terms of the smallest pictures that could be identified accurately. Of the nineteen children tested, ranging in age from twenty-one to sixty-two months, fifteen identified the smallest pictures correctly under binocular viewing conditions. Accordingly, they were assumed to have acuities of 10/10 or better. The youngest subject (twenty-one months) had the poorest acuity (10/30) while all subjects forty-five months or older were given Snellen ratings of 10/10. Since the older subjects were able to detect elements subtending ·a visual angle of one minute, Peckham interpreted these data as indicating that children under four years old tend to have visual acuity comparable to adults. The data do not really support this conclusion, however: the one-minute norm for adults applies to *minimum separable* acuity, whereas Peckham's picture-identification test (1933) involved something more like *minimum visible* acuity. In addition, other studies have shown that adults are able to detect lines subtending angles of the order of one minute (e.g., see Geldard, 1953).

Because of language factors, tests of acuity in children less than two years of age have relied heavily on estimates made on the basis of fixation and following of various size cubes (often black) moved against a background (often white) at a prescribed distance (usually less than two feet). Such tests, as summarized by Evans (1946), give values for acuity of 6/728 at three to four months, 6/288 at six months, and 6/72 at nine months to two years. Other tests, *E* charts and picture tests, give values of 6/12 to 6/9 at three to five years.

The usefulness, reliability, and possible equivalence of various acuity tests for children have also been investigated by Allen (1957) and Jonkers (1958). Allen discusses such issues as the importance of rapport between examiner and child, the intrinsic interest of the test, its sensitivity, the degree to which it permits uniformity of response, and conditions of illumination (he recommends 12 to 18 ft-c as a desirable level of illumination). For Allen, a primary object of testing acuity in preschool children is the detection of amblyopia, the failure of development of acuity in an eye free of organic disease, and a condition often missed in objective examinations. With these considerations in mind, Allen devised a picture identification test that consists of familiar pictures calibrated to the E chart. Jonkers' study (1958) of the relative reliability and accuracy of letter charts, figure charts, pictures, broken circles (Landolt Cs), and E-hooks is also of considerable interest although his subjects were somewhat older. Jonkers found that reliability was greatest for letter charts and least for pictures. If letter charts are considered as "standard," E-hooks give reasonably similar acuity estimates; Landolt Cs gave lower values, however, except at visual acuities of 1.0 and 0.9.

Evans (1946) devised a simple test that capitalizes on the infant's tendency to attend visually to specks and moving objects. The stimulus consists of movement of various sizes of iron filings and ball bearings over a white visual field; the movement is controlled by motion of a tiny magnet on the opposed side of the surface. Since the response is to movement, the test does not measure acuity *per se*, as Evans notes. He also points out that amblyopia can be detected with this test by first covering one eye and then the other. With the good eye covered, the child tries to move the covering hand away in order to watch the moving speck. Schwarting (1954) similarly takes advantage of early visual reflex and curiosity. The infant, in a darkened room, observes the movement of various sizes of steel wire across an illuminated frosted glass field at a distance of one meter, visual acuity being assessed in terms of the smallest wire eliciting smooth following movements.

Several studies have attempted to measure visual acuity by means of opticokinetic nystagmus or visual following. The methodological forerunner of these was McGinnis' study, described earlier, in which the nystagmus response was induced by a moving visual field carried by a rotating cylinder, the infant having been placed in a crib along the axis of rotation. The targets, consisting of one bar or ten bars, each subtending 5° to 6° at the eye, could be moved at various speeds— about 10°, 20°, and 40° per second. Opticokinetic nystagmus consists of slow visual movements in the direction of motion of the field and opposed quick jerks to new points of fixation. McGinnis (1930) found that it appeared at the slow and medium speeds, and that the number of responses varied with the number of bars.

Gorman, Cogan, and Gellis (1957) had been unable to elicit opticokinetic nystagmus with a vertically-lined kymographic drum. They then designed an apparatus based on that which McGinnis had used. It permitted the movement of a sixteen-foot roll of paper, nine inches wide, at a controlled speed of 8.5° per second. The first eight feet carried a pattern of white and black stripes each subtending 11.1' of arc and the second eight feet, similar stripes subtending 33.5' of arc. If there was no response to the finer pattern, the cruder pattern was used. The viewing distance, with the infant at the center of rotation, was six inches. Two 25-watt floodlights provided illumination. The one hundred subjects, with a single exception, were from one hour to five days old. Their responses were rated as excellent, good, fair, or negative (nystagmus absent). A positive response was indicated by widening of the palpebral fissure followed by slow, smooth following and saccadic returns to center. Of the ninety-three positive responses fifty-two were excellent, thirty-one were good, and ten fair. The response to the crude pattern was equivalent to a Snellen fraction of 20/670, and the authors considered it a minimal estimate of static acuity. The same authors (1959) found similar results for an increased range of line patterns and a second group of one hundred subjects under four days of age. All subjects responded to 20/450 patterns, and the majority to 20/350. (Reinecke and Cogan [1958] administered both the nystagmus test and Snellen test on a double-blind basis to a large number of older subjects. Snellen acuity was always greater than opticokinetic acuity although the correlation between the two was .664.)

Fantz, Ordy, and Udelf (1962) compared estimates of visual acuity obtained by opticokinetic nystagmus with those made by a "differential fixation test of visual acuity" (Fantz, 1959). Essentially, this test employs grid patterns of varying degrees of fineness paired with homogeneous gray areas of equivalent brightness, the response measure being preference, as indexed by relative fixation time or number of fixations. Location of target reflection in either pupil is taken as indicating fixation as long as the alternate target does not appear in the other pupil. (Such binocular disparity may occur during the first weeks of life when coordination is relatively poor.) Forty-six infants from one week to six months of age were compared on opticokinetic nystagmus and differential fixation tests of acuity. Both tests were run under similar conditions of illumination, with targets ten inches distant. Threshold values were lower for the opticokinetic nystagmus test only at one to two months; at three to four months, threshold values were lower for the differential fixation test. Fantz and his co-workers note, with respect to the opticokinetic test, that nystagmus was at times so fleeting and irregular in the younger subjects that the expected objectivity of the test was not achieved. According to them, the fixation method allows a much simpler criterion of acuity and a quantitative criterion of response on each test. Nevertheless, their data clearly indicate that a fixation time measure of acuity is considerably less sensitive, at least at the earliest age levels. (Compare the results obtained by Gorman *et al.* [1957] by means of an opticokinetic measure to those obtained by Fantz *et al.* [1962] using fixation time, for which the equivalent Snellen fraction was 20/825 for infants one month or younger.)

The observational difficulties reported by Fantz can be overcome by combining direct observation of the opticokinetic response with electro-oculographic recording of the component eye movements. Dayton *et al.* (1964a) used apparatus and stimuli similar to that already described to elicit nystagmus. Electrodes at the outer canthus (junction of upper and lower lids) of each eye and on the bridge of the nose recorded changes in resting corneal-retinal potential occasioned by eye movement. Nystagmus was recorded graphically as a "sawtooth" pattern. The subjects were 39 full term infants ranging in age from eight hours to eight days; most were one day old. Only thirteen records were of sufficient clarity to permit assessment of visual acuity. The analysis of these records suggested that binocular acuity in newborns is at least 20/150. The authors conclude that the combined recording technique produces a more reliable estimate of visual acuity in the infant than heretofore obtained.

COLOR DISCRIMINATION

Nearly a century of observations and formal experimentation has failed to provide consistent information on the development of color discrimination in the young child. Some ambiguity of findings has arisen from the diverse methods and responses used, but lack of stimulus control has also been to blame. One of the most serious problems facing the investigator is that of control for brightness. It is often assumed that luminosity curves are equivalent for infant and adult, although this assumption has been explicitly questioned by a number of researchers including Chase (1937), Holden and Bosse (1900), Munn (1955), and Riesen (1960). Peiper's study (1926) and, more recently, that of Trincker and Trincker (1955), have in fact provided behavioral data which support the assumption of similar scotopic and photopic luminosity curves for infant and adult.

Peiper (1926) used the ocular-neck reflex (or eye-on-the-neck reflex) as the indicator response; this consists in a throwing back of the head in reaction to light stimuli. Peiper found, in four premature infants, that the amplitude of the reflex depended on the color of the stimulus light and on whether the infant had been dark adapted or light adapted. Thus, while blue was twice as effective as red under dark adaptation, red was four times as effective as blue under light adaptation. Peiper concluded that he had demonstrated the Purkinje effect, that both the rods and cones of the infants were functional, and that the brightness values of the colors were similar for infants and adults.

Trincker and Trincker (1955) observed the ocular-neck reflex under conditions of dark and light adaptation. Their subjects were 18 premature and 20 full term infants. The former group was tested repeatedly from the first to the tenth week of life, and the latter group from the first to sixth week. Subjects were tested at least twice; most were seen three or four times. The light source for testing was a 200-watt "Osram-nitra" bulb. Stimulus color and intensity were controlled by colored and neutral filter combinations. Intensities of the spectral lights were equated with that of an unfiltered white light at 250 lux; they had the following wavelength limits: 430–465 mμ (violet), 465–500 mμ (blue), 550–560 mμ (green), 560–585 mμ (yellow), and 645–680 mμ (red). Threshold determinations for the various colors began at 250 lux: intensity was decreased by addition of neutral filters in 22 steps to 0.25

lux, all obtained threshold values falling within this range. The initial period of dark adaptation was thirty minutes; readaptation between tests was at least ten minutes. Similarly, initial light adaptation was for fifteen minutes at 1500 lux, with readaptation periods of five minutes. The results were evaluated in terms of threshold values translated into relative brightness values of the several colors, the lowest threshold value being taken as 100 per cent and the highest as 0 per cent.

With light adaptation, the brightness values for the colors were the same for all subjects at all ages and were similar to values typically obtained for adults, thus indicating similar photopic curves over the wavelengths tested. The cones, then, are apparently functional at birth and show little further development in the ensuing weeks. With dark adaptation, however, the "twilight" values for the newborn were different from those of the adult, and the Purkinje effect appeared to develop in three stages: (1) an increase in light value towards the yellowish-green part of the spectrum and a minor decrease in the red, (2) a significant decrease in red value which, however, remained greater than that for blue (a finding similar to Peiper's) and finally, (3) appearance of the normal Purkinje effect observed in adults, with blue having a greater brightness value than red. The first stage is observed in the first week, the second in the second and third weeks, and the last in the fourth to seventh weeks. The authors conclude that the cone apparatus has morphological and functional priority over that of the rods.

Zetterström's ERG data (1951, 1952, 1955) are not easily reconcilable with findings of Trincker and Trincker. The electroretingram, which is a record of the changes in electrical potential of the eye induced by changes in light stimulation, is composed of "negative" and "positive" components, the a-wave (or initial negative "dip") and the subsequent b-wave (the positive "rise"). These components presumably have their origins in processes occurring in the receptor and bipolar cells of the retina. Recent consensus is that each of these wave components has both photopic and scotopic elements; however, the a-wave appears to reflect primarily cone activity and the b-wave appears to be associated primarily with activity of rods. The electrical changes are recorded by use of an active electrode attached to a plastic contact lens applied to the cornea of the stimulated eye. A head band supports a neutral electrode in contact with the forehead. Some device, such as the spring speculum, is used to keep the eyelids separated. Riggs (1958) has noted that in the human eye the photopic response is overshadowed by the scotopic and that the ERG does not clearly register "the activity that is basic for the superb color vision and form perception that we know to be mediated by the human eye." He lists a number of techniques useful in obtaining ERGs; these include the use of flickering light of moderately high frequency, use of red light, and flashes of less than .04 second duration (to minimize rod participation).

Zetterström (1951, 1952, 1955) does not describe her method in detail but states that it is the method developed by Karpe (1948). Dilatation is induced by a drug such as homotropine, since pupillary constriction reduces ERG response. Karpe also uses a plastic contact glass, adjusted over the center of the cornea and filled with physiological saline, to carry the active electrode rod, a silver plate on the frontal head band that serves as the indifferent electrode. A spring speculum keeps the eyelids apart. A 25-watt bulb produces a stimulus of 1/7 sec duration, the weakly glowing lamp filament serving as the fixation point between tests. Intensity is changed by varying the distance between lamp and subject.

Zetterström (1951) presented stimuli of 20, 80, and 1,600 lux. The last was used with newborn infants who failed to respond to 80 lux. Thirty-five normal subjects were tested; of these, fourteen were retested every second or third month over the first year of life. During the first two or three days subminimal ERGs were obtained. The first b-waves to appear were of longer latency and duration but of lesser amplitude than in the adult. Adult values were only approached by the sixth month. An attenuated a-wave was observed in about 25 per cent of the subjects only at the end of the first year. Zetterström stated that no theories seemed available to explain this course of development and suggested that light, by stimulating the function of visual purple or rhodopsin, may trigger the appearance of the ERG. In a subsequent study (1952) with thirty premature newborns, Zetterström reports observations over the first three months of life. The first ERG appeared between three and forty-five days, the time of first appearance varying inversely with birth weight. The course of ERG development was similar to that observed in the first study. The fact that the ERGs appeared at similar postnatal times in both full term and premature infants led Zetterström to conclude that extrauterine factors are important.

Zetterström (1955) has also recorded flicker ERGs in thirty-five full term infants ranging from less than one week to eight weeks of age. The intensity of the white light used varied from .1 to 1,000 lux. Flicker was provided by a hand-rotated, four-sector disk, the light and dark periods being recorded synchronously with ERG by means of a photocell. *Fusion frequency* was the lowest frequency at which intermittent ERG was not produced at each flash.

Flicker ERG was absent during the first twenty-four hours after birth even with an intensity of 1000 lux. After two to three days, flicker was scotopic and maximum at 25/sec with 200–700 lux; this compares with 10–20/sec with .5–5 lux for adults. The rate increased to 35/sec with 5–10 lux by the second week and to 50/sec at less than 1 lux at six to eight weeks. Zetterström concludes that the flicker first observed (repeated small, rounded b-waves of low potential) is consistent with rod activity, and that the appearance of photopic flicker (small, negative a-waves between sharp b-waves) results from maturation of the macula (a central pigmented area of the retina). Zetterström's Fig. 7 however —a comparison of fusion curves for adults and infants over the range of .1 to 1000 lux—shows two clearly defined stages only for the adults. Some infant curves have less clearly defined turning points and briefer "scotopic" sections. On the other hand, the photopic portions of the curves for older infants and adults seem quite similar. The general picture is of cone rather than rod dominance.

Findings reported by Horsten and Winkelman (1960), Winkelman and Horsten (1962), and Barnet, Lodge, and Armington (1965) indicate that the ERG of the newborn is in fact similar to the adult ERG. Horsten and Winkelman, having noted that the ERG fails to appear in children with congenital blindness, attempted to correlate development of the ERG response in young dogs and human neonates with histological data on retinal development. Changes in the retina observed in the dog between birth and the third week of life take place in man between the fifth and eighth month of intrauterine development. The data obtained with the dogs over the first thirty-one days of life indicated that (a) electrical activity was demonstrable, given adequate dark adaptation and a stimulus of sufficient intensity at a relatively early stage of histological differentiation; and (b) that growth of rods and cones did not parallel the increase in b-potential. The latter starts to increase rapidly at the time receptor growth is slowing (about the twentieth day). These findings suggest that the ERG should certainly appear in the newborn child, given his comparatively advanced state of retinal differentiation.

Horsten and Winkelman obtained ERGs in both premature and full term infants within twenty-four hours after birth. The stimulus was produced by an electronic stroboscope of very high intensity (capacity 160,000 lux/sec) and a flash duration of .001 sec at a distance of 25 cm. In their second study (1962) they used a gas-discharge lamp with variable intensity as the light source. With a 60 lux flash, they found it was always possible to elicit ERG in newborn infants, whether premature or full term. The potentials were small and varied with light intensity and dark adaptation. Winkelman and Horsten conclude that, given a strong enough stimulus, electrical activity can be evoked in the normal infant eye and that the ERG is a valuable diagnostic and prognostic tool.

Barnet, Lodge, and Armington (1965) were particularly concerned with demonstrating the so-called x wave (the fast photopic component of the positive b-wave) in the ERG of infants because of its possible use as an index of maturation of photopic mechanisms. Barnet *et al.* assert that this wave, when elicited by light of long wavelength, is "clearly related to photopic vision." They recorded responses to a slowly flashing stimulus (three flashes per second) of long wavelength and variable intensity; these were then compared with responses to a similar series of white flashes. A Corning HR red-shade 34 filter was used to produce the colored stimulus. Since observations were made on sleeping infants, control data were obtained on adults with eyes both open and closed. The findings were as follows: ERGs obtained from infants were similar in form to the adult ERGs but smaller in amplitude. When light of long wavelength was used, a negative potential occurred soon after the stimulus and was followed by two positive deflections comparable in latency to the x wave and the b-wave of adult records.

The latency of the b-wave changed with shifts in intensity but that of the x wave remained relatively constant. In summary, the presence of the x wave in the ERG records of the infants supports the assumption that photopic vision is functional in the newborn while the b-wave itself indicates activity of the scotopic system. The findings of the last three studies are consistent, therefore, with the behavioral data reported by Trincker and Trincker (1955).

In summary, there is evidence that shortly after birth infants are sensitive to light changes under conditions of light adaptation and, by the age of one month, under conditions of dark adaptation. The Trincker and Trincker data, which receive considerable support from the recent ERG findings (particularly in regard to early photopic function), are at odds with some earlier conceptions of visual receptor cell development as well as with earlier ERG records obtained by Zetterström. Trincker and Trincker support their behavioral data by reference to the observed late development of the rods in the embryonic retina and to Walls' theory of cone-rod transmutations. In discussing Zetterström's data they point out that under certain pathological conditions the ERG may be absent in an adult possessed of relatively good vision.

We will review only a few of the studies attempting to assess color discrimination and preference over the first months of life. Chase (1937) tried to determine discrimination by recording pursuit of a colored target across a differently colored ground of equal brightness. His 24 subjects were from fifteen to seventy days old at the start of the experiment. Combinations of colors were projected, with a 500-watt tungsten lamp as the light source, against the back of a transparent paper screen parallel to and 15 inches from the subjects' eyes. The projected size of the target was 3 by 4.5 in., and the apparatus provided for target movement across but not out of the field. Chase found that infants could discriminate any one of the colors used—red, yellow-green, green, and blue-green—from any other. He was unable to equate completely the brightness of lights transmitted by the various filters for brightness (the maximum difference in brightness was 27 per cent between blue-green and yellow-green). Nevertheless the results of control tests in which brightness only of target and field was varied appear to support Chase's contention his infant subjects had discriminated color *per se*. (Note that the lack of response in the brightness control tests seems inconsistent with the Trincker and Trincker findings.)

The use of conditioning procedures and adaptation methods has produced data comparable to that obtained by preference and discrimination methods. Conditioned differentiation to colored conditional stimuli was first studied by Kasatkin and Levikova (1935). (This is discussed in Chapter 4.) Brackbill (1962) has reviewed the Soviet position that a fully stable, simple CR to a visual CS is only obtained around three months and a stable discrimination about six weeks later. She has also summarized a methodological comparison of the Bronshtein adaptation method and the classical conditioning approach reported by Zonova. In the former, onset of one stimulus produces initial suppression of ongoing nutritive sucking, followed by adaptation and renewed sucking as the stimulus is repeated. Introduction of a new (and discriminated) stimulus again leads to suppression. Hence, one may infer that the infant has discriminated between the first and second stimuli. Zonova used the adaptation method with infants from one and one-half hours to six months of age and the conditioning method with subjects from one to six months old. At four to six months the former produces a typical response (suppression of sucking) in only half the subjects, while fully stable discrimination was obtained by means of conditioning at fifty-five days in all subjects.

A number of studies have used the method of pair comparisons to measure color preference. McDougall (1908) combined the method with the grasping response in his study of two infants. Valentine (1913–14), who tested his son for a six-month period beginning when the child was three months old, noted that grasping is not sufficiently developed in early infancy to be useful as a response. He therefore adopted a method of measuring preference that had been devised by Marsden (1903) and that has since been used extensively even at the very youngest age levels. According to this method—usually called visual fixation time or, simply, fixation time—the experimenter tallies the number of seconds an infant spends looking at each of two visual stimuli of equal visibility. In Valentine's case, the stimuli were initially juxtaposed 12 inches in front of the child's face and then drawn slowly apart. Twenty years later, Staples (1932) used the fixation time method again—this time with Munsell colored papers—with infants ranging from sixty-nine days to twenty-four months. The results of these studies indicate that color preference may not even be consistent for any one child, and that there certainly is no consensual agreement among infants except a preference for colors over noncolors (unpatterned whites and grays).

In a more recent study of color preference, Spears (1964) used four Munsell papers for comparison, red 10R 4/6, yellow 5Y 5/6, blue 5B 5/6, and gray N/5. The papers were cut into bull's-eye shapes and pasted to white matteboard. Each of the ten four-month-old subjects received two presentations of a given pair. Stimulus position and order of presentation of pairs were randomized. Each pair was presented for 15 seconds during which fixation times of the stimuli were recorded on two electric clocks. An analysis of first presentation data, i.e., first viewing times for each pair for each subject, produced a significant preference only for blue over gray although eight of the ten subjects preferred red to gray as well. Second presentation data were similarly analyzed but no significant differences were found. The Kendall coefficients of group agreement for the orderings produced—blue, red, yellow and gray for first presentations and red, blue, yellow and gray for second presentations—were both significant.

At least two studies have tried to assess development trends in the relative potency or pull of color vs. shape as stimuli. The youngest subjects in an early study by Brian and Goodenough (1929) were fourteen months old. The stimuli consisted of two-dimensional and three-dimensional objects of various colors. Three of these objects were presented on each trial. One of the objects was arbitrarily designated the standard, and subject was told to choose one like it from the other two. Since two of the objects had the same color and two of them the same shape, subject could choose either on the basis of color or shape but not both. The results showed that up to the age of three, subjects matched largely on the basis of form; at four and five years, color was the predominant basis of choice; from six years on, form again predominated. In a later study, Spears (1964) used fixation time and pair comparisons to measure relative preference for two shapes and two colors (red vs. gray). His results suggested that shape dominates choice at the four-month age level.

SHAPE AND PATTERN PREFERENCE

Studies of shape or pattern discrimination and preference have a more difficult problem with stimulus definition than do those on color discrimination. In addition, concepts such as "complexity," "novelty," and "goodness" have been used with little attempt to relate them to objective stimulus properties. There exists, as Cantor comments, ". . . an imperative need for objective stipulation of stimulus properties, for unbiased stimulus presentation techniques, and for clearly delineated indices of stimulus selection behaviors" (1963, p. 29).

Fantz (1956) reported a procedure that he subsequently used to study the development of pattern preferences (1958), acuity (1959, 1962), and depth perception (1961a) in human infants. In that study he observed "ocular fixation" of a young chimpanzee to various pairs of stimuli. The measure, relative fixation time, was indicated by overlap of "reflected image and pupil," observable directly or from photographic records. To facilitate observation the subject was placed in a form-fitting crib that minimized head and body movements. The crib was then placed in an illuminated test chamber; an observation hole in the ceiling of the box permitted observation of fixations. In a second study Fantz (1958) reported data on the visual fixations (as indexed by corneal reflection) of twenty-two human infants ranging from one to fourteen weeks of age at the first of the ten weekly sessions. The four pairs of patterns or shapes were red figures of equal area on a white ground. These were presented against a gray background at a distance of one foot, one foot apart. Each pair was presented in each position for 30 seconds. Times of fixation to the left and to the right were cumulated. Over the ten weekly sessions neither the control pair, two identical red triangles, nor a cross vs. circle produced significant preferences. Of the twenty-two subjects, nineteen preferred a "checkerboard" pattern to plain red squares of equal or greater red area, and twenty preferred a red "bull's-eye" to a horizontally striped figure. This latter preference represented a reversal of initial direction of preference for subjects under seven weeks of age. Fantz suggested that the early preferences shown argue against the empiricist viewpoint on the development of vision and pattern discrimination. In writing on the "origin of form perception" (1961b) he states that while the effects of maturation are relatively clear, those of learning are more difficult to measure, and that there appears to be a complex interaction involved.

More recently (1963), Fantz has employed similar apparatus and the same response indicator with presentations of single stimuli rather than pairs. The measure was relative duration of initial gaze in successive and repeated presentations. The stimuli were circular, six inches in diameter and with nonglossy surfaces. They were presented in random order for each infant, with up to eight repetitions when possible. The eighteen subjects, from ten hours to five days of age, were selected for ability to keep their eyes open on two exposures of each of the six targets. The targets, patterned and unpatterned, were arranged in order of decreasing reflectance: yellow, white, newsprint, schematic face, concentric circles, and red. Blue felt lining provided a constrasting background, and illumination (10 to 15 candles) was produced by baffled lamps at the sides of the infant's head. The rankings for infants under forty-eight hours of age, infants from two to five days old, and infants from two to six months old were all significant and quite similar. For example, the preference ranking for the youngest group was face, circles, newsprint, white, yellow, and red. There was an obvious preference for patterned over unpatterned stimuli, while hue and reflectance, often thought to be "primary visual stimuli," were not particularly effective. Fantz believes that these and other data contradict the view that the visual world of the infant is initially formless and chaotic.

Berlyne (1958) used the method of pair comparisons, and a response measure of first fixations, in an attempt to determine the influence of albedo and complexity on visual fixation in fourteen subjects ranging from three to nine months of age. Complexity was equated with amount of contour. Berlyne's control for experimental bias is worth noting: the observer was unaware of the stimuli presented on experimental trials.

Spears (1964) also used a pair comparisons procedure, with relative fixation time, as indicated by direct observation of line of sight, as the measure of preference. Five groups of ten subjects each, all about four months of age, were presented with sets of stimuli varying in shape or in shape and color. Most of the basic stimulus shapes had been chosen from those used by Fantz and by Berlyne, and the apparatus was similar to that developed by Fantz. Complexity was operationally defined in terms of amount of contour, number of turns in the pattern, and degree of symmetry, both rotational and translational.

The results were analyzed separately by first and second presentations of pairs. The results of both analyses were quite similar: none of the quantifying measures proved to be consistently related to the response rankings, although contour showed a trend in this direction. Some "negative" evidence for the importance of contour is perhaps offered by findings from a subsequent study by Spears (1966) in which no preferences were obtained from a series of five regular polygonal figures, reasonably equivalent with respect to area and contour and identical in color.

Hershenson (1964) has reported on the preferences of newborn infants, two to four days of age, for stimuli varying in brightness or in complexity. Complexity was defined as the "number of dark-light transitions in a stimulus"; the three corresponding stimuli consisted of checkerboard patterns of varying degrees of fineness. The three stimuli for brightness, "patches of light projected onto the stimulus screen," were 3.56, 35.6, and 356 apparent ft-c, respectively. A pair comparisons method was used. Twenty subjects were used in the brightness study and sixteen in the study of complexity. Both studies were run in a completely dark condition, with corneal reflections as the indicator of fixation. The point of fixation was determined from infrared photographic records taken at 60 frames per minute. The results in brief were as follows: (1) In the brightness experiment, the stimulus of intermediate intensity was significantly preferred to the other two, as was the bright to the dim stimulus; (2) in the complexity experiment the least complex pattern was significantly preferred to the most complex.

Hershenson's study and findings are of considerable interest. His incidental observations of conjugate fixation and coordinated eye movement in these very young infants are in contradiction to a number of other findings but are possibly a matter of the experimental conditions, since the responses in this case were to light stimuli in a dark field. (See Dayton et al., however, 1964b.) It seems reasonable to question whether Hershenson's subjects were sufficiently dark adapted to give completely comparable data on the several brightnesses of stimuli. His data on complexity and preference are, of course, contrary to what has been generally found, but in view of the confusion as to what constitutes "complexity," it would be difficult to rule conclusively on their validity.

Stechler (1964) presented three stimuli, singly and in random order, for nine one-minute periods to twenty normal, full term babies, two to four days old. The stimuli were a plain sheet of white paper, a simple outline face, and an outlined square containing three dots along the diagonal. In terms of total looking time, attention to the face was significantly greater than to the dots and that, in turn, greater than to the blank stimulus. Infants from mothers given depressant drugs before delivery looked at the stimuli for a significantly shorter time than did infants from nonmedicated mothers.

Jennings (1936) explored several dimensions governing aesthetic preference for figures. Twenty-two children, age thirty to seventy-one months, were confronted with sets of picture cards and instructed to take the preferred card from each set and drop it in a nearby "mail box." The results indicated that about half of the choices were determined by stimulus properties and half by card position, with choice by position decreasing with age.

Daniels (1933) asked thirty-eight children, from about two to six years of age, to produce one of a pair of block models, one "balanced" and the other "unbalanced." Various complexities of models were used, from six to twenty-five blocks. Symmetrical figures were preferred by preschool children. Thompson (1946) randomly arranged twelve black rectangles, with width-length ratios ranging from .25 to .75, on a white background and presented them to subjects between two and twenty-three years of age. One hundred subjects from two to five years of age were asked to indicate which rectangle each liked best and then, with successive choices removed, which of the remainder, etc. The youngest age group showed no stable preferences.

There is little question that the discrimination of patterns and shapes is observable in the very young infant. However, it is also true that the stimulus dimensions and attributes governing preference are largely unknown. It may be that preferences form only at a relatively late stage of development. Little can be said about the aesthetic bases of preference in the first three years of life.

FORM PERCEPTION

The perception of form requires that the discrimination of a figure persist through changes in orientation, dimensions, and context of the figure. In human beings the mediational or symbolic processes relevant to form perception probably involve language.

Munn and Steining (1931) trained a fifteen-month-old male infant to discriminate between a two-dimensional black cross (the positive stimulus) and black square (the negative stimulus) mounted on similar white backgrounds, with chocolate as reinforcement for correct choices. Subsequent training involved 45° rotation of the cross, changes in background and/or stimulus figures and, finally, reversal learning. To all these the child adjusted easily and gave clear evidence of form perception, regardless of orientation of the stimulus figure. Much the same results were found by Gellerman (1933a, 1933b) and Ling (1941).

Form perception probably requires attention to details and cues beyond the capacity and experience of the very young infant. The ability to perceive form obviously precedes language ability although the latter undoubtedly extends the range of equivalence. By two years of age, the child clearly can discriminate certain shapes and forms despite changes in orientation, size, and context.

SIZE DISCRIMINATION

Studies of size determination can be divided into those in which judgment is of the relative size of equally distant objects and those, such as in studies of size constancy, in which the perception or judgment appears to be mediated by cognitive and situational factors. We will consider size constancy later, in connection with depth perception, and discuss at this point the available experimental data concerning discrimination of size of equally distant objects.

Welch (1939), using what he termed a conditioning method, concluded that it is difficult to establish a size discrimination at less than sixteen months of age. (See, however, the study by Misumi, 1951.) Welch's subjects were first trained to choose the smallest of a series of successively larger boxes for a candy reward and then tested with pairings of that box and other members of a graduated size series. Comparison of performances of an experimental group trained for some time on the task and a control group of the same age level produced no evidence for superiority of the former. Comparisons of tests for "larger," "smaller," and "middle-sized" indicate that the last was more difficult to acquire; only 20 per cent of the subjects passed this test at about three years of age.

Hicks and Stewart (1930) tested forty children, ten at each age level from two to five years, for their ability to select the middle-sized box from a set of three randomly positioned boxes. A small toy served as the reward. Although nine of the youngest group could not learn even the first of four such sets, the other three groups learned all of them. The middle-sized box was confused twice as often with the larger as with the smaller box. Thrum (1935) found his two- to four-year-old subjects made fewer errors in the identification of "big" than "small." "Middle-sized" was still the major source of mistakes. Graham *et al.* recently reported that the learning of absolute size concepts by young children was significantly more difficult than relative size concepts (1964).

CONSTANCY, SPACE PERCEPTION, AND DEPTH PERCEPTION

From the empiricist point of view it could be argued that objects are "built" from certain basic sensation units—color, shape, size, and so on—in association with cues from other modalities, e.g., kinesthetic and cutaneous, and, similarly, that space perception is the product of learned association of visual cues to distance and depth experienced in conjunction with cues from the other senses. Those who favor the "innate" view of object perception would contend that the organism is equipped from birth with the ability to appreciate distance, depth, shapes, and forms. A convenient statement of the status of the long controversy between environmentalists and hereditarians is provided by Hochberg's comment that "Actual research with humans and animals does not support either a nativist or empiricist position. Processes of maturation, deterioration, and learning all interact to form a very complex picture" (1962, p. 325).

There appear to be only four studies of the development of size constancy. In the earliest of these (Frank, 1925) thirty subjects from eleven months to seven years of age first learned to find a piece of chocolate (or a toy) under the larger of two boxes placed at the same distance. The movement of the boxes relative to one another produced some evidence that even at less than three years of age children could make choices on the basis of size constancy—that is, could still choose the larger box when retinal images were equal.

Beyrl (1926) tested fifty-five subjects of whom fourteen were between two and three years of age. (The remainder were between three and seven years of age.) The stimuli were wooden cubes and circular discs of different sizes. The method of constant stimuli was used: the standard cube or disc was placed at a distance of one meter, and the various sized comparison stimuli at 2 to 11 meters from the subjects. Each comparison disc was compared with the standard at least 10 times at each distance in order to determine which was bigger. Beryl noted that children at two to three years of age already understood the concepts of "bigger" and "smaller." Although younger subjects showed some size constancy, it was not equal to that shown by an adult, and it was always earlier for three-dimensional than for two-dimensional stimuli. An additional experiment with cubes and squares suggested that this priority did not depend upon shape difference. Findings obtained with a group of older children and adults indicated that size constancy is at an adult level by about ten years. In general, the tendency to underestimate the farther of two objects decreased with increasing age. At lower age levels there was less consistency as stimulus distance increased. Beyrl interpreted his results to mean that although perception of size constancy is basically innate it becomes better established with maturation. Cruikshank (1941) concluded from her study of infants ten to fifteen weeks old that size constancy is present by six months. This conclusion was based on a comparison of reaching responses of 73 infants to a small rattle presented at 25 or 75 cm and to a rattle three times as large presented at 75 cm. The retinal image of the larger rattle at the greater distance was thus equal to that of the smaller rattle at 25 cm, hence an infant showing complete absence of size constancy might be expected to reach equally often for the large distant and small near rattles, but less often for the small far rattle. Even the youngest infants tended to reach more frequently for the rattle presented at 25 cm than for either rattle at 75 cm, indicating that some degree of constancy is present as early as ten weeks of age. Infants up to five or six months still tended to reach occasionally for the distant rattles, however, with responses to the larger rattle predominating. These responses to the far stimuli tended to disappear at about six months of age and older infants would only reach for the rattle when it was realistically near.

Misumi (1951) started with the basic assumption that infants would naturally prefer the larger of two objects presented at the same distance. The tendency to reach for or manipulate the stimulus was considered as the response; visual attention only was recorded as a negative reaction. His subjects ranged from twelve to fifty-five weeks of age. Misumi demonstrated in his first experiment that with the exception of the youngest group (twelve to seventeen weeks), subjects at all ages did indeed prefer the larger of two red plastic goldfish (10 cm and 17.5 cm long) presented at the same distance (17 cm). In Exp. II, he then presented the same stimuli at distances that were different (17.5 and 31 cm) but produced equal retinal images. In Exp. III, he presented two large toy goldfish of equal size at 31 cm to forty infants ranging from twenty-one to fifty-nine weeks of age. Since the discrepancy in positive responses to large vs. small fish in Exp. II was significantly greater than the discrepancy in positive responses to the two large fish in Exp. III—all four fish having produced retinal images of equal size—he considered size constancy to have been definitely demonstrated in the former. Misumi replicated these experiments with red balls instead of fish and found substantially the same results. His last two experiments determined that "nearness" can be a determining factor in size constancy and that preference for the larger of two objects holds only within certain limits—for 2:1 ratios preference was obtained, while for 7:1 ratios it was not.

Altogether, the results of these studies indicate that size discrimination and constancy are present in early infancy but that size constancy may not reach the adult level until much later. Both Misumi's and Beyrl's studies indicate that the age of occurrence and extent of size constancy may depend on the properties of the visual stimulus.

Several studies have been concerned with the effects of manipulation of various cues, such as color, position, or context, on the ability to locate objects in space relative to each other and the perceiving organism. Skalet (1931) and Miller (1934) were especially interested in the effects of such manipulations on "delayed reaction." In Skalet's study, the delayed reactions of sixty children from two to five and one-half years of age were studied in four situations. The first, which tested delay to spatial cues, required that the subject remember the position at which a food reward was hidden. Delays ranged from one to thirty-four days. The middle of the three possible positions proved the most difficult. Maximum delay preceding correct response increased with age.

Miller (1934) investigated the effects of various cues on the ability of 98 subjects, ranging from about 11 to 162 months in ages, to delay reaction for 10 seconds. The experimenter placed the "bait" (a toy dog) in one of two boxes, one red and one yellow. Each box was aligned with the subject's shoulder, in one situation, or at double that distance, in another situation. Then a screen was interposed between the subject and the boxes for 10 seconds. When the screen was removed, the subject was asked to find the dog (graham crackers were used with subjects below 18 months of age). When the criterion of two successive correct choices was reached, tests involving lateral displacements and/or inversion of positions of the boxes were made in order to determine whether color, positions relative to each other or to the observer, or a combination of cues was the dominant factor. Position dominated choice below the age of three years, and color after that time; 6 per cent of the choices were made on the basis of a combination of the two cues. An increase in the distance between boxes did not affect color-based responses, but did shift 46 per cent of choices from position relative to other box as the significant cue to position relative to the subject. Miller was also able to show, when contrasting configuration to position, that except from eleven to twenty-four months, configuration was the more dominant cue. Configuration was also dominant for the situation in which the other cue was color difference. On the other hand, Leuba (1940) concluded from his study of delayed reaction in 18- to 66-month-old children that the probability of a correct choice was a function of the position of the positive stimulus within the configuration rather than the configuration *per se.*

Although stereoscopic vision is well developed at two years, if not before (Johnson & Beck, 1941), it does not come under cognitive control until much later. Meyer (1940) attempted to study the development of spatial relationships in 63 children, eighteen to sixty-six months of age, by administering a series of tasks that required spatial reorganization. Children less than three years of age were neither able to nest boxes properly nor fit rectangular blocks into the correct formboard holes. At three years, there was some trial-and-error learning. In a detour problem, the youngest subjects tried to reach through the barrier directly to obtain objects; only at three to four years did subjects start to reach over the barrier. Prediction of position for an object rotated through 180° was possible only at four years. Meyer discusses her results in terms of three stages of development of "space": *practical* space, in which the child neglects relations between objects (eighteen to thirty months); *empirical* space, in which the child profits from experience although motion is still understood mainly in relation to himself; and *objective* space, in which patterns of activity are adapted to objects, and the subject is part of the world rather than the center of it.

Fantz (1961a) measured the effects of several variables on depth perception, as inferred from a preference measure, in 52 infants from one to six months of age. He found that a sphere was preferred to a circle, and that infants less than six months of age could discriminate "solidity" through texture and brightness gradients even without binocular cues. These cues, however, became useful after the first few months of life.

Several of the well-known "visual cliff" studies (Gibson & Walk, 1960; Walk & Gibson, 1961; Walk & Dodge, 1962) have been concerned with the time of first occurrence and the subsequent development of depth perception in the young of various species, including man. Gibson and Walk (1960) reported the results of testing 36 infants, six to fourteen months of age, on the visual cliff. The visual cliff consisted of a sheet of heavy glass under half of which lay a checkerboard pattern in contact with the glass while the other half overlay a similar pattern placed at a distance of about four feet. This side represented the cliff. A board laid down the center, between the two sides, served as the starting platform which the infant, in response to calls from his mother, was invited to leave. In general, infants would not crawl over the cliff side but would respond to mothers by venturing out on the shallow side. The young of other terrestrial species performed similarly. The authors conclude that in general young human infants discriminate depth concomitantly with development of the ability to creep or walk. (On the other hand the authors also remarked that if it had not been for the glass some of the children would have fallen off the board.) In the most recent visual cliff study, Walk and Dodge (1962) report that a monocular infant about eleven months of age performed on the visual cliff in a fashion similar to that of binocular infants, thus, it seems that monocular cues can suffice for depth perception despite the obvious superiority of binocular depth perception.

Binocular vision shows considerable improvement in the first year of life. Depth perception, along with form perception and size constancy, is demonstrable by six months and is probably well developed soon thereafter. Young children tend to localize objects by position cues and, where special color cues are not involved, configuration cues. Spatial relationships are not completely understood by three years, and "objective" space is probably not realized until four or five years.

ATTENTION, DISTRACTION, AND NOVELTY

Taylor (1931) studied visual apprehension in thirty young adults and thirty preschool children who were thirty-four to fifty-eight months of age. His procedure called for the inspection of various arrays of objects presented for three seconds and an immediate oral report of the objects perceived. It was found that, on the average, children could name two objects and adults, six. Poyntz (1933) administered a pegboard task to forty children, from twenty-six to forty-four months of age. Five trials were given each day for five successive days. Records were kept of the time required for a trial as well as the interruption of attention as a function of several conditions of distraction: (1) no distraction; (2) the intermittent beating of a metronome; (3) the continuous presence of toys; (4) continuous music; and (5) a light flashing at 60 times a minute. The results indicated that both visual and auditory distraction lessened visual attention to the task but that conditions (3) and (5) were most disruptive. Saayman, Ames, and Moffett (1964) have recently used apparatus and procedures similar to those of Fantz (1959, 1961a) in order to study the effects of familiarization on fixation time in three-month-old infants for stimuli varying in shape (cross and circle) and/or color (black and red). An experimental session began with two 30-second trials, during which both stimuli were present, to determine prefamiliarization looking time and, hence, stimulus preference. This was followed by a four and one-half minute familiarization period during which the subject viewed either the preferred or nonpreferred stimulus. The final phase consisted of two 30-second test trials with both stimuli present again to determine the effects of the preceding familiarization procedure on differential fixation of the two stimuli. The authors found that visual exploration of the single stimulus presented during the familiarization period decreased as a function of viewing time. They also found that when the initially preferred stimulus had been familiarized, the infant looked at it significantly less during the postfamiliarization test trials.

VISUAL STIMULI OF A SOCIAL NATURE

In caretaking situations, the infant has "many opportunities for the development of social responsiveness on a purely perceptual basis," and the human face "is demonstrably an object complex and mobile enough to hold the infant's attention" (Walters & Parke, 1965). Walters and Parke reviewed a large number of studies concerned with the effect of various stimuli on "smiling" and "vocalization," as well as on orienting and exploratory behaviors. We will confine our discussion here to a few studies that have investigated the effects of social visual stimuli on smiling.

Gesell and Ames (1947) photographed children responding to their mirror images. Their subjects were seen at monthly intervals between the ages of sixteen and sixty weeks. The authors found some smiling at sixteen weeks, a decrease in rate at twenty weeks, and an increase subsequently.

Kaila (1932) studied the reactions of seventy infants to the human face. His subjects ranged from two to seven months of age at the beginning of experimentation, which lasted for periods of from one to nine weeks. He found that the first reaction to a face is a smile, the two- to four-month-old infant looking at the face as a whole and only the older infants focusing on the mouth and eyes. At five months the child looks at the adult's eyes and will not smile at the face in profile. At this age they also react to frowns (by crying), although an adult smile will reinstate smiling. Finally, at six months, the children would successfully mimic expressions, according to Kaila.

Spitz and Wolf (1946) observed over two hundred institutionalized infants at repeated and varied times over the first year of life. They found that the experimenter's nodding, smiling, full face would evoke a smiling response at about twenty days. The response was present from two to six months, after which it disappeared. Neither racial nor sociological variables affected the course of smiling. In one phase of their study, Spitz and Wolf presented a rictus face to their subjects, i.e., a nonsmiling but distorted facial configuration. Almost all subjects between three to six months responded as positively as they had to smiling. In another situation, the experimenter wore a mask and cap, substituting tongue movements and head nodding for smiling. This produced the same result. A "primitive, life-size" puppet proved similarly effective. A control series, involving use of facial profiles, novel objects, and various intensities of light and sound produced no smiling responses. Spitz and Wolf concluded that the full-face presentation and movement of elements of the human face, and not the face *per se*, is what elicits smiling, and that therefore the response is not to the Gestaltlike character of the stimulus as Kaila had suggested (1932). They further concluded that the development of smiling is an indicator of emotional as well as perceptual development.

Ahrens (1954) reported a series of observations on smiling in institutionalized infants from one to eight months of age. He investigated the effectiveness of a number of variables in eliciting smiling. In the first month, for example, dots and angles proved more effective in producing smiles than did lines or sketches of faces. The investigator's face was smiled at for the first time at about six weeks, and at two months it became the favored object. At four months, mouth movements had a positive effect while brow movements produced some negative reactions. At five months, the live adult became important, and the widened mouth and brow movements more effective. A month later, however, the only certain way of evoking smiling or laughter was by movements of the mouth. At eight months mimic experiments were difficult to elicit because of lack of attention, fear of strangers, and a tendency to treat facial changes as a game. The changes, as Ahrens notes, may take place earlier in children living in their own homes.

Ambrose (1961) comments that the studies of smiling have used mainly institutionalized infants as subjects and have emphasized presence or absence of the smiling response rather than variations and changes in response strength across or within subjects. His own study of smiling, as well as those of Brackbill (1958) on smiling and of Rheingold, Gewirtz, and Ross (1959) on vocalization, were primarily concerned with response and social reinforcement parameters.

Ambrose concludes that the smiling response to a motionless adult face is stronger in "home" infants than in institutionalized infants. He infers that the earlier and more frequent occurrence of smiling in "home" babies is the result of more frequent reinforcement for smiling. If Polak, Emde, and Spitz (1964a) are correct, the "exhaustibility" of the smiling response observed by some investigators may be partially the result of using a "motionless" rather than a "nodding" face as the stimulus. Their studies, described in two papers (1964a, 1964b), have attempted, first, to determine the relative efficacy of several measures of smiling as a preliminary step toward quantification and the tracing of the "natural history" of the smiling response, and second, to use the response itself to investigate the early development of visual discrimination and depth perception.

The two stimuli for Polak et al.'s second study consisted of the experimenter's face and a life-sized, cut-out, color photograph of the experimenter's face. Both were presented with a nodding motion at the rate of one nod per two seconds, latency being the response measure. It was hypothesized that time of development of visual discrimination and depth perception would be signalled by differential smiling to these stimuli. The investigators report that depth perception in this situation, i.e., smiling to the live face only, begins at about the eleventh or twelfth week of life. They caution, however, that certain differential cues, such as uncontrollable eyelid movements and color distortion in the photograph, could have affected discrimination.

The assumption of Polak et al. that the face becomes important by "virtue of direct association with tension-reducing and pleasureable stimuli" is not supported by findings reported by J. S. Watson (1964).

Watson states that face stimuli are ineffective when in other than an upright position, even though the infant has seen the face in other positions many times while being fed or diapered. Watson suggests that the development of smiling may be relatively independent of primary-drive reduction. His findings suggest that studies of the combined effects of orientations and motions of the face would be desirable.

There appears to be little doubt, as Walters and Parke note, that "social smiles are to a large extent elicited, maintained, and modified through the presentation of visual and auditory stimuli." Beyond that generality, however, there is little that can definitely be said as to the relative effectiveness for smiling of separate sensory stimuli. Certain patterns other than the human face are capable of eliciting smiling; indeed, in the first month of life, even dots may produce more smiles than facial representations.

Audition

When a pure tone is sounded, a train of waves of alternating compression and rarefaction is activated in the medium surrounding the source of the tone. A continuous measure of pressure at, say, the external receptor organ of an observer of the tone, plotted against time, would thus yield a curve showing pressure to be alternately above and below the ambient atmospheric pressure.

Two characteristics of a sound wave of most concern are its frequency—that is, the number of compression-rarefaction cycles per unit time—and its intensity. Frequency is nearly always expressed in cycles per second (cps); intensity, or energy delivered per unit time by the wave (acoustic power), is usually expressed in terms of a decibel (db) scale. The number of decibels expressing intensity level of a sound stimulus of acoustic power P, is equal to $db = 10 \log_{10} P/P_0$, where P_0 is some arbitrary reference intensity. When a sound intensity level is given in db in the present paper, the value for P_0 will be understood, unless otherwise indicated, to be 10^{-16} watts/cm², which is the acoustic power of a 1000-cps tone of .0002 dynes/cm² pressure amplitude. This is the approximate absolute hearing threshold for a normal adult observer.

A third characteristic of a sound wave is its phase angle, which designates the part of the waveform occurring at a particular instant in time. Phase angle is conventionally specified in terms of degrees or radians, where a full cycle of the wave, beginning and ending with the upward crossing of the zero line, is 360 degrees or 2π radians.

The subjective experience of pitch is primarily a function of frequency of the stimulus, while apparent loudness is primarily associated with intensity. Pitch is also influenced to some extent by intensity, however: as intensity is increased, the apparent pitch of higher-frequency tones (above about 3000 cps) gets higher, while that of lower-frequency tones (less than about 2000 cps) gets lower (Stevens, 1935). The pitch of tones of intermediate frequencies is relatively independent of intensity. Similarly, apparent loudness is not completely independent of frequency (Wever, 1949). Tones of fixed intensities appear loudest when their frequencies are in the 1000- to 2000-cps range, presumably because the human auditory receptor system responds optimally to frequencies of this order.

Most sounds occurring in nature are produced, not by a simple waveform of a single frequency, but by a complex wave consisting of a composite of a number of frequencies. As long as the component frequencies are constant such that the sound wave contains a repetitive pattern, however, the sound will still have a characteristic pitch. This pitch is primarily a function of the component frequency with the greatest amplitude, but other frequencies of lesser amplitude can be detected in the composite. Other sound stimuli contain no sustained frequencies at all. Such stimuli, produced by essentially randomly spaced pressure pulses, and containing approximately equal energy at all audible frequencies, are called *noise*.

THE RECEPTOR SYSTEM

Information contained in sound stimuli is transmitted to the central nervous system through a channel starting with the external ear. Sound waves are carried to the middle ear, where a mechanical lever arrangement transmits the pressure waves to vibration-sensitive receptors in the inner ear. Fibers of the acoustic nerve then conduct coded output of these receptors to various central neural structures.

Sound waves entering the external ear produce vibrations of the ear drum, or tympanum with a frequency and amplitude corresponding to those of the sound pressure waves. The first of three ossicles, the malleus, is attached rigidly to the tympanum, so that it is set in motion directly by vibrations of this membrane. Through lever action of the malleus on the remainder of the ossicle chain in the middle ear, sound vibrations are transmitted to a membrane (the oval window) separating the middle ear cavity from fluids in the cochlea of the inner ear. The middle ear thus serves effectively as an impedance-matching device enabling transmission of a pressure wave from air to the liquids of the inner ear without large energy losses. This is achieved through force or pressure amplification from two sources: mechanical advantage provided by the ossicle lever system, and "hydraulic press" action afforded by greater area of the tympanum compared to that of the oval window. The result is a force gain on the order of nineteen to one (Towe & Ruch, 1960).

Pressure pulses in the cochlear fluid, resulting from excursions of the oval window, produce displacements of the basilar membrane, which runs the entire length of the cochlea. The auditory receptor cells are located on the surface of the basilar membrane, and movement of this membrane provides stimulation of the receptors.

There is conclusive evidence that the region of the basilar membrane undergoing maximal displacement depends on the frequency of the sound wave (Stevens, Davis, & Lurie, 1935), but there has been some disagreement concerning the details of the processes leading to this correlation.

Considerable evidence has been advanced in support of each of several theories, but no single theory accounts for all available data (e.g., von Békésy, 1960). Whatever the explanation of the fact that different frequencies stimulate different receptors, this localization appears to be preserved in the acoustic nerve and in the auditory cortex, hence it is reasonable to suppose that frequency discrimination depends on differential activation of local cortical areas. Intensity discrimination and loudness experience presumably are correlated with variations in amplitude of basilar membrane displacements, which produce variations in the magnitude of receptor output.

Development of the Auditory System. Formation of the anatomical details of the human auditory system is essentially complete by the later stages of fetal development (Patten, 1953), but at the time of birth, the middle ear cavity is filled with a residue of connective tissue which severely restricts full movement of the ossicles. Absorption and drainage of this substance proceeds fairly rapidly, however, and after a few days the middle ear becomes partially functional. Within a few months the resorption process is complete, and movements of the ear drum are freely transmitted by the ossicles to the inner ear.

The initial immobility of the middle ear structures led a number of earlier writers (e.g., Meyer, 1912)—and some later ones as well (Martin & Vincent, 1960)—to conclude that newborn infants are deaf. This conclusion is correct in the sense that a neonate's hearing cannot be "normal"; nevertheless, a large number of studies—e.g., Richmond, Grossman, and Lustman (1953); Wedenberg (1956); Hardy, Dougherty, and Hardy (1959); Suzuki, Kamijo, and Kiuchi (1964); to cite a few—have reported observing a variety of reflex responses by newborn infants (including premature infants) to auditory stimuli. Other observations have indicated that loud sounds can even elicit responses from a human fetus *in utero.* Peiper (1924), for example, reported observing definite fetal movements in response to an automobile horn sounded near the mother's abdomen, and Forbes and Forbes (1927), studying a mother slightly less than a month before her normal-term baby was born, observed that a sharp rise of the maternal "anterior abdominal wall" would immediately follow a blow from a metal object on the edge of a bathtub full of water in which the mother was lying. The mother herself reportedly was not startled by the blow on the tub, nor did she detect any tactile experience of vibration accompanying the stimulus. Bernard and Sontag (1947) recorded reliable fetal heart rate accelerations following presentation of loud tones near the abdomen of each of three gravida in the last two and one-half months of pregnancy. Frequencies ranging from 20 to 6000 cps appeared to be equally effective in producing the cardiac response.

A number of investigators of fetus and neonate sensitivity to auditory stimuli have commented on the possibility that observed responses following presentation of sound stimuli are not reactions to stimulation of auditory receptors, but, rather, are responses to stimulation of tactile receptors by the sound pressure waves. This possibility seems rather remote: the intensity level required to excite tactile receptors in normal human adults has been shown repeatedly to be well over 120 db (Licklider, 1951), yet intensity levels well below 120 db reliably elicit responses in fetuses and neonates. The assumption that these responses are to tactile stimulation would thus imply that an infant's tactile threshold is below that of an adult. The interpretation of tactile stimulation is unnecessary, of course, since even without normal operation of the middle ear, it is possible for sound waves to reach the auditory receptors —albeit with reduced energy—via bone tissue surrounding the inner ear. In view of available evidence, therefore, it does not seem rash to suppose that the human auditory system, with the exception of the middle ear, is functional some weeks before birth. It must be expected, however, that an infant's hearing threshold will be very high until the impedance-matching function of the middle ear is available permitting more efficient transfer of sound energy from air to the cochlear fluids.

METHODS OF STUDYING INFANTS' HEARING

Behavioral Responses. A very large number of investigators have reported observations of infants' behavior to various auditory stimuli, but formulating generalizations from these studies is made somewhat difficult by the fact that so many of them either failed to measure and control important characteristics of the stimuli, or failed to obtain objective records of responses, or both. Typical procedures in studies investigating sensitivity of neonates to auditory stimuli, for example, might involve presentation of varied sounds such as a whistle or a bell, a clapping of the hands, an object falling on the floor, a toy gun, or a blow on a pan or a tin can. One or more observers then look for various somatic responses of the infant following presentation of the stimulus.

Probably the most reliably observed response is the auro-palpebral reflex (reflex blinking to a loud sound when the eyes are open, or tightening of the eyelids if the eyes are shut). Other responses include the Moro reflex, kicking, turning the head or eyes, and either onset or cessation of crying.

Among the earliest investigators to obtain objective records of newborn infants' responses to sounds was Canestrini (1913), who recorded kymographically respiration rate changes and fontanelle pressure changes at the accompanying presentation of the stimuli. The sound stimuli, however, were from such uncalibrated sources as a bell, a harmonica, hand clapping, voices of adults, and the noise of a falling book. Similarly, Pratt, Nelson, and Sun (1930) and Pratt (1934) obtained kymographic records of movements of infants in response to sound stimuli, using a stabilimeter (a moveable crib mounted on bearings and linked to a recording instrument in such a manner that slight movements of the crib produce deflections of a pen or stylus), but again, the stimuli in these studies were not well calibrated with respect to either intensity, frequency, or quality. (Relative intensities of the stimuli in the Pratt, *et al.* study, however, were roughly determined in terms of the distances at which they were audible to two adults with normal hearing.) On the other hand, Haller (1932) presented well controlled stimuli from a commercial audiometer (with the actual intensities not specified), but the responses reported were qualitative observations of general somatic movements from which "comfort" or "discomfort" of the subjects was inferred.

Two examples of early studies of newborn infants' behavior to auditory stimuli using both objective recording procedures and well-calibrated stimuli are those reported by Weiss (1934), who studied effects of continuous light and sound stimulation on infants' general activity, and by Stubbs (1934), who investigated variations in newborn infants' responses to different durations, intensities, and frequencies of sound stimuli. Both of these studies used pure tones as stimuli, with both intensity level and frequency controlled, and both obtained polygraph records of general activity of the subjects in stabilimeters. Stubbs also measured respiration rate by means of a pneumograph linked to the polygraph.

Most investigations of hearing in infants have had as a goal development of a convenient behavioral test of impaired hearing in infants. The proposed testing procedures range in complexity from simply sounding a loud (over 100 db) bell near the infant and observing whether some somatic startle reflex occurs (Richmond, Grossman, & Lustman, 1953), to a series of observations of responses to such stimuli sources as rattles, clackers, bells, xylophones, tonettes, and voiced consonants (Hardy, Dougherty, & Hardy, 1959). Use of these kinds of stimuli in the latter study was justified on the basis of evidence that infants respond more readily to "meaningful" stimuli than to the less familiar pure tones used in standard audiometry (Pratt, Nelson, & Sun, 1930; Ewing & Ewing, 1944; Froeschels & Beebe, 1946). Stimulus sources with dominant frequencies covering a wide range were selected in the hope that the test might provide some information concerning an infant's sensitivity to particular frequencies.

Also in the context of audiometry, several investigators have attempted to condition the galvanic skin response in young children to pure tones of various frequencies and intensities. (These studies are reviewed below.) In the "peep show" technique proposed by Dix and Hallpike (1947), attractive pictures are projected on a screen for the child to view if he moves a switch when a tone sounds. If a child is sufficiently motivated by the pictures, and he has been given sufficient training to ensure consistent responding, then failure to respond to a particular tone might be taken to indicate that the tone is below the child's threshold. A similar testing procedure was successfully used by Lowell, Rushford, Hoverstein, and Stoner (1956) and by Barr (1954) to obtain audiograms from partially deaf, preschool-age children. The technique has not been found satisfactory for children younger than two years old, however.

Physiological Responses. Most objective recordings of infants' responsiveness to tones have been measurements of physiological changes which follow presentation of the stimulus. Recordings of respiration rate, fontanelle pulsation, and heart rate have already been mentioned; other experimenters have investigated skin resistance (GSR) changes (e.g., Jones, 1930; Statten, Page, & Wishart, 1956) and electroencephalographic (EEG) measures (e.g., Gidoll, 1952) as possible indicator responses in studies of audition in infants. Detailed descriptions of techniques of observation and methods of analysis of data on autonomic functions in infants have been provided by Lipton, Steinschneider, and Richmond (1961a; 1961b), and by Steinschneider, Lipton, and Richmond (1964).

Most studies recording autonomic and EEG changes in response to sound stimulation have assumed that these changes are due to nonspecific "arousal" responses that are evoked by any sudden detectable change in the subject's environment (e.g., Marcus, 1951).

Bordley and Hardy (1949) and Hardy and Bordley (1952) have attempted to develop an "objective audiometry," recording GSR changes which have been conditioned to tones, with electric shock serving as an unconditioned stimulus. The procedure begins with presentation of loud tones of varying frequencies and intensities followed by a mild electric shock after four or five seconds. As soon as a consistent drop in skin resistance is observed following the tone, intensity level is reduced until no GSR is elicited. Shock is not given on those trials in which no GSR is observed, but the shock is re-introduced whenever a response occurs to the tone. In this way the intensity threshold can be determined for various frequencies and the same procedure can be used on any age subject. The method reportedly yields audiograms (curves showing intensity thresholds as functions of frequency) from adults that agree quite well with those obtained through standard subjective audiometric procedures. Audiograms have been obtained by Hardy and Bordley from children as young as seven months, but unfortunately, all the infants tested showed other evidence of hearing impairment, and hence no information was gained concerning normal hearing thresholds of young children; the results of the tests on infants were evaluated in relation to adult norms.

The conditioned GSR procedure has been applied and evaluated by Barr (1954) and by Goldstein, Ludwig, and Naunton (1954) in studies of children of various ages and with various hearing disorders. Both studies report considerable variability in the ease with which the necessary conditioned GSR could be established, with a number of children not responding at all. Barr (1954) also found that repeated audiograms sometimes showed quite poor agreement. When repeated audiograms did agree, however, the results showed good agreement with audiograms obtained from the same child using some variant of the "peep show" technique described above.

ABSOLUTE THRESHOLDS

Although it might be expected that infants—especially newborn infants—are less sensitive to sounds than older children and adults, very little data appear to be available indicating *how much* less sensitive infants might be; nor is unambiguous information available on the nature of changes in sensitivity as a function of age. The chief problem in obtaining these kinds of information seems to be that the only way intensity thresholds can be determined is in terms of some form of observable responses which must occur before perception of a stimulus by the subject can be inferred—and whether or not the particular response selected by the experimenter for observation is elicited by the stimulus might depend not only on the subject's sensitivity, but also on a variety of other factors influencing the subject's tendency to make this response.

One seemingly potent factor affecting response thresholds of infants for auditory stimulation is quality of the sound stimuli used. Pratt, *et al.* (1930), for example, found that newborn infants in a stabilimeter showed substantially more activity in response to sound from an electric bell than to a wooden bell, even though the latter bell appeared louder to adult observers. Froeschels and Beebe (1946) reported that out of thirty-three neonates observed between the ages of one-half to nine days, only one showed reflex somatic responses to tuning forks, whereas all thirty-three responded to a whistle. The relative intensities of the two kinds of stimuli were not reported. To make matters still more difficult, a series of observations by Ewing and Ewing (1944) of ninety-one presumably normal children between birth and five years of age suggest that the types of stimuli which most readily evoke responses in infants vary with age of the infants. During the first three months the infants gave reflex responses to percussion sounds more quickly than to a human voice, with this difference diminishing during the second three months. At about six months, reflex reactions began to be replaced with learned responses. The infants began to localize sounds by turning the eyes or head, and these responses were elicited most prominently by "meaningful" sounds such as voices. By the end of two years, quiet speech would attract the infants' attention more effectively than loud speech, and loud percussion sounds tended to be ignored.

The method devised by Bordley and Hardy (1949), involving observation of GSR changes conditioned to tones, would seem to overcome these problems, since the response would be common for all ages, and the tendency for the stimulus to elicit this response is controlled by the conditioning procedure. As suggested in the last section, however, the method does not appear to have been applied in studies of infants with normal hearing.

Although most studies of audition in neonates have only been concerned with the question of whether infants will respond at all to sound stimuli, the possibility that quantitative thresholds for pure tones can be determined with newborn infants has been well demonstrated by Wedenberg (1956). In this study Wedenberg constructed a special pure tone audiometer and loudspeaker system that could produce tones of 500 through 4000 cps with intensity levels up to 115 db. Tones of five different frequencies were presented to twenty infants ranging in age from one to ten days; and for each frequency, the minimum intensity level was determined that would elicit an auro-palpebral reflex. The mean obtained thresholds for pure tones of 500, 1000, 1500, 2000, and 4000 cps were 108, 105, 107, 108, and 112 db. These values, it should be noted, reflect thresholds for the specific response chosen for observation by the experimenter; selection of a different response would no doubt result in different threshold values. In fact, Suzuki, Kamijo, and Kiuchi (1964) found that a group of forty-five infants from five hours to seven days old all showed some response (blinking, jerking, crying, grimacing, and so on) to sound stimuli at intensity levels less than 80 db. The stimuli used were a 500-cycle pure tone and a "sound of a cow's moo," and in contrast to results described earlier, these stimuli appeared to be equally effective in eliciting somatic responses. In another experiment these same investigators recorded changes in respiration of infants in response to pure tones of 500 and 1000 cps. All sixty-one infants tested, ranging in age from one to thirty-three days, showed responses to tones under 90 db. The average minimum intensity level required to elicit a measurable change in respiration was 62.8 db.

That the typical hearing thresholds for neonates is of the order indicated by the Suzuki, *et al.* study is further suggested from a series of experiments reported by Bronshtein and Petrova (1952). Of thirty-three infants, ranging in age from two hours to eight days, twenty-nine showed disruption or inhibition of the sucking response when they were presented intermittent stimuli of medium intensity.

ADAPTATION AND HABITUATION

In common with other sensory systems, the human auditory mechanism undergoes a reduction in responsiveness with extended stimulation. This phenomenon can be demonstrated by leading a fatiguing or adapting tone into one phone of a set of earphones for various durations, and determining immediately after each duration, the intensity level that must be presented to the previously unstimulated ear to produce a loudness matching that of the adapting tone in the adapted ear. Data on adults reported by Wood (1930) suggest that, for a 1000-cycle tone, most of the adaptation occurs in the first 20 or 30 seconds of stimulation. More recent data (Thwing, 1955), however, indicate that continued stimulation results in further reductions in sensitivity for as long as three or four minutes.

A possible instance of auditory adaptation in infants is Haller's (1932) observation that, when pure tones of 10-seconds duration were presented to newborn infants, various somatic movements, initiated at onset of the tones, tended to decrease during the 10-second intervals.

An alternate interpretation of Haller's observations is that the reductions in responding were due to a process called "response habituation," a term used to describe the phenomenon of decreasing responsiveness with repeated stimulation where no sensory fatigue is involved. Canestrini (1913) found reductions in respiratory changes and fontanelle pressure changes with repeated presentation of sound stimuli to newborn infants, and Peiper (1924) observed declining frequencies of motor responses of a fetus *in utero* with successive presentations of an auto horn if the stimulations were separated by less than a few minutes. Both these investigators interpreted their findings in terms of "inhibition" rather than adaptation or fatigue. Pratt (1934) found that the number of movements per stimulus by infants in a stabilimeter—where the stimulus was a solenoid-operated plunger striking a tin can—decreased systematically over successive minutes of ten-minute observation periods and that the reductions were when the stimulus was presented more frequently (every 10, 30, or 60 seconds). Pratt also concluded that this was due to some kind of inhibition phenomenon. He reasoned that adaptation was unlikely because of the very short duration of each stimulus; even the 10-second interval between stimuli seemed to be sufficiently long to permit recovery from any fatigue effects.

In their experiment demonstrating inhibition of infants' sucking upon presentation of new or unusual auditory stimuli, Bronshtein and Petrova (1952) used as auditory stimuli the sound of organ pipes, a harmonica, a whistle, or a pencil tapping on a table. A stimulus presentation typically consisted of four identical, half-second sound impulses separated by one-second intervals. Orienting to the sound was initially accompanied by inhibition of the sucking response. However, with repeated presentations of any one stimulus, the orienting response extinguished, i.e., the infant no longer oriented toward the sound and the sound became ineffective in interrupting the sucking response.

Bronshtein and Petrova's interpretation in terms of response extinction (or habituation) rather than fatigue of the auditory mechanisms was based on two aspects of the data. First, after an auditory stimulus had been presented until the infant showed no reaction to it, a longer-than-usual intertrial delay tended to produce a recurrence of the reaction to the same stimulus. Second, following the disappearance of the responses to one stimulus, if a different sound was introduced, the original reaction, i.e., orienting and interruption of sucking, could be revived. Both these phenomena could be interpreted in terms of sensory adaptation, of course: recovery of the response following an extended intertrial delay could have been due to recovery from adaptation effects, and the renewed response to a tone containing different frequencies could have resulted from stimulation of fresh, unadapted receptors.

Bartoshuk (1962a) investigated changes in magnitude of heart rate accelerations with repeated stimulation in 120 infants one to four days old. The stimulus on each trial was a monophasic 85-db, 50-cycle (square wave) tone of one second duration. The magnitude of the cardiac response (difference between the durations of five beats preceding and five beats following the stimulus) decreased over 40 trials for each age group. This effect was the same whether the interstimulus intervals were 15, 30, or 60 seconds. These response decrements over trials were interpreted to be due to response habituation, since, if sensory or neural fatigue were involved, the longer intertrial intervals should have permitted greater recovery between trials. The data are not strongly supportive of this interpretation, of course, since it is based only on failure to obtain a significant interaction between trial and intertrial intervals. Besides, as mentioned above, Pratt (1934) did find greater reductions in general activity of infants over successive trials when the interstimulus interval was shorter.

In another experiment, however, Bartoshuk (1962b) demonstrated a reduction in responsivity as a function of number of stimulus presentations with sensory fatigue specifically ruled out as a possible interpretation. Twenty neonates (one to four days old) were presented a square-wave tone increasing from 100 cps to 1000 cps over an eight-second interval. Median intensity was 85 db above adult threshold. Means of 10-second samples of heart rates immediately preceding and following the rising-frequency tone indicated that cardiac accelerations occurred to this stimulus, but their magnitudes tended to decrease over trials. Immediately following a series of these eight-second trials, the tonal sequence was reversed so that on subsequent trials the frequency of the tone varied from 1000 to 100 cps during the eight-second intervals. For the ten infants showing the greatest amount of response decrement during the prereversal series, the reversed tonal sequence produced significant "dishabituation," or recovery of the cardiac response. Since the same frequencies were presented—and hence the same receptors and afferent neural channels were activated—during both the pre- and postreversal series, sensory fatigue could not have been responsible for the initial response decrement, for if this were the case, the tonal sequence reversal should not have produced a recovery of the response: the receptors or neural elements should have remained fatigued.

FREQUENCY AND QUALITY DISCRIMINATION

Considerable evidence suggests that even newborn infants respond differentially to sounds with different qualities. Studies by Pratt *et al.* (1930) and Ewing and Ewing (1944), as pointed out above, have shown that neonates might respond in various ways to one complex sound but not to another, even when the sound responded to is judged less loud by an adult. A possible explanation of these observations is that the frequencies to which young infants are maximally sensitive might be different from those maximally effective for adults, so that the relative apparent loudnesses of two sounds with different dominant frequencies would not necessarily be the same for an infant as for an adult. The observed differential responses to different stimuli might thus be simply greater responsivity to the stimulus of greater apparent loudness for the infant. Evidence against this interpretation is provided by data reported by Wedenberg (1956) on newborn infants' thresholds for pure tones (see above). The pattern of mean thresholds as a function of frequency for infants less than ten days old was quite like the well-established pattern found for adults—a minimum threshold near 1000 cps and higher thresholds for both higher and lower frequencies.

Data bearing more directly on frequency discrimination by newborn infants is somewhat meager. Haller (1932) presented three- to five-week-old infants with seven pure tones of the same intensity but varying in frequency from 64 to 4096 cps. The somatic movements which she interpreted as "indicating discomfort" increased continuously with frequency up to 2048 cps, then dropped off for a 4096-cycle tone. The decrement in these kinds of responses to the highest frequency was probably due to reduced apparent loudness, but this could not account for the overall relationship. Stubbs (1934), on the other hand, found that varying frequencies of pure tones from 128 to 4096 cps had essentially no effect on general activity of infants under ten days old when intensity was held constant. Whether the differences in results of these two studies were due to differences in ages of the subjects or to differences in the kinds of responses observed is not clear.

Bridger (1961) attempted to provide a direct demonstration of frequency discrimination in neonates one to five days old by using an "habituation technique." An "intense," 40-second pure tone of a given frequency was presented repeatedly, with a half-second interval between the successive tones. The infant's heart rate and somatic responses during the first five seconds of each presentation were recorded. These trials were continued until the subject showed no responses on three consecutive trials—that is, until the infant had habituated (adapted?) to the tone—whereupon the frequency of the tone was changed to a new value. Bridger tried to equate apparent loudness of the habituating and test tones by adjusting intensity of the test tone in accordance with the function relating apparent loudness to frequency for adults. If the infant showed signs of startle or a reappearance of accelerated heart rate in response to the initial presentations of the new frequency, then discrimination of the two frequencies was inferred. Response recovery upon introduction of the test tone was observed in fifteen out of fifty infants. For recovery to occur, the required magnitude of difference between the two tones varied among the subjects, with the finest discrimination observed being one infant's differentiation of tones of 200 and 250 cps.

Because of the prolonged exposure (40 seconds) of Bridger's subjects to the "habituation" tone, it would be expected that adaptation to this tone must have been maximal after very few trials; and since introducing the new, test tone presumably involved stimulation of different, unadapted receptor and neural elements, this new tone would be expected to appear substantially louder to the subject, even though the intensity level was such that the habituation and test tones would normally appear equally loud. An experiment reported by Thwing (1955) demonstrated precisely this phenomenon with adult subjects. The reappearance of startle and cardiac responses in Bridger's subjects could thus be interpreted as responses to a sudden change in apparent loudness of the stimulus.

Using a conditioning procedure, Kasatkin and Levikova (1935) demonstrated differentiation of organ tones by older infants two and a half to four months old. The conditioned response was anticipatory sucking. At ages two and a half to three and a half months the infants could learn to respond differentially to tones about one and a half octaves apart, and one child four months old apparently could discriminate a difference of five and one-half tones.

SOUND LOCALIZATION

Sound waves originating from a source located at any point not in a plane perpendicular to and bisecting a line between the ears of an observer must necessarily travel different distances to the two ears. When the ears differ in distance from the source, the two sets of receptors are differentially stimulated in two ways: the phase angles of the waves differ for the two ears, and the amplitude is greater at one ear than at the other. The intensive difference is due less to the distance difference *per se* than that for sounds originating from one side, the head acts as a barrier to a direct path for pressure waves to one ear.

That a human auditory system is capable of making use of these stimulus cues has been well established (Licklider, 1951), although it is also known that localization cues are not uniformly effective at all frequencies. The head acts more efficiently as a barrier against high frequencies (above about 3000 cps) than against low frequencies, and interaural phase differences appear to be most effective for frequencies below about 1500 or 2000 cps. This leaves a range of frequencies just under 3000 cps which are difficult to localize. Cues for localizing sounds that are initially equidistant from the two ears may be introduced by the observer, of course, by turning or tilting the head.

Since localization of sounds requires coordination of information from the separate receptor systems, it seems certain that higher centers of the central nervous system are involved in this function. Accordingly, an experiment testing capacity for sound localizations in infants carried out by Chun, Pawsat, and Forster (1960) was conceived as a test for normal function of the temporal lobes of the cortex.

Twenty-six infants aged two to forty-nine weeks were tested. During the testing period the infant lay on its back in a specially constructed apparatus with five buzzers positioned in different locations in the space surrounding the subject. One buzzer was located directly to the left, and one to the right of the head; three others were positioned in the midline axis from head to toe, with one near the feet, one above the head, and another directly in front of the subject's face. To determine whether the infants localized the source of the buzzer sounds, the experimenters observed whether any eye or head movements occurred in the direction of the buzzer sounded. That the subjects could hear the stimulus sounds was established by the fact that all twenty-six infants showed some type of reflex in response to the buzzers. All fifteen infants over twenty-six weeks old made at least one localizing response, whereas only one infant under this age did so. Of the fifteen older subjects showing some sound localization, twelve localized in both right and left directions, and ten appeared to locate the buzzer when sounded immediately in front of them. Localization of the other two buzzers in the midline axis appeared to be considerably more difficult.

The Chun *et al.* results are consistent with observations of Ewing and Ewing (1944) who noted that clear indications of sound localization in infants first appeared at around six months (with some signs appearing earlier). Gesell (1925) also reported that infants did not readily turn their heads indicating localization of a bell until they were about five months old. Wertheimer (1961), however, reported observing eye movements in the direction of a toy cricket sounded on the right or left of a single infant from three to ten minutes following birth. In view of the fairly large numbers of infants observed by Ewing and Ewing and by Chun *et al.*, Wertheimer's results must have been due either to a highly atypical subject or to some other special circumstances connected with the observations of this subject.

In each of the studies described, a capacity for sound localization was inferred only if the subjects showed eye movements in the direction of the sound source. Directional eye movements in this context would seem to represent a fairly complex instrumental response, requiring not only a capacity for discriminating spatial localization of sounds but also some degree of coordinated motor behavior. It should not be surprising, therefore, that such responses do not typically appear in very young infants. But this is not to say that discrimination of spatial location of sounds by newborn infants cannot be demonstrated. On the contrary, some experiments of Bronshtein and Petrova (1952) suggest that such discrimination can be shown in infants as young as two hours old. Orienting responses elicited by a sound in one location would habituate, but when the sound was moved to a new location the response would reappear. A recent experiment reported by Leventhal and Lipsitt (1964) appears to confirm the results with slightly older infants (twenty-three to one hundred hours). Ten-second, 75-db tones of 200 cps were presented repeatedly from a speaker near the right ear of each infant until no response was observed (respiration change, stabilimeter movement, or foot withdrawal) on three successive trials. For an experimental group the tone was then switched to a speaker near the left ear, while a control group was given additional trials under unchanged conditions. A significantly greater number of subjects in the experimental group showed response recovery with the shift in locus of the stimulus compared to the control group on corresponding trials. Although these results could be interpreted in terms of sensory adaptation, they suggest that the human auditory system, including the cortical components, is developed to a rather high degree of complexity at birth.

EFFECTS OF CONTINUOUS SOUNDS ON INFANT BEHAVIOR

Many years ago, Francis Warner (1887, 1888) reported that infants' movements decrease in frequency and intensity when they are "listening" to something. Canestrini (1913) observed that infants' heart and respiration rates become more regular when they hear "pleasant," continuously presented sounds. Very little research was done concerning the effects of continuous sounds on infant behavior for the next twenty years. At that time, Weiss (1934) under Orvis Irwin's direction, reported the first extensive and systematic study of the problem.

Weiss used a pure 50 db tone of 5 minutes' duration and a pure 75 db tone of 5 minutes' duration. She found that either tone reduced the gross motor activity far more than did a corresponding period of silence, and that the louder tone had a significantly greater pacifying effect than did the softer one.

Similar results have been obtained by Bartoshuk (1962a, 1962b), Stubbs (1934), and Birns, Blank, Bridger, and Escalona (1965). Birns et al. used both continuous and intermittent tones of varying frequencies. They reported that every continuous tone was more soothing—regardless of frequency—than any intermittent tone.

Recently Salk (1960, 1961, 1962) reported that he had presented a paired heartbeat of 72 beats per minute at 85 db to 102 neonates continuously for four days. These Ss were compared to 112 control Ss on weight gain, amount of crying, and food intake. Salk's results showed significant differences in weight gain: the experimental group showed a median increase of 40 grams compared to a median loss of 20 grams for the control group. Crying and general restlessness also were significantly greater in the experimental group than in the control group— presumably due to a higher level of activity and arousal. These results are consistent with the earlier findings of Weiss (1934). A question might, at this point, be raised. Would *any* continuously presented sound have resulted in similar reduction of activity level?

In an extension of his original experiment, Salk (1960, 1961, 1962) compared the effects of three different sounds (metronome, heartbeat, and lullabies) in putting two-year-olds to sleep at bedtime. For the results of this study to be consistent with the earlier research, there should have been no significant difference between the effectiveness of the different sounds in inducing sleep. *All* sounds should have been equally more effective than no sound at all. Instead, Salk found that the heartbeat was significantly more calming than any other stimulus condition—and, in fact, there was no difference between the no sound condition and either the lullaby or the metronome.

A subsequent study (Tulloch, Brown, Jacobs, Prugh, & Greene, 1964) repeated the essential features of Salk's experiment with neonates. There was, however, one major difference: the intensity level of the heartbeat was only 45 db. The failure of Tulloch et al. to replicate Salk's results could be attributed to the fact that 45 db is probably below the hearing threshold of newborn infants.

Recently Brackbill, Adams, Crowell, and Gray (1966) attempted to replicate Salk's results by using the sounds of paired heartbeats at 72 beats per minute, a metronome at 72 beats per minute, and lullabies in a foreign language. All were presented at 85 db to 24 full term, normal neonates. Four consecutive, 15-minute presentations of the auditory stimuli were given in random order to each neonate in a hospital laboratory. Such factors as temperature of room, degree of swaddling, amount of time since last feeding, and amount of food consumed at last feeding were controlled. Polygraph records were obtained for heart rate, respiration, and gross motor activity. In addition to these data, an observer recorded the amount of crying in seconds.

Brackbill *et al.* found no significant differences between heartbeat and other sound conditions in any of these measures. They did find, however, that there was a significantly greater amount of crying under the no sound condition than under any of the auditory stimulation conditions. The absence of sound also resulted in significantly higher and more irregular heart rate, more gross motor activity, and less regular respiration. These results all support Weiss' finding that *any* sound is more calming than no sound at all.

Brackbill *et al.* also studied 41 nursery school children whose mean age was thirty-four months. In an own-control design, the children were exposed to one of four conditions (heartbeat, metronome, lullabies, and no sound) immediately following lunch when all were bedded down for naps. All sounds were presented at approximately 20 db above ambient noise level of the nursery school. The four conditions were presented in a random order with a new condition presented at the beginning of each week; the same stimulus was presented for 60 minutes per day for four days. In sharp contrast to Salk's findings, Brackbill *et al.* found no significant difference in time to fall asleep between the heartbeat, lullabies, and metronome conditions. Any sound was more effective in putting the children to sleep than was no sound at all.

The results of Canestrini (1913), Weiss (1934), Stubbs (1934), Bartoshuk (1962), Birns *et al.* (1965), and Brackbill *et al.* (1966) all point to the conclusion that continuous auditory stimulation, like continuous light stimulation, reduces the level of activity and arousal in infants.

The Chemical Senses

OLFACTION

The physical characteristics that determine whether or not a substance has odor are not known precisely. A necessary condition for a substance to be odorous, of course, is that it be volatile, for it must be in a gaseous state to reach the appropriate receptors. Presumably, the gaseous form of the substance must also be soluble, since it apparently must enter the linings of the nasal cavities in order to stimulate the olfactory receptors. A substance can be both volatile and soluble in a variety of solvents, however, and yet not be odorous. Other physical characteristics of a material such as chemical composition, the manner in which it absorbs or reflects light, and so on, seem to be only partially correlated with odorousness. And, of course, if there is uncertainty concerning the physical properties distinguishing odorous from nonodorous substances, it must be expected that the relations of stimulus properties to differential odors is even more obscure.

The olfactory receptors are located in a small area (the olfactory epithelium) at the very top of each nasal cavity where they come in contact with a small portion of all air passing through the nostrils. Exactly how this contact with odorous materials in the air results in stimulation of the receptors is not known. The actual receptors, several million in number, are endings of the first cranial (olfactory) nerve; hence they serve as a kind of combination receptor and ganglion cell, i.e., they serve both as generators and conductors of nerve impulses. In addition to olfactory receptors, the olfactory epithelium contains endings of the fifth cranial (trigeminal) nerve. These nerve endings mediate the sense of touch, and are readily activated by various substances such as menthol, ammonia, and acetic acid. Moreover, it has been demonstrated that certain substances usually considered to be olfactory stimuli—e.g., phenylethyl alcohol—might, in high concentration, activate both the trigeminal and olfactory nerves (Tucker, 1961). It is thus sometimes difficult to determine whether a particular stimulus substance is an olfactory stimulus, an irritant of the trigeminal nerve endings, or both.

Absolute Thresholds. About the only agreement among studies prior to 1930 dealing with olfaction in newborn infants was that neonates do respond in some manner to substances such as ammonia and acetic acid and that these are responses to irritation of the trigeminal nerve rather than to stimulation of smell receptors. (For a complete review of these earlier studies, see Disher, 1934.) There was disagreement on whether infants would respond at all to "pure odors," much less discriminate among different odors or respond differentially to odors considered pleasant and unpleasant. Apparently, none of the earlier studies provided for systematic variations of intensity of stimulation, and few obtained objective recordings of the infants' responses.

One of the first studies to introduce a control stimulus (air) with which to compare responses to odorous substances was that of Pratt, Nelson, and Sun (1930). Movements of 48 infants ranging from birth to twenty-one days of age were recorded from a stabilimeter following presentation of valerian, oil of cloves, acetic acid, ammonia, or air. Only 48 per cent of all presentations of the odorants elicited more activity than air, and of these, almost all (91 per cent) were elicited by ammonia and acetic acid. No relationship was observed between frequency of response and age of the subject.

Disher (1934) used a procedure similar to that of Pratt *et al.* except that two observers noted movements of the subjects and recorded these movements manually. Seven relatively pure odors, in that stimulation of the trigeminal nerve was presumed to be negligible, were presented in five different concentrations: violet, asafoetida, citronella, turpentine, pyridine, and lemon. Air was also presented as a control stimulus. Disher observed a total of 91 infants, aged three hours to ten days. All seven odorants elicited movement responses more frequently than an air puff did, but these frequencies were approximately the same for the various odors. Furthermore, response frequency did not vary with subject's age. Responses did increase with stimulus intensity, but no attempt was made to determine intensity thresholds for these odors.

For nearly thirty years following Disher's study, the investigation of olfaction in infants was almost completely neglected. Recently, however, a group of experimenters at Brown University has carried out a series of studies in this area (Engen, Lipsitt, & Kaye, 1963; Lipsitt, Engen, & Kaye, 1963; Engen & Lipsitt, 1965). The Lipsitt *et al.* study (1963) seems to demonstrate conclusively that (a) infants do indeed respond to at least one odor (asafoetida) shortly after birth, and (b) the intensity threshold for this odor decreases systematically over the first few days of life. Lipsitt *et al.* tested ten apparently normal, newborn infants within twenty-four hours of birth and at twenty-four-hour intervals during the second, third, and fourth days. The infants were observed in a stabilimeter, with an additional device attached to one of the infant's legs for recording limb movements. Respiration changes were also recorded by means of a pneumograph attached around the infant's abdomen. Each of these response-sensing devices was linked to a separate channel of a polygraph. The stimulus odorant was tincture asafoetida in various percentages of concentration in solution with a nonodorous diluent, diethyl phthalate. The experimenters prepared concentrations of 1.5625, 3.125, 6.25, 12.5, 25, 50, and 100 per cent asafoetida and a control stimulus of 100 per cent odorless diluent. On each trial a piece of cotton saturated with one of the stimulus solutions was held just below the subject's nostrils for ten seconds, with about one minute allowed between trials. On each day the infant was presented first the control stimulus (0 per cent asafoetida), followed by an ascending series of percentage concentrations until a response detectably greater than that to the control stimulus was observed. The threshold for an infant on a given day was recorded as the percentage concentration in the series that first elicited a response greater than that to the preceding, control stimulus. The possibility of diminished sensitivity of the subjects due to adaptation was thus minimized in this study because no subject received more than one suprathreshold stimulus on any day. The results indicated there was a significant increase in olfactory sensitivity over the four days: the mean threshold percentage concentration, just under 60 per cent on the first day, decreased monotonically over successive days to about 15 per cent on day four.

That previous studies had indicated infrequent responses by infants to asafoetida and similar odors was interpreted by Lipsitt *et al.* as due to the fact that earlier studies typically presented the stimulus odors repeatedly within sessions; consequently, response habituation and/or decreasing sensitivity due to sensory adaptation resulted in failure to respond on large numbers of trials. Examination of a few studies on adaptation and habituation will support the tenability of this interpretation.

Adaptation and Habituation. That the olfactory sense undergoes adaptation is well known (cf. Geldard, 1953). Unlike visual and auditory sensations, however, a particular olfactory sensation tends to disappear altogether with prolonged stimulation—a fact which Geldard has described as "at once a blessing, in the case of the tannery worker, and a hazard, in the case of those whose 'best friends will not even tell them'!" (1953, p. 287).

Several studies have demonstrated response decrements in newborn infants with repeated olfactory stimulations, but it has not been clear in most cases whether the decrements were due to sensory adaptation or to response habituation. Bronshtein, Antonova, Kamenetskaya, Luppova, and Sytova (1958), for example, observed that when iodoform, peppermint, or anise oil was presented to infants actively sucking a pacifier, the sucking initially would be interrupted; but after a few presentations of the stimulus odors, this suppression of the sucking response decreased until eventually the stimuli had no effect at all.

Engen, Lipsitt, and Kaye (1963) recorded leg withdrawals, respiration, general activity, and heart rate of newborn (thirty-two to sixty-eight hours old) infants during successive presentations of full strength acetic acid, phenylethyl alcohol, asafoetida, or anise oil. A response to the stimulus was said to have occurred if at least two of three judges agreed that the polygraph records showed a greater response on a stimulus-presentation trial than on an immediately preceding control trial with no odorant presented. One group of subjects receiving both acetic acid and phenylethyl alcohol showed significant numbers of responses to both these stimuli, with acetic acid producing a much higher percentage of responses than phenylethyl alcohol. There was no reliable diminution of responses over the ten trials in either case. A second group received either ten presentations of anise oil followed by ten presentations of asafoetida, or the reverse (ten presentations of asafoetida, then ten of anise oil). In either case, the odorant presented during the first ten trials was reintroduced for two trials immediately following the ten presentations of the second odorant. Frequencies of responding decreased substantially over the ten trials for both anise and asafoetida. This was true for either odorant whether it was presented first or second, though the overall frequency of responding was lower for either odorant when it was presented second. Reintroduction of either stimulus odor following the intervening ten presentations of the other odorant resulted in recovery of response frequencies to levels observed during the early trials of its initial presentations.

The results of this study as well as the data reported by Bronshtein *et al.* are consistent with interpretations either in terms of sensory adaptation or response habituation. Some writers (Martin, 1964; Rheingold & Stanley, 1963) have argued that the distinction between adaptation and habituation is not a useful one, since operationally, they appear to be one phenomenon, namely, response decrements with repeated stimulation. Others (Bartoshuk, 1962a; 1962b; Thorpe, 1956) have emphasized that many instances of observed response decrements to repeated sensory stimulation might be interpreted as a kind of learning: the repeated stimulation results in extinction of responses not followed by reinforcement. (Bronshtein *et al.*, as well as other Pavlovian theorists, interpret response decrement with repeated stimulation in terms of external inhibition.) The need for such a hypothesis has arisen from experimental demonstrations of response decrements where the usual interpretation of sensory adaptation in terms of receptor or neural fatigue does not seem applicable (e.g., the study by Bartoshuk, 1962b, described above). A recent demonstration of this phenomenon with olfactory stimuli has been reported by Engen and Lipsitt (1965). Each of two groups of ten newborn infants was first presented, for ten trials, a mixture of 33.3 per cent amyl acetate, 16.7 per cent heptanol, and 50 per cent nonodorous diluent; then, on trials 11 and 12, one group was presented a solution of 33.3 per cent amyl acetate and 66.7 per cent diluent, while the other group received a 16.7 per cent heptanol–83.3 per cent diluent mixture. On each trial a response to the stimulus was defined as a change in the subject's regular breathing as recorded on a polygraph linked to a pneumograph around the infant's abdomen.

The average frequency of responses to the mixture decreased linearly over the ten trials, but on the posttest trials—when the component odorants were presented singly in solution with the diluent—a significant increase in response frequency was observed, both for amyl acetate and for heptanol. If the response decrements during the ten presentations of the mixture had been due to receptor adaptation, there should have been no recovery of the response on the posttest trials, since for each group, the posttest stimuli were present in the mixture during the pretest trials. Accordingly, the results were interpreted in terms of response habituation, and the response recovery, or dishabituation, on the posttest trials was assumed to have been the result of introducing a "novel" stimulus. That novelty was a relevant aspect of the posttest stimuli in producing dishabituation was suggested by the additional finding that amyl acetate on the posttest trials produced greater response recovery than heptanol. This interpretation was consistent with the judgments of a group of adults that amyl acetate was slightly more dissimilar to the amyl acetate-heptanol mixture than heptanol.

GUSTATION

It is generally agreed that there are four basic introspectively identifiable taste qualities: salt, sour, bitter, and sweet. And these qualities are somewhat more closely correlated with the chemical composition of the stimulus substance than is true for different odors. To be an effective stimulus for taste, a substance must be soluble in water since the substance must be in solution with saliva (or something equivalent) in order to come in contact with the taste receptors.

Most human taste receptors (taste buds) are located in small raised spots (papillae) covering the dorsal surface of the tongue, but areas sensitive to taste stimuli are also found on the palate, the tonsils and epiglottis, in the pharynx and larynx, and even on the mucosa of the cheeks and the floor of the mouth (Bornstein, 1940). Taste buds are distributed extensively over the mouth and throat regions early in prenatal life according to Parker (1922), but by the late fetal stages, they begin disappearing from regions other than the tongue. This suggests that the sense of taste might be well developed before birth. It seems unlikely that there is any adequate stimulation of the appropriate receptors until after birth, however, since the only source of stimulation would be amniotic fluid, and it is essentially unchanging during the prenatal period (Carmichael, 1954).

There was considerable lack of agreement among early behavioral studies concerned with the extent to which the sense of taste is developed in newborn infants (see review by Pratt, 1954). Some investigators (e.g., Peterson & Rainey, 1910) concluded that this sense is highly developed in neonates, while others (e.g., Blanton, 1917) believed that taste, smell, and touch are not differentiated for some time after birth. The conclusions of most of these studies were based on qualitative observations of such reactions as facial expressions of the infants; the discrepant results and conclusions thus might be attributable primarily to differences in observers in the various studies.

Pratt, Nelson, and Sun (1930) observed general activity as well as sucking and facial movements of newborn infants in response to salt, sugar, quinine, citric acid, and distilled water. By including water as a control stimulus these experimenters obtained some information concerning the extent to which responses to the various taste stimuli were increased by taste quality over the responses due simply to the presence of liquid in the subject's mouth. The results showed that frequency of responding to the four taste stimuli was only slightly higher than that to water, hence it was concluded that taste *per se* was a negligible factor in producing the observed responses.

In contrast to the Pratt *et al.* study, Jensen (1932), using a different method of recording responses, demonstrated clear discriminations among taste qualities by newborn infants. A special feeding bottle was constructed and linked to a manometer such that an infant's sucking responses could be measured and recorded on a polygraph. Sucking responses to water, acid, glucose, and various concentrations of salt solutions were compared to responses to milk as a control stimulus. Each presentation of an experimental stimulus was preceded and followed by a presentation of the control stimulus. The results indicated that responses to each of the experimental stimuli differed from those to milk, and the magnitude of the differences between responses to milk and to salt solutions varied with the percentage concentrations of salt.

That Jensen found differential responses to different taste stimuli by newborn infants although many previous investigators did not was probably due to the nature of the response variable observed in this study: it should not be surprising that differential taste stimulation should have more pronounced effects on sucking behavior than on any other motor movements. Evidence supporting this notion is provided by Jensen's finding that noticeable facial expressions occurred only with differential sucking responses, but differential sucking responses occurred 95 per cent of the time without marked facial expression changes.

SUMMARY OF THE CHEMICAL SENSES

Recent studies have established that newborn infants do respond to olfactory stimuli, and that the intensity threshold to such stimuli decreases over the first three or four days of life. Many early studies indicated a lack of olfactory sensitivity probably because repeated presentations of the stimuli within sessions resulted in reduced responsivity of the subjects due to adaptation and/or response habituation. Both of these processes have been demonstrated in infants.

By observing changes in sucking responses to various taste stimuli, one investigator (Jensen, 1932) established clear indications of discrimination among taste qualities by newborn infants. Sucking responses to water, acid, glucose, and various concentrations of salt solutions were clearly different from responses to milk as a control stimulus.

Somethesis and Vestibular Functions

By far the most intensively studied senses are vision and audition, and to a lesser extent, taste and smell; yet these might be viewed as having less biological significance for the human infant than several less frequently studied senses. It is quite possible for a person to function without vision, hearing, taste, or smell, but it is difficult indeed to survive without kinesthesis for sensing and controlling position and movements, without pain receptors to detect potential injury, or without a thermal sense to detect threats to maintenance of a stable body temperature. The present section will be concerned with these vital, though less well known senses. The cutaneous senses (touch, pain, and temperature), kinesthesis, and the vestibular senses will be considered in that order.

THE CUTANEOUS SENSES

Human skin shows sensitivity to a variety of stimuli: mechanical, thermal, electrical, and chemical. And since the discovery of different types of nerve terminations in the skin, it has been widely believed that the various cutaneous sensations result from differential sensitivity of these structures to specific forms of stimulation. Precise relations between the cutaneous sensations and particular types of nerve endings have not been well established, however. The simplest and most prevalent structure of the skin is the free nerve ending, which is found over the entire body; and the more complex end organs appear simply to be elaborations of this basic type (Geldard, 1953). A common assumption has been that the free nerve endings are exclusively receptors for pain, but evidence suggests that these endings probably mediate all cutaneous sensations while the more elaborate end organs have auxiliary functions (Morgan, 1965).

Pressure and Touch Sensitivity. It has been well established that pressure and touch sensitivity are present in newborn infants (Pratt, 1937) and even in fetuses several months before birth (Carmichael, 1954). Some writers, e.g., Irwin (1930), and Pratt, Nelson, and Sun (1930), have emphasized the gross undifferentiated characteristics of infants' responses to tactual stimulation; the more specific responses manifested by older children and adults are assumed by these writers to be the result of a gradual process of differentiation. By analyzing photographs of neonates' responses to tactual stimulation of each of the four limbs, Delman (1935) attempted to show that the differentiation process begins very early, however. Although stimulation of any extremity usually results in movements of both hands and both feet, movement of the stimulated limb occurs first with greater than chance frequency. Thus, although responses tend to be generalized, some patterning may be observed even in very young subjects.

Other writers have pointed out that a variety of stimulus-specific behavior patterns or reflexes such as sucking and swallowing, sneezing, palmar responses, and plantar responses are present even before birth. From a review of studies reporting demonstrations of such reflex response patterns in fetal subjects, Carmichael concluded that "given a stimulus just above the lower threshold and a quiescent fetus in a standard posture, there is typically *one behavior act* or *reflex* set off by the stimulation of each cutaneous area. These cutaneous 'push buttons' are remarkably specific in their behavioral relations when the complexity of the central nervous system is considered" (1954, p. 142). These reflexes tend to persist for some weeks following birth, but eventually they are replaced by voluntary movements. A study by Halverson (1937), for example, showed that light pressure stimulations of the palms of infants under sixteen weeks of age usually resulted in immediate closure and gripping; but as ages increased, these responses disappeared and were replaced by withdrawal of the hand from the stimulus.

Pain Sensitivity. The major concern of early research on pain sensitivity in infants was (a) determining the nature of sensitivity changes with age, and (b) determining whether different parts of the body were differentially sensitive to pain stimuli, with the pattern of this differential sensitivity changing with development of the infant. Sherman and Sherman (1925) studied both these phenomena by determining the number of pinpricks on the face and on the legs required to elicit startle responses in infants ranging in age from five to eighty hours. Whether the pinpricks were applied to the cheeks or to the calf of the leg, the number required to elicit a response decreased systematically with age of the subjects, but the infants were consistently more responsive to pinpricks on the face than on the legs. The greater sensitivity in the head region was interpreted as a continuation of the general pattern of cephalo-caudal development observed in growth of the fetus.

In apparent contradiction of the Sherman and Sherman findings, Dockeray and Rice (1934) found no differences in the vigor and speed of responses to pinpricks in infants ranging from one to five days of age, and among these subjects, the legs showed quicker and more vigorous reactions than the arms or head in response to the stimulus. Sherman, Sherman, and Flory (1936) replicated the earlier results of Sherman and Sherman (1925), however, and these investigators pointed out that sensitivity was better indicated by their measure of thresholds than by the speed and vigorousness of the responses in the part of the body stimulated.

A recent study by Lipsitt and Levy (1959) clearly demonstrated systematic decreases in response thresholds for electrotactual stimulation over the first four days of life. The threshold on each day was determined by delivering an ascending series of two-second electric shocks, consisting of 10-cps monophasic pulses of two-msec duration. The voltage was increased in five-volt steps over trials until a discrete extension of the toes or a leg withdrawal was observed immediately following application of the stimulus. The results were comparable for two separate experiments, one in which the same infants were tested repeatedly over days, the other in which different groups were tested separately at different ages. In either case, the mean thresholds decreased from about 85 to 90 volts on the first day following birth to around 70 volts on the fourth day.

Results of a study reported by Gullickson and Crowell (1964) appear on the surface to contradict the Lipsitt and Levy findings. These investigators used a procedure similar to that reported by Lipsitt and Levy (1959) except for a slightly different stimulus (half-second presentations of a four-cps monophasic pulse stimulus with pulse durations of 20 msec), and a somewhat more stringent response criterion for determining thresholds (foot movements of specific magnitude on two consecutive trials). Mean thresholds were determined for infants in two groups on each of the three days following birth, and both groups were given 15 suprathreshold electrotactual stimulations on each day following threshold determination (where the stimulations were paired with tones for one group but not the other). Both these groups showed significant *increases* in threshold over the three days. The intervening stimulation, rather than a difference in the nature of the stimulus, apparently was the critical factor producing results opposite those obtained by Lipsitt and Levy, since the mean threshold for a third group observed for the first time on the third day following birth was about 15 volts below the mean first-day threshold for the other two groups. This is a fairly close replication of the results of one of the experiments reported by Lipsitt and Levy (1959).

The Gullickson and Crowell study thus provides another instance, along with the habituation studies discussed previously, in which response threshold changes apparently do not reflect changes in receptor or neural sensitivity—in fact, in the present case, the evidence suggests that response thresholds were raised by the intervening stimulations in spite of *greater* sensitivity on the second and third days. An interpretation of these findings favored by the experimenters was that the electrotactual stimulations between the daily threshold determinations provided the infants an opportunity to learn not to respond to this stimulus—i.e., the responses were not reinforced. Of further interest, in view of this interpretation, is an additional finding that a group of infants exposed for 15 trials to loud tones (not accompanied by shock) following electrotactual threshold determinations on each of the first three days following birth showed neither a decrease nor an increase in response threshold over days. This suggests that possibly the observed reductions in responsivity were due in part to habituation of a general "arousal" response that tended initially to be elicited by the tone as well as by the electrotactual stimulus.

Thermal Sensitivity. That newborn infants are sensitive to temperature changes has been well established. (See Pratt, 1954, for a review of evidence.) Such findings, of course, should not be very surprising; sensitivity to temperature variation is necessary for regulation of body temperature, which is essential for survival—and infants do survive fairly diverse environmental temperatures. Mestyan and Varga (1960) have shown that the mechanisms for thermoregulation are not completely effective during the first few days of life, however. Several infants one to ten days old were placed in an airtight metabolic chamber and submerged in water of controlled temperatures, and continuous records were kept of oxygen consumption, rectal body temperature, and muscular activity. When placed in such an environment with temperatures at 20° to 22° C, infants under six days old showed increases in muscular activity and increases in oxygen consumption, but body temperatures tended to decrease somewhat from normal. The older subjects (six to ten days), on the other hand, tended to maintain a constant body temperature when placed in this cooled environment.

The influence of environmental temperature on food and water intake was reported by Cooke (1952). Six normal infants from 14 to 231 days old were observed for an extended period with the room temperature at either 81° or 91° F. There was an increase in water intake and a decrease in milk intake when the temperature was higher, with this relationship less marked among the younger subjects.

Quantitative data indicating infants' sensitivity to temperature stimuli applied locally have been reported by Pratt, Nelson, and Sun (1930), and by Jensen (1932). Jensen recorded sucking rate by neonates from a specially constructed bottle containing milk of various temperatures. For each infant the range of milk temperatures was determined where no sucking responses different from the response to milk at 40° C were observed. The mean upper and lower differential response thresholds for 17 infants were 53.5° and 18.1° C. Since these threshold values are very nearly symmetrical around the normal infant's body temperature, it might be supposed that a neutral temperature stimulus for an infant would be his body temperature, and temperature stimuli above or below this level would be increasingly effective in eliciting responses. But this expectation is not confirmed by data of Pratt *et al.* (1930). These investigators noted infants' motor reactions in response to drops of water applied to the tongue with a medicine dropper, when the temperature of the water was varied from 8° to 53° C. A plot of the mean numbers of reactions per stimulation as a function of temperature of the applied stimulus (data from all 30 subjects in their Table CXIV, p. 160) yields a curve with a minimum slightly above 40° C. The conclusion of Pratt *et al.* that "the infants reacted less strongly to the temperatures which are warmer than body temperature than to those which are colder" (p. 167) is thus supported by these data, notwithstanding Jensen's (1932) criticism that Pratt *et al.* had presented more stimulus temperatures below body temperature than above.

Both the Jensen and Pratt, Nelson, and Sun studies seem to lend support to the almost universal practice of warming babies' milk or formula to body temperature. It is somewhat surprising, therefore, that a recent study (Holt, Davies, Hasselmeyer, & Adams, 1962) demonstrated that no deleterious effects whatever result from feeding premature newborn infants milk formula taken directly from a refrigerator (at 7° to 11° C). (The investigators used premature infants in order to have a conservative test of their procedure.) Seventeen infants were given feedings of normal, approximately body temperature milk, while sixteen received cold feedings only. Over 2000 feedings of each group took place during the period of observation. The only statistically significant difference that could be found between the two groups was a slight average drop in body temperature (.2° F) immediately following feeding among the cold-milk infants. No differences were observed in weight gains, vocal behavior, sleep patterns, or frequency of regurgitation, nor were any observable differences noted in the behavior of the infants during feeding.

That infants may be relatively insensitive to cold—and increasingly so with age—is also apparent from Tur's description of the way in which infants are raised in his residential nursery, Department of Physiology, Medical Pediatrics Institution of Leningrad (Brackbill, 1962). Tur writes,

> From the age of one month, infants take air baths. At first, the baths are two minutes long, but gradually they are lengthened to from 10 to 15 minutes, for one-year-old infants, and to 30 minutes for three-year-old infants. The temperature of the room where the air baths are taken is 71.6° F for infants under one year and from

64.4° to 68° F for those between one and three years. During the summer, air baths are taken in the garden in the shade at the above temperatures. Air baths are never given directly after meals nor on an empty stomach. The infant having an air bath is quite naked, and should not necessarily be lying down, but may play quiet games.

The clinic uses fresh air in other ways to strengthen the infants; in winter they take walks up to four hours a day; in summer they are out of doors the whole day. They also sleep outdoors in the daytime at all seasons. In winter the infants sleep in special sleeping bags, if the temperature outdoors is not lower than 14° F. At lower daytime temperatures or in a strong wind they sleep indoors with the windows open.

The water strengthening treatment is both local and general. Local water strengthening means a daily sponging or douche of the feet with cool water once or twice a day, beginning at age one month. The temperature of the water is gradually decreased to that of tap water. This type of strengthening is a good prophylaxis for infants against colds, rheumatic illnesses, and aggravation of all chronic diseases connected with chilling.

A general water treatment for infants from six to twelve months of age is general sponging. At first, the temperature of the water is 96.8° F; every two or three days it is lowered by 1.8° F until it reaches 77° F. After the age of one year, infants receive showers instead of general sponging. The temperature of the water is also gradually lowered every two to three days by 1.8° F—from 86° to 77° F. In the summer time showers are taken out of doors (Brackbill, 1962, pp. 101–102).

THE SENSES OF MOVEMENT AND POSITION: PROPRIOCEPTION

All of the sensory systems examined thus far involved *exteroceptors,* or receptors sensitive to stimuli external to the organism. Another important group of receptors, called *proprioceptors,* are stimulated primarily by actions of the body itself.

Kinesthesis. The kinesthetic receptors, located in the muscles and tendons, are stimulated by both passive and voluntary movements of various parts of the body, thus providing continuous information concerning the positions of different body parts. Carmichael (1954) cites evidence that kinesthetic receptors are functional well before birth, and are rather highly organized by the time an infant is born. He concludes that "much of the 'movement of the organism as a whole' which so many writers refer to seems to be the result of rather specific proprioceptive stimulation. Such stimulation often leads to the 'spread' of what are really quite delicately timed families of specific responses which can easily be mistaken for 'vague' or 'diffuse' behavior" (p. 146). Research on kinesthesis in postpartum infants appears to have been limited to informal observations attesting to the ubiquity and importance of this sense (e.g., Blanton, 1917).

The Vestibular Senses. The inner ear contains not only the cochlea, in which auditory receptors are located, but also the vestibular apparatus consisting of receptor organs sensitive to acceleration and to position. Responses to rotational, and to some extent, linear acceleration (positive or negative) of the head are mediated by three semicircular canals in each ear. Stimulation of the appropriate receptors requires that the semicircular canal in which they are located be rotated in the plane in which it lies, but since the canals lie in three planes approximately at right angles to one another, rotation of the head in any direction results in appreciable rotation of at least one right and one left canal. Responses to position with respect to gravity, and sensitivity to linear acceleration depend on the otolith organs located at the base of the semicircular canals. These organs, along with the semicircular canals and the cochlea, are supplied by the VIIIth cranial (acoustic) nerve.

Almost all behavioral studies dealing with vestibular functions in human infants have been concerned with nystagmic eye movements (repeated slow movements of the eyes in one direction followed by fast return to the original position) as a function of stimulation of the semi-circular canal receptors. All studies appear to agree that nystagmus can be demonstrated in neonates, but there is little agreement on even the gross details of the actual form of infants' responses to rotation. Bartels (1910), for example, reported that if an infant was rotated in a hori-zontal position, head movements were in a direction opposite the rota-tion, while Alexander (1911) found that head movements were in the same direction as the rotation, with this direction reversed following rotation. Baldenweck and Guy-Arnaud (1940) concluded that nystag-mus in response to rotation in a newborn infant was the same as is observed in adults, yet McGraw (1941) reported observing distinct changes in nystagmic responses over the first two years of age. Most of these discrepancies are probably due to failure to control critical pro-cedural details. Studies of nystagmus in infants typically have used an adaptation of the classical procedure described by Bárány (1907): an experimenter holds the infant and observes its eyes while both experi-menter and infant are accelerated to a rotational velocity of about 180 degrees per second, with this velocity maintained for a short period—say, 20 seconds—whereupon the rotation is stopped somewhat abruptly. Two factors having definite effects on the results are (a) whether or not the subjects' eyes are open and light is present during rotation, and (b) the duration of constant-velocity rotation between the initial positive acceleration and deceleration (Heck, 1952). If a subject has his eyes open during the rotation there is a tendency for him to fixate points in his (apparently) moving environment, hence even in complete absence of vestibular stimulation, his eyes would very likely move slowly in a direction opposite the rotation with rapid returns to central fixation. The potential effect of duration of the acceleration-deceleration interval may be seen from consideration of the sequence of events observed in a well-controlled experiment with an eyes-closed adult subject (e.g., Wendt, 1951). Rapid onset of rotation initiates nystagmus, with the direction of the slow phase opposite that of rotation. This primary nystagmus continues at a decreasing rate for about 25 to 50 seconds (provided the rotation is continued at a constant velocity), whereupon the direction of the slow phase reverses (*secondary* nystagmus), and continues for several minutes. Since rotational deceleration affects the semicircular canals in exactly the same way as acceleration, the sequence of events following rapid cessation of rotation (postrotation nystagmus) is the same as that following onset except that the direction of eye movements is reversed. This is true, however, only if constant velocity of rotation is maintained sufficiently long following onset to permit completion of the sequence of nystagmic responses to acceleration. If the acceleration-deceleration interval is not sufficiently long, the postrotation nystagmus is altered by continuing responses to onset of rotation—in fact, since the directions of eye movements to acceleration and to deceleration are opposite, it is possible that the opposing responses will cancel one another, eliminating any indication of postrotation nystagmus.

As suggested above, studies of infants' vestibular functions typically have involved rotating the infant with its eyes open—thus confounding visual fixations with semicircular canal-related nystagmus in observations of response to acceleration—and typically have limited the acceleration-deceleration interval to times less than the probable duration of the response sequence to acceleration—thus corrupting observations of postrotation nystagmus. Nevertheless, though the details of vestibular responses of infants are not clear, the fact of vestibular functioning in newborn infants appears to have been well established. Lawrence and Feind (1953), for example, observed some form of postrotation nystagmus in every individual in a sample of 64 infants ranging in age from three hours to ten days. The infants were accelerated on a motor-driven turntable to 30 RPM in 180 degrees, rotated at this rate for 20 seconds, then braked to a stop in 45 degrees. A movie camera was mounted on the turntable so that eye movements of the subjects could be photographed both during and following rotation. Fifty-two of the 64 infants reportedly kept their eyes open during rotation—which was a necessary condition, of course, for obtaining eye movement data, but which, at the same time, precluded obtaining unambiguous indications of vestibular responses during rotation. The mean duration of postrotation nystagmus was 13.1 seconds. Whether this result would differ significantly with longer acceleration-deceleration intervals cannot be said; nystagmus following acceleration reportedly lasted only for "several turns," suggesting there were perhaps no residual effects on the postrotation responses; however, since the eye movements during rotation were observed under an eyes-open condition, the significance of their duration is difficult to assess. Completely unambiguous data on nystagmus as a function of dynamic vestibular stimulation presumably will require that the subjects be rotated in darkness, with eye movements recorded electronically.

SUMMARY OF SOMETHESIS AND VESTIBULAR FUNCTIONS

It appears that pressure and touch sensitivity are present in newborn infants and even in fetuses several months before birth. Some writers have emphasized the gross undifferentiated characteristics of infants' responses to tactual stimulation, with the more specific behaviors observed later considered to be the result of a gradual process of differentiation. Others have pointed to a variety of stimulus-specific behavior patterns or reflexes such as sucking, swallowing, and sneezing, which are present even before birth.

The response threshold for electrotactual stimulation apparently decreases over the first few days of life, provided no similar stimulation is experienced between the threshold determinations. Infants in one study involving presentation of suprathreshold electric shocks between daily determinations of electrotactual thresholds showed increases in the infants' thresholds over the first three days following birth.

Although newborn infants have been shown to respond differentially to small differences in temperature, no differences were demonstrated in a study comparing infants fed cold milk ($7–11°$ C) with infants given milk warmed to body temperature.

Vestibular functioning in infants, as indicated by observations of rotational and postrotational nystagmus, appears to be similar to that of adults. A complete description of the response sequence of infants to acceleration is not available, however, because of procedural problems in previous studies.

References

Adler, F. H. *Physiology of the eye.* St. Louis: Mosby, 1959.

Ahrens, R. Beitrag zur Entwicklung des Physiognomie- und Mimikerkennens. (Contribution to the development of recognition of physiognomy and mimicry.) *Z. exp. angew. Psychol.,* 1954, 2, 412–454. Alexander, G. Die Reflexerregbarkeit des Ohrlabyrinthes an Menschlichen Neugeborenen. (Excitability of the labyrinth in human neonates.) *Z. Psychol. Physiol. Sinnesort.,* 1911, 45, 153–196. Cited by K. C. Pratt, The neonate. In L. Carmichael (Ed.), *Manual of child psychology.* (2nd ed.) New York: Wiley, 1954.

Allen, H. F. Testing of acuity in pre-school children. *Pediatrics,* 1957, 19, 1093–1100.

Alpern, M. Movements of the eyes. In H. Davson (Ed.), *The eye.* Vol. 3, part 1. New York: Academic Press, 1962.

Ambrose, J. A. The development of the smiling response in early infancy. In B. Foss (Ed.), *Determinants of infant behaviour.* New York: Wiley, 1961.

Baldenweck, L., & Guy-Arnaud. Valeur fonctionnelle du labyrinthe vestibulaire chez le nouveauné. (Functional importance of the labyrinth in the neonate.) *La presse medicale,* 1940, 48, 47–49.

Bárány, R. Physiologie und Pathologie des Bogengang-apparates beim Menschen. (Physiology and pathology of the auditory canal in humans.) Vienna: Deuticke, 1907. Cited by R. S. Woodworth & H. Schlosberg, *Experimental psychology.* (Rev. ed.) New York: Holt, 1954.

Barnet, A. B., Lodge, A., & Armington, J. C. Electroretinogram in newborn human infants. *Science,* 1965, 148, 651–654.

Barr, B. Pure tone audiometry for preschool children. *Acta Otolaryng.,* 1954, Suppl. 110, 89–101.

Bartels, M. Über Regulierung der Augenstellung durch den Ohrenapparat. (Regulation of the position of the eyes by the apparatus of the ear.) *Graefes Arch. Ophthal.,* 1910, 76, 1–79. Cited by K. C. Pratt, The neonate. In L. Carmichael (Ed.), *Manual of child psychology.* (2nd ed.) New York: Wiley, 1954.

Bartoshuk, A. K. Response decrement with repeated elicitation of human neonatal cardiac acceleration to sound. *J. comp. physiol. Psychol.,* 1962, 55, 9–13. (a)

———. Human neonatal cardiac acceleration to sound: Habituation and dishabituation. *Percept. mot. Skills,* 1962, 15, 15–27. (b)

Beasley, W. C. Visual pursuit in 109 white and 142 Negro newborn infants. *Child Develpm.,* 1933, 4, 106–120.

Békésy, G. von. *Experiments in hearing.* New York: McGraw-Hill, 1960.

Berlyne, D. E. The influence of the albedo and complexity of stimuli on visual fixation in the human infant. *Brit. J. Psychol.,* 1958, 49, 315–318.

Bernard, J., & Sontag, L. W. Fetal reactivity to tonal stimulation: A preliminary report. *J. genet. Psychol.,* 1947, 70, 205–210.

Beyrl, F. Über die Grossenauffassung bei Kindern. (On size perception in children.) *Z. Psychol.,* 1926, 100, 344–371. Translated and reprinted in Y. Brackbill & G. G. Thompson (Eds.) *Behavior in infancy and early childhood: A book of readings.* New York: Free Press, 1967.

Birns, B., Blank, M., Bridger, W. H., & Escalona, S. K. Behavioral inhibition in neonates produced by auditory stimuli. *Child Develpm.,* 1965, 36, 639–645.

Blanton, M. G. The behavior of the human infant during the first thirty days of life. *Psychol. Rev.,* 1917, 24, 456–483.

Bordley, J. E., & Hardy, W. G. A study in objective audiometry with the use of a psychogalvanometric response. *Ann. Otol.,* 1949, 58, 751–760.

Bornstein, W. S. Cortical representation of taste in man and monkey. II. The localization of the cortical taste area in man and a method of measuring impairment of taste in man. *Yale J. Biol. Med.,* 1940, 13, 133–156.

Brackbill, Y. Extinction of the smiling response in infants as a function of reinforcement schedule. *Child Develpm.,* 1958, 29, 115–124. Reprinted in Y. Brackbill & G. G. Thompson (Eds.), *Behavior in infancy and early childhood: A book of readings.* New York: Free Press, 1967.

———. Research and clinical work with children. In R. Bauer (Ed.), *Some views on Soviet psychology.* Washington, D.C.: Amer. Psychol. Ass., 1962.

Brackbill, Y., Adams, G., Crowell, D. H., and Gray, M. L. Arousal level in neonates and older infants under continuous auditory stimulation. *J. exp. child Psychol.,* 1966, 4, No. 2, 178–188.

Brian, C. R., & Goodenough, F. L. The relative potency of color and form perception at various ages. *J. exp. Psychol.,* 1929, 12, 197–213.

Bridger, W. H. Sensory habituation and discrimination in the human neonate. *Amer. J. Psychiat.,* 1961, 117, 991–996.

Brindley, G. S. *Physiology of the retina and the visual pathway.* London: Edward Arnold Ltd., 1960.

Brodal, A. *The cranial nerves.* Oxford: Blackwell Scientific Publications, 1959.

Bronshtein, A. I., Antonova, T. G., Kamenetskaya, A. G., Luppova, N. N., & Sytova, V. A. On the development of the functions of analyzers in infants and some animals at the early stage of ontogenesis. In *Problems of evolu-*

tion of physiological functions. Acad. Sci., U.S.S.R., 1958 (Dept. of Health, Educ. & Welf., U.S.A. Translation Service).

Bronshtein, A. I., & Petrova, E. P. Issledovanie zvukovogo analizatora novorozhdennykh i detei rannego grudnogo vozrasta. (An investigation of the auditory analyzer in neonates and young infants.) *Zh. vyssh. nerv. Deiatel.*, 1952, 2, 333–343. Translated and reprinted in Y. Brackbill & G. G. Thompson (Eds.), *Behavior in infancy and early childhood: A book of readings.* New York: Free Press, 1967.

Brown, C. A. The development of visual capacity in the infant and young child. *Cerebral Palsy Bull.*, 1961, 3, 364–372.

Burnham, R. W., Hanes, R. M., & Bartleson, C. J. *Color: A guide to basic facts and concepts.* New York: Wiley, 1963.

Canestrini, S. Über das Sinnesleben des Neugeborenen. (Sensations of the neonate.) *Monogr. a. d. Gestamtgeb. d. Neur. u Psychiat.*, No. 5. Berlin: Springer, 1913.

Cantor, G. N. Responses of infants and children to complex and novel stimulation. In L. P. Lipsitt & C. C. Spiker (Eds.), *Advances in child development and behavior.* Vol. 1. New York: Academic Press, 1963.

Carmichael, L. The onset and early development of behavior. In L. Carmichael (Ed.), *Manual of child psychology.* (2nd ed.) New York: Wiley, 1954.

Chase, W. P. Color vision in infants. *J. exp. Psychol.*, 1937, 20, 203–222.

Chun, R. W. M., Pawsat, R., & Forster, F. M. Sound localization in infancy. *J. nerv. ment. Dis.*, 1960, 130, 472–476.

Cook, R. C., & Glasscock, R. E. Refractive and ocular findings in the new-born. *Amer. J. Ophthal.*, 1951, 34, 1407–1413.

Cooke, R. E. The behavioural response of infants to heat stress. *Yale J. Biol. Med.*, 1952, 24, 334–340.

Cruikshank, R. M. The development of visual size constancy in early infancy. *J. genet. Psychol.*, 1941, 58, 327–351.

Daniels, P. C. Discrimination of compositional balance at the pre-school level. *Psychol. Monogr.*, 1933, 45, No. 1.

Davson, H. (Ed.) *The eye.* New York: Academic Press, 1962.

Davson, H. *The physiology of the eye.* (2nd ed.) London: J. & A. Churchill Ltd., 1963.

Dayton, G. O., Jr., Jones, M. H., Aiu, P., Rawson, R. A., Steele, B., & Rose, M. Developmental study of coordinated eye movements in the human infant. I. Visual acuity in the newborn human: A study based on induced optico-kinetic nystagmus recorded by electro-oculography. *A. M. A. Arch. Ophthal.*, 1964, 71, 865–870. (a)

Dayton, G. O., Jr., Jones, M. H., Steele, B., & Rose, M. Developmental study of coordinated eye movements in the human infant. II. An electro-oculo-graphic study of the fixation reflex in the newborn. *A. M. A. Arch. Ophthal.*, 1964, 71, 871–875. (b)

Delman, L. The order of participation of limbs in responses to tactual stimula-tion of the newborn infant. *Child Develpm.*, 1935, 6, 98–109.

Disher, D. R. The reactions of newborn infants to chemical stimuli admin-istered nasally. *Ohio State Univer. Stud.*, 1934, 12, 1–52.

Dix, M. R., & Hallpike, C. S. The peep-show. A new technique for pure-tone audiometry in young children. *Brit. Med. J.*, 1947, 2, 719–723.

Dockeray, F. C., & Rice, C. Responses of newborn infants to pain stimulation. *Ohio State Univer. Stud.*, 1934, 12, 82–93.

Engen, T., & Lipsitt, L. P. Decrement and recovery of responses to olfactory stimuli in the human neonate. *J. comp. physiol. Psychol.*, 1965, 59, 312–316. Reprinted in Y. Brackbill & G. G. Thompson (Eds.), *Behavior in infancy and early childhood: A book of readings.* New York: Free Press, 1967.

Engen, T., Lipsitt, L. P., & Kaye, H. Olfactory response and adaptation in the human neonate. *J. comp. physiol. Psychol.*, 1963, 56, 73–77.

Evans, J. N. A visual test for infants. *Amer. J. Ophthal.*, 1946, 29, 73–75.

Ewing, I. R., & Ewing, A. W. G. The ascertainment of deafness in infancy and early childhood. *J. Laryng.*, 1944, 59, 309–333.

Fantz, R. L. A method for studying early visual development. *Percept. mot. Skills*, 1956, 6, 13–15.

――――. Pattern vision in young infants. *Psychol. Rec.*, 1958, 8, 43–47. Reprinted in Y. Brackbill & G. G. Thompson (Eds.), *Behavior in infancy and early childhood: A book of readings.* New York: Free Press, 1967.

――――. A visual acuity test for infants under six months of age. *Psychol. Rec.*, 1959, 9, 159–164.

――――. A method for studying depth perception in infants under six months of age. *Psychol. Rec.*, 1961, 11, 27–32. (a)

――――. The origin of form perception. *Scient. Amer.*, 1961, 204, No. 5, 66–72. (b)

――――. Pattern vision in newborn infants. *Science,* 1963, 140, 296–297.

Fantz, R. L., Ordy, J. M., & Udelf, M. S. Maturation of pattern vision in infants during the first six months. *J. comp. physiol. Psychol.*, 1962, 55, 907–917.

Forbes, H. S., & Forbes, H. B. Fetal sense reaction: Hearing. *J. comp. Psychol.*, 1927, 7, 353–355.

Frank, H. Untersuchung über Sehgrössenkonstanz bei Kindern. (A study of constancy of visually perceived size by children.) *Psychol. Forschung*, 1925, 7, 137–145.

Friderichsen, C., & Edmund, C. Studies of hypovitaminosis A. II. A new method for testing the resorption of Vitamin A from medicaments. *Amer. J. Dis. Children*, 1937, 53, 89–109.

Froeschels, E., & Beebe, H. Testing hearing of newborn infants. *Arch. Otolaryng.*, 1946, 44, 710–714.

Geldard, F. A. *The human senses.* New York: Wiley, 1953.

Gellermann, L. W. Form discrimination in chimpanzees and two-year-old children: I. Form (triangularity) per se. *Ped. Sem.*, 1933, 43, 3–27. (a)

――――. Form discrimination in chimpanzees and two-year-old children: II. Form versus background. *Ped. Sem.*, 1933, 42, 28–50. (b)

Gesell, A. *The mental growth of the pre-school child: A psychological outline of normal development from birth to the sixth year, including a system of developmental diagnosis.* New York: Macmillan, 1925.

Gesell, A., & Ames, L. B. The infant's reaction to his mirror image. *J. genet. Psychol.*, 1947, 70, 141–154.

Gibson, E. J., & Olum, V. Experimental methods of studying perception in children. In P. H. Mussen (Ed.), *Handbook of research methods in child development.* New York: Wiley, 1960.

Gibson, E. J., & Walk, R. D. The "visual cliff." *Scient. Amer.*, 1960, 202, 64–71.

Gidoll, S. H. Quantitative determination of hearing to audiometric frequencies in the electroencephalogram. *Arch. Otolaryng.*, 1952, 55, 597–601.

Goldstein, R., Ludwig, H., & Naunton, R. F. Difficulty in conditioning galvanic skin responses: Its possible significance in clinical audiometry. *Acta Otolaryng.*, 1954, 44, 67–77.

Gorman, J. J., Cogan, D. G., & Gellis, S. S. Apparatus for grading the visual acuity of infants on the basis of opticokinetic nystagmus. *Pediatrics*, 1957, 19, 1088–1092.

Graham, F. K., Ernhart, C. B., Craft, M., & Berman, P. Learning of relative and absolute size concepts in preschool children. *J. exp. child Psychol.*, 1964, 1, 26–36.

Guernsey, M. A quantitative study of the eye reflexes in infancy. *Psychol. Bull.*, 1929, 26, 160–161.

Gullickson, G. R., & Crowell, D. H. Neonatal habituation to electro-tactual stimulation. *J. exp. child Psychol.*, 1964, 1, 388–396.

Haller, M. The reactions of infants to changes in the intensity and pitch of pure tone. *J. genet. Psychol.*, 1932, 40, 162–180.

Halverson, H. M. Studies of the grasping reflex of early infancy: I. *J. genet. Psychol.*, 1937, 51, 371–392.

Hardy, J. B., Dougherty, A., & Hardy, W. G. Hearing responses and audiologic screening in infants. *J. Pediatr.*, 1959, 55, 382–390.

Hardy, W. G., & Bordley, J. E. Evaluation of hearing in young children. *Acta Otolaryng.*, 1951–52, 40, 346–360.

Haynes, H., White, B. L., & Held, R. Visual accommodation in human infants. *Science*, 1965, 148, 528–530.

Heck, J., & Zetterström, B. Electroencephalographic recording of the on- and off-response from the human visual cortex. *Ophthalmologica*, 1958, 136, 258–265.

Heck, W. E. Vestibular responses in the newborn. *Arch. Otolaryng.*, 1952, 56, 573.

Hershenson, M. Visual discrimination in the human newborn. *J. comp. physiol. Psychol.*, 1964, 58, 270–276.

Hicks, J. A., & Stewart, F. D. The learning of abstract concepts of size. *Child Develpm.*, 1930, 1, 195–203.

Hochberg, J. E. Nativism and empiricism in perception. In L. Postman (Ed.), *Psychology in the making.* New York: Alfred A. Knopf, 1962.

Holden, W. A., & Bosse, K. K. The order of development of color perception and of color preference in the child. *Arch. Ophthal.*, 1900, 29, 261–278.

Holt, L. E., Jr., Davies, E. A., Hasselmeyer, E. G., & Adams, A. O. A study of premature infants fed cold formulas. *J. Pediatr.*, 1962, 61, 556–561. Reprinted in Y. Brackbill & G. G. Thompson (Eds.), *Behavior in infancy and early childhood: A book of readings.* New York: Free Press, 1967.

Holst, E. von. Relations between the central nervous system and the peripheral organs. *Animal Behaviour*, 1954, 2, 89–94.

Horsten, G. P. M., & Winkelman, J. E. Development of the ERG in relation to histological differentiation of the retina in man and animals. *A. M. A. Arch. Ophthal.*, 1960, 63, 232–242.

Irwin, O. C. The amount and nature of activities of newborn infants under constant external stimulating conditions during the first ten days of life. *Genet. Psychol. Monogr.*, 1930, 8, 1–92.

———. Effect of strong light on the body activity of newborns. *J. comp. Psychol.*, 1941, 32, 233–236.

Irwin, O. C., & Weiss, L. A. The effect of darkness on the activity of newborn infants. *Univer. Iowa Stud. Child Welf.*, 1934, 9, No. 4, 163–175.

Jennings, F. Preferences of pre-school children for specific geometric figures. *Child Develpm.*, 1936, 7, 227–235.

Jensen, K. Differential reactions to taste and temperature stimuli in newborn infants. *Genet. Psychol. Monogr.*, 1932, 12, 361–479.

Johnson, B., & Beck, L. F. The development of space perception: I. Stereoscopic vision in pre-school children. *J. Genet. Psychol.*, 1941, 58, 247–254.

Jones, H. E. The galvanic skin response in infancy. *Child Develpm.*, 1930, 1, 106–110.

Jones, M. C. The development of early behavior patterns in young children. *J. genet. Psychol.*, 1926, 33, 537–585.

Jonkers, G. H. The examination of visual acuity in children. *Ophthalmologica*, 1958, 136, 140–144.

Kaila, E. Die Reaktionen des Säuglings auf das Menschliche Gesicht. (The reactions of the infant to the human face.) *Ann. Univer. Aboensis.*, 1932, 17, 1–114.

Karpe, G. Apparatus and method for clinical recording of the electro-retinogram. *Documenta Ophthalmologia: II.*, 1948, 28, 268–276.

Kasatkin, N. I., & Levikova, A. M. On the development of early conditioned reflexes and differentiations of auditory stimuli in infants. *J. exp. Psychol.*, 1935, 18, 1–19. (a)

Kasatkin, N. I., & Levikova, A. M. The formation of visual conditioned reflexes and their differentiation in infants. *J. genet. Psychol.*, 1935, 12, 416–435. (b)

Kistiakovskaia, M. Iu. Stability of visual reactions in infants during the first months of life. *Voprosy Psikhologii*, 1959, 5, 124–133.

Lawrence, M. M., & Feind, C. R. Vestibular responses to rotation in the newborn infant. *Pediatrics*, 1953, 12, 300–306. Reprinted in Y. Brackbill & G. G. Thompson (Eds.), *Behavior in infancy and early childhood: A book of readings.* New York: Free Press, 1967.

Leuba, C. Children's reactions to elements of simple geometric patterns. *Amer. J. Psychol.* 1940, 53, 575–578.

Leventhal, A. S., & Lipsitt, L. P. Adaptation, pitch discrimination, and sound localization in the neonate. *Child Develpm.*, 1964, 35, 759–767.

Lewis, J. M., & Haig, C. Vitamin A requirements in infancy as determined by dark adaptation. *J. Pediatr.*, 1939, 15, 812–823.

Licklider, J. C. R. Basic correlates of the auditory stimulus. In S. S. Stevens (Ed.), *Handbook of experimental psychology.* New York: Wiley, 1951.

Ling, B-C. Form discrimination as a learning cue in infants. *Comp. Psychol. Monogr.*, 1941, 17, No. 2.

———. I. A genetic study of sustained visual fixation and associated behavior in the human infant from birth to six months. *J. genet. Psychol.*, 1942, 61, 227–277.

Lipsitt, L. P., Engen, T., & Kaye, H. Developmental changes in the olfactory threshold of the neonate. *Child Develpm.*, 1963, 34, 371–376.

Lipsitt, L. P., & Levy, N. Electrotactual threshold in the neonate. *Child Develpm.*, 1959, 30, 547–554.

Lipton, E. L., Steinschneider, A., & Richmond, J. B. Autonomic function in the neonate. III. Methodological considerations. *Psychosom. Med.*, 1961, 23, 461–471. (a)

———. Autonomic function in the neonate. IV. Individual differences in cardiac reactivity. *Psychosom. Med.*, 1961, 23, 472–484. (b)

Lowell, E. L., Rushford, G., Hoversten, G., & Stoner, M. Evaluation of puretone audiometry with pre-school age children. *J. Speech Hear. Dis.*, 1956, 21, 292–302.

Mann, I. *The development of the human eye.* (3rd ed.) New York: Grune & Stratton, 1964.

McDougall, W. An investigation of the colour sense of two infants. *Brit. J. Psychol.*, 1908, 2, 338–352.

McEwen, W. K. Secretion of tears and blinking. In H. Davson (Ed.), *The eye.* Vol. 3. New York: Academic Press, 1962.

McGinnis, J. M. Eye movements and optic nystagmus in early infancy. *Genet. Psychol. Monogr.*, 1930, 8, 321–430.

McGraw, M. B. Development of rotary-vestibular reactions of the human infant. *Child Develpm.*, 1941, 12, 17–19.

Marcus, R. E. Hearing and speech problems in children. *Arch. Otolaryng.*, 1951, 53, 134–146.

Marsden, R. A study of the early color sense. *Psychol. Rev.*, 1903, 10, 37–47.

Martin, I. Adaptation. *Psychol. Bull.*, 1964, 61, 35–44.

Martin, P. C., & Vincent, E. L. *Human development.* New York: Ronald Press, 1960.

Mestyan, G., & Varga, F. Chemical thermoregulation of full-term and premature newborn infants. *J. Pediatr.*, 1960, 56, 623–629.

Meyer, E. Comprehension of spatial relations in pre-school children. *J. genet. Psychol.*, 1940, 57, 119–151.

Meyer, J. Weitere Beiträge zur Frage der Schallokalisation. Untersuchungen an Säuglingen und Tieren. (More contributions to the question of localization of sound. Research on infants and animals.) *Mostschr. f. Ohrenh.*, 1912, 46, 449–474.

Miller, N. E. The perception of children: A genetic study employing the critical choice of delayed reaction. *J. genet. Psychol.*, 1934, 44, 321–339.

Misumi, J. Experimental studies on the development of visual size constancy in early infancy. *Bull. Fac. Lit., Kyushu Univer.*, 1951, 1, 91–116.

Morgan, C. *Physiological psychology.* (3rd ed.) New York: McGraw-Hill, 1965.

Morgan, S. S., & Morgan, J. J. B. An examination of the development of certain adaptive behavior patterns in infants. *J. Pediatr.*, 1944, 25, 168–177.

Munn, N. L. *The evolution and growth of human behavior.* Boston: Houghton Mifflin, 1955.

Munn, N. L., & Steining, B. R. The relative efficacy of form and background in a child's discrimination of visual patterns. *Ped. Sem.*, 1931, 39, 73–90.

Parker, G. H. *Smell, taste and allied senses in the vertebrates.* Philadelphia: Lippincott, 1922.

Patten, B. M. *Human embryology* (2nd ed.) New York: Blakiston, 1953.

Peckham, R. H. Visual discrimination in pre-school children. *Child Develpm.*, 1933, 4, 292–297.

Peiper, A. Beiträge zur Sinnesphysiologie der Frühgeburt. (Contributions to the sensory physiology of the premature infant.) *Ann. Paediatr.*, 1924, 104, 195–199.

———. Über die Helligkeits- und Farbenempfindungen der Frühgeburten. (On the brightness and color perceptions of premature infants.) *Arch. Kinderheilkunde*, 1926, 80, 1–20.

———. *Cerebral function in infancy and childhood.* New York: Consultants Bureau, 1963.

Peterson, F., & Rainey, L. H. The beginnings of mind in the newborn. *Bull. Lying-In Hosp.*, 1909–1911, 7, No. 3, 99–122.

Pirenne, M. H. Rods and cones. In H. Davson (Ed.), *The eye.* Vol. 2. New York: Academic Press, 1962.

Polak, P. R., Emde, R. N., & Spitz, R. The smiling response to the human face. I: Methodology, quantification and natural history. *J. nerv. ment. Dis.*, 1964, 139, 103–109. (a)

———. The smiling response. II: Visual discrimination and the onset of depth perception. *J. nerv. ment. Dis.*, 1964, 139, 407–415. (b)

Polyak, S. L. *The retina.* Chicago: Univer. Chicago Pr., 1941.

Poyntz, L. The efficacy of visual and auditory distractions for pre-school children. *Child Develpm.*, 1933, 4, 55–72.

Pratt, K. C. The effects of repeated auditory stimulation upon the general activity of newborn infants. *J. genet. Psychol.*, 1934, 44, 96–116.

———. The organization of behavior in the newborn infant. *Psychol. Rev.*, 1937, 44, 470–490.

———. The neonate. In L. Carmichael (Ed.), *Manual of child psychology.* (2nd ed.) New York: Wiley, 1954.

Pratt, K. C., Nelson, A. K., & Sun, K. H. *The behavior of the newborn infant.* Columbus, Ohio: Ohio State Univer. Press, 1930.

Redfield, J. E. A preliminary report of dark adaptation in young infants. *Child Develpm.*, 1937, 8, 263–269.

———. The light sense in newborn infants. *Univer. Iowa Stud. Child Welf.*, 1939, 16, No. 2, 105–145.

Reinecke, R. D., & Cogan, D. G. Standardization of objective visual acuity measurements. *Arch. Ophthal.*, 1958, 60, 418–421.

Rheingold, H. L., Gewirtz, J. L., & Ross, H. W. Social conditioning of vocalizations in the infant. *J. comp. physiol. Psychol.*, 1959, 52, 68–73.

Rheingold, H. L., & Stanley, W. C. Developmental psychology. *Ann. Rev. Psychol.*, 1963, 14, 1–28.

Richmond, J. B., Grossman, H. J., & Lustman, S. L. A hearing test for newborn infants. *Pediatrics*, 1953, 11, 634–638.

Riesen, A. H. Receptor functions. In P. H. Mussen (Ed.), *Handbook of research methods in child development.* New York: Wiley, 1960.

Riggs, L. A. Human retinal responses. *Ann. New York Acad. Sciences*, 1958, 74, 372–376.

Saayman, G., Ames, E. W., & Moffett, A. Response to novelty as an indicator of visual discrimination in the human infant. *J. exp. child Psychol.*, 1964, 1, 189–198.

Salk, L. The effects of the normal heartbeat sound on the behavior of the newborn infant: Implications for mental health. *World ment. Health*, 1960, 12, 168–175.

——. The importance of the heartbeat rhythm to human nature: Theoretical, clinical, and experimental observations. *Proc. Third World Congr. Psychiat.* Montreal: McGill Univer. Press, 1961, 1, 740–746.

——. Mother's heartbeat as imprinting stimulus. *Trans. New York Acad. Sci.*, 1962, 24, 753–763.

Schneidemann, N. V., & Robinette, G. E. Testing the ocular dominance of infants. *Psychol. Clin.*, 1932, 21, 62–63.

Schwarting, B. H. Testing infants' vision. An apparatus for estimating the visual acuity of infants and young children. *Amer. J. Ophthal.*, 1954, 38, 714–715.

Sherman, M., & Sherman, I. C. Sensori-motor responses in infants. *J. comp. physiol. Psychol.*, 1925, 5, 53–68.

Sherman, M., Sherman, I. C., & Flory, C. D. Infant behavior. *Comp. Psychol. Monogr.*, 1936, 12, No. 4.

Skalet, M. The significance of delayed reactions in young children. *Comp. Psychol. Monogr.*, 1931, 7, No. 1.

Spears, W. C. Assessment of visual preference and discrimination in the four-month-old infant. *J. comp. physiol. Psychol.*, 1964, 57, 381–386.

——. Visual preference in the four-month-old infant. *Psychon. Sci.*, 1966, 4, 237–238.

Spitz, R. A., & Wolf, K. M. The smiling response: A contribution to the ontogenesis of social relationships. *Genet. Psychol. Monogr.*, 1946, 34, 57–125.

Staples, R. The responses of infants to color. *J. exp. Psychol.*, 1932, 15, 119–141.

Statten, P., & Wishart, D. E. S. Pure-tone audiometry in young children: Psychogalvanic-skin-resistance and peep-show. *Ann. Otol.*, 1956, 65, 511–534.

Stechler, G. Newborn attention as affected by medication during labor. *Science*, 1964, 144, 315–317.

Steinschneider, A., Lipton, E. L., & Richmond, J. B. Autonomic functions in the neonate. VI. Discriminability, consistency, and slope as measures of an individual's cardiac responsivity. *J. genet. Psychol.*, 1964, 105, 295–310.

Stevens, S. S., Davis, H., & Lurie, M. H. The localization of pitch perception on the basilar membrane. *J. genet. Psychol.*, 1935, 13, 297–315.

Stubbs, E. M. The effect of the factors of duration, intensity, and pitch of sound stimuli on the responses of newborn infants. *Univer. Iowa Stud. Child Welf.*, 1934, 9, No. 4, 75–135.

Suzuki, T., Kamijo, Y., & Kiuchi, S. Auditory tests of newborn infants. *Ann. Otol.*, 1964, 73, 914–923.

Taylor, C. D. A comparative study of visual apprehension in nursery school children and adults. *Child Develpm.*, 1931, 2, 263–271.

Thompson, G. G. The effect of chronological age on aesthetic preferences for rectangles of different proportions. *J. exp. Psychol.*, 1946, 36, 50–58.

Thorpe, W. H. *Learning and instinct in animals.* London: Methuen, 1956.

Thrum, M. A. The development of concepts of magnitude. *Child Develpm.*, 1935, 6, 120–140.

Thwing, E. H. Spread of prestimulatory fatigue of a pure tone to neighboring frequencies. *J. Acoust. Soc. Am.*, 1955, 27, 741–748.

Towe, A. L., & Ruch, T. C. Audition and the auditory pathway. In T. C. Ruch & J. F. Fulton (Eds.), *Medical physiology and biophysics.* Philadelphia: Saunders, 1960.

Trincker, D., & Trincker, I. Die ontogenetische Entwicklung des Helligkeits- und Farbensehens beim Menschen. I. Die Entwicklung des Helligkeitssehens.

(The ontogenetic development of brightness and color vision in man. I. The development of brightness.) *Graefe's Arch. Ophthal.,* 1955, 156, 519–534. Translated and reprinted in Y. Brackbill & G. G. Thompson (Eds.), *Behavior in infancy and early childhood: A book of readings.* New York: Free Press, 1967.

Tucker, D. Physiology of olfaction. *Amer. Perfumer,* 1961, 76, 48–53.

Tulloch, J. D., Brown, B. S., Jacobs, H. L., Prugh, D. G., & Greene, W. A. Normal heartbeat sound and the behavior of newborn infants—a replication study. *Psychosom. Med.,* 1964, 26, 661–670.

Updegraff, R. Ocular dominance in young children. *J. exp. Psychol.,* 1932, 15, 758–766.

Valentine, C. W. The colour perception and colour preferences of an infant during its fourth and eighth months. *Brit. J. Psychol.,* 1913–14, 6, 363–386.

Walk, R. D., & Dodge, S. H. Visual depth perception of a 10-month-old monocular human infant. *Science,* 1962, 137, 529–530.

Walk, R. D., & Gibson, E. J. A comparative and analytical study of visual depth perception. *Psychol. Monogr.,* 1961, 75, No. 15.

Walters, R. H., & Parke, R. D. The role of the distance receptors in the development of social responsiveness. In L. P. Lipsitt & C. C. Spiker (Eds.), *Advances in child development and behavior.* Vol. 2. New York: Academic Press, 1965.

Warner, F. *The children: How to study them.* London: Hodgson, 1887–1888.

Watson, J. S. Perception of object orientation in infants. (Unpublished manuscript), Merrill-Palmer Institute of Human Development and Family Life, 1964.

Wedenberg, E. Determination of the hearing acuity in the newborn. *Nordisk Medicin,* 1956, 50, 1022–1024.

Weiss, L. A. Differential variations in the amount of activity of newborn infants under continuous light and sound stimulation. *Univer. Iowa Stud. Child Welf.,* 1934, 9, No. 4, 9–74.

Welch, L. The development of size discrimination between the ages of 12 and 40 months. *J. genet. Psychol.,* 1939, 55, 243–268.

Wendt, G. R. Vestibular functions. In S. S. Stevens (Ed.), *Handbook of experimental psychology.* New York: Wiley, 1951.

Wertheimer, M. Psychomotor coordination of auditory and visual space at birth. *Science,* 1961, 134, 1692.

Wever, E. G. *Theory of hearing.* New York: Wiley, 1949.

Winkelman, J. E., & Horsten, G. P. M. The ERG or premature and full-term born infants during their first days of life. *Ophthalmologica,* 1962, 143, 92–101.

Wood, A. G. A quantitative account of the course of auditory fatigue. Unpublished master's thesis, Univer. Virginia, 1930. Cited by F. A. Geldard, The human senses. New York: Wiley, 1953.

Wright, W. D. *Photometry and the eye.* London: Hatton Press, 1949.

Zetterström, B. The clinical electroretinogram. IV. The electroretinogram in children during the first year of life. *Acta Ophthal.,* 1951, 29, 295–304.

———. The electroretinogram in premature children. *Acta Ophthal.,* 1952, 30, 405–408.

———. Flicker electroretinography in newborn infants. *Acta Ophthal.,* 1955, 33, 157–166.

Zubek, J. P., & Solberg, P. A. *Human development.* New York: McGraw-Hill, 1954.

Chapter 3

Infant Motor Development

DAVID H. CROWELL

This review was supported in part by Grant HD 00869 from the National Institute of Child Health and Human Development, and in part by the Pacific Biomedical Research Center, University of Hawaii.

Miss Frieda Kraetzer and Miss Laura Shiro assisted with the basic work graciously and patiently. Miss Dorothy A. Wright's original compilation of the references was of immense and immeasurable worth.

Infant motor development and motor behavior as a field of psychological research have attracted insufficient attention during the past two decades. Even though motor acts are the primary means of expression for the young human, this activity, until very recently, has been incorrectly regarded as playing a relatively minor role in total development. This conclusion stems from a variety of reasons. There is, first, the fact that early motor acts superficially appear simple and descriptively the same from infant to infant. Second, the behavior of the infant is without much content and seemingly involves little meaningful direction or purpose. This difficulty in relating motor activity to events in the environment is further compounded by characteristics of instability, evanescence, and rapid changes in early behavior. Even if it be granted that motor patterns are basic to complex psychological processes, it is still difficult to relate early overt responses in any meaningful way to later development. Notwithstanding this, the view has been advanced that developing motor patterns can and have served to ". . . acquaint the developmental psychologist with the behavioral potential of the organism he is studying and permitted him to plan and conduct research more efficiently; their informative function may eventually prove to be more valuable than the concepts, states, or processes inferred from these" (Rheingold & Stanley, 1963, p. 16).

The purpose of the present review is to evaluate the current status of knowledge and trends evolved from past investigations of infant motor development. The last general summary in this area was based on Dewey's (1935) survey of the literature from 1920–1935 which was completed for the purpose of describing what was known about the development of human behavior. Behavior in this context was limited to "the neuromuscular and glandular reactions of living human organisms." Since this 1935 publication other discussions relevant to motoric components of behavior have appeared in edited works (Murchison, 1931; Murchison, 1933; Carmichael, 1946; Carmichael, 1954). These have been limited to such special topics as maturation (McGraw, 1946, pp. 332–369; Gesell, 1954, pp. 335–373), eating, sleeping, and elimination (Wooley, 1931, pp. 28–70), locomotor functions (Shirley, 1933, pp. 236–270), or designed to cover behavior for select groups, as, for ex-

ample, neonates (Pratt, 1946) and twins (Gesell, 1931, pp. 158–203).
Inasmuch as Dewey's (1935) volume still represents the most comprehensive approach, it stands as a bench mark for evaluating trends in
motor research since the early thirties. For future comparison Dewey's
conclusion is worth noting.

> In conclusion, a summary of all the literature on infant be-
> havior indicates that it is impossible as yet to give an adequate
> picture of the total course of development of single patterns, or even
> definitely to state that the evidence conclusively supports any one
> of the current theories of behavior. The tendency at present is to
> discard *in toto* the older reflex-arc and behaviorist theories, and to
> support a Gestalt or organismic concept of growth processes, with
> great emphasis on the role of maturation of the nervous system. A
> careful perusal of all the evidence and a recognition of the great
> gaps that still exist in our knowledge of the correlation of structure
> and function suggest that the pendulum may have swung too far in
> this direction, and that complete data will eventually show that
> there is truth in both points of view (Dewey, 1935, p. 304).

The present review will trace the development of early motor patterns in normal infant humans as they relate to the asleep-awake cycle,
vision, oral behavior, postural and locomotor control, prehension, dominance, and other areas of specialized motor skill. In order to assure a
broad coverage and examine the effects of special characteristics or
conditions, such as prematurity and environmental enrichment, the
relationship of motor patterns to other variables will be described. Data
will, for the most part, be from studies involving normal infants whose
ages range up to three years of age (Brackbill, 1964). These materials
will be presented using the following general plan: there will be, first,
a resumé of trends in theoretical approaches; second, a discussion of
empirical studies in selected areas of motor development, and third, an
overview of the whole subject.

Theoretical Orientations
and Motor Development

BEHAVIORISM

In most areas of knowledge, research interest and productivity are
greatest under the stimulus of theory. It is therefore no surprise to note
the association of emerging interest and increased research effort in
motor development with two theoretical orientations, namely, behaviorism and the maturational approach. One of the central principles of
behaviorism was ". . . that all complex behavior is a growth or development out of simple resources" (Watson, 1925, p. 325). This progressive
development of behavior was reflected in the notion of "the activity

stream" of the individual. Within this activity stream behavior was originally observed as a set of unlearned acts, stimulus-response connections or innate reflexes, from which would evolve stabilized habits through conditioning. This emphasis on the genesis of behavior became the setting for infant laboratory investigations and the background for genetic psychology as a field of independent study.

Under the aegis of behaviorism infants, and, specifically, infant responses to stimulation, were the prime foci for research. The main task of the scientist was considered to be to determine the repertoire of innate characteristics that would later become the habit patterns of the individual. Early investigators operating out of this tradition, however, did not confirm the notion that the infant was only a set of reflexes embedded in the activity stream awaiting organization into stabilized habits. Their more solid and permanent contribution was the emphasis on a laboratory approach to understanding human behavior. In addition, these researchers soon recognized that any description of motor behavior had to include changes related to increasing age, that maturation of neural structures produces behavioral growth. The latter idea represented the introduction of organismic growth factors as important elements underlying behavior.

Early behaviorism has been traditionally associated with the role of learning in the acquisition of behavioral patterns with the corresponding exclusion of instinctive factors. Even though the behaviorists' position was usually interpreted as synonymous with the acquired pole of the innate-versus-acquired dichotomy, there is evidence to suggest that their stand was not "either-or." In an early statement (1925) Watson acknowledged that it was difficult to say how much of any motor response was due to training or conditioning and how much due to growth changes in structure. In spite of the recognition of organismic factors, the heavier emphasis on conditioning by behaviorists laid the foundation for rejection of their approach.

MATURATION HYPOTHESIS

Gesell, as the foremost proponent of the maturational hypothesis, definitively described the new view in his polemic against behaviorism:

> The extreme versions of environmentalist and conditioning theories suffer because they explain too much. They suggest that the individual is fabricated out of the conditioning patterns. They do not give due recognition to the inner checks which set metes and bounds to the area of conditioning and which happily prevent abnormal and grotesque consequences which the theories themselves would make too easily possible. Although it is artificial to press unduly a distinction between intrinsic and extrinsic factors, it must after all, be granted that growth is a function of the organism rather than of the environment as such. The environment furnishes the foil and the milieu for the manifestations of development, but these manifestations come from inner compulsion and

are primarily organized by inherent inner mechanics and by an intrinsic physiology of development. The very plasticity of growth requires that there be limiting and regulatory mechanisms. Growth is a process so intricate and so sensitive that there must be powerful stabilizing factors, intrinsic rather than extrinsic, which preserve the balance of the total pattern and the direction of the growth trend. Maturation is, in a sense, a name for this regulatory mechanism (Gesell, 1929, p. 318).

As critics of this new construct were quick to show, this was a restatement of the role of heredity and a new cloth for the older instinct view. Both instinct and maturation were determined by heredity. The only difference between the two was the dimension of time; if the phenomenon in question appeared later but was dependent upon prior biological factors, then it was maturational. Gesell firmly supported the idea that structure developed prior to function. Although he admitted two processes of development, maturation and learning, development during infancy was chiefly due to maturation.

There are five principles which Gesell advanced as basic in the ontogeny of infant motor behavior. These were the *principles of* (1) *individuating maturation*, (2) *developmental direction*, (3) *reciprocal interweaving*, (4) *functional asymmetry*, and (5) *self-regulatory fluctuation*.

The *principle of individuating maturation* states that ". . . the original impulse of growth and the matrix of morphogenesis are endogenous rather than exogenous. . . . Environmental factors support, inflect, and specify, but they do not engender the basic forms and sequences of ontogenesis" (Gesell, 1945, p. 163). Because of this biological and organismic factor the baby will grasp and the child walk. In other words, all individuals within a species are going to acquire certain motor patterns regardless of environmental influences.

The ontogenetic organization of behavior is specified by the *principle of developmental direction*. In line with this, motor development proceeds in a given order along the principal axes of the body primarily from head to foot (cephalo-caudal) and from more central to peripheral structures (proximo-distal). The cephalo-caudal gradient is illustrated by the attainment of postural control beginning at the head and ending with complete body coordination and locomotion. Forearm and wrist functioning earlier than the fingers in motor acts reflects the proximo-distal gradient. Likewise, the ulnar-radial shift accompanying forefinger-thumb opposition showed the operation of this principle in a slightly different fashion. An adjunct of this principle is the corollary that development follows an orderly sequence. In addition to reflecting the idea of randomness in the development of early human behavior, this corollary proposed an orderly emergence and succession of patterns. As a prelude to Shirley's (1929) more systematic demonstration of this idea, Gesell (1929) wrote:

The complex of behavior growth also has a longitudinal aspect. It is made up of strands or channels projected in a linear manner. The development of perception, of postural control, of prehension, of locomotion, of adaptive exploitation, of language comprehension and expression, of social behavior in general and in special aspects follow continuous lines of genetic sequence. The orderly study of these lines of sequence yields another quota of patterns for the interpretation of infant development (p. 634).

The mechanism which coordinates and organizes muscle groups, and presumably operates to preserve balance and coordination, Gesell described as the *principle of reciprocal interweaving*. In its simplest form the principle is demonstrated by alternating extension and flexion of the arms and legs so as to facilitate walking. Upon closer analysis of reciprocal interweaving Gesell concluded that mature behavior was attained in a spiral-like rather than a linear-like manner (Fig. 3.1).

Such a developmental spiral reflects the shifts from immature to mature behavior, and the reverse, as observed in the growing infant. In addition to illustrating the previously discussed principles, Fig. 3.1 shows the alternate occurrence of bilateral and unilateral activity as required in independent locomotion. The more mature pattern is unilateral action. The shift from a primitive bilateral use of arms and legs to unilateral action is readily apparent in the initial ten stages of the first cycle of Fig. 3.1. During the second cycle, which involves crawling and creeping, a temporary use of earlier and less mature patterns is evident. Although cycles three and four will culminate in walking, there are still occurrences of former immature action patterns.

Somewhat the same idea encompassed by reciprocal interweaving is incorporated in the *principle of self-regulatory fluctuation*. In this latter instance, the principle was developed to cover the oscillatory and more variable aspects of behavior, particularly with regard to the time spent in activities. For example, over a period of time the infant moves from frequent feedings during a 24-hour cycle to fewer but larger individual meals. The baby may show a lot of variation in naptime from day to day, but eventually there is an overall trend toward the adult asleep-awake pattern. Quantitatively, this may be as much as a drop from nineteen hours in the fourth week to thirteen hours in the fortieth week. Since the self-regulatory fluctuations may shift from immature to mature, and vice versa, this principle also reflects the operation of the developmental spiral concept.

Opposed to the integration implied in reciprocal interweaving was the observation that the individual ". . . develops monolateral aptitudes and preferences in handedness, eyedness, footedness, and other forms of unidexterity . . . (which do not so much represent an absolute difference in skill as a predilection for stabilized psychomotor orientations" (Gesell, 1946, p. 307). These phenomena demonstrate the *principle of functional asymmetry*, and reference is to the development of dominance or laterality in motor functioning. Throughout early human development there can be observed periodic instances of symmetric and asymmetric behavior patterns. The tonic neck reflex undergoes such sequential changes in the shift from the newborn asymmetrical fencing

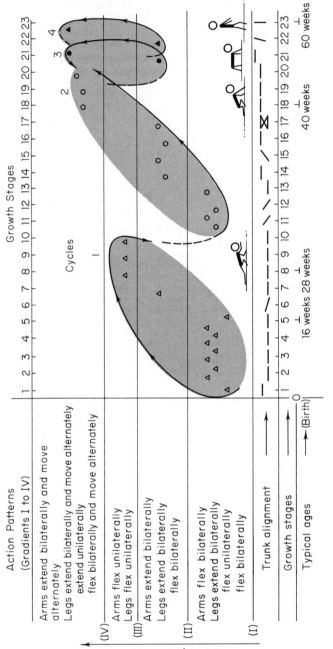

Figure 3.1. *Growth cycles in the patterning of prone behavior.*

(From A. Gesell & L. B. Ames. The ontogenetic organization of prone behavior in human infancy. *J. genet. Psychol.*, 1940.)

stance to the six-month symmetrical posture, with the head in a midline position and arms and hands used bilaterally, eventually ending in one-hand reaching, one-handed manipulation, and well-defined unidexterity.

The contributions from the maturational orientation are not to be lightly dismissed. Under this guidon much excellent systematic observation took place, establishing norms and cataloguing sequences of motor development. In a sharp departure from the earlier biographical or idiographic approach, these naturalistic observations were the first to classify by chronological age the appearance of specific motor behaviors. The Gesell Developmental Schedules (1947) were prepared from normative studies begun in 1919 and were categories which allowed appraisal of a child's development in four major areas: motor, adaptive, language, and personal-social behavior. The concept of developmental age represented as such, the child's level of development. The normative items, as well as the scaling, became the model for later standardized tests measuring early developmental progress. Though, with a few exceptions, the normative studies emphasized *when* specific behaviors would develop as opposed to *how* the behavior changed with age, some attention was directed toward this later problem. The cross-section methodology involved in the normative studies was later supplemented by a longitudinal approach, as seen in the work of Halverson (1937a, 1937b, 1937c) on prehension and Shirley (1931) on locomotion.

If Gesell and his colleagues had invested more energy in formal theory building, the adherents of the maturational hypothesis might have made a more extensive contribution. The principles were presumed to be synonymous with scientific laws and, as such, unqualified universal generalizations. These may have to be evaluated relative to this claim. While the principles were not experimentally determined, still they were derived from data based on multiple naturalistic observations. The principles of individuating maturation and developmental direction appear to have an adequate foundation in fact. Although it is true that Gesell initiated the co-twin method (1929) as one way of making a crucial test of the maturation hypothesis, it was, however, Shirley (1931) who provided a more definitive test and basic support for the validity of these two principles. In a deductive fashion she determined whether the general nature and features of motor development were consistent with "maturation at the helm." In analyzing her data Shirley questioned whether they met the basic assumptions of the maturation framework or were better explained by these alternative hypotheses: (1) a purely learning explanation, (2) chance factors, or (3) the interaction of learning, chance, and maturation.

Whether the term *principle* is applicable to reciprocal interweaving, functional asymmetry, and self-regulatory functioning is still open to question. At best the status of "law" for the principle of individuating maturation and the principle of developmental direction should be reserved for the domain of motor behavior. If, as Gesell seems to imply, the "laws of developmental morphology" account for trends not only in the motor sphere, but also in the adaptive, language, and personal-social areas, then there is unwarranted generalization.

The maturational phenomenon was presumed to be governed by the basic laws of developmental morphology or genetically predetermined development. For Gesell, "The growth of tissues, of organs, and of behavior is obedient to identical laws of developmental morphology" (Gesell, 1946, p. 297). This rationale represented the ultimate in reductionism and explanation with the net result of a stalemate in thinking. As a result, observed phenomena were left at a descriptive level requiring neither statements of systematic hypotheses for experimental analysis nor statements of interrelationships with other variables.

The inadequacy of behaviorism in explaining the intricate developmental changes in motor activities operated as a stimulus on the emergence of the maturational hypothesis. In turn, the maturational viewpoint focused attention on fundamental issues of ontogenetic development, namely (1) What neurological changes are associated with overt behavioral changes? (2) Does practice or training affect the rate of development of overt behavior? The second of these issues, succinctly referred to as the maturation versus learning controversy, will be referred to later and discussed in Chapter 4. Relative to the first problem, implicit in the maturational hypothesis was the corollary that behavior spontaneously emerged with the anatomical maturation of the nervous system. According to McGraw this was the real issue of the maturational theory: ". . . does function determine neural organization or does the neural organization form the framework within which function takes place" (McGraw, 1946, p. 347).

On the premise that motor changes should reflect the state of maturity or immaturity of the developing nervous system, McGraw attempted a partial answer to this question. After evaluations of developments in grasping, creeping, sitting, swimming, locomotion and other activities, she offered evidence to the effect that motor patterns progressively reflect the time (1) when the motor response is under subcortical control and (2) when cortical inhibitory influences are beginning to function, then (3) when cortical participation is involved in muscular movements, and finally, (4) when the cortex is dominant and voluntarily controls muscular activity. So that, for example, the appearance of independent walking in place of the early rhythmic stepping movements denotes a progressive lessening of subcortical influence and an increasing development of cortical maturity. Further, and perhaps, more importantly, she proposed an interaction of structure and function, stating:

> It seems fairly evident that certain structural changes take place prior to the onset of overt function; it seems equally evident that cessation of neurostructural development does not coincide with the onset of function. There is every reason to believe that when conditions are favorable, function makes some contribution to further advancement in structural development of the nervous system. An influential factor in determining the structural develop-

ment of one component may be the functioning of other structures which are interrelated . . . (McGraw, 1946, pp. 363–364).

Though her thinking did not result in any systematic theoretical position on the issue, her conclusions both modified the maturational hypothesis and provided a partial resolution of the nature and nurture problem. Since 1950 this interaction hypothesis has emerged as a trend with indications of having considerable influence on the study of motor behavior.

PIAGET'S INTERACTION HYPOTHESIS

Piaget's interest in sensorimotor background of intelligence avoided the maturation versus learning dilemma by conceptualizing development as the result of an interaction process. The emergence of this point of view was intimately tied to his methodological problems, for his earlier thinking on the development of logic and intellectual functions had been based upon explanation of events as given by his subjects, children. This *méthode clinique* had to be supplemented by observation and experimentation for, according to Piaget (1952), "It was only by studying the patterns of intelligent behavior of the first two years that I learned that for a complete understanding of the genesis of intellectual operations, manipulation and experience with objects had first to be considered" (Piaget, p. 247). In brief, the ways the child would perceive and cope with reality had to develop from interactive contacts between the organism and his environment. The most basic aspects of intellectual and cognitive functioning were intimately tied in with the actions or motor activity of the individual. As summarized by Flavell (1963), this conception of "intelligence-as-action" both linked simple sensorimotor adjustments of the neonate with adult abstract intellectual processes, and provided ". . . the rationale for carefully studying crude and habit-like sensory-motor actions as true if rudimentary forms of intelligence (as opposed to dismissing them as simple 'early motor behavior' or something of the sort). Since actions are the bricks of all intellectual edifices, it is especially important to investigate their earliest organizations (p. 83).

In detail this plan postulated that things, objects in the environment, as known to the adult do not exist for the child, but emerge after a process of modification by means of experience. At birth the organism's equipment is said to consist of reflexes and their associated schema. The reflex is the basic unit of behavior and, correspondingly, the schema is the basic unit of mental organization. The schema is known in terms of the behavior it involves; thus, for seeing, there is a schema of sight; for feeding, a schema of sucking. The schema developed by incorporating experiences, an act called *assimilation,* in turn alters and modifies the reflex schema itself. The process of modification or *accommodation* transforms the reflexive schema into a complex pattern for handling reality and at the same time forms a structure and a way for thinking about reality.

What warrants particular attention with respect to the continual assimilation-accommodation interplay is the developing knowledge of objects. In early infancy objects are intellectually indistinct from the simple act associated with them. Only when objects can be related to a number of different schemata do they become independent entities with distinct properties. Thus "ball" emerges as an object because it can be seen, held, and thrown. The network of schemata results in the definition of external reality and is crucial for cognitive development.

Three levels have been outlined in Piaget's taxonomy of intellectual development: the period of sensorimotor intelligence (birth to two years), the period of preparation for and organization of concrete operations (two years to eleven years), and the period of formal operations (eleven years to fifteen years). Most relevant to the present review is the sensorimotor period—the time for basic schema transformations and development of internalized modes of problem solving. Descriptive data for this period came from Piaget's observations of his three children.

Within the sensorimotor period are six stages. Even though extensive reflex activity is evident, genuine intelligent behavior is not assumed to exist in *Stage I*, which lasts from birth to one month of age. During *Stage II* (one to four months), reflexes become altered through accommodation and assimilation to form the first simple habits. Repetitive movements and routines are developed as a means of enlarging the range of experience. These are defined as *primary circular reactions* that will eventually serve to stimulate the recognition of objects and events. Within *Stage III*, four months to eight months, there are present several distinctive patterns, which are listed as *secondary circular reactions*. Among these are patterns that show a developing interest in the consequences produced by behaving in certain ways. Second, there is evidence of some recognition of previously contacted objects. Accompanying these are, third, patterns oriented toward maintaining the stimulus value or presence of novel objects. Finally, during Stage III, there is some evidence of intentional or goal-directed behavior. During *Stage IV*, eight months to twelve months, schemata are coordinated to facilitate voluntarily directed activity. Familiar schemata are used in new situations both as means to goals and as ends in themselves. Evidence suggests that new objects are explored in a way suggesting an attempt to know them and what they do. In addition, indications of anticipation of events can be often recognized. The distinguishing feature of *Stage V* is the *tertiary circular reaction*, a set of techniques for exploring and experimenting with new objects. The preconceptual phase is defined as *Stage VI* which covers the eighteen- to twenty-four-month interval. In this period are observed the child's earliest attempts at representation of events by means of symbols and thought processes.

In general, the sensorimotor period is marked by a shift from simple reflex functioning to a low level of symbolic activity. Correspondingly, there is a change in orientation from a body-centered or *egocentric* world to an object-centered or *allocentric* world. With the coordination of many sensory-perceptual impressions, the child derives a knowledge of objects and their properties as well as developing intellectual structures and cognitive processes.

Whether Piaget's theorizing will operate as a stimulus to more intensive motor development research remains to be seen. Up to now no systematic investigation has been initiated to evaluate infant behavior and development according to his categories. Notwithstanding this, the contributions of this "intelligence-as-action" system are impressive. There is, first, the provision of an assimilation-accommodation model, which puts emphasis on gradual cognitive growth; second, the demonstration of research fertility in infancy, a period generally considered inaccessible and devoid of possibilities for theory-construction; and, third, evidence ". . . that both [the] fact and form of development can be the raw materials for elaborate theorizing, [and] that there is nothing intrinsically atheoretical about the products of developmental-descriptive research" (Flavell, 1963, p. 424).

In summary, three major theoretical orientations—behaviorism, the maturational approach, and the interaction hypothesis—have been surveyed with a view to disclosing their influence on motor development research. On the surface behaviorism and the maturational view appear to have stimulated work in this area. In spite of this, both seem to have ultimately produced an impasse in conceptual and theoretical thinking about motor behavior. There is little doubt that the maturational hypothesis had considerable validity, but its dogma did not require nor permit the entry of behavior theory with its hypothetico-deductive framework and quantitative approach. Whether this type of concern would have produced imaginative research on motor development is difficult to decide. The theoretical problems of the 1930s that focused on learning made even less exciting what was already of limited and mild interest. It is interesting to observe that the potential contribution from the interaction hypothesis was also to remain dormant during this same era. In retrospect the impression emerges that much of the research effort, regardless of school of thought, has been essentially a survey or mapping of the motor area. The descriptive-normative involvement was a necessary preliminary step prior to the definition of other parameters and relationships.

Motor Responses

In spite of the inherent variability of early human behavior, past research has demonstrated that it may be systematically studied. Because of its primacy in the human repertoire, motor development in particular has furnished the most concrete area for observation and has been analyzed in terms of specific behaviors, interrelationships among items of behavior, length of duration for types of motor behavior, level of maturity, and behavioral sequences as, for example, demonstrated in the longitudinal study of locomotion (Shirley, 1931) and prehension (Halverson, 1932). Although all types of studies illustrative of these categories can be found, the casual impression is that specific items of behavior sequences in motor activity have received more attention. Regardless of the type of classification and the source of data—that is, whether the information was from a single biographical case or based on groups—the predominant experimental design, following Kessen's (1960) terminology, has revolved around simple age-function relationships. As such, the behavior response of interest has been described or measured as a function of age, $R = f(A)$, or as a function of age within a select sample, $R = f(A,S)$. The more sophisticated type of design involving the interaction of age and other manipulable antecedent stimuli, $R = f(A,S)$, has been less frequently used.

Historically, the baby biography as the earliest method of child study defined a period when facts on motor development were derived from purely descriptive accounts of naturalistic observations. Dennis (1936) has compiled the most complete bibliography of these biographies. These cover a wide spectrum of child behavior and exhibit a series of highly personalized hypotheses about the observed development. In spite of the alleged superiority of the biography in giving a fuller picture of development, the inescapable fact is that these data were based on a sample of one case and they were often of limited value because of problems of interpretation. The inherent limitation of generality is further compounded by the cultural class influence emanating from a group of sophisticated and literate biographers. Few comparative biographical studies exist (Jones, 1926; Shirley, 1931; Dennis, 1937). Based on comparisons of data from nine biographies, Jones (1926) noted that these infant case reports place the dates for appearance of smiling, eye coordination, blinking, thumb opposition, reaching, and sitting earlier than observed in her 365 cases. In 85 per cent of the biographical reports, the development was more rapid than in the average of her group. Searching eighteen biographies, Shirley (1931) found substantial agreement with her locomotor and visuomotor norms. Dennis (1937) compared median figures from forty biographies with Shirley's norms and found that, in general, they were similar. The biographical medians, however, tended to be earlier for two thirds of the behavioral items.

The early neonatal investigations which superseded the biographical approach and marked the beginning of experimental methods in laboratory evaluations of human behavior also opened a new area of developmental concern. These researches were primarily descriptive, designed to list responses present at birth and to record the changes with age. At the same time there was an associated if not always implied goal that the research was defining newborn behavior that was likely to show some continuity with later behavior. As Kessen, Williams, and Williams (1961) have suggested this problem required consideration of other interrelated issues: first, a demonstration of the relevance of newborn behavior to later behavior; second, the determination of behavioral sequences common to all humans, and third, the establishment of individual differences. Generally, one might conclude that all work on motor development was ultimately oriented toward answering these issues, and conversely, that these issues form the framework and background of motor development research.

Pertinent to the question of relevance of responses at one age period to a subsequent age is the fact that, provided pathological cases are excluded, there is no evidence as to which aspect of early motor behavior is most meaningful or most significant for later behavior. The past failure to establish antecedent-consequent relationships makes it difficult to eliminate any early behavior from consideration as a precursor of later development and, until demonstrated otherwise, all early motor behavior must be assumed to have some continuity with later behavior. Undoubtedly theory might have provided some direction for answering this question of significance. Since there is a voluminous literature on motor behavior and an immediate need for a definition of significance an arbitrary and common sense set of criteria can be used to select material for inclusion in the present review: (1) that the motor phenomenon must be reliably observed, and (2) the motor response or motor patterns must have a demonstrably important role in the total functioning of the organism. The basic assumption in evaluating these studies of motor patterns is the application of standards of scientific rigor. The immediate impression after perusal of these investigations is that they are largely naturalistic descriptions and the next stage of experimental manipulation and control has only been partially initiated.

ACTIVITY

The concept of activity has played an important role in attempts at understanding early developing behavior because it was observable and easily defined in its various manifestations. As an overt global index, it was something tangible that promised to provide evidence on individual differences and conceivably demonstrate behavioral continuity from one age level to another.

Four different ways of thinking about activity can be delineated in the literature. There is first of all the theoretical view of Watson (1925) on the human activity stream. As already noted, this matrix included reflexes that would essentially constitute the future conditioned habits and thus were the foundation of the later behavior of the organism. In retrospect, the activity stream notion is a picturesque expression, but at the same time, an unnecessary vehicle for calling attention to the large reflex repertoire of the human.

Second, evolving out of the impetus given by behaviorism, but antithetical to the specificity implied by the innate reflex position, were response patterns depicted as "mass activity" (Irwin, 1932). Even though many simple reflexes could be described, usually investigators reported the infant's behavior to be unorganized, random, and chaotic.

Irwin, for example, was of the opinion that mass activity was the infant's general primary response pattern and that through individuation and differentiation, this became more specific to stimuli. He wrote:

> The observations regarding irradiation, diffusiveness, and variability in the human fetus hold for the activity of the human newborn. It seems to be true in the newborn infant that when movements are slow they involve separate or isolated segments. But when segmental movements increase in rate they eventuate in an irradiation of activity until the entire infant is strenuously at work. The trunk is thrown about, curved, flexed, extended, arched, and rolled from side to side. The movements of arms and legs merge with those of the trunk with great variability, being slashed and kicked, flexed and extended, adducted and abducted incessantly. Ankle, wrist, elbows, knees, fingers, and toes as well as facial muscles are involved as part of the large movements. Crying usually accompanies them also. There are no regularities, no fine and precise gradations, little specificity in the reflex sense, and few effective coordinations in this activity. To designate the type of reaction involving the whole organism, whether proceeding at a high or at a low rate, I have used the expression "mass activity." It stands in striking contrast to the movements of single segments of the infant. The latter type of reaction is called specific. Then . . . it is not presuming too much to suggest that this behavior is due largely to internal factors. This is an important point in the organismic view. The organism itself furnishes factors which affect behavior (Irwin, 1932, p. 198–199).

Similarly, Pratt, Nelson, and Sun (1930) stated that,
Its behavior is generalized, that is stimulation of almost any group of receptors by almost any kind of stimulus will lead to a response in almost any part of the organism. The reaction tends, however, to manifest itself most strongly in that part of the organism which is stimulated, and from there spreads out with decreasing frequency and intensity to the other segments of the body (p. 208).

Jensen (1932) suggested that the reaction of the neonate to stimuli would appear in any part of the organism set to respond.

Although Dennis (1932a) was in agreement that the earliest human responses are total body responses, he denied that mass activity was the only such pattern exhibited by newborn infants. Based upon a summary of newborn behavior (Dennis, 1934), he differentiated fifteen separate responses which were specific to a definite range of stimuli under defined conditions. Further, these responses were thought to be not random, but patterned. In spite of the urgent need to analyze newborn responses and examine their organization only two investigators appear to have taken note of this issue. Sherman and Sherman (1929) stated that the initial response occurs in the stimulated area and spreads rapidly to other regions of the body so that the whole response, unless observed closely, appears to be generalized activity, particularly of the arms and legs. Though utilizing only three infants, Delman (1935) through motion film analysis concluded that responses did not occur in a chance fashion. Although responses were generalized there was some patterning which could be observed. More first responses occurred in the legs than in the arms, and with the second response to stimulation, there was a tendency for the arms to react together and similarly for the legs to respond together. A review of Delman's (1935) conclusions regarding gross behavioral patterns suggests that these served not only as a critique of the mass activity position, but also could have served as a valuable guideline for systematic research on motility. He wrote:

> In this study an attempt was made, by analyzing the time relations involved between the various components of the responses, to contribute toward a finer detail in the characterization of infant responses. Characterization of the neonate as behaving in a random manner implies a sedative finality which tends to halt analysis at the surface. It must be kept in mind that chance or randomness is nothing but a scientific construct, by which one characterizes phenomena which have not been successfully correlated with external conditions. The word random is an expression of the scientist's lack of knowledge of relationship. The aim of science is to substitute correlation for randomness.
>
> The results of this study indicate that the responses do not occur in a chance fashion. Considering the large number of factors which remained uncontrolled, it seems highly probable that further control would yield greater constancy in responses, and thus further knowledge of correlation between conditions and behavior.
>
> The next step indicated, therefore, would be to control factors, which were not controlled in this study, some of which have never to my knowledge, been controlled. Systematic control and variation of such factors as head position, flexion or extension of the limbs before stimulation, intensity of stimuli, together with further detail in analysis of behavior should establish fairly definite correlations between the behavior and the external conditions (Delman, 1935, pp. 107–108).

Though early investigations did not support the view of stimulus-response specificity, the direct consequence was an interest in activity of the organism *per se*. Correlates of mass activity were examined to determine what was responsible or related to motility changes.

No relationships have been found between motility and sex or race (Gatewood & Weiss, 1930), body temperature (Irwin, 1933a), change in environmental temperature and humidity (Pratt, 1930), physical measurements (Irwin, 1933b), or nutritional status (Irwin, 1933b).

Though there is the well-founded clinical opinion relating birth conditions to motility patterns, there is limited quantitative data to describe the effects of varying perinatal conditions on newborn activity. Prechtl (1965), using an observational scoring system, reports significant differences in type, amount, amplitude, and speed of activity between groups of babies with and without complications during pregnancy and delivery.

Discernible changes in motility have been related to feeding, greater increases appearing just prior to the time of feeding. When the period between feedings was divided into fifteen-minute periods, there was a constant increase in movement frequency from the first to the last fifteen-minute period of approximately 300 per cent (Irwin, 1932b). Because most babies appeared asleep near the middle of the interfeeding interval, Irwin (1930) concluded that the motility was due to hunger and not waking. Richards (1936) subsequently related activity to gastric activity. Breast-fed infants have been reported to be more alert and active (Davis, Sears, Miller, & Brodbeck, 1948; Newton & Newton, 1951). Significantly increased motility with increased crying was observed with unswaddled babies by Irwin and Weiss (1934a). From two separate samples of swaddled babies, Lipton, Steinschneider, and Richmond (1960, 1965) reported increased sleeping and less crying, leading them to hypothesize that motor restraint was responsible for these effects. Crowell, Yasaka, and Crowell (1964) in describing a stabilimeter using electronic instrumentation present data showing that motility increased with unswaddling.

Motility varies according to the intensity and duration of stimulation. Short intense visual stimuli are likely to evoke the pupillary or palpebral response or produce brief bursts of activity, as in the Moro reflex. Though more motility is produced under minimal light intensities, with continued illumination activity decreases with an increase in stimulus intensity (Weiss, 1934; Irwin & Weiss, 1934; Irwin, 1941). Females show more sensitivity to intensity differences (Weiss, 1934). Although differences in activity have not been associated with stages of dark adaptation, Redfield (1937) found increased sensitivity following long as opposed to short periods of darkness.

Comparable findings have been associated with the various parameters of auditory stimulation. Short, intense sounds evoke considerable activity but a continuous stimulus or repetition of discontinuous stimuli produces periods of quiescence (Pratt, Nelson & Sun, 1930; Weiss, 1934). This effect has been subsequently confirmed by Bartoshuk (1962), Birns, Black, Bridger and Escalona (1965), and Stubbs and Irwin (1934). Salk (1960, 1961, 1962) maintained that the heartbeat through intrauterine imprinting becomes more effective than any other sound in quieting infants. Offsetting this claim were the results of Brackbill, Adams, Crowell, and Gray (1966) demonstrating that prolonged auditory stimulation lessens activity and that the effectiveness of heartbeat in quieting is not superior to that of any other sound.

In spite of the information accumulated on mass activity, these data seemed only to remain as facts that are unintegrated with the larger body of psychological knowledge and, for the most part, to define parameters requiring experimental control. The critique of Gordon and Bell (1961) raises serious questions about the value of activity as measured and evaluated. From their review of published literature on motility and from their own data, they emphasize that,

> Even with activity recorded in such a gross fashion, it is apparent that research either on the general nature of the newborn's activity or individual differences must specify a large number of circumstances critical to comparability of results from study to

study or between infants in the same study. . . . Recent research suggests that qualitatively different components have been subsumed under the heading of mass activity. Further analysis of such components is recommended rather than a continuation of efforts to locate congenital characteristics which might assist explanations for the development of different symptom patterns and character structure. . . . It is possible that this area of research may yet yield positive results, but it will be necessary to carefully specify conditions of the infant's milieu, components of the activity involved, and the state of the infant or the point in the sleep, waking, and eating cycle involved (Gordon & Bell, 1961, pp. 113–114).

A third approach to activity is psychoanalytic in background and apparently conceives of the newborn as representing id function. In some unspecified manner this id role is said to be related to activity and tension release. Since empirical data are lacking for this type of theorizing, no further discussion of activity in this context will be undertaken.

SLEEP

Out of investigations on sleep and arousal has emerged the fourth type of thinking about activity. In this connection activity has been a variable of interest for determining depth of sleep and depicting position on the sleep-awake continuum. In the context of early experimental work, activity constituted a dependent variable. Even here, however, it was soon recognized that activity level fluctuated as a function of other background factors—in particular whether or not the subject was awake or asleep. In the ensuing discussion, focus will be on activity as one of an array of background variables that can be used as an index to the internal state of the organism.

In examining the ontogeny of sleep patterns it is evident that there are three types of events requiring examination: one referring to periodic activity and inactivity during sleep *per se,* another that is related to the former periodicity within sleep, but more concerned with position on the sleep-awake continuum, and last, phenomena of duration, night-day disparity in sleep and amount of sleep.

With regard to the first of these, there is broad agreement that there are two distinct phases of sleep. The sleep phase associated with rapid eye movements (REM sleep), as opposed to the nonrapid eye movement (NREM sleep), has attracted considerable interest following the initial observation and correlation with dreaming (Aserinsky & Kleitman, 1953, 1955a, 1955b). Encephalographic (EEG) changes support the idea that the REM phase is a distinctly different state. Along with EEG activity of short trains of sawtooth waves of 2 to 3 cycles per second and accompanying irregularity in heart rates and respiration cycles, REM sleep is generally accompanied by eye movements and an increase in gross body, facial, and sucking motions.

Except for an occasional gross body twitch and the respiratory excursions of the chest cavity, NREM sleep may be considered essentially devoid of muscular activity. The infant lies passive and motionless, in marked contrast to the almost continuous muscle contractions during the REM state. Grimaces, whimpers, smiles, twitches of the face and extremities are interspersed with gross shifts of position of the limbs. There are frequent 10- to 15-second episodes of tonic, athetoid writhing of the torso, limbs, and digits. Bursts of REM's commonly accompany the generalized muscle contractions, but the former are also present in the absence of other body movements (Roffwarg, Muzio, & Dement, 1966, p. 609).

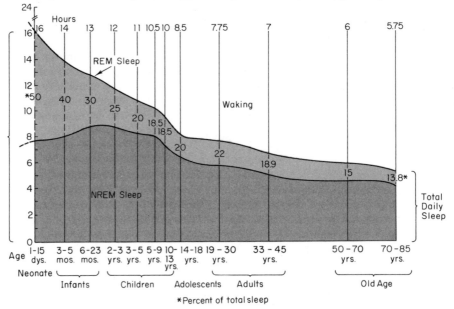

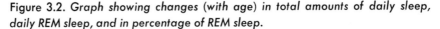

Figure 3.2. *Graph showing changes (with age) in total amounts of daily sleep, daily REM sleep, and in percentage of REM sleep.*

Note sharp diminution of REM sleep in the early years. REM sleep falls from eight hours at birth to less than one hour in old age. The amount of NREM sleep throughout life remains more constant, falling from eight to five hours. (From H. P. Roffwarg, J. H. Muzio, & W. C. Dement. Ontogenetic development of the human sleep-dream cycle. *Science*, 1966, 152, 604–617.)

Speculations regarding REM have led to studies on both the phylogeny of this type of sleep as well as its role in human ontogenetic development. Roffwarg, Muzio, and Dement (1966) report that a large proportion of the total sleep during the first few days following birth is REM sleep. This proportion diminishes with chronological age and maturation of the central nervous system (Fig. 3.2).

In infancy, when the proportion of time awake is smaller than in any other period of life, there is a large amount of REM activity. REM periods appear soon after sleep begins and are of random duration at any time of the night. Later, when the developing infant spends protracted intervals awake in increasingly active involvement with the environment (particularly when locomotive capacity is attained), the total amount as well as the percentage of REM sleep diminishes (Roffwarg, Muzio, & Dement, 1966, p. 607).

Roffwarg *et al.* recorded sleep tracings (EEG and electro-oculo-grams) from fourteen normal, full term infants during a succession of alternating REM and NREM periods. The sequence is different for newborns and adults. Whereas in adults the first REM period follows a fifty- to seventy-minute phase of NREM sleep, in newborns who have just fallen asleep, a REM period precedes the first NREM period. The fact that the EEG patterns for the REM sleep of newborns is related to the adult REM sleep phase has led Roffwarg, Muzio, and Dement (1966) to postulate first, that the REM state originates from endogenous proc-esses and second, that REM sleep is related to early development. With respect to the second point they hypothesize that

> REM sleep affords intense stimulation to the central nervous system, stimulation turned on periodically from within it by a mechanism capable of stimulating the rest of the central nervous system. This is probably the pontine REM mechanism which functions largely independently of factors external to the central nervous system. The intervals of intense activity during sleep would be available in great quantity to the developing organism *in utero* and later in its early extrauterine life when stimuli are limited (Roffwarg, Muzio, & Dement, 1966, p. 615).

A corollary implicit in this compelling hypothesis is that the developing fetus might show lags in central nervous system growth if deprived of the REM state.

Early concern with infant sleep appears to have arisen out of a need to describe the context within which stimuli were presented. Objective criteria of sleep are easily specified for the adult, but the infant, and more so the newborn, poses a special problem because of the lack of definite rhythms of quiescence and activity. In spite of this difficulty some estimate of sleep was incorporated in early studies and defined in terms of "eyes closed" (Pratt, Nelson, & Sun, 1930) or "eyes closed and quiet" (Irwin, 1930) or high electrical skin resistance (Richter, 1930), but it was Wagner (1937) who developed an operational defini-tion of depth of sleep. Based on the duration and extent of responses to pain, tactual, olfactory, and auditory stimuli, she established the first objective scale of states in depth of sleep. These relied on bodily ac-tivity, as well as breathing, eyelid, and mouth movements. The assign-ment of these behavioral characteristics to the particular step on the scale were reasonably congruent with neurophysiological theorizing and evidence established almost two decades later.

In recent years evidence has accumulated to indicate that atten-tion, consciousness, and sleep depend upon a common neurophysiolog-ical mechanism; ". . . it is known that certain differential electrical patterns (EEG) exist at any moment in widely dispersed regions of the brain, and that a certain amount of correlation has already been demon-strated between these electrophysiological patterns and the behavioral and subjective indices of attention, consciousness, wakefulness and sleep" (Lindsley, 1960, p. 1555). By a combined use of overt behavioral and physiological indices, position on the asleep-awake continuum has been inferred and, correspondingly, assumptions have been made about the relative "state" of awareness as well as the functioning efficiency of the individual. This state variable has come to be used synonymously with *level of arousal, level of excitation, activation level,* or *condition of the organism.*

Based upon continua related to heart rate, respiration, gross motor activity, ocular movement, and vocalizations, investigators report that a number of states can be differentiated in young infants. Table 3.1 is representative of scales for discriminating among states. Unfortunately the state variable has had only cursory attention. Brown's (1964) partial step in this direction only served to outline such significant parameters as the distribution of states, correlation between states, rate of change of states, type and direction of state changes, and stimuli associated with state changes.

Prechtl (1965) reports data on the frequency as well as duration of different states over the first nine days following birth. As defined by his scale, State 1 and State 2 are most prevalent during this period. With increasing age infants remain in State 2 longer than in other states. Fluctuations in states do not seem to occur in random order, but are sequential and periodic; that is, cycles of inactivity are followed by activity.

State in its most limited and specific sense implies position on the sleep-awake continuum. It has come to imply receptivity of the infant to stimulation and presumably is indicative of his responsiveness to stimulation. The difficulties of interpretation attending the definition of state have had little evaluation, but Prechtl (1965) has recommended that an exact specification be made whenever the term state is used and that the concept of state not be used as a casual explanation for other variables under examination.

Obviously the state variable presents a number of methodological problems. Bell (1963) has suggested that experimental procedures should be used to provide for comparability of state, or statistical adjustments made to partial out the effects of differences in state, or evidence collected to demonstrate that differences in state do not affect the behavioral response of interest.

The extent to which state does alter motor response level has been amply documented. Irwin (1932b) noted that spontaneous activity was almost six times as great during the waking period than during sleep. For Richmond, Grossman, and Lustman (1953) light sleep seemed to be optimal for testing hearing in newborns. Gentry and Aldrich (1948a) observed shifts in the oral behavior of their infants with changes in level of arousal. At the same time state itself may be related to and altered by other variables. Babies whose mothers received heavy medication during labor have been shown to be less attentive than their counterparts whose mothers received light medication (Stechler, 1964).

Table 3.1—Scales and Criteria Defining States In Young Infants

	State	Criteria
Wolff (1959)	Regular sleep	Breathing rhythm smooth and even; relatively little movement and frequent spontaneous startles
	Irregular sleep	Breathing rhythm irregular or alternating between rapid shallow, and slow deep breathing; relatively few spontaneous startles but many movements ranging from simple limb activity to writhing of body
	Drowsiness	Breathing rhythm irregular; spontaneous startles less frequent and motor activity greater than in regular sleep, but spontaneous startles more frequent and motor activity less than in irregular sleep; intermittent opening and closing of eyes
	Alert activity, Alert inactivity	Awake; eyes wide open, eyeballs "bright" and appear to be focused; relative mobility (activity) or immobility (inactivity)
	Crying	Precry grimace; cry of rhythmical braying quality with tandem kicking (before meals); arrhythmical shrill cry not synchronized with kicking (after meals)
Brown (1964)	S_3 Deep sleep	Motionless with closed eyes; regular respirations, no vocalizations, and unresponsive to external stimulation
	S_2 Regular sleep	Little movement, periodic discharges every two minutes through startles; skin mottled or pale; breathing raspy or wheezing and respiration regular, or passing from regular to irregular, with intervening Cheyne-Stokes character
	S_1 Disturbed sleep	Movement variable; eyelids closed, but may flutter; breathing irregular; no skin changes; vocalizations (squeaks, sobs or sporadic sighs)
	A_1 Drowsy	Eyes open or semiopened and glassy; little movement (startle or free type); breathing usually regular; skin mottled or pale, vocalizations more regular than in S_1
	A_2 Alert activity	Common "awake" state; eyes open and bright; often free movement, fretting, reddening of skin and irregular respiration with increased tension
	A_3 Alert and focused	Analogous to "attention" in older child, but uncommon in newborn; eyes open and bright; motor activity occurring is integrated around specific activity as listening or looking
	A_4 Inflexibly focused	Awake, but nonreactive to external stimuli as in concentrated sucking and wild crying
Prechtl (1965)	State 1	Regular respiration, eyes closed and no movements
	State 2	Irregular respiration, eyes closed, and slight movements
	State 3	Eyes open, alert, but inactive
	State 4	Eyes open, gross movements, and no crying
	State 5	Eyes open or closed, active and crying

The transition from the polycyclic patterns of sleep and wakefulness in the newborn to the monocyclic sleep-wakefulness rhythm of the adult has been considered related to a subcortically controlled wakefulness which gradually evolves into a cortically regulated advanced wakefulness of choice (Kleitman, 1963). The increased periods of wakefulness, leading to the eventual elimination of naps and predominant nocturnal sleeping have been of interest because of child-welfare implications. Questions about the amount, duration, and night-day disparity in sleep have been thoroughly investigated, providing considerable normative-descriptive material. Along with the practical application, these waking and sleeping patterns have become supporting data on the neurological functioning of the arousal mechanism.

In spite of the broad attention given to the topic of sleep, few studies, mostly limited to small samples, have been carried out with very young infants. Gesell and Amatruda (1945) using intensive observation of one infant over a fifteen-day period, found a mean duration of sleep of fourteen hours out of twenty-four. This mean figure was different from, but at the same time reasonably similar to, ones obtained from maternal recordings of the sleep-awake intervals of their infants during the first three days of life (Parmelee, Schulz, & Disbrow, 1961). These investigators found that babies were awake seven to eight hours per day or about 30 to 35 per cent of the day and asleep sixteen to seventeen hours or about 65 to 70 per cent of the time. Babies tended to retain their pattern of sleep duration over the first two days, but by day three, there was a shift to a common sleeping pattern for both groups. It was recognized that factors such as type of labor and delivery or analgesia and anesthesia might have influenced these sleeping patterns. Parmelee, Wenner, and Schulz (1964) recorded sleep and wake periods for 46 infants over the first sixteen weeks of life. There was an average total sleep per day of sixteen hours in the first week which decreased slightly to a mean total of 14.9 hours by the sixteenth week. Of practical significance was evidence that by the end of the third to fourth months, normal babies might show a sleep rhythm similar to that of the parents, sleeping for long periods and then primarily at night. No correlations were seen between age for beginning to eat solid foods and length of sustained sleep or the diurnal ratio, the ratio of day sleep to night sleep.

While generally confirming Gesell and Amatruda's findings, Kleitman and Engelmann (1953) extended them to the end of the first half-year of life. Basing their computations on maternal protocols and on continuous automatic recordings of crib movements, they found a mode of fourteen to fifteen hours of sleep for 19 infants. This decreased by about one hour over the first six months. Even though Thompson (1936) wrote that her figures probably erred in indicating more sleep than actually occurred, the mean duration of sleep at the end of twelve months was 13.5 hours. No significant sex difference was noted, though considerable variation in length of individual sleep was apparent. Prior to age twelve weeks, males were more irritable and had greater difficulty in establishing a schedule. Approximately one third of all infants deviated from the average by more than an hour and a half with respect to total sleeping time. Analysis of marked deviations showed that illness often preceded intervals of more than normal sleep, while teething, hyperactivity, and restlessness were associated with intervals of less than normal sleep. No correlations were evident at one year of age between individual sleep requirements and weight-length index, the ratio of lower extremity length to total vertex-heel length, nutritional, or growth-rate indices.

During the second year the total duration of sleep appears to fluctuate between thirteen to fourteen hours (Kleitman, 1963). According to Foster (1929), the subsequent decrease to twelve hours at five years is related to the diminishing and eventual elimination of the afternoon nap. Reynolds' (1935) data showed that the average amount of sleep between the ages of two to three was approximately eleven hours and a half. From questionnaire information on 78 cases, Flemming (1925) concluded that the amount of sleep decreased gradually from around eighteen months to six years. The decrease was most rapid between eighteen and twenty-four months, remained constant between two and four years, then dropped again. Sex differences in amount of sleep were observed, but seemed to be differences in rate of decrease with age and not a difference in amount of sleep. Boys decreased markedly from one to six years, while girls remained fairly constant in amount of sleep for the same period. Just as amount of sleep decreased with age, the length and number of naps decreased at a rate comparable to that of total sleep. In Flemming's (1925) sample all children took naps up to age two and one-half years, but between two and three years, 20 per cent took no naps and by five years of age no nap seemed to be the rule.

Relative to night-day disparity in sleep, Parmelee, Wenner, and Schulz (1964) observed that at birth almost equal amounts of sleep occurred during the day and night. By the sixteenth week, there was double the amount of sleep at night as compared to that seen during the day. Similarly, Kleitman and Engelmann's (1953) earliest records showed diurnal disparity; night sleep duration averaged 8.4 hours in contrast to the mean of 6.4 hours for day sleep. This disparity increased, ending with long sustained periods of night sleep and short morning and afternoon naps by the end of the first year. Related to the periodicity was detection of a fundamental rest-activity cycle of about one hour during the afternoon naps or long stretches of night sleep. Eye movements decreased, as did activity, at the onset of sleep. In this connection, Aserinsky and Kleitman (1955) correlated the activity cycles of sleeping infants with their eye movements. The patterning of both occurred in periodically recurring cycles. This material as well as data from older subjects have substantiated the existence of a basic rest-activity cycle which appears to be 50 to 60 minutes long in infants, later passes through a 60–70-minute cycle in the preschool child and eventually becomes the 85–90-minute adult cycle. From a study of 34 children, White (1931) concluded that length of night sleep did not decrease with increasing age. The data of Reynolds and Mallay (1933) suggested that over a period of time, longer than 24 hours, most children maintain some constancy in amount of sleep. White (1931), Shinn (1932), and Wagner (1933) have reported a negative relation between intelligence and sleep: the brighter child slept less than the duller child.

Time of going to sleep has been examined relative to both naptime as well as to effect on night sleep. Wagner (1933) found a mean length of time of going to sleep of approximately 24 minutes for young orphanage children, 25–72 months of age. Only a negligible correlation existed for time of going to sleep in the afternoon and time of going to sleep at night. White (1931) concluded that two-year-olds need more time than older children to fall asleep. The mean time to fall asleep reported for three- to four-year-olds was 20–27 minutes.

WAKING

In spite of evidence supporting the interdependence of sleeping and waking, Dittrichová and Lapackova (1964) suggest the development of sleep and waking are not entirely analogues. They studied the development of the waking state in infants, two to twenty-four weeks of age, through observations of hand movements and vocalizations. The waking state increased with age and was characterized by two distinct phases. During the initial period through two months of age the infants showed little manipulation of the toys, or babbled, but cried frequently. About two to three months, there was a significant decrease in crying and an increase in vocalization and manipulation. These data were interpreted as consonant with Kleitman's (1963) subcortical wakefulness of necessity and cortical advanced wakefulness of choice.

INDIVIDUAL DIFFERENCES

Interest in activity as a criterion of individual difference has extended back to the fetal period. Fetal movement is one behavioral measure that can be recorded with reasonable accuracy during pregnancy and analyzed for relationship with other variables in the postnatal period. Human fetal activity has been recorded with good reliability via mechanical devices (Sontag & Wallace, 1935; Sontag & Richards, 1938; Kellogg, 1941), as well as through introspective reports (Richards, Newbery & Fallgatter, 1938; Newbery, 1941; Harris & Harris, 1946; Walters, 1964). The Sontag and Richards (1938) study suggested that the mother-reporting technique is sensitive and permits measurement over a long time without the encumbrance of apparatus, but that it poses a psychophysical problem. Richards et al. (1938) found no significant differences in fetal activity which might be attributed to sex, age, maternal activity, basal metabolism, number of previous births, or time of day (diurnal rhythm). Trends suggested that there was a peak of activity during the eighth and ninth months of pregnancy which decreased near term.

Newbery (1941) concentrated on the last five months of pregnancy and reported that total activity increased significantly from the sixth to the last month. Three distinct types of activity were recorded and related to gestation. Significant differences were evident between kicking and squirming during the last months of pregnancy. Newbery's classification of *total activity, kicks, squirms, and hiccups* were later compared by Walters (1964), who concluded that (1) specific fetal movements differ significantly during pregnancy, and (2) that fetal activity decreases during the last month of pregnancy.

Among the first to report a discernible relationship between the amount of fetal activity and subsequent postnatal development were Richards, Newbery, and Fallgatter (1938). Fetal activity, based on the last two months of pregnancy with scores derived from introspective reports of minutes during which the fetus was active, was significantly correlated with performance on the Gesell Development Schedules for twelve subjects tested at six months of age. The correlation for six subjects at twelve months was .62. In concluding that ". . . these coefficients would indicate that from thirty to seventy per cent of the variance at six months is measured by the activity records during fetal life" Richards, Newbery, and Fallgatter (1938, p. 83), also acknowledged the possibility of unreliability in their finding.

Replication of this study, but with conflicting results, has been carried out by Bernard (1964) and Walters (1965). With a sample of 32 cases, Bernard (1964) computed separate correlations between fetal activity (slow, quiet, rhythmic, and total score) and the Gesell Developmental Schedules (at six, twelve, eighteen, and twenty-four months), the Merrill-Palmer (at twenty-four and thirty months), and the Stanford-Binet (at thirty and thirty-six months). He concluded that none of these data showed fetal activity significantly related to later test performance. Somewhat tangential to the primary issue was the observation that males were significantly larger and heavier at birth and showed more "quick" fetal movements. In contradistinction, Walters (1965) substantiated the Richards and Newbery results. She recorded fetal movements during the last three months of pregnancy. Correlations between fetal activity and postnatal development were based on weekly 1½-hour measurements of fetal activity. Walters concluded that (1) activity in each of the months of the last trimester was an indicator of postnatal motor and total Gesell scores, with the ninth month of fetal activity as the best indicator of development in all areas of behavior for all testing periods, and (2) the most significant relationships appeared between fetal activity and the 36-week test score. To explain this result Walters offers the hypothesis of Richards and Newbery that ". . . the amount of time a fetus is active is a criterion, during fetal life, of the developmental pattern or patterns of behavior responsible for rather specialized performances at six months postnatally" (1938, p. 85).

The only other published report dealing with behavioral data which incorporated activity as a dimension is that of Thomas, Chess, Birch, and Hertzig (1960). Postnatal, longitudinal data collected between birth and two years were subjected to content analysis and analyzed to determine the degree to which individual reactivity characteristics identified in early infancy persisted or changed. Nine characteristics of reactivity were identified in infancy and the first two years: (1) activity level, (2) rhythmicity of functioning, (3) adaptability, (4) approach or withdrawal, (5) intensity of reaction, (6) threshold or responsiveness, (7) quality of mood, (8) distractability, (9) attention span and persistence. Thomas *et al.* concluded that these primary patterns of reactivity were highly reliable and persistent individual characteristics.

POSTURAL CONTROL

Several generalizations bearing on the development of postural control have evolved from questions stimulated by the maturational approach. Concern with problems posed by the maturational framework is predominant in the general research on motor coordination and developmental sequences in motor coordination. From these can be derived generalizations with implications for developing postural control. The first set of these is grounded in McGraw's (1941) classifications of motor functioning into successive and overlapping stages of maturity. These phases of motor development suggest that subcortical movements predominate during the first postnatal month but eventually decline between the first and fourth months. Cortical inhibitory control is apparent between four and eight months and is noticed first in the upper part of the body. From eight to fourteen months of age cortical participation is clearly seen in the emerging voluntary control over activities of the lower body region.

The second set of generalizations emanates from the classic study of Shirley (1931) on the development of postural control and locomotion. In this study, which provided an important longitudinal overview of development, Shirley divided all motor reactions into five orders of skill. In the first order is passive postural control of the upper trunk region, which includes lifting the chin and chest when prone, making stepping movements, tensing the muscles for lifting, straightening the knees, and sitting when held. The median age for achieving this order is under twenty weeks. The second order involves postural control of the entire trunk and is represented by sitting alone momentarily, swimming activity, and standing with help; the median age for such achievement is twenty-five to thirty-one weeks. With the third order, active attempts at locomotion appear. This period shows considerable overlap with the second and fourth orders of skill. What characterizes this order is poorly coordinated activity when the infant is lying on his stomach. During the fourth order there is improved postural control of the body and locomotion through creeping or walking when led or supported. The median age for attaining these skills is forty to fifty weeks. In the fifth order (median age of sixty-two to sixty-four weeks), there is complete postural control during locomotion. The results of this investigation suggest that motor development is an orderly sequence and that each of the stages in the sequence—head control, sitting, swimming, creeping, and walking alone—is a prerequisite for the succeeding stages.

HEAD CONTROL

Roughly four groups of head control responses can be distinguished. In group one are responses, presumably reflexive, which consist of head-raising or head-turning to the side when the infant is lying prone and from side-to-side when he is in a supine position. The head-turning and head-raising acts have been reported to be present at birth (Bryan, 1930; Shirley, 1931). Shirley (1931) noted that these responses occurred in 88 per cent of her babies by the third week, and Gesell (1938) listed *lifting the head when prone* as fully established by four months. By this time the head-lifting action appears as a response of bringing the top of the head up and the mouth parallel to a horizontal surface. The reflex pattern seen at this time can be defined as the labyrinthine righting reflex of the head which Peiper says,

> . . . is decisive for the ability to bring the body into upright position, i.e., to adjust it to gravity and move it forward. This reflex has the task of adjusting the head to gravity; vertex up and mouth horizontal. . . . The reflex is only faintly demonstrable in the neonate, but during the first year of life it becomes an important prerequisite for the infant's ability to lift his head and later also the upper part of his body while in the prone position, thus reaching the starting position for locomotion in the abdominal position. With the help of this reflex the infant learns to sit and stand, a prerequisite for the upright and free gait. For this purpose the chain reflexes, which depend on the labyrinthine righting reflex of the head, are very important (1964, p. 175).

The side-to-side head turning behavior is usually considered as a head-orientation component of feeding. Discussion of this reaction will be reserved for the material on oral responses.

Bell and Darling (1965) studied the prone head reaction with the expectation that males would lift their heads higher and thus give some evidence for a congenitally determined difference in muscle strength. Although some support for this hypothesis was found, it was questioned whether the response was stable enough to warrant further generalizations. The prone head reaction appeared to have no relationship to tactile sensitivity.

Representative of a second group of responses involving the head, is the ocular-neck reflex (Peiper, 1963). The reflex is essentially a bending backward of the head to a light flash and has had little use as an experimental variable beyond the well-known studies by Peiper (1927) and Trincker and Trincker (1955) of brightness vision in infants.

The tonic-neck reflex (t-n-r) is a third type of head movement. The definition of this reflex was originally derived from observations on decerebrate animals. When the head was turned right or left, there was (1) an extension of the forelimb of the side toward which head is turned, and (2) a flexion of the opposite forelimb. In the human infant similar patterns were observed. Gesell (1938) stated that the t-n-r was normal during the first sixteen weeks, and by twenty weeks was replaced by a symmetro-tonic reflex (s-t-r). Initially the shoulder, pelvis, and leg on the same side of the body are involved in the response. From about eight weeks of age both legs are flexed in the t-n-r. According to Gesell the t-n-r is a pathologic sign if it persists beyond age six months. Under certain circumstances it is a good predictor of locomotion difficulties.

In 14 out of 19 cases the right- or left-face direction of t-n-r was predictive of later handedness. Generally, the t-n-r is to the right side.

In spite of Gesell's (1938) contention that marked persistence of the t-n-r beyond the age of six months was indicative of retarded, arrested, or defective development, Mehlman (1940) maintained that the reflex as a clinical test was of questionable value. His testing situation required that (1) infants be awake and quiet, and (2) show an extension of the forearm on the side to which the head is turned and flexion of the opposite forelimb for a period of 2 minutes. Forty per cent of 200 newborn infants showed a positive response. Twenty-seven infants who were tested on the first and eighth days showed inconstant responses. Even in two cases with the Down's syndrome, both negative and positive results were elicited.

The fourth type of head movements involves head control. There is an implied assumption in clinical situations that head control is an index of muscular tone and rate of development. Tensing of the neck muscle for control of the head is a relatively late development and is probably the first instance of infant body control. Most developmental inventories list this control as the first phase of the developmental sequence which will culminate in erect posture and walking. More specifically, the order of control progresses from lifting the head when prone to holding the head erect when sitting to lifting the head when on the back.

Based on a rationale that muscular energy was required to resist force, Knop (1946) proceeded to rate babies relative to their head lag when brought from a supine position to a sitting position and also on the ability to straighten the legs while in a supine position. From two evaluations of 689 infants, he concluded that this dynamic muscular energy was an inherent quality which did not change much over time. There was a prevalence of boys in the higher grades, but no correlation was apparent between weight and muscular energy. The effects of labor, delivery, and pathological conditions were inconclusive.

The data of Geber and Dean (1957) showed that 107 normal African newborns were advanced to the point that their performance showed little overlap with scores of Indian and European babies in control of the head, absence of primitive reflex activity, and degree of flexion. In a simple screening technique which involved hearing, listening attention, and good motor coordination, Hardy et al. (1959) selected directional head-turning as indicative of a normal response. They suggest that by the time the baby is eight months of age, he is expected to respond consistently with a full right-angle turn of the head, neck, and torso toward the side from which the sound is coming.

SITTING

Outside of age-normative data sitting behavior has been of little research interest. McGraw (1941) has analyzed independent sitting to identify structures regulating these antigravity muscles. Complete control over sitting involved getting from an erect to a sitting position as well as from a supine to a sitting position. She reported that, contrary to phases observed in other motor patterns of human infants, there was no definite reflex sitting posture comparable to the subcortical grasping or swimming or stepping movements. Because of this she concluded that sitting is of recent phyletic origin.

SWIMMING

As early as 1897 swimming actions of infants suspended in air were described by Mumford (1897). Later accounts of these movements were reported by Shirley (1931), Ames (1937), and McGraw (1935; 1939). Shirley listed the "swimming stage" as one example of the second order of motor skills. Somewhere around 25 to 35 weeks, these movements reflect completion of postural control over the whole trunk and emerging control over the pelvic and leg areas. Swimming behavior in this context ". . . consisted in drawing up the legs frog-like and in kicking them out suddenly as if swimming" (Shirley, 1931, p. 48).

The most intensive examinations of swimming movements were carried out by McGraw (1935, 1939). Observations extended from eleven days through two and one half years. McGraw found that when immersed in water the neonate makes coordinated swimming actions with both arms and legs. Around four months these movements become disorganized, but at the beginning of the second year voluntary movements become evident. Although swimming movements are more regular than stepping and crawling movements, the neuromuscular mechanisms that mediate all of these are presumed to be the same.

ROLLING OVER

Turning from a supine to a prone position is a precursor of the human righting response and a component in the later development of erect posture. For Shirley (1931) this action is also a second order skill, and is not the same behavior observed in newborns who, when prone and flexed in the fetal position, accidentally roll over. McGraw (1941) differentiated four phases in achievement of the ability to turn from prone to supine, and from her data concluded:

> It appears then that the righting response in an infant is composed of a complex series of reflexes developing in a cephalocaudal direction. After the series of reflexes attains a degree of integration at a nuclear level, the cerebral cortex gains dominance and the function becomes incorporated into the human mode of the righting response, viz., the assumption of an erect posture. Although observations on developmental changes in erect locomotion and the assumption of an erect posture were made under different conditions, the first signs of cortical participation in these activities occurred about the time deliberate rolling over was achieved, as revealed in these data. Evidence of cortical functioning was indi-

cated in these activities by most of the children between the eighth and ninth months. As the human righting response matures, rolling over becomes eliminated as an initial move in the performance (McGraw, 1941, p. 394).

CREEPING

Prone progression analysis is among the most completely covered sectors of motor development. The first detailed study is that of Burnside (1927) which was designed to show the sequences of movements involved in the stages of progression preceding walking. Though based on only nine babies, this study differentiated crawling from hitching and creeping. Hitching, defined as progression in a sitting posture, as well as rolling, may occur as the first mode of progression. In crawling the abdomen is in contact with a surface and the body is pulled along only by the arms with the legs dragging. Later the arms begin alternate action and the legs come into use.

In creeping, the posture is changed to hands and knees making contact with the ground while the trunk is free above the floor surface. Movements are often arrhythmic, with some cross-coordination. With complete cross-coordination, movements are rhythmic and one limb is moved at a time. Later yet, diagonal synchrony may be seen. Shirley (1931) reported that creeping activity was going on while sitting up behavior was progressing, and that creeping appeared at the same time the infant rolled over. She listed seven stages as making up the creeping sequence: chin up, chest up, knee push or swim, rolling, rock or pivot, scooting backward, and then creeping. According to her observations babies proceeded through these stages in the same sequence regardless of speed of development. There was a correlation of $+.84 \pm .05$ between the ages of walking alone and of creeping. When a baby creeps he has presumably covered about two thirds of the way toward walking.

McGraw's (1941a) summary of prone behavior was similar to that of Shirley's. Ames (1937) in a longitudinal analysis of 20 infants, outlined 14 steps in the development of prone progression: (1) one knee and thigh forward beside the body; (2) knee and thigh forward, inner side of foot contacting the floor; (3) pivoting; (4) inferior low creep position; (5) low creep position; (6) crawling; (7) high creep position; (8) retrogression; (9) rocking; (10) creep-crawling; (11) creeping on hands and knees; (12) creeping, near step with one foot; (13) creeping, step with one foot; and (14) quadruped progression (creeping on hands and feet).

Ames concluded that the development of prone progression proceeds from head to foot; during the first three stages of progression— pivoting, crawling, and retrogression—the arms are exclusively responsible for actual progression. Legs do not play an effective part in progression until stage 11 is reached.

ERECT POSTURE AND LOCOMOTION

The most complete study on the development of erect posture and locomotion is that by Shirley (1931). The steps she found in the development of the upright posture or position were (1) tensing the muscles when lifted; (2) sitting with support; (3) lifting the head when lying on the back; (4) sitting alone momentarily; (5) standing with support under the armpits; (6) sitting alone; (7) standing with support by holding; (8) sitting down from the standing position; (9) pulling self to the standing position; and (10) standing alone.

As soon as an erect posture can be maintained, walking ordinarily follows. In Burnside's (1927) early analysis the problems involved in weight distribution and muscular coordination were stressed.

> The stability of the body in erect posture depends upon the basis of support (which is the area enclosed by the two feet), the position of the center of gravity, and the weight of the body. In children the small size of the base of support and the relatively high situation of the center of gravity, combined with the slight weight of the body give an unstable equilibrium. The coordination of the muscles for the restoration of equilibrium is immature, hence the child frequently falls.
>
> In the very young child these factors are partially counterbalanced by the wide placing of the feet, which increases the area of the base of support, the slight flexion at the hip and knee which lowers the center of gravity, and the raising of the arms, which facilitates the muscular coordination required. It is to be noted that as the child's ease in walking increases, the arms are flexed at the elbows and only the forearms are held forward, to be followed at a still later period by the easy suspension at the side characteristic of adult walking. No alternative movement of the arms corresponding to the extension phase of the opposing leg is to be observed until this easy suspension at the sides is obtained (Burnside, 1927, pp. 328–329).

In addition the data suggested an age increase in speed and length of step in walking along with an age decrease in width and variability of steps.

Progress toward walking was presented by Shirley (1931) in terms of four stages: the early period of stepping, the period of standing with help, the period of walking when led, and lastly, the period of walking alone. Stepping records of 20 babies from seventeen to seventy-eight weeks showed that initially the babies danced or pranced with just the toes touching the floor when they were supported under the armpits. This was replaced by stepping acts when support was provided. In standing with support babies bore most of their weight but used outstretched arms to maintain balance. This period was important in Shirley's estimate for the sooner it was reached the earlier the walking. The rank order correlation between age of walking alone and standing with sup-

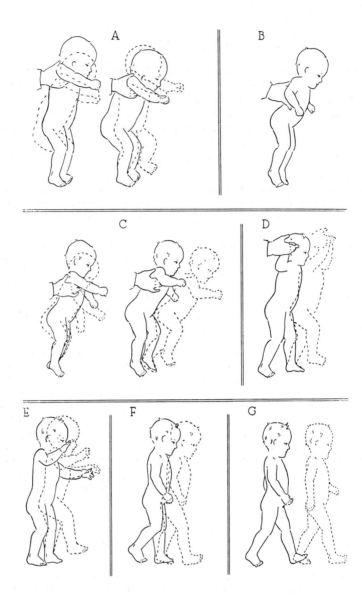

Figure 3.3. Line drawings showing infant neuromuscular development in the achievement of erect locomotion.

(From Myrtle B. McGraw. Neuromuscular development of the human infant as exemplified in the achievement of erect locomotion. *J. Pediatr.*, 1940, 17, 750, The C. V. Mosby Co., St. Louis.)

port was $+.80 \pm .06$. The third period was marked by progress in speed of walking, increase in width of step, and variability in size of the stepping angle. A correlation of $+.88 \pm .04$ was derived for the age at which babies walk with support and age of walking alone. In the stage of walking alone there was both an increase in speed of walking and length of step and a decrease in width and angle of step. A noticeable increase in straight as opposed to out-toeing steps also appeared. All these findings substantiated those previously reported by Burnside (1927).

Figure 3.3 outlines the seven phases of erect locomotion as defined by McGraw (1940b) and simultaneously illustrates the points discussed by Shirley (1931) and Burnside (1927).

The previous data on length, width, and angle of steps as well as speed of walking were attempts to quantify locomotor movements. McGraw and Breeze (1941) suggested that developmental change may be more profitably expressed and correspondingly more easily measured, in the following spheres: (1) progressive change in foot contact with the underlying surface; (2) changes in posture as reflected in base width, degree and type of flexion, extension, abduction, and adduction; (3) changes in weight bearing mechanisms; (4) changes in speed and length of step; (5) equilibrium control; and (6) rate in attaining motor efficiency.

Table 3.2—Median Ages for Stages of Motor Development
(Shirley, 1931)

Stage	Median age in weeks
First order skills	
On stomach, chin up	3.0
On stomach, chest up	9.0
Held erect, stepping	13.0
On back, tense for lifting	15.0
Held erect, knees straight	15.0
Sit on lap, support at lower ribs and complete head control	18.5
Second order skills	
Sit alone momentarily	25.0
On stomach, knee push or swim	25.0
On back, rolling	29.0
Held erect, stand firmly with help	29.5
Sit alone one minute	31.0
Third order skills	
On stomach, some progress	37.0
On stomach, scoot backward	39.5
Fourth order skills	
Stand holding to furniture	42.0
Creep	44.5
Walk when led	45.0
Pull to stand by furniture	47.0
Fifth order skills	
Stand alone	62.0
Walk alone	64.0

On the premise that quantitative measures would reflect developmental changes in postural configuration and also subtle changes of integration as well as increases in synergy, McGraw and Breeze (1941) studied the mechanics of locomotion through film analysis. Their data showed changes in the vertical height of the center of gravity of the leg, the horizontal distance covered during a step and the time consumed in making a step. The relationships between these were expressed in equations and demonstrated the feasibility of converting neuromuscular functions into measurable units.

Examining the development of independent motor performance in one baby girl, Shapiro (1962) noted that a period of 25 days intervened between independent standing and the first independent walking. Facility in walking was demonstrated to develop at an exponential and not a linear rate.

Normative data on locomotor development have been most comprehensively summarized by Aldrich and Norval (1946). The detailed longitudinal results of Shirley (1931) are presented in Table 3.2. Comparison of these with the figures of Aldrich and Norval (1946) or of Bayley (1965) suggest good consistency relative to age of achievement. The discrepancies in age of creeping, standing alone, and walking alone, may be a function of evaluation criteria, sampling error, or method of observation and recording.

MOTOR SKILLS

Studies of motor control in young children may be categorized into those dealing with gross motor as opposed to fine manual coordinations. Representative of the first group are activities involving the trunk and limbs or the hands and arms as shown in jumping or skipping, grasping or releasing, reaching or aiming. The fine motor coordinations usually require movements of the separate fingers as shown in dressing or writing activities.

Gross motor achievements for the ages of interest here are presented in the seriatim study by Bayley (1935) of 61 children and subsequently in standardization of the revised forms of the Bayley Scale of Motor Development (Bayley, 1965). Both the California Infant Scale of Motor Development (Bayley, 1935, 1936) and the Bayley Scale of Motor Development (Bayley, 1965) emphasize coordinations involving the whole body required in balancing, creeping, or walking. Table 3.3 is a modified copy of the latest standardization version.

Eye-hand coordination performance is usually inferred from the infant mental test scale results. These tests were designed to measure motor abilities from birth to three-and-a-half to four years. They cover prewalking behaviors and, starting at fourteen months, the motor coordinations of the walking child.

The 1935 version of the California Infant Scale of Motor Development was standardized on 61 children who were tested repeatedly. Scores for the first four months were least reliable in terms of split-

Table 3.3—Age Placement in Months for Motor Skill Items in the Bayley Infant Scale of Motor Development

Item number	Age in months	Item name	Item number	Age in months	Item name
1	0.1	Lifts head at shoulder	35	7.9	Partial finger prehension (Pellet) (inferior pincer)
2	0.2	Postural adjustment when held at shoulder	36	8.0	Pulls to standing position
3	0.3	Lateral head movements: prone	37	8.2	Raises self to sitting position
			38	8.4	Stands up
4	0.4	Crawling movements: prone	39	8.7	Combines cubes or spoons: Midline
5	0.5	Retains red ring			
6	0.7	Arm thrusts in play	40	9.0	Fine prehension: pellet (neat pincer)
7	0.8	Legs thrust in play			
8	0.9	Head erect-vertical	41	9.2	Stepping movements
9	1.7	Dorsal suspension—lifts head	42	9.9	Pat-a-cake: midline skill
10	1.8	Head erect and steady	43	9.9	Walks with help
11	2.2	Turns from side to back	44	10.2	Sits down
12	2.3	Prone—elevates self by arms	45	11.3	Stands alone
13	2.7	Sits with support	46	11.8	Walks alone
14	2.8	Holds head steady	47	12.5	Aufstehen I
15	2.9	Hands predominantly open	48	13.0	Throws a ball
16	3.7	Sits with slight support	49	13.5	Walks sideways
17	3.9	Cube: palmar prehension	50	14.2	Walks backward
18	4.0	Turns from back to side	51	18.3	Stands on right foot with help
19	4.5	Head balanced			
20	5.1	Effort to sit	52	18.3	Stands on left foot with help
21	5.2	Partial thumb opposition	53	18.7	Walks upstairs with help
22	5.3	Pulls to sitting position	54	18.9	Walks downstairs with help
23	5.4	Sits alone momentarily	55	20.9	Tries to stand on walking board
24	5.6	Unilateral reaching			
25	5.8	Rotates wrist	56	20.9	Aufstehen II
26	5.9	Attempts to secure pellet	57	22.7	Walks upstairs alone: marks time
27	6.0	Sits alone 30" or more			
28	6.9	Sits alone, steadily	58	22.9	Walks downstairs alone: marks time
29	7.0	Rolls from back to stomach			
30	7.2	Scoops pellet	59	26.0	Walks with one foot on walking board
31	7.2	Sits alone: good coordination			
32	7.3	Complete thumb opposition	60	26.4	Jumps off floor: both feet
33	7.6	Prewalking progression	61	27.6	Stands on left foot alone
34	7.8	Early stepping movements	62	27.7	Stands on right foot alone

half coefficients as corrected by the Brown-Spearman method. If these months are eliminated, the mean of the reliability coefficients is +.81. In the revised scale (1965) new items were added and directions clarified. Internal consistency reliabilities ranged from +.57 to +.97 with a median of +.89. The standardization sample was composed of 1409 infants, 680 of whom were boys and 728, girls. Approximately 55 per cent were white, 42 per cent Negro, and 2.3 per cent were from other racial or ethnic groups.

For the 1965 version, the following conclusions could be drawn. (1) Firstborn babies scored significantly higher than later born babies at five age levels (months 6, 7, 12, 14, and 15). Bayley (1965) postulated that amount of parent-child interaction might account for these differences. If rapid development did ensue, such differences were temporary and showed no cumulative effects. (2) There were no differences on the basis of educational level of either parent. (3) The means for the Negroes on the motor scale were higher at the early ages, but disappeared after 12 months. This superiority was not evident for any one class of behavior; two of the discriminating items involved midline arm and hand coordinations, and the others required muscular strength and tonus. Of these latter items, four related to antigravity: holds head steady, balances head when carried, sits alone steadily, and stands alone. The other five items related to locomotion: turns from side to back, raises self to sitting, makes stepping movements, walks with help, and walks alone.

For both the mental and motor scales, Bayley (1965) concluded:

> It would appear that the behaviors which are developing during the first 15 months of life, whether they are motor skills or the early perceptual and adaptive forms of mental abilities, are for the most part unrelated to sex, race, birth order, geographical location, or parental ability. The one possible difference is in motor development in which the Negro babies tend to be more advanced than the whites during the first 12 months. Although there is considerable overlap of scores among whites and Negroes of the same age, a genetic factor may be operating. That is, Negroes may be inherently more precocious than whites in their motor coordinations.
>
> It would appear that the advantage the Negro babies have is a pervasive one which may lie in a generally heightened muscle tonus (Bayley, 1965, pp. 408–409).

The 1935 publication on the development of motor abilities during the first three years (Bayley, 1935) suggested that motor functions over this period of time were less discrete and independent than motor skills measured at later ages, namely at the four-, five-, and six-year levels. McCaskill and Wellman (1938) looked at this question of increases in motor skill by means of achievement on steps and ladders activities, ball activities, and jumping, hopping, skipping, and balancing activities. No meaningful data were available on two-year-olds because of the small size of the group. Of general interest is the finding that there was a significant gain in ability from one age group to the next. In the context of this review the tentative age assignments according to the point at which 50 per cent of the group fail and 50 per cent succeed for the areas investigated are of interest. These, shown in Table 3.4, constitute an extension in the age range and cover activities for which data are not presently available.

Whether there is a general factor of motor ability has been examined by Goodenough and Smart (1935) in nursery school children. Reasoning that differential practice and motivation are less likely to be confounding factors in very young children and that individual differences are likely to be more evident, they administered a series of tests of motor abilities at annual intervals. With advancing age a general improvement in scores was seen. In the reaction-time test boys surpassed

Table 3.4

Months	Score	Item
71	4	Bouncing large ball, one hand, distance 1
68	6	Catching large ball, elbows at side of body, success on 2 or 3 trials
65	3	Bouncing large ball, both hands, distance 3
65	7	Throwing small ball, both hands or one hand, distance 7
63	5	Throwing large ball, both hands or one hand, distance 5
62	4	Descending large ladder, alternate feet, with facility
60	4	Hopping on one foot, 10 or more steps
60	3	Skipping, alternate feet
57	6	Throwing small ball, both hands or one hand, distance 6
56	3	Descending large ladder, alternate feet, with caution
55	5	Catching small ball, elbows at side of body, no success or success on one trial
55	4	Descending long steps, alternate feet, unsupported
55	3	Hopping one foot, 7 to 9 steps
53	4	Throwing large ball, both hands or one hand, distance 4
53	4	Descending small ladder, alternate feet, with facility
52	5	Throwing small ball, both hands or one hand, distance 5
51	3	Descending small ladder, alternate feet, with caution
51	5	Catching large ball, elbows at side of body, no success or success on one trial
50	4	Catching small ball, elbows in front of body, success on 2 or 3 trials
49	4	Descending short steps, alternate feet, unsupported
48	3	Descending long steps, alternate feet, with support
48	3	Descending short steps, alternate feet, with support
47	4	Ascending large ladder, alternate feet, with facility
46	2	Bouncing large ball, both hands, distance 2
46	3	Jumping 28 inches, alone, feet together
46	2	Hopping one foot, 4 to 6 steps
45	3	Ascending large ladder, alternate feet, with caution
45	3	Walking circle, no steps off
44	4	Throwing small ball, both hands or one hand, distance 4
44	4	Catching large ball, elbows in front of body, success on 2 or 3 trials
43	1	Hopping one foot, 1 to 3 steps
43	2	Jumping 28 inches, alone, one foot ahead
43	3	Throwing large ball, both hands or one hand, distance 3
43	2	Skipping on one foot
42	4	Hopping both feet, 10 or more steps
41	4	Ascending long steps, alternate feet, unsupported
41	3	Hopping two feet, 7 to 9 steps
40	2	Hopping two feet, 4 to 6 steps
40	5	Bouncing small ball, one hand, distance 2
38	2	Descending large ladder, mark time, with facility
38	4	Ascending small ladder, alternate feet, with facility
38	3	Catching small ball, elbows in front of body, no success or success on one trial
38	1	Skipping, shuffle
38	1	Hopping both feet, 1 to 3 steps
37	2	Catching small ball, arms straight, success on 2 or 3 trials
37	3	Jumping 18 inches, alone, feet together
37	3	Walking path, no steps off
36	1	Jumping 28 inches, with help
35	3	Catching large ball, elbows in front of body, no success or success on one trial
35	2	Walking circle, 1 to 3 steps off
34	2	Catching large ball, arms straight, success on 2 or 3 trials
34	2	Descending long steps, mark time, unsupported
34	3	Jumping 12 inches, alone, feet together
34	3	Ascending small ladder, alternate feet, with caution

Table 3.4—*Continued*

Months	Score	Item
33	2	Ascending large ladder, mark time, with facility
33	3	Throwing small ball, both hands or one hand, distance 3
33	3	Jumping 8 inches, alone, feet together
31	3	Ascending long steps, alternate feet, with support
31	4	Ascending short steps, alternate feet, unsupported
31	2	Jumping 18 inches, alone, one foot ahead
31	2	Walking path, 1 to 3 steps off
30	2	Throwing large ball, both hands or one hand, distance 2
29	2	Throwing small ball, both hands or one hand, distance 2
29	3	Ascending short steps, alternate feet, with support
29	2	Ascending long steps, mark time, unsupported
28	2	Descending short steps, mark time, unsupported
28	1	Walking circle, 4 to 6 steps off
28	1	Walking path, 4 to 6 steps off
24	4	Bouncing small ball, one hand, distance 1
24	2	Ascending short steps, mark time, unsupported
24	1	Jumping 18 inches, with help
24	2	Jumping 12 inches, alone, one foot ahead
24	1	Descending large ladder, mark time, with caution

girls at all ages, but girls were superior in fine manual coordination. Generally, though, sex differences were small. While reliability coefficients were high, test intercorrelations were low. From factor analysis of the results Goodenough and Smart proposed a common factor analogous to general motor maturity. Since chronological age had been controlled within groups, individual differences in this factor were interpretable as reflecting a more rapid rate of motor development in some children than in others. Detailed examination of factor loadings suggests that general motor maturity is more related to performance in fine manual coordination, reaction time, and repetitive manual activity at early ages than at later ages. Also, specific factors begin to play an increasingly greater role in motor activities. The second factor extracted from their data was listed as attentiveness or carefulness. As might be predicted this had a negative relationship to early locomotor speed and speed of tapping but a positive relationship to manual activity.

Rhodes (1937) used the Goodenough-Smart motor abilities material and data for comparison with 80 Negro children, two- to five-years of age. Similar racial comparisons were made with adult university students. She concluded,

As in the earlier study at least two group factors appeared to be present. Inspection of the loadings for the different tests lends support to the suggestion offered by Goodenough and Smart, that the first factor may best be called general motor maturity, while the second represents something akin to carefulness or attention.

Examination of the three tables leads to the conclusion that as far as motor abilities of the kind measured by these tests are concerned, there is little, if any, difference between Negroes and whites at any level of development. Considering the small number of cases studied, both the rate of motor development and the organization of motor abilities as brought out by a factor analysis are strikingly similar for the two races (Rhodes, 1937, p. 371).

Coordinated movements of the fingers, as required in manipulating scissors, have been studied with reference to chronological age and mental age (Karr, 1934). The weighted system of scoring resulted in a bimodal curve which was interpreted as probable evidence of a maturational factor; that is, the ability to oppose thumb and fingers in a scissors cutting motion appears when the hand has developed sufficiently. Among the tentative conclusions were the following: chronological age determines to a degree the ability to cut on the line; more intelligent children cut more accurately than less intelligent children of the same age; speed of cutting does not increase with age; consistency of use of the right hand increases with age; children who achieve highest on a test of finger coordination make higher cutting scores; and finally, methods of cutting show individual and personality differences. Girls performed slightly better than boys, and children who had practice at home made higher scores.

In the area of self-help skills, the dressing process has been experimentally attacked to throw light on "dressing readiness" and particularly "buttoning readiness" by Wagoner and Armstrong (1928). Performances on the Merrill-Palmer Performance tests, the Goodenough Drawing test and the Nest of Cubes test suggested the possibility of defining criteria of buttoning readiness. Ability to manipulate buttons and buttonholes improves with age. Other studies indicate that loops may be more satisfactory than buttons on clothing. Key, White, Honzik, Heiney, and Erwin (1936) developed a scale for measuring dressing ability. They reported individual differences and sex differences in favor of girls.

The domain of motor abilities has been investigated from many points of view in terms of interrelationships with other relevant variables such as physical condition, sex, race, and sociocultural factors. The important question as to whether motor skill represents a talent, with the implication that some genetic mechanism may be involved, has been raised by Shirley (1931). Shirley evaluated the talent hypothesis in terms of some quantitative, but mostly qualitative aspects of her data. In support of the hypothesis she offered evidence demonstrating individual differences in speed of development and general motor skill. Such differences were presumed attributable to training. Further support was adduced from observed persistence in motor activities and spontaneous involvement in motor play.

Pertinent to speed of development as a variable was Ames' (1940) motion picture analysis of manipulatory and locomotor behavior of eight infants to determine the constancy of speed of movement. In creeping and stair-climbing, the time for single-limb movement as well as for total four-limb patterns did not decrease with age or over extended periods. The time for combining one object with another remained constant from one age to another. The fact that new and often complex behavior patterns which were seen for the first time did not change the form or speed of the infant's movements led Ames to postulate that internal maturation rather than experiential factors were operative in the constancy of psychomotor tempo.

Toward eveluating the notion that birth order may exert discernible influences on early development, Jones and Hsaio (1933) investigated health during pregnancies, the incidence of prenatal casualties, delivery factors, neonatal condition, birth weight, duration of breast feeding, general health during the first year of life, and early locomotor and speech development. After analysis of samples that included varying numbers of sets of siblings, they concluded the results were negative for birth order differences which could be assumed to have a direct relevance for later development. Although individual cases might reflect some association with order of birth, it was felt that ". . . these factors are not distributed so as to produce on the average a favorable or unfavorable environmental weighting of any particular birth rank" (Jones & Hsaio, 1933, p. 147).

In somewhat the same vein as Jones and Hsaio's (1933) question, Solomons and Solomons (1964) investigated the influence of a primipara's previous experience in caring for an infant on the motor performance of her baby, as well as the quality of motor performance as associated with birth order, sex, race, and birth weight of the 168 babies tested. Fifty-three of these were firstborn; 115 ranged from the second to the twelfth ordinal position. Firstborn babies were definitely more advanced than subsequently born children. In agreement with Pasamanick (1946), no real racial difference was found. No sex difference was evident at the four-month level. Prematures were definitely retarded when compared with full term infants. Though the correlation between birth weight and motor score was extremely small, a parabolic relation was plotted: the motor score increased as birth weight increased, but for the group 9 pounds, 8 ounces and above, scores were lower than for the previous weight groups, that is, all babies weighing less than 9 pounds, 8 ounces. Abnormal and clinically suspicious babies had lower motor scores than the normal group, but the birth order difference was not apparent in the more impaired groups. Solomons and Solomons recognized that their hypotheses—that firstborns are not handled to the same extent as their later-born siblings and previous baby-care experience was not a factor in infant motor performance—were not supported. They did, however, speculate that being firstborn may mean more maternal attention which influences the superior gross motor ability of the four-month-old infant.

Few empirical data exist on the relationship between body growth and the development of motor skill. Gross assessments of anatomical and physical growth status and behavior were carried out by Crowell, Yasaka, and Crowell (1964). Measures of body weight, body length, metacarpal length, and phalangeal stockiness were related to behavioral status on sensorimotor items derived from Graham's (1956) scale. The subjects were 20 female, clinically normal neonates. Crowell concluded that anatomical status had dubious value for classification relative to behavioral status at birth. The lack of interrelationship was interpreted as evidence for the existence of independent systems with differential rates of development and is consonant with earlier findings showing low, positive correlations between physical and behavioral indices.

Weech and Campbell (1941) have shown a significant inverse relationship between per cent weight gain and motor performance in sitting, creeping, and walking: the infant who is expanding rapidly in physical size develops on the average more slowly in behavior than does the infant with a slow rate of gain. In one of the few quantitative studies based on serial observations of forty children, including five sets of twins, Campbell and Weech (1941) concluded,

> The results indicate that on the basis of behavior the individual is rather poorly differentiated from the group at the time of birth. Since it is also shown that girls are in advance of boys at birth, some of the slight degree of differentiation which was demonstrated may represent the contribution of the sex factor. In terms of rate of change in development (velocity of approach to average mature behavior), the individual is differentiated from the group up to the age of 150 days. At this age a rank order of arrangement of the 40 children disclosed twins in adjacent positions in four out of five instances: in the fifth instance the twins were separated by two other children. The data did not permit conclusions beyond the age of 150 days (Campbell & Weech, 1941, pp. 233–234).

The question of the relation of infant weight and body build to locomotor development has been commented on by Shirley (1931), who suggested that motor retardation may be a function of body size. Though only a very few of her subjects were implicated, she states, ". . . that thin muscular babies and small-boned babies walk earlier than short rotund babies and exceedingly heavy babies" (Shirley, 1931, p. 126). Peatman and Higgons (1942) examined this issue by first analyzing absolute weight and chronological age at the time of beginning to sit, stand, and walk. These relationships were reflected in positive correlations which only expressed the fact that infants increased in weight as they grew older. Thus, early sitters, standers, or walkers tended to be lighter since they were younger, and conversely late sitters and walkers tended to be older and heavier. Some evidence did suggest that the heavier boys tend to sit up earlier. The possibility of a slight sex difference arising out of a difference in body build was presumed to be related to a lower center of gravity in the larger boys.

An earlier study by Peatman and Higgons (1940) revealed that general health has little to do with time of sitting, standing, and walking. It also established that infant girls are consistently more accelerated than boys in sitting and walking. This sex difference is in accord with the findings of Smith, Lecher, Dunlap, and Cureton (1930) that girls walk two weeks earlier than do boys. These same authors found no significant racial differences in age of walking. Smith *et al.* (1930)

studied seven ethnic groups in Hawaii, as well as children in Iowa, New York City, and California. She reported that children in warmer climates walk earlier than those in colder regions, a difference of almost six weeks for comparable groups. Children from lower sociocultural levels and intellectual ranges walked at older ages than those in the higher levels.

A number of investigators (Curti, Marshall, & Stegerda, 1935; Pasamanick, 1946; Williams & Scott, 1953; Scott, Ferguson, Jenkins & Cutter, 1955) report relatively better motor performance in Negro infants as compared to that seen in white infants. With a group of British West Indies Negro infants Curti *et al.* (1935) found "precocity" in time of creeping, standing, and walking in comparison with New Haven white infants. For groups of New Haven infants, Pasamanick reported that the Negro infants were essentially equal in behavioral development to the white infants. Pasamanick (1946) subsequently observed superior gross motor behavior in Negro infants through two years of age. Williams and Scott (1953) demonstrated that the significant factor in the level of performance was attributable to socialization practices rather than race itself. Infants from lower socioeconomic levels were more accelerated in motor development than were middle-class infants. Further, Scott, Ferguson, Jenkins, and Cutter (1955) found that Negro infants from the lower socioeconomic groups showed acceleration from the eighth to the thirty-fifth week of life when compared to infants from a private medical practice. After the thirty-fifth-week period, both groups were similar in rate of development. The Negro sample in general showed more rapidity in motor development than is usually reported for white infants.

After clinical examination of 107 newborn African babies, Geber and Dean (1957) indicated that these infants were at a more advanced state of development than newborn European children. The superiority was shown in "remarkable" control of the head, absence of primitive reflex activity, and lesser general flexion. Other studies have established that development for the tested group of Africans was equal to that found in European children who were two or three times their ages.

The earliest observation incorporating intelligence and sex as related to walking and talking is that by Mead (1913). In comparing 50 normal children, equally divided as to sex, and 144 "schoolable" mentally retarded children, Mead found a median for normal children of 13.5 months for walking and 15.8 for talking. The median for retarded children was 21.6 months for walking and 34.4 for talking. The data indicated that walking appeared before talking and that boys both walked and talked later than girls. Data from the California Infant Scales for Mental and Motor Development (Bayley, 1935) indicated a correlation of about +.50 between intelligence and motor development at fifteen months of age. The size of the correlation decreased with age.

The extent to which childrearing practices may enter into facilitating early development has been raised by several investigators. Davids, Holden, and Gray (1963) dichotomized 50 eight-month pregnant women into high and low anxiety groups following assessment on adequacy of adjustment. High-anxiety mothers received less favorable ratings on mother-child interactions. Low-anxiety mothers had children with significantly higher developmental quotients on the Bayley Infant Mental Scale. No significant differences were present between infants on the high and low groups on the Bayley Infant Motor Scale. Uklonskaya, Puri, Choudhur, Luthura, Dang, and Kumar (1960) recommended the adoption of Soviet methods which rely on training by the mother that is assumed to facilitate psychomotor development. The recommendation was a result of the comparison of the motor achievement of normal, full-term Indian infants from low-income groups with Russian standard norms. This comparison revealed that the Indian infants were at par up to seven months but then became progressively retarded.

GRASPING, PREHENSION, AND REACHING

Early neonatal grasping is widely accepted as one motor act customarily present at birth. Though representative of an involuntary response, it is presumed to disappear between four and six months and to be supplanted by a voluntary grasping response. Halverson (1937a, 1937b, 1937c) suggests there is not so sharp a demarcation between the two, but rather a considerable choronological overlap. He describes two phases for the measure: a closure to pressure on the palm which disappears in sixteen to twenty-four weeks, and gripping or clinging as a proprioceptive response to stimulation of the finger tendons which wanes after twenty-four weeks. The change is accompanied by a decrease in pressure upon the object and a differentiation of digital function. The ulnar digits function for reflex grasping while in skilled prehension, the index finger and thumb are primary. Closure latency is about the same for all ages, approximately .5 second. Tightening time varies inversely with age but more grasping responses are shown by older infants within short intervals of time.

According to McGraw (1935, 1939), studies on the grasping reflex are in agreement that (1) the reflex can be elicited in almost all newborns; (2) it wanes after the first few months; (3) individual differences in both strength of grasp and age of diminution are apparent; (4) the reflex attains maximum strength some few weeks after birth; and (5) following the waning phase, voluntary or deliberate grasping is seen.

Although McGraw (1935, 1939) indicated that the literature indictates on appreciable difference in grasping strength between the right and left hands, some question can be raised about her conclusions. Reports on the strength of involuntary grasping vary. Chaney and McGraw (1925) found about 43.5 per cent of their neonates spontaneously gripped a stimulating rod, and 37 per cent could be lifted completely off the table. Little difference was seen in duration of grasp between both hands. Bryan (1930) noted that few infants could support their own weight, and, likewise, Sherman, Sherman, and Flory (1937) report that only about 10 per cent of infants can lift themselves with one hand. According to Halverson (1937c) the type of grasp the infant uses depends upon the length of digits, the neuromuscular maturation of the hand, the development of tactual perception by the digits and the ability of the infant to coordinate the arm and hand in reaching with visuospatial perception of the object. Similarly, the growth of body structure, length of body, trunk, and arms as well as proportion are important in the acquisition of motor skill. The state of activity of the infant also determines the character of the grasping response, that is, strong responses occur during heightened activity and weak reactions with low, general activity. In general, the grasping reflex can be considered variable in terms of readiness of response, speed of closure, duration of grip and strength of grip (Halverson, 1937c).

McGraw (1941a) has claimed that some confusion exists with respect to the grasping phenomenon both because of experimental procedural differences and because of definition differences. She suggests that the term "grasping reflex" has been applied indiscriminately to both reflex closure of the digits around an object and to what she would label the "suspension grasp phenomenon." McGraw (1940b) reported that the curves of single-hand suspension reflected individual differences in suspension time and in the age at which extinction of the response appeared. From these curves it is evident that suspension time is relatively low at birth, increases during the second month, then starts to decline, and eventually becomes extinct at the end of the fourth month. This ability to suspend the weight reappears near the end of the first or the beginning of the second year.

The most definitive work dealing with the sequence of prehensory development—the transformation of reaching patterns, the integration of arms and trend in reaching, the speed of movement and the patterning of errors in reaching from sixteen to fifty-two weeks of age—has been carried out by Halverson (1937a, 1937b, 1937c). Halverson's findings have been supplemented and extended to earlier ages by the study of White, Castle, and Held (1964) on the visually directed prehension of 34 infants during the first six months of life. Although basically normative in design, this study tested hypotheses on the role of experience in the growth and maintenance of sensorimotor coordination. It is evident that the authors' interest bore on the interaction viewpont of Piaget as well as the progressive neuromuscular maturation views of Halverson and Gesell. From a program of observation and testing designed to elicit visuomotor and prehension responses, White *et al.* describe the following normative sequence:

> In summary, then, given the proper object in the proper location and provided that the state of the subject is suitable, our subjects first exhibited object-oriented arm movements at about 2 months of age. The swiping behavior of this stage, though accurate, is not accompanied by attempts at grasping the object; the hand remains fisted throughout the response. From 3 to 4 months of age unilateral arm approaches decrease in favor of bilateral patterns, with hands to the midline and clasped the most common response. Unilateral responses reappear at about 4 months, but the hand is no longer fisted and is not typically brought directly to the object.

Rather, the open hand is raised to the vicinity of the object and then brought closer to it as the infant shifts his glance repeatedly from hand to object until the object is crudely grasped. Finally, just prior to 5 months of age, infants begin to reach for and successfully grasp the test object in one quick, direct motion of the hand from out of the visual field (White, Castle, & Held, 1964, p. 358).

Inherent in their analysis is an awareness of the distinct roles of visual-motor and tactual-motor behaviors which gradually become coordinated into visually directed reaching activity.

Progressive continuation and precision in reaching is implied by Halverson's (1931) film analyses based on the results of 12 or more infants at 16, 20, 24, 28, 32, 36, 40, and 52 weeks of age. Halverson detected three distinct recognizable forms of approach. Approach was defined to mean movement toward a cube while maintaining regard for it. The first or "sweeping" approach was usually seen under twenty-eight weeks of age. Here the hand swept inward or outward or both but did not necessarily approach the cube. The "circuitous" approach appeared between twenty-eight and thirty-six weeks of age. In these instances the hand moved outward laterally during the first part of the movement, then inward during the latter part, forming an arc. These two types of reaching were superseded by the "straight" approach or adult form of reaching. Lateral views of reaching disclosed *sliding,* whereby the infant slides the hand along the table top, *looping,* the hand rising high and moving forward or descending from the side sharply in the form of an arc, and *planing,* the pronated hand planing out toward the object on a broad low arc. The slide and loop usually occur in conjunction with the sweeping and circuitous forms of approach, and planing with the direct approach.

In a similarly detailed fashion Halverson (1933) has delineated the relative involvement of the parts of the body in reaching. During the initial forty weeks of life the shoulder appears to be relatively more important and effective in reaching than the trunk, elbow, wrist, or fingers. The elbow and fingers increase in participation, and by 40 weeks approximate the shoulder in usefulness in reaching. From thirty-two weeks on the trunk and wrist become more involved. From forty to sixty weeks all parts of the body contribute to the success of reaching activities. The majority of approaches before twenty-eight weeks occur with the forearm and hand in a straight line. The wrist, however, soon begins to assume an ulnar flexion so that a straight line through the elbow and wrist passes between the forefinger and thumb instead of through the middle finger. This observed change is concurrent with the development of thumb opposition appearing from thirty-two to fifty-two weeks of age (Gesell & Halverson, 1936).

ORAL RESPONSES

The newborn's lip and mouth movements are quite varied, ranging from opening and closing of the mouth to grimacing, licking, smacking, and pursing of the lips (Dennis, 1934). Those oral responses which are directly linked with feeding can be divided into four components, following Prechtl's (1958) outline: (1) side-to-side head movements or single-directed head movements to bring the mouth into contact with the breast; (2) opening of the mouth and grasping with the lips after tactile stimulation in these areas; (3) sucking movement with tactile stimulation in the mouth areas, and finally; (4) swallowing movements. Those dealing with orientation toward the breast or nipple, components 1 and 2 from above, have been also described under the terms *reactions des points cardinaux* (André-Thomas, Chesni, & Saint Anne-Dargassies, 1960), the search reflex (Pratt, 1930), or rooting reflex (Gentry & Aldrich, 1948). The most precise and objective description of the orientation movements or the so-called "search behavior" of the baby is contained in the analysis of Prechtl (1958). This study of both prematures and full term infants was designed to take into account state factors as well as stage of development. The background of the study reflects some theoretical concern for ethological concepts and thinking. Prechtl maintains that there are two distinct types of activity involved in the first feeding component—described one as a rhythmic, nondirected rooting activity—as opposed to the second, which is a directed searching for the breast. In rhythmic rooting, the head is turned to and fro, side-to-side, after the oral region has been touched and may appear in hungry infants without external stimulation. After two to three weeks these are replaced by a directed turning of the head toward the stimulus, i.e., a directed rooting reflex. Repeated turning of the head without stimulation has been observed in premature infants at twenty-eight weeks of gestation; it may persist until infants reach an age of approximately three months and a weight of about 3,000 grams.

Directed head turning is toward a stimulus. Repeated stimulation at short intervals produces "central adaptation." If stimulation is continued after the onset of central adaptation, the head may turn away from the stimulus, "central reset." As far as ethological theory goes Prechtl (1958) regards the automatic stereotyped motor pattern, the rhythmical side-to-side movement, as an *Erbkoordination*—an instinctive act which is also a "vacuum activity," that is, capable of occurring without external cause. Although learning was not invoked, he indicated that directed head turning is a nonstereotyped, environmentally controlled motor pattern that reflects a physiologically unique mechanism. He further proposes that directed head turning is a taxis or stimulus-directed behavior in the ethological sense.

Contrary to the conclusions of Prechtl (1958), an analysis by Turkewitz, Gordon, and Birch (1965) failed to find evidence for a stereotyped pattern of spontaneous head movements. Head-turning movements were restricted to the area to the right of the infant's midline in 85 per cent of the subjects, and variability in amplitude, frequency, and sequence was the most characteristic feature. Turkewitz *et al.* argue that because ". . . it is possible to account for the observed phenomena on the basis of the single-factor stimulus-determination hypothesis, it seems unnecessary to advance the additional (and largely untestable) hypothesis of patterned behavior that is solely dependent for its character upon features of central nervous system organization" (Turkewitz, Gorden, & Birch, 1965, p. 157).

Blauvelt (1960, 1962, 1964) has approached the feeding situation as a process which requires coordination of the mother's actions with the baby's reflex responses. Thus, the human neonate is described as having a capacity to "release maternal responses." Using observations and film analyses of the rooting reflex, Blauvelt demonstrated (1960) that the repetitive response pattern of the neonate to periodic stimulation matches the pattern of the stimulation. Subsequent data (Blauvelt, 1962) showed a sequential relationship among responses; later reactions were dependent upon the earlier occurring ones. These results were interpreted as indicating ". . . that the head orienting response of neonates can occur predictably to the complex stimulus of a human touch . . . that infants may learn to differentiate between stimulation as given by different individuals . . . [and] that infants learn to respond with readiness for feeding only when held as their parents hold them" (Blauvelt, 1962, p. 27). From further investigation, Blauvelt (1964) concluded that optimum stimulation for feeding is not the same for all babies. Without knowledge of an infant's action during a preceding sequence, the adult trying to feed an unresponsive baby cannot know whether the baby is unstimulated and requires much stimulation or whether the infant should have no stimulation.

Infant sucking behavior has been intensively investigated as a phenomenon *per se,* and, in the wake of psychoanalytic formulations, as a precursor of adult personality. Ordinarily the same stimuli which instigate the rooting reflex also evoke rhythmic sucking movements. Areas of sensitivity which will stimulate this search and sucking behavior have been generally defined as, first, the lips; then, the area above the lips; next, the area below the lips; and lastly, the cheeks. Head movements usually accompany the stimulation. The direction of the head movement is generally toward the area of stimulus application. That is, if contact is above the lips, then the head is thrown back as the mouth opens. Although practically any kind of stimulation will release searching and sucking behavior in the neonate, with increasing age the areas of stimulation start to diminish, and stimulation becomes effective only in the immediate region of the mouth.

Prechtl (1958) maintains that a strict correlation exists between the place of stimulation and the kind and form of head turning. In babies demonstrating the side-to-side pattern the response is elicited by stimulation around the mouth and lips. Directed head turning is a result of tactile stimulation to the area of the corners of the mouth. Stimulation of the cheeks up to and beyond 15 mm from the corners of the mouth is rarely effective. Premature infants and most newborn infants are observed to suck with their lips tightly closed around the nipple, so that each sucking movement causes a negative pressure in the oral cavity. After some weeks the sucking pattern changes so that the corners of the mouth are now open with the tongue taking over the whole sucking function and emptying the nipple by licking or stroking or other movements. These two sucking patterns are categorized as lip-sucking and pump-sucking patterns. They do not appear to be much different from the patterns of sucking and mouthing also described by Colley and Creamer (1958).

Attempts to record sucking activity objectively have been accomplished in a number of different ways. Jensen (1932) monitored sucking during bottle feeding by measuring pressure changes within the air space of the inverted nursing bottle. Halverson (1938, 1944, 1946) recorded the sucking pressure directly from the mouth while the infant was feeding from the nursing bottle. Colley and Creamer (1958) recorded mouth and nipple pressures during bottle feeding. These authors suggested that infants use two methods for obtaining nutrients via the nipple: (1) by developing negative pressure within the oral cavity, that is, by sucking; and (2) by squeezing out the nipple through compression between the jaw and other parts of the mouth, that is, mouthing or expression (Ardran, Kemp, & Lind, 1958). From these facts, Kron, Stein, and Goddard (1963) were able to design an apparatus which isolated sucking from mouthing to measure sucking behavior. Similarly, Sameroff (1965) has described an apparatus capable of simultaneously recording both the suction and expression components of the human newborn sucking response.

Jensen (1932), in comparing sucking reactions to experimental stimuli, noted that general activity was inhibited with sucking and that nonspecific stimulation other than oral would initiate sucking, e.g., pin pricks on the toes or sudden withdrawal of support were capable of setting off sucking movements. With a measuring system somewhat similar to Jensen's (1932), Halverson (1938) found a median value of 72 to 74 sucking movements per minute in healthy infants from birth to the age of eighteen weeks. Although there were interindividual differences, intraindividual rates were fairly stable, changing little during the course of development. Likewise, Balint (1948a, 1948b) reported that infants suck with approximately the same frequency. He observed a basic frequency of 48 to 80 sucks per minute. In terms of suction, Kron *et al.* (1963) detected rate changes in sucking between the second and third days of life which they attributed to age and not to learning.

The bulk of the work on sucking behavior has related to nonnutritive sucking activity. By means of a rubber nipple and a microswitch in combination with a polygraph, Kaye and Levin (1963) examined the effects of a 500 cps tone of moderate intensity on sucking rates. Tonal suppression of nonnutritive sucking could not be demonstrated in either a time-contingent or response-contingent series. Levin and Kaye (1964) found that individual sucking rates were highly consistent and correlated with wakefulness and stage of the feeding cycle. The methodological implications from their data indicated that one-minute samples of nonnutritive sucking rate were highly reliable, that repeated trials with rest periods showed little decrement in response level, and that rate of sucking could be predicted in gross terms by simply watching. They concluded, as did Bridger (1962), that neonates suck when they are awake or aroused, regardless of degree of hunger. Sucking rates have also been shown to vary with parameters of the oral stimulus (Lipsitt & Kaye, 1965).

The effects of type of infant feeding on oral behavior and on general motor development have some interest for both the researcher and parent. Breast-fed babies were reported to be more active by Davis, Sears, Miller, and Brodbeck (1948) and also by Newton and Newton (1951). Hoefer and Hardy (1929) also noted that breast-fed children tended to be more advanced in a number of measures; among these were muscle tone, age of walking and talking.

A fair number of studies have been designed to ferret out factors linked with the origin, continuation, and remission of nonnutritive sucking. Incidence figures on amount of nonnutritive sucking suggest that it occurs often and that the rates are high (Levy, 1928; Kunst, 1948; Yarrow, 1954; Brazelton, 1956; Traisman & Traisman, 1958; Honzik & McKee, 1962). Generally, the figures range from 25 to 50 per cent of a sample, with close to 50 per cent as a modal figure for all samples. Depending on the studies surveyed, some evidence for sex differences can be found (Kunst, 1948; Yarrow, 1954; Honzik & McKee, 1962). With the exception of Brazelton's (1956) most studies suggest little remission of the nonnutritive sucking pattern. In fact, Traisman and Traisman (1958) and Yarrow (1954) noted continuation of the act as late as two and four years, respectively, in a large number of children.

A large portion of the research on nonnutritive sucking behavior in children was inspired by Levy's (1928) observations and conclusion that inadequate oral drive satisfaction was associated with thumb and finger sucking. Basically the behavior was presumed to stem from changes connected with feeding. In support of Levy's thesis was evidence from Roberts (1944) and Levine and Bell (1950) who reported that amount of sucking and length of feeding were related to thumb-sucking. Klackenberg (1949) and Levine and Bell (1950) also observed that use of the pacifier was accompanied by less thumb-sucking.

Evidence contradictory to the position advanced by Levy (1928) has been shown by several investigators. Davis, Sears, Miller, and Brodbeck (1948) and Sears and Wise (1950) demonstrated that oral behavior is strengthened by continued nutritive sucking and that the strength of this drive influences both the reaction to weaning and the development of thumb-sucking. To some extent Bernstein (1955) and Traisman and Traisman (1958) supported this conclusion. In summary, this opposing viewpoint suggested that the strength of the oral drive rather than oral frustration was the precursor of thumb-sucking. As a reconciliation of these ideas, Yarrow (1954) has formulated a "phase-specific" hypothesis. According to this the oral drive is a function of the age of the child, so that, in early infancy fast feeding is tied with frustration, fixation, and nonnutritive patterns, but late weaning likewise produces fixation and nonnutritive sucking.

HAND-MOUTH BEHAVIOR

A number of responses linking the hand and mouth areas have been described and appear for the most part in the foreign literature. One of these, the hand-mouth reflex of Babkin (1958), has been fairly extensively examined by Parmelee (1963b) for maturational patterning. The Babkin reflex, which is elicited by pressure on the palms of the infant and consists of opening of the mouth, flexion of the forearm, flexion of the head and closing of the eyes, is obtained easily in small prematures, but appears to be state-dependent in larger infants. Smaller infants show some response on stimulation but larger infants respond only if somewhat aroused. Kaye (1965) suggests that the response may have usefulness as a test for differential conditionability of newborns.

Another response in the hand-mouth category is the palmomental reflex. This consists of a contraction of the mentalis muscle when the thenar eminence of the hand on that side is stimulated. Parmelee (1963b) has shown that the reflex is present in prematures, is not strongly dependent on arousal level, and is strongly correlated with presence of the Babkin reflex. Though the palmomental response may be "primitive," it has been generally found in full term newborns, gradually waning with age.

LATERALITY

Even though the body is bilaterally symmetrical, some degree of asymmetry can be seen in facial features and in eye and leg patterns of movement. Gesell's (1946) statement of the principle of functional asymmetry suggested the early appearance of a one-sided or lateral development in motor functioning. Whether this asymmetrical state always characterizes human embryonic and fetal development or represents a shift from perfect symmetry at some time during the prenatal period is still an open question. A considerable body of literature covers the development of laterality in eye patterns, chewing, smiling, prehension, and locomotion. Hand dominance, however, has been the focus of most investigations on laterality development. As summarized in Hildreth's comprehensive review (1949a, 1949b) developmental trends in handedness indicate a shift from bilaterality in earliest infancy to consistently unilateral preference around seven to nine months of age. Hand preference stabilizes around three years of age. Right-handedness appears earlier than left-handedness and becomes increasingly dominant from ages two to five.

The problem of establishing definitive criteria of handedness, that is, what is to be observed and measured, has led to the selection of motility indicators—strength of grasp and reaching—as evidence of usage. Within the neonatal period Watson's (1919) efforts seem among the first which attempted to get an experimental estimate of early hand dominance. Using twenty infants he recorded the length of time the subject could suspend himself by grasping a rod in daily five-minute trials over the first ten days following birth. No differences in hand preference were noted. Similarly, no trend in hand preference was observed for another group of 20 infants who ranged from 120 to 160 days in age. Chaney and McGraw (1932) concurred with these latter findings. Contrary to both these results is evidence for relatively greater strength in the left hand (Sherman, Sherman, & Flory, 1936; Halverson, 1937).

Using a tridimensional movement recorder Valentine and Wagner (1934) reported significantly greater right arm motility in 100 newborns. There were no sex differences. A follow-up of 31 of the original group showed that relative arm motility at birth was not associated with later hand preference. These data did not show any greater relationship between weight, strength of grip at birth, or family handedness with hand preference than was seen with relative arm motility. After observing greater right-arm and -leg movement in four infants throughout a ten-day interval following birth, Stubbs and Irwin (1933) concluded that there may be a significant difference in laterality development of the extremities. The relatively greater preponderance of right-arm movement observed by them also appeared in Valentine and Wagner's (1934) records. The latter investigators stated that this behavior was independent of sex and only slightly dependent upon race.

Giesecke (1936) seems to be the only investigator who has adopted motility as a hand-preference criterion and who also reported pronounced handed preferences over the first six months of life. From a study based on spontaneous activity of both hands she concluded that greater hand differentiation occurs throughout infancy. Though frequency of right-handed usage was always greater for her Ss, this dominance became more pronounced during the latter half of the first year. There were also frequent changes in dominance noted during this period. Most other researchers (Lippman, 1927; Halverson, 1931; Shirley, 1931), basing hand usage on reaching activity, have found no pronounced hand preference during the first six-month age period. For the second half year Lippman (1927), Halverson (1931), and Giesecke (1936) have reported dominance of the right hand in their subjects. In what was essentially an experimental situation, involving acceptance of objects by infants, Lippman (1927) observed a shift from equal use of both hands at four-and-one-half months to a 70 per cent right-handed preference at age twelve months. Likewise, Halverson (1931) found alternating hand preference in touching cubes up to thirty-six weeks; this then shifted and dominance remained with the right hand from forty weeks on.

Lederer (1939) contributed data which filled the gap of development during the second year. She found that infants six to eleven months of age were evenly distributed in terms of right- and left-handed tendencies. A larger segment of right-handed cases appeared in the twelve- to twenty-month-old age group. From these facts it was concluded that the establishment of right-handedness took place between twelve and twenty-four months. Noting that changes from left-handed preference occurred more often than changes from the right hand, Lederer (1939) inferred that environmental factors were responsible for such shifts. Postural development, nonnutritive sucking behavior, and social influences, such as waving good-bye with the right hand under direct tuition, were instances of such modifying factors.

Studies with nursery school children support the trend of increased right-hand usage in activities. In children eighteen to twenty-four months of age Gesell (1940) noted that right hand activity in picking up and scribbling increased from 68 per cent at eighteen months to 92 per cent at twenty-four months. Later handedness could not be predicted at this time. Handedness and footedness were more closely related than handedness and eyedness. Among Heinlein's (1930) group of 24 children ranging in age from twenty-four to sixty months two thirds were right-handed and one third were ambidextrous or left-handed. From data on 60 children ranging from eighteen to thirty-eight and one-half months in age, Jones (1931) computed work ratios for the two hands. Using the regression of dextrality on age he estimated a work ratio of .56 at birth and .59 at six months. He observed .66, .70, .75, and .80 ratios at 24, 36, 48, and 54 months, respectively. Dextrality ratios were not only higher, but also the rate of increase was greater for girls. Bimanuality increased with age, that is, older children more often tended to use two hands together. Updegraff's (1932) data from 40 children, ages two to six years, showed that over a two-day period children were more consistent in hand usage with activities that had been practiced previously or had been practiced over a long period of time.

These data on nursery school children were confirmed and also supplemented by Hildreth (1949a) who computed handedness indices to evaluate unimanual skills and choices in a group of 44 nursery school children, ages two to five years. Although the differences between indices were not subjected to statistical tests, the trend toward right-handedness appeared to increase from the two-year level to the three-year level. Left-handedness seemed to increase in the four-year-old group; the per cent of the left-handed cases was comparable to those seen by Updegraff (1932). For the age two and age three groups scores indicative of right-hand dominance were highest for eating with a spoon and fork, followed by ball throwing, then for using a shovel and crayons. Scores indicative of left-handedness or ambilaterality were obtained for eating with fingers, random activity in other spontaneous acts and drinking from a glass or cup. Hildreth (1949a) concluded that these laterality activities reflected the effects of training.

Any consistent relationship between eyedness and handedness is difficult to determine, particularly during infancy. Updegraff (1933) has presented some data on 74 children, two to six years of age which suggest that a right-eyed child is more likely to be right-handed than is a left-eyed child to be left-handed. The results of this study are in line with the earlier findings of Gordon (1931) and Eames (1957).

CRYING

Although infant crying is frequently mentioned as a behavioral response concomitant with some other variable of research interest, crying has not been the main focus of study in many investigations. There seems to be agreement that the birth cry is a reflexive response to the onset of breathing and that crying *per se* has some undefined relation to a state of distress. Outside these facts, speculation as to why babies cry has varied widely. There seems to be no agreed-upon period for the beginning of crying with tears though Taylor-Jones (1927) reported tears in newborns. Motor correlates of crying have been described by Ames (1941). As such, crying was characterized by intense limb activity which was more predominant in the legs, more unilateral than bilateral, and involved more flexor than extensor movements. Distinguishing patterns of crying activity have been associated with colic and brain-damaged infants. In the case of colic, attacks

> . . . begin suddenly with an agonizing, loud and more-or-less continuous cry, accompanied by a somewhat cyanotic appearance of the face. The abdomen is distended with legs flexed on the chest. Fists are clenched. The paroxysms end abruptly after minutes or hours, sometimes only to begin again. Food may be refused or taken eagerly, temporarily relieving the symptoms, but they may return with even greater intensity. Passage of flatus or feces may or may not give relief. In some cases the crying attacks are periodic and may occur at the same time daily, while in others no such periodicity is apparent. Commonly, some of the symptoms listed above are omitted (Lakin, 1957).

In comparing the normal child's cry with that of the brain-damaged, Karelitz, Karelitz, and Rosenfeld (1960) noted:

> A. There is a striking difference in the latent period from the time of stimulus to crying. The cry of the normal child is an immediate response to the pain stimulus and is sustained and vigorous; the abnormal requires repeated, almost constant stimulation to elicit the crying, and the cry is sporadic.
> B. The quality of the normal infant's cry changes progressively with age. The voice becomes larger, the cry more sustained, the pitch more varied, and the inflections suggest more meaningful purpose. A plaintive quality develops . . . in the first six months. . . . In the abnormals, the voice quality was recognizably different: in some guttural, in some piercing and shrieklike, in some very high pitched, weak and thin, but in all for a long time lacking the growing variety of sounds of the normal child's cry.
> C. The pre-speech sounds are delayed in the brain-defective child. In the normal child, as the sounds that precede speech develop, they are heard in the crying; in the abnormal, these sounds are not heard until later, and in some not at all (Karelitz *et al.*, 1960, p. 443).

Infants with diffuse brain damage required more stimulation to produce a standard one-minute crying response than did normal infants (Karelitz & Fisichelli, 1962; Fisichelli & Karelitz, 1963).

The most intensive study of crying, particularly of newly born infants is that of Aldrich, Sung, and Knop (1945). Based on 30 days of nursery observations, the crying activity of babies was analyzed in terms of average amounts of crying for the whole month, amounts of crying for single days, amounts of crying at single instants and relationships with barometric pressure. Diurnal variations in the amounts of crying had a reciprocal relationship to variations in the amount of nursing care and attention; i.e., the more attention, the less crying. Crying appeared to be an active, individual reaction to many undefined stimuli, however it was neither initiated or increased by the cries of other nursery babies.

With improved and individualized baby care, subsequent observations (Aldrich, Norval, Knop, & Venegas, 1946) indicated that average crying for babies diminished greatly—from 55 minutes in contrast to the 113.2 minutes tabulated earlier. (Actual amount of nursing care given each baby was 1.9 hours in contrast to the earlier study figure of .7 hours.) As noted before, hunger, unknown reasons, wet diapers, soiled diapers, and vomiting, in this order, were judged to be causes of crying. Once at home, the average baby had 4.0 prolonged crying spells during its first seven weeks of life as compared with the nursery figure of 11.9 crying episodes (Aldrich, Sung, & Knop, 1945). Again, hunger led the list of causes of crying, but unknown reasons diminished greatly as judged sources of crying. Wet or soiled diapers and vomiting were minor reasons, and loud noises or glaring lights were not important as causes for crying.

Babies of mothers with high prenatal anxiety levels have been noted to cry significantly more during the first four days of life when compared to babies of low anxiety mothers (Ottinger & Simmons, 1964). Ourth and Brown (1961) hypothesized that a deficiency in stimulation—particularly mild, firm support and rhythmical body stimulation at feeding times—would result in disturbed behavior. For the slightly older children, Bayley (1932) has demonstrated that the amount of crying is not related to mental scores, socioeconomic status, birth weight, birth order, or sex. The observed periodicity in the amount of crying was presumed to be due to the fact that children cry for different reasons at different ages. The fact that some stimuli were consistently effective may indicate the possibility of innate differences or the readiness with which emotional or affective conditioning occurred in some children. In line with this is Ellesor's (1933) observation that some visual stimuli cause crying when a child has reached a certain age or when there is a contrast between the familiar and unfamiliar (novelty). Thus, not all negative responses, that is, crying to visual stimuli, were acquired by conditioning. Repeated stimulation with these cry-producing stimuli was capable of causing the negative reaction to be replaced by positive responses.

DEFENSIVE OR PROTECTIVE REFLEXES

Originally the term *réflexe de défense* or "withdrawal reflex" or "shortening reaction of the leg" (Peiper, 1963) was applied to leg flexion at the hip and knee following stimulation of the sole of the foot. The term has become more inclusive, following Watson's (1919, 1925) classification which included (1) arm and hand movements in response to pressure stimulation of the face; (2) contralateral leg flexion to stimulation of the inside of the knee; and (3) extreme activity in reaction to restraint of the arms and body. The idea that Watson may have overgeneralized seems in order when studies on these defense reactions are examined in detail. Specifically, when the infant's nose was held or pinched Watson reported that the arms were raised or even struck at the experimenter's hands in from 2 to 18 seconds. Using essentially the same technique, however, with 67 infants, Pratt, Nelson, and Sun (1930) noted the typical reaction to consist of a retraction of the head, an arching of the back, and generalized body movements. Sherman, Sherman, and Flory (1936) elicited defense movements by applying pressure to the chin for 30 seconds. Defense movements of the hands increased in effectiveness and accuracy with age. In general, motions of the right or left arm appeared before combined coordinated movements of both hands. With a different stimulus and body area, in this instance a stethoscope, over the baby's heart, Shirley (1931) reported a left arm rotary movement touching the stethoscope or examiner's hand in 26.4 per cent of 181 examinations.

The observation that stimulation of the knee regularly brought the foot up to the site of contact (Watson, 1919, 1925) has, likewise, not been substantiated in the only known attempt to check on the reliability of this report. Shirley (1931) found that in about 25 infants, over a total of 260 reactions, more than one third of the babies did not react at all to the pinching stimulus. Those who did react responded with the same leg; less than one fifth reacted with the opposite leg. The leg and foot withdrawal act has also been utilized as a measure of response threshold to electrotactual stimulation (Sherman, Sherman, & Flory, 1936; Graham, Matarazzo, & Caldwell, 1956; Lipsitt & Levy, 1959; Gullickson & Crowell, 1964). Since the interpretation of these results has been directed to the threshold as an index of sensitivity, these studies fall somewhat outside the province of this review.

Relative to the restraint reaction, again, no support has been forthcoming to confirm the universality of Watson's (1919) claim (Pratt, Nelson, & Sun, 1930; Shirley, 1931; Dennis, 1940). Dennis (1940) offered the notion that stimuli eliciting rage are not determined solely by the structure of the individual, but also by past experiences. Moreover, reaction to frustration involves the prior acquisition of the response to be thwarted; in other words, a certain kind of learning is involved in reaction to frustration.

Representative of a somewhat broader theoretical approach to defense reflexes is material on the development of a protective-defensive conditioned reflex in premature children (Polikanina, 1961). This and other studies of conditioned defensive reflexes are reviewed in the chapter in this volume on conditioning and learning.

MORO REFLEX

As was true for the plantar response, the Moro reflex has had a long history of usage in behavioral observation on babies. Ordinarily the Moro has been used for evaluation of the neurological status of the infant. Published accounts suggest that the reflex can be elicited by intense stimuli, such as pounding the table surface near the infant's head, or by lifting the head and releasing it, or by pulling the baby from a supine to a sitting position and partially releasing the arms so the head drops backward suddenly. The responding infant usually flays both arms away from the body, spreading the fingers and bringing the arms back over the body in a clasping manner like forming a bow. Extension and adduction of the legs are often seen with the extension and flexion of the arms.

From analyses of motion picture frames which were based on stimulating 57 infants from birth through nine months, McGraw (1937) has described the developmental sequence of Moro reflex patterns. The *newborn phase* is characterized by extension and bowing of the arms, extension of the spine, extension and fanning of the digits in the form of a *C*, and extension of the legs followed by intense crying. These gross actions diminish during the second and third months, and the predominant features become extension and adduction of the arms and slight movement of the knees with less frequent crying. McGraw labeled this phase *transitional*. The final or *mature* phase is reflected in a body jerk with blinking and occurs in the largest percentage of babies when they are around 130 days of age.

Parmelee (1964) tried to determine in a systematic way the optimal stimulus and most adequate method for evaluating the Moro response pattern. From a series of three studies he concluded that allowing the baby's head to drop back suddenly, slapping the surface near the head, or the sudden jarring of a board to which the infant was strapped were equally effective stimuli for eliciting the reflex. Neck movement with accompanying proprioceptive stimulation was, however, necessary to produce an adequate Moro response. Relative to the response pattern, the bilateral spreading of the arms was present throughout the 12-week testing period, but the inward bowlike movement was absent at twelve weeks of age. No correlation was present between degree of Moro response and the state of arousal at the time of stimulation. In light of the obtained low interscorer reliability, Parmelee (1964) emphasized the need for precise observation and recording of the reflex, as with a camera. This suggests that intensity, latency, and duration of response may be the significant parameters to be quantified in any evaluation.

Some controversy has been generated over whether the Moro and startle reflexes are separate responses to stimulation or are age-related reaction patterns with the startle replacing the Moro in later life. Parmelee (1964) in reviewing this issue stressed, in the definition of a Moro reflex, the "extensor response of the fingers and of the arms at the elbows with movement of the extended arms away from the body and secondary movements of the arms toward the body." Evidence presented by Peiper and Isbert (1927), Strauss (1929), Hunt, Clarke, and Hunt (1936), Hunt and Landis (1936), Wagner (1938), Clarke (1939), and Wieser and Domanowsky (1957) justifies defining two independent responses: a startle reflex which may have a shorter latency but persists into maturity, and a Moro reflex of longer latency which is more dominant in early life, but wanes soon after birth. Contrary to the contentions of many others Dennis (1935) has contended that disappearance of the Moro in older children reflects conditioning and inhibition of the reflex.

It may generally be concluded that, first, the Moro is of diagnostic significance with an absent or asymmetric response considered abnormal (Gordon, 1929; Sanford, 1933); second, the persistence of a response beyond the age of four months may be considered indicative of retarded maturation (Gordon, 1929; McGraw, 1937); third, variations in the Moro may be of value in detecting milder disorders (Prechtl & Dijkstra, 1960); and fourth, the return of a good Moro during the newborn period is a positive sign.

POSTURAL ADJUSTMENT TO INVERTED POSITIONS

Developmental changes in adjustment to an inverted position, or suspension upside down by the knees or feet, have been described by Irwin (1936) and McGraw (1940). For both of these investigators the behavioral changes are developmentally significant and related to changes in the nervous system. After observing 77 children weekly over five years McGraw, in typical fashion, outlined four phases. The newborn phase was characterized by flexion and was most evident during the first thirty days of life. This phase was assumed to be controlled at the subcortical level and could extend over the first four months. A period of hyperextension (arching) of the vertebral column was most common between four to six months and presumably still reflected subcortical control. From eight to eighteen months the righting phase, or attempt to regain the upright posture, became predominant and suggested cortical participation in the adjustment. The relaxed or mature phase appeared as early as the end of the first year, but characteristically not until the second half of the third year. In the mature phase there was no marked flexion or extension but the head hung down in the same plane as the shoulder and pelvic girdles with arms extended toward the floor. Crying was more often associated with the newborn and righting phases.

FOOT AND TOE RESPONSES

The tremendous popularity of research on the foot and toes is undoubtedly due to Babinski's (1896) description of the extension of the great toe and fanning of the other toes with stimulation to the sole or plantar surface of the foot. This plantar pattern was assumed to be indicative of some pathology if seen in adults. In light of this observation there developed a spate of research to determine whether a similar sign, not of dysfunction but of immaturity of the corresponding neural pathways, existed in infants. Regardless of the voluminous literature on this topic, which as Richards and Irwin (1934b) state ". . . may possibly be due to a seeming necessity for the student of infant reactions at some time in his career to do an experiment on infantile plantar phenomena" (p. 9), this review questions whether the topic meets the criterion of having "a demonstrably important role in the total functioning of the organism." As long ago as 1933 Pratt questioned the significance of the plantar response in the life economy of the child. Nevertheless, primarily for historical reasons and the remote possibility that some principles of significance may be deduced from the material, a summary of research on the plantar reflex is presented.

The classic report on plantar responses of infants and young children is that of Richards and Irwin (1934b). From their general overview of published literature they concluded

> Studies of the development and maintenance of the plantar response in humans show generally that the earliest responses noted are at about two months of the gestation period. Here, if called out, they are inconsistent but perhaps predominantly extensor in character. By the time the infant is born, however, the response is of a clear flexor character. This response seems to change to one of extension of a variable character, the "infantile extension" pattern. Some time during the first three years this pattern gives way to the gradual development of a flexion type of response, which, perhaps concomitant with a general "integrative" process in the organism, is of a fairly clearcut character in the adult years. The flexor (or better "nonextensor") pattern predominates until senility sets in, at which time the flexion gives way once more to variability and inconsistency and perhaps to a greater amount of extension (Richards & Irwin, 1934b, pp. 37–38).

Turning to the early age span, in infants from birth to ten days, Pratt, Nelson, and Sun (1930) observed under all conditions more extension of the contralateral great toe with stimulation of the right foot. The left foot, however, showed significantly more extension. It was noted that plantar stimulation produced the greatest response in the toes, less in the feet, and least in the legs. The more specific reflexive reaction, such as isolated responses of the toes, were less frequent than were complex and generalized reactions involving leg, foot, and toes. Chaney and McGraw (1932) found that toe responses decreased with 'movement of the point of stimulation from the sole to the dorsum to the more proximad regions, respectively. More toe flexion responses during sleep and more toe extension during waking periods appeared as common findings in the investigations of Pratt *et al.* (1930), Waggoner and Ferguson (1930), Pratt (1934b, 1934c, 1934d), and Richards and Irwin (1934b). Twice as much toe extension as flexion activity was produced by stimulation in the posterior quadrants of the foot by Waggoner and Ferguson (1930), who also observed that 80 grams pressure elicited more toe extension from infants than 250 grams.

From their study of 264 infants, whose ages ranged from a few hours to sixty-six months, Richards and Irwin (1934b) concluded that plantar response patterns do not appear to be related to race, fatigue, type of delivery, type of anesthesia used at birth, prematurity of birth, weight or length, type of feeding in infancy, cephalic index, ability to stand and walk, bending of the knee, or being distracted by adults.

In addition, there was no evidence of a demonstrable correlation between sex (Feldman, 1922; Richards & Irwin, 1934b) and plantar response. Clarke, Hunt, and Hunt (1937) did find that plantar responses were elicited by a startle stimulus.

In general, research on the plantar response has followed two trends. The first has examined the development of the plantar response as an expression of neural maturation (McGraw, 1941). From a study of 75 children ranging in age from birth to five years, McGraw (1941) classified reactions into three developmental phases: The mass reaction or movement of the leg was typical of the first four months; the transitional phase involved fewer segments and was present about the end of the first year; and the segmental reflex was common after the age of two-and-one-half years.

The second investigative trend has focused on toe reflexes and plantar grasp reflexes. Gentry and Aldrich (1948) examined the relationship between the development of voluntary control and the disappearance of three reflexes: the toe grasp reflex, pressure foot reflex, and plantar reflex. The loss of the toe grasp reflex and the pressure foot reflex were more closely related to the acquisition of voluntary control of the feet and legs than to age. The negative findings for the Babinski or plantar-flexor reflex are in line with earlier reports (Richards & Irwin, 1934b). Dietrich (1957) concurred with the above results in noting that the plantar grasp reflex disappeared between six and twelve months of age and was related to the age of standing. His other conclusions, as based on periodic observations of the same 103 normal infants from birth through two years, essentially reconfirmed that (1) the spontaneously appearing Babinski, seen primarily in the neonate period, was not a symptom of pathology; (2) the Babinski is frequently and irregularly present during the first six months and thereafter relatively uncommon; and (3) lack of myelination is not a valid explanation for presence of the Babinski in the young infant. With a somewhat different objective Pacella and Barrera (1940) examined the relationship between the tonic neck reflexes and all grasping movements, primarily the grasp reflexes of the hand and foot. Although the authors concluded that some degree of concurrence exists between the two variables, their data leaves this point open to question.

BOWEL AND BLADDER CONTROL

Elimination control constitutes an important type of socialization training during infancy. This training, which required substituting a set of socially approved behaviors and restrictions in place of uncontrolled voiding and evacuation, is presumed to be basically a learning process. Notwithstanding this, the mere fact that neuromuscular structures underlie the behavior has heightened interest in the extent to which achievement of control is related to training (McGraw, 1940a). The review of Caldwell (1964) in this area indicated that research on elimination training has been concerned with (1) the relationship between training practices and reaction to training; (2) the relationship between training and clinical syndromes; (3) the association between training patterns and normal personality development, and (4) the extent to which "anal" traits are a function of toilet training.

A natural distinction exists between bladder and bowel functioning and probably should be maintained in research on these subjects. However, both acts seem to have been grouped together in past research. Reliable evidence indicates that bowel training occurs first. Davis and Havighurst (1946) determined that in a group of 567 children 40 per cent had training initiated at six months, and in 28 per cent bowel training was completed by twelve months. For a group of two-and-one-half-year-old children, Roberts and Schoellkopf (1951) reported that about 88 per cent had bowel control. A significantly larger proportion of boys than girls lacked control. Sears, Maccoby, and Levin (1957) found from maternal interview data that seven months was the average age for initiation of bowel training and eleven months the average time for completion of training.

Examining norms for bladder control, Davis and Havighurst (1946) found this training started by six months in 14 per cent of their sample and was completed by eighteen months in 49 per cent. Although about 40 per cent of their sample had daytime accidents or lack of urinary sphincter control, approximately 90 per cent of the girls and 79 per cent of the boys could signal and successfully manage their urinary needs.

A number of factors have been implicated and considered significant in understanding the development of elimination control. Hull and Hull (1919) presented for one subject probably the first analyses of the attainment of voluntary bladder control and its relationship to vocabulary development. Their data have been interpreted as evidence that learning to talk represented an interference phenomenon in elimination training. (The relationship of elimination control to language acquisition is discussed in Chapter 4.)

Attempting to determine the basic behavioral changes that accompany voluntary control of micturition, McGraw (1940a) studied two sets of identical twin boys. One infant from each set of twins, beginning at thirty days of age, was placed on a chamber seven times a day at hourly intervals. The corresponding twins were exposed to the same toilet training schedule at later ages. For both cases, trained and control achievement levels were the same. These data suggested that the optimum time for initiating training was not before the onset of the period of cortical participation. Lending support to the dominance of cortical and subcortical factors in micturition control are the observations of Illingsworth (1961), Knobloch and Pasamanick (1962), and Drillien (1965). Differences in the rate of maturation of the nervous system and probably myelination with related enzymatic processes (Illingsworth, 1961) are said to be reflected in delayed sphincter control. Drillien (1965) observed that smaller prematures (birthweights less than 4½ pounds) and twins showed later toilet control. Knobloch and Pasamanick's (1962) study of about 300 infants revealed that the more normal the neurologic diagnosis and status at forty weeks of age, the better the toilet control at three years of age.

DEVELOPMENTAL TESTING

From the early researches directed toward determining the behavioral functioning of the newborn (Watson & Watson, 1921; Jones, 1926; Bryan, 1930; Furfey, Bonham, & Sargent, 1930; Chaney & McGraw, 1932; Sherman, Sherman, & Flory, 1936) two basic generalizations seem in order: first, the human newborn is capable of a vast array of responses which are essentially representative of reflex activity and can be conveniently described in terms of the part of the body involved, and second, little was done to determine which, if any, of these reflexes were especially predictive of current or future behavior. For a long period Dennis' (1934) description and classification of responses of the newborn represented the best summary of responses of normal children over the first ten days. More contemporary references are listed and defined by Peiper (1963) whose book is probably the most comprehensive source available.

These earlier studies gave little consideration to factors to be controlled to facilitate comparisons between studies. Bell (1963) suggests these factors probably should have included (a) the level of arousal or state of the infant; (b) effects of being firstborn; (c) complications of pregnancy and delivery; (d) effects of analgesics and anesthetics; (e) effects of bottle-feeding versus breast-feeding and interaction effects with (d); and (f) age differences and their interaction with (c) and (d).

Based on an examination of 100 newborns, Yang's study (1962) has shown that a third-day evaluation is best for obtaining maximum performance and information.

Similarly, Prechtl (1964) recommends that examinations and experiments which will be affected by state fluctuations should not be carried out during the first three or four days, and for his laboratory such procedures are delayed until six to eight days. To establish what was normal or common among newborns and at the same time evaluate the prognostic value of neurological signs, Prechtl and Dijkstra (1960) compared 50 neonates without any history of complications with 218 neonates born with histories of complications. All babies were considered full term. Results from this examination revealed significantly different proportions of normal and pathological cases in boys and girls; boys were more vulnerable to damage. Birth weights below 3000 grams showed more complications. From the neurological examination indicators, fetal distress and prolonged labor cases had the worse prognoses. Singletons with histories of both prenatal and perinatal complications had poorer prognoses than their counterparts. The neurological abnormalities in the group with complications were classified as (1) Lateralization of tonus and intensity of responses, e.g., an asymmetrical Moro response. (2) Abnormalities of tonus and motility. (3) A syndrome of hyperexcitability characterized by hyperactivity, a very low threshold for the Moro reflex and, most importantly, a tremor of low frequency (4–6/sec) and high amplitude that is superimposed on spontaneous movements as well as on elicited responses, especially the Moro reflex. This syndrome may be present for the first few months. Mothers who do not know that their baby is neurologically abnormal think he is very easily frightened. (4) Epileptic manifestations. (5) Consistent absence of at least two obligate responses.

A follow-up examination, after two to four years, of 110 children from the group with histories of complications showed 52 per cent classified as normal and 48 per cent as pathological. Neurological conditions in the newborn period were especially predictive: the lateralization and hyperexcitability syndromes had a high prognostic value.

Graham, Matarozzo, and Caldwell (1956) have attempted to set up procedures for detecting the impact of prenatal, perinatal, and postnatal complications. They established five test procedures which were administered to 265 infants without perinatal complications and to 81 traumatized infants suffering from anoxia, mechanical birth injury, and diseases or infections associated with brain damage. These procedures consisted of a pain threshold test, a maturation scale, a vision scale, an irritability rating, and a muscular tension rating. Older subjects were found to be more sensitive on the pain threshold test and to perform better on the maturation and vision scale. Negro subjects were superior on both the maturation and vision scales, but there were no race differences on the other tests. When a cutting point was established, all tests identified some traumatized subjects as abnormal; the percentage increased with the seriousness of the trauma. These behavioral tests subsequently were administered to a group of 60 "anoxic" infants made up of those with observable postnatal anoxia and to a group of 62 normal infants. The degree of impairment in test performance reflected the severity of the clinical condition as determined by pediatric evaluation and medical history (Graham, Pennoyer, Caldwell, Greenman, & Hartmann, 1957).

Rosenblith (1961), in a further modification of the Graham scale, established that the maturation scores were significantly related to the age of the neonate; scores increased with age from day one to day three. Vision scores were less related to postnatal age during the four-day period of examination. From these facts came the hypotheses that, first, performance on day two or three may more accurately reflect the maturational level achieved at the time of birth than does the day one performance, and, second, that the difference between the maturational scores from day one and three may provide a measure of the degree of stress to which the infant was subjected at birth.

There is no question but that there is a clear interrelationship between mental and motor tests during the early periods of development. If anything it is difficult to decide whether a test is tapping motor or intellectual functions. As Stott and Ball (1965) have pointed out, there is developing a conceptual change concerning the nature of intelligence which fuses the old dichotomy of motor behavior versus mental behavior.

> The infant begins to know and cope with his environment through his motor responses to stimulation. His eyes follow a patch of color. He responds to the sound of a person's approaching steps. He kicks and thrashes about with his arms in a random, disorganized manner, bringing his hands in contact with objects within his reach. He grasps, mouths, shakes, and bangs them, and thus "experiences" them with his various senses. It is quite clear, however, that, in the beginning, these simple sensorimotor experiences do not involve the awareness of the objects from which the stimulation comes. There could be no central representation of them, as such, at first. But development change is rapidly taking place. Soon, with further maturation and experience, the child learns to differentiate objects, and to respond to them as objects as he sees, grasps, and tastes them, and hears them fall to the floor. His motor behavior now involves the cognitive awareness of things and persons. His functioning with respect to them, has become meaningful. All his motor manipulations—eye-hand, fine motor, and gross motor coordinations—appear now to be centrally mediated and are directed toward some kind of adjustment to, or coping with, the environment. In that sense, therefore, they are "intellectual" in nature. In short, the motor behavior of the young child is mental behavior (Stott & Ball, 1965, p. 2).

The view expressed by Stott and Ball is certainly analogous to and has overtones of the Piaget approach; in addition, some support for it can be found in Hofstaetter's (1954) factor analysis of the California Scales. He extracted two factors for ages under four years; the first, which showed up during the first two years, was labeled *sensory-motor alertness,* and the second, *persistence,* appeared during years two to four. After age four, the group factor was called *manipulation of symbols.*

To determine the kinds of things that infant and preschool mental tests evaluate, Stott and Ball (1965) took test protocols of 1926 infants and young children and examined the meaning and content of the tests.

Item intercorrelations were obtained for two levels each of the Cattell Infant Scale (Cattell, 1940), the California First Year Scale (Bayley, 1933), and the Gesell Developmental Schedules (Gesell, 1925); for five levels of the Merrill-Palmer Scale (Stutsman, 1931), and for three levels of the Stanford-Binet (Terman & Merrill, 1937). The data represented a tapping of developmental progress in mental ability from three months to five years. From each interitem correlation matrix, principle axes were extracted. For each factor in the various analyses, the items having factor loadings of .40 or over were studied to discover the similarity of meaning that functioned to bring them together in the same factor. Suggestions for factor names were made by three or more judges and agreement reached on the meaning in terms of the Guilford structure of intelligence (Guilford, 1956, 1957, 1959).

The results of these factor analyses were interpreted as follows: (1) The factors indicated that the test responses may be definitely intellectual in nature. There may be some question as to whether the factors represent the true "meaning" but it is óbvious that as young as three months of age some "thinking" processes occur. (2) The factor content of tests at different age levels vary, and one of the reasons for longitudinal changes in mental test scores is that the child is being tested for different abilities at age levels. (3) The content of the various scales also vary. (4) Of the test items analyzed, only those at the infant level contain items which are interpretable as involving divergent production, the factor most closely associated with creativity. (Stott and Ball [1965] conclude that one should not expect the scales at the preschool children level to select creative children since they do not contain items testing creativity.) (5) Some intelligence tests have items that yield large, general factors, but it is difficult to understand what is implied by this result. (6) The meaning of the test items is not necessarily related to the format and type of material used. That is, items containing painted blocks for manipulation may be just as effective as indications of cognition as are tests using verbal material.

Stott and Ball (1965) make an excellent case on the matter of meaning elicited by the test item operations:

> In the evaluation, of the operations elicited by the test items in our present study, we discovered cognition, memory, evaluation, and both divergent and convergent production, in addition to the hand dexterity and other psychomotor skills, for which we found no ready intellectual process name. It is felt that the resort to the naming of test performance as "psychomotor" is an acknowledgment of failure to analyze the behavior adequately and, thus, emphasizes the motor, rather than the psychological implications of the task. Most of the child's reactions require that intellectual processes accompany the movements involved. They are goal directed and examiner directed, and they involve discrimination, selection, and control of the neuromuscular responses to be used. They are more appropriately chosen actions for the age level studied than they would be for older ages when the behaviors have become more habitually performed. These tests, involving what seem like

simple motor responses at these young ages, are actually much more complicated and need more selective judgment and control than we realize. This is why they are indicators of intellectual ability. The habitual responses of children at more mature levels have not been developed at these younger ages. Superficial judgment about these responses, lumping them into a category called *psychomotor* or *performance,* constitute a very inadequate analysis of the behavior involved (Stott & Ball, 1965, p. 126).

Another recent development of importance is the standardization data of Bayley (1965) which not only provide a technique for comparative work on development but also establish central tendencies in early development, including the extent to which various subgroups in the population are similar or different.

PREMATURITY

Early birth offers an opportunity to study general problems of behavioral growth particularly pertinent to the late fetal period. As a clinical entity the term "prematurity" implies a lack of development or retardation in development with an assumption that special medical care is needed to insure survival of the individual. Various criteria of prematurity have been developed but the most widely accepted definition usually refers to ". . . an immature live-born infant with a birth weight of 5 lb 8 oz (2500 gm) or less, or live-born infant with a period of gestation of less than 37 weeks" (Dunham, 1955). Medical literature substantiates the fact that early birth is associated with generalized biological inadequacies. The effect of this immaturity on psychological development has similarly been extensively investigated and documented.

To date there have been two reviews (Benton, 1940; Wiener, 1962) on the psychological correlates of prematurity. Benton's (1940) comprehensive critique called attention to the variations in quality appearing in the research on mental development of prematurely born individuals. While there were a few sound studies, many others were obviously deficient. Within the latter groups the flaws not only tended to invalidate the conclusions drawn, but also contributed to the appearance of contradictory results in comparing one study to another. Among the methodological flaws were the use of subjective criteria as measures of performance, failure to equate for the influence of socioeconomic factors, inadequate and limited sampling, and biased sampling.

In addition to many of the weaknesses just enumerated, Wiener (1962) concluded that the studies on prematures since 1940 were marked by (1) a lack of theoretical framework; (2) an absence of statistical evaluation or data to complete such analyses; (3) a failure to use factorial designs both for control and study of interactions of age, birth weight, sex, and social class; (4) a disregard for the interaction of parental sociopsychological characteristics with low birth weight; (5) the use of questionable techniques in assessment, and, finally; (6) selection of age intervals for assessment which overlooked or minimized the influence of age-specific defects.

The data to be summarized can be cast as answers to the usual array of questions which are stimulated when an exceptional or a typical condition is presumed to be operative: what is the course of development of prematures during infancy, what is the relationship between behavior, birth weight, and type of birth, and what deviations are associated with immaturity? Even though this review has focused on studies involving infants, generalizations about prematurity must take into account the fact that most past studies have been retrospective in design. While this may highlight the significance of residual effects, it may also overlook the presence of age-specific defects and the contribution of these to behavior at older ages. For these reasons reference will be made both to subjects who were assessed during infancy and at older ages.

An analysis of the course of development of prematures during infancy raises problems. Although the main interest of this chapter is in motor development, it is obvious that there is considerable overlap between motor development and intellectual development during infancy. Thus information pertaining to the intelligence quotient or developmental quotient can be presumed to shed light on early motor patterning. Among the studies of prematurity initiated during infancy are those by Gesell (1925; 1928; 1933), Mohr and Bartelme (1934), Melcher (1937), Shirley (1938), Knobloch, Rider, Harper, and Pasamanick (1956), Lezine (1958), Harper, Fisher, and Rider (1959), and Drillien (1965). The investigation of Mohr and Bartelme (1934) is appraised as excellent because of the authors' concern for socioeconomic factors, the use of objective assessment, and the inclusion of a control sample. Their group of 250 prematurely born ranged in age from eight months to seven years when tested with the Gesell and Kuhlman-Binet. Generally, developmental quotient differences in mental growth of the prematures existed when comparisons were made of their scores with those of full term siblings or with the standardization data if degree of prematurity was taken into account. If degree of prematurity was not taken into account, retardation appeared present during the first two years for the prematurely born. Although no relationship was apparent between maternal condition or birth weight and intelligence of the prematures, those children with evidence of brain damage were retarded. The prematures were significantly retarded in time of walking, and they showed more speech difficulties along with a heightened dependency reaction.

Melcher's (1937) findings of superior development and accelerated rates of development in prematures have been open to question and criticism. Similarly criticized both because of the socioeconomic level of the comparison control group and uncertain standardization of the test instrument are the results of Shirley (1938). She reported that prematures were more retarded in manipulative development than in intellectual grasp and social responsiveness. If the general results of the tests were disregarded, there still remains evidence of a positive relationship between birth weight and developmental status, which concurred with Melcher's (1937) earlier result.

Knobloch *et al.* (1959) carried out a large scale study on 500 single-born prematures and 492 full term controls matched for race, season of birth, parity, and socioeconomic status. Neurological status and intellectual development were positively related to premature birth weight (Knobloch *et al.*, 1956). Subsequently, Harper *et al.* (1959) evaluated 900 Ss of this group at three to five years of age. Full term children were significantly less impaired than prematures at both 40 weeks and at three to five years. Small size at birth continued to be a hazard in terms of neurological development. This observed defective functioning with lower birth weights was not apparent at the three- to five-year period in terms of intelligence quotients. Lezine (1958) concluded that gestation time has a greater influence than does weight on psychomotor development—a conclusion somewhat difficult to interpret in light of the high correlation between birth weight and gestation time. This study also noted that premature males tend to be more impaired than premature females.

By far the most extensive investigations on prematurity have been those of Drillien. In one study, this investigator observed trends in developmental level and status (1959) in a sample of 600 subjects, two thirds of whom were prematures. These data were not statistically evaluated, but did permit some assessment of birth weight and its interaction with other factors. Data were derived from examinations between six months and two years. Results showed that the smaller the premature at birth, the more impaired he was at both six months and at two years. Although these smaller prematures tended to "catch up," still they were comparatively more impaired at two years than larger prematures. In line with Shirley's (1939) and Lezine's (1958) findings, Drillien (1959) reported that male premature infants did not show the acceleration, the so-called "catching up," as readily as females. Higher birth weights were associated with higher developmental quotients and socioeconomic levels (Drillien, 1961). Generally, it was observed that smaller prematures showed more defective functioning and seemed to come from the lower socioeconomic classes (Drillien, 1959). Whereas small premature infants from higher social class levels showed gains with age, small prematures from lower classes showed declining scores with age (Drillien, 1961). These latter data were obtained from sequential assessments of children from three to six years of age. In support of earlier findings (Kastein & Fowler, 1959) Drillien (1965) found that speech was more impaired in prematures than was general motor activity. Even sphincter control was later for those under four-and-one-half pounds at birth.

In summary, the evidence indicates that prematures are relatively impaired in intellectual functioning (Wiener, 1962); this conclusion is somewhat contradictory to that made earlier by Benton (1940). Behavior generally appears to reflect organic involvement (Lilienfeld,

Pasamanick, & Rogers, 1955) and perhaps is aptly classified as a prematurity syndrome (Shirley, 1938). In this connection Eames, from a series of studies (1945, 1954, 1955, 1957), concluded that mixed dominance, poor visual acuity, and perceptual and reading difficulties were sequelae of neurological damage correlated with immaturity and low weight. Retardation in development is demonstrable. Relative to the effects of degree of prematurity or size at birth, Wiener (1962) states that it is difficult to draw conclusions in light of conflicting results from the Drillien (1959, 1961) and the Harper *et al.* (1959) studies. The results cited in this review would tend to support the notion of increased impairment with decreasing birth weight.

The lack of any defined theory underlying research in prematurity is evident. Wiener (1962) proposes that some theoretical formulations may account for the observed facts and provide research guidelines. Among these would be a set of theories defined as functional or environmental that would be concerned with (1) impairment in premature performance as a function of early separation and sensory deprivation, or (2) the negative effects transmitted by maternal anxiety over producing a biologically inadequate child, or (3) premature behavior as a function of social class and psychosocial stresses inherent in the lower socioeconomic environment. Another group of theories would be oriented toward examining premature behavior in terms of biological factors and neurological deficits. Last, some combinatory theory would take into account the interaction of neurological and psychosocial factors as they operate to produce impairment, thus handling those observations which associate prematures of lighter birth weights with harsher environments and consequently, with greater behavioral deficits.

References

Aldrich, C. A., & Norval, M. A. A developmental graph for the first year of life. *J. Pediatr.*, 1946, 29, 304–308.

Aldrich, C. A., Norval, M. A., Knop, C., & Venegas, F. The crying of newly born babies. IV. A follow-up study after additional nursing care had been provided. *J. Pediatr.*, 1946, 28, 665–670.

Aldrich, C. A., Sung, C., & Knop, C. The crying of newly born babies. II. The individual phase. *J. Pediatr.*, 1945, 27, 89–96.

Ames, L. B. The sequential patterning of prone progression in the human infant. *Genet. Psychol. Monogr.*, 1937, 19, 409–460.

———. The constancy of psycho-motor tempo in individual infants. *J. genet. Psychol.*, 1940, 57, 445–450.

———. Motor correlates of infant crying. *J. genet. Psychol.*, 1941, 59, 239–247.

Anderson, R. B., & Rosenblith, J. R. Light sensitivity in the neonate: a preliminary report. *Biol. Neonat.*, 1964, 7, 83–94.

André-Thomas, Chesni, Y., & Saint-Anne Dargassies, S. *The neurological examination of the infant.* London: Medical Advisory Committee of the National Spastics Society, 1960.

Ardran, G. M., Kemp, F. H., & Lind, J. A cineradiographic study of bottle feeding. *Brit. J. Radiol.*, 1958, 31, 11–22.

Aserinsky, E., & Kleitman, N. Regularly occurring periods of eye motility and concomitant phenomena during sleep. *Science,* 1953, 118, 273–274.

――――. Two types of ocular motility occurring in sleep. *J. appl. Physiol.,* 1955, 8, 1–10. (a)

――――. A motility cycle in sleeping infants as manifested by ocular and gross bodily activity. *J. appl. Physiol.,* 1955, 8, 11–18. (b)

Babinski, J. Sur le réflexe cutané-plantaire dans certains affections organiques du système nerveux central. (On the cutaneous-plantar reflex in certain organic diseases of the C. N. S.) *C. R. Soc. Biol.,* Paris, 1896, 48, 207–208.

Babkin, P. S. The establishment of reflex activity in early postnatal life. *Fiziol. Zh. SSSR,* 1958, 44, 922–927.

Balint, M. Individual differences of behavior in early infancy, and an objective method for recording them: I. Approach and the method of recording. *J. genet. Psychol.,* 1948, 73, 57–79. (a)

――――. Individual differences of behavior in early infancy, and an objective method for recording them: II. Results and conclusions. *J. genet. Psychol.,* 1948, 73, 81–117. (a)

Bartoshuk, A. K. Response decrement with repeated elicitation of human neonatal cardiac acceleration to sound. *J. comp. physiol. Psychol.,* 1962, 55, 9–13.

Bayley, N. A study of the crying of infants during mental and physical tests. *J. genet. Psychol.,* 1932, 40, 306–329.

――――. Mental growth during the first three years: A developmental study of sixty-one children by repeated tests. *Genet. Psychol. Monogr.,* 1933, 14, 1–92.

――――. Development of motor abilities during the first three years. *Monogr. Soc. Res. Child Develpm.,* 1935, No. 1.

――――. *The California Infant Scale of Motor Development.* Berkeley: Univer. of Calif., 1936.

――――. Comparisons of mental and motor test scores for ages 1–15 months by sex, birth order, race, geographical location, and education of parents. *Child Develpm.,* 1965, 36, 379–411.

Bell, R. Q. Some factors to be controlled in studies of the behavior of newborns. *Biol. Neonat.,* 1963, 5, 200–214.

Bell, R. Q., & Darling, J. F. The prone head reaction in the human neonate: relation with sex and tactile sensitivity. *Child Develpm.,* 1965, 36, 943–949.

Benton, A. L. Mental development of prematurely born children: A critical review of the literature. *Amer. J. Orthopsychiat.,* 1940, 10, 719–746.

Bernard, J. Prediction from human fetal measures. *Child Develpm.,* 1964, 35, 1243–1248.

Bernstein, A. Some relations between techniques of feeding and training during infancy and certain behavior in childhood. *Genet. Psychol. Monogr.,* 1955, 51, 3–44.

Birns, B., Blank, M., Bridger, W. H., & Escalona, S. K. Behavioral inhibition in neonates produced by auditory stimuli. *Child Develpm.,* 1965, 36, 639–645.

Blauvelt, H. H. Capacity of a human neonate reflex to signal future response by present action. *Child Develpm.,* 1962, 33, 21–28.

――――. Differential latency of oral response on the first day of life. *J. genet. Psychol.,* 1964, 104, 199–205.

Blauvelt, H. H., & McKenna, J. Capacity of the human newborn for motor-infant interaction. II. The temporal dimensions of a neonate response. *Psychiat. res. Rep.,* 1960, 13, 128–147.

Bower, T. G. R. Discrimination of depth in premotor infants. *Psychonomic Science,* 1964, 1, 368.

Brackbill, Y. (Ed.) *Research in infant behavior: A cross-indexed bibliography.* Baltimore: Williams & Wilkins, 1964.

Brazelton, T. B. Sucking in infancy. *Pediatrics,* 1956, 17, 400–404. Reprinted in Y. Brackbill & G. G. Thompson (Eds.), *Behavior in infancy and early childhood: A book of readings.* New York: Free Press, 1967.

――. Psychophysiologic reactions in the neonate. *J. Pediatr.*, 1961, 58, 508–512.

Bridger, W. H. Ethological concepts and human development. *Recent advances in biol. Psychiat.*, 1962, 4, 95–107.

Brown, J. States in newborn infants. *Merrill-Palmer Quart.*, 1964, 10, 313–327.

Bryan, E. S. Variations in the responses of infants during first ten days of postnatal life. *Child Develpm.*, 1930, 1, 56–77.

Burnside, L. H. Coordination in the locomotion of infants. *Genet. Psychol. Monogr.*, 1927, 2, 279–372.

Caldwell, B. M. The effects of infant care. In M. L. Hoffman & L. W. Hoffman (Eds.), *Review of child development research.* New York: Russell Sage Foundation, 1964. Pp. 9–88.

Campbell, R. V. D., & Weech, A. A. Measures which characterize the individual during the development of behavior in early life. *Child Develpm.*, 1941, 12, 217–236.

Carmichael, L. (Ed.) *Manual of child psychology.* New York: Wiley, 1946.

――. (Ed.) *Manual of child psychology.* (2nd ed.) New York: Wiley, 1954.

Cattell, P. *The measurement of intelligence of infants and young children.* New York: Psychological Corp., 1940.

Chaney, B. L., & McGraw, M. B. Reflexes and other motor activities in newborn infants. *Bull. Neur. Inst. New York*, 1932, 2, 1–56.

Clarke, F. M. A developmental study of the bodily reaction of infants to an auditory startle stimulus. *J. genet. Psychol.*, 1939, 55, 415–427.

Clarke, F. M., Hunt, W. A., & Hunt, E. B. Plantar responses in infants following a startle stimulus. *J. genet. Psychol.*, 1937, 50, 458–461.

Colley, J. R. T., & Creamer, B. Sucking and swallowing in infants. *Brit. Med. J.*, 1958, 2, 422–423.

Crowell, D. H., Yasaka, E., & Crowell, D. C. Infant stabilimeter. *Child Develpm.*, 1964, 35, 525–532.

Curti, M. W., Marshall, F. B., & Steggerda, M. The Gesell schedules applied to 1, 2, and 3 year old Negro children of Jamaica British West Indies. *J. comp. Neurol.*, 1935, 20, 125.

Davids, A., Holden, R. H., & Gray, G. B. Maternal anxiety during pregnancy and adequacy of mother and child adjustment eight months following childbirth. *Child Develpm.*, 1963, 34, 993–1002.

Davis, A., & Havighurst, R. J. Social class and color differences in child-rearing. *Amer. Sociol. Rev.*, 1946, 11, 698–710.

Davis, H. U., Sears, R. R., Miller, H. C., & Brodbeck, A. J. Effects of cup, bottle, and breast feeding on oral activities of newborn infants. *Pediatrics*, 1948, 2, 549–558.

Delman, L. The order of participation of limbs in responses to tactual stimulation of the newborn infant. *Child Develpm.*, 1935, 6, 98–109.

Dennis, W. The role of mass activity in the development of infant behavior. *Psychol. Rev.*, 1932, 39, 593–595. (a)

――. Two new responses of infants. *Child Develpm.*, 1932, 3, 362–363. (b)

――. The age at walking of children who run on all fours. *Child Develpm.*, 1934, 5, 92–93.

――. The effect of restricted practice upon the reaching, sitting, and standing of two infants. *J. genet. Psychol.*, 1935, 47, 17–32. (a)

――. Laterality of function in early infancy under controlled developmental conditions. *Child Develpm.*, 1935, 6, 242–252. (b)

――. A psychologic interpretation of the persistence of the so-called Moro reflex. *Amer. J. Dis. Child.*, 1935, 50, 888–893. (c)

――. A bibliography of baby biographies. *Child Develpm.*, 1936, 7, 71–73.

――. Infant reaction to restraint: An evaluation of Watson's theory. *New York Acad. Sci. Trans.*, 1940, 2, 202–218.

Dennis, W., & Dennis, M. G. Behavioral development in the first year as shown by forty biographies. *Psychol. Rec.*, 1937, 1 (21), 348–361.

Dewey, E. *Behavior developments in infants; a survey of the literature on prenatal and postnatal activity, 1920–1934.* New York: Columbia Univer. Press, 1935.

Dietrich, H. F. A longitudinal study of the Babinski and plantar grasp reflexes. *Amer. J. Dis. Child.*, 1957, 94, 265–271.

Drillien, C. M. A longitudinal study of the growth and development of prematurely and maturely born children. Part III: Mental development. *Arch. Dis. Child.*, 1959, 34, 37–45.

————. A longitudinal study of the growth and development of prematurely and maturely born children. Part VII: Mental development 2–5 years. *Arch. Dis. Child.*, 1961, 36, 233–244.

————. *The growth and development of the prematurely born infant.* Edinburgh: Livingstone, 1964.

Dunham, E. C. *Premature Infants.* New York: Harper, 1955.

Eames, T. H. Comparison of children of premature and full term birth who fail in reading. *J. Educ. Res.*, 1945, 38, 506–508.

————. Correlation between birth weight and visual acuity. *Amer. J. Ophthal.*, 1954, 38, 850–852.

————. The relationship of birth weight, speed of object and work perception, and visual acuity. *J. Pediatr.*, 1955, 47, 603–606.

————. Frequency of cerebral lateral dominance variations among school children of premature and full term birth. *J. Pediatr.*, 1957, 51, 300–302.

Ellesor, M. V. Children's reactions to novel visual stimuli. *Child Develpm.*, 1933, 4, 95–105.

Fantz, R. L. A method for studying early visual development. *Percept. mot. Skills*, 1956, 6, 13–15.

————. Pattern vision in newborn infants. *Science*, 1963, 140, 296–297. Reprinted in Y. Brackbill & G. G. Thompson (Eds.), *Behavior in infancy and early childhood: A book of readings.* New York: Free Press, 1967.

————. Visual experiences in infants: Decreased attention to familiar patterns relative to novel one. *Science*, 1964, 146, 668–670.

Feldman, W. M. The nature of the plantar reflex in early life and the causes of its variations. *Amer. J. Dis. Child.*, 1922, 23, 1–40.

Fischer, L. K. The significance of a typical postural and grasping behavior during the first year of life. *Amer. J. Orthopsychiat.*, 1958, 28, 368–375.

Fisichelli, V. R., & Karelitz, S. The cry latencies of normal infants and those with brain damage. *J. Pediatr.*, 1963, 62, 724–734.

Flavell, J. H. *The developmental psychology of Jean Piaget.* Princeton, N.J.: Van Nostrand, 1963.

Flemming, B. M. A study of the sleep of young children. *J. Amer. Ass. Univer. Women*, 1925, 19, 25–27.

Foster, J. C. Hours spent in sleep by young children. *Proc. Ninth Internat. Congr. Psychol.*, 1929, 168–169.

Furfey, P. H., Bonham, M. A., & Sargent, M. K. The mental organization of the newborn, *Child Develpm.*, 1930, 1, 48–51.

Gatewood, M. C., & Weiss, A. P. Race and sex differences in newborn infants. *Ped. Sem.*, 1930, 38, 31–49.

Geber, M., & Dean, R. F. A. The state of development of newborn African children. *Lancet*, 1957, 272, 1216–1219. Reprinted in Y. Brackbill & G. G. Thompson (Eds.), *Behavior in infancy and early childhood: A book of readings.* New York: Free Press, 1967.

Gentry, E. F., & Aldrich, C. A. Rooting reflex in the newborn infant; incidence and effect on it of sleep. *Amer. J. Dis. Child.*, 1948, 75, 528–539. (a) Reprinted in Y. Brackbill & G. G. Thompson (Eds.), *Behavior in infancy and early childhood: A book of readings.* New York: Free Press, 1967.

————. Toe reflexes in infancy and the development of voluntary control. *Amer. J. Dis. Child.*, 1948, 76, 389–400. (b)

Gesell, A. L. *The mental growth of the pre-school child.* New York: Macmillan, 1925.

——. *Infancy and human growth.* New York: Macmillan, 1928.

——. Maturation and infant behavior pattern. *Psychol. Rev.,* 1929, 36, 307–319.

——. The developmental psychology of twins. In C. Murchison (Ed.), *A handbook of child psychology.* Worcester, Mass.: Clark Univer. Press, 1931.

——. The mental growth of prematurely born infants. *J. Pediatr.,* 1933, 2, 676–680.

——. The tonic neck reflex in the human infant: Its morphogenic and clinical significance. *J. Pediatr.,* 1938, 13, 455–464.

——. *The first five years of life.* New York: Harper, 1940.

——. The ontogenesis of behavior. In L. Carmichael (Ed.), *Manual of child psychology.* New York: Wiley, 1946.

——. The ontogenesis of behavior. In L. Carmichael (Ed.), *Manual of child psychology.* (2nd ed.) New York: Wiley, 1954.

Gesell, A. L., & Amatruda, C. S. *The embryology of behavior. The beginnings of the human mind.* New York: Harper, 1945.

——. *Developmental diagnosis.* (2nd ed.) New York: Hoeber, 1947.

Gesell, A. L., & Halverson, H. M. The development of thumb opposition in the human infant. *J. genet. Psychol.,* 1936, 48, 339–361.

Giesecke, M. The genesis of hand preference. *Monogr. Soc. Res. Child Develpm.,* 1936, 1, No. 5.

Goodenough, F. L., & Smart, R. C. Interrelationships of motor abilities in young children. *Child Develpm.,* 1935, 6, 141–153.

Gordon, K. A study of hand and eye preference. *Child Develpm.,* 1931, 2, 321–324.

Gordon, M. B. The Moro embrace reflex in infancy: Its incidence and significance. *Amer. J. Dis. Child.,* 1929, 38, 26–34.

Gordon, N. S., & Bell, R. Q. Activity in the human newborn. *Psychol. Rep.,* 1961, 9, 103–116.

Gough, D. The visual behavior of infants in the first few weeks of life. *Proc. Royal Soc. Med.,* 1962, 55, (4) 308–310.

Graham, F. K. Behavioral differences between normal and traumatized newborns: I. The test procedures. *Psychol. Monogr.,* 1956, 70, No. 20.

Graham, F. K., Matarozzo, R. G., & Caldwell, B. M. Behavioral differences between normals and traumatized newborns: II. Standardization, reliability, and validity. *Psychol. Monogr.,* 1956, 70, No. 21.

Graham, F. K., Pennoyer, M. M., Caldwell, B. M., Greenman, M., & Hartmann, A. F. Relationship between clinical status and behavior test performance in a newborn group with histories suggesting anoxia. *J. Pediatr.,* 1957, 50, 177–189.

Guilford, J. P. The structure of intellect, *Psychol. Bull.,* 1956, 53, 267–293.

——. A revised structure of intellect. *Rep. Psychol. Lab.,* Los Angeles: Univer. Southern Calif., 1957, No. 19.

——. Three faces of intellect. *Amer. Psychologist,* 1959, 14, 469–479.

Gullickson, G. R., & Crowell, D. H. Neonatal habituation to electrotactual stimulation. *J. exp. child Psychol.,* 1964, 1, 388–396.

Halverson, H. M. An experimental study of prehension in infants by means of systematic cinema records. *Genet. Psychol. Monogr.,* 1931, 10, 107–286.

——. The acquisition of skill in infancy. *J. genet. Psychol.,* 1933, 43, 3–48.

——. Studies of the grasping responses of early infancy. *J. genet. Psychol.,* 1937, 51, 371–449.

——. Infant sucking and tensional behavior. *J. genet. Psychol.,* 1938, 53, 365–430.

——. Mechanisms of early infant feeding. *J. genet. Psychol.,* 1944, 64, 185–223.

Hardy, J. B., Dougherty, A., & Hardy, W. G. Hearing responses and audiologic screening in infants. *J. Pediatr.,* 1959, 55, 382–390.

Harper, P. A., Fischer, L. K., & Rider, R. V. Neurological and intellectual status of prematures at three to five years of age. *J. Pediatr.*, 1959, 55, 679–690.

Heinlein, J. H. Preferential manipulation in children. *Comp. Psychol. Monogr.*, 1930, 7, No. 33.

Hildreth, G. The development and training of hand dominance: II. Developmental tendencies in handedness. *J. genet. Psychol.*, 1949, 75, 221–254. (a)

———. The development and training of hand dominance: III. Origins of handedness and lateral dominance. *J. genet. Psychol.*, 1949, 75, 255–275. (b)

Hoefer, C., & Hardy, M. Later development of breast-fed and artificially-fed infants. *J. Amer. med. Ass.*, 1929, 92, 615–619.

Hofstaetter, P. R. The changing composition of "intelligence," a study in *T* technique. *J. genet. Psychol.*, 1954, 85, 159–164.

Honzik, M. P., & McKee, J. P. The sex-difference in thumb-sucking. *J. Pediatr.*, 1962, 61, 726–732.

Hull, C. L., & Hull, B. I. Parallel learning curves of an infant in vocabulary and in voluntary control of the bladder. *Ped. Sem.*, 1919, 26, 272–283. Reprinted in Y. Brackbill & G. G. Thompson (Eds.), *Behavior in infancy and early childhood: A book of readings.* New York: Free Press, 1967.

Hunt, W. A., Clarke, F. M., & Hunt, E. B. Studies of the startle pattern: IV. Infants. *J. Psychol.*, 1936, 2, 339–352. Reprinted in Y. Brackbill & G. G. Thompson (Eds.), *Behavior in infancy and early childhood: A book of readings.* New York: Free Press, 1967.

———. The startle pattern in infants in response to non-auditory stimuli. *J. genet. Psychol.*, 1938, 52, 443–446.

Hunt, W. A., & Landis, C. Studies of the startle pattern: I. Introduction. *J. Psychol.*, 1936, 2, 201–205.

Illingsworth, R. S. Delayed maturation in development. *J. Pediatr.*, 1961, 58, 761–770.

Irwin, O. C. The amount and nature of activities of newborn infants under constant external stimulating conditions during the first ten days of life. *Genet. Psychol. Monogr.*, 1930, 8, 1–92.

———. The amount of motility of seventy-three newborn infants. *J. comp. Psychol.*, 1932, 14, 415–428. (a)

———. The distribution of the amount of motility in young infants between two nursing periods. *J. comp. Psychol.*, 1932, 14, 429–445. (b)

———. Infant responses to vertical movements. *Child Develpm.*, 1932, 3, 167–169. (c)

———. The latent time of the body startle in infants. *Child Develpm.*, 1932 3, 104–107. (d)

———. The organismic hypothesis and differentiation of behavior. I. The cell theory and the neurone doctrine. *Psychol. Rev.*, 1932, 39, 128–146. (e)

———. The organismic hypothesis and differentiation of behavior. II. The reflex arc concept. *Psychol. Rev.*, 1932, 39, 189–202. (f)

———. The organismic hypothesis and differentiation of behavior. III. The differentiation of human behavior. *Psychol. Rev.*, 1932, 39, 387–398. (g)

———. The relation of body motility in young infants to some physical traits. *J. exp. Educ.*, 1932, 1, 140–143. (h)

———. Motility in young infants: I. Relation to body temperature. *Amer. J. Dis. Child.*, 1933, 45, 531–533. (a)

———. Motility in young infants: II. Relation to two indexes of nutritional status. *Amer. J. Dis. Child.*, 1933, 45, 534–537. (b)

———. Qualitative changes in a vertebral reaction pattern during infancy: A motion picture study. *Univer. Iowa Stud. Child Welf.*, 1936, 12, 199–207.

Irwin, O. C., & Weiss, L. A. The effect of clothing on the general and vocal activity of the newborn infant. *Univer. Iowa Stud. Child Welf.*, 1934, 9. (a)

————. The effect of darkness on the activity of newborn infants. In O. C. Irwin, L. A. Weiss, & E. M. Stubbs (Eds.), Studies in infant behavior. I. *Univer. Iowa Stud. Child Welf.*, 1934, 9, 163–175. (b)

Jensen, K. Differential reactions to taste and temperature stimuli in newborn infants. *Genet. Psychol. Monogr.*, 1932, 12, 361–479.

Jones, H. E. Dextrality as a function of age. *J. exp. Psychol.*, 1931, 14, 125–143.

Jones, M. C. The development of early behavior patterns in young children. *Ped. Sem.*, 1926, 33, 537–585.

Karelitz, S., Karelitz, R., & Rosenfeld, L. S. Infant vocalizations and their significance. In P. W. Bowman & H. V. Mautner (Eds.), *Mental retardation: Proc. First International Medical Conf.* New York: Grune & Stratton, 1960. Pp. 439–446.

Karelitz, S., & Fisichelli, V. R. The cry thresholds of normal infants and those with brain damage. An aid in the early diagnosis of severe brain damage. *J. Pediatr.*, 1962, 61, 679–685.

Karr, M. Development of motor control in young children; coordinated movements of the fingers. *Child Develpm.*, 1934, 5, 381–387.

Kastein, S., & Fowler, E. P. Language development among survivors of premature birth. *Amer. med. Ass. Arch. Otolaryng.*, 1959, 69, 131–135.

Kaye, H., & Levin, G. R. Two attempts to demonstrate tonal suppression of non-nutritive sucking in neonates. *Percept. mot. Skills*, 1963, 17, 521–522.

Kellogg, W. N. A method for recording the activity of the human fetus in utero, with specimen results. *J. genet. Psychol.*, 1941, 58, 307–326.

Kessen, W. Research design in the study of developmental problems. In P. H. Mussen (Ed.), *Handbook of research methods in child development.* New York: Wiley, 1960. Pp. 36–70.

Kessen, W., Williams, E. J., & Williams, J. P. Selection and test of response measures in the study of the human newborn. *Child Develpm.*, 1961, 32, 7–24.

Key, C. B., White, M. R., Honzik, M. P., Heiney, A. B., & Erwin, D. The process of learning to dress among nursery-school children. *Genet. Psychol. Monogr.*, 1936, 18, 67–163.

Klackenberg, G. Thumbsucking frequency and etiology. *Pediatrics*, 1949, 4, 418–424.

Kleitman, N., & Engelmann, T. G. Sleep characteristics of infants. *J. appl. Physiol.*, 1953, 6, 269–282.

Kleitman, N. *Sleep and wakefulness.* (rev.) Chicago, Ill.: Univer. Chicago Press, 1963.

Knobloch, H., & Pasamanick, B. The developmental behavioral approach to the neurologic examination in infancy. *Child Develpm.*, 1962, 33, 181–198.

Knobloch, H., Rider, R. V., Harper, P., & Pasamanick, B. Neuropsychiatric sequelae of prematurity. *J. Amer. med. Ass.*, 1956, 161, 581–585.

Kron, R. E., Stein, M., & Goddard, K. E. A method of measuring sucking behavior of newborn infants. *Psychosom. Med.*, 1963, 25, 181–191.

Kunst, M. S. A study of thumb and finger sucking in infants. *Psychol. Monogr.*, 1948, 62, No. 3.

Lakin, M. Personality factors in mothers of excessively crying (colicky) infants. *Monogr. Soc. Res. Child Develpm.*, 1957, 22, 1–48.

Lederer, R. K. Studies in infant behavior. V. Part One: An exploratory investigation of handed status in the first two years of life. *Univer. Iowa Stud. Child Welf.*, 1939, 16, 8–103.

Levin, G. R., & Kaye, H. Non-nutritive sucking by human neonates. *Child Develpm.*, 1964, 35, 749–758.

Levine, M. L., & Bell, A. I. The treatment of colic in infancy by use of the pacifier. *J. Pediatr.*, 1950, 37, 750–755.

Levy, D. M. Finger sucking and accessory movements in early infancy: An etiologic study. *Amer. J. Psychiat.*, 1928, 7, 881–918.

Lézine, I. Le développement psychomoteur des jeunes prématurés. (The psychomotor development of young premature infants.) Etudes Neo-Natales, 1958, 7, 1–50.

Lilienfeld, A. M., Pasamanick, B., & Rogers, M. Relationship between pregnancy experience and the development of certain neuropsychiatric disorders in children. Amer. J. Publ. Hlth, 1955, 45, 637–643.

Lippman, H. S. Certain behavior responses in early infancy. J. genet. Psychol., 1927, 34, 424–440.

Lipsitt, L. P., & Kaye, H. Change in neonatal response to optimizing and non-optimizing sucking stimulation. Psychonomic Science, 1965, 2, 221–222.

Lipsitt, L. P., & Levy, N. Electrotactual threshold in the neonate. Child Develpm., 1959, 30, 547–554.

Lipton, E. L., Steinschneider, A., & Richmond, J. B. Autonomic function in the neonate. II. Physiologic effects of motor restraint. Psychosom. Med., 1960, 22, 57–65.

———. Swaddling, a child care practice: Historical, cultural and experimental observations. Pediatrics (Suppl.) 1965, 35, 521–567.

McCaskill, C. L., & Wellman, B. L. A study of common motor achievements at the preschool ages. Child Develpm., 1938, 9, 141–150.

McDowell, M. S. Frequency of choice of play materials by preschool children. Child Develpm., 1937, 8, 305–310.

McGraw, M. B. A comparative study of a group of southern white and Negro infants. Genet. Psychol. Monogr., 1931, 10, 1–105.

———. The Moro reflex. Amer. J. Dis. Child, 1937, 54, 240–251.

———. Neural maturation as exemplified in achievement of bladder control. J. Pediatr., 1940, 16, 580–590. (a)

———. Maturation of behavior. In L. Carmichael (Ed.) Manual of child psychology. New York: Wiley, 1946. Pp. 332–369.

———. Swimming behavior of the human infant. J. Pediatr., 1939, 15, 485–490. Reprinted in Y. Brackbill & G. G. Thompson (Eds.), Behavior in infancy and early childhood: A book of readings. New York: Free Press, 1967.

McGraw, M. B., & Breeze, K. W. Quantitative studies in the development erect locomotion. Child Develpm., 1941, 12, 267–303.

Mead, C. D. The age of walking and talking in relation to general intelligence. Ped. Sem., 1913, 20, 460–484.

Mehlman, J. The tonic neck reflex in newborn infants. J. Pediatr., 1940, 16, 767–769.

———. Neuromuscular development of the human infant as exemplified in the achievement of erect locomotion. J. Pediatr., 1940, 17, 747–771. (b)

———. Neuromuscular mechanism of the infant: Development reflected by postural adjustment to an inverted position. Amer. J. Dis. Child., 1940, 60, 1031–1042. (c)

———. Suspension grasp behavior of the human infant. Amer. J. Dis. Child., 1940, 60, 799–811. (d)

———. Development of neuro-muscular mechanisms as reflected in the crawling and creeping behavior of the human infant. J. genet. Psychol., 1941, 58, 83–111. (a)

———. Development of the plantar response in healthy infants. Amer. J. Dis. Child., 1941, 61, 1215–1221. (b)

———. Neural maturation as exemplified in the reaching prehensile behavior of the human infant. J. Psychol., 1941, 11, 127–141. (c)

———. Neural maturation of the infant as exemplified in the righting reflex, or rolling from a dorsal to a prone position. J. Pediatr., 1941, 18, 385–394. (d)

———. Neuro-motor maturation of anti-gravity functions as reflected in the development of a sitting posture. J. genet. Psychol., 1941, 59, 155–175. (e)

Melcher, R. T. Development within the first two years of infants prematurely born. Child Develpm., 1937, 8, 1–14.

Mohr, G. J., & Bartelme, P. F. Developmental studies of prematurely born children. In J. H. Hess, G. J. Mohr, & P. F. Bartelme (Eds.), *The physical and mental growth of prematurely born children.* Chicago: Univer. Chicago Press, 1934. Pp. 57–217.

Morgan, J. J. B., & Morgan, S. S. Infant learning as a development index. *J. genet. Psychol.*, 1944, 65, 281–289.

Mumford, A. A. Survival movements of human infancy. *Brain*, 1897, 20, 290–307.

Murchison, C. (Ed.) *A handbook of child psychology.* Worcester, Mass.: Clark Univer. Press, 1931; 2nd ed. rev., 1933.

Newton, N., & Newton, M. Recent trends in breast feeding: A review. *Amer. J. med. Sci.*, 1951, 221, 691–698.

Ottinger, D. R., & Simmons, J. E. Behavior of human neonates and prenatal maternal anxiety. *Psychol. Rep.*, 1964, 14, 391–394.

Ourth, L., & Brown, K. B. Inadequate mothering and disturbance in the neonatal period. *Child Develpm.*, 1961, 32, 287–295.

Pacella, B. L., & Barrera, S. E. Postural reflexes and grasp phenomena in infants. *J. Neurophysiol.*, 1940, 3, 214–218.

Parmelee, A. H. A critical evaluation of the Moro reflex. *Pediatrics*, 1964, 33, 773–778.

Parmelee, A. H., Wenner, W. H., & Schulz, H. R. Infant sleep patterns: From birth to 16 weeks of age. *J. Pediatr.*, 1964, 65, 576–582.

Pasamanick, B. A comparative study of the behavioral development of Negro infants. *J. genet. Psychol.*, 1946, 69, 3–44.

Peatman, J. G., & Higgons, R. A. Development of sitting, standing, and walking of children reared with optimal pediatric care. *Amer. J. Orthopsychiat.*, 1940, 10, 88–111.

——. Relation of infants' weight and body build to locomotor development. *Amer. J. Orthopsychiat.*, 1942, 12, 234–240.

Peiper, A. *Cerebral function in infancy and childhood.* New York: Consultants Bureau, 1963.

Peiper, A., & Isbert, W. Über die Körperstellung des Saüglings. (On body posture in the infant.) *Jb. Kinderhk.*, 1927, 115, 142.

Piaget, J. *The origins of intelligence in children.* New York: Int. Univer. Press, 1952; 2nd ed., 1965.

Polikanina, R. I. The relationship between autonomic and somatic components of a defensive conditioned reflex in premature children. *Pavlov J. high. nerv. Act.*, 1961, 11, 72–82.

Pratt, K. C. Note on the relation of temperature and humidity to the activity of young infants. *Ped. Sem.*, 1930, 38, 480–484.

——. The neonate. In C. Murchison (Ed.), *A handbook of child psychology.* (2nd ed. rev.) Worcester, Mass.: Clark Univer. Press, 1933. Pp. 163–208.

——. The effects of repeated auditory stimulation upon the activity of newborn infants. *J. genet. Psychol.*, 1934, 44, 96–116. (a)

——. Generalization and specificity of the plantar response in newborn infants. The reflexogenous zone: I. Differential sensitivity and effector-segment participation according to the area of stimulation. *J. genet. Psychol.*, 1934, 44, 265–300. (b)

——. Generalization and specificity of the plantar response in newborn infants. The reflexogenous zone: II. Segmental patterning of responses. *J. genet. Psychol.*, 1934, 45, 22–38. (c)

——. Generalization and specificity of the plantar response in newborn infants. The reflexogenous zone: III. The effects of the physiological state upon sensitivity, segmental participation, and segmental patterning. *J. genet. Psychol.*, 1934, 45, 371–389. (d)

Pratt, K. C., Nelson, A. K., & Sun, K. H. The behavior of the newborn infant. *Ohio State Univer. Stud. Contrib. Psychol.*, 1930, No. 10.

Prechtl, H. F. R. The directed head turning response and allied movements of the human baby. *Behavior*, 1958, 13, 212–242.

———, *The neurological examination of the full term newborn infant.* London: Spastics Soc. Med. Educ. & Info. Unit, 1964.

Prechtl, H. F. R., & Dijkstra, J. Neurological diagnosis of cerebral injury in the new-born. In B. S. Berge (Ed.), *Prenatal Care.* Gröningen, The Netherlands: P. Noordhoff, 1960. Pp. 222–231.

Redfield, J. C. A preliminary report of dark adaptation in young infants. *Child Develpm.*, 1937, 8, 263–269.

Reynolds, M. M., & Mallay, H. The sleep of young children. *J. genet. Psychol.*, 1933, 43, 322–351.

Reynolds, M. M. Sleep of young children in 24 hour nursery school. *Ment. Hyg.*, 1935, 19, 602–609.

Rheingold, H. L., & Stanley, W. Developmental psychology. *Annu. Rev. Psychol.*, 1963, 14, 1–28.

Rhodes, A. A comparative study of motor abilities of Negroes and whites. *Child Develpm.*, 1937, 8, 369–371.

Richards, T. W. The relationship between bodily and gastric activity of newborn infants. I. Correlation and influence of time since feeding. *Hum. Biol.*, 1936, 8, 368–380. (a)

Richards, T. W. The relationship between bodily and gastric activity of newborn infants. II. Simultaneous variations in the bodily and gastric activity of newborn infants under long-continued light stimulation. *Hum. Biol.*, 1936, 8, 381–386. (b)

Richards, T. W., & Irwin, O. C. Experimental methods used in studies on infant reactions since 1900. *Psychol. Bull.*, 1934, 31, 23–46. (a)

———. Studies in infant behavior. II. Plantar responses of infants and young children: An examination of the literature and reports of new experiments. *Univer. Iowa Stud. Child Welf.*, 1934, 11, 1–146. (b)

Richards, T. W., Newbery, H., & Fallgatter, R. Studies in fetal behavior: II. Activity of the human fetus in utero and its relation to other prenatal conditions, particularly the mother's basal metabolic rate. *Child Develpm.*, 1938, 9, 69–78.

Richmond, J. B., Grossman, H. J., & Lustman, S. L. A hearing test for newborn infants. *Pediatrics*, 1953, 11, 634–638.

Richter, C. P. High electrical resistance of the skin of newborn infants and its significance. *Amer. J. Dis. Child.*, 1930, 40, 18–26.

Roberts, E. Thumb and finger sucking in relation to feeding in early infancy. *Amer. J. Dis. Child.*, 1944, 68, 7–8.

Roberts, K. E., & Schoellkopf, J. Eating, sleeping, and elimination practices of a group of two and one-half-year-old children. IV. Elimination practices: Bladder. *Amer. J. Dis. Child.*, 1951, 82, 144–152.

Roffwarg, H. P., Muzio, J. N., & Dement, W. C. Ontogenetic development of the human sleep-dream cycle. *Science*, 1966, 152, 604–618.

Rosenblith, J. F. The modified Graham behavior test for neonates: Test-retest reliability, normative data, and hypotheses for future work. *Biol. Neonat.*, 1961, 3, 174–192.

Salk, L. The effects of the normal heartbeat sound on the behavior of the newborn infant: Implications for mental health. *World ment. Hlth.*, 1960, 12, 168–175.

———. Mothers' heartbeat as imprinting stimulus. *Trans. New York Acad. Sci.*, 1962, 24, 753–763.

Sameroff, A. J. An apparatus for recording sucking and controlling feeding in the first days of life. *Psychon. Sci.*, 1965, 2, 355–356.

Sanford, H. N. The Moro reflex in the newborn. *Amer. J. Dis. Child.*, 1933, 46, 337–340.

Schmeidler, G. R. The relation of fetal activity to the activity of the mother. *Child Develpm.*, 1941, 12, 63–68.

Sears, R. R., Maccoby, E., & Levin, H. *Patterns of child rearing*. Evanston, Ill.: Row, Peterson, 1957.

Sears, R. R., & Wise, G. W. Relation of cup-feeding in infancy to thumb-sucking and the oral drive. *Amer. J. Orthopsychiat.*, 1950, 20, 123–138.

Shapiro, H. The development of walking in a child. *J. genet. Psychol.*, 1962, 100, 221–226.

Sherman, M., & Sherman, I. C. *The process of human behavior*. New York: Norton, 1929.

Sherman, M., Sherman, I., & Flory, C. D. Infant behavior. *Comp. Psychol. Monogr.*, 1936, 12, No. 59.

Shinn, A. V. A study of sleep habits of two groups of preschool children, one in Hawaii and one on the mainland. *Child Develpm.*, 1932, 159–166.

Shirley, M. M. *The first two years, a study of twenty-five babies. Vol. I. Postural and locomotor development*. Minneapolis: Univer. Minn. Press, 1931.

———. Development of immature babies during their first two years. *Child Develpm.*, 1938, 9, 347–360.

Skinner, B. F. The phylogeny and ontogeny of behavior. *Science*, 1966, 153, 1205–1213.

Smith, M., Lecker, G., Dunlap, J. W., & Cureton, E. E. The effects of race, sex, and environment on the age at which children walk. *Ped. Sem.*, 1930, 38, 489–498.

Solomons, G., & Solomons, H. C. Factors affecting motor performance in four-month-old infants. *Child Develpm.*, 1964, 35, 1283–1296.

Sontag, L. W., & Nelson, V. L. Monozygotic dichorionic triplets: Part II. Behavior of a set of identical triplets. *J. genet. Psychol.*, 1933, 42, 406–422.

Sontag, L. W., & Richards, T. W. Studies in fetal behavior: I. Fetal heart rate as a behavior indicator. *Monogr. Soc. Res. Child Develpm.*, 1938, 3.

Sontag, L. W., & Wallace, R. F. The effect of cigarette smoking during pregnancy upon the fetal heart rate. *Amer. J. Obstet. & Gynecol.*, 1935, 29, 3–8.

Stechler, G. Newborn attention as affected by medication during labor. *Science*, 1964, 144, 315–317.

Stott, L., & Ball, R. S. Infant and preschool mental tests: Review and evaluation. *Monogr. Soc. Res. Child Develpm.*, 1965, 30, 1–151.

Strauss, H. Das Zusammenschiecken. (The startle pattern.) *J. Psychol. u. Neur.*, 1929, 39, 111–231.

Stubbs, E., & Irwin, O. C. Laterality of limb movements in four newborn infants. *Child Develpm.*, 1933, 4, 358–359.

Stutsman, R. *Mental measurement of preschool children*. New York: World Book, 1931.

Taylor-Jones, L. A study of the behavior of the newborn. *Amer. J. Med. Sci.*, 1927, 174, 357–362.

Terman, L. M., & Merrill, M. A. *Measuring intelligence*. Boston: Houghton Mifflin, 1937.

Thomas, A., Chess, S., Birch, H., & Hertzig, P. H. A longitudinal study of primary reaction patterns in children. *Comp. Psychiat.*, 1960, 1, 103–112.

Traisman, A. S., & Traisman, H. S. Thumb and finger-sucking: a study of 2,650 infants and children. *J. Pediatr.*, 1958, 52, 566–572.

Turkewitz, G., Gordon, E. W., & Birch, H. G. Head turning in the human neonate: A spontaneous pattern. *J. genet. Psychol.*, 1965, 107, 143–158.

Uklonskaya, R., Puri, B., Choudhuri, N., Dang, L., & Kumar, R. Development of static and psychomotor functions of infants in the first year of life in New Delhi. *Indian J. Child Hlth.*, 1960, 9.

Updegraff, R. Preferential handedness in young children. *J. exp. Educ.*, 1932, 1, 134–139.

———. The correspondence between handedness and eyedness in young children. *J. genet. Psychol.*, 1933, 42, 490–492.

Valentine, W. L., & Wagner, I. Relative arm motility in the newborn infant. *Ohio State Univer. Contr. Psychol.*, 1934, No. 12, 53–68.

Waggoner, R. W., & Ferguson, W. G. The development of the plantar reflex in children. *Arch. Neurol. Psychiat.*, 1930, 23, 619–633.

Wagner, I. F. The establishment of a criterion of depth of sleep in the newborn infant. *J. genet. Psychol.*, 1937, 51, 17–59.

———. The body jerk of the neonate. *J. genet. Psychol.*, 1938, 52, 65–77.

Wagner, M. A. Day and night sleep in a group of young orphanage children. *J. genet. Psychol.*, 1933, 42, 442–459.

Wagoner, L. C., & Armstrong, E. M. The motor control of children as involved in the dressing process. *Ped. Sem.*, 1928, 35, 84–97.

Walters, C. E. Reliability and comparison of four types of fetal activity and of total activity. *Child Develpm.*, 1964, 35, 1249–1256.

Walters, C. E. Prediction of postnatal development from fetal activity. *Child Develpm.*, 1965, 36, 801–808.

Watson, J B. *Psychology from the standpoint of a behaviorist.* Philadelphia: Lippincott, 1919.

———. *Behaviorism.* New York: The People's Institute Publishing Co., 1925.

Weech, A. A., & Campbell, R. V. D. The relation between the development of behavior and the pattern of physical growth. *Child Develpm.*, 1941, 12, 237–240.

Weiss, L. A. Differential variations in the amount of activity of newborn infants under continuous light and sound stimulation. In O. C. Irwin, L. A. Weiss, & E. M. Stubbs (Eds.), *Studies in infant behavior. I. Univer. Iowa Stud. Child Welf.*, 1934, 9, 9–74.

White, B. L., Castle, P., & Held, R. Observations on the development of visually-directed reaching. *Child Develpm.*, 1964, 35, 349–364.

White, M. R. Some factors affecting the night sleep of children. *Child Develpm.*, 1931, 2, 234–235.

Wiener, G. Psychologic correlates of premature birth: A review. *J. nerv. ment. Dis.*, 1962, 134, 129–144.

Williams, J. R., & Scott, R. B. Growth and development of Negro infants: IV. Motor development and its relationship to child rearing practices in two groups of Negro infants. *Child Develpm.*, 1953, 24, 103–121.

Wooley, H. T. Eating, sleeping, and elimination. In C. Murchison (Ed.), *A handbook of child psychology.* Worcester, Mass.: Clark Univer. Press, 1931.

Yang, D. C. Neurologic status of newborn infants on first and third day of life. *Neurology*, 1962, 12, 72–77.

Yarrow, L. J. The relationship between nutritive sucking experiences in infancy and non-nutritive sucking in childhood. *J. genet. Psychol.*, 1954, 84, 149–162.

———. Maternal deprivation: Toward an empirical and conceptual reevaluation. *Psychol. Bull.*, 1961, 58, 459–490.

Chapter 4

Conditioning

and

Learning

YVONNE BRACKBILL

and

M. M. KOLTSOVA

Preparation of this chapter was supported in part by NSF grant GB-4784 and USPHS grant K5-MH-5925 to the first author.

An account of learning is fundamental to any account of child development. The infant's genetic makeup will ultimately set the limits on the extent to which his behavior is modifiable, but at this time of life his susceptibility to the effects of environment, of experience, of *learning* is enormous. Indeed, it is larger during infancy and early childhood than it will be at any time in the future, for learning sets its own limits, too; by the age of eighteen months the human being has long since ceased to be just any infant, but is a Scandinavian or a Bulgarian infant who has already learned to be intolerant of warmth or of cold, who resonates to Germanic syntax or Slavic morphology, who can effectively manipulate the adults in his immediate family.

This chapter deals with learning—the principal way in which the human being comes to cope with the environment in which he finds himself and, in turn, to be molded by it. In accordance with academic tradition, our discussion of learning is divided into classical and instrumental studies of conditioning and learning.

Definitions of Learning and Conditioning

There is no standard definition of *learning* that is acceptable to all who use the term, principally because of the breadth of the process that must be defined. According to the most general definition, learning is reflected in changes of behavior that result from training, practice, or "experience." This definition is meant to exclude behavior changes due to genetic determination, maturation, or physical growth as well as those resulting from transitory changes in psychological or physiological states such as depression, sensory adaptation, or drug states.

Conditioning is easier to define, since it has traditionally been considered the simplest form of learning and has been specified in terms of experimental methodology. The first part of this chapter is taken up with classical conditioning—perhaps the simplest form of conditioning in infancy and certainly the first form of infant learning to have undergone investigation in the laboratory (Bogen, 1907; Krasnogorskii, 1907; Mateer, 1918). The second part of the chapter is devoted to instrumental learning.

Classical Conditioning

THE SENSORY ANALYZERS: THEIR FUNCTION AND DEVELOPMENT IN PAVLOVIAN THEORY

At the time Pavlov began his work on conditioned reflexes just before the turn of the century, the pioneering work on the reflex arc had already been done by such scientists as Magendie and Bell, Fritsch and Hitzig, Sherrington, Sechenov, and others. In fact, it was the results of these studies—or more particularly, their limitations, as Pavlov saw them— that provided both the impetus and direction for Pavlov's work. He was not interested in the response or efferent side of the reflex arc; that had already been studied enough, he thought. The really virgin territory for investigation was on the afferent side, and, especially, the middle part of the reflex arc, the cerebral connections between afferent and efferent. Thus it was that Pavlov took as his basic research interest the study of the sensory analyzing functions of the central nervous system. He called this the study of the *nervous analyzers*, but the term *sensory analyzers* or simply *analyzers* is more commonly used today.

Sensory analyzers, then, include both central parts and afferent or peripheral (in the sense of noncentral) parts. The peripheral parts are the afferent receptors that select the one type of physical energy to which they are singularly sensitive and that will initiate a nerve impulse in them. For example, the visual analyzer selects, from the entire electromagnetic spectrum, only those energies that fall between about 350 and 770 millimicrons. The central parts of the sensory analyzers are the ". . . sensory nerve cells which lie at the central termination of the nerve fibers" (Pavlov, 1960, p. 110). These central parts select [1] the effective stimuli from all the potentially effective stimuli. In general, *effective* stimuli are those that have biological significance for the organism. For example, of the many sounds that are received by the peripheral receptors of a sleeping mother during the night, only the sounds made by her infant awaken her. Although the peripheral components of the sensory analyzers are more "basic" in phylogenetic terms, the central components are more important, and complex, in higher organisms. The

---

1. Notice the term *select* in describing both peripheral and central components of analyzer activity. Pavlov was a very dynamic and forceful man, and there is nothing passive about any aspect of his theory. It is particularly well to remember this about such a term as *inhibition*, which in English is often used in such a way as to connote passivity. Pavlov meant *inhibition*, and *disinhibition* as well, to be altogether as active processes as excitation.

central parts are able to synthesize stimulus components into a whole as well as to analyze stimulation into its component parts. Moreover, they change functionally according to the experiences the organism acquires, i.e., in accordance with his repertoire of conditioned connections. As Pavlov said, ". . . only with the progressive development of the analyzing activity of the nervous system is the organism enabled to multiply the complexity of its contacts with the external world and to achieve a more and more varied and exact adaptation to external conditions" (Pavlov, 1960, p. 111).

In order to investigate analyzing functions experimentally, Pavlov made use of two methodological tools. The first of these was the orienting or investigatory reflex, a reflex that is not specific to any one sensory modality. The orienting reflex consists behaviorally in the organism's orienting itself physically toward the source of stimulation; it is usually accompanied by interruption of ongoing activity. For example, imagine a young infant in a quiet room who is sucking on a nursing bottle. A pencil is tapped on the table nearby; the infant immediately stops sucking, and his eyes search for the source of stimulation. In a few seconds, he resumes sucking (Bronshtein & Petrova, 1952). We can infer from this orienting response that the infant's auditory analyzer has selected the tapping sound, analyzed it, and triggered an afferent response appropriate to the results of that analysis.

The orienting reflex, however, has certain disadvantages as a tool in studying the analyzers. The chief disadvantage is that it extinguishes very rapidly with repeated presentations of the same stimulus, e.g., if one continues to tap the pencil, the infant will, in no time at all, continue to suck placidly, just as if he could not hear the tapping sound. (Behaviorally, extinction of the orienting response is equivalent to the American "habituation" and "adaptation.") At this point, in order to reinstate the orienting reflex, one must either introduce a new sound or wait a while before reintroducing the old one.

The more robust and generally satisfactory method that Pavlov adopted and developed for studying analyzer function is the conditioned reflex. The starting point for this procedure is an *unconditioned reflex* (UCR) that is always elicited by an *unconditioned stimulus* (UCS) but never elicited by the particular neutral or indifferent stimulus that one intends to use as a *conditional stimulus* (CS).[2] For example, in a young infant, the Babinski reflex is always elicited by firmly stroking the sole of the foot; it is never elicited by an auditory stimulus of mild intensity, e.g., a complex tone of 65 db. Now, however, we begin presenting the tone (CS) just before we begin stroking the sole of the foot (UCS). After a number of these temporally paired combinations we will find that presentation of the CS alone, unaccompanied by stroking, gives rise to the reflex (Malakhovskaia, 1959). At this point the response is properly termed a *conditioned reflex* (CR).

Pavlov was not interested in the conditioned reflex or any other

2. This explanation is something of an oversimplification, but qualifications will be added later on.

behavior for its own sake. For him, behavior was merely a means of making inferences about the physiological analyzing processes that determined the behavior. In the case of a simple CR, the fundamental concept in Pavlov's hypothetical physiology is *excitation*. Excitation is a cortical process that arises in response to afferent stimulation and that impels the organism to respond. Excitation arises at the point of cerebral representation of a particular sensory analyzer and *irradiates* or spreads throughout the brain, diminishing in strength with increasing distance from that point. Excitation at those points at which *unconditional* stimuli and responses are represented in the brain is relatively strong. Excitation at those points at which *conditional* stimuli are represented is relatively weak—at least initially. The mechanism underlying CR formation, according to Pavlov, is that the weaker excitation resulting from the initially neutral CS is drawn toward the locus of stronger excitation resulting from application of the UCS and becomes concentrated there. There is now a closed brain path from the point of C⁻ excitation to the point of UCS-UCR excitation, so that the former activates the latter.

There are several operational ways by which Pavlovian physiologists gauge the strength of excitation. Strong excitation is manifested behaviorally by (a) a strong UCR or CR; (b) a short latency period preceding either the UCR or CR; (c) the rapid elaboration, i.e., formation, of a CR; (d) the elaboration of a CR that is stable, i.e., occurs with maximum frequency over a series of test trials; and (e) the elaboration of a CR such that the action of the effector involved is clear-cut or "well-expressed."

Another name that Pavlov coined for the CR is *temporary connection*. This term emphasizes that certain contingencies are involved if the artificial connection between conditional stimulus and conditioned response is to be maintained, that the connection is not automatically stable nor immutable. The principal contingency is the extent to which the temporary connection is reinforced after its elaboration. If the UCS is no longer presented along with the CS, the CR begins to decrease in in frequency of occurrence, to decrease in amplitude, and to increase in latency until it finally *extinguishes* altogether.

Pavlov considered that extinction was one behavioral manifestation of a physiological process that he termed *inhibition*. The net behavioral effect of inhibition is to keep the organism from responding, just as its reciprocal process, excitation, impels the organism to respond. Thus, it has a definite protective function for the organism and is the key to homeostatic maintenance. Like excitation, inhibition is an active process (the Russian word for inhibition, *tormozhenie*, literally means "braking" or "putting a brake on"). Inhibition is also like excitation in that it irradiates over the cortex before becoming concentrated in one limited area; in the case of extinction, inhibition becomes concentrated in the area that was previously the focus of excitation from the conditional stimulus.

There are also certain differences between excitation and inhibition.

One of them is that inhibition is a less stable process than excitation (which led Pavlov to conclude that it represents a higher evolutionary process than excitation). Another difference between these two basic processes is that whereas excitation appears in but a single form, there is more than one form in which inhibition is manifested. The major forms of inhibition are external inhibition and internal inhibition. (Pavlov felt that these were probably one and the same process, differing only in behavioral manifestations.)

External inhibition is unlearned or innate response inhibition to unusual or new stimuli. It results from the depression of one reflex by another which is biologically of greater potential importance at the moment of its action. It is called "external" inhibition since its cause lies outside the reflex arc that is being inhibited. We have already given an example of external inhibition, without labeling it as such, i.e., if one presents a brief auditory stimulus to an infant when he is sucking rhythmically on a bottle he will orient toward this stimulus, and he will also stop sucking momentarily. The sucking response, in other words, has been externally inhibited (Bronshtein & Petrova, 1952). In the same way, external inhibition can take place during conditioning when something in the environment, external to the organism and foreign to the conditioning procedure, disturbs the course of conditioning, and the CR disappears or is disrupted for a brief period of time.

Internal inhibition occurs during conditioning as a result of altering the usual relationship between CS and UCS. There are several forms in which internal inhibition may appear. These are (1) extinction; (2) differentiation or discrimination; (3) conditional inhibition; and (4) delay, or the delayed reflex. *Extinction* has already been described; in this case the UCS is permanently withheld from further presentations of the CS. *Differentiation* occurs when the experimenter, having elaborated a CR to one CS, introduces a second CS that is typically similar but not identical to the first CS. He continues to reinforce the first or positive CS whenever it is presented, but does not reinforce the second or negative CS when it is presented. At first the CR occurs when either CS appears, i.e., the CR generalizes to the new CS. With successive trials, however, the response to CS— begins to extinguish, since it is not being reinforced. Finally, the point is reached at which the infant consistently responds to the CS+ and consistently fails to respond to the CS—. In other words, he has differentiated the two stimuli or discriminated between them.

Conditional inhibition occurs when E, having elaborated a CR to one CS, adds a second stimulus to the first—either simultaneously or just prior to the appearance of the established CS. The immediate effect of this arrangement is to inhibit the appearance of the CR. To establish a *delayed* reflex, E first elaborates a CR to some CS, e.g., a tone. He then gradually increases the length of time between the onset of the CS and the arrival of the UCS. Under this arrangement the usual appearance of the CR shortly after the onset of CS becomes inhibited, and the CR gradually moves forward in time until it appears just prior to CS offset. At present there is still no work to speak of, besides Koltsova's (1952), on either conditional inhibition or delayed reflexes in infants.

Aside from these forms of internal inhibition, Pavlov also concluded that ". . . internal inhibition and sleep are fundamentally one and the same process" (Pavlov, 1928, p. 307); ". . . *inhibition* is a partial, fragmentary, narrowly limited, strictly localized sleep, confined within definite boundaries under the influence of the opposing process —that of excitation; sleep on the contrary is an inhibition which has spread over a great section of the cerebrum, over the entire hemispheres and even into the lower lying midbrain" (Pavlov, 1928, p. 311).

Pavlov concluded that inhibition is caused by very weak stimulation, very strong stimulation, and unusual stimuli of any strength (in the cases of external inhibition and conditional inhibition).

A state of inhibition in the cortical cells may be produced by either very weak or by very strong stimuli; only with stimuli of average strength may the cells continue for a long time in a state of excitation without passing over into different degrees of inhibition. With weak stimuli the process of excitation passes over to inhibition only slowly, but with strong stimuli the change is rapid. These degrees of strength of stimulus are, of course, relative, i.e., a strong stimulus for one type of nervous system may be only of average strength for another type (Pavlov, 1928, p. 367).

THE IMPORTANCE OF THE CONDITIONAL STIMULUS IN PAVLOVIAN THEORY

Pavlovian theorists have always insisted that the important element in conditioning is the conditional stimulus—a position that is consonant with Pavlov's unqualified emphasis on sensory analyzing function rather than on effector function. At first Pavlov maintained that the strength of a CR was attributable exclusively to the strength of the CS used in its conditioning. Later, he recognized that the relationship between CS and UCS is important for the course of conditioning. For one thing, the intensity of the UCS must exceed the intensity of the CS for conditioning to occur. For another, the CS, with its resulting weaker excitation, must precede the arrival of the UCS. Given the reverse temporal order ("backward conditioning"), it is unlikely that conditioning will occur.

In a typical experimental arrangement—and the one most often used in infant conditioning—the CS begins first and then overlaps temporally with the UCS. (This temporal arrangement is sometimes called *actual conditioning.*) However, a CR can also be formed when the offset of the CS precedes the onset of the UCS; this is called *trace conditioning,* since the conditional signal is no longer actually present at the time reinforcement is delivered. Although trace conditioning in infancy has yet to be investigated systematically, it is much more nearly paradigmatic of all conditioning that occurs under natural circumstances, particularly with development from infancy to childhood. (Conditioning that occurs under natural circumstances is called *natural conditioning.* The counterpart of natural conditioning is *artificial conditioning.*)

Pavlov and his collaborators also found, from their extensive investigations of the role of conditional stimuli in sensory analyzing function, that certain modalities yield characteristically weak CSs, no matter what the absolute intensity of stimulation. In addition, according to those who followed Pavlov, certain modalities are developmentally slower than others in analyzing stimuli effectively enough to allow CR formation. (See Table 4.1.)

The most outstanding characteristic of conditional stimuli as far as human beings are concerned is the extent to which they become symbolic. Stimuli of all kinds may be divided into three levels of denotative abstractness. At the most primitive, and earliest developmental, level there are reflexes that are triggered by unlearned or hereditarily determined, *unconditioned stimuli.* As the infant develops, other stimuli, initially ineffective, become associated with these reflex arcs through conditioning. These *direct* conditional stimuli—the sound of approaching footsteps, the sight of mother's face, and so on—signal to the infant the imminent action of a UCS. This level, one of direct action by conditional stimuli on the sensory analyzers, is called the *first signal system.* The multiple couplings that result from linking large numbers of direct conditional stimuli to the effector components of unconditioned reflexes is the first basis in man—and the only basis in nonhuman animals—for functional adaptation to the environment.

In human beings, however, there is a higher functional level of stimulation—one composed of language signals. These *second signal system* stimuli do not act directly on the sensory analyzers but indirectly, by signaling CSs of the first signal system. That is to say, it is the *meaning* of a word that has signal significance, not its physical characteristics as an auditory or visual stimulus (Koltsova, 1949, 1956b).

Second signal system stimuli are acquired through *higher order conditioning,* a procedure whereby a well-established CS serves as UCS. Specifically, after a first order signal has been well established as a CS, its continued association with an appropriate verbal signal serves to reinforce the verbal signal as a second order CS, so that the chain of elicitation becomes: second order, verbal signal → first order, direct signal → CR. By means of these second signal system connections, the links between the human organism and his environment become enormously varied and complicated, allowing remarkably precise adaptation to the demands of his real world.

INDIVIDUAL DIFFERENCES IN PAVLOV'S THEORY

A primary goal among American experimenters when planning research is to reduce to the maximum extent, variance due to between-subject differences, and the tacitly understood policy when, despite all, individual differences in results do appear, is to ignore the fact. On the other hand, Soviet physiologists, Pavlov among them, have always stressed the individual differences that appear in the results of their studies. As a matter of fact, this is much more a part of the Russian tradition than is the use of central tendency measures to describe results. Pavlov never failed to be impressed by the behavioral differences among his dogs that appeared in both experimental and extraexperimental situations. (The same dogs, of course, were used for a great many experiments, so that Pavlov and his collaborators were well acquainted with the "personalities" and behavioral dispositions of each of them.) After several years' work on the conditioned reflex, Pavlov had observed a great many dogs in a great many situations, and it seemed to him that the individual differences among them were classifiable into types on the basis of three criteria relating to the constitutionally determined status of excitation and inhibition. These criteria were the degree of balance between excitation and inhibition, i.e., the extent to which one habitually predominated over the other; the strength of the two processes; and the mobility of the two processes, i.e., the ease with which a change in excitation or inhibition can be induced.

Pavlov agreed with Hippocrates that there seem to be four major temperamental types. At the extremes are the unbalanced types: the highly excitable organism, corresponding to Hippocrates' *choleric,* and the overly inhibited type, corresponding to Hippocrates' *melancholic.* In between are two types whose nervous systems are both strong and well-balanced but differ in respect to mobility. In the *sanguine* type, excitation and inhibition are relatively mobile processes; in the *phlegmatic* type these processes are inert or rigid, i.e., resistant to change.

Although the temperamental factors underlying individual differences in the conditioning of infants and children have never really been the focus of much systematic research in the Soviet Union, the reader should understand that temperament plays an important though largely unpublicized role as a background variable in infant conditioning studies —in the speculative thinking giving rise to the problem under investigation, the formulation of procedure, the selection of subjects, and the interpretation of results. In their conceptualizations, Soviet physiologists think not so much in terms of type as in terms of the criteria on which the types are based. One child is thought of as having a strong, well-balanced nervous system, another as being highly excitable, and so on

PSEUDOCONDITIONING CONTROLS

Most of the fine points of conditioning methodology are specific to the particular CS-UCS parameters used in any conditioning procedure and will be taken up, as appropriate, in later sections. The problem of pseudoconditioning, however, is one that is general to all conditioning procedures. Because of its generality—and its importance—we will discuss controls for pseudoconditioning as a separate issue at this point.

"Pseudoconditioning" refers to experimental outcomes that appear to reflect true conditioning but that actually reflect procedural artifacts which mimic conditioning in their effects. The most efficient way to describe and illustrate pseudoconditioning effects is by way of describing the procedures that may be used to control for their occurrence. Although most of the examples will be drawn from classical conditioning methods, the reader is reminded that the same general principles hold for instrumental conditioning procedures as well. (For examples of classical and instrumental studies using extensive pseudoconditioning controls, see Weisberg, 1963, and Kaye, 1966.)

The problem of pseudoconditioning controls is typically discussed in the abstract, as it were, without reference to such specific factors as the particular response being conditioned or the particular experimental design being used. The first four controls that will be discussed represent the abstract approach to the problem of pseudoconditioning. The next three represent less publicized, but more old-fashioned or common-sense approaches to control for pseudoconditioning.

PRESENTATION OF THE CS ALONE

This is a control for sensitization to the CS—in other words, a control for the possibility that the mere presentation of the CS alone will produce the same behavioral effects as the presentation of the CS followed by the UCS. In order to have a suitable comparison, the number of CS presentations for the control and experimental groups should be equal. In addition, for this pseudoconditioning control as for those that follow, the two groups should be matched on any characteristics that are potentially pertinent to conditioning—age, average length of interstimulus interval, and so on. If conditioning has been a real phenomenon for the experimental group, continued presentation of the CS alone, by comparison, has no significant effect on the elicitation of the UCR in the control subjects.

In general practice, even if this control is not used in a particular study, it is the custom to pretest the CS on each infant, prior to accepting him as an experimental subject. Hopefully, and theoretically, the CS is initially neutral and will not elicit the UCR at all. Every once in a while, however, one comes across a particular infant in whom, for unknown reasons, the CS does elicit a UCR. More typically, however, the CS initially elicits an orienting response; this extinguishes after a few repeated presentations of the CS.

PRESENTATION OF THE UCS ALONE

This is a control for sensitization to the UCS, and is altogether analogous to the CS sensitization control just described, including the need for test trials to CS only. In practice, however, it is probably true that the need to use this control is more limited, arising chiefly in connection with the use of intense, noxious reinforcement in defense conditioning. Electric shock is the prime example of a UCS that demands such a sensitization control. (See, for example, Wickens & Wickens, 1940.)

RANDOM PRESENTATIONS OF CS AND UCS

This procedure is a combination of the two controls just described. The rationale underlying it is that conditioning will not occur unless CS and UCS are presented in proper temporal arrangement. Under this control procedure, both exeprimental and control subjects receive the same number of CS and UCS presentations; however, in the case of the control subjects, the temporal programming for CS administrations is essentially independent of that for UCS administrations. Note that if pseudoconditioning effects do appear, one cannot decide on the basis of this procedure alone whether to lay the blame on the CS, on the UCS, or on both stimuli, since their presentation has been confounded.

BACKWARD CONDITIONING

Under this control procedure, the UCS is presented before the CS —a temporal order under which, presumably, conditioning can rarely if ever take place. If "conditioning" effects do appear, they are likely to be sensitization effects, but again, attribution to either CS or UCS is impossible, since the two stimuli have been confounded in presentation.

USE OF A UCR OF RARE NATURAL OCCURRENCE

If one took the trouble to do so, one could rank order all responses in the infant's natural behavioral repertoire along a continuum of frequency of occurrence. For a young infant, extension of the big toes and fanning of the small toes (common components of the Babinski reflex) would be near the low-frequency end of the continuum, while sucking and associated mouth movements would be on the high-frequency end of the continuum. Hence, the one reflex may be conditioned against a background of essentially zero occurrence (Malakhovskaia, 1959), whereas conditioning of the other reflex demands at least the use of a difference score measure (unconditioned frequency minus conditioned frequency of occurrence, e.g., Kantrow, 1937) if not an extra group to check the possibility that sensitization effects and unconditioned response frequency may increase together.

USE OF COMPLEX EXPERIMENTAL DESIGNS

In general, the more simple the experimental design used to study conditioning, the greater the need for a standard pseudoconditioning control; the more complex the design, the less such a control is needed. To illustrate this, consider the question: Are visual stimuli effective reinforcers of a given operant response in four-month-olds? The skeleton design needed to answer this question is a single comparison of operant level vs. conditioning performance for a single group of subjects. The direction of difference for the single comparison can be predicted, but still, there is ample room in which to make a Type I error, and, hence, ample need for whatever pseudoconditioning controls will help decrease the probability of a Type I error. Note, however, that the complexity of this design can be increased. For example, one might add an extinction procedure, thus yielding two comparisons, or one might elaborate upon this second design such that during a performance period following conditioning, the total group is divided into thirds: one third maintained on continuous reinforcement, one third switched to a variable ratio schedule, and one third switched to a fixed ratio schedule. Now there are six separate directional predictions—three mean response rates that increase as a function of conditioning and three that decrease as a function of extinction—and, in addition, there are two rank order predictions for response rate under performance and extinction, e.g., during performance, response rate under fixed ratio should be higher than that under variable ratio reinforcement which, in turn, should be higher than that under continuous reinforcement. If all these predictions are upheld, only a confirmed disbeliever would demand another form of pseudoconditioning control before agreeing with the conclusion that a visual stimulus can function effectively as a reinforcer.

REPLICATION

All other things being equal, the more often a particular conditional stimulus (or response or reinforcement) has undergone successful investigation in previous research, the less need there is to combine its use in present research with a control for sensitization or other pseudoconditioning effects. The first person to demonstrate conditioned heart rate in infants may well want to include one or more controls for pseudoconditioning, but no one would want to do so in current research on, say, instrumentally conditioned vocalization or classically conditioned sucking by way of questioning whether these responses can "really" be conditioned.

THE CONDITIONAL STIMULUS IN EARLY CLASSICAL CONDITIONING

DIFFERENTIAL DEVELOPMENT OF THE SENSORY ANALYZERS

As far as infant conditioning is concerned, the most important question to be asked about the stimuli that are potential activators of the various sensory analyzers concerns their relative effectiveness as conditional stimuli. There are several aspects of this question to be considered. One such is the matter of what we will call "stimulus saliency." To illustrate, there is an obvious advantage in the use of some types of stimuli over others in the extent to which they compel the subject to respond—or in the extent to which the subject can avoid them. For example, there is not much a child can do to avoid hearing an auditory stimulus, but he can avoid seeing visual stimuli by turning away from the source of stimulation or by closing his eyes.

Another consideration in choosing stimuli for infant conditioning studies concerns the extent to which the different sensory analyzers may mature at different rates. For many years Soviet physiologists have held that there is a definite developmental sequence in which conditioned responses may be established during infancy that is determined by the sensory modality of the CS used. Denisova and Figurin reported in 1929 that CRs to auditory stimuli appeared somewhat earlier than CRs to visual stimuli, and Kasatkin (1935) subsequently confirmed this. Since 1935, other sensory analyzers have been added to this developmental order of conditionability (Kasatkin, 1948, 1952a, 1957). The version

Table 4.1A—Developmental Sequence of Conditionability as a Function of Type of Conditional Stimulus. Ages appear as days (d) or months (m). The entries are based on Professor Kasatkin's estimates, personal communication, 1960.

		SENSORY ANALYZERS					
		Vestibular	Auditory	Tactile	Olfactory	Taste	Visual
		E.g. change of body position	E.g., complex, 65 db tone	E.g., tickle, sole of foot	E.g., oil of roses or lavender	E.g., 5% sugar solution	E.g., colored light
Simple CR	First appearance	8d	15d to 24d	28d	28d	35d	40d
Simple CR	Semistable response	15d	40d	45d	45d	45d	2m
Simple CR	100% stable response	20–24d to 1m	35d to 2m	2m	2m	2.5m	3m

that is commonly accepted in the Soviet Union today is shown in Table 4.1.

The reader should note two points in connection with Table 4.1. First, and most important, neither Kasatkin nor any other Soviet physiologist would insist that the absolute values of the tabled entries are immutable; rather, they are convinced that there is a rank order of conditional stimulus development, that the correct rank order is as shown in Table 4.1, and that no matter what changes in absolute values of the entries might in the future result from technological improvements in methodology, the rank order will remain the same. Second, Table 4.1 lacks both *elapsed time* and *temperature* as CSs; there should probably be at the very earliest end of the developmental scale, in the case of time, and at the latest end, in the case of temperature.

The most obvious difficulty in trying to establish the validity of such a developmental ordering as shown in Table 4.1, is that which plagues any attempt at quantitative comparison of qualitative differences, since response to conditioning procedures depends upon the intensity of stimulation. How can one say that because a CR to a 70 db tone appears earlier than a CR to a yellow, 40-watt light, auditory stimuli are effective at earlier ages than visual stimuli? The one way in which to meet the challenge posed to future investigation by the contents of Table 4.1 is to regard the ordering it contains as a null hypothesis awaiting proof. Logically, all that is needed to disprove the validity of any contention that there is an immutable rank order of CS development is one set of valid results in which, for example, a CR becomes established to a gustatory or visual stimulus of any intensity within the same age limits as vestibular or auditory CRs are established. (Actually, Polikanina and Probatova [1955, 1957] did find that a light CS required fewer trials than an auditory CS to both first appearance of an anticipatory sucking CR and to semistable conditioning, although they draw the reverse conclusion.)

Other methodologies than conditioning have already supplied rea-

Table 4.1B

		Vestibular	Auditory	Tactile	Olfactory	Taste	Visual
		E.g., up-down from sideways	E.g., 1 octave higher or lower from CS+	E.g., right from left foot	E.g., roses from lavender	E.g., 1% from 5% solutions	E.g., red from green or blue
Simple Discrimination	First appearance	1m	2m	2m	2m	2.5m	3m
	Semistable discrim.	1.5m	2.5m	2.5m	2.5m	3m	3.5m
	100% stable discrim.	2m	3m	3m	3m	3m	3.5m

sons for being skeptical about the immutability or extreme importance of a CS-ordered conditionability. Consider the visual modality, for instance, which Kasatkin ranks last as an effective conditional stimulus. We know that, all things considered, the newborn infant's visual acuity is remarkably good at four days of age (Gorman, Cogan, & Gellis, 1959). We also know that, under light adaptation, brightness values for week-old infants do not differ in any discernible way from those for adults (Trincker & Trincker, 1955), and that discrimination of basic hues, with brightness held constant, is excellent at least as early as fifteen days (Chase, 1937). Given, then, the facts that shortly after birth the infant is sensitive to a variety of visual stimuli and that he can make some distinct motor response, e.g., sucking, head turning, why should it *not* be possible to condition a motor response to a visual stimulus during the first few days of life? The alternatives seem to be that either this *is* possible and its demonstration simply waits upon sufficient technological advance, or that it is *not* possible because of a developmental lag in the facility with which connections can be established between occipital and motor areas of the cortex.

TEMPORAL ARRANGEMENTS INVOLVING THE CS

In actual practice, the extent of the interval between CS and UCS onset has been subject to wide variation, ranging from one second or less (e.g., Marum, cited by Lipsitt, 1963; Lipsitt & Kaye, 1964) to seven or eight seconds (e.g., Polikanina & Probatova, 1957). As yet, no studies have been made of optimal CS-UCS interval in infant conditioning.

Some investigators prefer to begin conditioning sessions with simultaneous onset of CS and UCS and, at some point after the first day's session, to delay the onset of the UCS. Mirzoiants, for example, used simultaneous CS-UCS onset during the first day's session, and a three-second delay beginning the second day (Brackbill, 1962). Kasatkin and Levikova (1935a) and Malakhovskaia (1959) have used similar discrete changes. Polikanina (1961) and Polikanina and Probatova (1957) have described a system of progressive delay in interstimulus interval. "In the early stages of the elaboration of a protective-defensive conditioned reflex the unconditioned reinforcement was delivered in the 3rd or 5th second of action of the conditioned stimulus. The tone was switched off immediately after a reaction to the smell of ammonia developed. As the development of the conditioned reflex progressed the time before delivery of the unconditioned reinforcement was gradually increased to 10–15 seconds" (Polikanina, 1961, p. 73).

Length of CS presentation has also seen considerable variation in past studies. Some investigators have used CS presentations as long as fifteen or twenty seconds (Denisova & Figurin, 1929; Marquis, 1931; Polikanina & Probatova, 1955, 1957), whereas others have presented stimuli affecting the same analyzers for as few as two or two and one-half seconds (Morgan & Morgan, 1944; Marum, cited in Lipsitt, 1963). The length of UCS presentation—and, thereby, the temporal relation of CS offset to UCS offset—depends to a great extent upon the nature of the reinforcement. An airpuff, or even a short series of them, last no more than two or three seconds, whereas the administration of milk typically takes from ten to twenty seconds, and is, moreover, subject to greater variation from trial to trial and from individual to individual.

AUDITORY CONDITIONAL STIMULI

In infant conditioning the most frequently used type of conditional stimulus is auditory stimulation. Within this generic category, the most popular species of stimulus are buzzers, bells, metronomes, and pure tones. In most experiments, the sound is continuous from onset to offset; occasionally, intermittent stimulation is used (Bronshtein & Petrova, 1952; Polikanina & Probatova, 1955). The auditory stimulus is typically delivered at 60 or 70 db, although sounds as loud as 90 db have been used (Lipsitt & Kaye, 1964).

Kasatkin advises that, "Unless it is a focus of study, frequency per se is not so important a consideration for infant study as is complexity . . ." (Brackbill, 1962, p. 112). Although most investigators do, in fact, use a complex sound rather than a pure tone as CS, there is insufficient evidence at present to show that a complex tone is indeed a significantly more effective CS than is a pure tone. Kasatkin's advice evidently stems from a study (1953) in which he conditioned an orienting response in subjects who were 46 to 222 days old at the beginning of experimentation. The mean age at which a stable response appeared was 205 days when the CS was a pure tone of 810 cps and 151 days when the CS was produced either by an organ pipe or a bell. These two means, however, are based on Ns of only four and two, respectively.

In an unpublished dissertation, Tomka (1957) compared, among other things, the speed with which a conditioned blinking reflex was elaborated to both verbal and nonverbal stimuli differing in complexity. The stimuli were all delivered at 70 db; the verbal stimuli were tape recorded. A bell was used as CS for five children with an average age of 5.2 months at the beginning of experimentation. The first clear CR appeared after an average of nine reinforced trials, and a stable CR after one more CS-UCS combination. For a second group of eleven children, with an average age of 2.5 months, a pure tone of 1450 cps was used as CS. In this case the first clear CR appeared after 5.5 reinforced trials and a stable CR after six additional combinations. There is a difference between the two groups—in favor of the pure tone CS—only for first appearance of the CR, which is a much less reliable measure than stable conditioning. Note also that the test is a conservative one for the pure tone stimulus, since the infants in that group were younger to begin with, and younger infants generally take longer to condition.

Tomka subsequently introduced the sound of a metronome at 120 beats per minute as a differential stimulus for the infants conditioned to the bell and a tone of 396 cps as CS- for the infants conditioned to 1450 cps. Here again, there was no advantage of complex over pure sounds in terms of the number of CS- presentations to either the first differentiation or to a stable discrimination.

On the other hand, Tomka did find a difference in CS effectiveness between two *verbal* stimuli that differed in complexity—the sounds corresponding to the Russian letters a and p. (The first of these is pronounced like a broad a in English [a]. The second letter is transliterated as r, but has no exact sound equivalent in English; it is a lingual-palato-fricative sound produced by vibrating the tongue against the front palate.) The results for Tomka's most nearly comparable age groups are shown in Table 4.2. There is clearly a difference in number of trials to stable conditioning that favors the more complex vocal sound.

Table 4.2—Speed of Conditioned Blinking Reflex Formation to Verbal Stimuli Differing in Complexity

	a USED AS CS				p* USED AS CS	
N	3	5	8	5	5	7
Age in months at beginning of experiment	9.3	9.0	10.0	13.0	9.5	11.5
Number trials to first CR	12	10	13	12	7	7
Σ number trials to stable CR	28	27	33(N = 6) 49(N = 2)	32	19	19

* p in Russian is pronounced as a lingual-palato-fricative, not as r in English.

There is very little other evidence that bears directly or indirectly on the relative efficacy for infant conditioning of complex vs pure auditory stimuli and that may be regarded as conclusive. For example, one can tally failures and successes in neonatal conditioning with auditory stimuli and see that pure tone CSs predominate among the failures, whereas complex sound CSs predominate among the successes. At the same time, however, the use of aversive conditioning procedures is also predominant among the failures, whereas the successes have almost exclusively used appetitional conditioning.

Auditory Conditioning as a Diagnostic Device. The use of conditioning methods to measure the infant's perception of pure tones has recently been turned to practical use by audiologists, following the example of Bordley, Hardy, and Richter (Bordley, Hardy, & Richter, 1948; Bordley & Hardy, 1949; Hardy & Bordley, 1951, 1951–1952), who in turn may well have been inspired by the early publication in which Aldrich (1928) used a classical aversive conditioning method to determine whether a three-month-old infant was deaf.

The stimuli that are usually used nowadays in such a procedure are pure tones at 512, 1024, 2048, and 4096 cps, and the response, change in GSR following shock. This conditioning procedure, suggested originally by Bordley *et al.* in 1948, has been perpetuated without change in subsequent studies by other investigators (Barr, 1954; Goldstein, Ludwig, & Naunton, 1954; Statten & Wishart, 1956; Grings, Lowell, & Honnard, 1960, 1961), although there is no reason why this particular UCS and response need be used.

The whole procedure as described by Statten and Wishart is typically as follows.

> Our first attempt at measuring hearing is by using sound as the direct or unconditioned stimulus. Sounds are made in the ear, beginning with a 512 cycle tone at 10 decibels. The intensity is increased in 10 db steps. When the sound becomes loud enough it nearly always shows graphically, clinically or both graphically and clinically. Graphic evidence of a response appears after a delay of one to three seconds. It is a characteristic wave imposed on the continuous record of skin-resistance activity. A child tends to hesitate in his play to listen for the next sound. The intensity is then lowered by steps until the response disappears. It is raised again until it shows.
>
> When it is certain that the child hears sound, conditioning is attempted. A 512 tone well above our estimated threshold is presented. This is followed in a few seconds by a shock. If there is no graphic or clinical indication of reaction to this shock, the intensity is increased. If a child will become conditioned it usually occurs after about ten sound-shock sequences. The interval between the sequences depends upon the reaction of the child and graphic evidence that the skin-resistance is stabilizing. The usual interval is 15 seconds. When conditioning occurs the shock is omitted. It may be necessary to use it again and perhaps at a higher intensity, for reinforcement.
>
> . . . When a response to sound is evident the intensity is lowered by steps until it fails to give a response; then it is raised until the response reappears. This is considered threshold for this tone.
>
> Similar tests are made for 1024, 2048, and 4096 cycle tones. The procedure is repeated for the other ear. Many sittings may be necessary to complete the threshold levels (1956, pp. 520–521).

Although exact figures on test-retest reliability are not available, it would seem from the frequency with which audiologists have suggested averaging several tests or at least those two which disagree by not more than 5 db, that the reliability of a single test trial is not of the highest order. It also appears that reliability varies directly with age, as does the probability of success in conditioning. Factors interfering with successful conditioning include the child's resistance to having ear phones or electrodes attached to him, his unwillingness to tolerate shock, and a poorly expressed UCR. For 39 cases of children under two years of age, Statten and Wishart (1956) report 2 successful, 31 partially successful, and 6 unsuccessful attempts to condition. For 64 cases between two and five years of age, there were 5 successful, 45 partially successful, and 14 unsuccessful attempts to condition. Only after the age of five years was there a noticeable increase in the number of successfully conditioned cases.

Bordley and Hardy, in describing their UCS, have minimized the aversive character of the shock and the child's response to it. "The shock annoys but does not hurt, startles but does not traumatize" (Hardy & Bordley, 1951, 1952, p. 350). Other investigators, however, have found that many young children hold a different opinion. Statten and Wishart describe their reactions as follows:

> The galvanic shock from the Harvard inductorium produces a sensation that may be uncomfortable or painful. We attempt to make it a mere discomfort and yet it may be disturbing to a child. Some children are so upset by the initial test procedures that we find it wise to omit the shock and make our observations from the unconditioned sound response alone. If the shock is not of sufficient strength it will not produce a graphic response; if it is too strong the child will become upset and rebel. As no two children have the same pain threshold, the proper intensity must be found for each, by gradually increasing the shock until it shows graphically. Some children feel the shock intensely, as evidenced by wincing and withdrawal of the leg, with no graphic change being produced; they respond clinically. In others a response to an initial shock may be recorded graphically, but later the same shock may have no obvious effect; increasing the intensity may again produce a response, but again it may disappear (1956, p. 526).

It is largely because of the drawbacks presented by using shock as a reinforcement and GSR as a response that Dix and Hallpike (1947) invented the peep-show—a play-audiometry technique modelled along the lines of instrumental reward conditioning. (A comparison of play and GSR conditioning methods may be found in Barr, 1954.) An alternative method, as yet untried, would be for audiometrists to use a classical conditioning procedure with a reliable response and a UCS that, if not positive, is at least less noxious in character, e.g., an air puff to the eye.

VISUAL CONDITIONAL STIMULI

Although visual stimuli have been quite popular CSs in classical conditioning research, this research, in contrast to research on auditory CSs, has revealed next to nothing about the development of the visual analyzer. This is probably because, in contrast to the situation for other sensory analyzers, there are many *un*conditioned reflexes that can be used successfully and at younger age levels to assess the development of the infant's visual system and visual-motor coordination. There are, for example, no auditory reflexes in the strict sense of the term, i.e., there is nothing an infant can do with his ears to indicate that he has heard a sound. There are, however, many such unconditioned reflexes as far as the visual and visual-motor systems are concerned. The infant fixates on compelling stimulus objects; he blinks his eyes by way of indicating that he perceives an object approaching him very rapidly; he follows with nystagmoid movements the path of a moving object within his visual field; his pupils change in size in accordance with the intensity of light stimulation and also in accordance with his affective response to specific visual stimuli (Eckhard Hess, personal communication). There are also nonvisual reflexes specifically connected with the reception of visual stimuli, such as the eye-on-the-neck reflex (Trincker & Trincker, 1955). Finally, there is the fact that the receptors for visual stimuli are open to study by electroretinographic methods. Almost all of these reflexes appear before conditioning to visual stimuli appears; in addition, practically any one of them is more efficient in assessing the development of visual capacities than is conditioning.

Among the classical conditioning studies that have used visual stimuli, the most frequently encountered form of the CS is a colored light (e.g., Kasatkin & Levikova, 1935b). The point in using a colored light is less often to study color discrimination than it is to have a stimulus that is maximally distinct from the stimuli ordinarily provided by the infant's environment. Zonova (1964), however, did study color discrimination, and found conditioning to be a significantly better measure at age two months than the Bronshtein orienting-inhibition method. Examples of other types of visual CSs that have been used include three-dimensional, colored objects (Koltsova, 1956) and the sight of the experimenter's hand (Morgan & Morgan, 1944).

One of the most elaborate infant conditioning studies using visual as well as auditory CSs was carried out by Degtiar (1962) in an attempt to find the limits of generalization for various age groups of first signal system stereotypes (sequences of CRs) as opposed to second signal system stereotypes. In children of 1-8 to 3-0 years, stereotypes could be elaborated without great difficulty to visual and auditory stimuli of the first signal system (the sound of a bell, the onset of a light) as well as to the *concrete* verbal or second-signal system designations for those stimuli ("bell," "lamp"). But for these youngest subjects, conditioning did not generalize to the *general* or abstract verbal designations ("sound," "light") of the first signal system stimuli that had been used, despite the fact that all children had been taught the meaning of these abstract words—or had given evidence of knowing their meaning already—before the conditioning procedure ever began.

ELAPSED TIME AS A CONDITIONAL STIMULUS

In connection with conditioned reflex formation, one of the most interesting stimuli available for study is that arising from the discrimination of duration, of regular temporal intervals. For shorthand purposes we will call this stimulus *elapsed time*, or simply, *time*. The discrimination of elapsed time as a conditional signal is no less important than it is interesting. For example, the role of time in forming and maintaining naturally conditioned physiological responses is one of considerable biological significance for animals. The regularity or periodicity of many physiological functions, and therefore their predictability, depends on the extent to which an organism can accurately discriminate standard time intervals. Nevertheless, there has been no American research to speak of on the signal significance for humans of time in natural or laboratory conditioning. (What little Western research there has been has stemmed largely from England and France and has used phenomenological or introspective methods.)

One probable reason for the lack of attention in the United States to elapsed time as a stimulus is that, unlike other stimuli, the physiological mechanisms by which it operates are unknown. Most American specialists in sensation and perception have a strong physiological bent, and have never liked pursuing a "phantom" variable—one for which there is abundant behavioral evidence but no physiological locus. Soviet physiologists, on the other hand, have always been happiest when constructing their own hypothetical physiologies out of behavioral data. (Pavlov concluded that time perception, like the orienting response, must be nonspecific, i.e., a common property of all sensory analyzers.) In consequence, time as a conditional signal has been much more extensively investigated by physiologists in the USSR than in any other country. Still and all, most of these investigations have concerned time discrimination in lower animals; there have been relatively few studies of this function in adult human beings, and almost none in infants.

Nevertheless, it is the infant who is the best object of study in temporal conditioning: it is only at this early age level that time discrimination can be studied in its most nearly "pure" form, behaviorally as well as physiologically. Within the relatively short space of a few years, second signal system development and special environmental factors come to exercise considerable control over behavior, with the consequence that time discrimination undergoes complex and dramatic changes. Various studies done on older children and adults have shown great differences between and within individuals in time estimation as a function of such factors as socioeconomic level, amount and type of activity within the period of estimate, psychological disease process, etc.

Of the four existing studies relevant to temporal conditioning in infancy, perhaps the most interesting research is Krachkovskaia's on interoceptive conditioning of neonates to a temporal CS (1959). (It might be noted that neither Krachkovskaia nor Marquis, whose study is reviewed below, actually conceived of their studies as research in temporal conditioning.) Krachkovskaia found that by the age of eight days, infant Ss on a rigid three-hour or four-hour feeding schedule showed definite signs of a conditioned rise in leukocyte count just prior to feeding. (There was also a rise after feeding, but that can be accounted for physiologically.) When three infants previously on a three-hour schedule were changed to a four-hour schedule, the usual extinction phenomenon took place in regard to the old schedule at the same time that a new CR became established to the new schedule. That is to say, the "anticipatory" leukocytosis that had been appearing about two and three-quarter hours after feeding now gradually disappeared, to be replaced by occurrences of the same phenomenon three and three-quarter hours after feeding. Similar research had previously been conducted by Soviet physiologists on lower organisms and has been reviewed by Dmitriev and Kochigina (1959).

Additional direct evidence, although of a less clear-cut nature, can be found in a much earlier study by Dorothy Marquis (1941). Marquis measured gross motor activity in two groups of infants who were fed on a three-hour and a four-hour schedule during the first eight days of life.[3] On day nine, the first of these groups was switched to a four-hour schedule. Relatively accurate time discrimination is suggested by the great excess of activity in group I over group II during the interval between hours three and four on day nine. A subsequent study by Bystroletova (1954) confirmed but did not extend Marquis' results. None of these studies included a counterbalanced group switched from four-hour feedings to three-hour feedings.

Additional testimony, albeit indirect, bearing on the compellingly strong nature of time as a conditional stimulus comes from the fact that in designing classical conditioning studies, learning psychologists routinely and without exception use intertrial intervals of randomly varied length unless they have purposely designated time as the CS. Were one to do otherwise, by presenting, for example, a visual CS every 60 seconds, one would soon find that the CR had formed to the 60-second interval rather than to the visual stimulus.

Brackbill, Lintz, Fitzgerald, and Adams (1967) have recently found young infants to be just as competent in discriminating short time intervals (fractions of minutes) as Krachkovskaia, Marquis, and Bystroletova found babies to be in discriminating intervals of three and four hours. Their research also demonstrates that conditioning to elapsed time is not contingent on using appetitional reinforcement. The Brackbill *et al.* study is one on the conditioning of the pupillary reflex, and is reviewed in connection with that subject, later in this chapter.

SOMESTHETIC AND VESTIBULAR CONDITIONAL STIMULI

Very little systematic work exists as yet on tactual, vestibular, and proprioceptive stimulation in conditioning, although it is clear from

3. Marquis' third group, on demand feeding, is not relevant to this discussion.

several studies done outside the conditioning paradigm that newborns do respond to these stimuli. (See, for example, Irwin and Weiss' study [1934] on the effects on activity level of tactual stimulation in the form of clothing, or Lipton, Steinschneider, and Richmond's study [1960] of the effects on arousal level of proprioceptive stimulation arising from swaddling.)

In the United States, the first work to appear on tactual-kinesthetic stimulation in infant conditioning was Wenger's (1936). Of his six miniature experiments, three used tactual vibration as conditional stimuli. The stimulation was delivered by a Hull tactile vibrator which was most frequently set at 120 vibrations per second. (An apparatus for administering nonvibratory tactile stimulation has been described by Brackbill, 1962, p. 108.) This was applied to the sole of the foot ($N = 3$) in an attempt to elicit conditioned blinking (with strong light as the UCS) or to the thorax ($N = 1$) in an attempt to elicit leg withdrawal (with shock as the UCS). Some success was found in conditioning blinking to vibration by the ninth day of age when the three experimental subjects were compared to the seven control subjects, but there was no evidence of success with the single subject to whom shock was administered.

Denisova and Figurin (1929) were the first investigators to have commented on the natural conditioning of anticipatory sucking movements to proprioceptive stimulation. They observed that when babies were picked up and placed in the usual position for feeding, they began to make sucking movements in advance of having been offered the breast. Ripin's similar study with similar results followed soon thereafter (1930). Several years later, Koltsova (1952) carried out an experimental study on the development of inhibition by means of proprioceptively conditioned feeding responses. On the basis of her results, she suggested that differential inhibition to sucking could be obtained between sixteen and twenty days, extinction of such a CR at two to two and one-half months, and delayed inhibition at five months.

Vakhrameeva (1964) has converted kinesthetic stimulation into an unusual form of CS. In her study, the CR was an eyeblink to an airpuff, and the CS consisted in the experimenter's moving the infant's arm from an extended to a fully flexed position. Aside from the fact that conditioning was obtained, Vakhrameeva emphasized that during the course of conditioning, her subjects initially generalized along the lines of the conditional stimulation. In other words, although the experimenter moved only one arm of the subject, both his arms flexed in a consensual response. This stage was succeeded by a differentiated stage in which only the mechanically flexed arm moved, but this occurred only in the four oldest subjects, who ranged from seven to nine months of age by this time; differentiation did not appear in the younger subjects, who ranged from three and one-half to seven months at the end of the experiment. A study carried out by Kaye (1965) was similar to Vakhrameeva's in the use of arm flexion as a CS. In this case, the subjects were neonates, and the CR was the Babkin reflex.

TEMPERATURE AS A CONDITIONAL STIMULUS

As Usoltsev and Terekhova noted in their review of the literature on temperature as a conditional stimulus in animal experimentation:

> . . . these conditioned reflexes are established slowly, are distinguished by their great instability and are rapidly extinguished. During the experiment, the animals developed a somnolent state at the time of extinction, all the conditioned reflexes were inhibited and the unconditioned secretion of saliva was reduced. The conditioned reflexes to temperature were widely generalized, with some relation to the strength and the place of application of the stimuli, and even after 300–500 combinations of the thermal stimulus to a localized area of skin with alimentary reinforcement, the action of a thermal stimulus on other points in the skin caused conditioned reflex secretion of saliva. Differentiation of thermal stimuli was not an easy task; the formation of the first stable differentiation was particularly difficult (1958, p. 174).

(Pavlov guessed that the principal reason for the inadequacy of temperature as a CS lay in the closely intermixed, peripheral distribution of warm and cold receptors.)

In spite of the discouraging results that had been obtained with dogs, Usoltsev and Terekhova undertook to try thermal conditioning with eight infants from one to four and one half months of age—and found much the same in the way of results as previous studies had found. These authors used varying methodology in respect to the parameters of the CS. In some cases tubes through which warm or cold water flowed were placed in contact with the skin of the abdomen or foot. In one case, an electric heating device was placed on the infant's abdomen. The temperature of the warm CS was 48–50°C (118–122°F) and that of the cold CS, 5–10°C (41–50°F). The UCS in all cases was an airpuff directed to the eye. Although, on the average, only 12.5 reinforced trials were necessary to elicit a first CR, conditioning never became stable even after several months of longitudinal conditioning on five of the subjects. The probability of getting a CR on test trials from children between two and three months of age was .28; it jumped to .47 between the third and fourth month of life, but from that point on changed very little (.57 between four and five months; .58 between six and seven months). The investigators noted that, aside from its instability, the conditioned temperature reflex was overly susceptible to external inhibition. Conditioned differentiation—either to a stimulus differing in temperature from one CS+ or to one differing in the site of application—showed about the same degree of success after three to four months.

It is interesting to speculate about the infant's development of sensitivity to temperature changes—first, whether there is a substantial difference in sensitivity to internal temperature changes, to generalized external temperature, and to localized external temperatures, and second, how soon after birth the effects of habituation or adaptation appear.

(The reader is referred, in connection with these questions, to Spears and Hohle's discussion, presented earlier in this volume, of thermal sensitivity in infancy.)

CONDITIONAL OLFACTORY AND GUSTATORY STIMULI

The chemical senses offer some interesting possibilities for conditioning that have only begun to be explored. In a study far more outstanding for its ingeniousness than for the rigor of its design, Irzhanskaia and Felberbaum (1954) tested the effects of prior familiarity with the CS on the subsequent course of conditioning. The subjects were 33 premature children ranging in age at the beginning of experimentation from one and one-half to two and one-half months. Two weeks prior to conditioning the children began to drink their milk from bottles with nipples which carried a distinct mint odor. Conditioning itself contrasted the relative effectiveness of the odors of mint and anise as conditional stimuli. The CR was eyeblinking to an airpuff. For the infants premature by only one month, twice as many reinforced trials were required to condition blinking to anise as to mint. This difference decreased somewhat as degree of prematurity increased.

THE UNCONDITIONED STIMULUS IN EARLY
CLASSICAL CONDITIONING

Exteroceptively conditioned responses can be divided into those for which the reinforcement is positive or rewarding, causing the subject to approach it, and those in which the reinforcement is negative or aversive, causing the subject to defend himself against it.

What is the relative effectiveness of the various positive and negative reinforcers suitable for use with infants in studies of classical conditioning? In keeping with the traditional Pavlovian emphasis on the conditional stimulus rather than the response and unconditioned stimulus, Soviet investigators have not as yet carried out any comprehensive, systematic studies to determine the possible differential effects on conditioning of different unconditional stimuli. The American literature is similarly lacking in such studies. There are a few studies, however, in which two or more different UCSs have been used, as well as some indirect evidence, that suggest that a simple answer will not soon be found to the question of UCS effects on conditionability.

Evidence for the null position (no difference as a function of UCS) comes from studies using conditioned blinking and conditioned sucking. In her study of color discrimination, Zonova (1964) included both of these responses. From the subject sample as a whole, it is possible to match 14 children in the two reinforcement groups for age at the beginning of experimentation (a mean of 68 days in both cases). The first CR appeared after 26.0 reinforcements for infants reinforced with an airpuff and after 18.5 combinations for those reinforced with milk. A strong CR appeared after 42.2 and 105.8 reinforcements, respectively. Neither difference is statistically significant, although the second difference approaches significance ($t = 1.98$, $df = 12$, $.10 > P > .05$). This trend is probably due to an age artifact, since the *un*conditioned sucking reflex was disappearing in the older subjects. (Only the two *youngest* subjects ever showed stable conditioning.)

Zonova's negative results agree with those of three previous studies using conditioned sucking and conditioned blinking. Kasatkin (1948) conditioned feeding responses in eight infants and blinking responses in six infants to sound as a CS. The mean ages for the two groups at the beginning of experimentation were 21 and 25 days, respectively; the mean ages upon reaching a semistable CR were 34 and 39 days. (Similar data were also reported by Kasatkin, 1962.) Dashkovskaia (1953) conditioned blinking and sucking in both normal and birth traumatized neonates, and found no differential conditionability in either group as a function of type of UCS used. Nechaeva (1954), interested primarily in the infant's developing ability to discriminate among tones differing in frequency, conditioned blinking in three infants and antici-patory sucking in another three. Following conditioning to the CS+, a tone of 810 cps, differential stimuli of 4010, 3010, 2010, and 1010 cps were introduced. No reliable differences appeared between reinforce-ment groups for any one of these conditioning procedures.

Using premature and full term infants of varying ages, Janoš (1965) conditioned blinking to a strong light in some of his subjects and blinking to an airpuff in others. There were no differences among groups attributable to the type of UCS used.

Evidence for the position that type of UCS does affect the course of conditioning comes from studies using shock and from one study using novelty as a reinforcer. Wenger (1936), using a tactile-vibratory CS on four young infants, could condition blinking in response to a strong light but could not condition leg withdrawal in response to shock. Fur-ther, all investigations to date whose purpose has been to establish whether conditioning is possible or not during the first ten days of life have found uniformly that it is not possible when shock serves as the UCS, although it is possible when appetitional reinforcement is used. (These studies are reviewed in greater detail in a later section on indi-vidual differences.) Finally, Koch (1965) found conditioned orienting to be stronger as a function of type and the degree of novelty of the reinforcing stimulation (Fig. 4.2, p. 235).

As far as general methodological considerations are concerned, there are certainly differences between reward and defensive condition-ing. For one thing, reward or approach conditioning has the disadvantage of being somewhat more dependent on the subject's motivational state than defense conditioning. To use anticipatory sucking or head turning with milk reinforcement means automatically that experimentation must be scheduled when the infant is hungry. In analogous fashion, to con-dition orienting, the infant must be "hungry" for novel stimuli.

On the other hand, strong aversive stimuli, such as electric shock, have several disadvantages, most of which are detailed elsewhere in this chapter. To summarize them here, highly noxious reinforcement increases the probability of pseudoconditioning effects and, hence, the need for pseudoconditioning controls; increases the probability of the infant's behaving in a negative, emotional manner or, if he is old enough, of leaving the field; and, probably, decreases the chances of obtaining successful conditioning (referring again to conditioning during the neonatal period).

REWARD CONDITIONING

Conditioned Sucking (and Related Mouth Movements). The classical measure of classical conditioning, when the reinforcement is appetitional, is salivation. When the subjects under investigation are, however, infants rather than dogs, it is not really feasible to use salivation as a dependent variable. For one thing, the salivary glands are not fully functional in neonates, and for another, the precision that characterizes salivation as a measure in animal conditioning depends upon the use of some operative intervention in order to collect the saliva. It is a rare thing to find an infant patient, as Bogen (1907) did, whóse medical state already demands the insertion of a gastric fistula.

Because of these considerations, investigators studying appetitional conditioning in infants have traditionally used, as a substitute, some overtly observable process associated with salivation, such as swallows or anticipatory sucking movements. Historically, swallowing was the first such substitute to be used (Krasnogorskii, 1907), but was soon replaced in popularity by anticipatory sucking movements, the first studies of which appeared in the 1920's (e.g., Denisova & Figurin, 1929). The typical method of recording sucking has been to record chin movements via a plethysmographic device (a Marey capsule or modification of one) strapped under the infant's chin (Brackbill, 1962, Fig. 8). However, a new method recently introduced by Kaye, Levin, and Lipsitt (Levin & Kaye, 1964; Kaye, 1966) offers more direct measurement of sucking responses through an automatic nipple-microswitch-polygraph recording sequence. (The article by Kaye presents convincing arguments for recording sucks continuously—whatever the particular method of recording—rather than simply during test trials.)

Anticipatory sucking and mouthing movements have been used more extensively than any other response in infant classical conditioning research to study the development of internal inhibition (Koltsova, 1952), the conditionability of premature infants (Polikanina & Probatova, 1957), the effect of drive level on conditionability (Kantrow, 1937), the effect of perinatal birth trauma and possible brain injury on conditionability (Dashkovskaia, 1953), and, of course, the development of the separate sensory analyzers and their discriminatory capacities: visual (Kasatkin & Levikova, 1935b), auditory (Kaye, 1966), olfactory (Irzhanskaia & Felberbaum, 1954), tactile (Kasatkin, 1952a), kinesthetic-proprioceptive (Koltsova, 1958), and time (Bystroletova, 1954).

With few exceptions the studies in which anticipatory sucking has been used have been of neonatal conditioning, and this points up the severest limitation on the use of anticipatory sucking as a CR measure

—its rapidly declining usefulness with increasing age. Papoušek (personal communication) has observed that by the age of 100 days, even the *un*conditioned sucking reflex cannot be elicited invariably and that by the age of 200 days, the conditioned sucking reflex cannot be reestablished even in subjects who had previously shown a strong, stable CR prior to extinction. For young infants, however, and for cross-sectional rather than longitudinal investigations, sucking may well be unsurpassed as an easily conditionable response. Rate of sucking shows considerable variability among infants, but as Levin and Kaye (1964) point out, individual sucking rates are highly consistent.

In an interesting study which demonstrates how complex discrimination can be, Papoušek (1961) remarked,

> We were able to demonstrate that even these emotional reactions have the nature of conditioned reflexes. In 11 infants (4–6 months of age) we used such a differentiation that the infant received sweet milk from the left after the bell signal and a bitter solution (quinine) from the right after the buzzer signal. Milk and quinine solution evoked completely different facial and vocal reactions. Soon the infant reacted facially and vocally similarly to the conditioning stimuli alone, without the reinforcement of sweet or bitter solutions. When the differentiation signals were reversed we found that by 4–6 months a conditioned signal of a certain significance overshadowed the immediate effect of an unconditioned object—i.e., the infants reacted quite inappropriately to milk or quinine. After the buzzer signal, the infant now was given milk rather than quinine, but repeatedly refused it and spat it out with every evidence of repulsion. On the other hand the infant would now quietly drink quinine solution for the whole 10 seconds of the bell signal. Gradually the infant's reactions on milk or quinine solution change to appropriate ones (personal communication).

Conditioned Head Turning. A response measure that Papoušek (1959, 1961) has recently introduced into infant conditioning combines aspects of both instrumental and classical conditioning. The infant is placed in an apparatus with a special, rotating head cradle (Fig. 4.5, p. 240). The CR is a turn of the baby's head from the midline not less than 30°—or 45°, or whatever the arbitrarily chosen CR criterion— toward a source of milk. The source of the CS is directly above the infant's head. At the beginning of experimentation, the CS is presented for a maximum of ten seconds before the UCS is presented. If the infant turns his head in the predetermined direction within this ten-second period, the assistant, who is sitting behind the child's head and is screened from his view, inserts a nippled bottle of milk into his mouth. If, however, the infant has not responded within ten seconds, the assistant touches the corner of the subject's mouth with the nipple. If the infant still does not turn his head, the assistant turns it for him and places the nipple in his mouth. After the infant has sucked for about three seconds, the CS is turned off. On subsequent, nonprompted trials the faster the infant responds, the sooner he is rewarded with milk.

(The results of Papoušek's research are reviewed in the sections on the course of conditioning and individual differences.)

Note that this procedure is instrumental conditioning in the sense that the response must occur *before* reinforcement is delivered, and that response latency controls the CS–UCS interval. On the other hand, Papoušek's procedure is characteristic of classical conditioning in that the infant receives the UCS or reinforcement on every conditioning trial, independent of the extent to which he responds voluntarily.

There are several advantages to the use of head turning as a conditioned response, as Papoušek has noted (1959, 1961, 1966, 1967). First, control of the neck muscles is much better developed at birth than is control of the muscles of the arms and legs. When the axis of rotation of the head cradle in Papoušek's apparatus is properly adjusted for a particular infant, even a three-day-old child can keep his head at midline, turn it easily to either side, and return it once more to the midline position. A second advantage is that head turning lends itself to objectivity in recording as well as to the measurement of response amplitude and latency, two valuable and often neglected conditioning parameters.

A third advantage is that since the response can be to either side, one may study the development of complex discrimination, using two different conditional stimuli. (It should be noted here that in the initial establishment of a simple CR, Papoušek uses a head turn to the left side. This is because most young infants show a strong tendency toward right-side turns.) A fourth advantage of head turning as a conditionable response is that it can be used with a variety of CSs and UCSs. Papoušek has to date used only auditory CSs (bells and buzzers), but there is no reason why visual or other types of sensory stimuli would be less happily joined to the head turning response. (Siqueland, 1964, has, in fact, used a tactile stimulus as CS for head turning.) As reinforcement, Papoušek has used formula, sweet solutions, and bitter solutions. Other reinforcing stimuli such as novel visual events could also be used.

The Conditioned Orienting Reflex. It was pointed out earlier that under some circumstances conditioning as a method for studying the sensory analyzers is not altogether suitable and that the orienting reflex can be—or sometimes must be—used as an alternative method of investigation. What was not pointed out at that time was that the orienting reflex itself may be conditioned.

Kasatkin, Mirzoiants, and Khokhitva (1953) were the first investigators to condition this reflex in 10 normal infants ranging in age at the beginning of experimentation from 46 to 292 days. As conditional stimuli they used various auditory stimuli, including both pure and complex tones. The source of reinforcement also varied, but appears to have consisted in the main of two flashing, 6-volt lamps of different colors separated by a few inches and situated to the right of the infant's head. An ingeniously simple mechanical device transmitted a record of response amplitude to a kymograph pen (Fig. 4.1). Mirzoiants (1954) followed up the conditioning procedure by establishing simple differentiations in two of the original infants as well as in two new subjects.

Later studies of conditioned orienting in infancy have been carried out by Karlova (1959) and Koch (1965).

From the point of view of its usefulness as a conditionable response, orienting does not have unlimited merit. In the first place, it extinguishes easily and quickly as the reinforcing stimulus loses its novelty; orienting is, as Pavlov pointed out more than once, a highly unstable response. Daily sessions must be limited to very few trials, and even then, one is likely to see, even within a short session, a decrease in response amplitude, an increase in latency, or even extinction.

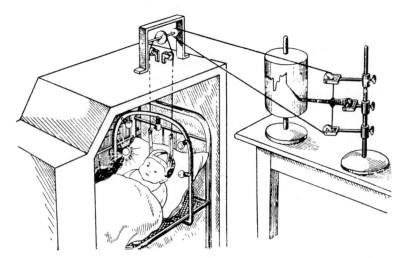

Figure 4.1. *A simply constructed and inexpensive device for eliciting and measuring orienting.*

The infant's head movement to the side displaces the kymograph pen, and the extent to which it is displaced is directly proportional to the extent of head movement from the median position. Source of UCS is an arch studded with ordinary light bulbs. These may be switched on and off in sequence, from top to side, or the sidemost light may be made to flicker. (From Kasatkin, Mirzoiants, & Khokhitva, 1953.)

One way of postponing the arrival of extinction, though not indefinitely, is to change the physical parameters of the reinforcing stimulus from trial to trial, as Koch has shown (1965). This investigator conditioned the orienting reflex to an auditory stimulus in three groups of two-month-old infants and three groups of three-month-old infants. The three groups at each age level differed according to the type of reinforcement they received and in the degree of its familiarity (or novelty). Ten trials a day were administered, the reinforcing stimulus appearing on every trial through an aperture in the side of the crib housing. For the infants in group *a*, reinforcement consisted in the sight of the mother's face and the sound of her voice; for those in group *b*, of a stranger's face and voice; and for those in group *c*, of the sight of a toy. The toys alone were changed from trial to trial. As might be expected, the relative effectiveness of these reinforcers in eliciting the orienting reflex was in direct proportion to their novelty value for the infants (Fig. 4.2).

Another consideration in choosing orienting as the response to be conditioned in any experiment is that it may turn out to be the case—although there is insufficient evidence at present to draw a firm conclusion—that orienting is affected by individual difference variables to a greater extent than are other responses. For example, it is known that there are marked age differences in the rapidity with which orienting

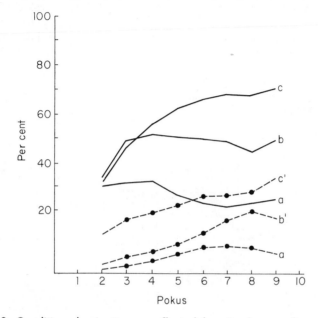

Figure 4.2. *Conditioned orienting as affected by stimulus novelty and infants' age.*

Solid lines indicate results for three-month-old infants, and broken lines, results for two-month-old infants. Reinforcing conditions were provided by (a) the mother, (b) one stranger, and (c) a variety of toys. (From Koch, 1966, "Activitos Nervosa Superior," 7. Published by Czechoslovak Medical Press, Prague.)

extinguishes among full term infants, one-month premature infants, two-month premature infants, and three-month premature infants (Polikanina & Probatova, 1957). Karlova (1959) also found marked age differences in the frequency and strength of orienting among normal children between one month and three years of age, and Koch (1965) found age differences between two- and three-month-old infants in the conditionability and resistance to extinction of the orienting reflex. There is no account as yet of conditioned orienting in neonates.

DEFENSE CONDITIONING

Shock-Induced Changes. Several attempts have been made by American psychologists over the last 40 years to condition infants by means of shock (e.g., Jones, 1930, 1931; Wenger, 1936; Wickens & Wickens, 1940; Lipsitt, 1963). Perhaps this represents the line of least resistance in adapting the more familiar animal conditioning techniques to use with infants, but in point of fact, the transplanted method does not seem to work well with infants. The use of shock during the neonatal period has not produced reliable evidence of conditioning, as Lipsitt (1963) has pointed out, although the administration of shock at later ages—virtually all of which has been done as a means of diagnosing deafness—has produced wide variability in behavior relevant to the experimental situation, a great deal of experimentally irrelevant behavior such as emotionality, and, given sufficient muscular maturity, a noticeable tendency to leave the field.

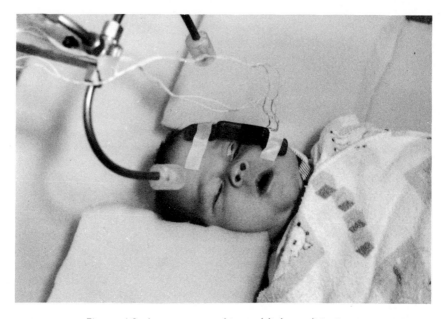

Figure 4.3. *Apparatus used in eyeblink conditioning.*

The magnet is taped to the upper eyelid, and the semiconductor is mounted on the plastic bridge over the eye. (From Lintz & Fitzgerald, 1966.)

Conditioned Eye Blinking. In the Soviet Union, aversive conditioning in infancy has been largely synonymous with conditioned eye blinking—such an extremely mild procedure, operationally, that it may not be meaningful to classify it in the same generic category as shock. In any event, use of the eyeblink as a CR has enjoyed considerable popularity with Soviet investigators. (For a partial bibliography of its use in Soviet research, see Brackbill, 1964, p. 232.)

Koltsova and her colleagues have been primarily responsible for methodological innovations in administering air puffs and recording blinks in older infant subjects. An apparatus suitable for use with children above the age of eighteen months to two years is illustrated in Brackbill (1962, pp. 158–159) and in Evdokimov and Zakliakova (1962). This is a carbon microphone capsule modified so that a small wire, brushed by the eyelash during a blink, affects the packing of the carbon granules. Typically, the force of the air puff is neither standard for all subjects nor automatically controlled, but is adjusted manually in response to the child's initial response. The usual procedure by which the experimenter accustoms an older infant or young child to this apparatus involves as many brief daily sessions as are necessary in the experimental room during which the experimenter becomes acquainted with the subject, tries on the head band himself, associates it verbally with Yuri Gagarin, allows the subject to play with a very attractive new toy, gives him a piece of candy, and finally sends him back to his nursery school group.

For younger infants, something is needed that the infant cannot inadvertently use to injure his eyeball. Figure 4.3 shows a recording apparatus quite recently devised by Lintz and Fitzgerald (1966) that meets these requirements. The air delivery part of the apparatus is modeled after the one Kasatkin devised many years ago for use with younger infants (Brackbill, 1962, Fig. 4, p. 109). The occurrence, latency, and duration of the eyeblink are recorded by means of a small permanent magnet, roughly 1 mm in diameter and 4 mm long, attached to the subject's upper eyelid, just above the eyelash, with a narrow strip of tape. With a steady 20-ma current flow across the short axis of the semiconductor, the voltage developed across the long axis (a function of the magnetic field) is fed to a low level DC polygraph channel.

The Conditioned Pupillary Reflex. Another mild form of defensive response is the adjustment of the size of the pupillary opening to light. The conditioning of this reflex has been studied only sporadically; of the dozen or so studies that have appeared since the 1920s, about half have found no evidence of pupillary conditioning, whereas the other half have reported that the pupillary reflex can be conditioned. Probably because of these discouraging results, pupillary conditioning has not been attempted with infants, even though the reflex is present at birth or shortly thereafter (Sherman & Sherman, 1925; Chaney & McGraw, 1932). Quite recently, however, Fitzgerald, Lintz, Brackbill, and Adams (1967), using a 2 × 3 design, have conditioned both pupillary dilation and constriction, using change in illumination as the UCS, to three different types of conditional stimuli: elapsed time, sound, and a compound CS consisting of time plus sound. For subjects receiving elapsed time as CS, the sequence was 20-second interval, 4-second UCS, 20-second interval, 4-second UCS, and so on. With time plus sound as CS, the temporal sequence was the same but the 4-second UCS interval was also the occasion for a 4-second presentation of a complex, 65 db tone. For conditioning with sound alone as CS, the same complex tone was presented coincident with the UCS, but the intertrial intervals were randomized within a 10- to 30-second range. The infant tends to fall asleep under this monotonous stimulation, so that a speculum or the more gentle services of an assistant are required to keep one of the infant's eyes open.

The UCS for pupillary conditioning was a change in illumination level: for conditioning constriction, a 100-watt blue bulb mounted in a reflector housing 15 inches in front of the subject was turned on, and for conditioning dilation, the same bulb was turned off. The pupillary response was continually recorded at one frame per second on infrared film.

In the experimental sessions for all six groups, 9 test trials were interspersed among 32 conditioning trials in a predetermined random sequence. Without interruption, 35 extinction trials followed the 41 conditioning and test trials. The entire procedure took place in one thirty-minute session.

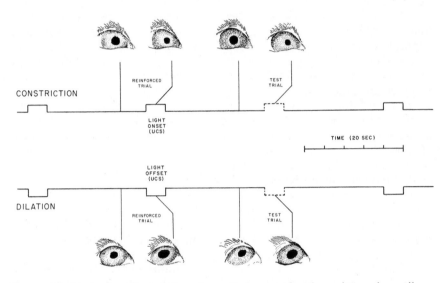

Figure 4.4. *Method and examples of results in a study of conditioned pupillary dilation in infants.*

(From Fitzgerald, Lintz, Brackbill, & Adams, 1967.)

Several control groups for pseudoconditioning are necessary in such a procedure. One group received 4-second presentations of the complex tone, spaced at 20-second intervals, as a check on whether this CS alone might elicit the UCR. A second group received 4-second presentations of either tone or UCS, mixed randomly but never paired, with intertrial intervals chosen randomly between 10 and 30 seconds. A third group received 4-second UCSs spaced at random intervals between 10 and 30 seconds. Notice that the traditional pseudoconditioning controls which involve temporal changes in CS administration cannot be used when the CS is elapsed time.

Figure 4.4 illustrates both the results and the procedure for the case in which elapsed time served as the CS. The photograph in Fig. 4.4a, illustrating conditioned dilation, was taken of a 57-day-old female infant with brown eyes. The pretest and posttest frames shown were taken on the third test trial, after 11 reinforced trials. Conditioned dilation is already occurring.

The photograph in Fig. 4.4b, illustrating conditioned constriction, was taken of a 54-day-old male infant with brown eyes. The pretest and posttest frames shown were taken on the fourth test trial, after 12 reinforced trials. Again, a CR has already made its appearance.

INTEROCEPTIVELY CONDITIONED REFLEXES

Whatever the original definition of interoceptive conditioning, it has generally come to mean the conditioning of physiological responses that are not normally under voluntary control. The possibilities for interoceptive conditioning of infants have just begun to be tapped. Bystroletova (1954) and Krachkovskaia (1959) have studied conditioned leukocytosis in infants, and various investigators have used conditioned GSR as a diagnostic measure. (These studies are detailed elsewhere in this chapter.) By our definition of interoceptive conditioning, one might also include the pupillary conditioning described above.

Tonkova-Iampolskaia has studied the susceptibility of vascular constriction to simple conditioning (1956), to differentiation (1956, 1961), and to the conditioning of a stereotype or sequence of CRs (1961). In her later study (1961), which in most respects parallels the earlier research (1956), Tonkova-Iampolskaia used 10 children ranging in age from twenty-eight to thirty-four months. The CSs were bells "of various tones" as well as the light of a 5-watt lamp; the UCS, ice, was applied to the child's arm. Vascular constriction was recorded by means of a plethysmograph. Under this procedure constriction is apparently conditioned rapidly in most children but has a strong tendency to remain unstable, and differentiation is obtained in only one out of two subjects. Interestingly, among those children who do not achieve a differentiation, paradoxical vasodilation sometimes appears on CS-trials (i.e., CS minus trials).

CHANGES IN RESPONSE PARAMETERS OVER THE COURSE OF CONDITIONING

In 1948, Kasatkin described four stages in conditioning: (a) indifference to the CS, i.e., no apparent behavioral reaction to the CS, (b) inhibition of general activity upon presentation of the stimulus, (c) appearance of an unstable CR (CR elicitation on approximately 50 per cent of test trials), and (d) achievement of a stable CR (CR elicitation on test trials approaches 100 per cent).

Recently, Papoušek (1967) has reached much the same conclusion —that the course of conditioning can be most meaningfully divided into four stages—although his description of the stages differs somewhat from Kasatkin's.

During the first phase of conditioning, the acoustic signal elicits non-specific orienting behavior in the form of inhibition of general movements, a change in breathing, and perhaps wider opening of the eyes. These responses extinguish quickly, and for some time the signals elicit no obvious changes in behavior.

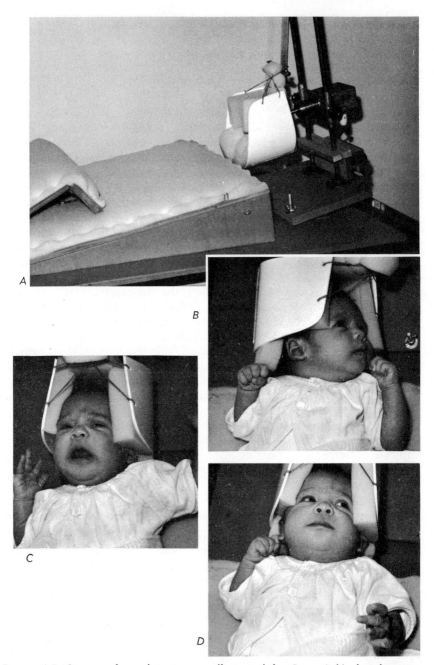

Figure 4.5. Stages of conditioning as illustrated by Papoušek's head-turning procedure.

(a) Head-turning apparatus; (b) gradual appearance of the first CRs; (c) emotionality during CS application; (d) the first CRs. (From Papoušek, 1967.)

This phase is succeeded by the gradual appearance of the first conditioned responses. At first CRs do not appear in an integrated form; one observes a gradual coordination of partial responses, such as increased general movements, unilateral contraction of the left corner of the mouth, or the turning of the eyes to the left prior to stimulation from the left side [Fig. 4.5b]. Eventually these individual responses become part of the head turn to the left. However, until coordination develops completely, the newborn may be upset, fussing and grimacing during the application of the conditioning stimulus [Fig. 4.5c]. Marked signs of this lack of coordination are observed in less than 1 per cent of the older subjects, but they are present in 50 per cent of the newborns.

Next comes the phase of unstable conditioned responses, during which CR frequency gradually increases. The newborn is typically unable to produce very many correct responses consecutively. This inability appears to be a function of age, since older infants show several consecutive correct responses as soon as they start responding at all. In newborns, 60.7% of the first ten conditioned responses appear as isolated CRs, while 32.9% appear in groups of two consecutive correct responses, and only 6.4% in groups of three or more. The first positive responses are frequently followed by signs of generalized inhibition—slow, regular breathing and a marked decrease in general movements [Fig. 4.5d].

The insufficient coordination that is still present during the phase of unstable conditioning has two characteristic features: there are frequent head turns to the left or to both sides during intertrial intervals, and, in addition, the CR assumes a generalized form, including movements of both trunk and extremities ("the newborn responds with the whole body") (Papoušek, 1967, pp. 269–272).

Papoušek has also described and illustrated the course of extinction —which he finds to be essentially a "mirror image" of the course of conditioning, in the same article (1967).

INDIVIDUAL DIFFERENCES IN CONDITIONING

NEONATAL CONDITIONING

Can infants be conditioned during the first ten days of life? Despite a good deal of skepticism on the part of both American and Soviet scientists, the present evidence is that conditioning can take place during the neonatal period. (Note that from the logical point of view, only one valid study with positive results is needed to disprove the premise that conditioning is *not* possible during the neonatal period.) Some of the positive findings in this area come from the studies of Marquis (1931, 1941), Dashkovskaia (1953), Bystroletova (1954), Krachkovskaia (1959), Lipsitt and Kaye (1964), and Kaye (1965, 1966). Failures to condition neonates have been reported by Wickens and Wickens (1940) and by Lipsitt (1963). In addition, Wenger's early attempt (1936) should also be considered a failure to condition, although he did not regard it so.

Whether by coincidence or not, the unsuccessful studies of neonatal conditioning have all used noxious stimuli as reinforcement—acetic acid vapor in one case and shock in the other cases—whereas the studies yielding positive results have almost uniformly used conditioning procedures that are intrinsic to the act or scheduling of feeding. Lipsitt (1963) has already suggested that aversive stimuli are not effective conditioners during the early neonatal period, and at present the only obstacle in the way of accepting this as a general conclusion is Dashkovskaia's reported success in conditioning first appearance of an eyeblink reflex in five eight-day-old infants (1953).

Aside from the question of neonatal conditionability, Papoušek has noted that there is a special advantage in using neonates as subjects. With neonates, conditioning proceeds slowly enough to enable the experimenter to observe the stages of conditioning in all their details and peculiarities with greater clarity than is possible with older infants in whom conditioning proceeds more rapidly.

CHRONOLOGICAL AGE DIFFERENCES

One of the questions most frequently asked in infant research on learning has concerned the extent to which it is affected by maturation. Is there a correlation between chronological age and speed of conditioning, extinction, differentiation, and so on? Except for investigations in which the age range is tightly restricted, as, for example, studies of conditioning during the first four or five days of life, there is generally found to be a substantial negative relationship between CA and the number of reinforced trials necessary to achieve a *stable* CR (Mateer, 1918; Kasatkin & Levikova, 1935a, 1935b; Kantrow, 1937; Morgan & Morgan, 1944; Kasatkin, Mirzoiants, & Khokhitva, 1953; Polikanina & Probatova, 1955; Kriuchkova & Ostrovskaia, 1957; Tomka, 1957; Karlova, 1959; Rendle-Short, 1961; Janoš, 1965; Papoušek, 1966, 1967; Irzhanskaia & Felberbaum, 1967).

Mateer concluded from her data that the number of trials required to condition an infant decreases with age up to sixty months but that the relationship of learning to age is less regular thereafter. On the other hand, there is apparently little or no relationship between CA and appearance of the *first* CR (Kasatkin et al., 1953; Polikanina & Probatova, 1955; Papoušek, 1966).

Age-based correlations are also smaller for procedures that follow simple conditioning, e.g., extinction, differentiation, and so on. Both Janoš (1959)[4] and Papoušek (1966) found nonsignificant correlations between age and trials to extinguish, although Mateer found a correlation of − .32 which is significant beyond the .01 level, but considerably smaller than the correlation of − .57 she reported between CA and trials to condition. Similarly, the majority of studies have found an insignificant relationship between CA and speed of differentiation (Kasatkin & Levikova, 1935b; Nechaeva, 1954; Tomka, 1957; Janoš, 1959; Papoušek,

4. In the 1959 article, a Russian-English translation, the author's name was transliterated as Ianosh instead of Janoš.

1961; Rendle-Short, 1961). Some contrary though not weighty evidence is provided by Vakhrameeva (1964), whose data show some difference in rate of differentiation when extreme age groups are compared, and by Kasatkin and Levikova (1935a), whose three subjects yielded a perfect correlation between age and speed of discrimination.

To some extent, the lower correlations between age and trials to extinction, differentiation, reversal, and so on, must be affected by the increased restriction in age range that occurs between the beginning and end of simple conditioning, since the youngest children have taken a relatively long time to condition and the oldest children, a relatively short time. Nevertheless, a less close correspondence between age and any conditioning procedure involving inhibition, such as extinction and differentiation, is consistent with Pavlovian theory. Pavlov considered inhibition to represent a higher evolutionary stage than excitation—an inference based on his observations of greater instability of the inhibitory than excitatory processes. Granting this to be the case, one might expect, first, that the attainment of full functional maturity of inhibitory processes would lag behind that of excitation and, second, that those conditioning processes involving inhibition would be marked by greater variability in inter-individual if not intra-individual performance.

CONDITIONING IN PREMATURE INFANTS

Pavlovian theorists are particularly interested in the conditioning of premature infants because the brains of these children are even less functionally mature at birth than are those of normal, full term infants —a condition that should be reflected in the premature's response to conditioning. Kasatkin's pioneer work on this problem (1936, 1948) led him to conclude that conditioned reflexes could be formed in prematures during the first half of the second month of life regardless of the degree of prematurity or the age at which experimental work was started (1936). In a later, more restrained description of these early findings, he said,

> . . . in children who are premature by 1–2 months, a blinking reflex to a sound stimulus is formed in the first half of the second month of life and sometimes even in the first week of the second month, depending upon the age at which experimental work is begun. Consequently, a conditioned reflex can be formed in premature children during the period between the moment of actual birth and the date of normal termination of intrauterine development. This face emphasizes the stimulating influence of the [extrauterine] environment surrounding the child (1957, p. 810).

From the results of subsequent research, however, investigators have maintained that degree of prematurity *does* affect the course of conditioning in prematures (Irzhanskaia & Felberbaum, 1954; Polikanina & Probatova, 1955, 1957; Janoš, 1959, 1965; Polikanina, 1961). There are two points at issue in the problem of conditioning premature infants. The first question is whether a prematurely born infant can be conditioned before the age at which this would be possible for a full term infant. The second question is why conditioning can or cannot proceed earlier for the premature. This question, rephrased in the minds of Pavlovian theorists, becomes: is the rate of cortical development affected by the abundant and varied stimulation the premature receives from the extrauterine environment—stimulation that he would not have received if pregnancy had proceeded normally?

With regard to the first problem, whether prematures can be conditioned "prematurely," the most formidable obstacle in the way of assessing the relative importance to conditioning of prematurity as opposed to chronological age—which we already know to affect conditioning—is that most studies in this area have allowed the two dimensions to vary to approximately the same extent. For example, in their first study Polikanina and Probatova (1955) used subjects who were premature by one to three months and who began serving as experimental subjects between eighteen and eighty days. Kasatkin (1936) almost succeeded in holding both variables constant: the range in degree of prematurity for nine of his ten subjects was fifteen days and the range in age at the beginning of experimentation, thirteen days. This no doubt accounts in large part for his initial conclusion that CR formation depended neither on degree of prematurity nor on CA at the beginning of experimentation. (The age range for attainment of stable conditioning was also 13 days.)

In terms of methodology, the best comparison to date of chronological age vs gestational age effects has been Janoš' use of matched groups (1959, 1965). Janoš used two groups of full term and one group of premature infants. He matched the prematures to one group of full term infants on the basis of actual CA at the beginning of conditioning; he also matched the prematures to a second group of full term infants on the basis of corrected age, i.e., the age the premature infants would have been had they been born at term. The matching was apparently on the basis of group means.

Table 4.3 shows that for the premature infants, the number of days' conditioning necessary to achieve five consecutive conditioned eyeblinks to a 1000 cps tone more closely approximates the number of days for full terms matched on corrected age than the number of days for full terms matched on CA. There is a significant difference between prematures and full terms in actual age upon reaching criterion under each conditioning procedure; the difference disappears when corrected age is used in the comparison.

One additional difficulty in comparing the conditioning performance of premature to full term infants is that prematurity is more often than not accompanied by physical or physiological abnormalities. The probability of such abnormalities increases markedly with degree of prematurity. (See, for example, Lubchenco et al., 1963.) Therefore, no matter how well an experimenter disentangles the problem of chronological vs. gestational age in comparing premature to full term infants, he is still faced with the very high probability of confounding differences in length of intrauterine development with differences in normal, postnatal body function.

Whether one concludes that premature infants can or cannot be prematurely conditioned, there is still the question of *why* to be disposed of. Kasatkin's evidence led him to conclude that premature conditioning does take place, and from this he inferred that the stimulating influence of the extrauterine environment speeds up the rate of cortical develop-

Table 4.3—Mean Age in Days for Premature and Full Term Infants upon Reaching Criterion in Successive Experimental Procedures (after Janoš, 1959).

| | | STAGES IN CONDITIONING | | | |
Group	Beginning of Experiment	CR Formation	Extinction	Reconditioning	Differentiation
Prematures, CA	54	112	123	141	157
Prematures, corrected age	21	80	87	106	121
Older full terms	48	76 ⎫			
Younger full terms	16	86 ⎬	88*	106*	121*

* Data for the two full term groups were combined following simple conditioning since there were no longer significant differences between them.

ment. As Janoš (1959) points out, however, even granting that premature conditioning occurs, it does not necessarily follow that there has been any postnatal change in rate of cortical development unless it can also be shown that fetal conditioning is either not possible during the last three intrauterine months or that its course is grossly inferior to that of conditioning in prematures during corresponding age periods.

Instrumental Learning

Whereas in classical conditioning the reinforcement elicits the response, in instrumental learning the reinforcement is delivered only when and if the response has already occurred. In other words, the emphasis in instrumental learning—or instrumental conditioning—is either on the response or on the reinforcement. The problems posed in instrumental learning studies center about two questions: which behaviors can be conditioned and which events are effective reinforcers in this conditioning? The emphasis in classical conditioning is on the conditional stimulus, while in instrumental learning situations, the stimulus may not even be identifiable.

Within the generic category, *instrumental learning*, there are two

Sequence, experimental stages and mean trials to criterion (in parentheses)		Nature of experimental stages	Number and order of presentation of discrimination in each stage of experimentation							
Group I	Group II		1	2	3	4	5	6	7	8
1 (35.80)	5 (30.33)	Simple, 2-choice simultaneous discriminations. (Circle correct)	○ ✚	○ △	○ ▢	○ ○				
2 (17.06)	4 (25.57)	Change in spatial orientation of negative stimulus. (Circle correct)	○ ✚	○ ✸	○ △	○ ▷	○ ▢	○ ◇	○ ○	○ ○
3 (12.80)	3 (16.71)	Change in size of the negative stimulus. (Circle correct)	○ ✚	○ ✚	○ △	○ △	○ ▢	○ ▢	○ ○	○ ○
4 (11.91)	2 (13.13)	Increase in number of negative stimuli. (Circle correct)	○ ✚	○ △	○ ✚ △	○ ▢	△ ✚ ○	○ ○	△ ▢ ○ ✚ ○	○ ○
5 (15.12)	1 (13.60)	Reversal learning.	✚ ○	✸ ○	△ ○	▷ ○	○ ▢	○ ◇	○ ○	○ ○

Table 4.4—Outline of Experimental Design and Procedure for Group I (N-10) and Group II (N-8) (After Ling, 1941.)

classes of studies that differ from each other principally in terms of methodology.[5] One class has never really acquired a proper, universally used name. It consists of studies that might be called "trial and error" or "discrete trial procedures," such as the Ling (1941) experiment described below. The other class consists of operant conditioning studies. Infant studies using discrete trial methodology outnumber operant studies by a large majority (Brackbill, 1964).

In a typical discrete trial procedure, the subject enters the experimental situation and quickly comes to understand what the learning task requires of him. This understanding is frequently mediated by verbal instructions from the experimenter or by some special features of the apparatus (which is apt to be more obtrusive and elaborate than is the usual case in operant conditioning procedures). The subject makes a predetermined number of responses (frequently only one) and is thereupon presented with the appropriate reinforcing consequences. The experimenter then separates the subject from the learning material while he rearranges the latter for the next trial. A typical response measure is the number of trials or errors to the predetermined criterion of learning.

A well-known example of discrete trial methodology in instrumental learning is the study by Bing-Chung Ling of form discrimination in infants (1941). Ling's subjects were children who ranged in age at the beginning of the experiment from 35 to 59 weeks. Half of these Ss, Group I, learned the series of form discriminations in what Ling described as an ascending order of difficulty, while the remaining Ss learned the same discriminations in a descending order. Table 4.4 indicates the design and stimulus material used. At the beginning of the experiment there were 13 Ss in each of these groups but at the end of seven month's work, after attrition had taken its toll, there were 10 Ss in Group I and 8 in Group II.

Each infant was seen individually. He was seated in front of a board on which could be hung the stimulus material—three-dimensional yellow blocks of various shapes. The board was adjusted so that the infant could reach the blocks easily. In each discrimination task, there was only one block that was not "locked" to the board. This removable block was the correct stimulus. When the infant removed it and brought it to his mouth, he was rewarded for his efforts by a sweet taste; the block had been soaked in a strong saccharine solution. A curtain was then inserted between the infant and the board, and the stimuli for the next trial were mounted on the board. The position of the correct stimulus was randomized across trials and the number of trials in any one session was determined by the length of time the infant was cooperative. There were three sessions per week for each subject.

It is difficult to say just how many form discriminations the infants actually did make. Ling presented each subject with 35 occasions on which to choose at criterion level before moving on to the next dis-

5. The points of methodological and theoretical distinction between the two classes are well described by Spiker, 1960, pp. 386–388.

crimination. However, some of these represented reintroductions of previously learned discriminations, and, too, 27 of the discriminations contained the same positive stimulus, a circle. The remaining 8 contained the same negative stimulus (See Table 4.4). The criterion for each discrimination was generally 8 out of 10 successively correct trials.

Ling's basic results showed that there was really no essential difference between the two groups in number of trials to criterion on all discriminations: the mean number of trials was 609 for Group I and 648 for Group II; the respective medians were 645 and 599. The means for each group's performance in each of the 5 successive stages of the experiment are also presented in Table 4.4.[6] None of the 5 between-group comparisons is significant. Thus, there was no clear evidence for a learning to learn phenomenon in these data, suggesting that the appearance of learning sets may have a lower age limit. The data in Table 4.4 also illustrate the fact that an experimenter's *a priori* assumptions about level of difficulty are not always endorsed by his subjects. Level of difficulty does not increase from Stage 1 to Stage 5, as Ling had assumed; it decreases.

In a typical operant conditioning procedure the subject is introduced into the experimental situation without any formally administered instructions—verbal or otherwise. In fact, it may not be at all clear to the subject what the experimenter wants of him. The experimenter, however, will probably have arranged the situation so as to maximize the probability that the criterion or operant response will occur. When the response occurs, it is rewarded, punished, or followed by no consequential event—in accordance with the experimenter's predetermined reinforcement schedule. A typical measure of conditioning is the rate of responding or number of responses per unit time.

Probably the best-known study of operant conditioning in infancy —even though it has sometimes been mistakenly cited as an example of classical conditioning—is that published by Watson and Rayner in 1920. The eleven-month-old subject of this study, known affectionately in the back rooms of child psychology as "Little Albert," was confronted with a rat toward which Albert had previously shown no fear. Thereupon, each time Albert reached out to touch the rat a loud noise was produced by striking a steel bar near the child. Watson and Rayner contend that a conditioned fear response was established with the administration of the second reinforcement. This was inferred from the child's ambivalent behavior on the third—and apparently unreinforced —trial one week later. Subsequently, five more negative reinforcements were delivered. Albert was then tested for generalization to blocks, the experimental room, a rabbit, a dog, a fur coat, cotton wool, human hair, and a Santa Claus mask. The conditioned fear reaction reportedly generalized to all of these things save the blocks. (The generalization aspect of these results is discussed further, below.) Additional reinforced trials and test trials were administered at an older age.

6. The means in Table 4.4 and the computations based upon those means are the present authors'.

THE ACQUISITION OF INSTRUMENTALLY LEARNED BEHAVIOR

Generally speaking, responses that lend themselves most readily to instrumental conditioning procedures begin to develop at a later age than do classically conditionable responses. Nevertheless, within a few months they are available in a variety and profusion that far exceed the limited range of classically conditionable responses.

In the area of conditionable changes in emotional and social behavior, the responses studied by instrumental learning methods have included crying, smiling, aggressive actions, and expressions of fear. In the area of linguistic development, the predominant studies are those of instrumentally learned vocalizations and vocabulary. Studies in the extensive area of conditioned motor responses have included such responses as bladder control, bowel control, selection of objects in a discrimination task, maze learning, locomotor responses, lever or panel pressing, dynamometer squeezing, and various perceptual-motor skills, such as buttoning and cutting with scissors. Representative studies in these areas will now be reviewed.

EMOTIONAL RESPONSES

There has been a great deal of inference and speculation concerning the learning of social and emotional responses—much of this in conjunction with the heredity-environment issue—but very little in the way of actual research has been done on the subject within the instrumental conditioning framework.

One of the exceptions, Watson and Rayner's demonstration of operantly conditioned fear in an eleven-month-old boy, was described briefly earlier in this section. The essence of the demonstration was that conditioned fear developed as a consequence of making a very loud noise behind the child whenever he reached out to touch an initially interesting rat, that the fear generalized to other furry objects, and that these data illustrated the "fact" that all human behavior is a learned elaboration based on three innate responses in infancy, one of which is a fear response to loud noises or loss of support.

Of the many protests against Watson's theory and the validity of his interpretations in regard to this particular study, one of the most interesting was made by Valentine, in an article resolutely entitled, "The Innate Basis of Fear" (1930). His thesis was that innately determined behaviors can appear at any time during the individual's lifetime, and that failure of a response to appear at birth is an invalid criterion of environmental determination. "The negative results gained by Watson in tests with cats and rabbits, on three infants of 4 and 5 months, have this disadvantage. The fact that the infants showed no fear of the animals at 4 or 5 months offers no proof that there was not, lurking within, the germ of an innate far which was not to ripen until 10 or 12 months" (1930, p. 397).

Valentine conducted several miniature demonstration-experiments with his own children to prove his point. For example, his daughter, Y, age twelve and one-half months, was seated on her mother's knee. A pair of opera glasses was given to Y for her brief inspection and then placed on a table in front of her. When she reached out to touch them, Valentine blew loudly on a whistle directly behind his daughter. Y showed no emotional disturbance toward the opera glasses either on this occasion or on subsequent trials (which included being shifted to her father's knee.)

Later that day Y was confronted with the same situation except that a fuzzy caterpillar had been substituted for the opera glasses. When Y turned to regard the caterpillar, the whistle was blown again.

> At once Y gave a loud scream and turned away from the caterpillar. This was repeated 4 times with precisely the same effect.
>
> It is remarkable that the blowing of the whistle, which that same morning had caused only a slight interest, should now so accentuate the reaction to the caterpillar. It can only be explained, I think, on the assumption that the attitude toward the caterpillar was a very *unstable* one, ready to be changed to great excitement and fear, or to calm acceptance, as seen later. The loud whistle, in itself undisturbing, provided just the slight shock to make the fear of the caterpillar burst forth (Valentine, 1930, p. 407).

In a more recent investigation, Brackbill studied the social smiling response in infants (1958). Her interest was not to determine whether smiling was innately or environmentally determined, but to see if smiling was subject to the same conditioning parameters that determine the frequency of occurrence of so many other responses. An operant methodology was used on eight four-month-old infants. Each subject was seen in his own home. A baseline rate for smiling was obtained while experimenter stood motionless and expressionless over the infant. During the conditioning period, the infant's smile obtained for him 30 seconds' worth of social reinforcement: the experimenter smiled at him, picked him up, and "held, jostled, patted, and talked to" him. Four of the subjects were reinforced on a regular schedule throughout. The other four were reinforced on a regular schedule initially, followed by a progressively thinner, randomized variable ratio schedule; by the end of the conditioning period, these subjects were receiving one reinforcement for every four smiles. The procedure during the subsequent extinction period duplicated that of the operant or baseline period.

There is little to be said about the main results of this study other than the fact that rate of smiling yielded to the conditioning and extinction procedures. More interesting results are to be found in the study's incidental results. In addition to recording smiling, Brackbill also recorded each occurrence of a "protest," a category that included all displays of unhappiness ranging from fussiness to out-and-out crying. According to the author,

> The data concerning protest show that during the conditioning period, as the rate of smiling increased, rate of protest decreased— or more properly, protest extinguished with the counterconditioning

of smiling. Specifically, there is a perfect rank correlation between number of trials taken to extinguish the protest response and number of trials to conditioning criterion on the smile response. Similarly, during the extinction period, as rate of smiling decreased, rate of protest increased (1958, p. 122).

Thus it would appear that smiling and crying are both instrumental responses that a young infant is able to use to get parental attention. However, by the time the infant is four months old, crying as an attention-getter is a much stronger response in his repertoire than is smiling, probably for two reasons. First of all, crying, unlike smiling, is both a visual and *auditory* stimulus; an infant with good lungs can reach a parent several rooms removed. Second, crying is a much more compelling stimulus to maternal action than is smiling. No action *has* to be taken when the baby smiles, but when he cries, his behavior carries all the force of a danger signal.[7]

VOCALIZATIONS AND LANGUAGE

Increasing the young child's verbal output through instrumental learning procedures has been the subject of several studies. With rare exceptions, the agent used to effect this increase has been some form of socially administered reinforcement.

Among studies using younger infants, the conditioning of *vocalizations* has naturally been the object of study (Rheingold, Gewirtz, & Ross, 1959; Smith & Smith, 1962; Weisberg, 1963). In the first of these (Rheingold *et al.*, 1959) the subjects were 21 three-month-old residents of an institution. The primary aim of this study was, of course, to see if vocalizations *could* be conditioned. Vocalizations were defined as all sounds produced by the infants other than protests (fussing, crying), straining sounds, coughs, whistles, squeaks, and snorts or noisy breathing. The reinforcement consisted of three simultaneous actions by experimenter: a smile, three "tsk" sounds, and a light poke at the infant's abdomen. The experiment was carried out on six consecutive experimental days devoted to baseline, conditioning, and extinction periods. In the majority of cases each conditioning day consisted of nine three-minute intervals. Vocalizations per three-minute period were raised by this simple procedure from a mean of 13 + to 25. By the end of the

---

7. It is interesting to note in this connection that crying had apparently been purposely extinguished in one of Brackbill's subjects prior to the experiment. This infant never once cried during operant and conditioning periods, nor was the first conditioning session over before she began to show clear indications that learning to smile was taking place. The mother, upon being asked if she could offer any explanation for this unusual behavior, readily avowed she could. She said that the child, her second, had at first had a particularly strong disposition to cry on any and all occasions. The problem was fast becoming a serious one for her and the rest of her family, so she consulted her pediatrician about it. The pediatrician advised the mother that the baby was "wrapping her around its little finger," and that this was both ridiculous and unnecessary. "When the child starts to cry," warned the pediatrician, "go set the kitchen timer for 10 minutes. If you can't stand the noise, close the child's door. *But on no account* go to the baby or pick her up before the end of 10 minutes." The mother followed this dictum, and after three heartrending 9-minute sessions the child cried for only seven minutes, then four, then two-minute periods—one each, as a matter of fact. Thereafter, she ceased crying altogether.

extinction period the mean number of vocalizations had decreased to about 15.

A subsequent experiment by Weisberg (1963) was carried out to see whether Rheingold *et al.* had *really* conditioned their subjects. His rather elaborate design involved two experimental groups and four control groups. The experimental groups differed on the basis of type of reinforcenment: one group ($N = 5$) was reinforced by experimenter's smile, vocalization, and tactual stimulation; the other ($N = 6$) was reinforced by a door chime. The control groups were as follows: one received the above social stimulation on a schedule that was not contingent on the infant's vocalizing behavior; one received the door chime on a noncontingent schedule; one received an extended baseline period with the experimenter present; and one, an extended baseline period without the experimenter present. The first, or socially reinforced, group was the only group to show evidence of conditioning and extinction. Apparently, Rheingold *et al.* had conditioned their subjects.

Smith and Smith (1962) attempted to reinforce vocalizations by physical rotation of their subjects. The infants in this study were twenty hospitalized children between four and thirty-seven months of age and five nonhospitalized children between six and thirty-six months. Each child was placed alone in a playpen that could be rotated $360°$ when a voice key was activated by the child's vocalizations. During a 10-minute "control" condition, the child's vocalizations were counted while he was rotated continuously in the playpen. During the 10-minute experimental condition, he effected his own rotation by vocalizing—or protesting?—with sufficient intensity to activate the voice key. For reasons not specified, the experimenters subjected one half of their hospital sample to the conditioning procedure immediately *prior* to the operant level procedure. (The authors apparently did not perceive of their method as operant conditioning.) The results are not presented separately for the two subgroups, although the authors claimed, as one would expect, that there were significant subgroup differences.

With older infants and young children, language research has concentrated on the conditioning of verbalizations, vocabulary training, the learning of serial and narrative material, and so on. Using an operant conditioning method, Lovaas (1961) conditioned verbalizations of a particular sort in young children. In his study, half the subjects were reinforced for making nonagressive statements and half for making aggressive statements. The reinforcement in both cases was not social, but rather the delivery of a trinket following each criterion response. Lovaas noted that conditioning resulted in his subjects' emitting "a very limited range of verbal responses." Nevertheless, the procedure was certainly effective in changing the frequency of aggressive and nonaggressive responses for the two groups. At the end of 14 minutes' worth of conditioning, the aggression-reinforced group of subjects was uttering, on an average, about 18 aggressive statements per minute and 0 nonaggressive statements per minute while the group reinforced for nonaggressive statements showed quite the opposite results.

Especially noteworthy in this study was Lovaas's attempt to assess the degree of generalization that might occur from a verbal conditioning situation to a nonverbal test situation. The latter was a specially contrived "doll play" procedure in which the child, by remote control, could have one doll hit the other doll on the head with a stick. Nonverbal aggression in this situation increased significantly for subjects who had previously been conditioned to utter aggressive verbalizations.

Attempts to teach words or sentences to very young children are reported by Watson (1925), Strayer (1930), Valentine (1930), and Liiamina (1960). The first of these represents a unique attempt to increase the vocabulary of infants in an institution. Liiamina's study, as well as Strayer's epic vocabulary training program, are described in Chapter 5.

More intriguing than the studies of direct training on language learning are those rare demonstrations of the effectiveness for subsequently developed linguistic skill of early exposure to verbal narrative. These studies indicate clearly that direct tuition—or linguistic training —is not the only way to increase linguistic skills in children. Mere exposure to and familiarization with verbal narrative has a marked and apparently long-lasting effect on the child's own verbal repertoire.

The classic study in this area is that of Harold Burtt (1932, 1937, 1941) who read Greek passages from *Oedipus Tyrannus* to his infant son every day for the better part of two years. At later ages—eight and one-half, fourteen, and eighteen years—the son learned matched familiar and unfamiliar passages from *Oedipus*. The numbers of trials to perfect recitation were compared for the familiar and unfamiliar material.

Burtt described his experimental design and material as follows:

> Each selection included approximately 20 lines or 240 syllables of iambic hexameter. The subject was a boy with an *IQ* of approximately 130. Beginning at the age of 15 months three of these selections were read to him once daily for a period of three months —a total of 90 repetitions. At the age of 18 months these selections were discontinued and three others read daily for three months. This procedure was continued until the subject was three years old and 21 selections had been presented. The 8½ year experiment utilized one-third (seven selections—one from each 3-month period) of the available material which had been presented in infancy, plus three new selections for control. The 14-year experiment utilized another third, and the present and final experiment [18 years] used the last seven selections plus three new controls (1941, p. 435).

Learning was carried out with a modified anticipation method.

The results are shown in Table 4.5. At the first test period, age eight years, there was a 27 per cent saving in learning the familiar material as compared to the unfamiliar. At the second test period, age fourteen years, the saving in learning the familiar material had been reduced to 8 per cent. By eighteen years, all effects of early familiarization had apparently vanished.

Of no less heroic proportion is the study by Irwin (1960) on the systematic verbal stimulation of infants by means of storybook reading. Irwin convinced mothers in 24 working-class homes to spend 15 to 20 minutes a day ". . . reading to their children from illustrated children's storybooks [The Little Golden Books], pointing out the pictures, talking about them, making up original, simple tales about them, and in general furnishing materials supplemental to the text so that the speech sound environment impinging upon the children would be enriched" (1960, p. 187). This continued for a year and a half, beginning when the infants were thirteen months old and continuing until they were thirty months old. Irwin took bimonthly samples of vocalizations from these subjects and from their 10 matched controls for a phoneme frequency analysis.

Table 4.5—Average Number of Trials to One Perfect Recitation *

	Age at Which Selections Were Learned		
	8 Years	14 Years	18 Years
Selections read to S between 15 and 23 months of age	340	150	191
Selections read to S between 24 and 36 months of age	299	148	187
Selections never previously encountered by S	435	162	191

* After Burtt, 1932, 1937, 1941.

The difference between experimental and control groups in vocalization rate was significant by the time the third sample was taken, at age seventeen to eighteen months, and grew progressively greater thereafter (Fig. 4.6). By the end of the experiment, age thirty months, the experimental group was vocalizing at a rate somewhat more than twice that of the control group.

Studies devoted to the instrumental conditioning of language parameters in infancy have been limited largely—and unnecessarily—to the conditioning of vocalizations and verbalizations (or vocabulary training). An example of some of the exciting psycholinguistic and paralinguistic variables that invite investigation was the attempt by Pike (1949) to train an infant to adopt the intonation contours of the English-speaking adult—a study that is described in Chapter 5. Such an investigation is all the more interesting when one considers that the intonation contour of one's native language or dialect is probably one of the earliest aspects of language to be learned and one of the most resistant to change in later life.

It should be noted that the Burtt, Irwin, and Pike studies were carried out with the subjects' parents as experimenters. An interesting consideration seems to have slipped past everyone's scrutiny save Valentine's (1930). Would it be possible in the indirect tuition situation to achieve the same results, or even to approximate them, if the experi-

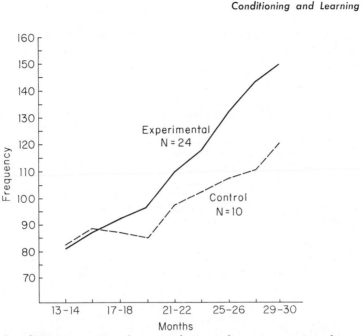

Figure 4.6. *Graphic presentation of mean phoneme frequency scores of two groups of young children.*

Children in experimental group were under a regimen of enriched reading. Children in control group were not. (From Irwin, 1960.)

menter were someone with whom the child did *not* have close emotional dependency ties? Valentine said,

> We see then, that, while Y [his infant daughter] will imitate many actions performed by others, it is her mother who "sets her off," as none other can. It is, I suggest, the mother whose actions are supremely interesting and with whom especially the child delights to be in accord.
>
> The others whom Y would sometimes imitate but sometimes refuse to imitate, were also members of the house. I have little doubt that the appearance of a relative stranger would usually so embarrass a child that the stranger would not be imitated to nearly the same extent—that is, at an age when the child is made shy by the presence of a stranger. This ignoring of the importance of the imitatee, weakens the observation of some experimenters that in the laboratory they have frequently tried to get imitation of simple movements (like putting two hands together) in children of from ten to eighteen months, without much success (Valentine, 1930, p. 129).

Jersild and Bienstock (1931) successfully trained a different order of vocalizations in young children—singing. Two groups of 18 children, age thirty-one to forty-eight months, were matched on pretest results for the accurate vocal reproduction of pitch and interval. The experimental group underwent ten-minute daily training in singing for six months, after which both groups were retested. Subjects in the experimental group sang both pitch and interval with significantly greater accuracy on both the posttest and a transfer test.

The Conflict Between Verbal and Motor Behavior in Early Development.

> While the child is learning to walk, there is very often a standstill, or even a retrograde movement in the matter of speech. After walking is mastered, the acquisition of language goes forward again with greater facility than ever.
>   During this third [6-month] period, marked progress is usually made in the understanding of words, and in their intelligent application, though the vocabulary is still very limited, and the pronunciation imperfect. Difficult sounds are omitted, or replaced by easier ones (Tracy, 1893, p. 116).

Here in a nutshell is a description of one of the most intriguing phenomena developmental psychology has to offer: the early cyclical relationship in the development of motor and language skills—a *competition*, one might say, for development of motor and language skills.

This early cyclical development has been described by many investigators in an incidental fashion, but it has altogether escaped a concentrated research effort. Perhaps the first to notice it was Schultze (1880) who observed that children appear to learn thoroughly only one thing at a time, and that this is exemplified by the reciprocity of learning to walk and learning to speak: when the child learns to walk, Schultze observed, he pushes aside the development of speech almost entirely and resumes his linguistic task only after the locomotor one has been finished.

Other investigators have confirmed these results. Brigance's daughter developed a vocabulary of four words during the eighth month (1934). During the next three months, while she was learning to walk, she added only three more to her vocabulary. Walking was fully developed by the end of the first year, and her vocabulary began to increase rapidly thereafter. By the age of fifteen months it consisted of seventy-five words. Jegi's child learned to walk in one day; there was no plateau in vocabulary acquisition for his child, as one might expect (1901). Shirley observed, during the developmental examination of her twenty-five babies, that the children vocalized much less during the periods in which they were mastering such motor skills as reaching for objects, sitting alone, and walking (1933). Her data also suggest that ". . . babbling is a type of play to which the baby resorts when there is nothing better to do or when the novelty of the new type of motor activity has worn off" (1933, p. 71).

Gross motor skills are not the only competitors of language development. The Clark Hulls submitted evidence many years ago that vocabulary acquisition is held in check while the child is struggling to achieve bladder control (1919). As Fig. 4.7 shows, there daughter's rapid increase in vocabulary began only after urination was more or less under the child's voluntary control.

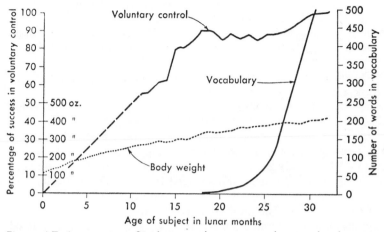

Figure 4.7. *Apparent conflict between language and motor development.*

Not until bladder control has been achieved does vocabulary growth begin to show rapid acceleration. (From Hull & Hull, 1919.)

MOTOR BEHAVIOR

Perceptual-Motor and Locomotor Responses. Psychologists have studied the responsiveness to training of a wide variety of locomotor and perceptual-motor responses in infancy. Gesell and Thompson, for example, began training twins T and C in climbing and in cube prehension at forty-six weeks of age (1941). Hilgard trained twenty-eight-month-old children to climb, button, and cut with scissors (1932). The results in this study indicate that the two perceptual-motor skills benefited more from training than did the locomotor skill, when the scores of the trained children were compared to those of their matched controls. (Presumably, the amounts of training for the three tasks were equal.) Moreover, of the two preceptual-motor skills, buttoning showed the greater relative improvement even though throughout training it had clearly been the task with the lowest motivational pull.

Ketterlinus (1931) confronted young children with one of the classic tasks of an earlier era in psychology—mirror reversals. The specific tasks required of her subjects, age 2–1 to 5–4, were (1) picking up objects and putting them in a cup, (2) pushing a disc with the foot from a starting point to an end point, and (3) pushing a toy cannon along a crooked path. In each case, the major components of the task were visible only through a mirror. All but two subjects completed the first two tasks, although there were noticeable age differences in the efficiency with which these were accomplished. However, difficulty level and frustration took its toll on the third task, which the four- and five-year-olds finished but which very few of the three-year-olds and none of the two-year-olds completed.

In several early studies, Hicks surveyed the effectiveness of training young children on a variety of perceptual-motor skills (Hicks,

1930a, 1930b; Hicks & Ralph, 1931). These included tracing the Porteus Diamond Maze, weight lifting via a pulley arrangement, tracing between lines of unequal width, punching circles in paper, and throwing balls at a moving target. In none of these did the trained children perform significantly better than their controls.

Watson (1966) has recently begun to study the possibility of conditioning infants' eye movements by operant procedures during brief intervals of time (30 to 90 seconds). This work is described below, in the discussion of visual and auditory reinforcements.

Maze Learning. A good example of the fads that arise in psychological experimentation is provided by the studies of infantile maze learning—whole body mazes, slot mazes, and so on. The publication of these studies began in 1929 and stopped in 1936. The majority of them were undisguised attempts to show that children can do it if rats can. One of the maze learning studies, however, went beyond such a demonstration to produce some interesting results concerning the need for novelty—or lack of it—at an early age.

Wenger (1933) ran 65 children between the ages of 1–0 and 4–9 in three types of body maze—a broken field maze, a four-choice maze, and a three-choice maze. Not all subjects learned all mazes. Each subject was given five trials on the maze to which he was assigned unless his path selection varied during those five trials; in that case he was given ten trials. The results showed that in all three mazes, a nonvariable path selection pattern predominated. Specifically, the same path was chosen over five successive trials by 64 per cent of the children running the broken field maze, sixty-four per cent of those running the four-choice maze, and 91 per cent of those running the three-choice maze. In addition, it was found that nonvariable choice was negatively correlated with CA; it may also have been correlated with the manner of rearing. Of the forty institutionalized orphan subjects used in this experiment, none under the age of forty-two months showed variable behavior; among the 25 home-reared children, variable behavior appeared at twenty-nine months. The confounding factor here is that variable path selection was apparently higher for brighter children.

Elimination Training. Although a large number of retrospective studies dealing with times and severity of bowel and bladder training as well as studies dealing with the relationship of these variables to personality development have been published, there are relatively few studies of elimination that actually inquire about training procedures and that use other than retrospective techniques of investigation. Of these few studies, most are descriptive in nature rather than experimental, and with one exception—Hull and Hull (1919), described above—they describe the general outcome of an unknown assortment of parental training practices.[8]

Of the studies that more nearly approximate experimental designs, two (Brazelton, 1962; Scoe, 1933) have used parents as the experi-

8. For reviews of the other types of studies of elimination the reader is referred to Caldwell (1964) and to Chapter 3, this volume.

menters to implement the authors' training programs. Brazelton's training program contains some unusual points, e.g., his advice that as soon as the infant understands what he is to do and can lower his own training pants the mother should leave him alone to manage his own toileting affairs. (This is counsel that complements Spock's concern with the infant's need for independence [1963].) Brazelton feels that training should not begin before eighteen months and points out that two thirds of the 108 children, out of a total sample of 1,170 who were not trained by age four years had been started before the age of eighteen months. The modal age for first achievement was twenty-four months, and that for completion of daytime training, thirty months. At these ages, 80 per cent of the children in his sample trained themselves on bowel and bladder control simultaneously.

Eighteen months may indeed be the optimal age to begin toileting, but it is not the age at which most Western mothers do, in fact, begin training their children. Sears, Maccoby, and Levin (1957) found that eleven months was the average age for beginning bowel training and that an average of seven months was required to complete training. Hetherington and Brackbill (1963) reported similar figures. Furthermore, unbelievable as it may seem to Americans, the typical British mother begins to toilet train her child within the first two weeks of its life (Douglas & Blomfield, 1958). In their sample of over 5,000 children, 60 per cent were "potted" within two weeks of birth. Of these, 83 per cent had completed training by 18 months.

One experimental study in the area of elimination training is that of McGraw (1940) who used the co-twin method in longitudinal fashion on two sets of identical twins. On four days a week, hourly potting was carried out for the trained member of each pair as soon as they were a few weeks old. Training for the trained twins began at ages 23 and 41 days; it ended at ages 470 and 800 days. Training for the control twins began at ages 430 days and 24 months; it ended for them, as it did for their trained brothers, at 470 and 800 days. Training appeared to have some beneficial effect in the younger set of twins, but not for the older set.

Yet to be done is the most obvious and obviously useful study—one that asks which of a variety of toilet training methods is the most efficient and least disturbing one for the child. Bowel training is the first situation of real consequence in which the mother attempts to get her child to learn something. It is also one of the most difficult training situations because the learner's motivations do not correspond to those of his mother and because unless the mother is consistently patient, watchful, and perceptive, the criterion response goes unrewarded. Furthermore, sooner or later the reinforcement system switches from reward for performance to punishment for lapses, with the concomitant increase in emotionality that punishment entails. When toilet training is viewed in these terms it is not even necessary to assume that erogenous activity is being interfered with in order to predict that the toilet training situation is one that may well disturb both child and parent.

THE LEARNING OF SEQUENTIAL MATERIAL

Serial Learning. Studies of the way in which young children learn ordered material are extremely scarce. The oldest and best of these rarities, Josephine Foster's, appeared in 1928. Foster used 29 children between the ages of two to seven and four to nine. The stimulus material consisted of eight children's stories approximately equal in length and difficulty. On the first presentation of each, the experimenter read the story to the subject at "an ordinary rate of speed with no pauses." On the subsequent nine readings of that story—given on the nine consecutive days following the first reading—

> . . . the reader paused at certain definite places (about 40 to each story), looked expectantly at the child and waited about two seconds. No directions were given but most of the children began to supply words during the fourth or fifth hearing of the first story. Children who had not begun to give words by the sixth repetition of this story were asked "What?" at the first ten hesitations. The child's completions were rewarded at first with a "Good!" and after that with a smile and nod. If incorrect completions were given, the reader repeated the correct words firmly enough to show the child that his completion had not been exactly right, but with no touch of a reproof which might discourage further efforts. The child was allowed to continue telling the story as long as he could, until he made some error, when the reader would interrupt and read on to the next "hesitation." The recorder, meanwhile, kept an exact record of everything the child said (1928, p. 28).

For stories 1 to 3 combined, the median number of correctly anticipated words rose steadily from 1.0 on the first anticipation trial (second reading) to 28.3 on the ninth anticipation trial. There were marked chronological and mental age differences in learning efficiency as well as a consistent sex difference for the last seven anticipation trials in favor of the boys, surprisingly enough, in spite of the fact that the girls as a group had a five-month edge in mental age. There were also large *positive* correlations between number of errors in anticipation and CA (.66) and between errors and MA (.74). Foster interpreted these to mean ". . . that the older and more mature children are more likely to remember the sense of a passage and so are more apt to stray from the verbatim reproduction. It might also mean that these children were more ready to guess at the next word than were the less mature children" (1928, p. 43). Interestingly enough, there was no correlation between the frequency of correct anticipation of individual words and the frequency of those words in the kindergarten child's vocabulary. In order to assess the importance of the cue word or words, i.e., those immediately preceding the word to be anticipated, Foster had thirty-four adults guess the missing words in each of the four stories. For all stories combined, the correlations between correct guesses by the adults and correct anticipations by the children was only .54, indicating the children's responses were only partially determined by conventional word orders already learned or by what seemed to adults to be logical sequences.

Learning Sets. Probably the earliest study to use a learning set methodology was that of Munn and Steining (1931), who confronted a fifteen-month old child with a series of two-choice, simultaneous discriminations. All discriminations following the first were typically presented for 10 trials on the same day. The discriminative stimuli were two-dimensional, geometric, black and white figures. When the infant chose correctly, he was able to retrieve a piece of candy from the compartment behind the correct stimulus.

Unfortunately, there is not very much that can be said for or against learning sets on the basis of these data, for the discriminations were too simple for the child from the outset. In the series of eight discriminations that followed the pretraining item there were only four errors in 86 trials, so that the modal score for the eight discriminations was 100 per cent correct. In addition, in six out of eight discriminations the same form was used as the positive stimulus.

Quite the same comment holds for a subsequent study by Gellermann (1933a) that was modeled closely after Munn and Steining's and in which he used two two-year-old subjects. However, in a companion study (1933b) using the same subjects, Gellermann introduced some diversity into his series of discriminations. Table 4.6 contains a description of the discriminative stimuli, along with a tabulation for both subjects of trials and errors to criterion, 10 consecutive correct choices. Despite the variation in stimuli there is no real evidence in these data to indicate that the children learned to learn.

Table 4.6—Pairs of Discriminative Stimuli, Listed in Order of Presentation, and Numbers of Trials and Errors to the Criterion of 10 Consecutive Correct Choices for Two Two-Year-Old Subjects (after Gellermann, 1933b)

DISCRIMINATIVE STIMULI		NANCY		JIMMY	
Positive	Negative	Trials	Errors	Trials	Errors
Star	Circle	0	0	0	0
Square	Cross	5	5	19	19
Diamond	Circle	0	0	0	0
Half-moon (point down)	Half-moon (point up)	18	8	50	23
Triangle (point down)	Triangle (point up)	2	2	–	–
Square	Diamond	1	1	–	–
Cross (rotated 45°)	Cross	1	1	6	5
Star (point up)	Star (point down)	30	15	50	29
Half-moon (point down)	Triangle (point up)	0	0	–	–
Circle	Cross	2	2	–	–

Skeels (1933) used 41 children ranging in age from fifteen to forty-six months in an early study of discrimination learning. Each of the form boards that served as the experimental material provided a four-choice simultaneous discrimination task; if the child picked up the correct form, he was rewarded with a bit of cookie. After the first correct form, a circle, had been learned to criterion, the child was told that his cookie would no longer be found under the circle and that another form would be correct from now on. This procedure was extended until all four forms had in turn been correct. Interestingly enough, and in harmony with Gellermann's data as well as Ling's results, the younger children showed no evidence of learning to learn. These children (mean CA = 26 months) took 1.29 trials to reach criterion on the first correct form, and 27.29 trials on the second correct form, whereas somewhat older subjects (mean CA = 37 months) took 4.13 and 3.20 trials, respectively.

The results of Hicks and Stewart's (1930) study of discrimination learning in two-, three-, four-, and five-year-olds also suggest that the phenomenon of learning to learn begins to appear toward the end of the period of infancy. In this study, the subjects were exposed to four three-choice simultaneous discriminations, the correct response in each case being the middle-sized stimulus. The majority of two-year-olds did not progress beyond the first discrimination, so that the data obtained from them are incomplete and inconclusive. At the three-year level, however, there is undeniably a systematic decrease in the mean number of errors to criterion over the 4 discriminations: 11.8, 2.0, 1.7, .3. (As far as the older groups are concerned, it would appear that half the four-year-olds and the majority of the five-year-olds were already acquainted with the concept *middle size* at the beginning of the experiment, so that they were not in a strict sense learning anything.)

Learning set formation in very young children has also been investigated by Kuenne (Harlow, 1949), using the Wisconsin General Test Apparatus, and by Koch and Meyer (1959), using two-dimensional stimuli for which color was the discriminative cue. In these two studies the subjects ranged in age from two to five years and from 2–5 to 5–6, respectively. The overall results in both cases showed a learning to learn effect; however, no separate analysis by CA was made in either study.

DISCRIMINATION LEARNING

In one of the earliest studies of infant discrimination learning Munn and Steining (1931) exposed a fifteen-month-old boy to a series of two-choice, simultaneous discriminations with two-dimensional black and white stimuli. The typical stimulus in this series was a black figure against a white background; the white background was mounted on a larger, black background. In the majority of discriminations the positive stimulus was a cross; it was changed from one discrimination to another in respect to its orientation or the contour of its background. The negative stimulus was changed in respect to shape, orientation, and background.

Munn and Steining summarize their results thus:

1. The positive stimulus (cross) was responded to with 45° rotation, with five changes in background, and with five different negative stimuli.

2. The negative stimulus was an effective element of the total situation only in [the case in which] the positive stimulus was an entirely new one.

3. When an entirely new situation was presented the child demonstrated that it could very readily adjust by making correct discriminations (1931, p. 85).

It might be noted that Ling reached much the same conclusion in her study of form discrimination as did Munn and Steining: "Change in the relative position, space orientation, or size of either or both positive and negative stimuli has a very slight effect on the discrimination performance of the infant" (1931, p. 60).

Gellermann's studies of discrimination learning in two two-year-olds are essentially replications of Munn and Steining's earlier study, although Gellermann did add two chimpanzee subjects and several more discriminations (1933a, 1933b). One interesting observation he made was that in the more difficult discriminations the subjects, chimp and child alike, resorted to tracing with their fingers the outlines of the figures, thus adding proprioceptive cues to the visual ones.

In the Hicks and Stewart (1930) study already mentioned, the investigators attempted to teach the concept *middle size* to two-, three-, four-, and five-year-olds by having them choose the middle size box out of three. Four sets of three boxes differing in absolute size were used as training stimuli. An analysis of errors made on each of the four sets indicates that in each instance, choice of the large box provided a far greater number of errors than choice of small box. For all subjects and all four sets combined, the large box was mistakenly chosen 165 times and the small, 82 times. The greater difficulty of learning "larger" than "smaller" has been confirmed for three-dimensional stimuli by Graham *et al.* (1964). These investigators further found that learning relative sizes was substantially easier for children age 2-0 to 4-6 years than it was for them to learn absolute sizes.

Spiker and Norcross (1962) have presented some interesting data relating to the effect on discrimination learning of prior discrimination training in which cue distinctiveness was manipulated. In their study 51 children, age 2-4 to 5-6, were exposed to a pretraining task followed by a transfer task. Both tasks were presented in the form of two-choice discriminations. The children were assigned to one of three procedures during pretraining; the transfer procedure was identical for all subjects.

The basic stimuli for both pretraining and transfer were line drawings of two girls' faces. On one half of the pretraining trials, both faces appeared as the discriminative stimuli; on the remaining trials, one or the other face was presented in duplicate. During pretraining, children in Group I (maximum distinctiveness) learned to a criterion of twelve consecutive correct trials to name one face "Jean" and the other face "Peg." Children in Group II learned to the same criterion that the two faces on any one trial were the "same" or "different." Children in Group III underwent the Group II procedure until they had made 12 correct choices; the pictures were then presented to them by a successive presentation method, one at a time. The number of stimulus exposures was matched across groups.

In the transfer task the two pictures were mounted on the front of small boxes. One of the pictures designated the "correct" box; when the subject chose it, he found a marble inside. After 30 transfer trials, the child exchanged his marbles for a toy of his choice.

The mean number of correct responses was, as predicted, significantly greater for Group I than for the other two groups—though only for the last 15 transfer trials. Although experimental emphasis was on the transfer task, it is interesting to note that for the three groups the mean number of errors to criterion in the pretraining task was 6.8, 1.7, and 2.0, respectively, indicating that Group I—those who learned the pictures by the names of Jean and Peg—was faced with a much more difficult task.

Other tasks that have been used to study the discrimination of infants and young children are learning to discriminate relative and absolute sizes of objects (Welch, 1939a, 1939b, 1939c), object shape (Ling, 1941), object shape and color (Hill, 1965), and such items as high versus low pitch, cans of different sizes, sticks of different lengths, pieces of silverware, and so on (Waring, 1927).

GENERALIZATION AND TRANSPOSITION

There has been very little work done within the instrumental conditioning paradigm on the generalization of conditioned responses—by which is meant, as in classical conditioning, the situation in which a response, conditioned to one stimulus, subsequently occurs in the presence of other stimuli as well. The clearest example of the simple generalization of a conditioned response is to be found in the Watson and Rayner study of conditioned fear (1920), described earlier. Once conditioned to fear the rat, Albert showed on test trials a generalized fear response to other furry objects in motion: a rabbit, a fur coat, the experimenter's hair, and a bewhiskered Santa Claus mask.[9]

An example of generalized extinction is to be found in Jones' (1924) parallel study of Peter. Whereas Albert ended up as a child with fears, Peter began to experiment in this condition. The process by which Peter's fears were extinguished is described in a later section. As far as generalization is concerned, interest attaches to the fact that once Peter's fear of a rabbit had extinguished, he also showed tolerance of rats, angle worms, frogs, and fur rugs when these were presented to him on test trials.

One of the few studies specifically concerned with simple, instrumentally conditioned generalization in infants is that of Welch (1939c). His four subjects were between eighteen and twenty months of age at

9. Little Albert's fear generalized to Watson's hair but not to the two observers' hair, with which he played. It was also Watson himself who wore the mask to which Albert responded negatively. Therefore, strictly speaking, the stimulus eliciting a generalized fear response may well have been Dr. Watson rather than hair and wool-festooned masks. (The extent to which Watson associated himself with the other stimuli is not made clear in the published presentation of this study.)

the beginning of training. The training material consisted of a set of blocks varying systematically in two dimensions from a square to a narrow rectangle. By means of pure repetition, Welch tried to establish an association between the training block and a "nonsense word," *ate*. On subsequent test sessions, this word was used to cue the selection of objects considered "ate-like" by the child from the assortment in front of him. Unfortunately, because of several factors, including procedural differences from subject to subject, very little can be said with certainty about the results of this study. Welch himself concluded, among other things, that the children seemed to be generalizing on the basis of form rather than color.

The experimental procedure called *transposition* is a special case of combined discrimination training and testing for generalization. The best-known developmental study of transposition in young children was carried out by Kuenne (1946). Kuenne's subjects ranged in age from thirty to seventy months. The stimuli used were two-dimensional white squares of varying sizes. Stimulus #1 was 2.0 sq. in.; #2, 3.6 sq. in.; #5, 21.0 sq. in.; #6, 37.8 sq. in.; and #7, 68.0 sq. in. There were no stimuli corresponding to the size that would have been numbers 3 and 4. Stimuli numbers 6 and 7 were used as training stimuli. Whenever the child chose the smaller of these two, he was rewarded with a toy. Training was continued to a criterion of 9 out of 10 correct choices. Then came the transposition tests. The child was confronted with the necessity of choosing either stimulus #1 or #2 for 10 unrewarded trials; this was followed by 10 test trials on #5 and #6. (The sequence was reversed for half the subjects.) Following Spence's theoretical formulations on relational learning, Kuenne reasoned that the younger children —those who had not yet learned the concepts of *bigger* and *smaller*— would respond on the "far" transposition test (stimulus #1 vs. #2) in a random fashion, while the older children, for whom choice behavior was verbally mediated, would choose in a manner consistent with their previous discrimination training, i.e., always the "smaller" stimulus.

As predicted, the younger group of children, with an average age of 37.6 months, chose stimuli #1 and 2 an equal number of times on the test trials, whereas the older group of children, with a mean age of sixty-five months, chose the smaller stimulus consistently. The four age groups did not differ on their choice of the smaller stimulus in the "near" transposition test. Kuenne's results have been replicated and extended in other developmental studies of transposition in young children by Alberts and Ehrenfreund (1951) and Cole *et al.* (1964).

EXTINCTION AND RETENTION OF INSTRUMENTALLY LEARNED RESPONSES

Withholding further reinforcement of a conditioned response leads, sooner or later, to a gradual weakening in the strength of that response and, ultimately, to its extinction. (When this process of learned response degradation takes place within the discrete-trial instrumental learning paradigm it is more traditionally referred to as "retention" than "extinction.") In research with animals and adult human beings, the rate of extinction has been found to depend on characteristics of the extinction procedure (e.g., drive level during extinction), on the relationship between extinction and the preceding learning situation (e.g., the extent of identity of the discrimination stimuli in both situations), and, indirectly, on the preceding learning situation in and of itself, since stronger habits are more difficult to extinguish. Accounts of the factors influencing conditioning and extinction or learning and retention may be found in Kimble (1961) and Deese (1958). Since considerably less research has been done on extinction and retention than on conditioning and learning, we do not yet know whether all of the variables that affect retention or resistance to extinction in animals and adult humans also affect this process in infants. The few conclusions that are available on extinction or retention in infancy are reviewed below.

In several early publications, M. C. Jones presented several suggestions, along with a few case demonstrations, that were concerned with the elimination of children's fears (1924a, 1924b, 1924c). She considered that her work was a sequel to Watson and Rayner's (1920) study of Little Albert. And indeed, Jones' prime example, Peter, age 2-10, might have been Albert reincarnated. Peter too was afraid of rats, rabbits, fur coats, cotton, and so on. Again, like Albert, Peter's fear had not generalized to nonfurry toys. According to Jones, of the strategies tried with Peter and with the other children showing similar fears, the following two were the most successful. (1) Vicarious adaptation or extinction. For example, the fearful subject watches a child who is not afraid of rabbits play with a rabbit. (2) Adaptation of extinction while the child is satisfying a need of compelling strength and one that is positive in nature. For example, as the fearful child hungrily consumes his meal, the rabbit is introduced into his line of vision, and is, meal by meal, moved ever closer to the child.

Young children's retention of learned material appears as a major variable in Foster's (1928) very interesting investigation of children's serial learning of stories by the anticipation method. Each story was presented to each child once a day for two weeks. Eight weeks later Foster had her subjects relearn all four stories in the same order as before—each story being presented once a day for five successive days. The savings scores for all four stories were not inconsiderable when one compares the first anticipation trial on relearning with that on learning. However, the fifth anticipation trial on relearning showed considerable divergence among the four stories in number of correctly anticipated words, so that the most influential determinant of the rate of relearning seemed to be the length of time intervening between learning and relearning.

In a more recent study of serial recall, in 210 children from two to five years of age Rossi and Rossi (1965) did not find a significant increase with age in number of words recalled in the same serial order in which they had been presented. (In the Rossi and Rossi procedure, unlike Foster's, the serial order of presentation varied from trial to trial.) The authors did find significant age increases, however, in the total number of words recalled and in the extent to which the words clustered associatively around the same conceptual category.

REINFORCEMENT SCHEDULE AND EXTINCTION

In work with animals and adult human beings, it has generally been found that resistance to extinction is greater following the use of intermittent reinforcement during conditioning, i.e., when more than one response is required for a reinforcement, than it is when every response is reinforced during conditioning, i.e., when only one response is required to elicit a reinforcement from the experimenter. The results from infant studies are not wholly in accordance with this finding, but, on the other hand, the data from infant studies are relatively meager and correspondingly less reliable.

As noted earlier, Brackbill (1958) demonstrated greater resistance to extinction of the smiling response in four-month old infants as a function of partial or intermittent reinforcement—or, to be precise, an increasingly thin, randomized variable ratio reinforcement schedule. (A randomized variable ratio reinforcement schedule is one in which the subject is reinforced, *on the average,* for every *n*th response. For example, on a VR3 ratio, over a series of 12 responses, the subject might be reinforced after, say, the 3rd, the 4th, the 8th, and the 10th responses.) The comparison group was maintained on continuous or regular reinforcement. A point of interest in these results is the fact that ". . . every member of the regularly reinforced group extinguished not to his previous, operant rate of response, but to a 0 rate."

The complement of a variable ratio reinforcement schedule is a fixed ratio schedule, according to which the subject is reinforced following every *n*th response. For example, on a FR3 ratio, over a series of 12 responses, the subject would be reinforced following the 3rd, the 6th, the 9th, and the 12th responses. Rate of responding is typically higher under fixed ratios than under variable ratios.

Rate of responding under progressively thin FR ratios (from FR3 to FR18) was the focus of a study by Rheingold, Stanley, and Doyle (1964). Of 20 children between 1-11 and 5-0 (mean age = 3.4 years), 15 showed increasing rates of response with advancing, i.e., higher, ratios. None of the 5 children maintained on continuous or regular reinforcement increased in response rate.

Warren and Brown (1943) tried a temporal conditioning schedule with their two- to five-year-old subjects. The response was lever pushing and the reinforcement, candy pellets. The temporal conditioning schedule was used in a reconditioning session, following both a period of regular reinforcement and one of extinction. Under this condition, a response was reinforced only if it occurred no less than 15 seconds after the previous response. Unfortunately, Warren and Brown do not report the degree to which reconditioning was successfully established for all nine children by this schedule.

NUMBER OF REINFORCEMENTS AND EXTINCTION

Pumroy and Pumroy (1961) included number of reinforcements as an independent variable in their study of resistance to extinction. They found as expected that more reinforcements during conditioning leads to significantly greater resistance to extinction.

Siegel and Foshee (1953) divided 80 subjects ranging in age from 2-11 to 5-8 into four groups that were matched for age and that differed in terms of the total number of reinforcements (candy) in a simple bar pressing task. Following two reinforced trials, the mean number of responses to extinction was 32.9; following four, 41.0; following eight, 51.6; and following sixteen, 94.9.

THE ROLE OF REINFORCEMENT IN EARLY INSTRUMENTAL LEARNING

If the choice of reinforcer is important to the course of instrumental conditioning in adults, it is doubly so in infants, for in using infants instead of adults one forfeits a bonus—the general motivation to cooperate with people, including an experimenter. The hardy college sophomore absorbs considerable verbal abuse or even physical pain in the name of scientific investigation, but the unsocialized infant simply leaves the field or, if he is not yet able, sets about screaming when the situation becomes unpleasant for him. The pros and cons of reinforcers that investigators have chosen to use in past research will be discussed in this section.

POSITIVE REINFORCEMENT

Social Reinforcement. Of the positive reinforcers available to experimenters, that which is most effective with young infants is social reinforcement. The age at which it ceases to be the most effective reward is probably the age at which the child has gained the ability to discriminate between principal caretaker and strangers, and is now developing an attitude toward strangers that may vary between distinct coldness and active antipathy.

The use of social reinforcement in the operant conditioning of infant behavior has been studied by Brackbill (1958), Rheingold, Gewirtz, and Ross (1959), and Weisberg (1963). Of these three studies, Weisberg's was the only one primarily concerned with reinforcement effectiveness as an independent variable. He found that vocalization rate could be increased by social reinforcement but not by nonsocial reinforcement, as represented by the sound of a door chime.

It might be noted that to date the social reinforcement used in such operant conditioning studies as those noted above has been a thing compounded of many elements: the experimenter moves his body, nods his head, zooms toward the infant, smiles, vocalizes, and makes some sort of bodily contact with the child. The study that begs to be done now is one showing which of these reinforcing elements, or combinations of elements, are the effective ones.

The use of social reinforcement in discrete trial learning is illustrated by Waring's early study (1927), described below.

Verbal Reinforcement. Verbal reward was made the focus of an early and very interesting study by Waring (1927, Experiment 1). Two groups of subjects ranging in age from 2-6 to 5-7 and matched on pretest scores, were trained on several discrimination tasks and several perceptual-motor tasks. Children in one group received a nod and a smile from the experimenter for responding correctly to any of the tasks. For children in the other group, the experimenter nodded, smiled, and said "Benito." (Waring wished to use a meaningless verbalization as reward.)

The author predicted that not only would the verbally reinforced group show higher scores on the final or transfer task, but also that the verbally rewarded group would show relatively greater improvement on the discrimination tasks than on the perceptual-motor tasks. Her reasoning behind this prediction was that, "In the gross motor situations the child's success is so obvious to him that the factor of approval, which is adult recognition of his success, is not so powerful" (1927, p. 60). The results supporting this prediction are shown in Table 4.7. It will be noted that the social reinforcement received by the second group of children was certainly instrumental in effecting improvement in both perceptual-motor and discrimination tasks. However, it was not as effective as social and verbal reward combined—particularly on the disciimination task.

Table 4.7—Mean Scores on Pretests and Posttests for Five Verbally Reinforced and Five Nonverbally Reinforced Subjects of Experiment 1 (after Waring, 1927)

Group	PERCEPTUAL-MOTOR TASKS		DISCRIMINATION TASKS	
	Pretests	Posttests	Pretests	Posttests
Verbally reinforced	2.4	6.8	1.6	8.6
Nonverbally reinforced	2.0	5.2	1.6	5.2

Appetitional Reinforcement. As one might expect, the use of a food or foodlike substance as a reward has been very popular in instrumental as well as classical conditioning studies with infants. Rewards that have been used in instrumental studies—all of them discrete trial procedures —have included candies (Munn & Steining, 1931; Warren & Brown, 1943; Hunter & Bartlett, 1948), cookies (Skeels, 1933), raisins (Jackson *et al.*, 1938), and jam and honey (Myers, 1908; Valentine, 1913–1914). All of these, by virtue of their caloric content, have the disadvantage of reducing drive with each additional trial. Valentine, for example, did not obtain any conclusive evidence that his seven-month-old son could learn to discriminate blue from green when consistently rewarded with jam or honey for choosing blue. We know from other studies that any normal child could make such a distinction were his motivation at a reasonably high level. Another disadvantage in attempting to use carbohydrate rewards nowadays is that news of their contribution to tooth decay has finally reached the ears of teachers and parents.

Without a doubt, the most ingenious "food" reward was the sac-charine-coated object used by Ling (1941) to denote to young infants the correct one of two or more objects in a series of simultaneous dis-criminations. Apparently, the infant's eagerness to suck on the correct stimulus did not decrease significantly with repeated trials, and despite the excessive experimental time required of each infant in this study, there are no data to show that the reinforcing effectiveness of saccharine was markedly reduced by the end of the experiment.

Visual and Auditory Reinforcement. Smith and Smith attempted unsuccessfully to reinforce panel pushing by means of visual reinforce-ment (1962). Their seven subjects, age nine to thirteen months, had to touch a contact plate on the side of the experimental crib in order to advance a film strip showing colorful country scenes. According to the authors, "Only two of these infants displayed any real interest in the colored pictures, and none established the connection between the con-tact plate and the projection on the screen" (1962, p. 281).

Rheingold *et al.* (1964) have reported that for children between the ages of two and five years three-second sequences of a color motion picture accompanied by music provide reinforcement effective enough to increase a touching response to a significant extent over operant levels —as long as reinforcement is delivered on an intermittent basis.

Purely auditory reinforcement in the operant conditioning of in-fants has been used by Basan (1960), Simmons and Lipsitt (1961), Smith and Smith (1962), Weisberg (1963), and Watson (1966). Sim-mons and Lipsitt (1961) reported findings for two infants, age ten and twelve months, who were confronted with two panels, only one of which operated a door chime when pressed. Both infants strongly preferred to press the panel that operated the chime, no matter whether that panel was to the child's left or right.

Weisberg, on the other hand, was unable to increase vocalizations in three-month-old infants by using a door chime (1963). The difference in the two sets of results may be attributable to the difference in sub-jects' ages. However, there was also a slight difference in methodology that may also have been a principal determinant of the differences in the two sets of data. In the Simmons and Lipsitt procedure, the child was left alone with the apparatus,[10] whereas in Weisberg's procedure, an unresponsive adult remained in the child's visual field during the attempt to condition. It may well be that such an auditory stimulus as a door chime is effective as a reinforcer only when it is not in competition with a more compelling stimulus, such as the actions or potential actions of adult human beings.

Smith and Smith (1962) also tried auditory reinforcement with their panel-pushing procedure described earlier. In this case, each con-tact with the panel produced two to three minutes' worth of a recorded female voice singing nursery songs. The ten subjects ranged from four to twenty-two months of age. In spite of the fact that the children all reacted "positively" to the music, only one of the children ". . . seemed

10. Lipsitt, L. P., personal communication (1966).

to form a limited connection between the contact plate and the activation of the recorder, even though at least six of the children controlled the recorder many times by making contact with the plate" (1962, p. 281).

Basan (1960), in an article having chiefly to do with methodology in operant conditioning, notes the use of verbal and musical reinforcement, but gives no empirical data regarding their effectiveness.

Watson (1966) has recently tried conditioning eye movements or, more specifically, the direction of visual regard in two experiments involving fourteen- and ten-week-old infants. In both, the infant was placed in an experimental bassinet with a ceiling about 12 in. above the infant's eyes. In the ceiling were two circles, separated by 3 in. in the horizontal axis, on which visual stimuli could be projected. The criterion response consisted in the infant's fixating one of these circles, and when this occurred during a conditioning period, which lasted a total of 90 seconds, he received one of two reinforcers: either the circle was illumined by a schematic red face or a speaker behind the infant's head emitted a soft tone of approximately 1000 cps. The measure of conditioning was derived from the distribution of fixation during the last 30 seconds of conditioning as compared to the distribution of fixation during the preceding operant period. In both studies, each infant received both auditory and visual reinforcers, in sequence. In the second study, a combined auditory plus visual conditioning was added.

According to the results of the first study, boys conditioned under visual reinforcers but not under auditory, whereas the opposite was true for girls. Only the latter finding was replicated in the second study: both the auditory reinforcer and the auditory plus visual reinforcer were effective in conditioning girls; the visual reinforcer alone was not. Boys did not condition under any one of the three treatments.

Token Reinforcement. Various kinds of token rewards have been used with infants in instrumental conditioning studies, e.g., a trinket on every reinforced trial (Bijou, 1957; Lovaas, 1961; Pumroy & Pumroy, 1961), a colored paper cut-out every five trials (McGinnis, 1929), a toy on every correct trial (Kuenne, 1946), and a marble on every correct trial, the accumulated horde of marbles being traded at the end of the session for a previously selected toy (Spiker & Norcross, 1962). Kendler *et al.* (1960) offered their subjects a choice of working for trinkets, raisins, candy, or nuts—a procedure shown to reduce intragroup variability in learning at the kindergarten level (Brackbill & Jack, 1958).

There are not enough data to draw an unassailable conclusion about the effectiveness for infant learning of token rewards as opposed to other types of rewards. However, one might guess that the younger the infant subject, the more necessary it would be that a reinforcer possess some intrinsic value and that, once given the child, it remain in his possession. To illustrate, in a study of discrimination learning, Heidbreder (1927) used a doll as a token solely to indicate to her subjects that they had made a correct response. The doll was not to be played with or taken home. Heidbreder's youngest subjects, age 2-6 to 3-6, could not learn to discriminate between two boxes—an achievement that Ling's six-month-olds *could* accomplish—and the investigator observed that the children really didn't seem to care when they made a mistake. In other words, they had been provided with insufficient motivation to learn.

Chase (1932), in a study of 259 children age twenty-four to thirty-six months, compared the reinforcing effectiveness of (a) apparent success only, (b) success and praise from the experimenter, and (c) success and a gold star reward. Although all these groups were superior to a control group who had no knowledge of results, they did not differ significantly from each other.

NEGATIVE REINFORCEMENT

The frequency of use of positive reinforcers in classical conditioning is about equal to that of negative reinforcers. In instrumental conditioning, however, the use of positive reinforcers is many times the frequency of use of negative reinforcers. This discrepancy reflects the fact that it is more difficult to cope with uncooperativeness in an instrumental learning situation than in classical conditioning. In instrumental learning, the appearance of the response is to an extent perhaps unappreciated by experimenters under the subject's control. In classical conditioning, it is much more nearly the case that the experimenter causes the response to be elicited whether the subject likes it or not.

Both Eigler (1932) and Johnson (1936), using older infants as part of their subject sample, tried to apply shock in connection with errors on a performance task. Eigler had the perspicacity to eliminate shock from her procedure before her subjects quit; Johnson didn't.

In addition to the reward conditions outlined above, Chase (1932) also investigated the effectiveness for performance of apparent failure plus either reproof or withdrawal of reward. The reproof consisted of such statements as, "Well, I thought you were a big, strong boy, but I guess not. You didn't make the bell ring, did you?" (following the first trial) and, "You haven't made the bell ring at all, have you? You certainly haven't done at all well" (following the sixth and last trial). The punishment condition was initiated by giving the child a paper gingerbread boy, after which the experimenter said, "You see the little boy has pretty red buttons on this side of his jacket, but he hasn't any down this side. Now every time you make the bell ring I'm going to put a little red button on your little boy's jacket. Of course, if you don't make the bell ring I can't put a red button on your little boy's jacket, can I? I'll have to cut one of these little buttons off" (1932, p. 68). There were six buttons and six failure trials. Chase found no significant difference between reproof and withdrawal of reward in their relative effectiveness for performance.

A second type of negative reinforcement to have been used in instrumental learning studies is a loud sound of sudden onset; this was used by Watson and Rayner (1920) and by Valentine (1930) to condition avoidance responses. These studies were described earlier; it might be noted here that they are apparently the only two operant conditioning studies to have used negative reinforcement.

INDIVIDUAL DIFFERENCES IN INSTRUMENTAL LEARNING

Although the largest number of studies concerned with chronological age differences in learning indicate that learning efficiency increases with CA (e.g., Graham *et al.*, 1964), there are many that, for artifactual or other reasons, find none (e.g., Skeels, 1933). There are even occasional studies showing reversed trends (Stevenson, Iscoe, & McConnell, 1955; Weir & Stevenson, 1959).

One of the few studies that has compared learning parameters across the full developmental scale—from infancy to adulthood—is that of Guillet (1909). The two subjects in this experiment—Guillet and his two-year-old son—learned the names of sets of birds and mammals in a paired associate arrangement. The child learned the English, French, or German name for each animal, while his father learned its Japanese name. On the basis of his results, Guillet concluded that he learned his words nearly twice as fast as the two-year-old, that after a six-week interval he retained more than twice as many words as the child, and that he relearned the set of words in one third the number of repetitions required by the child.

There are fewer studies showing definite positive relationship between MA and learning efficiency than between CA and learning. This is attributable in part to the enormous discrepancy in reliability between the two age measures at this time of life; i.e., during infancy and early childhood, CA as a measure is no less reliable than it is at any other time of life, while MA as a measure is at its least reliable.

Another general point that suggests itself in considering all intelligence-learning comparisons available for this age level is that studies showing definite positive relations between MA and learning have used, more often than not, cognitive or verbal tasks rather than motor or performance tasks. For example, Foster (1928) found a correlation of .74 between Minnesota Preschool Test scores and number of correct anticipations in serial learning; Matheson (1931) found a correlation of .42 between MA and problem solutions. On the other hand, Wenger (1933) found no consistent relation between MA and time to run mazes, while Batalla (1934) found that subjects with lower MAs were better maze performers.

Heredity, Environment, and Learning

The question of the degree to which behavior can be modified by environmental events as opposed to the degree to which it is predetermined by internal factors of hereditary or constitutional origin is a question that has been raised in various forms and with varying degrees of feeling since the time of Aristotle. In the history of *child* psychology, it was raised with great intensity of feeling during the late 1920s and early 1930s in a battle between the Stanford and Minnesota hereditarians and the Iowa environmentalists over the issue of externally induced changes in IQ scores. Most of the children who were being argued over were older than the birth to three-year age range considered here.

In infant psychology the heredity-environment issue was raised, with great clamor and invective, by John B. Watson in the 1920s. Watson dedicated his book of 1928, *Psychological Care of Infant and Child,* "To the first mother who brings up a happy child," with the clear implication—to be supported by the text that followed—that (a) *no* mother had yet raised a happy child, and (b) since only environmental, not genetic, forces shape behavior, every mother *should* be able to bring up a happy child.

Watson said of his behaviorism,

> This doctrine is almost the opposite of what is taught in the schools at the present time. Professor John Dewey and many other educators have been insisting for the last twenty years upon a method of training which allows the child to develop from within. This is really a doctrine of mystery. It teaches that there are hidden springs of activity, hidden possibilities of unfolding within the child which must be waited for until they appear and then be fostered and tended. I think the doctrine has done serious harm. . . . The behaviorists believe that there is nothing from within to develop (1928, pp. 40–41).

At a later point in his text, however, Watson modified his strictly Aristotelian stand by allowing that there are three instinctive responses present at birth. He steadfastly maintained, however, that all subsequently manifested behavior derives from conditioned connections elaborated on the basis of those three instincts. The three instincts are (1) fear—elicited by either a loud sound or by loss of support; (2) rage—elicited by restraint of the child's movements; and (3) love—elicited by stroking and touching the infant's skin, lips, and sex organs.

Watson's uncompromising position on environmentalism—not to mention the aggressively propagandistic way in which he publicized his position—spurred hereditarians to the front lines of battle. The defense was led by Arnold Gesell, who put the term "maturation" into the vocabulary of developmental psychology. This was his new name for innately determined behaviors, for the ". . . powerful stabilizing factors, intrinsic rather than extrinsic, which preserved the balance of the total pattern and the direction of the growth trend" (1933, p. 232).

As McGraw (1946) has pointed out, the hereditarians' prime objection to the inflexible dogma of behaviorism stemmed from their conviction that there were aspects of infant development that could not be explained as products of conditioning—principally, those behaviors that appeared suddenly in the infant's response repertoire and those that appeared to be universal in occurrence. In McGraw's terms, "the sponsors of maturation theory" were concerned with ". . . the appearance of particular abilities without the benefit of practice; . . . the sudden appearance of new behavior items; . . . the consistency of behavior patterns in different subjects of the same species; . . . an orderly sequence in the manifestation of different patterns; and . . . the gradual or saltatory course of growth" (1946, p. 336).

The defenders of maturation theory, again under the leadership of Arnold Gesell, developed a particular kind of experimental methodology by which they hoped to prove their point. The core of this was the co-twin control technique. By this technique one member of a pair of identical twins, usually called *T*, was given training or practice on a task for a period of time beginning at *x* weeks of age.[11] At the end of *T*'s training period, the control twin, *C*, was trained for a shorter period of time. The comparison between *T* and *C* was in terms of gain per training day.

Of the maturation vs. training or practice studies to appear in the war-against-Watson campaign, the most heroic was Strayer's (1930) study of language training in twins *T* and *C*—the second and last published study of those famous twins made during the period of their infancy. For a period of nine weeks Strayer confined herself, the twins, and one nurse in a nine-room suite. Her plan was to give twin *T* intensive vocabulary training for five weeks, from age 84 through 88 weeks, and then to give twin *C* four weeks of training, beginning with age 89 weeks. Daily sessions involved both formal training, e.g., "What is this?," "Bring me the . . . ," and informal training, e.g., spontaneous conversation relating to the daily routine and to games. The twins were kept apart during the nine-week period; the experimenter spent some time with each twin daily while the nurse babysat with the other twin.

By the end of four weeks of training, *T* had acquired 23 words; by the end of five weeks of training, she had acquired 35 words. During *C*'s four weeks of training, she acquired 30 words. On the basis of the 23/30 comparisons the author concludes that maturation is of greater importance than training to vocabulary acquisition.

But if Strayer's efforts were heroic, they were not unbiased. (In this respect also her study is not unrepresentative of many that were done to prove the cause of internally or externally determined behavior.) For one thing, the twins apparently did not have equal amounts of training. Strayer says, "It should be pointed out that differences in the frequency of repetition of a given word did occur between *T* and *C*. After careful consideration, it was decided that in an experiment of this kind any attempt to hold the number of repetitions entirely constant would create a highly artificial situation. With length of training time and forms of training kept constant, number of repetitions depended upon the child's own receptivity. If Twin *C* showed a capacity to progress faster, it did

---

11. Under what we think of as "practice" today, the children were free to manipulate the experimental materials as they wished, but no feedback, correction, or verbal reinforcement was given. Under "training" these were provided. The two terms were not always used consistently.

not seem justifiable to limit arbitrarily her tendency to do so" (1930, pp. 224–225).

In addition, Twin C may well have been more highly motivated for training than Twin T, for in the first place, the experimenter spent only half as much social contact time with C as with T during T's training, and, in the second place, C was deprived of all social speech save her own during the entire five-week period of her sister's training—a procedure that had a marked effect on both her verbal and nonverbal behavior.

The same conclusion, with respect to the dominant role of maturation over learning, was drawn by Gesell and Thompson (1929) and by Hilgard (1932). In both cases the conclusion is not fully supported by the data.

Other well-known studies by proponents of maturation theory are those by Jersild et al. (1932), McGraw (1935), and Valentine (1930). In all these studies learning, training, or practice has been an intrinsic part of the study rather than an inferred event.

In spite of the number and scope of the "maturation" studies, none satisfactorily tested the relative contribution of heredity and environment to the acquisition of a skill. What they did demonstrate was that, for the particular skills under study, the older the infant at the beginning of training, the less time it takes to train him.

The heredity-environment issue is never dormant for very long in psychological research, and at the present time it is with us again, garbed in various concepts borrowed from ethology; such as *sign stimulus, innate releasing mechanism, imprinting,* and *critical period.* A marked tendency to use these constructs can be seen in the writings of psychoanalytically oriented child research workers—particularly those who are concerned with the effects of maternal separation and deprivation.

As was the case thirty-five years ago with the hereditarian-maturationists in child psychology, the criteria for labeling behavior as innately determined rather than learned that are being used by many hereditarian-ethologists in child psychology, are sudden appearance and universal occurrence. As subjectively compelling as these criteria may be to the hereditarian, they carry no objective weight whatsoever as "proofs" of innate behavior. With respect to the first criterion it simply cannot be demonstrated conclusively that a response appears without observable precursory behavior. Nor is it generally the case that a response makes its initial appearance in its final form, i.e., undergoes no subsequent modification in terms of refinement. With regard to the criterion of universality, Tinbergen (1951) points out that,

> . . . identity of behaviour of many individuals by no means indicates that their behaviour is entirely innate. For instance, many European songbirds have to learn that wasps of the genus *Vespa* are inedible. Inexperienced individuals capture a wasp as readily as a fly. The repellent taste of the wasp's entrails and, in some cases, the wasp's sting, usually condition them on the very first occasion

and teach them to avoid wasps, and, in fact, all flies of similar colour as well. . . . As was mentioned already, Heinroth has shown that many male songbirds have to learn their song from males of the same species. Young nightingales, for instance, do not develop their typical song when reared in isolation and they imitate any members of other species which have been singing in their neighbourhood. Wild males, however, having been raised by their own species, all have the song of the species, and without experiments it would be impossible to know that the song has to be learned (1951, page 145).

References

Alberts, E., & Ehrenfreund, D. Transposition in children as a function of age. *J. exp. Psychol.*, 1951, 41, 30–38.

Aldrich, C. A. A new test for hearing in the new-born: The conditioned reflex. *Amer. J. Dis. Child*, 1928, 35, 36–37.

Anderson, H. H. Motivation of young children: Further studies in success and failure, praise and blame. *Child Develpm.*, 1936, 7, 125–143.

Anderson, H. H., & Smith, R. S. Motivation of young children: The constancy of certain behavior patterns. *J. exp. Educ.*, 1933, 2, 138–160.

Babska, Z. Formirovanie otozhdestvleniia vida predmetov u detei vtorogo i tretago goda zhizni. (The formation of object identification in one- and two-year-old children.) *Voprosy Psikhologii*, 1959, No. 6, 131–138.

Barr, B. Pure tone audiometry for preschool children. *Acta Oto-laryng.*, 1954, Suppl. 110, 89–101.

Basan, L. I. A method for the examination of higher nervous activity in infants under natural conditions. *Pavlov J. high. nerv. Act.*, 1960, 10, 853–857.

Batalla, M. B. An experimental study of children's behavior in a spatial complex. *J. genet. Psychol.*, 1934, 44, 127–138.

Bijou, S. W. Patterns of reinforcement and resistance to extinction in young children. *Child Develpm.*, 1957, 28, 47–54.

Bogen, H. Experimentelle Untersuchungen über psychische und assoziative Magensaftsekretion beim Menschen. (Experimental investigations on psychic and associative secretion of stomach fluids in the human.) *Jb. Kinderheilkunde*, 1907, 65, 733–740. Translated and reprinted in Y. Brackbill & G. G. Thompson (Eds.), *Behavior in infancy and early childhood: A book of readings*. New York: Free Press, 1967.

Bordley, J. E., & Hardy, W. G. A study in objective audiometry with the use of a psychogalvanometric response. *Annals of Otology, Rhinology, and Laryngology*, 1949, 58, 751–760.

Bordley, J. E., Hardy, W. G., & Richter, C. P. Audiometry with the use of galvanic skin-resistance response. *Bull. Johns Hopkins Hosp.*, 1948, 82, 569.

Brackbill, Y. Extinction of the smiling response in infants as a function of reinforcement schedule. *Child Develpm.*, 1958, 29, 115–124. Reprinted in Y. Brackbill & G. G. Thompson (Eds.), *Behavior in infancy and early childhood: A book of readings*. New York: Free Press, 1967.

———. Research and clinical work with children. In R. Bauer (Ed.), *Some views on Soviet psychology*. Washington, D.C.: Amer. Psychol. Ass., 1962.

———, (Ed.) *Research in infant behavior: A cross-indexed bibliography*, Baltimore: Williams and Wilkins, 1964.

Brackbill, Y., & Jack, D. Discrimination learning in children as a function of reinforcement value. *Child Develpm.*, 1958, 29, 185–190.

Brazelton, T. B. A child-oriented approach to toilet training. *Pediatrics*, 1962, 29, 121–128.

Brigance, W. N. The language learning of a child. *J. appl. Psychol.*, 1934, 18, 143–154.

Bronshtein, A. I., & Petrova, E. P. Issledovanie zvukovogo analizatora novoro-zhdennykh i detei rannego grudnogo vozrasta. (An investigation of the auditory analyzer in neonates and young infants.) *Zh. vyssh. nerv. Deiatel.*, 1952, 2, 333–343. Translated and reprinted in Y. Brackbill & G. G. Thompson (Eds.), *Behavior in infancy and early childhood: A book of readings.* New York: Free Press, 1967.

Burtt, H. E. An experimental study of early childhood memory. *J. genet. Psychol.*, 1932, 40, 287–295.

———. A further study of early childhood memory. *J. genet. Psychol.*, 1937, 50, 187–192.

———. An experimental study of early childhood memory: Final report. *J. genet. Psychol.*, 1941, 58, 435–439. Reprinted in Y. Brackbill & G. G. Thompson (Eds.), *Behavior in infancy and early childhood: A book of readings.* New York: Free Press, 1967.

Bystroletova, G. N. Obrazovanie u novorozhdennykh detei uslovnogo refleksa na vremia v sviazi s sutochnym ritmom kormleniia. (The formation in neonates of a conditioned reflex to time in connection with daily feeding rhythm.) *Zh. vyssh. nerv. Deiatel.*, 1954, 4, 601–609.

Caldwell, B. M. The effects of infant care. In M. L. Hoffman & L. W. Hoffman (Eds.), *Review of child development research.* New York: Russell-Sage Foundation, 1964.

Chaney, B. L., & McGraw, M. B. Reflexes and other motor activities in new-born infants. *Bull. Neurol. Inst. New York*, 1932, 2, 1–56.

Chase, L. Motivation of young children. An experimental study of the influence of certain types of external incentives upon the performance of a task. *Univer. Iowa Stud. Child Welf.*, 1932, 5, No. 3.

Chase, W. P. Color vision in infants. *J. exp. Psychol.*, 1937, 20, 203–222.

Cole, R. E., Dent, H. E., Eguchi, P. E., Fujii, K. K., & Johnson, R. C. Transposition with minimal errors during training trials. *J. exp. child Psychol.*, 1964, 1, 355–359.

Dashkovskaia, V. S. Pervye uslovnye reaktsii u novorozhdennykh detei v norme i pri nekotorykh patologicheskikh sostoiniiakh. (The first conditioned reactions in newborn infants under normal and in certain pathological conditions.) *Zh. vyssh. nerv. Deiatel.*, 1953, 3, 247–259.

Deese, J. *The psychology of learning.* (2nd ed.) New York: McGraw-Hill, 1958.

Degtiar, E. N. Sravnitelnaia kharakteristika fiziologicheskikh uslovnii pri vyrabotke stereotipa v pervoi i vtoroi signalnoi sistemakh. (Comparative characteristics of physiological conditions for the elaboration of a stereotype in the first and second signal systems.) *Zh. vyssh. nerv. Deiatel.*, 1962, 12, 63–68.

Degtiar, E. N., Znamenskaia, A. N., & Koltsova, M. M. Fiziologicheskie mekhanizmy nekotorykh form obobshcheniia u detei rannego vozrasta. (Physiological mechanisms of some forms of generalization in young children.) *Trudy Instituta Fiziologii im. Pavlova*, 1959, 8, 35–38.

Denisova, M. P., & Figurin, N. L. K voprosu o pervykh sochetatelnykh pis-chevykh refleksakh u grudnykh detei. (An investigation of the first combinative feeding reflexes in young infants.) *Voprosy geneticheskoi reflek-sologii i pedologii*, 1929, 1, 81–88.

Dix, M. R., & Hallpike, C. S. The peep-show. A new technique for pure-tone audiometry in young children. *Brit. Med. J.*, 1947, 2, 719–723.

Dmitriev, A. S., & Kochigina, A. M. The importance of time as stimulus of conditioned reflex activity. *Psychol. Bull.*, 1959, 56, 106–132.

Douglas, J. W. B., & Blomfield, J. M. *Children under five.* London: George Allen & Unwin Ltd., 1958.

Eigler, P. The effect of unusual stimulation on motor coordination in children. *Child Develpm.*, 1932, 3, 207–229.

Evdokimov, S. A., & Zakliakova, V. N. Pribor dlia registratsii migatelnogo refleksa u detei. (An apparatus for recording the eye blink reflex in children.) *Zh. vyssh. nerv. Deiatel.*, 1962, 12, 354–357.

Fitzgerald, H. E., Lintz, L. M., Brackbill, Y., & Adams, G. Time perception and conditioning an autonomic response in human infants. *Percept. mot. Skills,* 1967, 24, 479–486.

Foster, J. C. Verbal memory in the preschool child. *Ped. Sem.*, 1928, 35, 26–44.

Fudel-Osipova, S. I., & Khokhol, E. N. Narushenie uslovnoreflektornoi deiatelnosti u detei, bolnykh zatiazhnoi dispepsiei. (The disturbance of conditioned reflex activity in children showing prolonged dyspepsia.) *Zh. vyssh. nerv. Deiatel.*, 1953, 3, 260–266.

Gellermann, L. W. Form discrimination in chimpanzees and two-year-old children: I. Form (triangularity) *per se. Ped. Sem.*, 1933, 42, 3–27. (a)

——. Form discrimination in chimpanzees and two-year-old children: Form versus background. *Ped. Sem.*, 1933, 42, 28–50. (b)

Gesell, A., & Thompson, H. Learning and growth in identical infant twins: An experimental study by the method of co-twin control. *Genet. Psychol. Monogr.*, 1929, 6, 1–124.

——. Twins T and C from infancy to adolescence: A biogenetic study of individual differences by the method of co-twin control. *Genet. Psychol. Monogr.*, 1941, 24, 3–121.

Goldstein, R., Ludwig, H., & Naunton, R. F. Difficulty in conditioning galvanic skin responses: Its possible significance in clinical audiometry. *Acta Otolaryng.*, 1954, 44, 67–77.

Gorman, J. J., Cogan, D. G., & Gellis, S. S. A device for testing visual acuity in infants. *Sight Saving Rev.*, 1959, 29, 80–84. Reprinted in Y. Brackbill & G. G. Thompson (Eds.), *Behavior in infancy and early childhood: A book of readings.* New York: Free Press, 1967.

Graham, F. K., Ernhart, C. B., Craft, M., & Berman, P. W. Learning of relative and absolute size concepts in preschool children. *J. exp. child Psychol.,* 1964, 1, 26–36.

Grings, W. W., Lowell, E. L., & Honnard, R. R. Electrodermal responses of deaf children. *J. speech hear. Res.*, 1960, 3, 120–129.

——. GSR Conditioning with pre-school-age deaf children. *J. comp. physiol. Psychol.*, 1961, 54, 143–148.

Guillet, C. Retentiveness in child and adult. *Amer. J. Psychol.*, 1909, 20, 318–352.

Hardy, W. G., & Bordley, J. E. Special techniques in testing the hearing of children. *J. speech hear. Disord.*, 1951, 16, 122–131.

——. Evaluation of hearing in young children. *Acta Oto-laryng.*, 1951–1952, 40, 346–360.

Harlow, H. F. The formation of learning sets. *Psychol. Rev.*, 1949, 56, 51–65.

Heidbreder, E. F. Reasons used in solving problems. *J. exp. Psychol.*, 1927, 10, 397–414.

Hetherington, E. M., & Brackbill, Y. Etiology and covariation of obstinacy, orderliness, and parsimony in young children. *Child Develpm.*, 1963, 34, 919–943.

Hicks, J. A. The acquisition of motor skill in young children: A study of the effects of practice in throwing at a moving target. *Child Develpm.*, 1930, 1, 90–105. (a)

——. The acquisition of motor skill in young children: II. The influence of specific and general practice on motor skill. *Child Develpm.*, 1930, 1, 292–297. (b)

Hicks, J. A., & Ralph, D. W. The effects of practice in tracing the Porteus Diamond Maze. *Child Develpm.*, 1931, 2, 156–158.

Hicks, J. A., & Stewart, F. D. The learning of abstract concepts of size. *Child Develpm.*, 1930, 1, 195–203.

Hilgard, J. R. Learning and maturation in preschool children. *J. genet. Psychol.*, 1932, 41, 36–56. Reprinted in Y. Brackbill & G. G. Thompson (Eds.), *Behavior in infancy and early childhood: A book of readings.* New York: Free Press, 1967.

Hill, S. D. The performance of young children on three discrimination-learning tasks. *Child Develpm.*, 1965, 36, 425–435.

Hull, C. L., & Hull, B. I. Parallel learning curves of an infant in vocabulary and in voluntary control of the bladder. *Ped. Sem.*, 1919, 26, 272–283. Reprinted in Y. Brackbill & G. G. Thompson (Eds.), *Behavior in infancy and early childhood: A book of readings.* New York: Free Press, 1967.

Hunter, W. S., & Bartlett, S. C. Double alternation behavior in young children. *J. exp. Psychol.*, 1948, 38, 558–567.

Irwin, O. C. Infant speech: Effect of systematic reading of stories. *J. speech hear. Res.*, 1960, 3, 187–190. Reprinted in Y. Brackbill & G. G. Thompson (Eds.), *Behavior in infancy and early childhood: A book of readings.* New York: Free Press, 1967.

Irwin, O. C., & Weiss, L. A. The effect of clothing on the general and vocal activity of the newborn infant. *Univer. Iowa Stud. Child Welf.*, 1934, 9, No. 4, 149–162.

Irzhanskaia, K. N., & Felberbaum, R. A. Nekotorye dannye ob uslovnoreflektornoi deiatelnosti nedonoshennykh detei. (Conditioned reflex activity in premature children.) *Fiziologicheskii Zhurnal SSSR*, 1954, 40, 668–672. Translated and reprinted in Y. Brackbill & G. G Thompson (Eds.), *Behavior in infancy and early childhood: A book of readings.* New York: Free Press, 1967.

Jackson, T. A., Stonex, E., Lane, E., & Dominguez, K. Studies in the transposition of learning by children. I. Relative vs. absolute response as a function of amount of training. *J. exp. Psychol.*, 1938, 23, 578–600.

Janoš, O. (Ianosh, O.) Development of higher nervous activity in premature infants. *Pavlov J. high. nerv. Act.*, 1959, 9, 760–767.

———. *Věkové a individuální rozdíly ve vyšši nervové činnosti kojencie. (Age and individual differences in higher nervous activity of infants.)* Hálkova Sbírka Pediatrických Prací, No. 8. (Halek's Collection of Studies in pediatrics, No. 8.) Prague: Státní Zdravotnické Nakladatelství, 1965.

Jegi, J. I. The vocabulary of a two-year-old child. *Child Stud. Monogr.*, 1901, 6, 241–261.

Jersild, A. T., Bennett, W., Bush, R., Ortlieb, R., & Bienstock, S. *Training and growth in the development of children.* New York: Teachers College, 1932.

Jersild, A. T., & Bienstock, S. F. The influence of training on the vocal ability of three-year-old children. *Child Develpm.*, 1931, 2, 272–291.

Johnson, B. Variations in emotional responses of children. *Child Develpm.*, 1936, 7, 85–94.

Jones, H. E. The retention of conditioned emotional reactions in infancy. *J. genet. Psychol.*, 1930, 37, 485–498.

———. The conditioning of overt emotional responses. *J. educ. Psychol.*, 1931, 22, 127–130.

Jones, H. E., & Jones, M. C. Fear. *Childh. Educ.*, 1928, 5, 136–143.

Jones, M. C. A laboratory study of fear: The case of Peter. *Ped. Sem.*, 1924, 31, 308–315. (a)

———. Conditioning and reconditioning—an experimental study in child behavior. *Proc. Nat'l. Educ. Assoc.*, 1924, 62, 585–590. (b)

———. The elimination of children's fears. *J. exp. Psychol.*, 1924, 7, 382–390. (c)

Kantrow, R. W. An investigation of conditioned feeding responses and concomitant adaptive behavior in young infants. *Univer. Iowa Stud. Child Welf.*, 1937, 13, No. 3.

Karlova, A. N. Orientation reflexes in young children. *Pavlov J. high. nerv. Act.*, 1959, 9, 31–37.

Kasatkin, N. I. Razvitie slukhovykh i zritelnykh uslovnykh refleksov i ikh diferentsirovka u mladentsev. (The development of visual and acoustic conditioned reflexes and their differentiation in infants.) *Pediatriia*, 1935, No. 8, 127–137.

——. Slukhovye uslovnye refleksy u nedonoshennykh detei. (Conditioned reflexes to sound in premature children.) *Biulleten Vsesoiuznogo Instituta Eksperimentalnoi Meditsiny*, 1936, No. 3–4, 54–63.

——. Rannie uslovnye refleksy v ontogeneze cheloveka. (*Early conditioned reflexes in human ontogenesis.*) Moscow: Izdatelstvo Akad. Med. Nauk SSSR, 1948.

——. Uslovnye refleksy i khronaksiia kozhi detei. (Conditioned reflexes and skin chronaxie in children.) *Fiziologicheskii Zhurnal SSSR*, 1952, 38, 434–443. (a)

——. Rannie uslovnye refleksy rebenka. (Early conditioned reflexes in the child.) *Zh. vyssh. nerv. Deiatel.*, 1952, 2, 572–581. (Reprinted in *The central nervous system and behavior*, translations from the Russian medical literature collected for participants of the third Macy conference on the central nervous system and behavior, Princeton, N. J., Feb. 21–24, 1960, 330–342. Prepared and distributed by the Russian scientific translation program, National Institutes of Health. (b)

——. Ranii ontogenez reflektornoi deiatelnosti rebenka. (The early ontogenesis of reflex activity in the child.) *Zh. vyssh. nerv. Deiatel.*, 1957, 7, 805–818.

——. Ontogenez funktsii golovnogo mozga rebenka. (The ontogenesis of cerebral function in the child.) *Acta. Universitatis Carolinae Medica*, 1962, No. 7, 657–664.

Kasatkin, N. I., & Levikova, A. M. On the development of early conditioned reflexes and differentiations of auditory stimuli in infants. *J. exp. Psychol.*, 1935, 18, 1–19. (a)

——. The formation of visual conditioned reflexes and their differentiation in infants. *J. gen. Psychol.*, 1935, 12, 416–435. (b)

Kasatkin, N. I., Mirzoiants, N. S., & Khokhitva, A. Ob orientirovochnykh uslovnykh refleksakh u detei pervogo goda zhizni. (Conditioned orienting responses in children in the first year of life.) *Zh. vyssh. nerv. Deiatel.*, 1953, 3, 192–202. (Reprinted in *The central nervous system and behavior*, translations from the Russian medical literature collected for participants of the third Macy conference on the central nervous system and behavior, Princeton, N. J., Feb. 21–24, 1960, 343–358. Prepared and distributed by the Russian scientific translation program, National Institutes of Health.)

Kaye, H. The conditioned Babkin reflex in human newborns. *Psychon. Sci.*, 1965, 2, 287–288.

——. The conditioned anticipatory sucking response. In L. P. Lipsitt & C. C. Spiker (Eds.), *Advances in child development and behavior.* Vol. 3. New York: Academic Press, 1966.

Kendler, T. S., Kendler, H. H., & Wells, D. Reversal and non-reversal shifts in nursery school children. *J. comp. physiol. Psychol.*, 1960, 53, 83–88.

Ketterlinus, E. Learning of children in adaptation to mirror reversals. *Child Develpm.*, 1931, 2, 200–223.

Kimble, G. A. *Hilgard and Marquis' conditioning and learning.* (2nd ed.) (Rev.) New York: Appleton-Century-Crofts, 1961.

Koch, J. The development of the conditioned orienting reaction to humans in 2–3 month infants. *Activitas nervosa superior*, 1965, 7, 2, 141–142.

Koch, M. B., & Meyer, D. R. A relationship of mental age to learning-set formation in the preschool child. *J. comp. physiol. Psychol.*, 1959, 52, 387–389.

Koltsova, M. M. O vozniknovenii i razvitii vtoroi signalnoi sistemy u rebenka.

(The appearance and development of the second signal system in the child.) *Trudy Fiziol. Inst. im. Pavlova*, 1949, 4, 49–102.

——. O razvitii vnutrennego tormozheniia u rebenka. (The development of internal inhibition in the child.) *Fiziologicheskii Zhurnal SSSR*, 1952, 38, 27–32.

——. Fiziologicheskie usloviia razvitiia slova kak "signala signalov." (Physiological conditions of development of the word as a signal of signals.) *Trudy Fiziol. Inst. im. Pavlova*, 1956, 5, 384–390. (a)

——. O fiziologicheskikh mekhanizmakh razvitiia protsessa obobshcheniia u rebenka. (The physiological mechanisms of development of the process of generalization in the child.) *Zh. vyssh. nerv. Deiatel.*, 1956, 6, 201–211. Translated and reprinted in Y. Brackbill & G. G. Thompson (Eds.), *Behavior in infancy and early childhood: A book of readings*. New York: Free Press, 1967. (b)

——. O formirovanii vysshei nervnoi deiatelnosti rebenka. (*The formation of higher nervous activity in the child.*) Leningrad: MEDGIZ, 1958.

——. Rol vremennykh sviazei tipa assotsiativnykh v razvitii sistemnosti. (The role of temporary connections of the associative type in the development of systems.) *Zh. vyssh. nerv. Deiatel.*, 1961, 11, 56–59.

Krachkovskaia, M. V. Reflex changes in the leukocyte count of newborn infants in relation to food intake. *Pavlov J. high. nerv. Act.*, 1959, 9, 193–199.

Krasnogorskii, N. I. Opyt polucheniia iskusstvennykh uslovnykh refleksov u detei rannego vozrasta. (An attempt to form artificial conditioned reflexes in young children.) *Russkii Vrach*, 1907, 36, 1245–1246. Translated and reprinted in Y. Brackbill & G. G. Thompson (Eds.), *Behavior in infancy and early childhood: A book of readings*. New York: Free Press, 1967.

Kriuchkova, A. P., & Ostrovskaia, I. M. O vozrastnykh i individualnykh osobennostiiakh vysshei nervnoi deiatelnosti detei pervogo goda zhizni. (Age characteristics and individual differences in the higher nervous activity of children during the first year of life.) *Zh. vyssh. nerv. Deiatel.*, 1957, 7, 63–74.

Kuenne, M. R. Experimental investigation of the relation of language to transposition behavior in young children. *J. exp. Psychol.*, 1946, 36, 471–490.

Levin, G. R., & Kaye, H. Nonnutritive sucking by human neonates. *Child Develpm.*, 1964, 35, 749–758.

Liiamina, G. M. Mechanism by which children master pronunciation during the second and third year. *The central nervous system and behavior*, translations from the Russian medical literature collected for participants of the third Macy conference on the central nervous system and behavior, Princeton, N. J., Feb. 21–24, 1960, 509–528. Prepared and distributed by the Russian scientific translation program, National Institutes of Health.

Ling, B.-C. Form discrimination as a learning cue in infants. *Comp. Psychol. Monogr.*, 1941, 17, No. 86.

Lintz, L. M., & Fitzgerald, H. E. Apparatus for eyeblink conditioning in infants. *J. exp. child. Psychol.*, 1966, 4, 276–279.

Lipsitt, L. P. Learning in the first year of life. In L. P. Lipsitt & C. C. Spiker (Eds.), *Advances in child development and behavior*. Vol. 1. New York: Academic Press, 1963. Pp. 147–194.

Lipsitt, L. P., & Kaye, H. Conditioned sucking in the human newborn. *Psychon. Sci.*, 1964, 1, 29–30.

Lipton, E. L., Steinschneider, A., & Richmond, J. B. Autonomic function in the neonate. II. Physiological effects of motor restraint. *Psychosom. Med.*, 1960, 22, 57–65.

Lovaas, O. I. Interaction between verbal and nonverbal behavior. *Child Develpm.*, 1961, 32, 329–336.

Lubchenco, L. O., Horner, F. A., Reed, L. H., Hix, I. E., Jr., Metcalf, D., Cohig, R., Elliott, H. C., & Bourg, M. Sequelae of premature birth. *Amer. J. Dis.*

Children, 1963, 106, 101–115. Reprinted in Y. Brackbill & G. G. Thompson (Eds.), *Behavior in infancy and early childhood: A book of readings.* New York: Free Press, 1967.

McGinnis, E. The acquisition and interference of motor habits in young children. *Genet. Psychol. Monogr.,* 1929, 6, 203–311.

McGraw, M. B. *Growth: A study of Johnny and Jimmy.* New York: D. Appleton-Century Co., 1935.

———. Neural maturation as exemplified in achievement of bladder control. *J. Pediatr.,* 1940, 16, 580–590.

———. Maturation of behavior. In L. Carmichael (Ed.), *Manual of child psychology.* New York: Wiley, 1946. Pp. 332–369.

Malakhovskaia, D. B. Interaction between the conditioned and unconditioned plantar reflex in young children. *Pavlov J. high. nerv. Act.,* 1959, 38–44.

Marquis, D. P. Can conditioned responses be established in the newborn infant? *J. genet. Psychol.,* 1931, 39, 479–492.

———. Learning in the neonate: The modification of behavior under three feeding schedules. *J. exp. Psychol.,* 1941, 29, 263–282.

Mateer, F. *Child behavior: A critical and experimental study of young children by the method of conditioned reflexes.* Boston: R. G. Badger, 1918.

Matheson, E. A study of problem solving behavior in pre-school children. *Child Develpm.,* 1931, 2, 242–262.

Mirzoiants, N. S. Uslovnyi orientirovochnyi refleks i ego differentsirovka u rebenka. (The conditioned orienting reflex and its differentiation in the child.) *Zh. vyssh. nerv. Deiatel.,* 1954, 4, 616–619.

Morgan, J. J. B., & Morgan, S. S. Infant learning as a developmental index. *J. genet. Psychol.,* 1944, 65, 281–289.

Munn, N. L., & Steining, B. R. The relative efficacy of form and background in a child's discrimination of visual patterns. *Ped. Sem.,* 1931, 39, 73–90.

Myers, C. S. Some observations on the development of colour sense. *Brit. J. Psychol.,* 1908, 2, 353–362.

Nechaeva, I. P. K funktsionalnoi kharakteristike slukhogo analizatora rebenka rannego vozrasta. (The functional character of the auditory analyzer in the young child.) *Zh. vyssh. nerv. Deiatel,* 1954, 4, 610–615.

Papoušek, H. Conditioned head rotation reflexes in infants in the first months of life. *Acta Paediatr.,* 1961, 50, 565–576.

———. Experimental studies of appetitional behavior in human newborns. In H. W. Stevenson, E. Hess, & H. Rheingold (Eds.), *Early behavior: Comparative and developmental approaches.* New York: Wiley, 1966.

———. Conditioning during early postnatal development. In Y. Brackbill & G. G. Thompson (Eds.), *Behavior in infancy and early childhood: A book of readings.* New York: Free Press, 1967.

Papoushek, G. A method for the investigation of food-conditioned reflexes in infants up to the age of six months. *Pavlov J. high. nerv. Act.,* 1959, 9, 124–129.

Pavlov, I. P. *Lectures on conditioned reflexes.* Translated by W. H. Gantt. New York: International, 1928.

———. *Conditioned reflexes: An investigation of the physiological activity of the cerebral cortex.* Translated and edited by G. V. Anrep. New York: Dover, 1960.

Pike, E. G. Controlled infant intonation. *Language Learning,* 1949, 2, 21–24.

Polikanina, R. I. The relationship between autonomic and somatic components of a defensive conditioned reflex in premature children. *Pavlov J. high. nerv. Act.,* 1961, 11, 72–82.

Polikanina, R. I., & Probatova, L. E. Stanovlenie i razvitie pishchevogo dvigatelnogo uslovnogo refleksa na zvuk u nedonoshennykh detei. (The formation and development of the conditioned feeding movement reflex to sound in premature children.) *Zh. vyssh. nerv. Deiatel.,* 1955, 5, 237–245.

———. Razvitie orientirovochnoi reaktsii i dvigatelnogo pishchevogo uslovnogo refleksa na svet u nedonoshennykh detei. (Development of the orienting reaction and conditioned feeding movement reflex to light in premature children.) *Zh. vyssh. nerv. Deiatel.*, 1957, 7, 673–682.

Pumroy, D. K., & Pumroy, S. S. Effect of amount and percentage of reinforcement on resistance to extinction in preschool children. *J. genet. Psychol.*, 1961, 98, 55–62.

Rendle-Short, J. The puff test. An attempt to assess the intelligence of young children by use of a conditioned reflex. *Arch. Dis. Childh.*, 1961, 36, 50–57.

Rheingold, H. L. Controlling the infant's exploratory behaviour. In B. M. Foss, (Ed.), *Determinants of infant behaviour*. II. New York: Wiley, 1963. Pp. 171–175.

Rheingold, H. L., Gewirtz, J. L., & Ross, H. W. Social conditioning of vocalizations in the infant. *J. comp. physiol. Psychol.*, 1959, 52, 68–73.

Rheingold, H. L., Stanley, W. C., & Cooley, J. A. Method for studying exploratory behavior in infants. *Science*, 1962, 136, 1054–1055.

Rheingold, H. L., Stanley, W. C., & Doyle, G. A. Visual and auditory reinforcement of a manipulatory response in the young child. *J. exp. child Psychol.*, 1964, 1, 316–326.

Ripin, R. A study of the infant's feeding reactions during the first months of life. *Arch. Psychol.*, 1930, No. 116.

Rossi, E. L., & Rossi, S. I. Concept utilization, serial order and recall in nursery-school children. *Child Develpm.*, 1965, 36, 771–778.

Schultze, F. *Die Sprache des Kindes. (The speech of the child.)* Leipzig: E. Gunther's Verlag, 1880.

Scoe, H. F. Bladder control in infancy and early childhood. *Univer. Iowa Stud. Child Welf.*, 1933, 5, No. 4.

Sears, R. R., Maccoby, E. E., & Levin, H. *Patterns of child rearing*, Evanston, Ill.: Row, Peterson, 1957.

Sherman, M., & Sherman, I. C. Sensori-motor responses in infants. *J. comp. Psychol.*, 1925, 5, 53–68.

Shirley, M. M. *The first two years, a study of twenty-five babies. Vol. 2. Intellectual development*. Minneapolis: Univer. Minnesota Press, 1933.

Siegel, P. S., & Foshee, J. G. The law of primary reinforcement in children. *J. exp. Psychol.*, 1953, **45**, 12–14.

Simmons, M. W., & Lipsitt, L. P. An operant-discrimination apparatus for infants. *J. exp. Anal. Behav.*, 1961, 4, 233–235.

Siqueland, E. R. Operant conditioning of head turning in four-month infants. *Psychon. Sci.*, 1964, 1, 223–224.

Skeels, H. M. The use of conditioning techniques in the study of form discrimination of young children. *J. exp. Educ.*, 1933, 2, 127–137.

Smith, K. U., & Smith, W. M. Infant control of the behavioral environment. *Perception and motion*. Philadelphia: W. B. Saunders, 1962. Pp. 277–290.

Spiker, C. C., & Norcross, K. J. Effects of previously acquired stimulus names on discrimination performance. *Child Develpm.*, 1962, 33, 859–864.

Spiker, C. C. Research methods in children's learning. In P. H. Mussen (Ed.), *Handbook of research methods in child development*. New York: Wiley, 1960. Pp. 374–420.

Spock, B. The striving for autonomy and regressive object relationships. *Psychoanalytic study of the child*, 1963, 18, 361–364. Reprinted in Y. Brackbill & G. G. Thompson (Eds.), *Behavior in infancy and early childhood: A book of readings*. New York: Free Press, 1967.

Statten, P., & Wishart, D. E. S. Pure-tone audiometry in young children: Psycho-galvanic-skin-resistance and peep-show. *Ann. Otol. Rhinol. Laryngol.*, 1956, 65, 511–534.

Stevenson, H. W., Iscoe, I., & McConnell, C. A developmental study of transposition. *J. exp. Psychol.*, 1955, 49, 278–280.

Strayer, L. C. Language and growth: The relative efficacy of early and deferred vocabulary training, studied by the method of co-twin control. *Genet.*

Psychol. Monogr., 1930, 8, 209–319. Reprinted in Y. Brackbill & G. G. Thompson (Eds.), *Behavior in infancy and early childhood: A book of readings.* New York: Free Press, 1967.

Tinbergen, N. *The study of instinct.* Oxford: Clarendon Press, 1951.

Tomka, I. *Izuchenie razvitiia uslovnykh sviazei na zvuki rechi u detei rannego vozrasta. (A study of the development of conditioned connections to sound in young children.)* Unpub. dissertation, Candidacy in Med. Sci. Leningrad: Pavlov Inst. Physiol., 1957.

Tonkova-Iampolskaia, R. V. K kharakteristike sosudistykh uslovnykh refleksov u detei mladshego vozrasta. (Characteristics of vascular conditioned reflexes in young children.) *Zh. vyssh. nerv. Deiatel.*, 1956, 6, 697–701.

———. The features of vascular conditioned reflexes in children in the third year of life. *Pavlov J. high. nerv. Act.*, 1961, 11, 89–93.

Tracy, F. The language of childhood. *Amer. J. Psychol.*, 1893, 6, 107–138.

Trincker, D., & Trincker, I. Die ontogenetische Entwicklung des Helligkeits- und Farbensehens beim Menschen. I. Die Entwicklung des Helligkeitssehens. (The ontogenetic development of brightness and color vision in man. I. The development of brightness.) *Albrecht Graefe's Arch. Ophthal.*, 1955, 156, 519–534. Translated and reprinted in Y. Brackbill & G. G. Thompson (Eds.), *Behavior in infancy and early childhood: A book of readings.* New York: Free Press, 1967.

Usoltsev, A. N., & Terekhova, N. T. Functional peculiarities of the skin-temperature analyzer in children during the first six months of life. *Pavlov J. high. nerv. Act.*, 1958, 8, 174–184.

Vakhrameeva, I. A. Osobennosti obrazovaniia i protekaniia bilateralnykh uslovnykh dvigatelnykh refleksov u detei rannego vozrasta. (Characteristics of the formation and development of bilateral, conditioned movement reflexes in young children.) In N. I. Kasatkin (Ed.), *Ot prostogo k slozhnomu. (From the simple to the complex.)* Leningrad: Izdatelstvo "Nauka," 1964. Pp. 115–126.

Valentine, C. W. The colour perception and colour preferences of an infant during its fourth and eighth months. *Brit. J. Psychol.*, 1913–14, 6, 363–386.

———. The psychology of imitation with special reference to early childhood. *Brit. J. Psychol.*, 1930, 21, 105–132.

Waring, E. B. The relation between early language habits and early habits of conduct control. *Teachers College Contr. Educ.*, 1927, No. 260.

Warren, A. B., & Brown, R. H. Conditioned operant response phenomena in children. *J. gen. Psychol.*, 1943, 28, 181–207.

Watson, J. B. *Psychological care of infant and child.* New York: Norton, 1928.

———. Talking and thinking. In J. B. Watson, *Behaviorism.* New York: The People's Institute Publishing Co., 1925.

Watson, J. B., & Rayner, R. Conditioned emotional reactions. *J. exp. Psychol.*, 1920, 3, 1–14.

Watson, J. S. Personal communication. Detroit: Merrill-Palmer Institute, 1966.

Weir, M. W., & Stevenson, H. W. The effect of verbalization in children's learning as a function of chronological age. *Child Develpm.*, 1959, 30, 143–149.

Weisberg, P. Social and nonsocial conditioning of infant vocalizations. *Child Develpm.*, 1963, 34, 377–388. Reprinted in Y. Brackbill & G. G. Thompson (Eds.), *Behavior in infancy and early childhood: A book of readings.* New York: Free Press, 1967.

Welch, L. The development of discrimination of form and area. *J. Psychol.*, 1939, 7, 37–54. (a)

———. The development of size discrimination between the ages of 12 and 40 months. *J. genet. Psychol.*, 1939, 55, 243–268. (b)

———. The span of generalization below the two-year age level. *J. genet. Psychol.*, 1939, 55, 269–297. (c)

Wenger, M. A. An investigation of conditioned responses in human infants. *Univer. Iowa Stud. Child Welf.*, 1936, 12, No. 1.

————. Path-selection behavior of young children in body-mazes. *J. exp. Educ.*, 1933, 2, 197–236.

Wickens, D. D., & Wickens, C. A study of conditioning in the neonate. *J. exp. Psychol.*, 1940, 26, 94–102.

Zonova, A. V. O tsvetovom zrenii detei pervykh mesiatsev zhizni. (Color discrimination in children during the first months of life.) In N. I. Kasatkin (Ed.), *Ot prostogo k slozhnomu. (From the simple to the complex.)* Leningrad: Izdatelstvo "Nauka," 1964. Pp. 135–153.

Chapter 5

Language Development: The First Four Years

FREDA G. REBELSKY

RAYMOND H. STARR, JR.

ZELLA LURIA

The birth cry signals the entrance of the human into a complicated social world in which language is the primary tool of communication. At birth the child has some of the physical rudiments that enable him to speak, but it is several years before he becomes a fully active member of the community.

As McCarthy (1954) noted, the word "infancy" itself is derived from Latin and means the period without speech.

As a child moves from mere vocalizing to creative, meaningful, purposeful language use during his first four years, he moves out of his infancy. He produces new sentences never heard before, going well beyond imitation of those around him. How language is acquired and what such acquisition means for the development of thinking are the concerns of this chapter, concerns that the available data can answer only partially.

Because our knowledge of children's understanding of language is based on either their own speech or their reactions to speech, much of this chapter is about speaking. However, other aspects of communication —such as vocalization, which includes not only speaking, but also screaming, laughing, babbling, and nonsense sounds—are also covered.

Before 1950 studies of language development were usually observational descriptions, often made by parents who used their own children as subjects. Later observational studies were done on more extensive samples and relied on more complicated instrumentation.

The early 1950s, perhaps under the seminal influence of the Social Science Research Council, saw new lines of communication opened between psychologists and linguists. The October 1954 supplement of the *Journal of Abnormal and Social Psychology* (Osgood & Sebeok, 1954) represented an attempt to see where the study of language behavior had arrived and to pose questions of interest to psychologists and linguists, in the hope that new methods of analysis and insights into the language acquisition process would be generated. The collaboration between the two disciplines continues to date and has been fruitful.

The 1954 review of McCarthy, a very complete review of the status of language research for that time, shows clearly the tendency of psychologists in what may be called the "prelinguistic" phase to focus on developmental norms for vocabulary, sentence length, and phonetic elements, conceived to be the building blocks of language.

Phonemes and words were typical units of measurement for psychologists. Linguists have led psychologists to the study of morphological and syntactic elements as new language units for study, e.g., Brown & Bellugi (1964), Miller (1964). The preoccupation with norms, which characterized earlier work, has been replaced with more difficult and, perhaps, more fundamental questions.

Linguists' reliance on the competence of individual informants to induce the grammar of any language attacks the problem of grammar in a manner which has helped psychologists to pose new and meaningful questions. In early work, the question posed by psychologists was of the form: How does a child of age x measure up against the codified grammar? The answer was then in the form: nouns present, verbs not; active present, passive not; simple sentences present, complex not.

The new kind of question, exemplified by recent work by Brown and by Ervin (see Bellugi & Brown, 1964), is of the form: Given the way a child of age x speaks, what is his implicit grammar? The answer is then in the form: plural rule present, overregularization occurring; plural morpheme eliminated in words ending in s. Thus, the child becomes the informant, telling the psychologist what his rules are. Successive ages reveal rule changes, which may have no necessary correspondence to the adult grammar, but reveal a great deal about the cognitive process in language acquisition.

The linguist's definition of language competence (as distinct from performance) requires, however, that competence be assessed from more than a child's speech production. Some intriguing records of a twenty-eight-month-old's spontaneous speech play in "dialogues with himself" suggest how the child is actively processing language rules (Weir, 1962).

Chomsky has suggested that there is

. . . a general tendency to oversimplify drastically the facts of linguistic structure and to assume that the determination of competence can be derived from description of a corpus by some sort of sufficiently developed data-processing techniques. My feeling is that this is hopeless and that only experimentation of a fairly indirect and ingenious sort can provide evidence that is at all critical for formulating a true account of the child's grammar. . . . Consequently, . . . some of the research in this area (should) be diverted from recording of texts towards attempting to tap the child's underlying abilities to use and comprehend sentences, to detect deviance and compensate for it, to apply rules in new situations, to form highly specific concepts from scattered bits of evidence, and so on. . . . Thus, for example, the child's ability to repeat sentences and nonsentences, phonologically possible sequences and phonologically impossible ones, etc., might provide some evidence as to the underlying system that he is using. There is surely no doubt that the child's achievements in systematizing linguistic data, at every stage, go well beyond what he actually produces in normal speech. Thus it is striking that advances are generally "across the board" (Chomsky, 1964, p. 39).

Theory and Methodology in the Study of Language Development: Some Theoretical Considerations

A comparison of theories and current knowledge of language acquisition leads to the conclusion that the major questions about the appearance of language still cannot be answered definitively. Why does a child babble? How does a word acquire meaning? How or why does a child move beyond single words? How does he acquire grammatical forms? How, then, does language develop?

Few psychologists today would propose a simple associational model for language acquisition. That the model of a finite state Markov process could explain language without more complex requirements, was disproved by Chomsky (1957). Miller described the proof as follows:

> The fact that English grammar permits sentences to be embedded inside sentences means that it must be able to deal with parenthetical structures. . . . These are, of course, just the sentences in Chomsky's language. . . . Since no limit is imposed by the grammar on the number of left parentheses, and since each different number of left parentheses implies a different state of the assumed Markovian system (so that it can remember how many right parentheses are required to complete the string grammatically), it follows that the number of states must be denumerably infinite. But this is absurd, because a grammar with an infinite number of rules cannot be learned in a finite childhood or stored in a finite nervous system. An infinitely long grammar is, in fact, no improvement over an exhaustive list of all grammatical sentences, so the whole purpose of a grammar is vitiated. The only reasonable conclusion is that languages should not be characterized by structures having a finite number of states with specific transitions among them (Miller, 1964b, p. 257).

Early models for language learning assumed it to be another example of higher order conditioned responses and their generalization. Learning was expandable by systems of conditioning, chaining, generalization, and habit-family hierarchies. Thus to explain language no recourse to "mental structures" of any sort was to be needed and no new laws of learning were to be needed to account for language.

Modern models based on mediation, often highly complex, are dealt with in this chapter in the section on mediation only insofar as the studies have been made on young children. The decision to focus on some aspects of psycholinguistic theory rather than view the whole field of theory is, in part, a space consideration. We believe, in addition, that some recent formulations of a psycholinguistic theory pose new and important questions that might be overlooked by more traditional learning approaches. Chomsky (1959) has pointed out some unanswered questions in typical learning theory formulation of language acquisition. At this time, it is questionable if anyone has adequate answers to the central question of what transforms a nonverbal infant into a fluent speaker. But psycholinguistic theory appears to us to present a model with heuristic merit.

There is, in addition, evidence that a convergence is beginning among theorists of different persuasions at least on the nature of some of the phenomena of language structure to be explained (Deese, 1964; Jenkins & Palermo, 1964; Kagan, 1964; Moore, 1964).

The acquisition of phonemes as building blocks for speech as the first step in producing language and speech has been described by Jakobson (1941, 1956) in his theory of "distinctive features." He suggests that there is a developmental order in which a child learns the phonological system by learning to distinguish single features or properties of phonological contrasts (discussed in detail later in this chapter). This view of phonological development is based on the notion that phonemes have distinctive articulatory and acoustic features, for example, voiced or voiceless, oral or nasal, etc. The consonant-vowel distinction is supposedly learned first by the child, and the other distinctive features are learned in a regular developmental sequence.

We may assume that children throughout the world originally have the capacity for making all speech sounds, some of which are encouraged by the specific language heard and some of which drop out because they are not part of the child's environment.

From the early steps of word acquisition and naming—the base of all symbolization—to complex sentence development, psycholinguists view the child more as a "rule inducer" than as a learner of discrete items. Brown and Bellugi (1964) have stated the hypothesis well:

> There must be some kind of distinctive mechanism, peculiar to the human brain, which is appropriate to the processing of speech. One must somehow account for the fact that, when children have heard a lot of speech, they start to talk, whereas, if apes hear the same noises, they do not talk. A "language generator" must be built into the brain and set to operate independent of any natural language. The character of possible language, or the set of possible grammars, must somehow be represented in the brain. In the broadest sense, the language generator must contain the information-processing procedures which any human organism will use when exposed to some speech community. The language generator is either initially or through maturational processes primed to go off when suitable samples of speech are presented to it, and this has little to do with learning. This is not to say that man has *a priori* knowledge of any particular language. The particular language, particular grammar and phonological system, are learned. When we talk of language acquisition, it is often in the sense of the child's internalization of

the particular grammar to which he has been exposed (1964, p. 113).

The genetic mechanism assumed to be behind this formulation is spelled out and some evidence is presented by Lenneberg (1964). He judges from some case material that there is a genetic mechanism which enables and protects language comprehension and is quite distinct from language production. The reasoning is based on more current statements of the relation of heredity and environment, such as is presented in Chapter 8 of this volume. Assumed are (1) that the young child is specially adapted biologically for language acquisition and (2) that rules, not items, are built up in the child. Therefore, the developmental psychologist properly will be studying how the child's rules evolve.

One model of use to the developmental psychologist is proposed by Chomsky (1957). He has taken as his task as a linguist the development of the most parsimonious set of rules which will generate all possible grammatical sentences in English and no ungrammatical ones. He assumes that, starting with a small set of basic sentences ("terminal strings"), other sentences can be derived by single transformational rules. By a series of stepwise transformations, more complex sentences and finally inflected sentences will appear.

This thesis does not mean that children necessarily go through Chomsky's economical steps. But he raises a question of importance to developmentalists: What steps does the child use? This is a question which is relevant for the child as a decoder as well as an encoder.

Methodology

How should one study language development? Should one follow children about and observe what naturally occurs? Obviously, this is impossible. In observing, one automatically structures data, especially since the listener is a member of a linguistic community. For example, we tend to call certain linguistic units "words," but with a young child a "word" may have the implications that "sentence" has for an adult.

When a linguist analyzes a new language, he gets a native informant to provide him with a "corpus" from which informant and linguist together, by questioning and contrasts, work out the language's structure and rules. However, a child's language may not be as coherent or stable as a usual language, and a young child is a poor informant since he rarely answers questions appropriately.

Another approach is to subject the child to experimental intervention to see what the child knows linguistically, though he might not emit this knowledge in daily usage. As Chomsky has said, "The description which is of greatest psychological relevance is the account of competence, not that of performance . . . the kinds of structures the person has succeeded in mastering and internalizing, whether or not he utilizes them in practice" (1964, p. 36). However, children respond to subtle cues in presently nonpredictable ways, so that much teaching might occur during testing. If one is interested in experimenting on linguistic readiness such teaching is not necessarily prohibitive. A child who can learn from the cues in the testing situation may be ready to take the next linguistic step, or perhaps on further experimental questioning, the apparent step is not really made consistently. Both kinds of findings add information on competence.

In general, then, the problem is to study what the child has learned linguistically, in what sequence, and how. We are not at present certain what the elements of language are for which we should look. Words and sounds are one thing; complex grammatical forms, inflections, and sentence formation are quite another. Linguists are at this time debating the "essential" aspects of language (Bellugi & Brown, 1964). This section summarizes methods used to study language development. Many of the methods will be presented in more detail later in the chapter.

OBSERVATION

As in other areas of child development, observation has been one of the earliest techniques used in studying language development. Parents have been notable data collectors (see, e.g., Darwin, 1877; Preyer, 1889; Stern & Stern, 1909; Nice, 1917; Leopold, 1939). Most of these offer the usual positive and negative features of baby biographies. On the positive side, the studies are longitudinal, with the children being seen in a variety of activities. However, on the negative side, the reports are usually of one or two children and are based only on emitted responses unsystematically collected. While the results are often valuable, questions of generalization to other possible samples of children are hard to answer.

When such data have been systematically collected, the technique sometimes raises questions. For example, Leopold (1939) followed his daughter's speech development by recalling her sounds from notes which he transcribed in the evening by means of the International Phonetic Alphabet. Though as a highly trained linguist he used careful definitions of all his linguistic units, he was not concerned with the problems of storage and retrieval of his data. Psychologists would tend to feel that there might have been distortion during the time lapse. Also, the use of the International Phonetic Alphabet might have led to regularizing some infant noises which could not be adequately described by such a tool, e.g., some of the grunts collected by Lenneberg and his associates (Lenneberg, Rebelsky & Nichols, 1965).

Many observational studies have been done by nonparents. Most of these studies focused upon single aspects of language, e.g., adjectives (Carroll, 1939), speech sounds in crying (Irwin & Chen, 1941), cry latencies (Fisichelli & Karelitz, 1963), syntactic structures (Menyuk, 1963), repetitions (Winitz, 1961), and varieties of baby noises (Lenneberg, Rebelsky, & Nichols, 1965).

More recent observational studies have relied on instruments such as the tape recorder (e.g., Parmelee, 1955) or movie camera (Bullowa, Jones, & Bever, 1964). Tape recorders have been used in a variety of ways: intermittently (Chan, Lenneberg, & Rebelsky, 1964) or continuously (Brown & Bellugi, 1964); for short periods of time (Miller & Ervin [1964] recorded for ¾ hour) or long periods (Lenneberg, Rebelsky, & Nichols [1965] recorded for 24 hours); and timing of recording has often depended on some cut-off point, such as units emitted, e.g., in Brown and Fraser's work (1964), 500 different utterances was the limit chosen. Tape recorded data have been collected at least since 1935 (Mandell & Sonneck).

In addition, many observational studies have been accomplished through intelligence tests, vocabulary tests, and articulation tests. These will be described in detail later in the chapter.

All of the studies cited above concern emitted data. However, there have been attempts to study language competence through a variety of means, such as repetition of sentences (Lenneberg, Nichols, & Rosenberger, 1962); responses to pictures (Berko, 1958); and responses to questions (Brown & Fraser, 1964).

Observational data, collected either by human or mechanical means, must of course be analyzed. Some data, as noted above, have been subjected to simple frequency counts. Irwin (1941) and others have used the International Phonetic Alphabet for description. Brown and his co-workers (Brown & Bellugi, 1964; Brown & Fraser, 1964) have attempted to reconstruct the speech corpuses of children from tapes and have induced probable grammars from such corpuses. Lenneberg and his associates (Lenneberg, Rebelsky, & Nichols, 1965) employed the spectrograph (see Miller, 1951, and Irwin, 1960, for a description of this technique) using broad categories of sound (e.g., fussing, cooing, etc.) for analysis of taped records as well as measuring visual polygraph displays of sound (Chan, Lenneberg, & Rebelsky, 1964). In many instances reliability of observations from tape-recorded data have not been noted, though reliability studies have been done (e.g., Irwin, 1941; Fisichelli, 1950). While most modern observers of tape-recorded data are aware that problems of interpretation do not disappear when sounds are mechanically recorded, sound retrieval problems are markedly diminished.

EXPERIMENTATION

The recent "call for a change of method of investigation, from naturalistic observation to experimental intervention in the process of language acquisition" (Bellugi & Brown, 1964, p. 185) leaves open the question of methodology.

Most of the experimental studies of language with children have been done with older children of four years and more partially because, as many have noted (e.g., Luria, 1961), research on infants using our present techniques leaves something to be desired. Or as Brown and

Bellugi put it very well, by way of example, "Another week we noticed that Adam would sometimes pluralize nouns when they should have been pluralized and sometimes would not. We wondered if he could make grammatical judgments about the plural. 'Adam,' we asked, 'which is right, "two shoes" or "two shoe"?' His answer on that occasion, produced with explosive enthusiasm, was 'Pop goes the weasel!' " (Brown & Bellugi, 1964, p. 135). The two-year-old does not make a perfectly docile experimental subject.

As noted earlier, some interventions have been attempted to study language competence. The story of Adam is an example of such. In the 1920s and 1930s many studies were done using increased stimulation or attempts to teach language, especially words (Gesell & Thompson, 1929; Strayer, 1930; Hilgard, 1933). Such studies relied upon controlling the child's language environment, by, e.g., increasing casual and planned verbal interaction with one child while minimizing such interaction with the twin of the experimental child (Strayer, 1930). One major issue with all these studies, as with the recent conditioning studies, reviewed below, is that the previous stimulation history of the experimental children is unknown.

Recently several studies have attempted to understand language or sound acquisition through conditioning. Rheingold, Gewirtz, and Ross (1959) demonstrated that one can increase the number of positive vocalizations through social reinforcement of three-month-old infants. However, in this study, crying increased during extinction, so it may be that vocalization was generally increased, with positive vocalizations replaced by negative (crying). Weisberg (1963), following this work, demonstrated that vocalization at this age is conditioned by contingent social stimulation. Ruled out as positive conditioners by this study were a blank face of an adult, noncontingent social stimulation, and both noncontingent and contingent nonsocial stimulation (a door chime). Casler (1965), using children from six to sixty-six weeks of age, found that human, but impersonal, noncontingent stimulation did not induce further vocalization. It is difficult to conceive as "verbal stimulation" an impersonal human, gazing fixedly at the middle portion of a baby's body, repeating numbers up to five over and over for one minute and then saying "hello, baby." One of the important research problems is, obviously, to ascertain what is verbal stimulation for an infant. It has been well demonstrated by now that contingent human reinforcement can induce a baby to make more sounds, but everyone agrees that one must start with the sounds a baby is already capable of emitting.

The Russians have been notably clever in devising techniques to ascertain what children understand linguistically, though they have concentrated primarily on general understanding and not on particular linguistic forms.

In conclusion, the nature of research on language is becoming increasingly scientific, and, in general, investigators are becoming more aware of methodological problems in studying language, particularly in infancy. This awareness has, of necessity, led to refinements of methodology to describe better and understand better the development of language. It should be obvious, however, that this is a rich area for still further methodological improvements.[1]

The Development of
Vocalization and Language

The purpose of this section is to integrate the findings of almost a century of research and observation of language development in normal children and to show how, in the comparatively brief period of the first four years of life, children acquire language. The discussion is divided into five major areas: prelinguistic vocalization, articulation, vocabulary, semantics, and grammar.

PRELINGUISTIC VOCALIZATION

CRYING

The child's first vocalization is the birth cry. Although several psychoanalytic theorists attach great importance to the nature of the birth process and the birth cry, it is probable that the birth cry has little relation to later personality development. Hooker (1952) reports that respiratory and vocal organs are functional long before full term birth, e.g., crying has been heard in a fetus as young as twenty-three and a half weeks upon its exposure to air.

Ruja (1948) has attempted to test Rank's hypothesis that the birth cry is an indicator of trauma. He found no significant correlation between length of labor as measured by the time elapsed from the mother's admission to the hospital and delivery, and percentage of time the infant spent in crying during the first eight days.

Lynip (1951) performed a spectrographic analysis of the birth cry of a newborn girl. He found a resonance pattern which was in no way similar to spectrographic analyses of adult vowel sounds. (Four trained phoneticians were unable to agree on what sounds in the International Phonetic Alphabet were present in the birth cry.) Irwin and Chen (1943) state that the birth cry differs little from other cries of the newborn.

Other studies of infants' cries have considered the nature of crying, the causes of crying, and behavioral correlates of crying. Fairbanks (1942), in a longitudinal investigation of the pitch of infant hunger cries, found that during the first four months there is a rise in mean pitch followed by a leveling off in the second half of the first nine

---

1. See Berko & Brown (1960) and Irwin (1960a, 1960b) for further details on methodology. Although many of the methods noted in these two reviews are applicable only after the child has gained many language skills, and is older than the age of four, the top age covered by this review, we cite them for their potential relevance even to this age group.

months. He found increasing variability in pitch with increasing age. The changes were attributed to an increased tension in the vocal cords and to increased neuromuscular control of the infant over his vocal cords. Lynip (1951) found that crying in one child became more rhythmic and less intense during the first day of life; pitch rose with increasing intensity of crying.

Tonkova-Yampolskaya (1962) also performed an acoustic analysis of the crying of 18 newborns from one to six days of age. She found that cries consist of six or seven formant areas which correspond fairly well with the lines of the speech organs. The middle part of the sound spectrum is more intense than the upper or lower sections. She concluded that neonatal cries are not under cortical control and serve no communicative purpose. Similar results are reported by Lenneberg (1964a, 1964b) who spectrographically analyzed vocalizations of infants less than three months old and found they are acoustically quite different from speech sounds although formant patterns are present.

Various types of stimulation influence crying. The most general finding has been that continuous stimulation of moderate to high intensity levels has a marked quieting effect on children's behavior. Thus, Aldrich, Sung, and Knop (1945a, 1945b) found that light and heat tend to decrease crying. Irwin and Weiss (1934a), Smith (1936), and others have found that less crying occurs under illumination than in the dark. Stubbs (1934), varying intensity and duration of pure tone stimuli, found that long, intense sounds inhibit crying more than short, soft ones. Pratt (1930) found that temperature, when varied through a relatively limited range—between 74° and 88°F.—causes a decrease in crying. Humidity variations, however, are apparently without effect. Irwin and Weiss (1934b), Wolff (1959), and Lipton, Steinschneider, and Richmond (1960) have studied the effects of restraint on crying. According to Irwin and Weiss (1934b) infants cry less when clothed than when unclothed. They are also quieter when swaddled than when unswaddled (Lipton et al., 1960) or when partially swaddled (Wolff, 1959). In addition, Keitel, Cohn, and Harnish (1960) found infants who are kept on their backs cry more than those who are kept in a prone position.

Cries have been an object of study in and of themselves because they are the newborn's best means of influencing and acting on his environment. Many people claim to be able to know what is wrong with an infant by the type of cry. Sherman (1927) studied the ability of observers to determine what emotion was present in the crying of neonates. Four conditions of stimulation were used. There was little relation between the stimuli and judgments in the absence of information or stimulus cues. Lynip's (1951) spectrographic analysis confirmed these results by showing that judgments of the cause of crying are most likely due to knowledge of the state of the infant at the time of crying, not to the nature of the cry.

There are, however, marked individual differences in crying. A series of studies by Aldrich and his associates (Aldrich, Sung, & Knop,

1945a, 1945b; Aldrich, Sung, Knop, Stevens, & Burchell, 1945; Aldrich, Norval, Knop, & Venegas, 1946) has investigated crying in the hospital and home as well as after the infant received additional care. In one study of fifty neonates Aldrich *et al.* (1945a) found that the time spent crying in the hospital over an eight-day period ranged from 48.2 minutes to 117 minutes per day. Hunger appeared to be the main cause of crying; unknown causes were next in frequency when total crying time was considered. Aldrich, Sung, and Knop (1945b) found that 42 babies less than seven weeks old who had left the hospital and returned home cried less than nursery babies. The average baby at home had 4.0 prolonged crying spells a day, whereas nursery babies had almost three times as many. Clearly, crying induces search behavior in mothers, the success of which reduces crying frequency.

In a third study Aldrich *et al.* (1946) increased the amount of time spent in caring for nursery babies in the first eight days of life from 0.7 hours a day to 1.9 hours. The mean amount of crying dropped from 113.2 minutes to 55 minutes a day. Hunger was again the most commonly attributed cause with unknown causes next in frequency. Minor causes of crying were wet or soiled diapers or vomiting.

Karelitz and Fisichelli (1962) and Fisichelli and Karelitz (1963) examined cry thresholds and latencies of normal and brain damaged infants. A rubber band snapped against the sole of the foot was the painful stimulus used to elicit crying. It was found that greater stimulation was needed to make the abnormal infants cry. Moreover, crying was more easily induced in the older infants in both groups (Karelitz & Fisichelli, 1962). In a study on response latency (Fisichelli & Karelitz, 1963) normal subjects showed a significantly shorter latency than abnormal subjects.

SPEECH SOUNDS IN PRELINGUISTIC VOCALIZATIONS

The appearance of speech sounds is one of the first steps in the child's progress toward language acquisition. Orvis Irwin and his associates have performed the most thorough normative analysis of speech sound acquisition with the aim of providing a complete, systematic record of speech sound development.

Irwin and Curry (1941) examined vowel elements in the cries of infants less than ten days old. They transcribed manually the speech sounds uttered by each of 40 subjects in 25 consecutive respirations according to the International Phonetic Alphabet. They determined that the analysis of sounds occurring during a unit of behavior, a single breath in this case, is a more reliable measure than the analysis of sounds appearing in a given time period. (The method of breath unit analysis was adopted by Irwin in all his subsequent studies.) Irwin and Curry found little consonant vocalization among their neonate subjects, and only 4 vowels were commonly used. All 40 subjects used [æ], while [ɛ, I, ʌ] were less common.[2] For the sample as a whole, 92 per cent of

2. For a description of the International Phonetic Alphabet and of the way in which vowels and consonants are formed, see Irwin (1960a, 1960b).

the utterances were front vowels, 7 per cent were middle vowels and 1 per cent were back vowels.

Irwin (1948b) investigated the percentages of different vowel speech sounds according to place of articulation during the first two and a half years of life and found that the frequency of front vowels decreases from 72 per cent at two months to 47 per cent at thirty months. During the same period middle vowels decrease in frequency from 25 per cent to 17 per cent and back vowels increase from 2 per cent to 37 per cent of all speech sounds uttered. In the first year of life the vowel speech sounds vocalized by the infants are composed mainly of front and middle vowels. By thirty months, however, the distribution of percentages is similar to that for the English-speaking American adult.

There is a different pattern for consonants. In a study on the manner of consonant articulation Irwin (1947b) found that young infants use mainly voiceless, fricative, and plosive sounds, and that nasals, semivowels, and glides are rare. At thirty months, again the upper age limit of his sample, the consonant profile resembles that of the adult. Plosives are most common, and there is a decrease in the percentage of fricatives.

An analysis of the percentage occurrence of consonants by place of articulation also shows a gradual approximation of adult percentages by thirty months (Irwin, 1947c). For the first ten months, however, rear consonants are dominant. At two months 87 per cent of all consonants are glottals and almost 12 per cent are velars. These percentages decrease to 47 per cent and 6 per cent, respectively, at ten months. On the other hand, the percentage of postdentals rises from less than 1 per cent at two months to 53 per cent at thirty months, while labials and labiodentals increase from less than 1 per cent to 26 per cent. Linguadentals remain fairly constant at less than 2 per cent of all consonant vocalizations. Thus, unlike vowels, consonants can be said to develop from back to front.

In several studies Irwin presents combined data for vowels and consonants (Chen & Irwin, 1946a, 1946b; Irwin & Chen, 1946a, 1946b; Irwin, 1947a, 1949). Chen and Irwin (1946a) found that at two months the average infant uses 4.5 different vowel and 2.7 different consonant types. At thirty months 11.4 vowel and 15.8 consonant types are in use. This compares with the 35 phonemes in adult speech. The curve for speech sound type development is approximately parabolic. Vowel sounds exceed consonants for the first year, but thereafter there are more consonant than vowel types. At two and a half years almost all vowel sounds used by the adult and about two thirds of the consonants used by adults are present.

Data on phoneme frequency show that in the first month the mean number of vowels per 30 breaths is 49.0 and of consonants is 11.3. At thirty months there is an average of 75.3 vowels and 73.5 consonants (Irwin & Chen, 1946b).

In an interesting study Irwin (1960a) had mothers of twenty-four infants of lower socioeconomic status spend from 15 to 20 minutes a day reading stories to their children from the time the children were thirteen months old until they were thirty months old. Ten children in a control group were not systematically read to although they did receive environmental stimulation typical of their homes. Results on speech sound frequency were collected at bimonthly intervals. The experimental group showed a significantly higher frequency of vocalization by eighteen months, and the differences became larger with increasing age. Phonemic output can be increased, but whether the increased vocalization has any influence on language development is not known.

Lynip (1951) has questioned the validity of using direct observation to assess the presence of speech sounds in infancy. His conclusion that his subject did not use any speech sounds comparable to those of adults until she was almost a year old has been criticized (Winitz, 1960). Winitz claims that the sound spectrograph is a means of analyzing the physical aspects of language while phonetic transcription analyzes the linguistic aspects. The physical measures may or may not represent the phonetic transcription. Winitz obtained half-hour-long records of the vocalizations of five infants from nine to fifteen months old. Clear vowel speech sounds were selected from the tapes, and graduate students were asked to transcribe the sounds. Those vowel sounds agreed on by seven of ten students were analyzed spectrographically, and the resulting spectrograms were compared to adult spectrograms. Winitz agreed with Lynip that the vowel sounds made by young infants, although definitely vowel sounds to an observer, are not acoustically comparable to adult sounds.

From the conflicting research results in this area it can be concluded that the speech sounds uttered by the preverbal child, although similar to those used by adults, differ in several aspects, notably in pitch and volume. In addition, it should be remembered that the child is undergoing a process of motor maturation during which the muscles involved in speech production are increasing in coordination and there is more than one way to produce what is to the native listener the same phoneme.

BABBLING AND IMITATION

The infant moves in a remarkably short time period from a stage of vocalizing to one in which he possesses language. The first stage in the acquisition of language is marked by the appearance of babbling. According to Jespersen (1922) babbling may start as early as the third week of life but usually starts around the seventh or eighth week. The first babbling sounds probably have no referent but are merely muscular exercises. It has been found that deaf children make speech sounds even though they cannot hear them and that during the first three months the vocalizations of deaf and hearing children are identical. From the fourth through the twelfth month the sounds uttered by deaf and hearing children are similar, although deaf children use a more limited range of babbling sounds after six months (Lenneberg, 1964). Babbling continues until the child starts to use words in a meaningful manner and persists more than a year after the child starts to talk. Norman (1936) described one child who babbled well into her third year.

Babbling is most likely a period of practice during which the child perfects and completes his phonemic repertoire. Latif (1934) set forth the popular explanation that babbling is a period in which the child refines those phonemes used by the adults with whom he associates and drops those phonemes that are unnecessary in the language he will soon speak, a phenomenon called *phonemic contraction*. Tischler (1957) found that the greatest variety of sounds are produced between eight and twelve months with a decline after twelve months when the sounds begin to assume an intentional and communicative character. One reason these results differ from Irwin's may be that Irwin was concerned only with *phonemic expansion*, the acquisition of the sounds used in a particular language.

One of the earliest studies on babbling was by Wolfflin (1901) who concluded that the duplication of syllables in babbling was a natural part of children's speech. Winitz (1961) has reanalyzed some data of Irwin's in an examination of repetitions in the speech of children less than two years old. He identified several classes of repetitions. The results indicated that repetition was indeed a common occurrence. From 25 to 33 per cent of the breath units analyzed by Irwin contained repetitions of sounds or sound patterns. A peak of repetition was reached at about one year, and frequency then declined. However, this may have been due to the increasing number of words used in the second year.

The transition of babbling into more wordlike forms, or word approximations, was studied by McCurry and Irwin (1953). A word approximation was considered to be ". . . a phonetic pattern which is interpreted by the observers at the time of the transcription as an attempt by the infant to pronounce a standard word" (1953, p. 133). They found a significant increase in the number of approximations and the number of words attempted between nineteen to twenty-two months of age. There was, however, no significant increase in the number of correct pronunciations.

Several investigators have tried by training to increase phonemic output. Fedorov (1962) repeated syllables to a hospitalized 16-month-old boy who babbled but did not talk. The child showed comprehension but still could not produce meaningful words. At eighteen months word and object were finally associated. In his second year the boy could hear complex words but repeated only the strong syllables. Similarly, when asked to repeat sentences the boy responded only to the familiar word. Between two and three years he was able to give short sentences and could associate objects with the past. Training was, in this case, helpful. Ervin and Miller (1963) report a study by Shvarchkin who taught eleven- to twenty-two-month-old Soviet children Russian words that differed from each other by only one phoneme. The Russian phonemes were learned in a set order, and the children learned to distinguish all of them by the end of the second year.

These studies, by making use of the young child's propensity to imitate, have shown that it is possible to accelerate phonemic development in both normal and retarded children. In addition to articulation *training,* articulation *enrichment,* as noted earlier, is also effective in increasing speech sound output (Irwin, 1960a).

Guillaume (1925), in an extensive analysis of imitation in two children, proposed that there are four stages in the development of imitation: (a) no imitation, up to two or three months of age, (b) weak imitation, up to about twelve months, (c), echolalia, from twelve to twenty-four months, and (d) opposition toward new linguistic acquisitions and fixation of pronunciation, beginning about twenty-four months of age. Guillaume concluded from his analysis that imitation plays a role equally as great as physical development in the mental functioning of the child.

Lewis (1951) has divided imitation during the first year into three stages which correspond roughly to Guillaume's (1925) categories. The first stage starts at about one month and ends at around four months. It is characterized by a vocal response to speech. (Valentine [1930], for example, found imitation in one of his sons at one month when the son crooned in response to Valentine's croons.) The second, or abeyance, stage consists of a diminution or even a complete cessation of imitation. Lewis stated that this is due to the child's increased responsiveness to the meaning of what he heard. Remarks made by adults for the sole purpose of eliciting imitative behavior do not yield an imitative response when they have no contextual meaning for the child.

The third stage is identified by the appearance of true imitation and usually starts in the ninth month. According to Lewis, five changes mark this stage: "(i) A readier imitation of sounds drawn from the child's own vocabulary. (ii) The more certain imitation of intonational form. (iii) The appearance of delayed imitation. (iv) The more definite imitation—perhaps the first imitation—of sound-groups new to the child. (v) The development of 'echolalia'" (1951, p. 88). Imitation at this stage implies a certain degree of comprehension. Language, for the child, has meaning. Through the process of imitation the child is gradually brought to a stage where he is able to utter remarks with meaning. From the evidence provided by Lewis, it is apparent that some sort of comprehension begins to appear about the end of the ninth month at a point coincidental with the appearance of the third stage of imitation. This pattern of comprehension before use holds for more complex linguistic structures as well as for simple words, as will be seen in the studies of complex grammatical structures.

How a child manages to make a match between his sounds and those of speakers in his environment is still an open and interesting question. All things considered, such as the infant's immature vocal and brain structures, it is an enormous feat for a baby to match his sound to that produced by another human being. (See Merleau-Ponty, 1964, for further discussion of this point.)

ARTICULATION

NORMATIVE STUDIES

This section is concerned with the child's use of phonemes in his own language, the accuracy of his articulation of these phonemes, and tests that have been used to study articulatory ability. Although most studies are concerned with articulation *per se*, a few have considered other aspects of speech sound production such as pitch and loudness.

Early biographical studies of articulatory development were concerned mainly with errors in the child's pronunciation. Over a period of years a body of literature was established, and authors started comparing their own children with those of other authors. About 1930, there was a shift in the direction of research, and true normative studies appeared in which there were groups of children and in which the children were tested under standardized conditions rather than observed under variable conditions.

Since the debut of psycholinguistics in the early 1950s another question has been raised: why the child speaks as he does. To the degree that the psycholinguist's concern is with the individual's language development in relation to his linguistic environment this approach is also biographical.

Darwin's (1877) study of the development of a child contained the earliest analysis of articulatory development. Other nineteenth century investigations were made by Taine (1877), Pollock (1878), Humphreys (1880), Champneys (1881), Lukens (1894–1896), Moore (1896), Hall (1896–1897), Buckman (1897), and Mickens (1897–1898). Many of these early studies concentrated on the errors in articulation that children made, but made no further analysis of utterances (Lukens, 1894–1896; Combes, 1900–1905a, 1900–1905b; Chamberlain & Chamberlain, 1904a, 1904b; Pelsma, 1910; Bohn, 1914; Hills, 1914; Brandenburg, 1915; Miller, Miller, & Nice, 1923).

In a few studies, such as one by Holmes (1927), there has been a major concern with the development of articulation. Holmes devised his own phonetic notation to use in recording the speech of his daughter, Mollie. At eighteen months Mollie used no intervocalic consonants, and words of more than one syllable were articulated as though they were two separate words with each syllable having equal stress. He also noted an inability to pronounce final consonants. Four months later final consonants were slightly prolonged but polysyllabic words were beginning to be treated as one word. At twenty-three months Mollie tended to reduce words of more than two syllables to two syllables, and few consonant blends were noted at any time.

Humphreys (1880) made the interesting observation that when a child directly imitates words spoken by an adult he articulates them correctly, but when speech is spontaneous the child adopts the usual infant misarticulations.

One of the earliest experimental examinations of articulation was by Foulke and Stinchfield (1929) who studied four children until they were two years old. Responses were elicited from the children by showing objects and toys from a speech test devised by Blanton and Stinchfield. The next study, and the first truly detailed one, was by Wellman, Case, Mengert, and Bradbury (1931). Their sample consisted of 204 children from two to six years, with a mean Stanford-Binet IQ of 115.9. Responses, obtained by using questions and pictures, were recorded in the International Phonetic Alphabet with additional notation for the position of the sound in the word. The test covered 133 sounds—66 consonant elements, 48 consonant blends, 15 vowels, and 4 diphthongs. McCarthy (1935) has criticized the Wellman *et al.* test, stating that it is too long, contains unnecessarily rare sounds, and that the response words are not common in the speech of preschool children.

Williams, McFarland, and Little (1937) modified the test devised by Wellman *et al.* (1931) in their construction and analysis of an analytical scale of language achievement. Their test consisted of 98 sounds and consonant blends and was administered to part of a sample of 70 children between two and a half and six and a half years old. Phonetic transcriptions of actual speech were also used to obtain additional information on the accuracy and completeness of pronunciation. The final section of the Williams *et al.* monograph contains norms on the Analytical Scale of Language Achievement for 87 preschoolers, 91 babies in an infant clinic, and 107 orphans; subjects' ages ranged from one to eighty months. Their articulation test contains only 85 of the speech sounds studied by Wellman *et al.* (1931); it does not include sounds in the medial position of words; those peculiar to a particular geographic region; and sounds not commonly used by children, according to the International Kindergarten Union Word List (1928).

In the same study Williams *et al.* analyzed erroneous speech sound substitutions. They found that there was great variability in the occurrence of substitution; that easier sounds were substituted for more difficult ones; that there was a tendency for sounds which were acoustically similar to the correct sound to be substituted; and that pure vowels tended to be substituted for diphthongs.

A number of other studies have been done using a variety of pictorial and observational techniques to assess articulation. Poole (1934) tested, at four-month intervals, the articulation of 140 children from two and a half to five and a half years of age. She used objects, pictures, and questions requiring a single-word response. The most common sounds were the best articulated, and ability to articulate was related to physical development. The most comprehensive study in this area is Templin's (1957). This study, as was the case with the Williams *et al.* (1937) study just discussed, was not limited to articulation but considered also the development of and intercorrelations among a number of linguistic parameters. Templin's sample of 480 children was subdivided by sex, by parental occupation, and by age (3, 3½, 4, 4½, 5, 6, 7, and 8 years). Articulation, sound discrimination, sentence development, and vocabulary were measured. The articulation test was designed to examine the ability to use speech sounds correctly in words rather than the ability to utter the sounds. A total of 176 different sounds were studied: 69 consonant sounds in different positions within words; 71 double-consonant blends; 19 triple-consonant blends; 12 vowels; and 5 diphthongs. Different tests were used for children between three and five years than for children between six and eight years. The younger subjects either repeated the words after the experimenter or said them in response to pictorial stimuli. (One of Templin's many early studies of articulation had examined the question of the effect of different experimental conditions on articulation [1947]. She had found no differences in ability to articulate a selected sound in two different words or between words uttered in imitation or as a spontaneous utterance.)

Templin reported both a total articulation score and a score for each of the five sound categories. The number and percentage of correct consonant sounds according to place in the word and type of sound were also computed. Errors of various types were measured against the International Phonetic Alphabet. No reliability data were given; however, Templin stated that she felt the reliabilities reported in previous studies using the same methods were high enough that no new figures were needed.

Templin found statistically significant differences in total articulation score between ages three and three and a half; three and a half and four; five and six; and six and seven years. At three years the mean articulation score was 53 per cent of maximum and at eight years it was almost 95 percent. Significant score differences were found between three and three and a half years and between three and a half and four years for consonant elements and for double and triple blends but not for vowels and diphthongs. For different types of consonants in the three- to four-year age range she found that nasals in all positions of the test words were articulated best; then, in decreasing order of accuracy of articulation, came initial plosives, medial and final plosives, semivowels, fricatives, and combinations. In most cases initial consonant sounds were articulated better than medial sounds and medials were better articulated than final sounds.

From the analysis of errors Templin reported that substitution errors occur ten times as often as errors of omission and are 4.5 times as common as defective sounds. From three to four years omission errors decrease in frequency from 13 per cent to 9 per cent whereas the frequency of defective speech sounds increases from 13 per cent to 17 per cent and that of substituted sounds remains constant at 74 per cent.

The typical normative study of articulation elicits verbal responses from the subjects by use of pictorial stimuli. On occasion toys are used or questions are asked in the absence of stimulus materials. It has been found that the method used to elicit vocalizations is of little significance, so that the type of test that takes the least amount of time and covers the sounds desired is generally the best choice. Articulation in general is fairly well developed by four years of age, and the rate of increase slows from then until eight years when almost all sounds are articulated correctly.

PSYCHOLINGUISTIC STUDIES

Recently investigators have started to apply the methods of descriptive linguistics to psychological problems related to language. One area frequently studied by *psycholinguists* is language acquisition. Their primary aim is to see how the language of the growing child conforms to his model language, i.e., to the language of the adults around him. To this end both the child's comprehension and his production of language have been studied, using both detailed biographical records and experimental methods.

The development of language as a system is studied by examining the verbal behavior of the child. This approach has implications for cognitive as well as linguistic development, and, in fact, there can be no real separation of the two. This section examines the development of the child's phonological system—the way in which he acquires and differentiates the speech sounds of his language. The question is not whether the child can hear the difference between [b] and [p] and pronounce the two different phones, but whether such a phonetic distinction is of any meaningful import to him. Conclusions about the phonemes and speech sounds used to convey differences in meaning are the important variables in these studies—not ability to distinguish between the various phones which make up the same phoneme.

According to Berko and Brown (1960), many linguists feel that the onset of phonemic development occurs after the end of the babbling period. Until then phonetic development alone can be examined. It is only at this point that meaning appears; phonemes are meaningful units of speech.

Jakobson (1941) hypothesized that phonemic development is patterned according to a system of phonemic contrasts. Those phonemes which are maximally different in their means of articulation should be the ones to appear first. Thus, the first contrast is between vowel and consonant (Jakobson & Halle, 1956). Then come the finer contrasts between labial and nonlabial consonants, stops and fricatives, and so on. According to this theory the child doubles the number of phonemes in his repertoire each time he acquires a new contrast. Therefore, instead of gradual progress in phonemic development, rapid jumps should occur with each acquisition of a new set of contrasts.

Early investigators, e.g., Lukens (1894–1896), noted regularities in the process of speech sound acquisition, but Jakobson was the first to integrate these ideas. Studies by Leopold (1939–1949) and Velten (1943) have tested Jakobson's hypothesis of the patterning of phonemic development. Leopold, in his extensive diary account of the language development of his daughter, Hildegard, partially confirmed Jakobson's hypothesis. In his analysis of the acquisition of consonant contrasts Leopold used the time of permanent acquisition of a phoneme rather than the time of first appearance. This process insured against the inclusion of accidental utterances. Leopold concluded that most aspects of Jakobson's hypothesis could be upheld; the hypothesis was more fully confirmed for vowels than for consonants. In connection with ease of articulation Leopold reported a high correlation between the development of phoneme contrasts and the degree of motor skill required for articulation. Williams, McFarland, and Little (1937), however, in their tabulation of articulatory difficulty for various sounds, obtained results which did not entirely agree with Jakobson's hypothesis.

One factor which Leopold discussed (and that Jakobson neglected) is the effect of the position of a sound in a word on the development of contrasts. Thus, when Hildegard whispered "pretty" the stops [p] and [t] were articulated correctly until she was twenty months old. Then, at twenty-three months, when she said "pretty" aloud, the voicing of the vowels extended to [p] and [t] which were uttered as voiced rather than voiceless stops.

As a number of studies have noted, before any meaningful contrasts can exist the child must be able to hear differences between phonemes. Leopold (1939–1949), for example, stated that when he talked to Hildegard using her own baby talk she did not understand him. This shows that even though a child cannot yet articulate sounds correctly he can perceive whether or not something which is spoken to him is articulated correctly. Thus, Berko and Brown cite an example of an adult's using the child's mispronunciation of "fish": "the observer said, 'That is your *fis*?' 'No,' said the child, 'my *fis*.' He continued to reject the adult's imitation until he was told, 'That is your *fish*.' 'Yes,' he said, 'my fis.' " The child was able to hear the contrast between [S] and [s] even though he used only [s] (1960, p. 531).

Whereas early studies gave the impression that the process of speech sound acquisition is one in which chaos rather than order prevailed, Jakobson's hypothesis has provided an orderly analysis of the acquisition of contrasting speech sounds. It must be remembered, however, that this order is not the same for all children, since different children will acquire contrasts at different ages and in slightly different ways.

EFFECTS OF TRAINING

A number of authors have tried to improve articulation by using various types of training. One of the earliest studies was made by Nice (1915a, 1915b) who tried to improve the articulation of a left-handed girl by training. At three and a half years of age the little girl's speech consisted mainly of vowels, whereas a year later her speech was almost normal for her age. Strayer (1930) used the method of co-twin control to investigate vocabulary development; she included articulation as an incidental variable. The twin who received the earlier training articulated more correctly and produced a wider variety of sounds. Practice effects as a result of the earlier training might have been a factor in this superiority. Sommer (1932) examined the effect of training articulation in a group of preschoolers with articulatory defects. A control group consisted of normal children with no speech defects. The Blanton-Stinchfield Speech Measurement Articulation Test was used to divide the subject pool into the two groups. Training consisted of telling stories, various other activities, and speech and tongue exercises. Sommer found that the articulation of both the experimental and control groups increased during the 12-week experimental period. When percentage improvement in articulation was considered the trained group improved 57 per cent and the control group 28 per cent. Needless to say, there was more room for improvement in the former group.

Liiamina (1960) studied the way fourteen- to thirty-four-month-old children master pronunciation by the manner in which they repeated the name of an object when asked "Say. . . ." and in answer to the question "What is this?" There were two experimental conditions. In the first the child learned to pronounce the word at the same time he associated it with the appearance of the object the word represented. In the second he learned to repeat the word in the absence of the object. During the course of the study the words were made more complex. At fourteen months 39 per cent of the reactions made by the children in response to "What is this?" were speech responses, but only 2.3 per cent of these were deemed appropriate or "adequate" answers. These figures increased to 62 per cent and 3 per cent, respectively, at sixteen months; 70 per cent and 14 per cent at eighteen months; 86 per cent and 46 per cent at twenty months; 96 per cent and 78 per cent at twenty-two months; and 100 per cent and 89 per cent at two years. Adequate responses were found to be slightly more frequent at all age levels when subjects were asked to "Say . . ." thus imitating the adult. It was also found that the names of objects with which the children were in everyday contact were better articulated than those which were unique to the experimental situation. No analysis was made with respect to specific speech sounds, but it was noted that there were wide variations in a child's ability to articulate a word from moment to moment. Also, the more complex the stimulus, the greater was the distortion in naming it. The author suggests that in training articulation simple words should be used at first, and that attention should be directed toward articulation of words in sentences as well as the phonemes in individual words.

Pike (1949) studied the training of intonation contours in a young girl with the intent of changing the rising intonation contour of a child's early words to the falling intonation characteristic of adult speech. The girl was restricted with respect to her language environment in that the family lived in Mexico, and the only English in her environment was spoken by her parents. The girl's first word was "baby," and she used a falling intonation in pronouncing it. The parents, on the other hand, were careful always to use a falling intonation for the word "baby" when in the presence of the child. Next, the mother started calling the father "daddy"—again being careful to use a falling intonation. The girl again adopted the falling contour. The child was then left with another family who did not know about the experiment, and four days later she was using "baby" with the rising intonation that is characteristic of baby talk, although she still uttered "daddy" with the falling intonation previously used. The family she had been left with had often used "baby" in the child's presence giving it a rising intonation contour, but had not used "daddy" in her presence. After a few weeks with her parents the girl partially readopted a falling intonation with "baby."

VOCABULARY

The appearance of a child's first word is a much recorded event. Almost every baby biography contains the date of the first word although the observations of one person may not agree with those of another because of differences in the definition of a word. It is difficult to state whether the child is actually using an utterance meaningfully—as a word—or whether the utterance is merely part of normal babbling with no definite referent intended.

There are two types of data about the first word. From baby biographies it appears that a normal child may utter his first true word as early as eight months or as late as sixteen months of age with a median of about eleven months for children coming from higher socioeconomic levels (McCarthy, 1954).

The second source of data is retrospective reports, usually by the mother. Darley and Winitz (1961) have summarized 26 studies in which retrospective reports were obtained about the age at which the child speaks his first word. According to these maternal reports, the average child utters his first word by about one year. In addition, if the appearance of the first word is delayed beyond 18 months it may indicate the presence of physical, mental, or auditory pathology.

It is generally agreed that there is a hiatus between the first word or words and further vocabulary development. The Sterns (1922) reported a period of two months between the first and second words spoken by their daughter. Preyer's (1893) son had a two-word vocabulary for six months before a third word was added. Yet during this period, while usage remained constant, there appeared to be an enormous development of understanding.

A major problem occurs in comparing the results of vocabulary acquisition studies because different authors define a "word" in different ways. Many do not even supply a definition. If a child says *did, do,* and *does* one author may credit him with only one word, while another maintains the child has used three different words. A second problem in analyzing differences in vocabulary size is the difference between spoken and recognized vocabulary. Spoken or active vocabulary, or vocabulary of use, consists of the number of word types used by a person and is smaller than his recognition or passive or understood vocabulary which consists of the number of words he can comprehend even though these words may not appear in his spontaneous speech.

A pioneering study in vocabulary acquisition was made by an astronomer, E. S. Holden, who analyzed the vocabularies of three children who were less than two years old (1877). Holden defined a word as ". . . a symbol occurring in capital letters in Webster's Unabridged Dictionary, edition of 1852" (1877, p. 58). The vocabulary size of his subjects ranged from 173 to 399 words. (More interesting, however, is

Holden's count of the number of words in his own vocabulary: 33,456, with a probable error of 1 per cent.) Other early investigations included studies by Tracy (1893), Bateman (1914, 1915, 1916), Drever (1915–1916, 1919), Nice (1915a, 1015b, 1917, 1920), and Hull and Hull (1919). A bibliography of vocabulary studies has been compiled by Dale (1949).

Two methods have been used in more recent years to investigate vocabulary development systematically. The first involves controlled observation to study vocabulary of use, whereas the second uses some type of test materials or involves questioning the child to arrive at an estimate of recognition vocabulary. Often, in earlier studies using tests, recognition vocabulary was multiplied by a constant to obtain an estimate of total vocabulary. Both methods have defects. Long periods of observation are expensive and time consuming if a large sample is used. In addition, if the observation period is too extended there is the risk that new words not in the child's vocabulary at the start of the study will have been added. On the other hand, it has been demonstrated that the shorter the observation period the smaller the estimate of vocabulary size.

Problems of reliability and validity occur with the use of tests. Validity is especially important if the test score is to be multiplied by a constant to obtain an accurate estimate of total vocabulary size. Irwin (1960b) states that in addition to reliability and validity, other factors which should be considered in constructing and choosing a test are (a) an age progression in scores and (b) the range of difficulty, the discriminating power, and the uniqueness of the items. It was not until the 1920s that tests were devised for the sole purpose of examining vocabulary development. About 1921 Alice Descoeudres published a series of tests of language development. Recognition vocabulary was measured with pictures and, in addition, the child was questioned about his knowledge of other words. The multiplier used to obtain an estimate of complete vocabulary size was derived by comparison of test results with written records of the spoken vocabulary of three children.

Smith (1926), in the first extensive American study of vocabulary development, devised her own test from Thorndike's (1921) list of the most common English words and from 77 parental records of vocabulary acquisition in individual children. For most items in the test there were two questions. In the first question the experimenter tried to elicit the word without having said it, and in the second the experimenter used the word in a sentence. The child had to understand the word to respond to the sentence correctly. Split-half test reliability after the Spearman-Brown correction for attenuation was .97. The results of the test after multiplication by a constant correlated + .88 with Descoeudres' (1921) partial test of language development and + .84 with Cobb's (1922) revision of Terman's vocabulary test. A consistent age progression was found. Further validity was shown by a correlation of + .91 between order of difficulty as found in the 77 actual vocabularies and the results of the test. Smith estimated average vocabulary size and found a mean of one word at ten months which increased to 3 words at one year, 19 at one and a quarter years, 22 at one and a half years, 118 at one and three quarter years, 272 at two years, 446 at two and a half years, 896 at three years, 1222 at three and a half years, and 1540 at four years. The rate of increase reached a maximum between two and a half and three years. These figures are not outrageously different from the earlier tabulations of vocabulary size made by Nice (1926–1927) and Shirley (1933).

The Smith Test has had a profound influence on the construction of other vocabulary tests. Williams, McFarland, and Little, in their monograph (1937), include an abbreviated revision of the Smith Test. They developed two forms of the test, each with 42 items and abandoned use of the multiplier for estimating total vocabulary. The results of the 2 forms of the test correlated + .96 with each other and + .98 with the longer Smith Test.

Van Alstyne (1929) examined comprehension vocabulary by a multiple-choice technique. Cards were made up with pictures of four items on each card. The subjects, 75 three-year-old children, were asked to point to the correct picture when the experimenter named an object. The same method was used by Ammons and Ammons (1948) in developing what is today the most commonly used vocabulary test. The complete test consists of 16 plates with four pictures on a plate. A number of different words are applicable to any plate, depending on the question asked the subject. The construction of the test is discussed in Ammons and Huth (1949). Ammons and Holmes (1949) present norms for two-, three-, four-, and five-year-old boys and girls in a sample controlled for sex, race, and occupational status. Reliability of the two equivalent forms is .93.

Templin (1957) included a vocabulary test as part of her analysis of language development. She used the Ammons Test as well as a measure of vocabularly of use with subjects who were less than five years old. Her scores for the Ammons Test, when scored by annual rathͽr than semiannual intervals showed good correspondence with the results reported by Ammons and Holmes (1949). However, Templin found semiannual norms more useful than general norms during periods of rapid increase in vocabulary. Vocabulary of use was determined by number of words used in a sound discrimination test and by the number of word types in 50 utterances. Both measures also showed a consistent age progression. (The type-token ratio remained relatively constant at about .5 over the age range tested.) Correlation coefficients between the number of different words used and the Ammons vocabulary ranged from + .40 to + .57, with no apparent age trend. For the number of different words and the sound discrimination vocabulary the correlation ranged from + .27 to + .47; in this case there was a slight downward trend with increasing age. A similar, but better defined, downward trend appeared in the correlation of the Ammons vocabulary with the sound discrimination vocabulary; coefficients ranged from + .66 to + .36.

The Ammons Test (1948) has often been used as an indicator of intelligence. It is possible to convert the Ammons vocabulary scores directly to IQ scores. Templin (1957) reported that IQ equivalents as determined by the Ammons Test for her four and a half- and five-year-old subjects were very similar to Stanford-Binet scores for her six- to eight-year-old subjects. (There was, however, a steady decrease in the IQ equivalents from three to five years of age.) Verbal factors may be a more valid indicator of intelligence at still later ages.

GRAMMAR

This section deals with the process by which children acquire grammatical structures and how these structures develop into the grammar of the adult. The studies reviewed are arbitrarily divided into those that are normative in nature and those that examine grammatical development as the acquisition of different linguistic systems or as a process whereby the child's grammatical rules gradually shift toward an approximation of adult grammar.

NORMATIVE STUDIES

Normative studies of grammatical development have traditionally examined syntactical development from the viewpoint of the time the first sentence is spoken, the development of the sentence as indicated by changes in sentence length and complexity, and the function of the sentence for the child. There is, however, little in the way of normative data on morphological development other than studies of vocabulary already discussed.

If one classifies the child's first sentence as holophrastic, i.e., one word functioning in the place of several, then first sentence is coincident with the first word. It is probably more useful to define a sentence as a grammatically correct utterance of two or more words. After the child utters his first two-word sentence there appears a definite developmental sequence with respect to both sentence length and structural complexity.

McCarthy (1954) has summarized the data from a large number of studies concerning sentence length. The studies all show considerable agreement as to sentence length at various ages; length increases steadily through maturity. She concludes ". . . that the child of 18 months is still essentially in the one-word-sentence stage and . . . he is just beginning to combine words. A year later, sentences of 2 or 3 words are most typical, and by 3½ years complete sentences averaging about 4 words each are used" (p. 550).

Results from studies dealing with sentence complexity are not as clear. The main reason is the wide variety of definitions of complexity that have been used by various authors. Thus, Boyd (1913) in an early study considered sentences using connecting words, qualifying phrases, subordinate clauses, elliptical constructions, inversions, and inflections. Smith (1926) in analyzing the spontaneous sentences of children from two to five years of age performed three types of analyses: *Complete-*

ness, examined by separating sentences into complete, incomplete, or single words; *complexity,* by division into simple, complex, or compound; and *type,* as indicated by imperative, declarative, interrogative, or exclamatory sentences. Declarative sentences were most common at all ages. Other trends with increasing age were greater complexity, more questions, and fewer exclamatory sentences. The most significant age trend found was in increasing completeness of sentences.

McCarthy (1930) devised a system of analysis which has been used by a number of other investigators. She grouped responses according to whether they were complete or incomplete. Complete responses could be functionally complete but structurally incomplete, simple sentences without a phrase, simple sentences with a phrase, compound sentences, complex sentences, or elaborated sentences. Incomplete sentences were classified by type of omission. In her study of 140 children from eighteen to fifty-four months old, 50 consecutive verbal responses were collected while the child played with toys in the presence of the experimenter and the child's mother.

Results for complete responses showed a decrease with age in the percentage of functionally complete but structurally incomplete sentences; an increase in the frequency of simple sentences until thirty-six months and then a slight decrease; and an increase in simple sentences with phrases from twenty-four to forty-two months followed by a leveling-off period. Finally, compound, complex, and elaborated sentences became more frequent although they were never commonly used. There was a general decrease with age in incomplete responses and in specific types of omissions. The per cent of functionally complete but structurally incomplete sentences decreased from slightly less than 80 per cent at eighteen months to about 35 per cent at thirty months and remained fairly stable until fifty-four months. Day (1932a, 1932b) used twins in a replication of McCarthy's (1930) study and found them to be retarded with respect to most of the measures, although the age trends were basically the same.

In her monograph on language skills in children Templin (1957) used McCarthy's (1930) categories for sentence analysis. The main difference between McCarthy's and Templin's results is a relatively large decrease in the frequency of structurally incomplete and functionally complete sentences after three years for Templin's subjects; McCarthy had found a slight increase. Templin also found fewer incomplete sentences at older age levels and more simple sentences with phrases. On the whole, Templin's subjects were slightly more advanced than McCarthy's. This is part of a general trend found by Templin that shows modern children to be slightly more mature linguistically than children in the early 1930s.

When complete sentences were classified as declarative, interrogative, imperative, or exclamatory, Templin (1957) found the percentage of declarative sentences increased from 68 per cent at three years to 78 per cent at four and a half years. Interrogative sentences decreased from 18 per cent to 16 per cent; imperative from 12 per cent to 5 per cent; and exclamatory from 1.9 per cent to 1.3 per cent at three and four and a half years, respectively. The use of subordinate clauses increased at all age levels with adverbial clauses occurring most frequently, nominal clauses next, and adjectival clauses least frequently. When syntactical errors were examined almost half of the responses at three years were grammatically correct. The use of slang was the only type of "error" that did not decrease in frequency with age.

Other studies of the development of sentence type and complexity in young children have been made by Stalnaker (1933), Fisher (1934), and Smith (1939). In summary, about 25 per cent of the sentences of a four-year-old child are functionally complete but lack structural completeness, 38 per cent are simple sentences without phrases, 13 per cent are simple sentences with phrases, 7 per cent are compound or complex, 5 per cent are elaborated, and only 9 per cent are incomplete. The sentence uttered by the average four-year-old is relatively well developed as far as grammatical correctness is concerned, but is not nearly so complex as it is in the adult.

A common index of grammatical development is division of vocabulary by parts of speech. The basic problem in such an analysis is determining the part of speech of a word when it is used by a child. Some experimenters use the most common dictionary use of the word, whereas others assign parts of speech on the basis of the child's use of the word. Young (1941) has tried to reconcile differences in the reported frequencies of parts of speech by using the method of analysis developed by Jespersen (1933). Young's records consisted of about 444 hours of observation of children from average and below average socioeconomic status in a variety of situations. She found that the situation had a significant effect on the incidence of given parts of speech. Results showed stability in the frequency of parts of speech over the age range of her sample, from thirty to forty-eight months. Pronouns and verbs were most common, each comprising about 26 per cent of all words. Nouns were next in frequency, 17 per cent, and were followed by adverbs, 10 per cent; adjectives, 7 per cent; prepositions, 4 per cent; infinitives and interjections, 3 per cent each; and conjunctions, 1.5 per cent.

McCarthy (1930) and Smith (1926) found the largest changes in frequency of use of all parts of speech except adverbs occurred between one and a half and two and a half years. The percentages of pronouns, adjectives, verbs, prepositions, and conjunctions increased during this period while the percentage of nouns and interjections decreased. McCarthy found little change in percentage frequency of adverbs at any age, while Smith found a decrease after two and a half years. The stability in the use of parts of speech at older ages may well be due to the fact that the child who speaks in complete sentences is forced to adhere closely to correct syntax, and the parts of speech he uses are determined largely by English grammar.

Other studies have dealt with the pattern of development within parts of speech and for specific types of words. In general, these studies show that the more specific the function examined the greater the age differences found. Topics that have been studied include pronouns (Cooley, 1908; Goodenough, 1938; Young, 1942b), verb forms (Ames, 1946; Lewis, 1951), prepositions (Grigsby, 1932; Sokhin, 1959), adjectives (Carroll, 1939), words relating to space (Ames & Learned, 1948), and quantity (Martin, 1951). The basic aim of these studies has been to gain insight into the thought processes of the child through examination of his vocabulary. Most of these studies, however, have examined only the production of words, not the ability of the child to understand them.

One exception is an interesting study by Sokhin (1959) on the ability of children from twenty-three to forty-one months of age to understand prepositions. Each of Sokhin's 43 subjects was tested individually. The child sat at a small table with a ring and a block or two small blocks in front of him. He was told to put the ring on the block or one block on top of the other. Three stages of understanding were found. In the first stage there was no understanding of the preposition "on"; the children merely placed the objects side by side. This was the limiting stage for 11 subjects from twenty-three to twenty-eight months old. Eighteen subjects from twenty-six to thirty-six months old were able to place the ring on the block but could not cope with the more difficult task of placing one block on the other (stage 2). The remaining 14 subjects, all at least thirty-eight months old, were able to complete both tasks (stage 3). Understanding developed later than use in this situation.

PSYCHOLINGUISTIC STUDIES

The discovery by psychologists of the methods of descriptive linguistics and, to a lesser degree, by descriptive linguists of the methods of psychology has given rise to a new direction in research. With respect to language development the psycholinguists are concerned with the development of language as a system. Both observational and experimental methods have been used to examine the development of passive or understood and active or spoken language systems in the child. The rules a child uses in formulating his speech, how they develop, and how well they approximate the adult modal language are of primary concern in psycholinguistics.

Morphemic development will be considered before syntactic development, although syntax develops before morphology in English-speaking children. Leopold states, on the basis of observation of his daughter, that "In the field of grammar, syntax comes before morphology. The student of child language becomes very conscious of the fact that the morphological devices are a luxury of fully developed languages. The small child gets along quite well without them, for a short or long time" (1953–1954, p. 10). However, Burling (1959) found that both systems developed at about the same time in his son who spoke both Garo and English. The answer to such contradictions lies in the relative importance of morphological and syntactical systems in the particular language under consideration. For example, in Slavic languages morphology is more important than syntax, so that one might well expect morphology to develop first, the opposite result would be expected for speakers of English or German (including Leopold's daughter)—two languages in which syntax is more important than morphology.

It has been observed that the child systematizes his language first, and that irregularities inherent in the adult language usually appear later. Thus, a child may well say "foots" instead of "feet," showing that he is aware of a standard plural ending in English which he uses instead of the relatively rare, irregular plural. If instead, he had said "feet" one could not be certain that the plural rule was understood. The child could actually know the plural as an irregular form or he could just be imitating an adult. Such observations of "errors" have been helpful in studying grammatical development. The main disadvantage of observation in this area is that such "errors" occur infrequently in the child's speech so that the amount of speech that has to be examined in order to gain a thorough knowledge of the child's morphological rules is very large. In an effort to avoid this problem Berko (1958) devised a method for testing a child's knowledge of grammatical rules involved in forming plurals, past tenses, diminutives, derived adjectives, third person singulars, possessives, comparatives and superlatives, progressive and derived compounds, and compounded or derived words. Pictures were presented, and the child was told something about the picture and given a sentence to complete. One example, designed to test the child's understanding of the past tense, consisted of showing the subject a picture of a man standing on the ceiling and telling the child: "This is a man who knows how to *bing*. He is *binging*. He did the same thing yesterday. What did he do yesterday? Yesterday he _____." In an example used to test plurals the child was shown a picture of a birdlike object and then a picture of two of them. He was told: "This is a *wug*. Now there is another one. There are two of them. There are two _____." Variants of the plural morpheme were tested by using different nonsense names. Thus *wug* should elicit [-z] while *tass* should elicit [əz]. The subjects included children from four to seven years and adults.

Berko's results indicated that children have clearly demarcated, regularized morphological rules, so that their answers are not always correct with respect to English—particularly infrequently occurring, irregular forms in English. Little difference was found between preschoolers and first graders; both used basically the same morphological rules. Subjects were able to form plurals, verb forms, and possessives with a relatively high degree of skill but were not so successful in inflecting adjectives, deriving and compounding new words, or analyzing compound words. Differences were found in the children's ability to handle different variants of the plural and possessive in which [-s] and [-z] were used with new words. The more complicated [-əz] ending was generally not used when required. Similarly, while the children could apply [-t] and [-d] as allomorphs of the past they did not have a rule for using [-əd] when it was required.

Miller and Ervin (1964) used Berko's testing technique as part of a longitudinal study of grammatical development. Their 25 subjects were about two years old at the start of the study. Tests using both familiar and nonsense words were devised to examine plurals, possessives, and nominative pronouns. With respect to plurals, the results confirmed Berko's (1958) findings, i.e., subjects usually had rules for the formation of plurals by the time they were three years old although there were large individual differences. The children were able to give the plurals of familiar words at least a month before they could give them for nonsense words. In addition, a tendency was found to extend regular plural endings to irregular forms.

In another report, Ervin (1963b) presented data on past tense inflection. She still found a strong tendency to regularize the past tense in spite of the fact that irregular verb forms were quite common in children's language. There were, however, exceptions such as the learning of *did*, an irregular past tense form, rather than *doed* which would be expected if the subjects always regularized endings. Only when the subjects were older did they analogize past tense endings to irregular forms and say *doed* as well as *did*.

Thus, as far as morphological development is concerned, there is a definite tendency in the child to regularize and to analogize in his speech. Only later do less common irregular and unusual forms appear, although common irregular forms may be used correctly at an early age.

It has been stated that morphology is relatively unimportant in English, while syntax is quite important. A child can express himself quite adequately by using syntactic devices and, in many situations, the use of morphological signs is only redundant, increasing the probability of being understood without increasing the amount of information in the statement. Thus, English-speaking children can say "five boy" instead of "five boys" and still be understood; however, ambiguity as to meaning would result if he had said "boys five."

The question of passive as opposed to active control of language appears again with respect to syntactical development. Before the child utters his first two-word sentence there is a long period during which he passively understands sentences although he does not use them.

Fraser, Bellugi, and Brown (1963) have studied the active-passive development of grammar in children from three to four years old. They devised an Imitation, Comprehension, Production Test consisting of ten grammatical contrasts such as singular-plural and subject-object. The purpose of the study was to examine the development of comprehension, imitation, and production of a set of contrasting utterances in an effort to see if children understand before they are capable of reproducing utterances verbally. Verbal production was examined in two ways, since imitation and true production were conceived of as different processes. For any given contrast the sentences and pictures representing the contrasts were identical except for the contrast. Thus, for the subject-object contrast in the active voice one set of sentences was

"The train bumps the car" and "The car bumps the train." In the comprehension task the child merely had to point to the correct picture for each sentence. The pictures were not present during the imitation task; the child merely had to imitate the crucial contrast feature correctly. In the production situation subjects were given the contrasting sentences twice by the experimenter and then had to give the correct sentence when the experimenter pointed to a picture. Correct production of the elements essential to the contrast, not correct reproduction of the entire sentence, was required. Results showed that imitative production was most advanced, comprehension next most advanced, and true production least developed. Thus, the hypothesis that passive speech develops before active speech was accepted with respect to spontaneous speech and rejected when direct imitation was considered.

The child's first true sentence is a shortened, telegraphic version of adult speech. These sentences usually contain only content words and require the listener to add the function words he considers necessary on the basis of his knowledge of the child and the situation. The utterance "I go" could mean "I am going" or "I want to go," depending on whether the child is getting ready to go someplace with his parents or is watching them go someplace without him. Kahane, Kahane, and Saporta (1958), in an analysis of published records of children's language development, have used such utterances to infer the child's awareness of different verbal categories before he uses them in his speech.

There is evidence, however, as noted earlier, that even young children follow certain rules in formulating sentences although the rules used by different children may vary considerably and need not be the same as the rules used by adults. Braine (1963), Brown and Fraser (1963), Ervin (1963a), and Miller and Ervin (1964) have all formulated grammars for early child language. A grammar is a set of rules used by a child to generate sentences. Given a grammar it should be possible to specify all possible word combinations that a child commonly uses. Braine (1963), Brown and Fraser (1963), and Miller and Ervin (1964) all follow different methods in their constructions and analyses of children's grammars but arrive at similar conclusions. The main conclusion—that the child's first sentences are telegraphic versions of adult sentences—has been discussed. The difficulty with this conclusion is that not all sentences can be expanded to make sensible adult sentences, as Miller and Ervin (1964) point out. Brown and Fraser (1963) try to account for such utterances by expanding their model to include them. Brown *et al.* (1964) discuss the problems involved in deriving a model that is capable of predicting grammatical sentences while excluding nongrammatical sentences. For the single subject examined, the authors devised some sentences that according to the child's grammar should have been grammatical and some that were not explainable by the grammar. They then asked the child if he thought the sentences were "silly," but were unable to obtain any judgments. Information about the child's opinion of grammaticality would be useful if it could be obtained.

Brown and Fraser (1963) pursued the concept that a child's grammar is simply an abbreviated form of adult grammar. Using the mean number of morphemes per response they state: "In general, it appears that children whose speech is not yet English are using grammars which are systematic derivatives of adult grammar and that the particular features of the derivative grammar are predictable from the mean length of utterance" (p. 189). They tested this assumption by having children from 25.5 to 35.5 months of age repeat sentences. Omitted words were noted, and it was found that the imitated sentences became more like the original ones with increasing age. There was also a strong tendency for the same morphemes to be omitted by different children, indicating a core of language beyond the individual differences which have been found in generative grammars. Brown and Fraser hypothesized that a basic factor in telegraphic speech is a shorter memory span, but that a short memory span alone cannot account for the consistencies that appear in the morphemes dropped by different children. In addition, a very strong tendency to preserve word order was found—another indicator of the strength of syntax in English.

All authors who have tried to construct generative grammars have used frequency of occurrence in determining the classes of words a child uses. A first step in the construction of a generative grammar is the construction of tables indicating the frequency relations of word pairs. Miller and Ervin (1964), and Brown, Fraser, and Bellugi (1964) have developed their models around conventional parts of speech, whereas Braine (1963) has omitted reference to conventional parts of speech. Thus, although Braine's model is not so complex as the others, he deals more often with simple structures.

The presence of classes in children's speech indicates a degree of linguistic sophistication. Examination of the words within various classes shows that they are grouped in accordance with semantic similarity and that certain classes appear in certain positions in sentences. The young child's sentences usually consist of some combination of a content word such as a noun, adjective, verb, and, often, adverbs, and a function word, such as a pronoun, preposition, or conjunction. The child uses relatively few function words but adds a large variety of content words in connection with the function words. Braine (1963) in his analysis of the syntax of one of his subjects, Steven, found two parts of speech: *P* or pivot words which were of two types according to whether they appeared at the beginning or end of a sentence, and *X* words which appeared as either single word sentences or in connection with *P* words. The pivots corresponded to function words and were relatively rare whereas there were many *X* words that corresponded to content words. Thus, Braine found sentences such as *Want baby*, *Want horsie*, and *It horsie*. One could predict from this grammar that Steven might use the sentence *It baby* in the future; once there are a few function words, a wide variety of content words can be used in connection with them.

From this elementary base the child's language and the grammar needed to describe it become more complex. The child gradually approximates adult grammar by building upon his condensed sentences. Redundancies in structure appear in the form of form-class markers. The process by which the child acquires suffixes such as *-ed* to indicate past tense inflection and *-s* to indicate plurals has already been discussed. The words to which these suffixes are added are verbs and nouns, respectively. Suffixes need not be used, however. A child can say either *two dog* or *two dogs* and be understood.

Brown (1957) has examined the development of parts of speech in children between three and five years old. He was concerned with the linguistic definition of classes as formal parts of an analysis of structure rather than classes as determined by the more vague criterion of semantic usage. In the first part of the study he examined records of the speech of nursery school children which had been analyzed for parts of speech. He found that the nouns used as responses were semantically consistent names of objects. This contrasts with the wider adult use of nouns to include abstract nouns. Similarly, verbs also had more consistent semantic implications than verbs used by adults. In an effort to examine how well children were aware of the implications of particular and mass nouns and verbs, all of which were used correctly in everyday speech, an experiment was designed in which three sets of four pictures each were used to see how well the child understood the functions of the three syntactic categories. Using nonsense words Brown asked the children to find a picture that represented "sibbing"—a verb represented by a kneading like motion; a "sib"—a particular noun represented by a container; or some "sib"—a mass noun represented by a mass of confettilike material. Children correctly associated picture and nonsense word a significant amount of the time. Of the sixteen children tested, ten correctly chose the movement picture, eleven chose the proper object picture representing a particular noun, and twelve made the correct choice when the word was a mass noun. Thus, children knew that *some* indicated a mass noun, *a* a particular noun, and the suffix *-ing* a verb. Between three and five years, the age range of Brown's subjects, morphological features appeared with increasing frequency.

Although the function words used by different children differ, syntactic rules are developed at an early age. There is, however, a tendency for children to regularize more than adults by choosing the most probable correct solution in any linguistic situation. This, of course, is a maximizing strategy.

Chomsky (1963) has published an analysis of English syntax that is based on transformations from a simple basic sentence. There are several different types of English sentences: negative, interrogative, exclamatory, and so on, all of which have a common core. In such a system a relatively small number of rules can be used to generate a large number of sentences. For example, once the rule for a negative sentence is learned a person can easily transform the base sentence "He is washing" into "He is not washing." The transformation from the affirmative to the negative involves the addition of "no" or "not" to the sentence. Just as a person can transform tense or number, he can also transform one form of a sentence into another. Ervin (1963b) has discussed the appearance of transformations involving forms of the word "do" in children's speech. She found that "do" appeared early in negative and eliptical constructions, but only several months later in questions.

Menyuk has done a series of studies (1963a, 1963b, 1964) involving the child's use of transformations. In one study (1963b) she analyzed by Chomsky's technique samples of speech taken from nursery-school and first-grade children in three different situations. Most of the sentences fit Chomsky's model, and all the basic structures used by adults to generate sentences were found to be present in the sentences of preschoolers. With respect to age differences, Menyuk found that most structures were used consistently by both groups of subjects. Those structures which were not perfectly developed in the preschool subjects were not fully developed by the time they reached first grade.

In a later study (1964) Menyuk found that even by thirty-four months of age children are already using most of the syntactic rules used by adults. The main developmental trend was a relatively steady rise in the percentage of children using transformations.

In another study Menyuk (1963a) was concerned with the question of whether children actually derived sentences on the basis of grammatical rules or whether the sentences produced were merely imitated. Children were asked to repeat sentences containing various transformations and sentences that were not strictly grammatical (they contained restricted forms). She concluded that three-year-old children used rules to generate sentences and that their utterances were not merely imitations of adult sentences.

SEMANTICS

Acquisition of meaning in the young child is concept formation of a high order. At the center of language learning is the difficult question of how meaning develops. Linguists interested only in the structure of language can escape the semantic problem. For psychologists, however, it remains a difficult, central, and inescapable problem with its overload of subjective intent.

As the Kendlers (1962) have pointed out, the hope of S–R theorists is to explain such phenomena as meaning within a nonmentalistic framework. They assume, in agreement with Skinner (1957) and Staats (1961), that the objectivity of S–R language will help to clarify the issue; and that the theory and date already derived from the animal laboratory will show its predictive rather than *post hoc* capacity for a mentalistic constructlike meaning.

Meaning becomes, for such theorists, internalized S–R sequences of varying orders of complexity: Hull's pure stimulus act; Osgood's $r_m\text{-}s_m$ (1952); Goss' one- and two-stage paradigms of generalization (1961); the Staatses' varieties of verbal habit-families (1963). All these have in common the learning of a common mediating response, usually verbal in nature. Although there are significant differences among the above theorists on the nature of meaning (Staats & Staats, 1959), almost all the conceptions require some form of chaining of S–R units or higher order conditioning. Although higher order conditioning has been highly unstable in the laboratory, in the field of concept formation and meaning acquisition it plays an important theoretical role.

This chapter cannot do credit to the variety of S–R theory and experimentation on concept formation and meaning but will focus on those mediation issues which have appeared in work with children, particularly those relevant to mediation as a language phenomenon in children during the first four years.

What springs immediately into view is that although children of three to four have mastered, albeit imperfectly, most of the major forms of their language and show great flexibility in constructing novel, meaningful sentences, the experimental literature on mediation suggests that a mediational deficiency is the rule in the young preschooler. This has led a variety of workers (Kuenne, 1946; Luria, 1959; Kendler, Kendler, & Wells, 1960) to conclude that appropriate verbal responses are available to young children for some time before their verbalizations or those of others control their overt choice behavior, or, in Luria's terms, before language takes on a clearly directive or regulatory function (1959).

REVERSAL AND NONREVERSAL SHIFTS

A method for the test of the use of single unit S–R discrimination learning vs. that of mediation has been developed by Kendler, Kendler, and Wells (1960). The behavior of most of their three- to four-year-old subjects on the reversal and nonreversal shift problem suggested that these subjects solved the problem by use of a single unit S–R process. In contrast, the behavior of their five- to seven-year-old subjects suggested that some subjects had used the single unit approach as others had already changed to the mediational approach which seems to be characteristic of older children.

The typical procedure used in reversal and nonreversal shift research is to train subjects to respond consistently to one of two cues on a "relevant" stimulus dimension. Two cues on an "irrelevant" stimulus dimension are also present on each discrimination trial. For example, a subject might be trained to choose a black rather than a white cue when the black cue is the larger of the two on 50 per cent of the trials. Once this training is completed, the experimenter introduces a second discrimination task. This second task may differ from the first only in the contingency of reinforcement, e.g., subjects may now be reinforced for responding consistently to white (a reversal shift) or to one of the size cues (a nonreversal shift).

If the experimenter wishes to control for partial reinforcement of the original correct response (response to black) during learning of the second discrimination task, he may hold one stimulus dimension constant or introduce new cues on the stimulus dimensions that were employed on the first discrimination task. In either case the subject is reinforced for response to a cue other than the one which was "correct" during learning of the first task.

Figs. 5.1 and 5.2 from Kendler and Kendler (1962) show the processes assumed to underlie reversal and nonreversal shifts. According to single unit theory diagrammed in Fig. 5.1 a nonreversal shift should be made more readily than a reversal shift. This prediction comes about

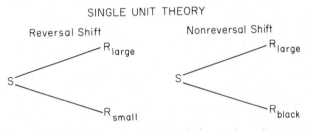

Figure 5.1. *An S–R representation of classical conditioning.*

(From H. H. Kendler & T. S. Kendler. Vertical and horizontal processes in problem solving. *Psychol. Rev.*, 1962.)

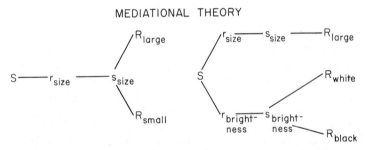

Figure 5.2. *Examples of a reversal and a nonreversal shift.*

(From H. H. Kendler & T. S. Kendler. Vertical and horizontal processes in problem solving. *Psychol. Rev.*, 1962.)

because a reversal shift would require subjects to begin responding to a stimulus which was consistently nonreinforced during the first discrimination task whereas the nonreversal shift requires responding to a cue which was nonreinforced only half of the time during the first task.

In contrast, the mediational notion depicted in Fig. 5.2 leads to the prediction that a reversal shift would be made more readily than a nonreversal shift. This follows from the conception that during the learning of task 1 subjects form a chain of covert responses specific to the "correct" stimulus dimension on task 1. Subjects making a nonreversal shift would seem to have to build a new chain during task 2 learning whereas subjects making a reversal shift would seem only to have to replace the overt response which occurs at the end of the covert chain. That is, the covert chain established during task 1 should be useful to subjects making a reversal shift but not to subjects making a nonreversal shift.

Results of the optional shift experiments indicate that the non-reversal shift is more frequent for rats, while for college students as well as older children the reversal shift is easier. Between ages three and four 37.5 per cent of Kendler's subjects used reversal shifts. With increasing age, the frequency of reversal shifts went up steadily. Children using reversal shifts verbalized the basis for their judgments more frequently than did those choosing nonreversal.

Results from experiments using the standard paradigm discussed earlier show that kindergartners who were slow learners on the first discrimination task made nonreversal shifts more readily than reversal shifts whereas just the opposite effect was observed for fast learners. Preschoolers are seen as being like the slow learners, cognitively somewhere between rats and older children (Kendler, Kendler, & Wells, 1960). The Kendlers see these results as suggesting that the mediational process is related to an increasing ability to relate words and actions. Further research indicates that simply furnishing a child with names for the relevant and irrelevant stimulus cues does not necessarily result in behavior predicted by mediational theory (Kendler & Kendler, 1962). Although this conclusion agrees with that of Luria (1957) cited above, it should be noted that Luria's experiments were quite different. They required that subjects obey complex commands involving some conflict of excitation and inhibition. Luria (1961) concluded that successful verbal mediation does not occur until ages 4–6 to 5–6.

Gollin and Liss (1962) found that learning of reversal shifts was significantly more difficult for children 3–6 to 4–0 than for children 5–6 to 6–0 years. Overlearning (at least in subjects between 5–9 and 8–0) facilitates reversal shifts but not nonreversal shifts (Youniss & Furth, 1965). In contrast, for younger children, 3–6 to 4–0 years, over-training on a reversal task results in a detrimental effect, whereas for older children, 4–6 to 5–0 years, it has a facilitating effect (Gollin, 1964).

TRANSPOSITION

Transposition experiments provide another experimental test of verbal mediation. Kuenne (1946) has found evidence for verbal mediation in children whose mental ages were between three years and six years. She trained children to select the smaller of a pair of squares, then shifted to an even smaller pair of squares (near transposition), and then to a still smaller pair (far transposition). Although almost all children made the near transposition, the far transposition was accomplished by only 50 per cent of the children with MAs of three. Verbalization (either spontaneously or in response to questioning) of the cues necessary for solution of the problem correlated with ability to perform the far transposition. Alberts and Ehrenfreund (1951) confirmed Kuenne's results regarding both verbalization and far transposition as these relate to age. These results appear to support the conclusion that mediational capacity increases with age and that this is a function of the increasing importance of language.

Rudel (1958), using even younger children than used in the two studies described above, reported far transposition, especially under conditions of negative direction, i.e., where during training the *smaller* of the stimuli was positive and transposition was to stimuli *larger* than the larger member of the training pair. Children between twenty-one and thirty-three months (shown by pretest to be preverbal) achieved transposition on both far and near stimuli but less transposition on intermediate stimuli. This resulted in a U-shaped curve for transposition. Although the younger, preverbal group required twice as much training on the initial discrimination as did the older, verbal group (thirty-four to forty-five months), verbalization capacity did not appear to be significantly related to transposition. Extension of this work to older subjects yielded results challenging the importance of verbalization as the source of mediation of relational responses and focusing attention on the subject's opportunity to compare stimuli during training and testing (Rudel, 1951, 1960; Gonzalez & Ross, 1958; Johnson & Zara, 1960). Hunter (1952) has demonstrated far transposition behavior in children as young as fourteen to thirty-two months who were carefully screened to eliminate any verbal subjects. Kendler (1950) has found U-shaped curves for transposition in rats. This is not unlike Rudel's curves described above.

In view of the accumulated research findings, the conclusion of Gonzalez and Ross (1958) is perhaps the most tenable one: Transposition can be most readily mediated by verbalization but it can be mediated also by some mechanisms of a preverbal nature. As a test of verbal mediation verbalization is, therefore, imperfect.

ACQUIRED DISTINCTIVENESS OF CUES

Spiker and his colleagues have been conducting a research program meant to test the hypothesis first proposed by Dollard and Miller (1950) that,

> . . . if an individual first learns to make discriminal responses to two or more similar stimuli, his subsequent learning to make different discriminal responses to these stimuli will be facilitated. . . . [This] type of transfer makes use of the concepts of mediating responses and response-produced stimuli. . . . [First] the individual learns to make distinctive responses (R_a and R_b) to the experimental stimuli (S_1 and S'_1). These responses produce distinctive stimuli (s_a and s_b). During the second (criterion) task, the experimental stimuli elicit the responses acquired in the first task. The stimulation produced by these responses thus forms a part of the total stimulus complexes to which the individual must learn new responses (R_1 and R_2). If the response-produced stimuli are highly distinctive, the stimulus complexes of the second task will be distinctive, and, the more distinctive these complexes, the more readily the new set of responses will be acquired (Spiker, 1963, p. 55).

In practice, acquired distinctiveness is produced in subjects by the learning of different verbal responses, whereas the final criterion task demands differential motor response to different stimuli. Presumably the verbal cue mediates the motor response.

Spiker (1963) reviews experiments performed largely on preschool subjects. Results support the facilitative effect of the learning of distinctive names. Some doubt exists, however, whether *any* names sufficiently well learned regardless of similarity or distinctiveness may not have positive transfer effects, similar to what is now attributed to distinctive cues. The converse may also be true: poorly learned distinctive names may interfere. Spiker suggests the possibility of verbal rehearsal playing a role even in transfer to motor tasks. Stevenson and Brackbill explore simpler explanations like direct reinforcement of verbal responses and direct motor mediation as explanations of the results (see Spiker, 1963). Verbal cues of names facilitated discrimination learning at ages three, five, seven, and nine in a study by Weir and Stevenson (1959).

A nonsense syllable, although used successfully as a common mediating response in Shepard's experiment (1956), was not found to be an effective aid to four- to five-year-olds in a sorting task. Familiar words were found to help preschool subjects sort a height-size category whereas nonsense syllables did not (Carey & Goss, 1957). Distinctive nonsense syllables did no better than self-induced verbalization in facilitating acquisition of a discrimination motor task (Smith & Goss, 1955). Why nonsense syllables seem to mediate well as a common mediating response in one context and not well as a distinctive cue in another remains a question. To invoke inadequate acquired distinctiveness *post hoc* fails to resolve the problem. Parametric problems yet to be solved (effects of overlearning, specific nature of cues, changes in reinforcing conditions, and so on) complicate the issue currently. Obviously, considerations influencing transfer play an important role here (Norcross & Spiker, 1958).

Analysis of evidence for the mediational deficiency hypothesis among younger preschool subjects based on these studies of acquired distinctiveness of cues (stimulus pretraining) leads Reese (1962b) to question whether mediation need be involved at all.

ACQUIRED EQUIVALENCE OF CUES

It is questionable if this category of mediation ever exists without acquired distinctiveness also. In cases of acquired equivalence, a common mediation response (rather than distinctive, different ones) is inferred. Typically, the experiments on acquired equivalence have some stimuli given distinctive names as well as some with shared, equivalent names.

Jeffrey (1953) found that both motor and verbal mediation responses (turning a handle and naming "black" or "white" respectively) facilitated the learning of a motor response based on the equivalence of the name given two of three experimental stimuli (white and gray; black and gray). Verbal mediation was superior to motor mediation which was in turn, superior to an inhibited motor mediation. Although younger preschoolers with MAs between 3–3 and 5–5.5 performed less well (mediational deficiency?) than those between 5–6 and 7–10, the relative ordering of the effectiveness of the various mediational forms is still borne out: verbal mediation is superior.

Shepard (1956) has reported significant increases in generalization of a learned response to colors by preschool children when test stimuli are given a verbal name shared by a stimulus to which the children have already learned a response. This study randomizes children of various ages in the experimental groups. The resultant skewness of the data suggests the possibility that the various age groups may not be mediating equally well. For maximal usefulness in testing the mediational deficiency hypothesis, age subgroups are preferable to designs such as Shepard's that combine children between 3–0 and 6–0.

DOUBLE ALTERNATION

Although double alternation problems are sometimes cited as potential measures of mediation, no developmental studies with children using the technique reach clear-cut conclusions. Hunter & Bartlett (1948) found no child below five years of age in a group between 2–0 and 6–9 who could verbalize the solution of the double alternation problem, although two children aged 3–7 and 3–9 solved the problem to criterion. Extension of the length of the series (*llrr* to *llrrllrr*) as well as delayed reaction tests might be closer to the study of "symbolic processes" and also might be better "adapted to the behavior characteristics of the young child" (Hunter & Bartlett, p. 567), according to these authors (who appear to have suffered at the hands of uncooperative two-year-olds). The rate of learning double alternation problems shows a peculiar phyletic order with ranking of superiority going from raccoon to rabbit to cat to monkey (Warren, 1965). Given the animal results and the confusion of interpretation of results even with adult subjects, use of double alternation problems as requiring mediation for solution may be questionable. The results lead to a conclusion similar to that reached on transposition behavior: verbal mediation is more frequently available in the ages where children more frequently solve double alternation problems, but there also appear to be other routes than mediation to solution.

SUMMARY

The idea that verbal mediation represents a developmental step whereby language organizes the child's behavior is widely held. The specific hypothesis that the young child (usually taken to mean the preverbal child) is deficient in ability to mediate, and therefore will perform in experiments said to require verbal mediation, like infrahuman subjects rather than like older human subjects appears to be at best controversial. Early results on reversal shift, transposition, acquired equivalence of cues, and double alternation appeared to support the mediation-deficit hypothesis; but later work has uncovered conditions under which mediation deficit in preverbal children is not the rule. The hypothesis has certainly had heuristic value, but the evidence is far from conclusive.

Factors Influencing the Rate of Language Development

Studies concerned with the way in which the child learns to speak and the importance of language to the child have been discussed in the preceding sections. A major finding of these studies is the presence of large individual differences in the rate of development of linguistic ability. A number of variables other than age have been examined in an effort to gain knowledge about individual differences in language development. The most common are sex differences, bilingualism, socioeconomic class, institutionalization and deprivation of social contact, family composition, multiple births, and race.

SEX DIFFERENCES

The most commonly noted, although not the most striking, differences in language acquisition occur in comparisons of children of opposite sexes. If any sex differences exist with respect to a given language measure, girls have usually been found to be developmentally superior, though not always to a statistically significant extent.

Sex differences do not appear until the child has started to talk with a reasonable degree of facility. Thus, Karelitz and Fisichelli (1962) found no significant sex differences in cry thresholds for newborns, and Fisichelli and Karelitz (1963) reported the same results for cry latencies. Irwin (1947a) and Irwin and Chen (1946a) analyzed data on phoneme type and frequency from birth to two and one half years of age for sex differences. They found a tendency for girls to use more phoneme types after twenty-six months; before then there was little difference. An opposite trend was found for frequency. Boys had higher phoneme frequencies in spite of the fact that girls developed at a faster rate during the first eighteen months of life.

Both the Sterns (1922) and Valentine (1930) have found girls to be more imitative than boys, and Valentine stated that the difference is largest for linguistic imitation. McCurry and Irwin (1953) found no significant differences between boys and girls in number of word approximations.

Girls are also superior with respect to overall comprehensibility of speech. Young (1941) found girls were superior regardless of social class and McCarthy (1930) reported that over 99 per cent of the remarks of three-year-old girls were comprehensible, a level not reached by boys for another year. There is, however, little difference between the sexes with respect to the development of articulation in early childhood. Children of both sexes develop at about the same rate until around five years of age (Poole, 1934; Williams *et al.*, 1937; Templin, 1953; Templin, 1957) although Wellman *et al.* (1931) found girls were superior with respect to consonant articulation and boys were slightly superior with respect to vowel articulation at three and four years. These differences disappeared by five years. Templin (1957) reported that girls were about a year ahead of boys after four and one-half years, but these differences were not significant until seven years and had disappeared a year later. Sommer (1932), in training children with articulatory defects, found that girls scored higher than boys on the pretest and showed the greatest degree of improvement during training.

Doran (1907) and Smith (1926) found girls to have larger vocabularies at two and three years of age but not thereafter. In examining the spontaneous speech of children from eighteen to fifty-four months, McCarthy (1930) found that girls used more word types and word tokens at all ages except at thirty months. On the other hand, Moore (1947), Ammons and Holmes (1949), and Templin (1957) found no significant sex differences in tests of recognition vocabulary. According to Darley and Winitz (1961) girls tend to start talking before boys do, and this superiority lasts until two to three years of age. Olson and Koetzle (1936) and Jersild and Ritzman (1938) also found a tendency for boys to talk less than girls, but Goodenough (1930) and Fisher (1934) found no significant difference. Olson and Koetzle (1936) found that when the boys did speak they spoke at a more rapid rate than the girls. Young (1941) reported a statistically reliable tendency for girls to talk more than boys. Apparently, girls are superior to boys in the early development of a vocabulary of use though not in the growth of a recognition vocabulary.

Davis (1939) found that boys tended to repeat syllables more than girls, but there were no sex differences for word or phrase repetitions.

Girls are also superior with respect to the development of various parts of speech (McCarthy, 1930; Fisher, 1932; Goodenough, 1938; Young, 1941, 1942a). Fisher (1932), Goodenough (1938), and Young (1942b) have found girls to be superior to boys in the acquisition of pronouns. They use the first person plural pronoun earlier and more often (Fisher, 1932), but differences are less for possessive than personal pronouns (Young, 1942b). Young felt this may indicate an increased social awareness on the part of girls. Contradictory findings have been reported by Berko (1958) who found no sex differences in mastery of the inflectional items used in her study. Her results, however, apply only to children four years old or older.

Most experimenters report girls are more advanced in all areas of sentence development. McCarthy (1954) has tabulated the results of 14 studies of sentence length. Of 64 comparisons of children of the same age but differing with respect to sex, 43 favor girls, 18 favor boys, and 3 show no difference. There is a clear superiority of girls with respect to sentence complexity (McCarthy, 1930; Fisher, 1932; and Templin, 1957). When sentences are classified according to structural or grammatical type, however, there are no clear sex differences (Smith, 1935a; Templin, 1957). Boys also tend to make more grammatical errors, especially at younger ages (Smith, 1933), but differences are minimal (Templin, 1957).

Although not all of the sex differences reported in this section are statistically significant, the large number of replicated studies showing girls to be superior lend credence to the real existence of small but consistent sex differences in language development. Kagan and Lewis (1965) suggest what might prove to be an explanation of these differences. They found that six- and thirteen-month-old girls had a greater capacity for sustained attention than boys of the same age.

SOCIOECONOMIC DIFFERENCES

The American concern with class mobility and equality has led to the inclusion of analyses for class differences in many normative investigations of language development. Results are usually analyzed according to upper and lower class status as defined either by paternal occupation or by use of a scale of socioeconomic status based on such variables as occupation, education, residence, and/or income.

Marked class differences have been found. It is generally the case that children from a higher socioeconomic background are linguistically more advanced than those from a lower class. The earliest significant class differences appear at about eighteen months. Irwin (1948a, 1948c), examining the children of laboring and nonlaboring parents, found that parental occupation was a significant factor in both phoneme type and frequency from eighteen months. He also found that when mothers of laboring class children read to their children each day phoneme frequency increases (Irwin, 1960a).

Templin (1953, 1957) found that upper class subjects tended to score higher on an articulation test with significant differences at four and four and a half years. She stated that this may be due to the presence of a better speech model for the upper class subjects. Templin (1957) also found that upper class children had a significantly larger vocabulary as measured by the Ammons Test. Similar results were reported by Smith (1926).

Young (1941) examined children from a superior soscioeconomic background and compared them with children whose families were receiving some form of government aid. The subjects from an above-average background used longer sentences, talked more, and were more advanced with respect to the use of different parts of speech. Studies by McCarthy (1930), Stalnaker (1933), Fisher (1934), Smith (1935a), and Templin (1957) confirmed Young's results regarding sentence length. General agreement with Young's findings regarding sentence type and complexity is not as clear. Templin (1957) found only a slight superiority in upper class children, whereas McCarthy (1930) found a marked one. Templin reasoned that this may be due to a recent decrease in class differences in verbal stimulation. Finally, Young (1941) found that sex differences were greater for lower class than for upper class children.

Gesell and Lord (1927) found children of professional men to be superior to those from lower classes in most aspects of verbal, practical, and emotional development, with the greatest difference appearing in the area of verbal development.

DIFFERENCES IN FAMILY COMPOSITION

The results of early biographical studies of children of the same sex and family were inconclusive with respect to the superiority of only children as opposed to children with older siblings. Gheorgov (1908), and Nice (1917, 1918) found that older children were linguistically superior. Holden (1877), Gale and Gale (1902), Bateman (1915), and Stern and Stern (1922), on the other hand, found the younger child was more advanced.

Later experimental and normative studies have shown with fair consistency that there is no reliable difference in language development as a function of the number of singly born siblings in the family. Irwin (1948d) found no difference between only children and those with older siblings on either phoneme type or frequency in the first two and one-half years of life. Wellman et al. (1931), in their study of speech-sound development from two to six years, found, with one exception, no significant correlations between number of sibs and speech-sound measures at any age level.

Studies of vocabulary development, response length, and loquacity as related to family composition have also yielded negative results. Young (1941) concluded that number of siblings did not influence mean response length in a consistent manner. Neither Goodenough (1930) nor Young (1941) found a reliable influence of number of siblings on number of words spoken. Smith (1926) found that the average vocabulary for first-born and later-born children was approximately the same on same-age comparisons.

It appears, then, that at least until four years of age there is no consistent or reliable difference between single children and children with siblings or between first- and later-born children. This does not mean, however, that at older ages only children may not be superior to those with siblings, as Davis found to be the case (1937).

On the other hand, there is a consistent superiority of singletons over children of multiple births. Luchsinger (1953) noted that twins started to speak at a later age than singletons. In an extensive study of twins' language development, and a replication of McCarthy's earlier study (1930), Day (1932a, 1932b) found twins to be retarded in all the phases of language development studied: function, construction, spoken vocabulary, and, especially, response length. Day also found that retardation increased with age (her subjects ranged from two to five years).

Five-year-old twins were using shorter sentences than McCarthy's (1930) three-year-old singletons. Sex differences in mean response length favored girls, but they were not so great as differences between singleton boys and girls. Singleton boys were, however, superior to twin girls. Socioeconomic differences showed upper class twins to be superior to lower class twins but inferior to both upper and lower class singletons. The same results were found for most aspects of sentence complexity and work analysis. In general, the greatest retardation in twins was found for those aspects of language development that showed the largest change with age. Measures of language development taken from identical twins correlated +.53. Results for like-sex and unlike-sex fraternal twins correlated +.31 and +.41, respectively.

Howard (1946), in a study of language development in 82 triplets [*sic*], compared her results with McCarthy's (1930) for singletons and Day's (1932a, 1932b) for twins. She found triplets to be more retarded than singletons or twins. The differences, as might be expected, were not as great between triplets and twins as between twins and singletons. It is interesting to note that 42 per cent of the triplets' parents noted their children used some sort of jargonlike, secret language.

A report on the Dionne quintuplets (Blatz, Fletcher, & Mason, 1937) showed even greater retardation than that shown by triplets. Only by twenty-two months were all the quintuplets using words. When the total spoken vocabulary of the quintuplets was compared with the results of the McCarthy (1930) and Day (1932a, 1932b) studies, the quintuplets were found by their fourth year to be from sixteen to eighteen months retarded with respect to number of different words used. Blatz *et al.* (1937) concluded that one reason for the severe retardation was the extensive use of gestures by the quintuplets. No pressure to acquire language was placed on the quintuplets, since all their needs were so well satisfied on the basis of gestures.

INSTITUTIONALIZATION

The effects of institutionalization on a variety of infant behaviors has long been a topic of concern. With respect to language in particular, authors agree that its development is retarded by institutionalization; however, they disagree as to the age at which language retardation becomes evident and the extent to which it is reversible. Gesell and Amatruda (1941) found speech retardation between twelve and fifteen months but believed the effects were reversible. Freud and Burlingham (1944) found children under one year who were separated from their parents used speech sounds as much as other children "because of the drive to gain oral erotic pleasure." During the second year, the family infant used more speech than the infant in an institution. This was attributed to the absence of opportunity for imitation because there was no mother with whom the child might identify.

Brodbeck and Irwin (1946) studied 94 institutionalized infants from birth to six months and found they were inferior to a control group in speech sound type and frequency as recorded in crying and noncrying situations. When socioeconomic differences were considered the control subjects were still superior to the orphanage infants. The authors concluded that identification may be crucial as early as six months. Koch (1961) compared 74 institutionalized children from four to twelve months of age with 74 family-reared infants and found speech retardation to be greater than retardation in any other area of development.

Provence and Lipton (1962) found that speech development in 75 institutionalized infants showed signs of maldevelopment early, became progressively worse, and was the most severely retarded of all functions measured on either the Gesell Developmental Examination or the Hetzer-Wolf Baby Test. Vocalizations began to diminish by the second month, and none of the subjects had used any specific words by the end of the first year. Comprehension of language was not retarded to the same extent as language production.

Pringle and Bossio (1958) found "environmentally deprived children," those from residential institutions, were more deficient in language development than in any other aspect of development and achievement. Early first separation from mother and subsequent deprivation had a significant effect on language development, but sheer length of residence in the orphanage did not. Pringle (1959) matched 18 pairs of children for age, sex, and intelligence. All attended preschool, but one group lived in an orphanage and the other at home. The family group was found to be from five to fifteen months ahead of the institutional group on all language measures used, although the *course* of development was similar for the two groups.

Williams *et al.* (1937) found small differences that increased with age and that favored family-reared over orphanage subjects with respect to speech sounds used, intelligibility, and organization of speech. Spitz (1946) observed 21 children from two to four years old who had spent nearly all their lives in an institution. Of the 21, 6 could not talk, 13 had vocabularies of 5 words or less, 1 had a vocabulary of 12 words, and only 1 used sentences.

Rheingold and Bayley (1959) followed up 14 children from an earlier study in which Rheingold (1956) had given "maximum daily attention" to 7 of the subjects. The extra attention was given from the time the subjects were six months old until they were eight months old. All subjects were institutionalized until about ten months of age when they were sent to foster homes. They were retested at twenty months, and the only significant difference between the groups was a superiority of the subjects who had received maximal care with respect to the amount of vocalization.

Moore (1947) studied the speech content of 11 orphanage children and 40 family children forty-nine months old. All subjects attended the same preschool. When differences in MA were controlled, the orphans were found to use significantly fewer words; however, differences between groups were not significant.

Lowrey (1940) found speech defects in "over half" of 21 children admitted to an institution before they were a year old, transferred to foster homes between three and four years, and studied at five years or older. Goldfarb (1943a) found speech problems in 50 per cent of a group of children who had spent most of their first three years in an institution compared to only 10 per cent of a group reared in foster homes. In a second study (1943b) he paired 30 children for age, sex, and socioeconomic status of parents. Institutionalized subjects, on the average, entered an institution at four and one half months and a foster home at forty-three months. The second group averaged fourteen months with their families before being placed in foster homes. All were tested at about twelve years. For the institutional group, 80 per cent were rated below average in speech, while only 7 per cent of the foster home group were below average. Similar results were found for speech fluency. In a third study Goldfarb (1945) matched, on the basis of age and sex, 15 children in foster homes with 15 children who had spent their first three years in an institution. Both groups were tested at thirty-four and forty-three months. (The institutionalized subjects were transferred to a foster home at thirty-seven months.) The foster home group surpassed the institutionalized group in IQ, speech sounds used, speech intelligibility, and level of language organization. There was a slight decrease in differences on the final test.

The summarized research leads to one definite conclusion: institutionalization retards language development. There is, however, controversy over how early differences appear and the extent of reversibility of the effects. One reason for the lack of agreement on these points has been differences in the institutions themselves: orphanages differ widely in the amount and type of care given. Other factors of importance are the intelligence of the natural parents, the circumstances of separation, age at separation, length of stay in the institution, age at testing, foster parents' economic status and intelligence, and so on.

ENRICHMENT

The effects of one type of severe environmental deprivation, institutionalization, have just been discussed. At the opposite extreme there are cases in which the experiences of the child have been enriching. In general, the few studies that have dealt with enrichment show the child to have improved in his language skills.

Children coming from upper class backgrounds may be superior to those from lower classes because their environment is enriched in ways that facilitate and improve language development. (This does not mean, however, that other factors, such as genetic differences in intelligence, do not also contribute to differential language achievement.) Upper class backgrounds appear to be enriching through increased contact with adults and through broadened experiences. In the first case the child has more speech directed to him by adults. Second, the language of an upper class adult is likely to provide a better imitative model for the child, although this hypothesis has not been systematically investigated.

A number of studies have examined the effects of specific kinds of enrichment. Skeels, Updegraff, Wellman, and Williams (1938), in an extensive study on the effects of institutionalization, matched 21 pairs of orphans on CA, MA, IQ, sex, nutritional status, and length of residence in the orphanage. Ages ranged from eighteen months to five and one half years; the mean IQ was 82. The experimental group attended a preschool in the orphanage, and the control subjects remained in the normal orphanage environment. Language was evaluated by the Smith-Williams Vocabulary Test and the Williams-Little Scale for Language Usage and Achievement. On the latter test, both groups were below average for family children, and both lost ground, when compared to family children, over the course of the experiment. Preschool attendance decreased the amount of language retardation, but did not entirely compensate for the deprivation present in the orphanage environment. With respect to vocabulary, both groups were below norms for family children, although a year of preschool helped markedly. A similar study was carried out by Dawe (1942) who found that a relatively limited amount of training had a significant influence on the language development of orphans at the preschool and kindergarten level.

Strayer (1930), using the method of co-twin control, examined the effectiveness of early as opposed to delayed vocabulary and language training for a pair of twins who had not yet begun to talk and who were isolated from each other in experimental living quarters. Twin T received intensive vocabulary training from eighty-four through eighty-eight weeks of age, and twin C was given the same training in a more concentrated dose starting at eighty-nine weeks. (The caretaking adults, by the way, did not speak in the presence of twin C from the eighty-fourth through the eighty-eighth week.) Training activities consisted of having the child repeat names, eliciting responses from objects and pictures, and informal language stimulation. The main result was that later language training was more effective.

Most of our information about the environmental factors that influence language development comes from studies of deprived children. Aside from a few observational biographies and the limited number of training studies, we know more about what the child needs to keep him from becoming retarded in language development than what we can do to improve the language of a normal child.

RACIAL DIFFERENCES

Few specific racial differences have been found in language development. In fact, studies consistently show that children, regardless of their native tongue, tend to follow the same sequence of language development. Studies in which matched subjects of different races are examined are too few and too contradictory to allow valid conclusions. Thus, while Gatewood and Weiss (1930) showed greater frequency of vocalization in white than in Negro children, Irwin (1949) found no such difference. An interesting reversal of sex differences was found by Anastasi and D'Angelo (1952) in a study of sentence length and complexity in the speech of five-year-old Negro children. There was little difference between the white and Negro subjects until they were separated both by race *and* sex. The results then showed that white girls were superior to white boys and Negro boys were superior to Negro girls. These reversals were more marked in racially segregated neighborhoods.

BILINGUALISM

The problem of bilingualism has long been of educational concern. The basic problem is whether the learning of a second language interferes with the acquisition of the first language. There have been a number of excellent biographical studies of bilingual children (Ronjat, 1913; Pavlovitch, 1920; Leopold, 1939–1949) but their results provide little basis for valid generalization or comparison with monolingual children.

The most comprehensive examinations of the effects of a bilingual environment on young children have been made by Madorah Smith. Her extensive monograph (1939) is the most complete normative study of bilingualism. In earlier studies (1931, 1935b) she examined records of children raised in bilingual environments. In Smith's study (1935a, 1935b) of the biographical records of the speech of eight bilingual siblings conclusions were reached that were upheld by her later studies. She found that it was preferable for children to receive instruction in each language from a different source, that a change from a monolingual environment to a bilingual one had a greater influence on a child's speech than did the reverse change, that bilingualism did not hinder the early development of speech, and that bilingual children were inferior to monolingual children in some aspects of speech.

In her later study Smith (1939) examined six groups of 125 children from two to six years of age who were living in Honolulu and were of Chinese, Filipino, Hawaiian, Japanese, Korean, and Portuguese ancestry. A seventh group consisted of 125 children of Filipino ancestry living in a rural area. Two other groups of mixed racial background were also studied. Records of speech were made while the child was playing at home with siblings or friends. Conversations were analyzed in terms of the proportion of English used, errors in the use of English, length of sentence, form and function of sentence, parts of speech, sex differences in English mastery, home influence in the children's speech, the influence of pidgin English as opposed to English, and most frequently occurring English and non-English words.

Smith's major finding was that children from non-Caucasian homes were linguistically retarded by several years at the time of school entrance. She attributed this retardation to extensive use of pidgin English as well as to bilingualism: incorrect English usage appeared to be linked to the use of pidgin English although bilingualism was responsible for the delay in language development. The results also indicated that children whose parents used more or better English in the home mastered English more easily than those whose parents spoke different languages, that the child whose parents spoke different languages at home mastered English at an earlier age, that nursery school and kindergarten attendance was beneficial to the bilingual child, that the amount and correctness of a child's English usage were related to the length of time his ancestors had had contact with English, and that English was the preferred language among the majority of the preschool population.

In a later study Smith (1949) examined the vocabularies of a group of bilingual children and found that, although the total number of words was only slightly less than a comparable group of monolingual children, total vocabulary size, discounting duplicate words, was much less than the mean vocabulary size of the monolingual children. Only a superior bilingual child was found to be capable of attaining a vocabulary equal in size to that of a normal monolingual child. Smith suggested that training in a second language be delayed until after preschool unless the subject were a child of exceptional ability.

A portion of this study was repeated with children of Chinese ancestry and the results showed that bilingual children who came from a background in which both English and Chinese were spoken equally used fewer different words than those from an environment where one language dominated. Monolingual children used a greater variety of words than bilinguals (Smith, 1957).

In 1961 Smith did a follow-up study of the three most severely retarded groups in her 1939 study. New groups of rural and urban Filipino and urban Japanese children between four and six years old were matched for age and socioeconomic status with the subjects used in the original study. Subjects in the new sample were found to be almost completely monolingual although the prevalence of pidgin English was still a problem.

A major concern of people interested in bilingualism is the influence of bilingualism on intelligence test performance. Darcy (1946), after matching subjects for age and socioeconomic level, compared monolingual and bilingual children from two and one half to four and one half years of age on the Stanford-Binet and Atkins Object-Fitting Tests. She found significant differences between monolingual and bilingual boys on both tests. On the Stanford-Binet the monolingual boys had higher scores, whereas on the Atkins Test the bilingual boys had higher scores. Comparable results were found for monolingual and bilingual girls except that the superiority of bilingual girls was not statistically significant. She concluded that the bilingual children suffer from a language handicap on intelligence tests, such as the Stanford-Binet, that rely heavily on verbal factors.

Nonverbal Communication

Little is known about the child's use of nonverbal methods of communication. Few experimental investigations have been done on the role of kinesic and paralinguistic variables in children's language. Most of our knowledge consists of information from observational records.

KINESICS

Gestures are more important in many languages than they are in English. Indian sign language has reached highly developed stages and has been used to compensate for deficiencies in the spoken language of certain Indian tribes (Latif, 1934). Latif also reports findings by Stout that the Bubis cannot communicate in the dark and that among the Fans it is customary to be near a fire to see what other people are saying.

The normal child often uses gestures to communicate for a brief period before he can communicate verbally, e.g., as Gesell (1925) pointed out, an infant typically waves "bye-bye" before he can say "bye-bye." Sometimes however, infants develop strong gesture languages that persist with time. These cases are usually retarded with respect to language development. Nice (1925) reported that her two-year-old daughter had a vocabulary of only five words but was able to communicate by changes in pitch and gestures. The Dionne quintuplets (Blatz, Fletcher, & Mason, 1937) communicated mainly by using gestures. Blatz *et al.* concluded that the quintuplets had no need for verbal language since their needs were well attended to and since they could communicate well enough to satisfy their needs by use of gestures.

PARALINGUISTICS

Slightly more is known about the second aspect of nonverbal communication, paralinguistics, than is known about kinesics. Most reports in this area have been concerned with fluency variables such as number of seconds speaking, number of words, and rate of speaking (Shah, 1960). Records of amount and rate of talking are obtained by sampling either an absolute number of utterances or the number of utterances over a certain time unit. Most studies using the first method follow McCarthy's (1930) lead in recording 50 consecutive responses; studies using the second use some type of time sampling.

Mean response-length changes are discussed in the section on grammatical development. Studies present varying results concerning the amount and rate of talking. Olson and Koetzle (1936) used 30 one-minute sampling periods and found that their four-year-old subjects used an average of 1,000 words an hour. However, when they spoke, it was at a mean rate of over 11,000 words per hour. Little correlation was found between amount and rate of talking: boys talked less than girls but at a faster rate. Smith (1926), using one-hour records of speech in a free-play situation, found a steady increase from 78 words per hour at two years to 400 words per hour at four years. More striking was the wide variability she found. Some subjects did not speak at all while one used 1,100 words in the hour-long sample. Others have found individual differences of a similar magnitude (McCarthy, 1930; Fisher, 1934; Olson & Koetzle, 1936).

The results of the Smith (1926) and Olson & Koetzle (1936) studies also show that there is variability in empirical findings. This may have been due to differences in methods of sampling. Ellesor (1934) found that for a three-year-old girl restrained and unfamiliar situations produced fewer vocalizations than did familiar free-play situations. Nice (1920) summarized the results of ten children's rate of talking at home and found rates varying from 10 to 21 words per minute. The children ranged in age from two to five years. Nice also noted wide variation in her daughter's talkativeness in different situations. Young (1941) observed nursery school children in four situations: outdoors, indoors, at dinner, and looking at pictures. She found that the situation was related to the amount of language used in a ten-minute period. Williams and Mattson (1942) found that nursery school children talked more when in a group composed of several children and an adult than when they were alone with an adult. Although one can draw no conclusions about the relationship between amount and rate of talking and actual communication, these studies are important in pointing out the need for precise control of the situation in studies of language variables.

Studies examining hesitation variables are also relatively scarce. Most common are studies dealing with repetitions. On the basis of reports of repetition it appears that a certain amount of repetition is normal in young children and should not be considered pathological. Kirkpatrick (1891) hypothesized that children repeat themselves because they are not certain they have been understood. Most studies fail to define what is meant by repetition and have examined it only as an incidental phenomenon or in relation to stuttering. The most extensive investigation was made by Davis (1939, 1940) who examined syllable, word, and phrase repetition in 62 children from twenty-four to sixty-two months of age. With respect to syllable repetition, a highly skewed distribution was found; 16 of the 62 subjects repeated no syllables at all. Phrase repetitions were most common and were followed by word and then syllable repetitions. There was a tendency for repetition to decline with age—the greatest change appearing in the two- and three-year-old subjects. This tendency was, however, diminished for syllable repetition. Amount of syllable repetition was found to be unrelated to language maturity although it was related to the situation; the greatest amount of repetition was found in situations in which the child was excited over his own activity or wanted to direct the activity of another child.

Baldwin and Baum (*personal communication*) have examined the interruptability of words in nursery school children from three to five years of age. The subjects repeated a number of sentences after the experimenter and were told that the light bulb in a Santa Claus face which illuminated the room would be turned off. At this point they were "not to make another sound." They were to stop talking even if the light went out in the middle of a word and when the light came on they were to finish the sentence. There were 26 test sentences, each with 11 syllables. The interruption occurred at about the middle of the sentence. In some cases two-syllable words were interrupted at the start, in the middle, and at the end of the word; in others two-word phrases like "show me" were interrupted at the start of the first word or between the two words. Six of the twelve subjects between three and four years were not able to stop talking before the end of the sentence and were discarded. Results showed that two-syllable words were usually completed regardless of the time of interruption although some subjects stopped talking before uttering the word and about 25 per cent stopped before finishing the word. Subjects who were able to interrupt the word in the middle usually started talking again by using the next word in the sequence rather than by beginning at the point of interruption. When cessation occurred at the end of the word, subjects usually resumed with the following word. When their phrases were interrupted, the children tended to complete the entire phrase regardless of the point of interruption, and they almost always finished one-syllable words before they stopped talking.

It appeared that the word functioned as a unit for most of the subjects although it was likely that the sentence was the elementary unit for some of the younger subjects. This finding was substantiated by the fact that subjects who did interrupt a word in the middle did not resume at the point of interruption but at the start of the next word. Certain phrases did, however, tend to form a unit.

Abnormalities in
Language Development

Only those studies of abnormal language development that are relevant to normal development will be cited in this section. Some limitations in the available data need to be noted: most data have been gathered on the language abnormalities of children older than the four-year-old limit of this review because of the greater notice taken by medical and school authorities as the child nears school age; many studies are merely descriptive; many investigators have studied abnormal development as a means of understanding normal development, but often there are no comparative normal data.

Various causes for language disorders have been suggested, though the major diagnostic categories are not well defined. Lenneberg (1964, p. 152) suggests the following causes: deafness, mental retardation, childhood psychosis, congenital inarticulation, aphasia, and structural abnormalities concerned with speech, e.g., deviation from the normal anatomy of lips, teeth, palate, or tongue. In addition, institutionalization has been associated with language disorders (Yarrow, 1961). McCarthy (1961) stressed emotional disturbance, not psychosis, as a cause for many language disorders in children, and many studies have concerned themselves with this issue (e.g., Isaacs, 1932; Hattwick, 1937; and the bibliography cited by McCarthy, 1961). Stuttering has been ascribed to many causes, including the critical ears of the listener (Johnson, 1945).

The effects on language development of each of these causes, of

Table 5.1—Important Points for Differential Diagnosis of Speech and Language Disorders *

Diagnosis	Medical History	Developmental History	Symptomatology	Management	Prognosis
Peripheral deafness	In ⅔ of cases: family history or infectious disease.	Normal milestones; normal vocalization during first 6 months. Abnormal persistence of babble and complete absence of words.	Normal affect; gestures only but eager to communicate; plays constructively and with concentration; no reaction to sounds.	Establish diagnosis by audiogram; hearing aid; special training.	Good for written language. Oral communication usually poor but depends on age of onset and depth of deafness; no intellectual limitations.
Mental retardation	Signs and symptoms of central-nervous-system disease.	Slow but steady; motor development sometimes better than cognitive.	Comprehension slightly ahead of speech production. Language is consistent with that of a younger child and free from bizarre stereotypes. Understanding, vocabulary, syntax suffer to an equal extent.	No special measures for language habilitation; speech therapy is of little value.	Good if IQ is 50 or above by chronological age seven.
Childhood psychosis	Typically, non-contributory.	Normal for motor milestones. Progress is irregular with surprise advances or regressions; socialization defective.	Usually mutism with occasional indications that language has been acquired but motivation to speak is lacking; sometimes well developed language but bizarre use of it; normal communication process interrupted.	Treatment is restricted to psychiatric disease. Amplification of sound is contraindicated. Articulation exercises are irrelevant.	Potentially good for speech and language but subordinate to prognosis of primary psychiatric disease.

Table 5.1—Continued

Diagnosis	Medical History	Developmental History	Symptomatology	Management	Prognosis
Congenital inarticulation	Perinatal stress with cranial nerve signs after birth. Family (paternal) history of similar disorder or dyslexia common.	Normal milestones, except for development of vocalization.	Intelligent or slightly dull child with normal affect and good motivation for communication; certain consonants consistently omitted or distorted; voice and intonation pattern intact. In severe cases no intelligible speech at all but in all cases understanding of language is normal.	Pre-school child: prevention or correction of secondary mental health problems in patient and parents. School child: assure proper instruction in reading and writing by enlightenment of teachers. Speech correction in second or third grade.	Depends on severity of defect but some spontaneous improvement in nearly all cases. Except for severest defects, disorder is outgrown by early teens.
(Acquired) Aphasia	Trauma, cerebral vascular accidents, Status epilepticus.	Within normal limits.	Under four years: short period of complete loss of language followed by rapid relearning. After four years: well-formed words but apraxia, word-finding difficulty, inappropriate utterances, confusion, jargon, telegraphic style.	After first six months of spontaneous recovery, speech rehabilitation often helps to encourage patient and restore self-confidence. If learning difficulties are associated with aphasia, academic help ought to precede articulation drill.	Dependent upon age at cerebral insult: recovery is complete in children under ten with the recovery period lasting three months or less in preschoolers and up to a year in older children. In teenagers residua become increasingly likely with advancing age. In the young adult symptoms present a year after injury are usually irreversible.

* From Lenneberg, E., Language disorders in childhood. *Harv. Educ. Rev.*, 1964, 34, 175-176.

course, differ, as might be expected. Major effects are delayed speech, delayed understanding of language, and stuttering. Table 5.1 summarizes present knowledge of various prognostic effects for various language disorders.

The delayed acquisition of language with institutionalization helps point to the environmental factors associated with normal development. Data on psychotic and neurotic children suggest, as did the institutionalization studies, that some parent-child interactions, presently not completely specifiable, can interfere with normal language development, especially in influencing production of speech, with understanding less often damaged. McCarthy (1961, p. 28) suggests that "either extreme of maternal behavior," i.e., overprotection or rejection, "seems to prevent healthy ego development and lead to some form of language disorder." Even the amount of crying in early infancy has been found to be related to the mother's behavior (Stewart, 1953, 1954; Lakin, 1957), especially to psychological disturbance manifested in problems centered about the female role and feelings of inadequacy as a mother.

Deaf and blind children appear to develop adequate language skills, though obviously not in the missing modalities. This suggests that hearing sounds or seeing things is not absolutely essential for language development. So, too, having physical or motor limitations on speech production does not necessarily diminish a child's ability to understand and use language (Scripture, 1915; Lenneberg, 1962).

Work on retarded children suggests that a high level of intelligence is not needed for language development, though such development is markedly retarded below an IQ of 50 at age seven (Lenneberg, Nichols, & Rosenberger, 1962). Mongoloid infants babble and make noises approximating the phonemes and the intonation of English. However, few later acquire adequate language skills, suggesting that the babble may be a necessary but not a sufficient condition for the acquisition of later language abilities. On the other hand, some sparse data (Lenneberg, 1964) show that the sounds (spectrographically analyzed, as well as listened to) make in the first year of life by deaf children differ from those produced by normal children. The deaf children babble until about a year of age, at which time they stop, probably because of lack of stimulation from the outside. However, we are not certain why they continue babbling normally for so long without stimulus input from without. That they start at all may be of significance ultimately for understanding how language starts biologically. That deaf children develop language skills without speech is well known, suggesting again, as above, that normal babbling is not an absolute essential for language development.

From the above argument it can be seen that babbling or early speech sounds may be in some cases neither necessary nor sufficient for language development. Many theories of language development suggest otherwise, i.e., that language is shaped from these primitive noises by some sort of reinforcement. Data from abnormal children thus help to raise questions about what is essential for normal language development.

It is not inconceivable, however, that the very young child is sufficiently plastic to find different routes to language development, if the normal one is blocked.

The material in this section is typical of research on abnormalities, in that the data are tantalizing and suggestive. No one has yet attempted, through the naturally occurring abnormalities, to relate systematically the environmental and biological necessities for language development in the normal child.

Conclusion

The review of language development in this chapter shows clearly that psychologists are now studying problems very different from those posed as recently as twenty years ago, chiefly because of structural linguistics. It is hoped that further cooperation between psychologists and linguists will produce better understanding of the processes underlying language acquisition. The need for more experimental research into language is strongly felt because language development is still so poorly understood.

References

Alberts, E., & Ehrenfreund, D. Transposition in children as a function of age. *J. exp. Psychol.*, 1951, 41, 30–38.

Aldrich, C. A., Norval, M. A., Knop, C., & Venegas, F. The crying of newly born babies: IV. A follow-up study after additional nursing care had been provided. *J. Pediatr.*, 1946, 28, 665–670.

Aldrich, C. A., Sung, C., & Knop, C. The crying of newly born babies. II. The individual phase. *J. Pediatr.*, 1945, 27, 89–96. (a)

———. The crying of newly born babies. III. The early period at home. *J. Pediatr.*, 1945, 27, 428–435. (b)

Aldrich, C. A., Sung, C., Knop, C., Stevens, G., & Burchell, M. The crying of newly born babies. I. The community phase. *J. Pediatr.*, 1945, 26, 313–326.

Ames, L. B. The development of the sense of time in the young child. *J. genet. Psychol.*, 1946, 68, 97–125.

Ames, L. B., & Learned, J. The development of verbalized space in the young child. *J. genet. Psychol.*, 1948, 72, 63–84.

Ammons, R. B., & Ammons, H. S. *Full-range picture vocabulary test.* Missoula, Mont.: Psychological Test Specialists, 1948.

Ammons, R. B., & Holmes, J. C. Full-range picture vocabulary test: III. Results for a preschool-age population. *Child Develpm.*, 1949, 20, 5–14.

Ammons, R. B., & Huth, R. W. Full-range picture vocabulary test: I. Preliminary scale. *J. Psychol.*, 1949, 28, 51–64.

Anastasi, A., & D'Angelo, R. A comparison of Negro and white preschool children in language development and Goodenough draw-a-man IQ. *J. genet. Psychol.*, 1952, 81, 147–165.

Bandura, A., & Huston, A. Identification as a process of incidental learning. *J. abnorm. soc. Psychol.*, 1961, 63, 311–318.

Bateman, W. G. A child's progress in speech, with detailed vocabularies. *J. educ. Psychol.*, 1914, 5, 307–320.

——. Two children's progress in speech. *J. educ. Psychol.*, 1915, 6, 475–493.

——. The language status of three children at the same ages. *Ped. Sem.*, 1916, 23, 211–240.

Bellugi, U., & Brown, R. (Eds.) The acquisition of language. *Monogr. Soc. Res. Child Develpm.*, 1964, 29, No. 1.

Berko, J. The child's learning of English morphology. *Word*, 1958, 14, 150–177.

Berko, J., & Brown, R. Psycholinguistic research methods. In P. H. Mussen (Ed)., *Handbook of research methods in child development*. New York: Wiley, 1961. Pp. 517–557.

Blatz, W. E., Fletcher, M. I., & Mason, M. Early development in spoken language of the Dionne Quintuplets. *Collected studies on the Dionne Quintuplets*. Toronto: Univer. Toronto Press, 1937.

Bohn, W. E. First steps in verbal expression. *Ped. Sem.*, 1914, 21, 578–595.

Boyd, W. The beginnings of syntactical speech: A study in child linguistics. *Child Study*, 1913, 6, 21–24, 47–51.

——. The development of a child's vocabulary. *Ped. Sem.*, 1914, 21, 95–124.

Brackbill, Y., & Thompson, G. G. (Eds.) *Behavior in infancy and early childhood: A book of readings*. New York: Free Press, 1967.

Braine, M. D. S. The ontogeny of English phrase structure: The first phase. *Language*, 1963, 39, 1–13.

Brandenburg, G. C. The language of a three-year-old child. *Ped. Sem.*, 1915, 22, 89–120.

Brodbeck, A. J., & Irwin, O. C. The speech behavior of infants without families. *Child Develpm.*, 1946, 17, 145–156.

Brown, R. Linguistic determinism & the part of speech. *J. abnorm. soc. Psychol.*, 1957, 55, 1–5.

——. *Words and things*. New York: Free Press, 1958.

Brown, R., & Bellugi, U. Three processes in the child's acquisition of syntax. *Harv. Educ. Rev.*, 1964, 34, 133–151.

Brown, R., & Fraser, C. The acquisition of syntax. In C. N. Cofer & B. S. Musgrave (Eds.), *Verbal behavior and learning: Problems and processes.* New York: McGraw-Hill, 1963. Pp. 158–201.

——. The acquisition of syntax. In U. Bellugi, & R. Brown (Eds.), The acquisition of language. *Monogr. Soc. Res. Child Develpm.*, 1964, 29, No. 1. Pp. 43–79.

Brown, R., Fraser, C., & Bellugi, U. Explorations in grammar evaluation. In U. Bellugi & R. Brown (Eds.), The acquisition of language. *Monogr. Soc. Res. Child Develpm.*, 1964, 29, No. 1. Pp. 79–92.

Buckman, S. S. The speech of children. *Nineteenth Century*, 1897, 793–807.

Bullowa, M., Jones, L. G., & Bever, T. G. The development from vocal to verbal behavior in children. In U. Bellugi & R. Brown (Eds.), The acquisition of language. *Monogr. Soc. Res. Child Develpm.*, 1964, 29, No. 1 (Whole No. 92). Pp. 101–107.

Burling, R. Language development of a Garo and English speaking child. *Word*, 1959, 15, 45–68.

Carey, J. E., & Goss, A. E. The role of mediating verbal responses in the conceptual sorting behavior of children. *J. genet. Psychol.*, 1957, 90, 69–74.

Carmichael, L. The early growth of language capacity in the individual. In E. H. Lenneberg (Ed.), *New directions in the study of language*. Cambridge, Mass.: M.I.T. Press, 1964.

Carroll, J. B. Determining and numerating adjectives in children's speech. *Child Develpm.*, 1939, 10, 215–229.

Casler, L. The effects of supplementary verbal stimulation on a group of institutionalized infants. *J. child Psychol. Psychiat.*, 1965, 6, 19–27.

Chamberlain, A. F., & Chamberlain, I. C. Studies of a child. I. *Ped. Sem.*, 1904, 11, 264–291. (a)

———. Studies of a child. II. *Ped. Sem.*, 1904, 11, 452–483. (b)

Champneys, F. H. Notes on an infant. *Mind*, 1881, 6, 104–107.

Chan, C. H., Lenneberg, E. H., & Rebelsky, F. G. Apparatus for reducing playback time of tape recorded, intermittent vocalization. In U. Bellugi & R. Brown (Eds.), The acquisition of language. *Monogr. Soc. Res. Child Develpm.*, 1964, 29, No. 1 (Whole no. 92). Pp. 127–130.

Chen, H. P., & Irwin, O. C. Infant speech vowel and consonant types. *J. speech Disord.*, 1946, 11, 27–29. (a)

———. Development of speech during infancy: Curve of differential percentage indices. *J. exp. Psychol.*, 1946, 36, 522–525. (b)

Chomsky, N. Review of B. F. Skinner's *Verbal Behavior. Language*, 1959, 35, 26–58.

———. *Syntactic structures.* The Hague: Mouton, 1963.

———. Discussion. In U. Bellugi & R. Brown (Eds.), The acquisition of language. *Monogr. Soc. Res. Child Develpm.*, 1964, 29, No. 1 (Whole No. 92). Pp. 35–39.

Cobb, M. V. Tentative order of difficulty of the Terman vocabulary with very young children. *J. educ. Psychol.*, 1922, 13, 357–362.

Comes, L. Quelques observations sur le langage des enfants. (Some observations on the language of children.) *Bull. Soc. Libre pour l'Étude Psychol. de l'Enfant*, 1900–1905, 1–5, 452–454. (a)

———. Quelques observations sur le langage des enfants. (Some observations on the language of children.) *Bull. Soc. Libre pour l'Étude Psychol. de l'Enfant*, 1900–1905, 1–5, 571–577, 594–599. (b)

Cooley, C. H. A study of the early use of self-words by a child. *Psychol. Rev.*, 1908, 15, 339–357.

Dale, E. *Bibliography of vocabulary studies.* Columbus, Ohio: Bureau of Educational Research, Ohio State Univer., 1949.

Darcy, N. T. The effect of bilingualism upon the measurement of the intelligence of children of preschool age. *J. educ. Psychol.*, 1946, 37, 21–44.

Darley, F. L., & Winitz, H. Age of first word: Review of research. *J. speech hear. Dis.*, 1961, 26, 272–290.

Darwin, C. A biographical sketch of an infant. *Mind*, 1877, 2, 285–294.

Davis, D. M. The relation of repetitions in the speech of young children to certain measures of language maturity and situational factors. Part I. *J. speech Disord.*, 1939, 4, 303–318.

———. The relation of repetitions in the speech of young children to certain measures of language maturity and situational factors. Parts II and III. *J. speech Disord.*, 1940, 5, 235–246.

Davis, E. A. The mental and linguistic superiority of only girls. *Child Develpm.*, 1937, 8, 139–143.

Dawe, H. C. A study of the effect of an educational program upon language development and related mental functions in young children. *J. exp. Educ.*, 1942, 11, 200–209.

Day, E. J. The development of language in twins. I. A comparison of twins and single children. *Child Develpm.*, 1932, 3, 179–199. (a)

———. The development of language in twins. II. The development of twins: their resemblances and differences. *Child Develpm.*, 1932, 3, 298–316. (b)

Deese, J. Comments and conclusions. In U. Bellugi & R. Brown (Eds.), The acquisition of language. *Monogr. Soc. Res. Child Develpm.*, 1964, 29, No. 1 (Whole No. 92). Pp. 177–183.

Descoeudres, A. *Le développement de l'enfant de deux à sept ans. (The development of the child from two to seven years.)* Paris: Delachaux & Niestle, 1921.

Dollard, J., & Miller, N. E. *Personality and psychotherapy.* New York: McGraw-Hill, 1950.

Doran, E. W. A study of vocabularies. *Ped. Sem.*, 1907, 14, 401–438.

Drever, J. A study of children's vocabulary. I & II. *J. exp. Pedag.*, 1915–1916, 3, 34–43, 96–103, & 182–188.

———. The vocabulary of a free kindergarten child. *J. exp. Pedag.*, 1919, 5, 28–37.

Ellesor, M. V. The relation between situation and response in vocalization of a three-year-old child. *Child Develpm.*, 1934, 5, 158–164.

Erickson, E. *Childhood and society.* New York: Norton, 1950.

Ervin, S. M. Imitations in the speech of two-year-olds. Paper read at Amer. Psychol. Ass., Philadelphia, August, 1963. (a)

———. Structure in children's language. Paper read at Int. Congr. Psychol., Washington, 1963. (b)

Ervin, S. M., & Miller, W. R. Language development. In H. W. Stevenson (Ed.), *Child psychology: The sixty-second yearbook of the National Society for the Study of Education. Part I.* Chicago: Univer. Chicago, 1963. Pp. 108–143.

Fairbanks, G. An acoustical study of the pitch of infant hunger wails. *Child Develpm.*, 1942, 13, 227–232.

Fedorov, V. K. Nekotorye fiziologicheskie mekhanizmy nachalnogo razvitiia psikhicheskoi zhizni rebenka. (Physiological mechanisms in the early stages of the child's psychological development.) *Voprosy Psikhologii*, 1962, 149–154.

Fisher, M. S. Language patterns of preschool children. *J. exp. Educ.*, 1932, 1, 70–85.

———. *Language patterns of preschool children.* New York: Teachers College, 1934.

Fisichelli, R. M. An experimental study of the prelinguistic speech development of institutionalized infants. Unpublished doctoral dissertation, Fordham Univer., 1950.

Fisichelli, V. R., & Karelitz, S. The cry latencies of normal infants and those with brain damage. *J. Pediatr.*, 1963, 62, 724–734.

Foulke, K., & Stinchfield, S. M. The speech development of four infants under two years of age. *J. genet. Psychol.*, 1929, 36, 140–171.

Fraser, C., Bellugi, U., & Brown, R. Control of grammar in imitation, comprehension, and production. *J. verbal Behav. verbal Learning*, 1963, 2, 121–135.

Freud, A., & Burlingham, D. *War and children.* New York: Int. Univer. Press, 1943. Reprinted in Y. Brackbill & G. G. Thompson (Eds.), *Behavior in infancy and early childhood: A book of readings.* New York: Free Press, 1967.

———. *Infants without families.* New York: Int. Univer. Press, 1944.

Gale, M. C., & Gale, H. The vocabularies of three children in one family at two and three years of age. *Ped. Sem.*, 1902, 9, 422–435.

Gatewood, M. C., & Weiss, A. P. Race and sex differences in newborn infants. *Ped. Sem.*, 1930, 38, 31–49.

Gesell, A. L. *The mental growth of the pre-school child: A psychological outline of normal development from birth to the sixth year, including a system of developmental diagnosis.* New York: Macmillan, 1925.

Gesell, A. L., & Amatruda, C. S. *Developmental Diagnosis.* New York: Hoeber, 1941.

Gesell, A. L., & Lord, E. A psychological comparison of nursery-school children from homes of low and high economic status. *J. genet. Psychol.*, 1927, 34, 339–356.

Gesell, A. L., & Thompson, H. Learning and growth in identical infant twins: An experimental study by the method of co-twin control. *Genet. Psychol. Monogr.*, 1929, 6, 1–124.

Gheorgov, J. A. *Ein Beitrag zur grammatischen Entwicklung der Kindersprache. (Contributions to the development of grammar in children's language.)* Leipzig: Engelmann, 1908.

Goldfarb, W. Infant rearing and problem behavior. *Amer. J. Orthopsychiat.*, 1943, 13, 249–265. (a)

——. The effects of early institutional care on adolescent personality. *J. exp. Educ.*, 1943, 12, 106–129. (b)

——. Effects of psychological deprivation in infancy and subsequent stimulation. *Amer. J. Psychiat.*, 1945, 102, 18–33.

Gollin, E. S. Reversal learning and conditional discrimination in children. *J. comp. physiol. Psychol.*, 1964, 58, 441–445.

Gollin, E. S., & Liss, P. Conditional discrimination in children. *J. comp. physiol. Psychol.*, 1962, 55, 850–855.

Gonzalez, R. C., & Ross, S. The basis of solution by preverbal children of the intermediate-size problem. *Amer. J. Psychol.*, 1958, 71, 742–746.

Goodenough, F. L. Inter-relationships in the behavior of young children. *Child Develpm.*, 1930, 1, 29–47.

——. The use of pronouns by young children: A note on the development of self-awareness. *J. genet. Psychol.*, 1938, 52, 333–346.

Goss, A. E. Verbal mediating response and concept formation. *Psychol. Rev.*, 1961, 68, 248–274.

Grigsby, O. J. An experimental study of the development of concepts of relationship in pre-school children as evidenced by their expressive ability. *J. exp. Educ.*, 1932, 1, 144–162.

Guillaume, P. *L'Imitation chez l'enfant. (Imitation in children.)* Paris: Alçan, 1925.

Haggerty, L. C. G. What a two-and-one-half-year-old child said in one day. *J. genet. Psychol.*, 1930, 37, 75–101.

Hall, W. S. The first five hundred days of a child's life. *The Child Study Monthly*, 1896–97, 2, 330–342; 394–407; 458–473; 522–537; 536–608.

Halle, M. & Jakobson, R. *Fundamentals of language.* The Hague: Mouton & Co., 1956.

Hattwick, L. A. Sex differences in behavior of nursery school children. *Child Develpm.*, 1937, 8, 343–355.

Hebb, D. O. *The organization of behavior.* New York: Wiley, 1949.

Hilgard, J. R. The effect of early and delayed practice on memory and motor performances studied by the method of co-twin control. *Genet. Psychol. Monogr.*, 1933, 14, 493–567.

Hills, E. C. The speech of a child two years of age. *Dialect Notes*, 1914, 4, 84–100.

Holden, E. S. On the vocabularies of children under two years. *Trans. Amer. Philol. Ass.*, 1877, 8, 58–68.

Holmes, U. T. The phonology of an English-speaking child. *Amer. Speech*, 1927, 2, 219–225.

Hooker, D. *The prenatal origin of behavior.* Lawrence: Kansas Univer. Press, 1952.

Howard, R. W. The language development of a group of triplets. *J. genet. Psychol.*, 1946, 69, 181–188.

Hull, C. L., & Hull, B. I. Parallel learning curves of an infant in vocabulary and in voluntary control of the bladder. *Ped. Sem.*, 1919, 26, 272–283. Reprinted in Y. Brackbill & G. G. Thompson (Eds.), *Behavior in infancy and early childhood: A book of readings.* New York: Free Press, 1967.

Humphreys, M. W. A contribution to infantile linguistics. *Trans. Amer. Philol. Ass.*, 1880, 11, 5–17.

Hunter, I. M. L. An experimental investigation of the absolute and relative theories of transposition behavior in children. *Brit. J. Psychol.*, 1952, 43, 113–128.

Hunter, W. S., & Bartlett, S. C. Double alternation behavior in young children. *J. exp. Psychol.*, 1948, 38, 558–567.

Hymes, D. Formal discussion. In U. Bellugi, & R. Brown (Eds.), The acquisition of language. *Monogr. Soc. Res. Child Develpm.*, 1964, 29, No. 1 (Whole No. 92). Pp. 107–111.

International Kindergarten Union. *A study of the vocabulary of children before entering the first grade.* Baltimore: Williams & Wilkins, 1928.

Irwin, O. C. The profile as a visual device for indicating tendencies in speech data. *Child Develpm.,* 1941, 12, 111–120.

——. Infant speech: Consonant sounds according to manner of articulation. *J. speech Disord.,* 1947, 12, 402–404. (a)

——. Infant speech: Consonant sounds according to place of articulation. *J. speech Disord.,* 1947, 12, 397–401. (b)

——. Development of speech during infancy: Curve of phonemic frequencies. *J. exp. Psychol.,* 1947, 37, 187–193. (c)

——. Infant speech: Development of vowel sounds. *J. speech Disord.,* 1948, 13, 31–34. (a)

——. Infant Speech: Speech sound development of siblings and only infants. *J. exp. Psychol.,* 1948, 38, 600–602. (b)

——. Infant speech: The effect of family occupational status and of age on use of sound types. *J. speech hear. Disord.,* 1948, 13, 224–226. (c)

——. Infant speech: The effect of family occupational status and of age on sound frequency. *J. speech hear. Disord.,* 1948, 13, 320–323. (d)

——. Infant speech. *Sci. Amer.,* 1949, 18, 22–24.

——. Infant speech: Effect of systematic reading of stories. *J. speech hear. Res.,* 1960, 3, 187–190. (a) Reprinted in Y. Brackbill & G. G. Thompson (Eds.), *Behavior in infancy and early childhood: A book of readings.* New York: Free Press, 1967.

——. Language and communication. In P. H. Mussen (Ed.), *Handbook of research methods in child development.* New York: Wiley, 1960. Pp. 487–516. (b)

Irwin, O. C., & Chen, H. P. A reliability study of speech sounds observed in the crying of newborn infants. *Child Develpm.,* 1941, 12, 351–368.

——. Speech sound elements during the first year of life; a review of the literature. *J. speech Disord.,* 1943, 8, 109–121.

——. Development of speech during infancy: Curve of phonemic types. *J. exp. Psychol.,* 1946, 36, 431–436. (a)

——. Infant speech: Vowel and consonant frequency. *J. speech Disord.,* 1946, 11, 123–125. (b)

Irwin, O. C., & Curry, T. Vowel elements in the crying vocalization of infants under ten days of age. *Child Develpm.,* 1941, 12, 99–109.

Irwin, O. C., & Weiss, L. A. Differential variations in the activity and crying of the newborn infant under different intensities of light: A comparison of observational with polygraph findings. *Univer. Iowa Stud. Child Welf.,* 1934, 9, 137–147. (a)

——. The effect of clothing on the general and vocal activity of the newborn infant. *Univer. Iowa Stud. Child Welf.,* 1934, 9, No. 4, 149–162. (b)

Isaacs, S. Some notes on the incidence of neurotic difficulties in young children. *Brit. J. educ. Psychol.,* 1932, 2, 71–91.

Jakobson, R. C. *Kindersprache, Aphasie und allgemeine Lautgesetze.* (*Children's language, aphasia, and general phonetic laws.*) Uppsala: Almqvist & Wiksell, 1941.

Jakobson, R. C., & Halle, M. Fundamentals of language. The Hague: Mouton, 1956.

Jeffrey, W. E. The effects of verbal and nonverbal responses in mediating an instrumental act. *J. exp. Psychol.,* 1953, 45, 327–333.

Jenkins, J. J., & Palermo, D. S. Mediation processes and the acquisition of linguistic structure. In U. Bellugi & R. Brown (Eds.), The acquisition of language. *Monogr. Soc. Res. Child Develpm.,* 1964, 29, No. 1 (Whole No. 92). Pp. 141–168.

Jersild, A. T., & Ritzman, R. Aspects of language development: The growth of loquacity and vocabulary. *Child Develpm.,* 1938, 9, 243–259.

Jespersen, O. *Language: Its nature, development, and origin.* London: Allen & Unwin, 1922.

————. Essentials of English grammar. New York: Holt, 1933.

Johnson, R. C., & Zara, R. C. Relational learning in young children. J. comp. physiol. Psychol., 1960, 53, 594–597.

Johnson, W. (Ed.) Stuttering in children and adults. Minneapolis: Univer. of Minn. Press, 1945.

Kagan, J. Formal discussion. In U. Bellugi, & R. Brown (Eds.), The acquisition of language. Monogr. Soc. Res. Child Develpm., 1964, 29, No. 1 (Whole No. 92). Pp. 169–172.

Kagan, J., & Lewis, M. Studies of attention in the human infant. Merrill-Palmer Quart., 1965, 11, 95–127.

Kahane, H., Kahane, R., & Saporta, S. Development of verbal categories in child language. Int. J. Amer. Linguistics, Part II, 1958, 24, 1–65.

Karelitz, S., & Fisichelli, V. R. The cry thresholds of normal infants and those with brain damage. An aid in the early diagnosis of severe brain damage. J. Pediatr., 1962, 61, 679–685.

Keitel, H. G., Cohn, R., & Harnish, D. Diaper rash, self-inflicted excoriations, and crying in full-term newborn infants kept in the prone or supine position. J. Pediatr., 1960, 57, 884–886.

Kendler, H. H., & Kendler, T. S. Vertical and horizontal processes in problem-solving. Psychol. Rev., 1962, 69, 1–16.

Kendler, T. S. An experimental investigation of transposition as a function of the difference between training and test stimuli. J. exp. Psychol., 1950, 40, 552–562.

————. Development of mediating responses in children. Monogr. Soc. Res. Child Develpm., 1963, 28 (86). Pp. 33–48.

Kendler, T. S., Kendler, H. H., & Wells, D. Reversal and non-reversal shifts in nursery school children. J. comp. physiol. Psychol., 1960, 53, 83–88.

Kirkpatrick, E. A. The number of words in ordinary vocabularies. Science, 1891, 18, 175.

Koch, J. An attempt to analyze the influence of the environment of children's homes on the neuropsychic development of 4- to 12-month-old children. Cesk. Pediatr., 1961, 16, 322–330. (Child Develpm. Abstr., 36:556)

Kuenne, M. R. Experimental investigation of the relation of language to transposition behavior in young children. J. exp. Psychol., 1946, 36, 471–490.

Lakin, M. Personality factors in mothers of excessively crying (colicky) infants. Monogr. Soc. Res. Child Develpm., 1957, 22 (Whole No. 64).

Latif, I. The physiological basis of linguistic development and the ontogeny of meaning: I, II. Psychol. Rev., 1934, 41, 55–85, 153–176.

Lenneberg, E. H. Language, evolution, and purposive behavior. In E. Diamond (Ed.), Culture in history. New York: Columbia Univer. Press, 1960.

————. Language disorders in childhood. Harv. Educ. Rev., 1964, 34, 152–177. (a)

————. Speech as a motor skill with special reference to nonaphasic disorders. In U. Bellugi & R. Brown (Eds.), The acquisition of language. Monogr. Soc. Res. Child Develpm., 1964, 29, No. 1 (Whole No. 92), 115–127. (b)

Lenneberg, E. H. (Ed.) New directions in the study of language. Cambridge, Mass.: M.I.T. Press, 1964. (c)

Lenneberg, E. H., Nichols, I. A., & Rosenberger, E. Primitive stages of language development in mongolism. Disorders of communication, 1964, 42, 119–137. Published by the Assoc. Research in Nervous & Mental Disease, Dec., 1962.

Lenneberg, E. H., Rebelsky, F. G., & Nichols, I. A. The vocalizations of infants born to deaf and to hearing parents. Human Develpm., 1965, 8, 23–37.

Leopold, W. F. Speech development of a bilingual child: A linguist's record. Northwestern Univer. Stud. Humanities, 1939–49, No. 6, 11, 18, 19. 4 vols.

————. Patterning in children's language learning. Language Learning, 1953–1954, 5, 1–14.

Lewis, M. M. Infant speech. (2nd ed.) New York: Humanities Press, 1951.

————. *How children learn to speak.* London: George G. Harrap, 1957.

————. *Language, thought and personality.* New York: Basic Books, 1963.

Liiamina, G. M. Mechanism by which children master pronunciation during the second and the third year. *The central nervous system and behavior,* translations from the Russian medical literature collected for participants of the third Macy conference on the central nervous system and behavior, Princeton, N. J., Feb. 21–24, 1960, 509–528. Prepared and distributed by the Russian scientific translation program, National Institutes of Health. Library of Congress Catalog card number: 5960785.

Lipton, E. L., Steinschneider, A., & Richmond, J. B. Autonomic function in the neonate. II. Physiological effects of motor restraint. *Psychosom. Med.,* 1960, 22, 57–65.

Lowrey, L. G. Personality distortion and early institutional care. *Amer. J. Orthopsychiat.,* 1940, 10, 576–585.

Luchsinger, R. Die Sprachentwicklung von ein- und zweieigen Zwillingen und die Vererbung von Sprachstörungen. (Language development in monozygotic and dizygotic twins, and the inheritance of speech disturbances.) *Acta geneticae medicae et genellologaie,* 1953, 2, 31–48.

Lukens, H. T. Preliminary report on the learning of language. *Ped. Sem.,* 1894–1896, 3, 424–460.

Luria, A. R. The directive function of speech in development and dissolution. *Word,* 1959, 15, 341–352.

————. *Role of speech in the regulation of normal and abnormal behavior.* New York: Liveright, 1961.

Luria, A. R., & Yudovich, F. *Speech and the development of mental processes in the child.* London: Staples Press, 1957.

Lynip, A. W. The use of magnetic devices in the collection and analysis of the preverbal utterances of an infant. *Genet. Psychol. Monogr.,* 1951, 44, 221–262.

McCarthy, D. A. The language development of the preschool child. *Univer. Minn. Inst. Child Welf. Monogr.,* 1930, No. 4.

————. A preliminary report on a new articulation test for young children. *Psychol. Bull.,* 1935, 32, 699.

————. Language development in children. In L. Carmichael (Ed.), *Manual of child psychology.* (2nd ed.) New York: Wiley, 1954. Pp. 492–630.

————. Affective aspects of language learning. Presidential address, Division of developmental psychology, Amer. Psychol. Ass., Sept., 1961.

McCurry, W. H., & Irwin, O. C. A study of word approximations in the spontaneous speech of infants. *J. speech hear. Disord.,* 1953, 18, 133–139.

Mandell, S., & Sonneck, B. Phonographische Aufnahme und Analyse der ersten Sprachäusserungen von Kindern. (Phonograph recording and analysis of the first verbal manifestations in children.) *Arch. ges. Psychol.,* 1935, 94, 478–500.

Martin, W. E. Quantitative expression in young children. *Genet. Psychol. Monogr.,* 1951, 44, 147–219.

Menyuk, P. A preliminary evaluation of grammatical capacity in children. *J. verbal Behav. verbal Learning,* 1963, 2, 429–439. (a)

————. Syntactic structures in the language of children. *Child Develpm.,* 1963, 34, 407–422. (b) Reprinted in Y. Brackbill and G. G. Thompson (Eds.), *Behavior in infancy and early childhood: A book of readings.* New York: Free Press, 1967.

————. Syntactic rules used by children from preschool through first grade. *Child Develpm.,* 1964, 35, 533–546.

Merleau-Ponty, M. La conscience et l'acquisition du language. (Conscience and language acquisition.) *Bull. Psychol.,* 1964, 18, 226–259.

Mickens, C. W. Practical results of child study. *Child Study Mon.,* 1897–1898, 3, 198–205.

Miller, G. A. *Language and communication.* New York: McGraw-Hill, 1951.

———. Language and psychology. In E. H. Lenneberg (Ed.), *New directions in the study of language.* Cambridge, Mass.: M.I.T. Press, 1964. (a)

———. *Mathematics and psychology.* New York: Wiley, 1964. (b)

———. Some preliminaries to psycholinguistics. *Amer. Psychol.,* 1965, 20, 15–20.

Miller, G. F., Miller, M. D., & Nice, M. M. A boy's vocabulary at eighteen months. *Proc. Okla. Acad. Sci.,* 1923, 3, 140–144.

Miller, N. E., & Dollard, J. *Social learning and imitation.* New Haven: Yale Univer. Press, 1941.

Miller, W., & Ervin, S. The development of grammar in child language. In U. Bellugi & R. Brown (Eds.), The acquisition of language. *Monogr. Soc. Res. Child Develpm.,* 1964, 29, No. 1 (Whole No. 92). Pp. 9–34.

Moore, J. K. Speech content of selected groups of orphanage and nonorphanage preschool children. *J. exp. Educ.,* 1947, 16, 122–133.

Moore, K. C. The mental development of a child. *Psychol. Rev. Monogr. Suppl.,* 1896, 1, No. 3.

Moore, O. K. Comments and conclusions. In U. Bellugi & R. Brown (Eds.), The acquisition of language. *Monogr. Soc. Res. Child Develpm.,* 1964, 29, No. 1 (Whole No. 92), pp. 181–186.

Mowrer, O. H. *Learning theory and personality dynamics.* New York: Ronald Press, 1950.

———. Hearing and speaking: An analysis of language learning. *J. speech hearing Disord.,* 1958, 23, 143–151.

———. *Learning theory and symbolic processes.* New York: Wiley, 1960.

Mullahy, P. The theories of Harry Stack Sullivan. *Oedipus myth and complex.* New York: Hermitage Press, 1948. Reprinted in Y. Brackbill & G. G. Thompson (Eds.), *Behavior in infancy and early childhood: A book of readings.* New York: Free Press, 1967.

Nice, M. M. The development of a child's vocabulary in relation to environment. *Ped. Sem.,* 1915, 22, 35–64. (a)

———. The speech of a left-handed child. *Psychol. Clinic,* 1915, 9, 115–117. (b)

———. The speech development of a child from eighteen months to six years. *Ped. Sem.,* 1917, 24, 204–243.

———. Ambidexterity and delayed speech development. *Ped. Sem.,* 1918, 25, 141–162.

———. Concerning all day conversations. *Ped. Sem.,* 1920, 27, 166–177.

———. A child who would not talk. *Ped. Sem.,* 1925, 32, 105–142.

———. On the size of vocabularies. *Amer. Speech,* 1926–1927, 2, 1–7.

Norcross, K. J., & Spiker, C. C. Effects of mediated associations on transfer in paired-associate learning. *J. Exp. Psychol.,* 1958, 55, 129–134.

Norman, E. Some psychological features of babble. In D. Jones & D. B. Fry (Eds.), *Proceedings of the second international congress of phonetic sciences.* London: Cambridge Univer. Press, 1936.

Olson, W. C., & Koetzle, V. S. Amount and rate of talking of young children. *J. exp. Educ.,* 1936, 5, 175–179.

Osgood, C. E. The nature and measurement of meaning. *Psychol. Bull.,* 1952, 49, 197–237.

Osgood, C. E., & Sebeok, T. A. (Eds.), Psycholinguistics: A survey of theory and research problems. *J. abnorm. soc. Psychol.,* 1954, 49 (Whole No. 4, Part 2.).

Parmelee, A. H., Jr. Infant speech development: A report of a study of one child by magnetic tape recordings. *J. Pediatr.,* 1955, 46, 447–450.

Pavlovitch, M. *Le langage enfantin: Acquisition du serbe et du français par un enfant serbe.* (Child language: The acquisition of Serbian and French by a Serbian child.) Paris: Champion, 1920.

Pelsma, J. R. A child's vocabulary and its development. *Ped. Sem.,* 1910, 17, 328–369.

Penfield, W., & Roberts, L. *Speech and brain-mechanisms.* Princeton: Princeton Univer. Press, 1959.

Piaget, J. *The language and thought of the child.* New York: Harcourt Brace, 1926.

Pike, E. G. Controlled infant intonation. *Language Learning,* 1949, 2, 21–24.

Pollock, F. An infant's progress in language. *Mind,* 1878, 3, 392–401.

Poole, I. Genetic development of articulation of consonant sounds in speech. *Elem. Eng. Rev.,* 1934, 11, 159–161.

Postal, P. M. Underlying and superficial linguistic structure. *Harv. Educ. Rev.,* 1964, 34, 246–266.

Pratt, K. C. Note on the relation of temperature and humidity to the activity of young infants. *Ped. Sem.,* 1930, 38, 480–484.

Preyer, W. *The mind of the child.* New York: Appleton, 1888.

Pringle, M. L. Comparative study of the effects of early deprivation on speech development. *Percept. mot. Skills,* 1959, 9, 345.

Pringle, M. L., & Bossio, V. A study of deprived children. Part II: Language development and reading attainment. *Vita Humana,* 1958, 1, 142–170.

Provence, S., & Lipton, R. C. *Infants in institutions: A comparison of their development with family-reared infants during the first year of life.* New York: Int. Univer. Press, 1962.

Reese, H. W. Transposition in the intermediate size problem by preschool children. *Child Develpm.,* 1961, 32, 311–314.

———. The distance effect in transposition in the intermediate size problem. *J. comp. physiol. Psychol.,* 1962, 55, 528–531. (a)

———. Verbal mediation as a function of age level. *Psychol. Bull.,* 1962, 59, 502–509. (b)

Rheingold, H. L. The modification of social responsiveness in institutional babies. *Monogr. Soc. Res. Child Develpm.,* 1956, 21, No. 2.

Rheingold, H. L., & Bayley, N. The later effects of an experimental modification of mothering. *Child Develpm.,* 1959, 30, 363–372. Reprinted in Y. Brackbill & G. G. Thompson (Eds.), *Behavior in infancy and early childhood: A book of readings.* New York: Free Press, 1967.

Rheingold, H. L., Gerwirtz, J. L., & Ross, H. W. Social conditioning of vocalizations in the infant. *J. comp. physiol. Psychol.,* 1959, 52, 68–73.

Ronjat, J. *Le développement du langage observè chez un enfant bilingue.* (*Language development in a bilingual child.*) Paris: Champion, 1913.

Rudel, R. G. Transposition of response by children trained in intermediate-size problems. *J. comp. physiol. Psychol.,* 1951, 50, 292–295.

———. Transposition of response to size in children. *J. comp. physiol. Psychol.,* 1958, 51, 386–390.

———. The absolute response in tests of generalization in normal and retarded children. *Amer. J. Psychol.,* 1959, 72, 401–408.

———. The transposition of intermediate size by brain-damaged and Mongoloid children. *J. comp. physiol. Psychol.,* 1960, 53, 89–94.

Ruja, H. The relation between neonate crying and length of labor. *J. genet. Psychol.,* 1948, 73, 53–55.

Scripture, E. W. Speech without using the larynx. *J. Physiol.,* 1915, 50, 397–403.

Shah, I. S. An investigation of linguistic decision points and encoding segments in spoken English. Unpublished doctoral dissertation, Cornell Univer., 1960.

Shepard, W. O. The effect of verbal training on initial generalization tendencies. *Child Develpm.,* 1956, 27, 311–316.

Sherman, M. The differentiation of emotional responses in infants: II. The ability of observers to judge the emotional characteristics of the crying of infants, and the voice of an adult. *J. comp. Psychol.,* 1927, 7, 335–351.

Shirley, M. M. *The first two years. A study of twenty-five babies. Vol. II. Intellectual development.* Minneapolis: Univer. Minn. Press, 1933.

Skeels, H. M., Updegraff, R., Wellman, B. L., & Williams, H. M. A study of environmental stimulation; an orphanage preschool project. *Univer. Iowa Stud. Child Welf.*, 1938, 15, No. 4.

Skinner, B. F. *Verbal behavior.* New York: Appleton-Century-Crofts, 1957.

Smith, J. M. The relative brightness values of three hues for newborn infants. *Univer. Iowa Stud. Child Welf.*, 1936, 12, No. 1.

Smith, M. E. An investigation of the development of the sentence and the extent of vocabulary in young children. *Univer. Iowa Stud. Child Welf.*, 1926, 3, No. 5.

————. A study of five bilingual children from the same family. *Child Develpm.*, 1931, 2, 184–187.

————. Grammatical errors in the speech of preschool children. *Child Develpm.*, 1933, 4, 183–190.

————. A study of some factors influencing the development of the sentence in preschool children. *J. genet. Psychol.*, 1935, 46, 182–212. (a)

————. A study of the speech of eight bilingual children of the same family. *Child Develpm.*, 1935, 6, 19–25. (b)

————. Some light on the problem of bilingualism as found from a study of the progress in mastery of English among preschool children of non-American ancestry in Hawaii. *Genet. Psychol. Monogr.*, 1939, 21, 119–284.

————. Measurement of vocabularies of young bilingual children in both of the languages used. *J. genet. Psychol.*, 1949, 74, 305–310.

————. Word variety as a measure of bilingualism in preschool children. *J. genet. Psychol.*, 1957, 90, 143–150.

Smith, M. E., & Kasdon, L. M. Progress in the use of English after 20 years by children of Filipino and Japanese ancestry in Hawaii. *J. genet. Psychol.*, 1961, 99, 129–138.

Smith, S. S., & Goss, A. E. The role of the acquired distinctiveness of cues in the acquisition of a motor skill in children. *J. genet. Psychol.*, 1955, 87, 11–24.

Sokhin, F. On the formation of linguistic generalization in the course of speech development. *Voprosy Psikhologii*, 1959, 112–123.

Sommer, A. T. The effect of group training upon the correction of articulatory defects in preschool children. *Child Develpm.*, 1932, 3, 91–103.

Spence, K. W. *Behavior theory and conditioning.* New Haven: Yale Univer. Press, 1956.

Spiker, C. C. Verbal factors in the discrimination learning of children. *Monogr. Soc. Res. Child Develpm.*, 1963, 28 (Whole No. 86). Pp. 53–69.

Spitz, R. A. Hospitalism: A follow-up report on investigation described in volume 1, 1945. *The psychoanalytic study of the child*, 1946, 2, 113–117.

————. *No and yes.* New York: Int. Univer. Press, 1957.

————. *La première année de la vie d'enfant. (The first year in the life of the child.)* Paris: Presses Universitaires de France, 1958.

Staats, A. W. Verbal habit-families, concepts, and the operant conditioning of word classes. *Psychol. Rev.*, 1961, 68, 190–204.

Staats, A. W., & Staats, C. K. Meaning and *m*: Separate but correlated. *Psychol. Rev.*, 1959, 66, 136–144.

————. *Complex human behavior.* New York: Holt, Rinehart & Winston, 1963.

Stalnaker, E. Language of the preschool child. *Child Develpm.*, 1933, 4, 229–236.

Stern, C., & Stern W. *Monographien über die seelische Entwicklung des Kindes. II. Erinnerung, Aussage und Lüge in der ersten Kindheit. (Monographs on the mental development of the child. II. Memory assertion and lying in early childhood.)* Leipzig: Verlag von Johann Ambrosius Barth, 1909, 111–160.

————. *Die Kindersprache. (The language of the child.) (3rd ed.) Monogr. über die seelische Entwicklung des Kindes*, 1922, 1.

————. *Die Kindersprache. (The language of the child.)* Leipzig: Barth, 1928.

Stern, W. *Psychology of early childhood.* New York: Holt, 1930.

Stewart, A. H. Excessive crying in infants—a family disease. In M. J. Senn (Ed.), *Problems of infancy and childhood.* Transactions of sixth conference, Josiah Macy, Jr., Foundation, 1953.

Stewart, A. H., Weiland, I. H., Leider, A. R., Mangham, C. H., Holmes, T. H., & Ripley, H. S. Excessive infant crying (colic) in relation to parent behavior. *Amer. J. Psychiat.,* 1954, 110, 687–694.

Strayer, L. C. Language and growth: The relative efficacy of early and deferred vocabulary training, studied by the method of co-twin control. *Genet. Psychol. Monogr.,* 1930, 8, 209–319. Reprinted in Y. Brackbill & G. G. Thompson (Eds.), *Behavior in infancy and early childhood: A book of readings.* New York: Free Press, 1967.

Stubbs, E. M. The effect of the factors of duration, intensity, and pitch of sound stimuli on the responses of newborn infants. *Univer. Iowa Stud. Child Welf.,* 1934, 9, No. 4.

Sullivan, H. S. *Collected works.* New York: Norton, 1965.

Taine, H. M. Taine on the acquisition of language by children. *Mind,* 1877, 2, 252–259.

Templin, M. C. Spontaneous versus imitated verbalization in testing articulation in preschool children. *J. speech Disord.,* 1947, 12, 293–300.

———. Norms on a screening test of articulation for ages three through eight. *J. speech hear. Disord.,* 1953, 18, 323–331.

———. A note on a screening test of articulation of speech sound. *J. Pediat.,* 1954, 45, 443–445.

———. Certain language skills in children: Their development and interrelationships. *Univer. Minn. Inst. Child Welf. Monogr.,* 1957, No. 26.

Thorndike, E. L. *The teacher's word book.* New York: Teachers College, 1921.

Tischler, H. Schreien, Lallen und erstes Sprechen in der Entwicklung des Säuglings. (Crying, babbling and first speech in the development of the infant.) *Z. Psychol.,* 1957, 160, 210–263.

Tonkova-Yampolskaya, R. V. On the question of studying physiological mechanisms of speech. *Pavlov J. high. nerv. Act.,* 1962, 12, 82–87.

Tracy, F. The language of childhood. *Amer. J. Psychol.,* 1893, 6, 107–138.

Valentine, C. W. The psychology of imitation with special reference to early childhood. *Brit. J. Psychol.,* 1930, 21, 105–132.

Van Alstyne, D. The environment of three-year-old children: Factors related to intelligence and vocabulary tests. *Teachers College Contr. Educ.,* 1929, No. 366.

Velton, H. V. The growth of phonemic and lexical patterns in infant language. *Language,* 1943, 19, 281–292.

Vygotskii, L. S. *Thought and language.* Cambridge, Mass.: M.I.T. Press, 1962.

Warren, J. M. The comparative psychology of learning. *Ann. Rev. Psychol.,* 1965, 16, 95–118.

Watson, J. B. *Behavior.* New York: Holt, 1914.

———. *Behaviorism.* New York: Norton, 1930.

Weir, M. W., & Stevenson, H. W. The effect of verbalization in children's learning as a function of chronological age. *Child Develpm.,* 1959, 30, 143–149.

Weir, R. H. *Language in the crib.* The Hague: Mouton, 1962.

Weisberg, P. Social and nonsocial conditioning of infant vocalizations. *Child Develpm.,* 1963, 34, 377–388. Reprinted in Y. Brackbill & G. G. Thompson (Eds.), *Behavior in infancy and early childhood: A book of readings.* New York: Free Press, 1967.

Wellman, B. L., Case, I. M., Mengert, I. G., & Bradbury, D. E. Speech sounds of young children. *Univer. Iowa Stud. Child Welf.,* 1931, 5, No. 2.

Werner, H., & Kaplan, B. *Symbol formation.* New York: Wiley, 1963.

Williams, H. M., McFarland, M. L., & Little, M. F. Development of language and vocabulary in young children. *Univer. Iowa Stud. Child Welf.,* 1937, 13, No. 2.

Williams, R. M., & Mattson, M. L. The effect of social groupings upon the language of preschool children. *Child Develpm.*, 1942, 13, 233–245. Reprinted in Y. Brackbill & G. G. Thompson (Eds.), *Behavior in infancy and early childhood: A book of readings.* New York: Free Press, 1967.

Winitz, H. Spectrographic investigation of infant vowels. *J. genet. Psychol.*, 1960, 96, 171–181.

———. Repetitions in the vocalizations and speech of children in the first two years of life. *J. speech hear. Disord., Monogr. Suppl.*, 1961, No. 7, 55–62.

Wolff, P. H. Observations on newborn infants. *Psychosom. Med.*, 1959, 21, 110–118.

Wolfflin, E. Reduplikation in der Kindersprache. (Reduplication in the language of the child.) *Z. deutsche Wortforschung*, 1901, 1, 263–264.

Yarrow, L. Maternal deprivation: Toward an empirical and conceptual reevaluation. *Psychol. Bull.*, 1961, 58, 459–490.

Young, F. M. An analysis of certain variables in a developmental study of language. *Genet. Psychol. Monogr.*, 1941, 23, 3–141.

———. Certain social indices in the language of preschool subjects. *J. genet. Psychol.*, 1942, 61, 109–123. (a)

———. Development as indicated by a study of pronouns. *J. genet. Psychol.*, 1942, 61, 125–134. (b)

Youniss, J., & Furth, H. G. Discrimination shifts as a function of degree of training in children. *J. exp. Psychol.*, 1965, 70, 424–427.

Chapter 6

Cognition in Infancy and Early Childhood

DAVID ELKIND

$\mathbb{C}$ognition has to do with knowledge and with the processes by which it is acquired and utilized. Research on the development of cognition has gone in several different directions depending upon the theoretical orientation of the investigator in question. These orientations can be loosely grouped within two broad categories. On the one hand there is the orientation which starts from the assumption that knowledge and the capacity to acquire it exists in some amount and can be measured. This is the *mental test* approach. A second orientation starts from the premise that knowledge and the processes of acquisition change or develop with age and the task of psychology is to describe and explain this development. This second orientation might be called *developmental*. It should be said that these two approaches do not necessarily contradict one another. The mental test approach is concerned with assessing individual differences whereas the developmental approach concerns itself with normative trends. Yet individual differences can only be assessed with reference to norms while norms are always abstractions from individual variations. In fact, many of the tasks which appear on intelligence tests are also used in the study of the nature and content of cognitive processes. In short, the difference between the orientations is relative rather than absolute and is more a matter of differing emphasis rather than differences in kind.

Defined in this broad fashion, these two orientations with respect to cognition in infancy and early childhood encompass a tremendous amount of research. Selection is obviously necessary not only because of the sheer amount of material but also because few investigators abide by the age limits of our present concern, so that many studies deal with age groups which overlap the infancy and early childhood periods. In the present chapter no attempt has, therefore, been made to be encyclopedic. On the contrary, the aim has been to select issues and areas of research that seem important and whose examination might lead to reevaluation and/or new insights into problems of theory or fact. Such an approach will, of necessity, involve some new categorizations and terminology as well as a moderate amount of speculation. Hopefully it will be of more use and interest than a single compilation of the available literature.

361

The first section of the chapter will deal with the mental test approach to cognition in infancy and early childhood. Three issues will be taken up: the prediction of later mental ability on the basis of infant tests of intelligence, infancy as a critical period in intellectual development, and, finally, the many faces of causality with respect to intelligence in young children. The second section of the chapter will deal with the developmental approach and will take up problem solving, memory, and conceptualization during the early years of life.

Intelligence

THE PROBLEM OF INFANT INTELLIGENCE

If any psychological finding has a claim to being axiomatic it is the observation that so called infant tests of intelligence are poor predictors of later intellectual level. Virtually everyone who has reviewed the research in this area (e.g., Goodenough, 1949; Jones, 1954; Bayley, 1955; Cronbach, 1962; Landreth, 1962) agrees that the usefulness of infant tests as predictors of later intelligence varies as a joint function of (a) age of initial testing; (b) the time interval between initial examination and retest (including the events which occur within that interval). By and large the earlier the test is given, the lower the correlation with later tests of mental ability and the shorter the interval between test and retest, the larger the correlation. Tests, for example, given prior to the third year are of little predictive value with respect to intelligence scores attained in middle childhood (Bayley, 1940). On the other hand tests given during the third year correlate significantly with IQs attained at age six (Ebert & Simons, 1943; Honzik, et al., 1948).

Reactions to this state of affairs have been of two sorts. On the one hand there are those who accept these findings as inevitable because of the different capacities assessed by infant as opposed to noninfant tests of intelligence. These writers reject the notion of intelligence as a fixed capacity or quantum of mental energy that remains relatively constant throughout life. As Bayley (1955) writes, "I see no reason to think of intelligence as an integrated entity or capacity which grows throughout childhood by steady accretions" (Bayley, 1955, p. 807). In a similar vein Goodenough suggests that it may not even be justified to speak of intelligence in infancy and speaks of "The unsettled question as to whether or not true intelligence may be said to have emerged before symbolic processes exemplified in speech have become established. Attempting to measure infantile intelligence may be like trying to measure a boy's beard at the age of three" (1949, p. 310).

Other writers, however, have reacted differently to this anomalous situation. While granting the validity of the findings regarding quantitative prediction of intellectual standing from infant tests, they claim that qualitative estimates of intelligence made in infancy may still be of value. That is to say, although one may not be able to predict the later quantitative scores on the bases of scores attained in infancy, one can make successful predictions from the infants' general level of functioning. Thus if infants were categorized in gross terms as mentally retarded, below average, average, above average, and superior with respect to intellectual ability and on the bases of infant tests, the predictive power of these tests for later intellectual standing would be considerably improved. From a practical standpoint, such predictions would be of value to institutions, as adoption agencies, which are in great need of infant predictive indices.

The evidence for the predictive validity of such qualitative evaluations, although not overwhelming, is sufficiently impressive to warrant further exploration. Since these studies are less well known than those which demonstrate the lack of quantitative relationship between infant and later intelligence, a few of them will be reviewed here. In one study, Illingworth (1961) sought to demonstrate that at the low end of the intelligence continuum a diagnosis of mental level in infancy will have considerable predictive value with respect to later ability. Illingworth found that in a sample of 122 infants given a diagnosis of mental inferiority in infancy, 30 died and 65 out of the 87 survivors had an IQ score of less than 70 when tested several years later. Despite these findings, however, Illingworth does not believe that, with the exception of mental subnormality, there will ever be a high correlation between infant tests of intelligence and IQ scores attained at later age levels.

This pessimism is not entirely shared by Simon and Bass (1956) who studied 56 infants tested before the age of one year and again prior to school age. When the infant test scores and the scores attained at the preschool level were grouped according to three categories—dull normal and defective; average; above average and superior—a significant relationship between the two sets of categorizations was obtained. These writers found, however, that this relationship was largely a function of having included children at the two extremes of retardation and superiority in the sample. Macrae (1955) using more subjects (102) and more categories (superior, above average, average, below average, and mentally defective) obtained similar results. The children were initially tested before the age of three with the Gesell Schedule and were retested after the age of five with the WISC. Of the 102 cases examined, only five cases deviated more than one category, and there was not a single instance of a deviation of more than one category. Furthermore, in striking contrast to all of the findings using quantitative scores, the predictive value of the infant tests was affected neither by the age at which the infant test was given nor by the interval between test and retest.

Escalona and Moriarity (1961) introduced clinical appraisal of total test performance into their calculations of the predictive value of infant intelligence tests. The subjects were 58 infants selected for "normalcy" on the bases of medical, social, and developmental criteria. Infant measures were (a) Gesell Schedule scores, (b) Cattell IQ scores, and (c) clinical appraisal based on total test performance. The subjects were again tested between the age of six and nine years with the WISC. The results indicated that for this sample, no method of appraisal predicted later intelligence range when utilized prior to the age of twenty weeks. For tests administered between twenty and thirty-two weeks of age there was a positive but not significant relationship with later measures of IQ. When clinical appraisal of test scores made during this same age period (twenty to thirty-two weeks) were related to later intellectual standing, significant correlations were obtained. The authors conclude, "When infant assessments were examined for their ability to distinguish between subjects who would later be of average or above intelligence, clinical appraisal (but neither of the test scores) achieved these discriminations at a highly significant level" (1961, p. 604).

Knobloch *et al.* (1963) also found that clinical assessment was a successful way of predicting later intellectual level and argued for giving up the test-score method of infant evaluation.

Although these studies are not free from methodological defects—a statement which also holds true for the studies dealing with quantitative scores—the results do suggest that if the full range of intellectual variation is taken into account and this variation is dealt with categorically rather than numerically, then the assessment of infant intelligence can predict intellectual level at later ages. Put differently, one might say that infant examinations may be useful in predicting gross differences in later intellectual level and particularly at the extremes (superior and mentally retarded range). For practical purposes, such as advising adoptive parents, such gross discriminations are much better than nothing and seem to justify the continued use of infant assessment methods for predicting later intelligence.

Do these findings refute the axiom that infant tests are poor predictors of later ability? Not necessarily. If intelligence is conceived in strictly quantitative terms as a score on a particular test, then the axiom still holds true. Infant tests cannot apparently predict later intelligence test *scores*. If, on the other hand, intelligence is conceived as a *ranking* relative to other children of the same age, then infant tests do seem to be able to predict the child's later standing with respect to his peers. Considering the fact that all intelligence scores are in reality ranks since they do not represent units—recalling six digits does not mean that one has two units more of memory than the person who recalls only four—the question boils down to just how much precision one is willing to settle for. If one is adopting a child even some precision is better than none.

INFANCY AND EARLY CHILDHOOD AS A CRITICAL PERIOD IN INTELLECTUAL GROWTH

The concept of the "critical period" seems to derive mainly from the work of ethologists such as Konrad Lorenz (1957) who used the term to describe some extraordinary circumstances of animal behavior. What Lorenz and others have observed is that there is a period during infancy when social attachments need to be made if they are to be lasting. Apparently these attachments are made regardless of species and Lorenz and other ethologists tell of chicks who follow them around as if they were the mother hen. Extensive work on this phenomenon has been done by Scott (1963) with dogs. Scott has shown that for dogs the period of socialization begins at approximately twenty days of age and continues for a few weeks thereafter. If social relationships are not established during this period it becomes increasingly difficult to do so later. Dogs with no experience of humans during this period are "wild" whereas those handled by humans during the same period are "tame."

It seems likely that something similar is apt to hold for the human infant. Schaffer and Emerson (1964) have, for example, shown that evidences of social attachments among infants begin to appear during the third quarter of the first year. The signs of such attachment are evidences of distress when a familiar person leaves the room, or when a stranger enters it. Infancy is not only a period when the child establishes social attachments, it is also a period in which it establishes a fundamental feeling tone about the social world. Erikson (1963) describes this attitude as one of *basic trust,* the feeling that the social world is reliable and that one's needs will be met. This attitude derives from the normal experiences of infancy in which the baby is cared for on an unconditional acceptance basis. In the absence of this unconditional acceptance and care, the child develops a sense of mistrust, the feeling that the world is a dangerous, fearful, and unreliable place, which then undermines all his later attempts to establish healthy interpersonal relationships.

These conditions, the establishment of emotional attachments and basic trust, thus seem to have their critical periods during the first year of life. If this is true then cognitive development must also have a critical period in infancy. This follows because for the infant, much more than for the older child and adult, intellectual and affective functions are undifferentiated. That is to say, anything which affects the child's affective equilibrium also affects his cognitive functioning. For the adult, whose intellectual abilities are fully developed, even severe neuroses may only dampen intellectual functioning. But for the growing organism whose intellectual capacities are in the process of development, emotional disturbance can be catastrophic. As the work of Ribble (1943), Goldfarb (1945), and Spitz (1945) suggests, lack of appropriate social and affective stimulation in infancy leads to devastating consequences in both the personality and intellectual spheres. It is for this reason that infancy can be regarded as a critical period in intellectual development. At this age social and emotional deprivation are equally intellectual deprivation.

It is not, however, simply deprivation which affects later personality and intellectual development. On the contrary, research is beginning to show that the nature and quality of the stimulation provided infants may have enduring effects. Although such research is only now gaining momentum, it promises to reveal much about the early influences on intellectual growth. To illustrate this line of research and some of the most interesting conclusions several representative studies will be reviewed in detail.

In one of the continuing reports from the Berkeley growth study Bayley and Schaefer report on the intercorrelations between maternal and child behaviors and intelligence over an age span of eighteen years. The patterns of correlations for the 61 subjects tested repeatedly during the first eighteen years of their lives were complex and varied with the age and the sex of the individuals involved. What emerged from the study was the importance of what might be called "parental emotional temperature"—from extreme warmth to extreme coldness—shown during the early years of the child's life for later intellectual development:

> Hostile mothers have sons who score high in intelligence in the first year or so, but have low IQs from age 4 through 18 years. The highly intelligent boys, in addition to having loving mothers, were characteristically happy, inactive and slow babies who grew into friendly, intellectually alert boys and well adjusted, extraverted adolescents. The girls who had loving, controlling mothers were happy, responsive babies who earned high mental scores. However, after three years, the girls' intelligence scores show little relation to either maternal or child behavior variables, with the exception of negative correlations with maternal intrusiveness. The girls' childhood IQs are correlated primarily with education of the parents and with estimates of the mother's IQ (1964, p. 71).

Bayley and Schaefer conclude that these results support the hypothesis of genetically determined sex differences. Their results suggest that the effect of the environment, particularly maternal behaviors, exerts a constant influence on the developing mental capacities of boys but not of girls. Apparently this study presents some empirical evidence for the proverbial hardiness of the female sex in comparison to males. If these results are accepted, the boy would seem to be much more susceptible to environmental influence than are girls. From a clinical point of view, this might explain why many more boys than girls have learning problems and get into trouble with the law.

Another study concerned with parent-child relationships has been reported by Kagan and Freeman (1963) on the basis of data from the Fels longitudinal research investigation. As in the Bayley and Schaefer report, the obtained relationships were complex and varied with age and sex. Kagan and Freeman, however, were concerned with a different parameter of parental behavior. This parameter, which might loosely be called *parental control*, involved such activities as restriction, coercion, protectiveness, criticism, acceptance, and affection. On the basis of their findings, Kagan and Freeman concluded that "Maternal justification of discipline during the ages 4 through 7 continued to be associated with higher IQ scores for both boys and girls even when mother's education was controlled. Moreover, for girls, early criticism was positively associated with IQ at ages 3½ ($r = .52$), 5½ ($r = .51$), and 9 ($r = .46$) with maternal education held constant" (1963, pp. 905–906).

Both Bayley and Schaefer and Kagan and Freeman are careful to point out the dangers of interpreting correlation as causation. It may be the case, for example, that the obtained correlations are mediated by other variables not directly studied. What does seem clear is that there is a host of parental behavior dimensions such as emotional temperature and control which may influence intellectual growth. When these dimensions begin to be combined in the same investigation we can expect the results to be even more involved and complex. And that, after all, is as it should be since human behavior is no simple matter.

In some cases, the parental parameters are bound to overlap. It is hard to imagine a warm mother who is also critical. But such conflicting, or apparently conflicting, patterns do seem to occur as in the cold, hostile mothers who breast feed their babies out of a sense of duty rather than affection (Heinstein, 1963). Children who receive this kind of double communication often develop serious emotional difficulties in later life. We are thus now only beginning to appreciate the variety of parental behavior dimensions which may influence intellectual growth. It is still too early to say with assurance that warmth or coldness, coercion or affection will have this or that effect upon the child until we can measure the whole spectrum of parental behaviors in combination. Although the two studies reported here are only a start in that direction, they do underscore the intricate chain of causation that underlies what were once thought to be simple and straightforward relationships between the intelligence of parents and their children.

Before closing this section on infancy as a critical period in the development of intelligence, it might be well to point out that some writers, namely Fowler (1962), have stressed the positive aspects of this hypothesis. Fowler's point is that infancy and early childhood have been neglected by educators and parents out of, to Fowler's view, a mistaken belief that education was not appropriate during the early years and that it might even interfere with the child's personality development. Quite the contrary, claims Fowler. He argues that gifted persons have routinely shown early cognitive skills such as reading or playing instruments prior to the age of three. Fowler claims that this is due to earlier intellectual stimulation and training experienced by such persons. To substantiate his claim, Fowler reports work with his daughter whom he taught to read at an early age and who at the age of eight had an IQ of 150 to 170. Fowler admits that the girl does manifest mild emotional problems although in general she gets along quite well. Fowler, like Watson (1928) and, apparently, Bruner (1960) seems to take an extreme environmentalist position which asserts that one can after all make a silk purse out of a sow's ear. The current revival of interest in the Montessori methods (1964) suggests that Fowler is not alone in his belief in the importance of early education.

The issues raised by Fowler are of extreme importance. Assuming that one can train children earlier than we have been accustomed to doing, what would be the purpose of such training? Is intellectual development purchased at the expense of something more valuable? And if it is not, is the educational system prepared to handle children who read and do mathematics when they enter kindergarten? In short the matter is not just a philosophical or scientific one, but an eminently practical issue. For the early education of children presupposes a fundamental change in the hierarchy of the educational system. What sense does it make to provide early education for children if they will then only be bored when they go to school. Those who wish to educate at an early age must face the fundamental fact of educational existence, to wit, that the wheels of change regarding educational practice grind exceedingly slowly.

We began this section with the statement that infancy and early childhood are a "critical period" in the development of intellectual functioning. Research dealing with emotional deprivation and with maternal interaction patterns does seem to indicate that intelligence is vulnerable in the early years just because it is not yet differentiated from affective components of personality. This is not to say that infants are mere passive lumps to be molded by experience and parental behaviors—far from it. Considering the variety of parental behaviors one has to assume that infants are surprisingly hardy critters who will develop relatively well under an amazingly wide variety of conditions. What we need to know are the lethal parental behavior combinations and dosages as well as the optimal ones. Research such as that of Bayley and Schaefer and of Kagan and Freeman is a start in the direction of attaining that knowledge.

THE MANY FACES OF CAUSALITY

The environment of the infant and of the young child can vary in so many different ways that it is possible to find a multitude of factors which may have an effect upon his intellectual development. There is no point in going over all of these materials in detail inasmuch as they have been frequently summarized in books and articles. There does, however, seem to be some value in reviewing the research on those factors which are particularly pertinent to the infancy and early childhood period. The three factors to be briefly considered here are prematurity, nursery school experience, and nutrition.

PREMATURITY

Does the child who does not develop to full term prior to birth develop normally thereafter? This is an extremely pressing question for parents of premature infants. Unfortunately, there is no simple answer to it. Indeed, there is not even complete agreement on what constitutes prematurity. Although most writers agree on the international criterion of 2500 grams (5½ pounds) others regard this standard as being too exclusive, inexact, and incomplete to meet the actual situation. Not only is the definition of prematurity in dispute, but the effects of early birth are particularly difficult to evaluate since premature children differ in many other ways from their full term cohorts.

"Their families tend to be poor and their mothers have often failed to use ante-natal services, have worked late in pregnancy or have had no help with the housework. They are also more likely to be girls, to be first born or to have mothers who are either much younger or older than average" (Douglas & Blomfield, 1958, p. 133). Differences between premature infants and full term youngsters are thus difficult to interpret since so many sociocultural differences are confounded with low birth weight.

One finding that does seem to hold across most studies of prematurity (e.g., Alm, 1953; Knobloch *et al.*, 1956; Drillien, 1958, 1964; Lubchenco *et al.*, 1963) is the negative prognosis for children of low birth weight (under 4 pounds). Such children are least likely to survive and, if they do, show a high incidence of retarded growth, physical illness, and handicaps as well as a high incidence of mental retardation and emotional disorders. Children with relatively high birth weights (above 4½ pounds) seem to have a better chance for normal growth and development (Capper, 1928; Mohr & Bartelme, 1930; Melcher, 1937; Alm, 1953; Knobloch *et al.*, 1956; Harper, 1959). Even in the case of high birth weight, however, the possibility of residual neurological deficit seems to be a possibility, and Douglas and Blomfield (1958) in a carefully controlled study found a higher incidence of reading difficulties among premature children than among normal controls matched for socioeconomic level, maternal age, and birth order. These investigators found no correlation between the incidence of such reading difficulties and birth weight. Thus, even among those prematures who seem to catch up with their peers in weight, height, and overall intellectual prowess, the possibility of residual deficit in specific intellectual areas such as reading is a very real consideration.

Apparently then, the outlook for premature children is not entirely reassuring. Parents of such children should probably be counselled in a realistic fashion as to the possibilities of illness and handicaps so as to be better prepared for them. It would probably also be helpful if school personnel were alerted to the special difficulties encountered by premature youngsters.

NURSERY SCHOOL EXPERIENCE

In retrospect, the effort expended in attempting to determine the effects of nursery school experience upon intelligence appears as so much wasted labor. Not only are the experimental difficulties enormous as Jones (1954) has pointed out, but the results have been for the most part negative. As Goodenough (1940) concluded "The attempts to demonstrate the differential effects of different kinds of school practice upon child achievement have been disappointingly meager when suitable controls have been employed" (1940, p. 330). The troubling fact about these studies is the apparent assumption that the nursery school environment and experience is necessarily more enriching than a home environment. Anyone who has spent time in nursery schools knows that the quality of nursery school teaching and practice is extraordinarily wide. The physical plants also vary tremendously. Given a finding that nursery school did improve IQ in a particular instance, one could hardly generalize from this to all nursery school experience. What is important is not going or not going to nursery school but rather what goes on within the nursery school or home setting.

In this connection it is interesting that no one has as yet attempted to compare children attending Montessori nursery schools with those attending schools with nonspecialized programs. In contrast to most nursery school programs the Montessori schools have a very structured regime (cf. Rambusch, 1962) which is quite directly aimed at facilitating cognitive development. With the revival of interest in the Montessori schools, research on the effects of nursery school experience may well be revived. The writer has heard of several studies of this kind in the planning stage. Such research would make sense, since it is reasonable to ask whether one system is more effective than another. Obviously many experimental difficulties are still involved, but the attempt to determine whether specific types of experience have an effect upon intellectual development seems more surely founded than an attempt to find whether a general difference in experience such as attendance or nonattendance at nursery school affects mental growth.

NUTRITIONAL FACTORS IN INTELLECTUAL DEVELOPMENT

The present-day concern with the underprivileged in America may well produce a spate of studies dealing with such factors as nutrition and intellectual development. Some are already available. As in all investigations dealing with IQ changes, they must be accepted with caution because of the numerous experimental difficulties such investigations must overcome. In an early study of this type Kugelmass (1944) attempted to determine the effect of nutritional improvement on Kuhlman-Binet scores of 182 children two to nine years of age, for a period of 14 years. Kugelmass reports that children undernourished at the time of first testing showed an average rise of ten points for those who were initially retarded and an average rise of ten points for those who were initially normal. For children well nourished initially and at the time of retesting, the mean gain in IQ was zero. Kugelmass stated that the chance of improvement of mental function is greatest if the child is young when nutritional therapy is instituted, since the IQ rise is insignificant if therapy is started after four years of age. Similarly, less well documented results were reported by Poull (1938) and Knobloch and Pasamanick (1953).

An interesting new tack in this type of research was recently taken by Stock and Smyth (1963) in Cape Town, South Africa. They explored the effects of undernutrition during infancy upon brain growth as measured by the circumference of the head. The subjects were two groups of 21 colored children. One group was severely undernourished during the first year and more or less so thereafter. The undernourished lived in abominable conditions, many were illegitimate and the mothers were neglectful and apathetic. The well nourished children came from homes where the mothers were much more adequate as persons. All of the children were followed from the first through the eighth year of life. Head circumference, height and weight, and IQ were all significantly less in the undernourished as opposed to the well nourished children. While the authors are aware that the IQ differential could well be accounted for in terms of the difference in emotional and cognitive climate experienced by the two groups, they nonetheless point out that the difference in head circumference could not reasonably be attributed to these factors, and that this head circumference difference does seem to support the hypothesis of a direct relationship between intelligence and nutrition. Obviously we need to know much more in this area before reaching any definite conclusions, but in a general way there does seem to be some relationship between nutritional status and intellectual development.

The Developmental Approach

COGNITIVE ACTIVITIES IN INFANCY

Although the sphere of cognitive activities is much more limited and much less differentiated in infancy and early childhood than it is among older children and adults, it is still possible to distinguish—at least for heuristic purposes—such activities as problem solving, memory, and conceptualization. The difficulty with making such distinctions is already familiar from the earlier discussion of intelligence. What we mean by memory, problem solving, and conceptualization in the very young person may be operationally and factually different from what we mean by these terms for the adult. There is thus always the question as to whether we are really talking about similar or parallel phenomena or phenomena which are epigenetically distinct from one another. What are needed are criteria that bypass the particular differences at each developmental level and which demonstrate the continuity of mental development across age levels. Such criteria are still lacking so that when we speak of problem solving, memory, and conceptualization below, the reservation that we may be talking about qualitatively different phenomena going under the same name must be kept in mind.

PROBLEM SOLVING IN INFANCY AND EARLY CHILDHOOD

Generally speaking, problem solving situations are those in which the subject is desirous of attaining some goal, the direct access to which is blocked in some way. When, for example, a child sees a box of candy on the top shelf of a cupboard, he is confronted with a problem situation. He desires the candy but is prevented from reaching it because of its height. If he recognizes that he can utilize the kitchen stool to climb to the top of the cupboard, he has solved the problem.

Several things should be noted about this situation. First of all, the solution clearly depends upon the child's past experience and learning. Without having experienced the sweetness of candy, it would not have been desired and there would have been no problem to be solved. Likewise, without having previously learned that stools, chairs, and benches could be used not only for sitting but also for climbing and jumping, their relevance to the problem solution would probably not have been recognized. Second, the attainment of a solution amounts to a kind of learning (Gagné, 1964). Once the child has discovered how to use the stool to mount to the top of the cupboard, he is likely to continue to use this solution whenever he wants to get things outside of his immediate reach. His behavior has thus been modified by past experience, he has therefore *learned* in the broad sense of that term.

The third characteristic of problem solving is that the goal can be attained in any number of different ways. In lieu of using the stool, the child could have pulled out drawers and constructed a stairway, or he might have used a stick to knock the candy off its perch. This last point is very important because it distinguishes problem solving from other types of learning in which the goal can only be attained in a manner prescribed by the experimenter. Problem solving allows for innovation and this is why it is frequently used to study the higher mental processes.

One of the issues that dominated problem solving research for many years was the question of trial and error versus insight. Do solutions to problems come suddenly as the cognitive field is reorganized or do the solutions emerge gradually as a result of trying out a variety of alternatives? An eclectic resolution of this conflict has been offered by Harlow (1949) who has described what he called "learning sets." After an animal or human subject has learned a great number of similar problems he becomes an expert with this type of problem and can solve them readily sometimes in a single trial. If the subject's past experience were unknown one might say that the solution was insightful when in fact it was based upon considerable previous experience. The data on problem solving in infancy seem to support a learning set hypothesis. Both trial-and-error and sudden insightful solutions have been observed in the very young and often are observed in one and the same child. In short, trial and error and insight are, in all likelihood, not mutually exclusive patterns but rather probably represent different phases of the problem solving process.

In the following discussion of problem solving the work done with infants will be presented separately from that done with young children. Investigators have seemed to use either infants or preschool children in their studies so that in order to deal with the problem solving of three-year-olds it is necessary to introduce investigations that employ children beyond the age brackets which are our primary concern. Rather than leave out the work with the three-year-olds, the studies with preschool children will be included here.

PROBLEM SOLVING IN INFANTS AND TODDLERS

In a study using infants and toddlers from six to twenty-seven months of age McGraw (1942) observed a variety of behaviors which ranged from gross emotional reaction to trial-and-error and sudden "insightful" solutions. McGraw placed her subject on one side of a sheet of plate glass and put a desired object, such as a bell, on the other. In one situation the child had to reach *over* the glass to reach the goal, in another it had to reach *around* the glass and in the third situation it had to *climb* over the glass to attain the goal object. McGraw's careful observations of infants' performances in this situation not only point up the difficulties of studying problem solving at this age level but also the wide variety of behaviors elicited by problem solving situations even in infancy and early childhood.

Using a different problem situation with children of approximately the same age, seven to twelve months, Richardson (1932) also found a wide variety of behaviors. Richardson employed a series of string problems of varying complexity. Each setting was constructed behind a screen so that the child could not view it until the task was presented. One of the strings was always attached to the goal object but the problem of determining which string was in fact attached was made easy or difficult depending upon the patterning of the strings.

In describing his results Richardson listed what he called five types of *perceptive attitudes* which he grouped according to whether or not insight was involved in the solution. Successful solutions without insight were described as (a) interest in the string rather than in the lure and (b) interest in the lure and apparent accidental contact with the string. Successful solutions with incomplete insight were described as (c) awareness of both lure and string without evident purposive utilization of the string and (d) experimentation. Success with insight was described as (e) definite utilization of the string as a means to bring the lure into reach. With increasing age more of the infants demonstrated "e" type solutions and were able to solve more complex string problems.

A rather simple problem, but interesting nonetheless, has been used by Gesell *et al.* (1950). It involves having the child put a pellet in a bottle and then retrieve it. The behavior trends noted by Gesell and his associates were as follows. At fifteen months the child dropped the pellet into the bottle and tried to extract it by shaking the bottle. If he did not succeed, he inserted his finger into the bottle so as to "hook it." Some children turned over the bottle to let the pellet fall out. Similar behavior was observed at eighteen months. At two years, however, the child dropped the pellet into the bottle and immediately tipped it over in order to retrieve the pellet. This is probably a situation where "learning sets" play an important role since pouring sand or water is a frequent play activity at this age level and the older children may have readily seen the relevance of this play activity to the problem situation.

What is important to note about these studies is how dependent the child's behavior is upon the nature of the problem situation as well as upon the age of the child. The one-year-old child who can solve Richardson's string problems straightaway might have trouble with getting the pellet out of the bottle. Whether or not the child shows insight or trial and error will thus depend upon the nature of the problem situation as much as it will upon the child's level of development. The child who fumbles and bumbles with one task may solve another quickly and with apparent insight. To be sure, the infant and toddler do not have all the mental tools available to the older child and adult, but with problems attuned to their capacities they can be quite efficient problem solvers.

PROBLEM SOLVING IN PRESCHOOL CHILDREN

The preschool child (two and a half to five) is energetic, verbal, and highly imaginative. Problem solving takes up not a little of his time. The adult is hardly aware of the many problems the child actually encounters. The writer, for example, was amazed to see the difficulty his thirty-four-month-old son had with a pair of children's scissors. He could not manage to hold the scissors with one hand and so had to use both. But then he had nothing to hold the paper with so that it never remained at right angles to the cut and merely slipped between the blades. After several attempts he became infuriated and nearly threw the scissors to the floor. He finally arrived at a solution by getting his father to hold the paper for him!

If there is any characteristic that seems at all unique to this age group with respect to problem solving it would seem to be that *although the preschooler can respond to and solve problems posed verbally, he is not able to verbalize his solutions*. This point, as well as others, is illustrated in a variety of studies some of which are described below.

In a study instigated by Piaget's (1951a) contention that children cannot make an exception to a rule, Hazlitt (1930) carried out several studies with three- to seven-year-old children. In one study she employed a Russian egg which is an egg-shaped shell made of wood and gaily painted to resemble a doll. The egg is hollow and opens at the midline. Within the shell is another egg which also opens up, and within it is still another egg, and so on. Some of these eggs contain as many as six or seven smaller eggs. Hazlitt took out all of the eggs and told the child to put all *except* the green one back together. The youngest child to respond successfully to this command was three to four years of age, well below the age Piaget had claimed children were unable to make an exception. In addition, when Hazlitt substituted the word *but* for the word *except* many more children made a successful response.

Using different materials Hazlitt asked children to put on a tray all those cards except the ones with a moon and a star. In this slightly

more complex situation the youngest child to make a correct exception
was 4.8 years. The difference between being able to respond to the
instruction to make an exception and being able to verbalize the exception was shown in Hazlitt's third experiment. The material consisted of
colored and ornamented cards mixed with twelve cards of the same
size and five smaller black cards. Hazlitt told the child that he was to
watch her and to notice what she called K_____. K_____ was called
out when each of the large black cards was put down. After this
experience the child was told to pick Ks out of the whole set of cards.
Many children who succeeded on this task in the sense of being able to
pick out the Ks were nonetheless unable to verbalize the solution, i.e.,
"All the black cards except the little ones are Ks." These children were
then given the sentence, "All the black cards _____ the little ones are
Ks" and were asked to fill the blank with one of the three words "although," "except" or "but not." Among the children who could not verbalize the rule not many were able to choose the word *except*. Similar results
with respect to verbalization were obtained by Roberts (1932) who found
that although children could find which of three doors always led to
the falling of an airplane, they could not verbalize the solution.

The ability of preschool children to understand verbal instructions
without being able to verbalize problem solutions was also illustrated in
the work of Harter (1930). Harter worked with three- to six-year-old
children and adults. Three performance tests, an obstacle peg test, a
canal box test, and a pulley test were the problems. In each of the tests
the solution of the problem consisted in recognizing that for a solution to
be attained, a series of moves had to be made in a prescribed sequence.
Thus, in the pegboard test there was a grooved path with side alleys. At
the end of one of the alleys and close to the center of the circular path
was a red hole. With the path were three styluses, one of which was
green, one of which was yellow, and one of which was red. The yellow
and green styluses were placed in the groove between the red stylus
and the red hole. A solution involved recognition of the fact that both
the yellow and green styluses had to be sidetracked into the short alleys
in order for the red stylus to be moved into the red hole.

Harter found that the average number of moves needed to attain
a solution decreased from a mean of 36.0 at age three years to a mean
of 17.6 at six years. This decrease in errors with age suggests that as
the child grows older he relies increasingly upon mental manipulation
of materials rather than upon overt trial and error behavior. It is not
far-fetched to suppose that at least some of this mental manipulation
is verbal in nature and that the ability to mentally manipulate things
increases as the child is able to internalize and utilize inner language.

Several other examples point to the same conclusion. Hamilton
(1911, 1916) presented subjects from twenty-six months to adulthood
with an insoluble problem. The subjects were presented with four doors
only one of which was unlocked on each trial. The task was to find
which door was unlocked on succeeding trials. There was, however, no
rational solution since Hamilton merely locked at random one of the

three doors that had previously been unlocked. For the unwitting subject this procedure suggests that there is a pattern or rule governing the procedure and he must discover what it is. The subject thus had to set up hypotheses, or in modern parlance, strategies, in order to solve the problem. In such a situation the optimum strategy is the one that maximizes the possibility of success, namely, to choose any door but the one that was previously locked. Hamilton described five different strategies that were employed by his subjects:

A. Trying three inferentially possible doors and avoiding the one that was previously locked.

B. Trying all four doors, each in irregular order.

C. Trying all four doors in regular order, right to left or the reverse.

D. Trying a given door more than once with intervening attempts to open some other door.

E. Repeated attempts to open a given door without intervening attempts at other doors, or persistent avoidance of a given door while attempting all others.

As might be expected, "A" or maximizing solutions, tended to appear more frequently with increasing age with 76 to 86 per cent of the adult subjects giving the maximizing pattern. It is at least possible that the ability to formulate some verbal rule was of importance for a maximizing solution in this insoluble problem.

Before closing this section on the problem solving behavior of young children it might be well to present a study in which the actual behavior of the child in the situation is described in some detail. Such descriptions convey better than anything else the variety and complexity of the behaviors elicited by problem solving situations.

Alpert (1928) used problems that were very similar to those employed by Kohler with the exception that she substituted toy for fruit as the goal objects or lures. In her study Alpert employed stacking problems, construction problems in which the child had to put together sticks to reach a toy, and tool problems in which the child had to use some object such as a stick in order to reach the goal. Among her nineteen- to forty-nine-month-old subjects Alpert noted a wide variety of behaviors from trial-and-error to sudden insightful solutions. The latter type of solution, however, generally appeared only after the child had been exposed to the problem several times. Here is the record of a child of thirty-eight months whose behavior depicts such a transition with a two stick problem.

First exposure. S examined one of the sticks and tried to reach objective with it over the top of the pen; examined the other stick and used it in the same way, repeating "I can't" over and over; tried out the stick between the bars, over the top of the pen, finally striking it viciously against the floor; complained bitterly, and tried again to reach as before, stretching and straining; tried to climb out and whined, "I can't." E terminated exposure to avoid fatigue.

Second exposure. S reached for objective as above and in ten seconds said, "Look, I can't," but continued her efforts; fitted sticks up against bars of pen, banged them together, etc. S tried to reach objective with her hand through the spaces, to force her way out, to shake the pen, etc.; said, "Dolly does not want me to get him."

Third exposure. As above, complaining intermittently and finally giving up.

Fourth exposure. S stretched for objective over top of pen, striking out angrily with stick, complaining and asking E to move object closer. S said, "Let's try big stick on little one," picked up the other stick, examined ends carefully and succeeded in fitting them with a shout of "bang." S angled for objective, reached it exultantly and repeated stunt several times (Alpert, 1928, p. 11).

For Alpert the criteria of insight were changes of facial expression and posture, tempo and precision of work, and verbalization of the solution. The most important factor in problem solution, according to Alpert, was the nature of the problem situation. In addition, emotional, temperamental. and mental factors all seemed relevant to the successful attainment of a solution. To this catalogue it is only necessary to add the wealth of the child's previous experience in general and the experience with the particular problem in particular.

Problem solving in preschool children thus has many of the characteristics to be found in problem solving at all age levels. The one outstanding characteristic of this age seems to be the ability to follow instructions without at the same time being able to verbalize the problem solution effectively. This suggests that verbal mediation is not an important factor in problem solving at this age level.

MEMORY PROCESSES

In the broadest sense, memory is involved in all psychological activity. To the extent that previous experience affects current behavior, to that extent is memory operative. Put differently, memory is the retention of what has been learned or experienced. Different forms of memory, however, need to be distinguished. One of the most elementary forms of memory and the form that is perhaps most prominent in infancy and early childhood is what might be called *sensorimotor memory*. This involves the retention of sensorimotor coordinations learned in the course of adapting to the immediate environment. Sensorimotor memory includes the retention of a variety of motor coordinations such as those involved in swimming and skating which may be learned in early childhood and not practiced for many years but whose traces nevertheless seem to remain and to facilitate relearning. Exposure to foreign languages in early childhood also seems to have lasting effects with respect to relearning and could be included in sensorimotor memory. Another type of memory that makes its appearance in the early years of life might be called *representative memory*. This type of memory involves the retention of certain means-end relationships. Representational memory is revealed, for example, when the child seeks objects that are no longer present to perception. Still a third form of memory that begins to appear as the child's language skills develop has often been called *rote memory*. This form of memory involves the repetition of heard language sequences which may but usually do not have an adaptive function. A fourth type of memory and one about which there is much disagreement as to whether it occurs in infancy might be called *historical memory* and involves the retention of experiences and images that fit within a spatial-temporal conceptual framework.

SENSORIMOTOR MEMORY

It is generally observed that motor skills acquired in early childhood are retained to some degree throughout life. Youngsters who learn to swim, ski, sail, or ride horseback as youngsters are usually more proficient in these skills as adults than are persons who attempt to learn them once they are grown up. Although this is probably due in large part to motor coordinations which are established early, it is probably also attributable to the emotional attitudes established in childhood. The adult who is relearning a childhood skill probably has fewer fears and inhibitions than another adult who has had no previous experience with the skill in question. Although these foregoing generalizations are common observations there has been little systematic research in this area.

In the area of language learning, which in the very young child is as much sensorimotor as it is symbolic, the efficacy of early experience has been demonstrated by the classic studies of Burtt (1932, 1937, 1941). Burtt was concerned with the effects of reading Greek passages to his infant son who was then taught these passages and others of equivalent difficulty as a child and as an adolescent. Learning the passages to which he had been exposed as a toddler was significantly more easy than learning new passages of equivalent difficulty at eight or fourteen years of age, but the effects had dissipated by the age of eighteen. Since Burtt's son did not understand the Greek passages that were read to him as an infant, the memory could not have been mediated by content or meaning and must have been mediated by some form of sensorimotor process or trace left by the early exposure to the passages.

REPRESENTATIONAL MEMORY

One of the classic ways of studying representational memory in young children is by means of the delayed reaction experiment. This is a variant of a game that most parents spontaneously play with their children. In essence the game involves hiding an object which is currently attracting the interest of the child to determine whether he can make use of the cues provided in the situation in order to find the object. A variant of the delayed reaction experiment is found on many infant intelligence scales and is a second-year item on the Stanford-Binet (Terman & Merrill, 1960). In the Binet test the materials consist of three small pasteboard boxes and a small toy cat. The child is told, "I am going to hide the kitty and then see if you can find it again." The cat is then hidden under the right, left, and middle boxes on successive trials to insure that successful responses do not occur by chance. For one trial the probability of a chance success is $\frac{1}{3}$ whereas for three trials the probability of success on all three on the basis of chance drops to $\frac{1}{27}$.

An early study of the delayed reaction was carried out by Hunter (1917) and is of interest primarily because Hunter postulated that prior to language acquisition the child employs "kinesthetic sensory ideas" as a means of finding the hidden object. An elaborate study by Miller (1934) gives some support to this kinesthetic ideas hypothesis in the sense that Miller's youngest subjects (11½ to 24 months) used position cues in bridging the delay interval whereas the older children tended to use color. Recent research by Soviet psychologists (Zaporozhets, 1965) and by Piaget and Inhelder (1956) seems also to suggest that kinesthetic imagery plays a considerable role in the mediation of problem solutions.

In addition to the question of what it is that mediates the delayed reaction, psychologists have been concerned with the length of the delay interval and its relation to age. Like so many similar psychological questions, the answer would seem to be that "it depends." First of all it seems to depend upon the nature of the discriminative response required. In a test employed by Charlotte Bühler (1930) a ball containing a chicken that pops out is given to the child. As the child plays with the ball, pressure upon it makes the chicken pop out. Later a second ball, similar to the first but without a chicken, is given to the child. If the child shows by its facial expression and associated behaviors that he expected something which did not occur, then the child is credited with a memory of the chicken. Using this procedure, the time interval between the presentation of the first and second balls can be varied to test for length of memory. The length of interval that produced a surprise reaction with this procedure ranged from one minute at ten or eleven months to seventeen minutes at twenty-one to twenty-four months.

Other studies concerned with the delay interval have used goal seeking responses as evidence of representative memory processes. In studies by Hunter (1917), Allen (1931), and Skalet (1931) the correct response was an actual uncovering of the hidden object. With this type of procedure, comparable to that of the Binet test described earlier, the length of the delay interval is somewhat shorter than that obtained by Bühler. One possible reason for this difference may lie in the fact that the Bühler procedure required only the recognition of an absent object whereas finding an object which is hidden, as in the standard delayed reaction procedure, requires a more active recall. The difference in underlying processes called upon in the two procedures could, in part at least, explain why children can delay longer on the Bühler apparatus. As children get older, longer delays are probably mediated by language elements as Skalet (1931) has suggested. Even some of her two-year-old subjects were able to find a goal object after a day-long interval. Such lengthy delays are unlikely to be mediated by transitory kinesthetic imagery, and a more likely possibility is verbal mediation.

It is perhaps well to point out here, however, that the utilization of language as a mediating mechanism is still quite elementary in the pre-school child and is apparently used in a systematic way only after the age of five or six, by which time language has to some extent become internalized (Kendler & Kendler, 1959). Among young children verbal signs may only serve to prolong the kinesthetic imagery rather than replace it as it seems to do among older children. In complex problem solving situations (Harter, 1930; Kendler, Kendler, & Wells, 1960) young children seem unable to use verbal mediation in an effective way. Nevertheless, it is perhaps well to recognize that verbal mediation has levels and degrees and that far from being a phenomenon that occurs only after school age, some forms of it may appear as early as the second year.

HISTORICAL MEMORY

Few people seem to be able to remember experiences that occurred prior to the third, fourth, or even fifth years of their lives. Different sorts of explanations have been given for this routine observation. Psycho-analytic authors often write as if they assumed that early experiences are retained and play an important part in later development. Freud's (1953a) notions regarding fixation at the early levels of development and Rapaport's (1954) model of thinking both imply that experiences during infancy and early childhood affect later development and be-havior and to that extent are retained or remembered. So long as such memories are regarded as sensorimotor in nature then there is some evidence, cited above, to the effect that such memories can be retained and have lasting effects.

On the other hand, if these memories are regarded as being com-parable, say, to an adult's memory of his last visit to the dentist, or of a dinner at a restaurant, the developmental psychologist would raise serious objections. That early experiences are sometimes thought of in these terms is reflected in the fact that some hypnotists argue that they can "regress" adults back to a preverbal level and uncover memories of the infantile period. Such a view flies in the face of our knowledge about cognition during the infantile period. True historical memory requires a spatial-temporal conceptual context. One can only remember an event by associating it with some particular place or time. Questions about past experience invariably contain temporal or spatial cues. We ask "What did you do last Saturday night?" or "How did you like Hawaii?" and without these spatial-temporal cues recall could not occur.

Now we know very well that the spatial-temporal concepts of in-fants and children are limited pretty much to the here and now or at most to the immediate past and the immediate future. It is not without reason that children's stories begin with the indefinite "Once upon a time" and usually occur in a spatial-temporal limbo. It is not until mid-dle childhood that children begin to have a true appreciation of historical time (Ames, 1946) as is evidenced by their language, their reading interests, and by the age at which history is introduced in the school curriculum.

The developmental psychologist thus does not deny that sensori-motor memories such as fixations persist throughout life nor that they may determine later behavior. What he does insist upon is that such memories are not cognitive in the sense of being labeled and dated and that they exist outside of the spatial-temporal conceptual context of cognitive memory. Freud himself (1953b) came to recognize that memories of childhood brought to him by his adult patients were in fact untrue when these were checked by objective sources. Such memories turned out to be "screens" for the real events which had occurred. Even screen memories, however, seldom date back before the fourth year. In short, truly cognitive or historical memory is probably not present until the school years and is not fully developed until later childhood and adolescence.

CONCEPT FORMATION IN INFANCY AND EARLY CHILDHOOD

Within psychology, concepts are generally thought of in behavioral terms as "the acquisition or utilization or both of a common response to dissimilar stimuli" (Kendler, 1961, p. 447). A child, for example, who calls a variety of differently shaped and colored objects "apples" is said to have a concept of apple if his designations are correct by adult standards. It is in this behavioral sense that animals can be said to have concepts since they too make common responses to diverse stimuli. In fact, however, concepts always have two aspects. On the one hand they have an *extension,* the population of objects, properties, or relations, to which the concept applies. On the other hand, they also have an *intension,* which corresponds to the feature or element that all of the objects, properties, or relations have in common.

From a developmental point of view, it would appear that during infancy the extensive aspect of a concept is cognitive whereas the intension is affective. Infants can, for example, distinguish between different geometric forms even when these are varied in size and orientation (Zaporozhets, 1965). By the end of the first year, the child recognizes his parents and a variety of objects despite changes in their appearance and this reveals a large store of extensive concepts. The meaning of these concepts or their intension is, however, affective rather than cognitive. The mother means warmth and affection, and the intension of the many objects the child can distinguish is measured by their positive or negative feeling tone.

With the development of language the child's conceptual sphere expands tremendously as he discovers that everything has a name. During the second year the child also discovers another form of representation, namely, pictures. The response to pictures is of importance because it reflects a new level of conceptual differentiation and an expansion of conceptual thinking to include pictures as well as things. According to Karl Bühler (1930) there are three steps in the development of pictorial recognition. At first pictures are no more than pieces of paper to be grasped and torn. A little later the child begins to recognize the picture and to treat pictured objects as if they were real. During this stage the child may be as frightened by a picture of a dog as of a dog itself. At the third stage the child appears to clearly grasp the notion of the picture as a representation of the real object. Bühler claims that this occurs at about the same age as the use of language and represents still another manifestation of the representational function which emerges at about the end of the first year of life.

Although the child does form a wide range of extensional concepts during these years it is necessary to point out that these concepts are less differentiated than those of older children and adults, even though they may appear to be quite similar. Every word that stands for a concept is ambiguous in the sense that it can stand either for an example of the class or for the class as a whole. The word *man*, for example, can mean a particular person or men in general. Older children and adults use both words appropriately, depending upon the context. Young children, on the other hand, fail to distinguish between individual and class designations of words. Piaget (1951b), for example, tells of his daughter who, on a walk, saw a slug and said, "There is the slug we saw yesterday," demonstrating that she did not distinguish between the particular slug and other exemplars of the class. Mothers whose children call strange men "daddy" are victims of the same phenomenon.

As children grow older, the intention of concepts gradually expands to include functional as well as affective meanings. Objects come to mean "what they can be used for" in addition to "how they make one feel." While these functional meanings are already implicit in the child's behavior during the second and third years of the child's life, they are not verbalized until much later. Indeed, the verbalization of intensive meanings seems to follow a parallel development to that reflected by the child's behavior with the exception that it occurs several years after the extensive development which it parallels. When at the age of four and five, children begin to be able to give verbal definitions, these are often perceptual-affective in nature. An apple is "red" or "sweet" and only later is it "something to eat" or a bicycle something to ride. The verbalization of intensive meaning thus lags behind its comprehension as evidenced by behavior, but follows the same developmental sequence.

With these general remarks as a starting point it might be well to make them concrete by describing the development of a few concepts in more detail.

It appears that children have conceptualized a variety of simple geometric forms by the age of two, the age at which the three-hole form board (square, triangle, circle) is placed on the Stanford Binet (Terman & Merrill, 1960). Recognition of these same forms in a rotated position occurs at a slightly later age, indicated by its being placed at the two-year, six-month level on the Binet. The difference would seem to be entirely due to the triangle since neither the square nor the circle are altered by rotation. Simple number concepts are also present by about the age of two years and most children can utilize "one" and "two" without much difficulty (e.g., Beckmann, 1923; Giltay, 1936). These are primitive numerosity concepts, however, since animals can make similar discriminations (Dantzig, 1954) and no one would claim that animals have a concept of unit which is necessary for a true conception of number.

Of particular interest with respect to children's concepts are those which Kant called *categorical*. These concepts—space, time, and causality—are imperative in the sense that regardless of the nature of "true reality" we can only experience within these categories. These are not innate ideas but rather principles according to which our experience is organized without our being able to help it. From a developmental point of view it is of interest to inquire how these organizing concepts change with age. We owe to Piaget (1954) the first intensive study as to how these organizing concepts develop in infancy. Piaget's observations and interpretations are impressive and have engendered considerable research (e.g., Wolff, 1959; White *et al.*, 1964).

CATEGORICAL CONCEPTS DURING
THE FIRST TWO YEARS OF LIFE

Kant wrote that although one could not deny the reality of the external world, one could not at the same time deny that everything regarded as external was at least in part dependent upon the thinking and perceiving subject. That is to say, the world we know is always limited by our organs of knowing. There are, for example, many forms of stimulation, such as high-frequency sounds, that are not within the sphere of our experience but are very much within the sphere of certain animal species such as dogs. Many other such examples could be cited, and von Uexküll (1957) has given vivid illustrations of perceptual worlds other than our own. Our knowledge of the world is, according to Kant, not simply limited by the sense organs but also by the innate organizing tendencies of the mind. Just as we cannot escape being sensitive to some stimuli and not to others, so can we not escape organizing our world within a spatial, temporal, and causal framework. We have, in Kant's view, really no choice in the matter, and all our experience is organized within such a framework. Kant, however, wrote as if these categories were the same in children as in adults, i.e., a priori. What Jean Piaget (1954) has shown is that although the child does seem to organize his experience within the categories described by Kant, the categories themselves go through a gradual process of construction.

This is not to say that the infant is aware of space, time, and causality as we know them. Far from it! On the other hand, it is possible for an observer to see in the infant's actions a causal, temporal, or spatial framework of which the infant is probably not aware. The situation is a little analogous to certain computers that can be programmed to play chess or write novels. To say that the computer operates in an intelligent way is not the same thing as saying that it is conscious of its intelligence, but only that it behaves *as if* it were. The same is true for infants in whom we can observe intelligent behavior without, at the same time, having to assert that the infant is aware of its intelligence. With these cautionary remarks in mind we can proceed to the development of the categorical concepts in infancy.

THE CONCEPT OF THE OBJECT

Although not a categorical concept in the Kantian sense, the concept of the object is one of the fundaments of all categorical thinking and of all later conceptual developments and so must be dealt with. Although to the adult objects such as a chair or a table seem to be "out there" and to be separate from their physical properties (hardness, texture, color) and action properties (to be sat upon, leaned against, stood on), this is not the case for the very young infant.

In his brilliant studies of his own three infants during their first years of life, Piaget (1954) has provided evidence of the enormous labors involved in constructing the concept of an object. For Piaget the infant does not have a true object concept until he can represent it as evidenced by his pursuit of that object in its absence. This point is not reached, however, until the middle of the second year of life and is prefaced by a series of behaviors that gradually lead up to this representation. During the first few months after birth objects are really not distinguished from the actions associated with them. An object is simply something to suck, to grasp, to push, or merely to look at. When the object disappears, say the bottle removed before the infant has satisfied his hunger, he may continue to suck as if the sucking would reconstitute the object. Likewise, when the mother leaves the room, the infant continues to look at the point where the mother disappeared as if watching would bring the image back.

Between the third and seventh and eighth months after birth the child comes increasingly to differentiate the object from his own actions and to recognize that it has movements or trajectories of its own. One evidence of this differentiation is that the older infant now looks at the place where an object will land, after it has been dropped, rather than its position before it has dropped. Still another evidence of this differentiation is the recognition at this age level of an object from seeing only a part of it. This does not mean, according to Piaget, that the child conceives of a whole object, part of which is hidden. On the contrary, Piaget believes that the infant regards an object emerging from behind a screen to be in the *process of formation*. Still another interesting behavior at this age level is the child's ability to neglect an object and then return to it after an interval of time. All of these observations suggest that the object is coming to be regarded as something which exists independently of the infant's perceptual and motor activity. This point is not fully reached, however, until several additional skills are mastered.

One of the next advances in attainment of the object concept, which Piaget says occurs between the age of eight and ten months, occurs when the infant begins to search for objects that have been hidden behind a screen. What marks this stage distinctively is that the child actually removes the screen himself. Piaget, for example, describes hiding a cigar case under a cushion after which his son Laurent (age nine months, seventeen days) immediately raised the cushion in order to find the object. (Prior to this age the child ceased to pursue an object hidden before his eyes.) The behavior of this stage was, however, governed by a very important restriction which Piaget describes as follows: "The child looks for and conceives of the object only in a special position, the first place in which it was hidden and found" (1954, p. 50). That is to say, if the object is first hidden under one screen and then under another, both displacements visible to the child, the child nonetheless looks under the first and not the second screen.

During the second year of life the child gradually advances to the stage where he can recognize the position of an object even after it has been hidden in three successive positions. This ability, to take account mentally of the successive displacements of a hidden object, is for Piaget the mark of a true object concept. Such behavior suggests that the child can deal with objects as independent of his own perception and as having independent positions and trajectories in space.

SPACE CONCEPTS

Many of the observations that Piaget used to describe the development of the object concept can equally well be employed to illustrate the attainment of space concepts. In the development of space, however, Piaget makes it clear just how complex and intricate are the unconscious coordinations by which the infant gradually orients himself and things within a spatial framework. One can get a rough idea of some of the difficulties involved by imagining oneself in a strange city whose narrow, winding streets are unmarked and for which there is no map or guide available. To learn the plan of the city one would have to make one's own map in a sort of trial-and-error fashion. Constructing a kind of map space is only one of the many problems of space conceptualization faced by the infant.

According to Piaget (1954) the infant progresses during the first two years of life from an initial sense of *practical space* to a *subjective space* and eventually to an *objective space*. To understand the differences between these three forms of spatial concept, we must begin by noting that any spatial concept involves the coordination of positions in a systematic way. These positions may either be of things or of the child in relation to things. Practical, subjective, and objective space correspond to different levels of differentiation and integration of these two kinds of positions.

Up to about the age of three months the infant can be observed to move his glance from one to another of a series of objects. From the point of view of the observer this type of visual behavior already implies a notion of space. It is still a practical notion because the child deals with positions in terms of his activity, looking, and the positions of objects are still not separated from the movement needed to perceive those positions. There are thus as many practical spaces or positions as different activities. The child might thus be said to have a buccal (mouth) space, a tactile space, a visual space, kinesthetic space, and so on. Practical space is revealed whenever the child shows an awareness of the position or displacement of things with respect to a particular activity as in the following example:

> From 0;2 Laurent knows how to carry to his mouth an object grasped independently of sight and how to adjust it empirically. . . . At 0;3 he puts a clothespin in his mouth, adjusting its position so that he may suck it (Piaget, 1954, p. 107).

Beginning about the fourth month of life and extending until about the tenth, the child evolves what Piaget calls a *subjective* space. What seems to occur is that the various practical spaces begin to be coordinated one with the other. In Piaget's view the central condition for the establishment of these coordinations is the development of prehension, the ability to deal with things manually. Once prehension emerges, the child begins to grasp for what he sees, tastes, or feels and in this way gradually begins to bring together the spatial information obtained from each of the different sensory avenues. As a result he is able "to relate certain of his own movements to those of the environment" (Piaget, 1954, p. 114). Here is an example of this type of coordination:

> At 0;6 he (Laurent) directs his eyes towards an object after having touched it. But he cannot see it because of various screens (Piaget, 1954, p. 115).

From the age of about nine or ten months and extending into the second year the young child gradually elaborates what Piaget calls an *objective* space. At this age the coordination of positions and displacements of subjective space come gradually to be divorced from the child's activity as a whole and to be regarded as independent of his own influence. At the same time the child also begins to see himself and his positions as but one object among many objects in the spatial field. The crucial evidence for the attainment of objective space is that the child's recognition of the movements and displacements of things in the environment is reversible. This means simply that the child recognizes that an object moved from one position to another can be moved back again. Although this would seem to be the simplest of ideas, it is in fact extraordinarily complex. When the child does demonstrate the recognition of this, it indicates a fundamental change in spatial organization. Instead of regarding objects as having fixed positions, he suddenly comes to see positions as more or less temporary *states* of objects. This transition from a static to a dynamic way of viewing reality also occurs in the verbal and logical plane, as we will see later.

Although Piaget derived his notions of practical, subjective, and objective space from his observations on his three infants, older children seem to manifest similar stages in the mastery of more complex spatial problems. In a study by Meyer (1940) preschool-age children's spatial concepts were tested by having them fit wooden forms together and by determining their understanding of the rotations of a pivoted bar. With these tasks Meyer claims to have found Piaget's stages repeated between the ages two and five. In brief, Meyer found that up to the age of two or two and a half, children showed only a *practical* space in the sense that they regarded objects only as something to satisfy their needs. Between the ages of three and four Meyer found what resembled Piaget's *subjective* space in the sense that although the children were still centered on their own activities, they also manifested some interest in the objects themselves, independent of their own immediate needs. After the age of four Meyer reported that the children manifested *objective* space in the sense that they considered themselves as but one object among many and that they attempted to adjust their own behavior to the position of objects.

TIME CONCEPTS

As in the case of the object and space, Piaget finds a gradual development in infancy from a practical time to a subjective and finally to an objective time by the end of the second year of life. During the first few months of life the infant shows a practical grasp of time in the sense that it knows how to coordinate its movements in time and how to perform certain actions before others in a regular order. Piaget notes, for example, that even at two months the infant turns its head when it hears a sound and tries to perceive what it has heard. These sequences, although suggesting some temporal ordering, do not imply that the child has any awareness of time. This is to say, the actions could occur in a reflex fashion without any sense of causal connection between the two.

Beginning about the age of three months the infant begins to construct what Piaget calls a *practical* time series. By this he means that the child begins to perform a series of actions that are not determined entirely by the external stimulations acting upon him. At this stage the infant adds to the simple reflex series of the previous stage the results of his past experience so that his action no longer appears reflexive but rather purposive. Consider the following illustration:

> abs 169 At 0;3 (13) Laurent, already accustomed for several hours to shake a hanging rattle by pulling the chain attached to it . . . is attracted by the sound of the rattle (which I have just shaken) and looks simultaneously at the rattle and at the hanging chain. Then while staring at the rattle, (R), he drops from his right hand a sheet he was sucking, in order to reach with the same hand for the lower end of the hanging chain (C). As soon as he touches the chain, he grasps and pulls it, thus reconstructing the series C-R (Piaget, 1954, p. 330).

What this illustration shows is that the child knew he had to drop one thing in order to attain another just as he knew he had to pull the chain in order to shake the rattle. It is the use of intermediary means to a goal that differentiates the purposive from the pure reflexive act and that suggests a temporal as well as a causal series. Piaget also argues that it is at this stage that one sees the beginning of memory formations. The child now not only recognizes the mother but also localizes her in the recent past. If she comes into the room and sits down while the infant is playing, the infant may note this and return to its play. Moments later it may again look toward where the mother is seated giving evidence of a recent memory.

From about the eighth or ninth month and extending through the second year, the child gradually constructs what Piaget calls an *objective* time. Some of the observations relevant to the attainment of the object-time notion are significant here. First of all, the child begins to search for hidden objects, which means he has ordered a series of perceptions of memories within a temporal sequence. As he grows older the child begins to be able to take account of successive displacements of the hidden object which implies a still more elaborate temporal organization of perceptual memories. Finally, toward the middle of the second year a "true" objective sense of time appears to the extent that the child begins to symbolize or represent temporal sequences and durations by means of words.

CAUSALITY

The development of elementary causal conceptions in the infant follows the pattern we have become familiar with in discussing the other categories. Beginning as practical causality in which psychological efficacy and physical force are undifferentiated, the infant progresses to the more or less complete practical separation of physical and psychic causality by the end of the second year. During the first few months of life the child's reflex behaviors are the only indices of causal connections. As Piaget puts it:

> Whether the nursling at the age of one or two months succeeds in sucking his thumb after having attempted to put it into his mouth or whether his eyes follow a moving object, he must experience, though in different degrees, the same impression: namely, that without his knowing how a certain action leads to a certain result, in other words that a certain complex of efforts, tension, expectation, desire, etc., is charged with efficacy (1954, p. 229).

For Piaget then, causality during the early months of life consists in little more than the feeling of effort experienced in connection with the resistance of things.

From about the third to the seventh or eighth month a new level of causal behavior emerges which Piaget calls *magico-phenomenalistic causality*. This it will be recalled is the period in which active prehension emerges and, hence, the coordination of vision and other sense modalities with movement. At this stage the infant becomes witness to, and takes interest in, three types of action: movements of the body, movements which depend upon body movements, and movements that are independent of the child's actions. In Piaget's view, the infant begins to discover causal relations in the process of observing the three types of movement. Children at this level of development "find their hands" and begin to associate the feeling of efficacy with the visual perception of hand movements. Likewise, the feeling of effort when pushing or shaking a rattle comes to be associated with the sight of the movement of the rattle and with its sound. Piaget calls this stage "magico-phenomenalistic" because the child fails to distinguish the sphere of its efficacy from the sphere of movements wherein it lacks efficacy. The infant, for example, may shake its leg on seeing a doll at a distance as if this act would move the doll. Piaget also argues that even when the child of this stage pulls a string to make a toy rattle, he does not realize that there is an intermediary between his action and the effect. It is the fact that the infant behaves as if his gestures alone could produce physical results that accounts for Piaget's attaching the magico-phenomenalistic label to this period. (Traces of this kind of causality can still be seen in adults who try to influence the course of a bowling or billiard ball with "body English.")

Beginning at about the seventh or eighth months of life and extending to the latter half of the second year Piaget found what he regarded as the gradual attainment of an objective sense of causality. By objective with respect to causality Piaget means that the child comes to distinguish between physical and psychological causes. At the outset of this period the child only dissociates causality from his own actions without at the same time attributing causality to objects. Then, at about one year of age, "the child recognizes causes that are entirely external to his activity and for the first time he establishes among events perceived links of causality independent of the action itself" (Piaget, 1954, p. 279). Here is an example:

> At 1; (28) Jacqueline touches with her stick a push cat placed on the floor, but does not know how to pull it to her. The spatial contact between the stick and the cat seem to her sufficient to displace the object. . . . Finally at 1;3 (12) Jacqueline utilizes the stick correctly; objective and spatialized causality are therefore applied to the physical conditions of the problem (Piaget, 1954, p. 284).

Finally, toward the middle of the second year of life the objectification of causality is completed with the beginnings of representation. What this means is that at this point the child begins to take account of causes that are outside his immediate sphere of perception, something he did not do heretofore. He comes at this final point in the development of practical causality to be, in Piaget's words, "capable of reconstructing causes in the presence of their effects alone." Here is one example of representative causal behavior:

> At 1;4 (4) Laurent tries to open a garden gate but cannot push it forward because it is held back by a piece of furniture. He cannot account either visually or by any sound for the cause that prevents the gate from opening, but after having tried to force it he

suddenly seems to understand; he goes around the wall, arrives at the other side of the gate, moves the armchair which holds it firm and opens it with a triumphant expression (Piaget, 1954, p. 296).

At this final point the child shows clearly that causality is no longer merely perceptual and that by means representation he can reconstruct causes and anticipate consequences not immediately present.

It might be well, at this point, to summarize in a general way the process of conceptualization that occurs during the first two years of life as disclosed by the work of Piaget. What Piaget argues is that the infant begins in an egocentric universe in which there is nothing other than that which directly concerns his own activities and needs. It is thus a world that, in terms of the object and space, does not transcend the images and spatial relations that are immediately given in perception. It is a world, moreover, in terms of time and causality, that does not go beyond the immediate present. With increasing age the child gradually becomes aware of a world that is independent of his perception and action and that manifests laws and sequences that are independent of his will. By the end of the period, with the aid of representation, he recognizes the existence of objects not present to perception and the relativity of spatial position while his notions of time and causality expand backward to the past and press forward to the future. The egocentric universe has thus been transformed into an objective world.

At the same time, however, it must be recognized that this achievement holds only on the plane of perception and action. For, at the age of about two, the child begins to construct a new universe on the level of verbalization and representation. And, in the process of constructing this verbal, representational universe he again begins egocentrically and only gradually extricates himself to discover the objective verbal and representational world. For Piaget, each new, higher level of conceptual functioning demands a new structuring of experience. This is as arduous as that undertaken at the previous level of mental functioning.

Summary

This chapter began with the distinction between two broad approaches to the study of cognition in infancy and early childhood. Within the mental measurement approach three separate issues were taken up. The first issue was that of the usefulness of predicting IQs on the basis of infant tests. It was concluded that there is some promise of effective prediction if projections are based on categories of ability rather than upon numerical scores *per se*. A second issue dealt with the hypothesis of infancy as a critical period in intellectual development. This hypothesis was held to be supported by the literature which suggests that infancy is a critical period with respect to healthy personality growth. Since the infant is particularly vulnerable to deviations from a normal expectable emotional environment and since, during infancy, cognitive and affective factors are closely intertwined it follows that if infancy is a critical period from the affective point of view, then it must as a matter of course also be a critical period from the point of view of cognition. The third issue taken up dealt with several of the many causative agents affecting infant intelligence including prematurity, malnutrition, and nursery school experience.

With respect to the second, developmental approach, three issues were again taken up. The first of these concerned problem solving in infancy and the issues of insight vs. trial and error as well as the role of verbal mediation. It was concluded that in infancy problem solving behavior was dependent pretty much upon the nature of the task and that both trial and error as well as insight could be observed and could well represent different phases of the problem solving process. It was suggested that verbal mediation in problem solving may operate at different levels and make its first appearance at about two years of life. A second developmental issue was that of memory. Different forms of memory were distinguished and work upon them summarized. It was concluded that all forms of memory, sensory, motor, rote, and representational were present in early childhood with the exception of historical memory which does not make its appearance until middle childhood. The final issue taken up was that of concept formation in infancy. After distinguishing between the intensive and extensive aspects of concepts, the emergence of several fundamental concepts was described. The section was closed with a detailed summary of Piaget's work on the development of the categorical concepts during the first years of life.

The aim of this review was not to summarize all the available literature on the topic of cognition in infancy, but rather to point to issues that seem worthy of further research and exploration. The scientific study of cognition is only in the present day coming into its own right as a field of investigation and dogmatism is unwarranted. As we saw with respect to the question of the value of infant tests in predicting later IQ levels, today's truth can be tomorrow's fallacy. It is in this spirit that the present discussion has been offered.

References

Allen, C. N. Individual differences in delayed reaction in infants. *Arch. Psychol., New York*, 1931, 19, No. 127.

Alm, I. The long term prognosis for prematurely born children. A follow-up study of 999 premature boys born in wedlock and of 1002 controls. *Acta Paediat.*, 1953, Supplement 94.

Alpert, A. The solving of problem-situations by preschool children. *Teach. Coll. Contrib. Educ.*, 1928, No. 323.

Ames, L. B. The development of the sense of time in the young child. *J. genet. Psychol.*, 1946, 68, 97–125.

Bayley, N. Mental growth in young children. *Yearb. nat. Soc. Stud. Educ.*, 1940, 39, Part II.

———. On the growth of intelligence. *Amer. Psychol.*, 1955, 10, 805–818. Reprinted in Y. Brackbill & G. G. Thompson (Eds.), *Behavior in infancy and early childhood: A book of readings.* New York: Free Press, 1967.

Bayley, N., & Schaefer, E. Correlations of maternal and child behaviors with the development of mental abilities: Data from the Berkeley growth study. *Monogr. Soc. Res. Child Develpm.*, 1964, 29, No. 97.

Beckmann, H. Die Entwicklung der Zahlleistung bei 2–6 jährigen Kindern. (The development of number achievement in two- to six-year-old children). *Z. angew. Psychol.*, 1923, 22, 1–72.

Bruner, J. S. *The process of education.* Cambridge: Harvard Univer. Press, 1960.

Bühler, C. *The first year of life.* New York: Day, 1930.

Bühler, K. *The mental development of the child.* London: Rutledge & Kegan Paul, Ltd., 1930.

Burtt, H. E. An experimental study of early childhood memory. *J. genet. Psychol.*, 1932, 40, 287–295.

———. A further study of early childhood memory. *J. genet. Psychol.*, 1937, 50, 187–192.

———. An experimental study of early childhood memory: Final report. *J. genet. Psychol.*, 1941, 58, 435–439. Reprinted in Y. Brackbill & G. G. Thompson (Eds.), *Behavior in infancy and early childhood: A book of readings.* New York: Free Press, 1967.

Capper, A. The fate and development of the immature and of the premature child. *Amer. J. Dis. Child.*, 1928, 35, 262–288; 443–491.

Cronbach, L. J. *Educational psychology.* (2nd ed.) New York: Harcourt, Brace & World, 1962.

Dantzig, T. *Number, the language of science.* New York: Macmillan, 1954.

Douglas, J. W. B., & Blomfield, J. M. *Children under five.* London: George Allen & Unwin, 1958.

Drillien, C. M. Growth and development in a group of children of very low birth weight. *Arch. Dis. Childh.*, 1958, 33, 10–18.

———. *The growth and development of the prematurely born infant.* Baltimore: Williams & Wilkins, 1964.

Ebert, E., & Simons, K. The Brush Foundation study of child growth and development. I. Psychometric tests. *Soc. Res. Child. Develpm. Monogr.*, 1943, 8, No. 2.

Erikson, E. H. *Childhood and society.* (2nd ed.) New York: Norton, 1963.

Escalona, S. K., & Moriarity, A. Prediction of school age intelligence from infant tests. *Child Develpm.*, 1961, 32, 597–605.

Fowler, W. Cognitive learning in infancy and early childhood. *Psychol. Bull.*, 1962, 59, No. 2, 116–152.

Freud, S. Character and anal erotism. *Collected papers.* Vol. II. London: Hogarth, 1953. (a)

———. Screen memories. *Collected papers.* Vol. V. London: Hogarth, 1953. (b)

Gagné, R. M. Problem solving. In A. W. Melton (Ed.), *Categories of human learning.* New York: Academic Press, 1964.

Gesell, A., & Ames, L. B. Tonic-neck-reflex and symmetro-tonic behavior. *J. Pediatr.*, 1950, 36, 165–176.

Giltay, M. Sur l'apparition et le développement de la notion du nombre chez l'enfant de deux à sept ans. (Concerning the appearance and development of the notion of number in children from 2–7 years.) *J. Psychol. Norm. Pathol.*, 1936, 33, 673–688.

Goldfarb, W. Psychological privation in infancy and subsequent adjustment. *Amer. J. Orthopsychiat.*, 1945, 15, 247–255.

Goodenough, F. L. New evidence of environmental influence on intelligence. *Yearb. nat. Soc. Stud. Educ.*, 1940, 39, No. 1, 307–365.

———. *Mental testing.* New York: Rinehart, 1949.

Hamilton, G. V. N. A study of trial and error behavior in mammals. *J. Animal Behav.*, 1911, 33–36.

———. A study of perseverance reactions in primates and rodents. *Behav. Monogr.*, 1916, 3, No. 2.

Harlow, H. F. The formation of learning sets. *Psychol. Rev.*, 1949, 56, 51–65.

Harper, P. A., Fischer, L. K., & Rider, R. V. Neurological and intellectual status of prematures at three to five years of age. *J. Pediatr.*, 1959, 55, 679–690.

Harter, G. L. Overt trial and error in problem solving of preschool children. *J. genet. Psychol.*, 1930, 38, 361–372.

Hazlitt, V. Children's thinking. *Brit. J. Psychol.*, 1930, 20, 354–360.

Heinstein, M. I. Behavioral correlates of breast-bottle regimes under varying parent-infant relationships. *Soc. Res. Child Develpm. Monogr.*, 1963, 28, No. 4.

Honzik, M. P., MacFarlane, J. W., & Allen, L. The stability of mental test performance between two and eighteen years. *J. exp. Educ.*, 1948, 17, 309–324.

Hunter, W. S. The delayed reaction in a child. *Psychol. Rev.*, 1917, 24, 74–87.

Illingworth, R. S. The predictive value of developmental tests in the first year, with special reference to the diagnosis of mental subnormality. *J. child Psychol. Psychiat.*, 1961, 2, 210–215.

Jones, H. The environment and mental development. In L. Carmichael (Ed.), *Manual of child psychology.* New York: Wiley, 1954.

Kagan, J., & Freeman, M. Relation of childhood intelligence, maternal behaviors and social class to behavior during adolescence. *Child Develpm.*, 1963, 34, 899–911.

Kendler, T. S. Concept formation. In P. R. Farnsworth, O. McNemar, & Q. McNemar (Eds.), *Annual review of psychology*, 1961, 12, 447–472.

Kendler, T. S., & Kendler, H. H. Reversal and non-reversal shifts in kindergarten children. *J. exp. Psychol.*, 1959, 58, 56–60.

Kendler, T. S., Kendler, H. H., & Wells, D. Reversal and non-reversal shifts in nursery school children. *J. comp. physiol. Psychol.*, 1960, 53, 83–88.

Knobloch, H., & Pasamanick, B. Further observations on the development of Negro children. *J. genet. Psychol.*, 1953, 83, 137–157.

———. Predicting intellectual potential in infancy. *Amer. J. Dis. Childh.*, 1963, 107, No. 1, 43–51.

Knobloch, H. Rider, R., Harper, P., & Pasamanick, B. Neuropsychiatric sequelae of prematurity, a longitudinal study. *J. Amer. med. Ass.*, 1956, 161, 581–585.

Kugelmass, I. N., Poull, L. E., & Samuel, E. L. Nutritional improvement of child mentality. *Amer. J. med. Sci.*, 1944, 208, 631–633.

Landreth, C. *The psychology of early childhood.* New York: Knopf, 1962.

Lorenz, K. Comparative study of behavior. In C. H. Schiller (Ed.), *Instinctive behavior.* New York: Inter. Univer. Press, 1957.

Lubchenco, L. O., Horner, F. A., Reed, L. H., Hix, I. E., Jr., Metcalf, D., Cohig, R., Elliott, H. C., & Bourg, M. Sequelae of premature birth. *Amer. J. Dis. Child.*, 1963, 106, 101–115. Reprinted in Y. Brackbill & G. G. Thompson (Eds.), *Behavior in infancy and early childhood: A book of readings.* New York: Free Press, 1967.

MacRae, J. M. Retests of children given mental tests as infants. *J. genet. Psychol.*, 1955, 87, 111–119.

McGraw, M. B. Appraising test responses of infants and young children. *J. Psychol.*, 1942, 14, 89–100.

Melcher, R. T. Development within the first two years of infants prematurely born. *Child Develpm.*, 1937, 8, 1–14.

Meyer, L. E. Comprehension of spatial relations in preschool children. *J. genet. Psychol.*, 1940, 57, 119–151.

Miller, N. E. The perception of children: A genetic study employing the critical choice delayed reaction. *J. genet. Psychol.*, 1934, 44, 321–339.

Mohr, G. J., & Bartelme, P. Mental and physical development of children prematurely born. *Amer. J. Dis. Childh.*, 1930, 40, 1000–1015.

Montessori, M. *The Montessori method.* New York: Schocken, 1964.

Piaget, J. *Judgment and reasoning in the child.* London: Routledge, & Kegan Paul, Ltd., 1951. (a)

——. *Play, dreams and imitation in childhood.* New York: Norton, 1951. (b)

——. *The construction of reality in the child.* New York: Basic Books, 1954.

Piaget, J., & Inhelder, B. *The child's conception of space.* New York: Humanities Press, 1956.

Poull, L. E. The effect of improvement in nutrition on the mental capacity of young children. *Child Develpm.*, 1938, 9, 123–126.

Rambusch, N. M. *Learning to learn.* Baltimore: Helicon Press, 1962.

Rapaport, D. On the psychoanalytic theory of thinking. In R. P. Knight & C. R. Friedman (Eds.), *Psychoanalytic psychiatry and psychology.* New York: Inter. Univer. Press, 1954.

Ribble, M. A. *The rights of infants.* New York: Columbia, 1943.

Richardson, H. M. The growth of adaptive behavior in infants: An experimental study of seven age levels. *Genet. Psychol. Monogr.*, 1932, 12, 195–359.

Roberts, K. E. The ability of preschool children to solve problems in which a simple principle of relationship is kept constant. *J. genet. Psychol.*, 1932, 40, 118–135.

Schaffer, H. R., & Emerson, P. E. The development of social attachments in infancy. *Soc. Res. Child Develpm. Monogr.*, 1964, 29, No. 3.

Scott, J. P. The process of primary socialization in canine and human infants. *Soc. Res. Child Develpm. Monogr.*, 1963, 28, No. 1.

Shirley, M. Development of immature babies during their first two years. *Child Develpm.*, 1938, 9, 347–360.

Simon, A. J., & Bass, L. G. Toward a validation of infant testing. *Amer. J. Orthopsychiat.*, 1956, 26, 340–350.

Skalet, M. The significance of delayed reactions in young children. *Comp. Psychol. Monogr.*, 1931, 7, No. 34.

Spitz, R. A. *Hospitalism: An inquiry into the genesis of psychiatric conditions in early childhood on the psychoanalytic study of the child.* New York: Inter. Univer. Press, 1945.

Stock, M. B., & Smyth, P. M. Does undernutrition during infancy inhibit brain growth and subsequent intellectual development? *Arch. Dis. Childh.*, 1963, 38, 546–552.

Terman, L. M., & Merrill, M. A. *Stanford-Binet intelligence scale. Manual for the third revision, form L-M.* Boston: Houghton Mifflin, 1960.

von Uexküll, J. A stroll through the world of animals and men. In C. H. Schiller (Ed.), *Instinctive behavior.* New York: Inter. Univer. Press, 1957.

Watson, J. B. *Psychological care of infant and child.* New York: Norton, 1928. Reprinted in part in Y. Brackbill & G. G. Thompson (Eds.), *Behavior in infancy and early childhood: A book of readings.* New York: Free Press, 1967.

White, B. L., Castle, P., & Held, R. Observations on the development of visually directed reaching. *Child Develpm.*, 1964, 35, 349–364.

Wolff, P. H. Observations on newborn infants. *Psychosom. Med.*, 1959, 21, 110–118.

Yale University, Clinic of Child Development. *The first five years of life: A guide to the study of the preschool child.* New York: Harper, 1950.

Zaporozhets, A. V. The development of perception in the preschool child. In P. H. Mussen (Ed.), European research in cognitive development. *Monogr. Soc. Res. Child Develpm.*, 1965, 30, No, 2, 82–101.

Chapter 7

The Development
of Social Behavior

DARRELL K. ADAMS

$\mathbb{S}$ocial behavior is essentially a descriptive concept referring either to the interaction of two or more individuals or to the influence of one individual upon another. Defined broadly in this way, the applicability of this concept to early human development is limited because relatively few psychological phenomena would fail to qualify for inclusion. Additionally, this kind of definition fails to specify a criterion for the acquisition of new social responses. Investigators in this area have therefore tended to use more specific definitions of social behavior. Fortunately, perhaps, the descriptive concept of social behavior lends itself to classificatory analysis, which permits the researcher to coordinate more specific aspects of the concept to observable behavior.

Traditionally, the concept has been subdivided into fairly major categories of behavior. Four categories are frequently used: (1) behavior that is influenced by the presence and/or the behavior of other persons (e.g., various forms of behavior subsumed under the label of "social reinforcement"); (2) behavior that is aimed at influencing other people (e.g., a child's dominant behavior in a free-play situation, or "showing off" antics when company visits the home); (3) behavior associated with and peculiar to membership in identifiable groups (e.g., interaction patterns as affected by group size, group composition, use of materials, physical facilities, and the like); and (4) behavior that is directed or controlled by organized society and its institutions (e.g., family, church, school).

The first two of these classifications correspond to the individual, the third to the group, and the fourth to the social-structural, institutional, or cultural levels of analysis. The focus of the present chapter is on the social behavior of the individual child (that is, what he *does* rather than what is done to him) within the context of these levels of analysis. Each level will be treated independently and, when appropriate, developmentally.

Whenever an examination of a particular research area is attempted, there are limitations in the scope and content that are necessarily imposed. The major limitation here is one of age: all studies include at least one subject under thirty-six months of age. As much of the literature on the social behavior of children has focused on subjects from four- to six-years-of-age, and older, an important limitation upon coverage was thus produced. Nonetheless, adherence to this criterion came to serve an important purpose—that of demonstrating the relative paucity of research in the area of early social behavior.

Individual Social Development

The bulk of information about the sequential aspects of early social behavior has come from studies now some three decades old. Most of these studies were observational in nature and many lacked controls that would now be expected. Formal theory—or even systematic conceptual orientations—played minor roles in shaping this research. Typically the researcher proceeded in one of two ways. According to the first approach, a particular aspect of behavior that seemed social (e.g., laughing, crying, smiling, and so on) was selected, occurrences of that behavior in a standardized situation were observed, the apparent cause of the behavior was noted, and then extensive tabulations of the findings were presented, frequently subject by subject. According to the second approach, gross behavior was observed, recorded, categorized (social, emotional, motor, and so on, with subdivisions of each), and developmental trends were established for the categories on a longitudinal or a cross-sectional basis. Despite frequent methodological inadequacies, these studies have provided a general view of the development of social behavior in the early years that remains valuable.

Specific manifestations of social behavior, as such, are not present at birth. As Murphy, Murphy, and Newcomb (1937, p. 554) observed:

> The newborn infant may smile, but this smile is no more social than a Babinski reflex or his ability to support his body suspended in mid-air by grasping a pencil. The newborn baby can breathe, cough, hiccough, blink, smile, cry in different tones and with different forms of mouth opening, sneeze, yawn, move his head, hands, arms and legs, as well as show a wide range of specific reflexes from sucking and avoiding to cries and starts. Yet neither the smiling nor the crying, nor any of the multitudinous combinations of skeletal behavior that appear in his repertory, are specifically social responses.

The development of social behavior requires that responses be elicited by a social stimulus—one in which another person is an integral component. As the infant grows and matures, his ability to discriminate between social and nonsocial sources of stimulation increases. Simultaneously, the inventory of different responses increases as the infant develops physiologically. It is the new association between responses or patterns of responses and social stimuli that constitute early social development rather than the emergence of new kinds of responses.

Rudimentary social behavior has been observed in young children and described in a number of early studies. Bühler (1927) studied the reactions of children of the same age to one another in a play situation through the first eighteen months of life. Observation of individual differences in reactions to these situations led Bühler (1933) to distinguish between "socially blind," "socially dependent," and "socially independent" behavior even at these early ages.

A procedure similar to Bühler's was used by Maudry and Nekula (1939) in a study of ninety-two children from six to twenty-five months of age. The subjects were paired with a partner within three months of the same age to form a "baby party" in a playpen. For the first four minutes no play material was present. During the second four minutes a hollow cube was given to each child and a third cube was placed midway between them. At the beginning of the third four-minute period the cubes were removed and a bell was given to one child. Next a drum was placed between them and drumsticks were provided. Finally, during the last four-minute period, a ball was introduced and the subjects were shown how to roll it from one to the other. Except when the play materials were being changed, the subjects were alone together. Their responses were observed from behind a screen, recorded in diary fashion, and coded into categories of contact and positive or negative social interaction. To analyze trends in development during these ages, the records were examined with special emphasis on the initial reaction to the situation, the reactions to the partner, and "fights and games" during the interaction. The trends in social responsiveness were noted as follows:

Six to eight months: Approximately as many positive contacts as negative contacts were made; little attention was paid either to the partner or to the play material; nearly half of the social overtures were ignored; interference was as often devoid of social intention as it was a positive or negative social reaction; friendly contact was limited to looking, smiling at, and grasping for the partner; the partner was treated about the same as the play material; fighting was equally impersonal, and consisted of socially blind attempts to secure materials.

Nine to thirteen months: Play materials became important and were responded to first; as the partner became an obstacle to their possession, negative interaction increased and fighting attained its highest level (this was the most frequent behavior throughout the situation). Free materials (those available to both) were preferred, and conflict became personal for the first time when play materials were in the possession of the partner.

Fourteen to eighteen months: There was a tendency to shift attention to the partner when the desire to play with the materials had been satisfied. There was also less conflict over play materials.

Nineteen to twenty-five months: There was increasing recognition of the opportunity for social contact and integration of social and play material interests. Positive social relations predominated during this period: play was personal, with each subject adjusting his behavior to his partner's activity, and the play materials became the means for establishing positive social relations rather than a source of conflict.

Of particular interest was the changing role of the partner in the situation. As Maudry and Nekula pointed out, the partner's role was ". . . successively that of play material (6–8 months), obstacle to play material (9–13 months), and playmate (19–25 months)" (1939, p. 215).

The general sequence of social perception and response indicated by Maudry and Nekula has been supported in the work of a number of investigators. The summary of observations of 62 infants from three weeks to twenty-four months of age provided by Bridges (1933) indicates a comparable expansion of awareness of adults as well as of other children as social stimulus objects. Mengert's (1931) study of ten two-year-olds in a paired, free-play situation, found a preponderance of "friendly" rather than "unfriendly" behaviors which corresponds to the changes in the nineteen- to twenty-five-month category of Maudry and Nekula. Washburn and Hilgard (1934) studied 76 subjects from eighteen to fifty-four months of age in a free-play situation. As age and experience increased, a general development away from the individual types of play and toward the social was noted.

During the first year of life it is particularly difficult to isolate specific responses in a way that permits a clear distinction between social and nonsocial behavior. The rapid changes in the physical characteristics, perceptual and motor abilities, and the learning and gradual emotional differentiation that occur, all interact to produce the patterns of responses which ultimately will be meaningfully characterized as social. For most infants the principal source of continuing social stimulation is an adult—usually the mother. Bühler and Hetzer (1930) provided extensive observational examples of children's responses to adults occurring during their first year of life. Although the reactions noted are interesting, the sample was small enough at each age level so that the generality of the findings remains uncertain. As motor development occurs so that crawling and walking become possible, the number and variety of stimuli impinging upon the child increase substantially. Necessarily then, the opportunities for contact with social stimulus situations increase. Both social awareness and social responsiveness are accelerated as the child moves into the preschool years.

The increased association with peers either in informal, spontaneous play or in more structured nursery school situations provides both the opportunity and the necessity for social interaction. A number of investigators (Loomis, 1929; Barker, 1930; Arrington, 1932; Beaver, 1932; Van Alstyne, 1932; Parten, 1933b; Robinson & Conrad, 1933; Updegraff & Herbst, 1933; Manwell & Mengert, 1934; Mallay, 1935a; Mallay, 1935b; Heathers, 1955) have studied the social processes that occur in groups in play situations.

Beaver (1932) studied the different ways that preschool children in group situations initiated social contacts. Five-minute observation records were made on 32 children between the ages of twenty-six and forty-five months. There were between twenty-four and thirty-three separate observations of each child during periods of spontaneous play.

The mode of social contact was analyzed into the following categories: *material verbal,* involving an exchange of both an object, e.g., toy and conversation; *material nonverbal,* an exchange of only an object; *nonmaterial verbal,* a verbal exchange only; and *nonmaterial, nonverbal,* in which neither objects nor words were exchanged. Beaver provides a graphic example of the latter category: "Two babies stood about a foot apart, solemnly inspecting each other. Suddenly one raised his arm and struck at the other without warning. He was within easy reach of the other child, but he did not touch his person. Baby Number Two blinked and batted his eyes, but raised his arm and returned the gesture. Though not a word was spoken nor either person touched, no one could deny for a moment that something in the nature of social intercourse was taking place" (1932, p. 5). Beaver found a distinct tendency for the number of social contacts to increase with age $(r = .69)$. Younger children used more material contacts in their initiations, whereas older children relied on the use of verbal contacts. With increasing age, the preschool child increasingly attempts to initiate social interaction, and is less reliant upon materials, e.g., toys, to mediate the initiation of interactions.

A number of investigators (Barker, 1930; Arrington, 1932; Van Alstyne, 1932; Updegraff & Herbst, 1933) were concerned with the effects that different play materials might have upon the nature of social interaction. Van Alstyne observed preschool children from two to five years of age in a free-play situation. Records were made of choice and subsequent use of play materials. Clay seemed to sustain interaction and be associated with cooperative interaction. Updegraff and Herbst studied the same problem. They observed and recorded the social behavior in dyads of subjects ranging in age from two to four years. The relative superiority of clay in sustaining cooperative social interaction was not supported. It would seem that understanding the dynamics of social interaction is not likely to be advanced substantially by the study of effects of play materials upon that interaction.

Techniques for analyzing the quality of social interaction in play situations have been varied. Loomis (1929), for example, observed nursery school subjects in a free-play situation for the number and types of physical contacts as indicators of social behavior. More extensive coding systems were used by Parten (1933a; 1933b), and by Manwell and Mengert (1934).

Parten (1933b) studied the social play of thirty-four children between two and five years of age. The coding system used a dimension from minimum to maximum degree of social involvement. Six specific categories were defined: *unoccupied,* no apparent activity; *solitary,* independent play with materials different from those in use around him; *onlooker,* watching other children but not engaged physically or verbally with them; *parallel activity,* playing alongside other children with similar materials; *associative activity,* play with other children in which turns are taken or materials are exchanged; and *cooperative play,* in which all children are working toward a common goal and there is some social organization. Social participation scores were obtained for each subject by algebraically summing weights from -3 (unoccupied) to $+3$ (cooperative play). Parten found these scores to be positively correlated with age ($r = .61$), indicating that more time is spent in associative and cooperative kinds of activity as age increases.

Manwell and Mengert (1934) studied thirty-five subjects from twenty-one to forty-five months of age. These investigators were concerned with age and sex differences in choice of play activities, the changing interests in play activities, the relationship between use of language and types of play, and the relationship between group play and types of play activities. Differences were found between the two- and three-year-old children in language frequency, imaginative play, group play, manipulative play, and watching others. The three-year-olds had higher scores on the first three items and lower scores on the last two. In the choice of play activities, sex differences were found only for physical play, with boys scoring higher. Speech occurred with equal frequency in all types of play except constructive activity (where the frequency was lower). The two-year-old subjects talked as much alone as when playing with others. The three- and four-year-old subjects talked more in groups.

The data collected by Parten (1933b) and Manwell and Mengert (1934), then, along with the findings of Goodenough (1930), Robinson and Conrad (1933), Heathers (1955), and Mallay (1935b) provide evidence that between the ages of two and three there is a rapid increase in both the variety and the complexity of social behavior patterns. There seem to be substantial positive correlations between practically all overt social behavior patterns. Individual differences, however, may be large, and they probably reflect both differences in intellectual ability and maturational level, as these variables affect the play interaction situation.

Other aspects of social behavior in various play settings have been studied by Bridges (1927), Arrington (1932), Parten (1932), Staples (1932), Isaacs (1933), Kellogg and Kellogg (1933), Washburn and Hilgard (1934), Mallay (1935a, 1935b), Bernhardt, Millichamp, Charles, and McFarland (1937), Fales (1937a, 1937b), Durkin (1939), Janus (1943), and Morgan and Morgan (1944).

Group Process and Structure

Play is not the only process that characterizes interaction among preschool children. Disputes, quarrels, and other forms of conflict occur, patterns of competition and cooperation appear, companionships and friendships arise, and there is the necessity for some degree of compliance or obedience to authority. Each of these topics has received the attention of investigators working with children in group settings.

In general, the needs of group members, or *demand-input,* increase as the size of the group increases and as the likelihood of immediate gratification of demand diminishes. It is not surprising then that as the child moves out of the family setting (ordinarily a small group) and into nursery school groups the immediate gratification of his needs and desires becomes less likely. He will encounter the necessity of subordinating some of his needs and desires to those of others, and this process not infrequently produces conflict.

Green (1933a, 1933b) studied the relationship between friendship, group play, and quarreling among forty nursery school children between the ages of twenty-five and sixty-five months. Green made time-sampling observations of thirty seconds a day for forty days. Some degree of positive relationship between friendship and quarrelsomeness was found ($r = .30$). Close friends were the most quarrelsome. This finding probably reflects the fact that "friends" are likely to spend more time together, thus increasing the probability of conflicting demands. A difference in the sex composition of groups was also related to quarrelsomeness. Boy-boy groups were most quarrelsome, boy-girl groups next, and girl-girl groups were the least quarrelsome. In general, boys quarreled more than girls. Age differences also appeared. Children under thirty months of age were least often the aggressor and most often passive, but tended to rely most upon physical behavior in disputes. Three-year-old subjects tended to be most quarrelsome, and the older children relied upon verbal behavior in conflicts.

Another study of conflict behavior was that of Jersild and Markey (1935). Each of their fifty-four subjects, age two to five years, from three nursery school groups that differed in socioeconomic status, were observed in free-play situations during ten fifteen-minute periods. Outdoor play situations accounted for eight of the ten periods, while the other two were indoors at times when the observed subject was with at least four other children. Observers recorded all behavior in diary fashion. These diary data were coded for nature, frequency, and intensity of conflicts. The conflicts were then analyzed by age, sex, IQ, height, weight, national background, group differences, and the role of adults in the conflict. The results indicated that although conflicts occurred frequently (approximately every five minutes), they were usually no longer than twenty to thirty seconds in duration. Although the number of conflicts declined irregularly with increasing age, the duration of conflict increased with age. Again, boys were found to engage in more conflicts than girls, as did children from lower socioeconomic groups. Practically all aspects of conflict behavior were positively related, e.g., frequency of instigation and frequency of reception of aggression, the number of conflicts won and the number lost. Twenty-four subjects were followed up a year later and observed in the same way. A high degree of consistency in individual behavior for both conflicts and frequency of aggression was found. The relationships between height and weight and conflict behavior, and those between conflict and national background were generally inconclusive.

A number of studies have, in part or in whole, dealt with conflicts, disputes, quarrels, and anger in young children (cf. Bott, 1928; Berne, 1929; Goodenough, 1931; Greenberg, 1932; Etziony, 1933; Isaacs, 1933; Ricketts, 1934; Koch, 1935; Jersild & Fite, 1937; Andrus & Horowitz, 1938; McFarland, 1938; Roff & Roff, 1940; Landreth, 1941; Blood, 1961).

While Green (1933a, 1933b) and Jersild and Markey (1935) used time-sampling techniques, Dawe (1934) used behavior sampling in a study of the quarrels of nursery school children. The group studied included 40 subjects (19 girls, 21 boys) ranging in age from twenty-five to sixty months. Observers stationed themselves daily in the playground and watched for quarrels to develop. Quarrels were timed and observation forms were completed as soon as the quarrels ended. The findings from 200 quarrels suggest a summary of the generalizations which can be made about children's conflicts.

First, the duration of young children's conflicts is short, generally lasting one minute or less. This finding probably reflects the interaction of such factors as a short span of attention, differential ages of those involved, the tendency of adults to move in quickly, and so on.

Second, boys quarrel more frequently and tend to be more aggressive during quarrels than girls. This finding reflects the tendency in our society to reinforce assertive behavior in males and acquiescent, dependent behavior in females.

Third, quarrelsomeness tends to decrease with age. This is probably the result of negative reinforcement for quarrelsomeness as well as the child's ability to delay gratification.

Fourth, quarrels tend to become less physical and more verbal with increasing age, although when physical conflict occurs in older subjects it is more violent. Increasing verbal fluency is probably the central reason for this change. When words fail, however, affective involvement is usually substantial and the physical manifestations correspondingly extreme.

Relatively few studies have directly confronted the processes of competition and cooperation at the preschool level, although a number of studies (Bott, 1928; Berne, 1929, 1930; Van Alstyne, 1932; Isaacs, 1933; Klein & Wander, 1933; Updegraff & Herbst, 1933; McFarland, 1938) have touched upon either competition or cooperation or both processes in the context of other concerns.

The studies which have dealt directly with competition (Greenberg, 1932; Leuba, 1933; Hirota, 1951) have found surprisingly few manifestations of the process in preschool peer groups. Greenberg studied pairs of children two to seven years of age in a building-block situation. At first the subjects were simply invited to use the building blocks; both sharing the same pile of blocks. After they had finished their constructions, the children were asked which was prettier. Finally, they were instructed to see who could build the prettier arrangement. Observations were made of both verbal and behavioral indications of competition. For the subjects as a whole, competition increased with age; however, in the two- to three-year-old category no competition was observed. A pegboard test was used by Leuba (1933) in a study of rivalry in subjects ranging in age from twenty-one months to six years. Subjects were observed alone at the pegboard task and then paired with another subject on the basis of age and original pegboard performance. Although pegboard performance and rivalry responses both increased with age, rivalry responses from the youngest subjects were infrequent. (The two-year-old children usually merely looked at each other.) Hirota (1951), in an extensive study of competitive and noncompetitive situations, using 343 subjects from two to seven years of age, found little evidence for either cooperative or competitive responses among the two-year-old children.

Wolfle and Wolfle (1939) studied the development of cooperative behavior in monkeys and young children. Eight monkeys and eight children thirty to sixty-eight months of age were placed by pairs (monkey-monkey, child-child) in separate, adjoining cages. Levers were provided whereby the subjects could alternately provide one another with food. In general, the monkeys showed little cooperation whereas the children's cooperation increased with increasing age. The difference in cooperation were attributed largely to the presence of verbal communication in the children.

The results of these studies seem to indicate that competition between members of peer groups is quite infrequent at the preschool level. However, the limited situations covered by these studies necessarily restrict the range of competitive behaviors which can be evoked. A number of alternative explanations for such findings are possible.

First, behavioral manifestations of competition in young children are frequently negatively reinforced. Learning that there is a socially acceptable *and* a socially undesirable way to engage in competition, as well as the frequently subtle distinctions between the two, is a difficult process. An experimental situation including an adult observer is not likely to evoke competitive behavior if—as is likely—the child expects punishment as a consequence. The use of one-way observation windows, which is standard practice in much current research, would largely eliminate this kind of difficulty.

Second, the situation may be too artificial for the child at that level to provoke feelings of competition.

Third, the pairing of subjects may have neglected a crucial variable —the degree of personal relationship previously existing between them. At this level of development, competition may require something more than a superficial relationship—a degree of affective involvement not present in casual acquaintances. It is, of course, possible that it is too early in development to have learned the general competitive attitude prevalent in our society. Most nursery schools actively discourage overt competition. If it is too early in development, the generalization implied by the results of the studies cited above is valid. It would seem that more imaginative research in this area is necessary before accepting such conclusions.

Fourth, competitiveness is a complex process in children of any age. There has to be the right mixture of individual propensities and situational requirements to produce competitive behavior. If the child is reticent enough, few situations will be sufficiently compelling to arouse competition. If the stakes are not high enough, the child is unlikely to compete. The rivalry that frequently occurs between siblings provides an illustration of a situation where the stakes often prove to be high enough to arouse competitive behavior. A number of studies (Foster, 1927; Ross, 1930; Sewall, 1930; Smalley, 1930; Sperling, 1952; Thomas, Birch, Chess, & Robbins, 1961) have shown that competition between siblings for parental love and attention not only occurs at these age levels, but also is demonstrated in many different ways ranging from jealousy and ignoring to physically aggressive behaviors. If investigators of competition in preschool peer groups could devise situations which had at stake something as significant as adult love or affection, there is little doubt that competitive behaviors could be evoked.

As preschool children interact in group situations, patterns of mutual attraction will gradually be established. The process and nature of friendship formation and related positive social relationships have received the attention of a number of investigators (Mengert, 1931; Challman, 1932; Green, 1933a, 1933b; Jersild & Fite, 1937; Shirley, 1939; Slama-Cazacu, 1961). In its most frequent usage, the term "friendship" refers to sustained, mutually rewarding social interaction between two individuals. This usage is not totally appropriate when applied to preschool children because of the relatively short duration of friendships at these ages. Additionally, as Thompson points out, friendships at this age level are not always reciprocal:

> A child may seek the company of another child, call him his friend, and meet a number of his social needs through associating with him, whereas the second child may find the first child's company boring, unpleasant, or downright painful. Although such unilateral friendships are usually temporary attachments, they may persist for long periods of time in some social situations. Thus, we see that friendship is an extremely nebulous concept, ranging all the way from parasitic social attachments to social symbiosis. This vagueness of definition does not, however, negate the importance of friendships in the child's social development. The confidant, the "buddy," the "chum," and the "pal" have been appropriately eulogized in modern song and ancient verse. A close friend gives the child a type of social-emotional support which is unlike that found in any of his other personal relationships (1962, p. 487).

There is ample evidence of apparently substantial need for social contact even among young children. As the child grows there is less opportunity for sustained interaction with those such as parents who earlier provided most of the social contact and reward. It is generally accepted that it is desirable for the child to cut the close ties to his mother and to broaden his base of interaction to include those outside the immediate family. This process is often painful, and children frequently seek supplementary forms of social stimulation. This is illustrated by Ames and Learned (1946) who studied 210 children between the ages of two years and three months, and five years and ten months. They found that there was a substantial use of spontaneous fantasy play including the use of imaginary companions, impersonation of animals or humans, animation or personalization of objects, and general imaginative play. For some children, then, the need for social contact produces interaction at the fantasy level if either the peer companions are unavailable or the child feels too insecure in real peer interaction.

One frequently used technique for studying friendship is to observe children's selections of companions while they are engaged in free play. Under such circumstances the constraints upon spontaneous selection are less imposing than they would be in more structured activities such as classroom or adult-supervised games. Hagman (1933), for example, used a quantitative coding system in observing the companionships of a two-year-old and a four-year-old group of preschool children. The most and the least frequent companions were paired in a standard interaction analysis situation. Differences in interaction indices were correlated with such variables as sex, chronological age, mental age, height, and weight. While most of these variables were essentially uncorrelated, some individual differences and differences between the two groups proved to be important. First, the individual variation in choice of companions was large: some children selected companions very much like themselves whereas others spent most of their time with very dissimilar children and in the interaction situation some reacted to a companion more than 40 per cent of the time while others reacted less than 5 per cent of the time. The principal difference between the age groups was the sex preference in companions. The two-year-olds showed no sex preference, whereas the four-year-olds preferred to be with their own sex. A slight difference was found in the time spent in companionship reactions, with the older subjects devoting 58 per cent of their time to companions and the younger group only about 50 per cent. This latter finding suggests that as children grow older there is a decreasing dependence upon adults for emotional and social support and a corresponding increase in peer orientation. The results of Heathers' (1955) study of nursery school play in two groups of subjects (two-year-olds vs. four- to five-year-olds) in which emotional dependence, emotional independence, play categories, and social interaction were studied over a year's time, supported the same conclusion—an increasing focus on peer interaction and subsequent decrement in dependency relations upon adults.

While the studies by Challman (1932), Mallay (1935a, 1935b), and Heathers (1955) used observational techniques where subjects were aware they were being observed, studies by Mengert (1931) and Cockrell (1935) were among the earliest to use indirect observational techniques, so that subjects were not directly aware of the fact that their behavior was being observed. Mengert used time-samplings of the friendship behavior of ten two-year-olds paired behind a one-way screen for twenty-minute periods. As in the Hagman (1933) study, differences in individual behavior were found with a considerable amount of consistency. Positive social relations predominated for the group as a whole, with more friendliness than unfriendliness exhibited. One interesting finding of this study was the relationship between the giving and receiving of friendly overtures. The total overt friendly behavior manifested by the subject was negatively related to the total overt friendly behavior manifested toward him by the rest of the group ($r = -.60$). This relationship suggests that there is an optimal level of friendly behavior for maximally reciprocated friendly gestures. Behavior above this level may be regarded as being too aggresively friendly or "pushy." At the other end of the continuum a shy, withdrawn child may evoke sympathetic, helpful behavior from his peers.

As has already been noted, friendship requires a fairly sustained amount of interaction. Closer friends are apt to spend far more time together than will more distant friends. With sustained interaction, the probability of situations involving mutually competitive needs increases. It is not surprising, therefore, that these close cooperative relations often involve conflict (Green, 1933a, 1933b; Jersild & Markey, 1935; Jersild & Fite, 1937).

Generally, then, there is support for the belief that positive, friendly social relations do exist among preschool children's groups. But as Murphy, Murphy and Newcomb point out:

> Among young children there is ample evidence that close cooperative relations involve both conflict and integration: positive correlations are found between "friendship" and "quarrels" and between sympathizing and attacking, and close friends frequently quarrel most. We may infer that at this age friendship does not imply any responsibility to inhibit resistant or antagonistic responses to the specific behavior of a friend. Or is it indeed assuming too much to suppose that friendship at an older level would not be accompanied by a large proportion of quarrels? Insofar as amount of time spent with another individual affords more opportunity for conflicts, we might expect the same relation at any age level. Insofar as the transitoriness of early relationships gives place to sustained patterns of mutual support, understanding, and participation, we should expect the proportion of conflict in relation to time spent together to decrease (1937, pp. 513–514).

Early patterns of acquiescence to authority are established within the context of the family setting. Control of the child's fate is at first entirely in the hands of the child's parents. As more time is spent outside the immediate confines of the home, either in informal neighborhood play groups or in the more structured nursery school, the means of external control over a child's behavior become more differentiated. In school the teacher assumes the type of control which previously had been restricted to parents. Definite patterns of dominance-submission and leadership-followership evolve within the play groups of these preschoolers. Such changes in the child's social relationships require him to restructure his sources of authority. These readjustments are complex.

Differentiations between adults as sources of power must be learned. Although the teacher has control legitimized by parents (e.g., "You do what the teacher tells you"), other adults do not (e.g., "Don't talk to strangers on the way home from school"). Temporal and situational limitations upon legitimized fate control also become important. Teacher control begins when the child arrives at school, continues through the variety of situations encountered during school, and largely terminates when school is over, at which time the parent reassumes authority. Compliance and obedience are the principal nature of the response typically demanded of the child during these times. (It should be noted that these terms have different referents when applied to adult behavior. Suggestions usually produce compliance whereas orders produce obedience. This distinction is rarely applied rigorously to child behavior.) From the child's point of view, such demands must appear to be arbitrary—and even capricious— but he must either comply or be prepared to receive any one of a large number of sanctions that adults are able to impose.

The nature and degree of obedience or compliance have been studied by a number of investigators (Berne, 1929, 1930; Klein, 1932; Weiss, 1934; Koch, 1935; Shirley & Poyntz, 1941; Meyers, 1944).

Klein (1932) found the concept of authority present in children up to two years of age which was evidenced in their recognizing, accepting, and obeying adult persuasion, coercion, and influence attempts.

Weiss (1934) provided a more systematic examination of factors involved in compliance behavior. In this study, both the nature of the situation and the complexity of the command were varied. Eight commands were given to 77 subjects from two years, five months to five years, eight months in three situations: "control," "toy," and "social." In the "control" situation the child was not provided with anything to do between the commands. In the "toy" situation a variety of toys were provided and the experimenters encouraged the subject to play with them. The "social" situation included the presence of both toys and another child of the subject's age. Each subject was tested in all three situations in a counterbalanced manner. The complexity of the commands was varied both in the comprehension and in the motor ability demanded. Data consisted of observational records of subjects' behavior, latency, and the overall time required to complete the response after it began. Whereas the time required for response completion decreased with increasing age, there was a consistent increase in preresponse latency for all subjects as the complexity of commands increased. The three situations produced significant differences in speed of compliance, with time increasing from the control to the play to the social situation.

Berne's (1930) study of social behavior patterns employed experimental, observational, and rating assessments of obedience, as well as a large number of other kinds of behavior traits. This study was one of the early attempts to obtain multiple measures of the same concept, thus reflecting a methodological concern that is still important. A five-point scale was used to rate obedience which was defined by either submission to restraint or submission to command imposed by authority. Experimental tests of obedience were performed upon individual children. Each child was given a simple, but arbitrary, command, e.g., "lie down on the floor," that was repeated ten times at regular intervals unless the child complied before then. The investigator recorded the child's behavior during this process. The ratings and experimental scores for obedience were substantially related ($r = .64$). The tendency to obey generally increased from the two- to three-year-old subjects. At the same time, the children showed a decrease in dependency on adults providing activity.

Meyers (1944) studied the effects of adult authority on the constructiveness of nursery school children's play. A series of commands was given by two adults. The commands varied from positive to negative, from vague to specific, and from agreement between the adults to disagreement. The rated constructiveness of play decreased more with negative commands than with positive, and more with vague than with specific commands. While conflicting orders produced a substantial decrease in constructiveness of play, the most damaging effect occurred when the adults agreed but the commands were negative. The constructiveness of play also decreased when the adults' orders agreed and were positive. Too frequent interference with the child's play was most likely responsible for the latter finding.

The results of these studies point to but a few of the interrelated effects of maturational and experiential factors involved in the development of compliant and obedient behavior. It is not surprising to find a general increase in obedient behavior with increasing age, though substantial individual differences are apparent throughout the findings.

Several interesting questions remain unanswered. How does the process of sequential and differential allocation of authority to different individuals such as parents, older siblings, grandparents, babysitters, and teachers occur? What are the different dynamic effects of commands to cease ongoing behavior as opposed to beginning new activities? What are the age, sex, and individual difference variables most relevant to these processes?

Problems of a related nature occur when differential patterns of individual authority are considered in the context of peer groups without respect to adult-child interactions. As Thompson points out,

> When one takes a careful look at the interaction of different kinds of organisms, he is immediately impressed by the fact that there is a "king," a "boss," or a "top kick" in every social grouping. Bees have a queen. Hens have a well-established "pecking order." Wolves have a leader of the pack. And man has kings, prime ministers, presidents, governors, bosses, champions, and bullies who, either by the nature of their positions or their personal powers, cause other people to do certain things. The social groupings of children also reflect this hierarchy of individual authority. The ascendant patterns of behavior through which children satisfy their social needs are varied and complex. Some patterns of ascendant behavior are socially acceptable and desirable in our culture, and others are

distinctly frowned upon. Most parents encourage their children to become leaders but *not* bullies. Very young children often fail to discriminate between such closely related patterns of social behavior. Ascendant behavior in which the child is sensitive to his companions' as well as his own social needs does not appear on the basis of maturation alone. It needs to be encouraged by precept and example . . . (1962, p. 496).

Ascendancy, then, whether manifested in socially acceptable or socially undesirable forms refers to the tendency of a child to take the lead in determining the behavior of another person or the actions of a group. As such, ascendancy is closely related to the way that the concept of leadership is frequently thought of in relation to adult behavior. At the preschool level, however, the complex interactions of social skills and group situations necessary to the leadership process are rarely, if ever, present. Klein and Wander (1933), for example, found that interaction of a limited nature among subjects up to two years of age could be maintained only in dyads. A group of three quickly degenerated to dyadic interaction. Among dyads where there was a substantial age difference (six months to one year) dominance-submission relations were established, and the interaction then became one-way. The concept of leadership is inapplicable with such young children, although Parten (1933a) was able to distinguish leadership "types" with slightly older subjects.

The processes variously referred to as ascendancy, dominance-submission, and leadership occurring among preschool children have been studied by a number of investigators from various perspectives (e.g., Stern & Stern, 1909; Arrington, 1932; Day, 1932; Parten, 1932, 1933a; Caille, 1933; Page, 1936; Anderson, 1937; Stone, 1941; Wolf, 1952; Tyler & Whisenhunt, 1962).

Page (1936) extended an earlier study by Jack (1934) and attempted to modify ascendant behavior of even younger children. Page used training methods aimed at increasing the self-confidence of 73 three- and four-year-old children from the Iowa Child Welfare Research Station preschool laboratory and 34 preschool age subjects from an orphan's home. Each subject was sequentially paired with five other children. While watching through a one-way-vision screen, observers scored the ascendant responses according to Jack's scoring system. On the basis of these scores subjects were divided into ascendant, moderately ascendant, and nonascendant groups. Each group was then given training in specific situations involving a story book, clay flowers, puzzles, and so on. This training was designed to increase self-confidence. The subjects were paired again with subjects who had not received the training, and ascendance responses were recorded. The training was generally effective in increasing ascendant responses in both nonascendant and moderately ascendant subjects. The control subjects showed a mean loss in ascendancy, which suggests that as one member of a dyad demonstrates competence and self-confidence there is a tendency for the opposite reaction in the other member. The orphanage group was subdivided into those who had received nursery school experience and a control group of those who had not. Neither of the latter two groups received ascendancy training, and the question was whether or not the nursery school experience itself facilitated ascendancy. Pre-school subjects were found to be relatively stable with respect to as-cendancy over a period of time, whereas the control group showed losses. The general findings of Page's study were, then, that the training de-signed to increase self-confidence resulted in an increased expression of ascendant behavior above and beyond the effects of nursery school attendance alone.

The categories of ascendant behavior used by Page (1936) were those formulated by Jack (1934). These categories did not differentiate between socially desirable and socially undesirable forms of ascendant behavior. Anderson (1937) refined the concept of ascendant behavior by distinguishing between "dominative" and "integrative" forms of behavior. Both forms of behavior reflect attempts by one person to achieve a personal goal by interacting with another. Dominating be-havior results when neither alternative courses of action nor the desires of the other person are considered. Integrative behavior is more flexible and usually involves an attempt to simultaneously satisfy the goal-directed behavior of both individuals.

Anderson (1937) used an experimental situation very similar to Page's (1936) in a study of dominative and integrative behavior of 128 children from twenty-eight to seventy-nine months of age. He found a distinct tendency for dominative behaviors by one child to elicit like responses from the other. Similarly, integrative overtures tended to evoke integrative responses. The discrepancy between these results and those obtained by Page, where increased ascendancy by the trained subjects elicited decreased ascendancy by the nontrained subjects, probably reflects the conceptual refinement provided in the distinction between socially acceptable and socially undesirable modes of ascendant behavior. Anderson also found more integration among the older subjects than with the younger subjects. This result is not surprising in view of the fact that it is easier for the younger child to use the more direct dominative modes of behavior. Integrative behavior requires foresight, planning, and an awareness of the needs of others rarely found in very young children.

The development of Anderson's concepts of dominative and in-tegrative behavior into notions of leadership seems rather straight-forward. It would be expected that the dominative leader would function in a dictatorial manner, imposing his will by physical or verbal attack. The integrative individual, on the other hand, ought to be more flexible and democratic, seeking compromise whenever possible.

At least a rough parallel of these processes was found in a study by Parten (1993a). Spontaneous free play situations provided the set-ting for observation of thirty-four children ranging in age from two years to four years and five months. Each subject was observed during one-minute periods, 60 times over the course of a year. "Leadership" was defined by the intensity of social participation shown in "independent pursuing of own will" as well as by the ability to direct others. Two different kinds of leaders were identified: the "bully" and the "diplomat." These designations correspond well to the "dominative" and "integrative" behaviors noted by Anderson. However, the parallel is difficult to sustain. Parten found more variability than stability in "leadership," over both long and short periods of time. Those children most involved in following were also rated high on leading. The amount rather than the qualitative nature of social participation seemed to be the crucial variable. "Bullying" and "diplomatic" leading also occurred in the same child. Apparently leadership among preschool children is frequently a combination of integrative and dominative behaviors, as Thompson (1962) notes. He further points out in this context: "The child's limited perceptual-response abilities often prevent his finding an integrative solution to a social relations problem. The dominative approach is usually an easy second choice. This intermingling of dominative and integrative behavior in the leadership concept, . . . as it applies to children's social behavior, confounds its descriptive properties" (1962, p. 499). The difficulty in applying the concept of leadership to children's behavior is further amplified by the transitory nature of role systems within children's groups. Role occupancy, when defined, depends upon which children happen to be present in the group at a given time, and even stabilized roles change markedly from one year to the next (cf. Arrington, 1932; Jersild & Markey, 1935; Murphy, 1937).

Only one level of analysis—the individual—is reflected when the psychologist conceives of processes like leadership that occur in group interaction in terms of "ascendancy" or even the more refined "dominative" and "integrative" forms of behavior. It is well known that the process of interaction between adults is affected not only by the personal characteristics of the interacting individuals, but also by both the specific context and the wider sociocultural environment within which such interaction occurs. Thus the emergence of "leadership" in a group setting is a consequence of the joint interplay of situational and dispositional, i.e., personality, variables. Given the personal propensity to become involved in directing either the behavior of others or the group as a whole, the actual occurrence of such behavior may depend upon a plethora of "social structural" variables, such as the size of the group, the degree of structural elaboration of the group, e.g., status or role differentiation, communicative accessibility, and composition, in terms of sex, age, race, or socioeconomic class.

Although it is probably true that the effect of such variables upon the interaction of young children is less substantial than upon adult interaction, the actual effects remain largely unexplored. Both the degree of influence and the ages at which the influence of these variables first occurs are of interest not only to those concerned with the individually developing child, but also to those concerned with the processes *per se*. Swift (1964), in her review of the effects of early group experience, emphasizes the potential importance of the study of the effects of those variables traditionally associated with adult small group research on preschool group research. She says:

> The development of a group identity with values and mores of its own is a subject which has received considerable attention with respect to children in the elementary and high school years. Less attention has been accorded the subject in regard to the preschool years. The existence of some group identification in the preschool child, however, cannot be doubted by anyone who is familiar with groups of children of this age (1964, p. 274).

A case of extreme group identification was reported by Freud and Dann (1954). The subjects of this study were six refugee children who, after having been separated from their parents during their first year of life, spent approximately their next two years together in a concentration camp. After the camp was liberated at the end of World War II, the group of children was taken to live in England. The degree of group feeling which developed as a consequence of common exposure to a harsh environment was described as follows:

> The children's positive feelings were centered exclusively in their own group. It was evident that they cared greatly for each other and not at all for anybody or anything else. They had no other wish than to be together and became upset when they were separated from each other, even for short moments. No child would consent to remain upstairs while the others were downstairs, or vice versa, and no child would be taken for a walk or on an errand without the others. If anything of the kind happened, the single child would constantly ask for the other children while the group would fret for the missing child.
>
> This insistence on being inseparable made it imposible in the beginning to treat the children as individuals or to vary their lives according to their special needs (1954, p. 407).

While the identification with the group was thus very high, the amount of status differentiation within the group was minimal. Leadership varied with the momentary nature of the activity and particular qualities of specific individuals. Thus, one child was the "leader" at mealtimes—when he finished eating all the others also stopped. Another child (the youngest in the group) led and directed all the games, an activity at which he was both skillful and imaginative. There was also a striking lack of competition, rivalry, and jealousy within the group; they were a solid, cohesive whole, functioning interdependently in the context of what previously had been a very unrewarding environment.

Although such extreme group identification is unusual, it is interesting to note that attempts are being made in Israel to institutionalize this process in the collective settlements, or *Kibbutzim*. Within the Kibbutz the role of the individual is subordinated to the collective's goals and orientations. The children's mothers work all day, so much of the child care is performed by the caretaker, or *metapalet*. Traditional patterns of family relationships are thus substantially altered, and primary peer contact is maximized even at the very early ages. Evidence suggesting substantial and enduring group identification is provided in the studies and reports of numerous investigators (Irvine, 1952; Rabin, 1957, 1958a, 1958b; Faigin, 1958; Spiro, 1958).

It is clear that the process of identifying with a group can occur in very young children. However, both the nature and implications of such identification are largely unknown. As Swift (1964) states:

> Further research on social development in the preschool years is needed to provide a fuller understanding of the meaning of this identification in the development of the young child. Still unanswered is the question of whether it represents a positive extension of the individual's capacity for forming relationships through identification with others, or whether it tends to interfere with the development of personal goals and standards, thus strengthening conformity at the expense of individuality (1964, p. 275).

The process of identifying with a group, whether it results in the positive extension of interpersonal relationships or in the restriction of individuality through conformity, requires the acceptance of the purpose and values of a group (or of another person) as one's own. The overt manifestations of such identification are found in the imitation of outward behavior. Thus a close link between the processes of identification with a group and imitation of group standardized behavior seems likely. The learning of socially significant forms of behavior by imitation has received considerable attention recently, particularly in the well-conceived and executed work of Bandura and his associates.

Bandura, Ross, and Ross (1961), for example, exposed a group of nursery school children to adult models who used a number of toys and other objects in an aggressive fashion. A control group was exposed to models who behaved in an inhibited, nonaggressive manner. Posttests of both groups showed that the experimental group showed significantly more aggressive play with the toys and equipment. A later study (Bandura, Ross, & Ross, 1963a) demonstrated that aggression following mild frustration was facilitated as much by observation of human models and cartoon characters portraying aggression on film as by living models. The effects of such exposure, however, were to some extent a function of the sex of the model, sex of the child, and the reality cues of the model. For example, male subjects exhibited more total aggression, imitative aggression, aggressive gun play, and nonimitative aggression than female subjects. Exposure to the aggressive male model produced significantly more aggressive gun play than did exposure to the aggressive female model. Boys who viewed the male model expressed far more aggressive gun play than girls who were exposed to the female model. Both the sex appropriateness of the model's behavior and the sex of the subject, then, were important determiners of the model's influence in promoting social learning. Other studies (Bandura, Ross, & Ross, 1963b; 1967) showed that imitative responses are at least partially contingent upon the status of the model and the consequences of the behavior for the model. From these studies it appears that imitation can have an effective role in transmitting some classes of social responses. Investigation of the degree to which a group might provide a model for imitation learning of aggression, as well as other classes of social responses, such as sex-role, achievement, and dependency behaviors, would appear to be a fruitful area for further research.

Social structural variables—so extensively studied with adult groups —represent an area of investigation largely neglected with preschool children. The potential effects that the size of the group, for example, might have on the nature of the interaction raises some very interesting questions. How large can a preschool group be and still maintain a sense of group identity? To the extent that identification with a group normally occurs at these ages, how does it vary with the size of the group? What is the relationship between the size of the group and the effectiveness of the group in working toward different kinds of goals, either those imposed by teachers or those which spontaneously emerge during group activity? How does the size of the group interact with the level of individual social development to facilitate emotional growth and adjustment? Would the educational and adjustment functions of the nursery school class be facilitated by smaller groups than are usually found? Such questions are of both practical and theoretical significance.

It is interesting to note that although this (size) variable has received very little direct attention from investigations of preschool children, the dyad composed of two children has been used extensively as the structural unit in the investigation of other processes. For example, studies by Mengert (1931), Greenberg (1932), Bridges (1933), Green (1933a), Klein and Wander (1933), Updegraff and Herbst (1933), Page (1936), Anderson (1937), McFarland (1938), Wolfle and Wolfle (1939), Janus (1943), Ames (1952), relied either in part or totally upon dyads. Similarly, the three-child triad has occasionally been used (e.g., Klein & Wander, 1933; Williams & Mattson, 1942; Ahrens, 1954). Still other studies have utilized the structural unit of an adult-child dyad (Bridges, 1933; Goodenough, 1938; Williams & Mattson, 1942; Arsenian, 1943; Morgan & Morgan, 1944; Ames, 1952; Antonovsky, 1959). It would seem that whatever the specific nature of the process under investigation, very different dynamic components of interaction are evoked as a consequence of the number of members involved in that interaction. The nature and extent of such effects deserve far more attention than has thus far been accorded them.

Group composition is another social structural variable having a direct impact on the nature of interaction. When the differences between homogeneity and heterogeneity of group composition upon activity in free-play situations are considered, for example, a group composed totally of girls would probably be differently engaged than a group of all boys. Imagine, however, the possible differences between groups homogeneous with respect to sex, but including wide age differences. The differential effects of homogeneity and heterogeneity with respect to age, sex, social class, ethnic group, and their combinations upon the child's development of a positive self-image need to be explored systematically. As Swift points out:

> While we know that the child's concept of himself and his evaluation of himself and his abilities during the preschool years are fashioned in large part by parental attitudes toward him, there can be no doubt that he also develops an image of himself in relation to his peers, based on their reactions to him. How he is perceived by the children and adults around him will influence his own perception of himself as a social person. Hence, behavior which leads to unpopularity in the group, despite its relative harmlessness otherwise, may need to be considered seriously by those working with the child, and modified where possible (1964, p. 277).

It seems probable that the nature of interaction, and hence the kinds of reactions to himself that the individual child will receive, will be significantly affected by the social structure of the interaction group.

It is apparent that more research on children's groups and their functioning is needed. But what of the methodological issues of advantage and disadvantage to such research? Thompson has cogently presented the problems and issues as follows:

> There is a hard core of American psychologists who believe that research progress can best be expedited by concentrating our efforts first on the behavior of infrahuman subjects by constructing an explanatory model for "simple" organisms and then revising and expanding this model, as subsequent research may dictate, to explain the more "complex" behavior of man. These psychologists have traditionally selected the white rat as an appropriate experimental subject. If one accepts the validity of this approach, he can make an equally strong case for studying the dynamics of children's groups prior to the presumably more difficult task of identifying and measuring the dimensions of social functioning within groups composed of adults.
>
> An argument can be made that the psychological defenses of children will have been less frequently practiced than those of adults. Hence the available behaviors from which the scientist must make his inferences will be more direct and spontaneous. Although this may in fact be a defensible argument, it is practically and operationally not demonstrable at our present state of ignorance about the functioning of social groups at any level of maturity.
>
> Another methodological advantage that is sometimes claimed for the study of children's groups is their greater availability and greater ease in manipulating the conditions important to their functioning. There seems to be some justification for the first part of this claim, although college sophomores may still be preferred as subjects for the study of group behavior because of their greater proximity to the typical university laboratory. The second alleged advantage seems unwarranted. Children are generally less tolerant than adults about anything that bores or frustrates them. If group conditions become uninteresting or unduly frustrating, they are more prone than adults to withdraw (either overtly or covertly)

from the group. For example, in one of Lewin's authoritarian groups a boy who became a scapegoat for his companion's aggression quit the group (Lewin, Lippitt, & White, 1939). In addition, there are some ways of manipulating the social conditions of adult groups that no one has, as yet, been ingenious enough to adapt for use in the study of children's groups. A good example is the introduction of a "ringer" or "stooge" into the adult group, either to make un-detected observations or to play a social role important to the group's functioning (Festinger, 1953).

In general, it may be concluded that there are no *demonstrated* advantages for furthering scientific knowledge by the study of child as contrasted with adult groups. The investigator who elects to do research with children's groups may be legitimately influenced in this direction by any of the following conditions: he may be most interested in studying developmental variables affecting social groups during the accelerated growth period of the early years of life; he may have readier access to child subjects; he may find it more personally rewarding to do research with children; or he may wish to throw light on some pressing social problem whose solution would help to advance the happiness and adjustment of many children (1962, pp. 823–824).

Thompson (1962) then summarizes major techniques for the study of groups including problems of group selection or creation, experi-mental manipulation, important dimensions of group functioning (in-cluding both process and structural variables), observational techniques, and the measurement of social structure and social roles.

Other methodological discussions of either direct or potential relevance to the study of the social interaction of young children are available in Mussen (1960) including Wright's thorough presentation of observational techniques, Lambert's discussion of interpersonal be-havior, Marian Radke Yarrow's chapter on the measurement of attitudes and values, Leon Yarrow's chapter on interviewing children (a useful but all too infrequently used adjunct to interaction study), and the discussion by Hoffman and Lippitt of family variables. These discus-sions are useful in presenting not only research techniques, theoretical and methodological issues, and unanswered questions, but also many of the frustrating practical problems which are likely to be encountered. The psychologist concerned with children's social relationships who becomes familiar with the material presented by these authors will find his research path considerably smoothed and shortened.

Individual Behavior in the Larger Social Context

During the first three years of life the most pervasive and influential forms of social contact occur within the family setting. Normally, of course, the mother is the first human with whom the child has sustained contact. The predominant form of early mother-child interaction is uni-directional: the mother directs her behavior to the child, meeting his specific needs as they arise. In this caretaking role, which is fundamentally life sustaining in nature, as the mother feeds, burps, and cleans the infant, she also provides much of the sensory stimulation important to the infant's development. Gradually the caretaking process merges into a training process, wherein more specific behavioral responses on the part of the child are sought. As this transition occurs, the unidirectional interaction pattern becomes more reciprocal and the child begins responding to cues from the mother. With this change, it becomes appropriate to speak of truly social behavior.

A great deal of attention, mostly inspired by psychoanalytic contentions, has been given to the effects of different aspects of infant care during early development. However, the bulk of the concern has been with the potential effects of such care on personality and emotional development. Although it seems difficult to separate emotional and personality development from social behavior, the focusing of infant care research on emotional and personality development to the exclusion of social behavior renders most of it inappropriate to the present emphasis. The interested reader is directed to Caldwell's (1964) comprehensive review of the research on the effects of varying infant care procedures.

The family is the group in society to which the initial task of preparing the child for active societal participation is relegated. This means that the family is expected not only to provide for the physical care and well-being of the child but also to begin the inculcation of norms and values which are deemed important to society's functioning. The specific contents of normative standards and value concerns vary widely between societies and within subcultures as do the favored techniques for achieving them. To the extent that patterns of social behavior developed early in life and within the matrix of social relations existing within the family come to provide the individual with basic ways of structuring his social world, those patterns are of signal importance. It is essential, then, to understand the normal nature of the child's social behavior as it develops within the familial setting.

Unfortunately, however, information about the nature of normal social behavior developing in the family setting is sparse. The vast literature on the effects of maternal deprivation has focused principally upon abnormal social relations and their effects on intellectual, social, and emotional behavior. A number of thorough reviews of this literature have been published (e.g., Casler, 1961; Yarrow, 1961, 1964; World Health Organization, 1962) which point out the considerable degree of re-evaluation of conclusions regarding the effects of maternal deprivation and separation that has occurred in recent years. Such re-evaluations appear to be the result of extensive conceptual elaboration as well as new research findings. Ainsworth (1962), for example, distinguishes between three major dimensions of mother-child interaction which had previously been included under the term "maternal deprivation." Her dimensions are: (a) interaction insufficiency, or the kind of deprivation that occurs when an infant or young child is institutionalized under circumstances where he has insufficient opportunity for interaction with a mother-figure; (b) interaction distortion, where the character, rather than the quantity, of interaction is adverse (e.g., rejecting, hostile, over-indulgent, and so on); (c) interaction discontinuity, where the child is separated from the mother after an attachment had been formed. The result of these refinements has been a more differentiated view of maternal deprivation, and a more balanced view of the effects. However, the understanding of the positive aspects of maternal-child interaction has been little advanced by the research on material deprivation.

As the social structure of a group affects the nature of the inter-action that occurs within that group, so do the social-structural attributes of the family affect the processes which occur within the family. Clausen and Williams (1963) have recently provided a review of the major sociological influences upon child behavior. Their review covers the processes of social differentiation and socialization, specific social con-texts and behavior settings, age and sex-role differentiation, the inter-related effects of family structure and functioning, family size, sibling order, the patterning of parental authority and family ties, father-absent families, and maternal employment. In addition to Clausen and Wil-liams' comprehensive review, Becker (1964) has covered recent research relating to the consequences of different kinds of parental discipline, and Kagan (1964) has provided a stimulating review of studies con-cerned with the development of sex typing and sex-role identity. The recency and thoroughness of these reviews eliminate the need for further (and necessarily repetitive) consideration here.

In this chapter the attempt has been to provide an overview of research on the development and functioning of the social behavior of infants and young children. The emphasis has been upon the social behavior of the individual child first, as social awareness and responsive-ness develop, and second, as these processes are manifested in group situations. Two general observations can be made in concluding this discussion.

First, the social behavior of young children represents an area of study which has in the main been woefully neglected in child psychol-ogy. Hartup (1965) states that since 1958 more than half of the litera-ture in child psychology has been concerned with some aspect of social behavior. Unfortunately, little of this resurgent interest in social be-havior has filtered down to the ages between the neonatal phase and nursery school age. Additionally, there is a need to replicate many of the studies which have already been done, not only because of the methodological advances that have been made during the past three decades but also because of the differences between the world of today and that of thirty years ago. The patterns that social stimuli present in the young child's environment, for example, are of a very different character (cf. Maccoby's [1964] chapter on the effects of mass media). To the extent that the social behavior of the young child is dependent upon the stimulating conditions present in the general environment, changes in both the character and the rate of development might well be expected.

Second, there is the lack of a parsimonious set of integrating concepts appropriate to the social behavior of young children. There are concepts appropriate at the individual level of analysis (e.g., dominative and integrative behavior, social awareness, social responsiveness, and so on), and there are concepts at the social group level of analysis (social-structural concepts). However, adequate conceptualization of individual social behavior logically requires accounting for the interaction of both situational and dispositional factors. Hence concepts of individual social behavior should be located at the intersection of the individual and social group levels of analysis. At the present time there are few, if any, concepts so uniquely situated, and there is therefore no overall theory of social development. Considering the rapid growth of research interests in social behavior of children in general (disregarding the specific ages involved in the present concern), it seems unlikely that such a state of affairs will long continue. During the interim period the utilization of presently available information is a necessary, if dissatisfying, procedure, for as Thompson notes, even the knowledge of the ". . . descriptive, correlational aspects of social development permits better understanding of, and some measure of control over, the social behavior of children" (1962, p. 465).

References

Ahrens, R. Beitrag zur Entwicklung des Physiognomie- und Mimikerkenness. (Contribution on the development of physiognomy and mimicry recognition.) *Z. exp. angew. Psychol.*, 1954, 2, 412–454.

Ainsworth, M. D. The effects of "maternal deprivation": A review of findings and controversy in the context of research strategy. In *Deprivation of maternal care.* Public Health Paper No. 14. Geneva: World Health Organization, 1962.

Ames, L. B. The sense of self of nursery school children as manifested by their verbal behavior. *J. genet. Psychol.*, 1952, 81, 193–232.

Ames, L. B., & Learned, J. Imaginary companions and related phenomena. *J. genet Psychol.*, 1946, 69, 147–167.

Anderson, H. H. Domination and integration in the social behavior of young children in an experimental play situation. *Genet. Psychol. Monogr.*, 1937, 19, 341–408.

Andrus, R., & Horowitz, E. L. The effect of nursery school training: Insecurity feelings. *Child Develpm.*, 1938, 9, 169–174.

Antonovsky, H. F. A contribution to research in the area of the mother-child relationship. *Child Develpm.*, 1959, 30, 37–51.

Arrington, R. E. *Interrelations in the behavior of young children.* New York: Teachers College, 1932.

Arsenian, J. M. Young children in an insecure situation. *J. abnorm. soc. Psychol.*, 1943, 38, 225–249.

Bandura, A., Ross, D., & Ross, S. A. Transmission of aggression through imitation of aggressive models. *J. abnorm. soc. Psychol.*, 1961, 63, 575–582.

――――. Imitation of film-mediated aggressive models. *J. abnorm. soc. Psychol.*, 1963, 66, 3–11. (a)

――――. Vicarious reinforcement and imitative learning. *J. abnorm. soc. Psychol,.* 1963, 67, 601–607. (b)

――――. A comparative test of the status envy, social power, and secondary reinforcement theories of identificatory learning. *J. abnorm. soc. Psychol.*, 1963, 67, 527–534. Reprinted in Y. Brackbill & G. G. Thompson (Eds.), *Behavior in infancy and early childhood: A book of readings.* New York: Free Press, 1967.

Barker, M. *A technique for studying the social-material activities of young children.* New York: Columbia Univer. Press, 1930.

Beaver, A. P. *The initiation of social contacts by preschool children: A study of technique in recording social behavior.* New York: Teachers College, 1932.

Becker, W. C. Consequences of different kinds of parental discipline. In M. L. Hoffman & L. W. Hoffman (Eds.), *Review of child development research,* I. New York: Russell Sage Foundation, 1964.

Berne, E. V. C. An investigation of the wants of seven children. *Univer. Iowa Stud. Child Welf.*, 1929, 4, No. 2, 1–61.

――――. An experimental investigation of social behavior patterns in young children. *Univer. Iowa Stud. Child Welf.*, 1930, 4, No. 3.

Bernhardt, K. S., Millichamp, D. A., Charles, M. W., & McFarland, M. P. An analysis of the social contacts of preschool children with the aid of motion pictures. *Univer. Toronto Stud. Child Develpm.*, 1937, No. 10.

Blood, R. O., Jr. Social class and family control of television viewing. *Merrill-Palmer Quart.*, 1961, 7, 205–222.

Bott, H. Observations of play activities in the nursery school. *Genet. Psychol. Monogr.*, 1928, 4, 44–88.

Bridges, K. M. B. Occupational interests of three-year-old children. *Ped. Sem.*, 1927, 34, 415–423.

――――. A study of social development in early infancy. *Child Develpm.*, 1933, 4, 36–49.

Bühler, C. Die ersten sozialen Verhaltungsweisen des Kindes. (The first social behavior patterns of the child.) *Quellen und Studien zur Jugendkunde,* 1927, 5, 1–102.

――――. The social behavior of children. In C. Murchison (Ed.), *Handbook of child psychology.* Worcester: Clark Univer. Press, 1933.

Bühler, C., & Hetzer, H. Inventar der Verhaltungsweisen des ersten Lebensjahres. (Behavior patterns in the first year of life.) In C. Bühler, *The first year of life.* New York: Day, 1930.

Caille, R. K. *Resistant behavior of preschool children.* New York: Teachers College, 1933.

Caldwell, B. M. The effects of infant care. In M. L. Hoffman, & L. W. Hoffman (Eds.), *Review of child development research,* I. New York: Russell Sage Foundation, 1964.

Casler, L. Maternal deprivation: A critical review of the literature. *Monogr. Soc. Res. Child Develpm.*, 1961, No. 26.

Challman, R. C. Factors influencing friendships among preschool children. *Child Develpm.*, 1932, 3, 146–158.

Clausen, J. A., & Williams, J. R. Sociological correlates of child behavior. In H. W. Stevenson (Ed.), *Child psychology: The sixty-second yearbook of the National Society for the Study of Education.* Chicago: Univer. Chicago Press, 1963.

Cockrell, D. A study of the play of children of preschool age by an unobserved observer. *Genet. Psychol. Monogr.*, 1935, 17, 377–469.

Dawe, H. C. An analysis of two hundred quarrels of preschool children. *Child Develpm.*, 1934, 5, 139–157.

Day, E. J. The development of language in twins. II. The development of twins: Their resemblances and differences. *Child Develpm.*, 1932, 3, 298–316.

Durkin, H. E. Dr. John Levy's relationship therapy as applied to a play group. *Amer. J. Orthopsychiat.*, 1939, 9, 583–917.

Etziony, M. A method of studying the character traits of the preschool child. *J. genet. Psychol.*, 1933, 42, 184–205.

Faigin, H. Social behavior of young children in the *Kibbutz. J. abnorm. soc. Psychol.*, 1958, 56, 117–129.

Fales, E. A rating scale of the vigorousness of play activities of preschool children. *Child Develpm.*, 1937, 8, 15–46. (a)

——. A comparison of the vigorousness of play activities of preschool boys and girls. *Child Develpm.*, 1937 8, 144–158. (b)

Festinger, L. Laboratory experiments. In L. Festinger, & D. Katz (Eds.), *Research methods in the behavioral sciences.* New York: Dryden, 1953.

Foster, S. A study of the personality make-up and social setting in fifty jealous children. *Ment. Hyg.*, 1927, 11, 53–77.

Freud, A., & Dann, S. An experiment in group upbringing. *Psychoanalytic Stud. Child*, 1951, 6, 127–168. Reprinted in Y. Brackbill & G. G. Thompson (Eds.), *Behavior in infancy and early childhood: A book of readings.* New York: Free Press, 1967.

Goodenough, F. L. Inter-relationships in the behavior of young children. *Child Develpm.*, 1930, 1, 29–47.

——. *Anger in young children.* Minneapolis: Inst. Child Welf. Monogr., Univer. Minnesota, 1931, No. 9.

——. The use of pronouns by young children: A note on the development of self-awareness. *J. genet. Psychol.*, 1938, 52, 333–346.

Green, E. H. Friendships and quarrels among preschool children. *Child Develpm.*, 1933, 4, 237–252. (a)

——. Group play and quarreling among preschool children. *Child Develpm.*, 1933, 4, 302, 307. (b)

Greenberg, P. J. Competition in children: An experimental study. *Amer. J. Psychol.*, 1932, 44, 221–248.

Hagman, E. P. The companionships of preschool children. *Univer. Iowa Stud. Child Welf.*, 1933, 7, No. 4.

Hartup, W. W. Social behavior of children. *Rev. Educ. Res.*, 1965, 35, 122–129.

Heathers, G. Emotional dependence and independence in nursery school play. *J. genet. Psychol.*, 1955, 87, 37–57.

Hirota, K. Experimental studies of competition. *Jap. J. Psychol.*, 1951, 21, 70–81.

Irvine, E. E. Observations on the aims and methods of child rearing in communal settlements in Israel. *Hum. Relat.*, 1952, 5, 247–275.

Isaacs, S. *Social development in young children: A study in beginnings.* New York: Harcourt, Brace, 1933.

Jack, L. M. An experimental study of ascendant behavior in preschool children. *Univer. Iowa Stud. Child Welf.*, 1934, 9, 7–65.

Janus, S. Q. An investigation of the relationship between children's language and their play. *J. genet. Psychol.*, 1943, 62, 3–61.

Jersild, A. T., & Fite, M. D. Children's social adjustments in nursery school. *J. exp. Educ.*, 1937, 6, 161–179.

Jersild, A, T., & Markey, F. V. *Conflicts between preschool children.* New York: Bureau of Publications, Teachers College, 1935.

Kagan, J. Acquisition and significance of sex typing and sex role identity. In M. L. Hoffman & L. W. Hoffman (Eds.), *Review of child development research, I.* New York: Russell Sage Foundation, 1964.

Kellogg, W. N., & Kellogg, L. A. *The ape and the child: A study of environmental influence upon early behavior.* New York: McGraw-Hill, 1933.

Klein, R. Die Autorität als eine Form der sozialen Beeinflussung. (Authority as a form of social influence.) Z. *Kinderforschg.*, 1932, 39, 249–299.

Klein, R., & Wander, E. Gruppenbildung im zweiten Lebensjahr. (Group formation during the second year of life.) Z. *Psychol.*, 1933, 128, 257–280.

Koch, H. L. An analysis of certain forms of so-called "nervous habits" in young children. *J. genet. Psychol.*, 1935, 46, 139–170.

Landreth, C. Factors associated with crying in young children in the nursery school and the home. *Child Develpm.*, 1941, 12, 81–97.

Leuba, C. An experimental study of rivalry in young children. *J. comp. Psychol.*, 1933, 16, 367–378.

Lewin, K., Lippitt, R., & White, R. K. Patterns of aggressive behavior in experimentally created "social climates." *J. soc. Psychol.*, 1939, 10, 271–299.

Loomis, A. M. A preliminary study of the physical contacts of nursery school children. In D. S. Thomas (Ed.), *Some new techniques for studying social behavior.* New York: Teachers College, 1929. Pp. 55–75.

Maccoby, E. E. Effects of the mass media. In M. L. Hoffman, & L. W. Hoffman (Eds.), *Review of child development research, I.* New York: Russell Sage Foundation, 1964.

McFarland, M. B. *Relationships between young sisters as revealed in their overt responses.* New York: Teachers College, 1938.

Mallay, H. A study of some of the techniques underlying the establishment of successful social contacts at the preschool level. *J. genet. Psychol.*, 1935, 47, 431–457. (a)

———. Growth in social behavior and mental activity after six months in nursery school. *Child Develpm.*, 1935, 6, 303–309. (b)

Manwell, E. M., & Mengert, I. G. A study of the development of two- and three-year-old children with respect to play activities. *Univer. Iowa Stud. Child Welf.*, 1934, 9, 69–111.

Maudry, M., & Nekula, M. Social relations between children of the same age during the first two years of life. *J. genet. Psychol.*, 1939, 54, 193–215.

Mengert, I. G. A preliminary study of the reactions of two-year-old children to each other when paired in a semi-controlled situation. *Ped. Sem.*, 1931, 39, 393–398.

Meyers, C. E. The effect of conflicting authority on the child. *Univer. Iowa Stud. Child Welf.*, 1944, 20, 31–98.

Morgan, S. S., & Morgan, J. J. B. An examination of the development of certain adaptive behavior patterns in infants. *J. Pediatr.*, 1944, 25, 168–177.

Murphy, G., Murphy, L. B., & Newcomb, T. M. *Experimental social psychology.* (Rev. ed.) New York: Harper & Brothers, 1937.

Murphy, L. B. *Social behavior and child personality.* New York: Columbia Univer. Press, 1937.

Mussen, P. H. (Ed.) *Handbook of research methods in child development.* New York: Wiley, 1960.

Page, M. L. The modification of ascendant behavior in preschool children. *Univer. Iowa Stud. Child Welf.*, 1936, 12, No. 3.

Parten, M. B. Social participation among pre-school children. *J. abnorm. soc. Psychol.*, 1932, 27, 243–269.

———. Leadership among preschool children. *J. abnorm. soc. Psychol.*, 1933, 27, 430–440. (a)

———. Social play among preschool children. *J. abnorm. soc. Psychol.*, 1933, 28, 136–147. (b)

Rabin, A. I. Personality maturity of kibbutz and non-kibbutz children, as reflected in Rorschach findings. *J. proj. Tech.*, 1957, 21, 148–153.

———. Behavior research in collective settlements in Israel. 6. Infants and children under conditions of "intermittent" mothering in the kibbutz. *Amer. J. Orthopsychiat.*, 1958, 28, 577–584. (a)

————. Some psychosexual differences between kibbutz and non-kibbutz Israeli boys. *J. proj. Tech.*, 1958, 22, 328–332. (b)

Ricketts, A. F. A study of the behavior of young children in anger. *Univer. Iowa Stud. Child Welf.*, 1934, 9, No. 5.

Robinson, E. W., & Conrad, H. S. The reliability of observations of talkativeness and social contact among nursery school children by the "short time sample" technique. *J. exp. Educ.*, 1933, 2, 161–165.

Roff, M., & Roff, L. An analysis of the variance of conflict behavior in preschool children. *Child Develpm.*, 1940, 11, 43–60.

Ross, B. M. Some traits associated with sibling jealousy in problem children. *Smith Coll. Stud. Soc. Work*, 1930, 1, 364–376.

Sewall, M. Two studies of sibling rivalry. I. Some causes of jealousy in young children. *Smith Coll. Stud. Soc. Work*, 1930, 1, 6–22.

Shirley, M. A behavior syndrome characterizing prematurely-born children. *Child Develpm.*, 1939, 10, 115–128.

Shirley, M., & Poyntz, L. Development and cultural patterning in children's protests. *Child Develpm.*, 1941, 12, 347–350.

Slama-Cazacu, T. A study of dialogue among preschool children. *Voprosy Psikhologii*, 1961, 97–106.

Smalley, R. E. Two studies in sibling rivalry. II. The influence of differences in age, sex and intelligence in determining the attitudes of siblings toward each other. *Smith Coll. Stud. Soc. Work*, 1930, 1, 23–40.

Sperling, M. Animal phobias in a two-year-old child. *The psychoanalytic study of the child*, 1952, 7, 115–125.

Spiro, M. E. *Children of the kibbutz.* Cambridge, Mass.: Harvard Univer. Press, 1958.

Staples, R. Some factors influencing the afternoon sleep of young children. *J. genet. Psychol.*, 1932, 41, 222–228.

Stern, C., & Stern, W. *Monographien über die seelische Entwicklung des Kindes. II. Erinnerung, Aussage und Lüge in der ersten Kindheit. (Monographs on the mental development of the child. II. Memory, assertion and lying in early childhood.)* Leipzig: Verlag von Johann Ambrosius Barth, 1909, 111–160.

Stone, L. J. Experiments in group play and readiness for destruction. Part II. In E. Lerner & L. B. Murphy (Eds.), Methods for the study of personality in young children. *Monogr. Soc. Res. Child Develpm.*, 1941, 6, No. 4.

Swift, J. Effects of early group experience: The nursery school and day nursery. In M. L. Hoffman & L. W. Hoffman (Eds.), *Review of child development research, I.* New York: Russell Sage Foundation, 1964.

Thomas, A., Birch, H. G., Chess, S., & Robbins, L. Individuality in responses of children to similar environmental situations. *Amer. J. Psychiat.*, 1961, 117, 798–803.

Thompson, G. G. *Child psychology.* Boston: Houghton Mifflin, 1962.

Tyler, F. B., & Whisenhunt, J. W. Motivational changes during pre-school attendance. *Child Develpm.*, 1962, 33, 427–442.

Updegraff, R., & Herbst, E. K. An experimental study of the social behavior stimulated in young children by certain play materials. *J. genet. Psychol.*, 1933, 42, 372–391.

Van Alstyne, D. *Play behavior and choice of play materials of preschool children.* Chicago: Univer. Chicago Press, 1932.

Washburn, R. W., & Hilgard, J. R. A quantitative clinical method of recording the social behavior of young children. *Ped. Sem.*, 1934, 45, 390–405.

Weiss, L. A. An experimental investigation of certain factors involved in the preschool child's compliance with commands. *Univer. Iowa Stud. Child Welf.*, 1934, 9, 127–157.

Williams, R. M., & Mattson, M. L. The effect of social groupings upon the language of preschool children. *Child Develpm.*, 1942, 13, 233–245. Reprinted in Y. Brackbill & G. G. Thompson (Eds.), *Behavior in infancy and early childhood: A book of readings.* New York: Free Press, 1967.

Wolf, K. M. Observations of individual tendencies in the first year of life. In M. J. E. Senn (Ed.), *Problems of infancy and childhood.* New York: Josiah Macy, Jr. Foundation, 1952. Pp. 97–137.

Wolfle, D. L., & Wolfle, H. M. The development of cooperative behavior in monkeys and young children. *J. genet. Psychol.,* 1939, 55, 137–175.

World Health Organization. *Deprivation of maternal care.* Public Health Paper No. 14. Geneva: Author, 1962.

Yarrow. L. J. Maternal deprivation: Toward an empirical and conceptual re-evaluation. *Psychol. Bull.,* 1961, 58, 459–490.

———. Separation from parents during early childhood. In M. L. Hoffman & L. W. Hoffman (Eds.), *Review of child development research, I.* New York: Russell Sage Foundation, 1964.

Chapter 8

Emotional Behavior and Personality Development

DANIEL G. FREEDMAN

CHARLOTTE B. LORING

ROBERT M. MARTIN

Charlotte B. Loring is responsible for the section on emotional behavior; Robert M. Martin, for the section on personality development: psychoanalytic theory; Daniel G. Freedman, for the section on personality development: a biological approach. The work by Charlotte B. Loring was supported in part by a Neurological and Sensory Disease Traineeship Award from the U.S. Public Health Service.

Emotional Behavior

At all times research in this field has been concerned with the origin and ontogenesis of emotion and emotional expression. A number of theoretical issues have influenced the direction of research. Some issues were distinctive of a particular period, others have persisted through the years, yet developing and changing with advances in scientific sophistication.

Darwin was one of the first scientists to study the emotional expression of infants. In 1877 he published *A Biographical Sketch of an Infant*. Further observations and a more extensive treatment of his views appeared in his well-known book, *The Expression of Emotions in Man and Animals* (1898). Darwin introduced at least four areas of inquiry which command much attention today.

1. Innate behavior with respect to emotion.
2. Emotional expression that is distinctively human: crying and smiling.
3. Anatomical structure and function relative to emotional expression.
4. Comparative behavior of animals and human beings in regard to the development of emotional behavior.

During the first decades in which early emotional behavior was studied, the first two of the above issues were considered. The third and fourth issues have become increasingly important in recent years, although all of them are currently of vital interest. These concepts were, of course, of interest to Darwin as integral aspects of his theory of evolution. Today there are many who find renewed interest in bringing evolutionary concepts to bear on these and other aspects of behavior.

Watson initiated a period of infant study relevant to the issues of emotion such as fear, rage, and love, as well as studies of smiling and crying (Blanton, 1917; Jones, 1926). He is perhaps best known for his introduction of the issue of learned emotion (1925a, 1925b); for Watson all emotion was elaborated from the basic unit of emotional development, the reflex. Watson and his associates published on these matters for over a decade, from 1917 to 1928.

In the following decade there were not only attempts to replicate Watson's studies, but there were also ontogenetic studies of emotional behavior. These studies were influenced by the new emphasis on processes of normal development. Work in comparative development by Coghill (1929) and others introduced the concept of progressive differentiation from massive to finite response patterns. Clearly, this view was in marked contrast to the reductionistic reflexology which had influenced Watson's methods and his interpretation of his work with infants. Sherman (1927a, 1927b), Irwin and Weiss (1930), and Pratt, Nelson, and Sun (1930), who were among those who challenged Watson's views, investigated broad ranges of newborn behavior and interpreted their findings in terms of mass behavior as the distinctive characteristic of the newborn.

In 1926 Freud published his theories of the origin of anxiety and since that time there has been increasing interest in various aspects of anxiety in infants and throughout childhood. There has also been increasing interest, as a consequence of the psychoanalytic theory, in the effect of early experience on subsequent emotional development. Study of mother-child interaction in infancy has led to a current interest in the ontogenesis of smiling, fear of strangers, and separation anxiety.

DEFINING AND CONCEPTUALIZING EMOTION
IN THE YOUNG INFANT

Woodworth (1928) suggested three criteria which must be considered before attempting the identification of emotion: the significance of the environmental situation as it is perceived by the individual; the overt expression; and finally the occurrence of autonomic reactions. Woodworth maintained that emotion can be identified only if all three components can be found to occur together.

Studies of midbrain development, function, and contribution to emotion in infancy have been well reviewed by Scheibel and Scheibel (1964). Histological studies show that subcortical centers associated with emotion in the human newborn are intact at birth. The stages of development of many of these structures have been carefully presented by Conel (1939, 1963). Unfortunately, it is not yet possible to determine the extent to which all centers are functional or how they function in the young infant. However, there are autonomic reactions functioning at birth and it is these that have been selected for systematic and extensive study by a number of investigators in recent times.

A notable example is the work of Lipton, Steinschneider, and Richmond (1960, 1961a, 1961b, 1966) who have been conducting extensive systematic studies of autonomic function of the newborn in relation to sensory stimulation. Others have taken a similar course so that today there is a growing literature on relationships between autonomic responsiveness as a measure of arousal under varying conditions of stimulation and in terms of individual differences in reactivity.

The instability of states of arousal remains a major concern for any investigation of newborn behavior. Bell (1960, 1963) and Wolff (1959, 1963) attempted systematic ratings of level of arousal in the newborn. This has also been done by Bridger, Birns, and Blank (1965) who have found correlations between such ratings and heart rate measures in the neonate.

EARLY RESEARCH

Watson (1925a, 1925b) and Watson and Morgan (1917) provide accounts of what Watson interpreted as unlearned emotional behavior in the newborn. Watson and Rayner (1920) described learned and generalized fear in an infant of eleven months. According to Watson, unlearned emotion is limited to the newborn, although he speculated on the possibility of habit formation *in utero*. Demonstrations of this view were made primarily with respect to what Watson interpreted as unlearned responses that were really precursors of emotional expression in more mature infants. While systematic observations of newborns were conducted under Watson's direction (Blanton, 1917), he himself attempted what he described as experimental studies, but which today we would be more inclined to regard as demonstrations. During his experiments with newborns from one to ten days of age, Watson kept records of respiratory and vasomotor responses, but controlled measurements were not taken.

Watson claimed that there are three instinctive, unlearned emotions: fear, rage, and love. *Fear* was said to be elicited by a very loud, sudden sound, or by sudden removal of support, to which the infant responded with random clutching of arms and hands, sudden closing of eyelids, puckering of the lips, and crying. *Rage* was said to be produced by restraining the infant's arms and holding the head, or pressing the legs together. The infant responded by stiffening the body, holding his breath until he became blue in the face, and sometimes by slashing or striking movements of the arms and hands. *Love* was said to appear in response to gentle tactile stimulation, including stroking of erogenous zones. The young infant was said to respond by quieting, gurgling, relaxing, and smiling.

Watson's demonstration of learned fear in the eleven-month-old Albert as well as related studies conducted by M. C. Jones (1924a, 1924b), by Jones and Jones (1928), and by H. E. Jones (1931) are discussed by Brackbill and Koltsova in the chapter on conditioning and learning in this volume.

Understandably, Watson's work was controversial. His dogmatic, propagandistic pronouncements inevitably kindled negative reactions in the scientific community. The controversies, however, served the cause of developmental study by generating further research with infants. There were a number of attempts to replicate his work under more controlled conditions and with larger groups of infants (Pratt *et al.,* 1930; Irwin, 1932; Taylor, 1934; Stoffels, 1940–41). None of these attempts at replication was successful.

A stereotype of anger in newborns was created by Watson (1925a) with the description of slashing and defensive arm movements when head, arms, and legs are severely restricted. Levy (1944) noted that prolonged restraint by swaddling from birth does not elicit rage reactions. He suggested that restriction occurs only when freedom has been experienced previously or when purposive responses are interrupted. Stirnimann (1937) made a study of reactions to restraint of hand movements in newborns and reported varied responses. Levy's (1944) attempt to replicate this study produced similar findings of wide individual differences among infants. Levy attributed the differences to constitutional predispositions, some of which may be due to perinatal events. Taylor (1934) suggested that Watson's handling of his infant subjects may have been unduly rough and was probably painful.

Sherman and Sherman (1925) and Sherman, Sherman, and Flory (1936) conducted an extensive series of studies of newborn responses to a variety of stimuli including restraint. These responses varied with increase in the duration of restraint. Initially there was head withdrawal or retraction; then there was an approach response described as attack. (Possibly what Watson described as defensive movements, the Shermans described as attack. Operational descriptions of procedures were very incomplete in early studies, and the Sherman's account of intensity and duration as important stimulus characteristics represents a step forward.) It may be of some passing interest to note that this observed progression from retraction to active approach suggests Schneirla's theory of innate tendencies of withdrawal and approach (1959).

In spite of the many apparent semantic confusions in the early studies, Irwin (1932) recognized the resemblance between the Moro reflex in the newborn and the reactions elicited when replicating Watson's "fear" experiment with 24 infants. Pratt (1954) suggested that he may also have been eliciting this reflex. Irwin's reference to the Moro reflex is notable in view of his position with respect to the issue of mass vs. discrete activity in the newborn:

> Reflexes and behavior patterns may be later specializations of individualizations of aspects of mass activity. The view that the reflex is the unit from which all complex behavior is built seems to be losing its high status both in physiology and psychology (1930, p. 79).

Pratt *et al.* noted in their 1930 publication: "The fact that seems most pronounced in our own investigations is that any stimulus may release any reaction" (p. 211).

Irwin and Pratt were impressed with Coghill's reports (1929) that in Amblystoma (salamander) larvae, independent activity of limbs and gills follows general, diffuse, total body movements. Movements of limbs were believed to acquire independence through a process of "individuation," having first moved in association with movement of the trunk. From diffuse developmental trends of the organism as a whole comes a gradual individuation of the independent movements of the parts. The early notion that the newborn is both physiologically as well as psychologically undifferentiated in every respect has now been revised in recognition of a group of discrete reflex responses.

Bridges (1932) apparently found in the then current interest in the ontogenesis of behavior, dominated as it was by the concept of gradual differentiation, another means of challenging Watson's views of unlearned and learned emotion. Her study of the development of emotion over the first fifteen months of life is widely quoted and appears consistently in both introductory and advanced psychological textbooks. It is infrequently noted, however, that Bridges' study consisted of somewhat less than ideally systematic observations of institutionalized infants. The study offers very little evidence of systematic procedures or systematic operational definitions of emotional states; nor is there a report of observer reliability.

The Bridges study combined both short-term longitudinal and cross-sectional design. Infants from two weeks through twenty-four months were each observed for three-month periods. Three infants were followed from the second week of life. There was an N ranging from 11 to 25 infants at each age level from one through fifteen months, while there was an N of two to eight among the older infants. Observations appear to have been based chiefly on running records of daily behavior under a variety of daily routine situations. From such observations Bridges briefly sketched the behavior characteristic of each age. This behavior was labeled in terms of various emotions.

Bridges also made a schematic analysis of differentiation from an "original emotion" of general excitation at birth to increasingly distinct affect states appearing during the course of the first two years. She labeled all emotional expression at three months as either distress or delight. At six months, according to Bridges, distress differentiates into fear, disgust, and anger, although generalized distress is observed through the first two years. This is true also for generalized delight. Sometime in the last half of the first year delight differentiates into elation and affection. Shortly after twelve months jealousy becomes apparent as well as a distinction between affection for adults and affection for peers.

Bridges wrote of "evolution" of subjective emotional states as well as the progressive differentiation and "consolidation" of overt "reactions." Inferences about the former were apparently made quite freely from unsystematic observations of the latter.

FIRST YEAR

CRYING

Blanton (1917) and Wolff (1959) gave detailed descriptions of the facial expression of newborns, just prior to their crying, that involved very discrete muscular movements. In one of the earliest accounts of newborn crying, Blanton observed 15 infants and reported preparatory muscular changes prior to crying as early as ten and thirty minutes after birth. The corners of the mouth turn down, or the lower lip rolls down, or there is pouting. These "expressions" are sustained for a while before crying. Wolff described a "precry face" in the newborn during irergular sleep. These observations are of interest because they run counter to the concept of purely massive response in the newborn.

Two well-known studies of crying by Sherman (1927a, 1927b) were among the first to employ certain experimental controls. They were devised as yet another challenge to Watson's assertions about early emotional behavior in the newborn. Sherman chose to demonstrate the difficulty in making judgments of differential emotional responses in the newborn. Three groups of observers, without knowledge of the stimuli, were shown motion pictures of the responses of infants under twelve days of age. The crying occurred as a consequence of sudden dropping, restraint, hunger, and pain. There was no agreement among observers as to the meaning of the response. They failed to guess correctly either the nature of the stimulus or to agree among themselves as to what specific emotion was expressed. There was similar disagreement in identifying the cries of infants to whom stimuli were administered when a screen separated the judges from the infants. This procedure tested the operational definition necessary for identification of emotional response suggested by Woodworth.

Bayley (1932) made one of the most systematic studies of crying during the course of mental and physical tests given monthly to each of the 61 infants in the Berkeley Growth Study. Judgments were based on mutual agreement of the two experimenters who saw the infants at different times during the hour-long procedures; there is no report of tests of reliability.

The most frequent cause of crying was physical restriction and handling during examination and testing. Only about one third of the infants cried under these circumstances, however. Strangeness was the next most frequent cause of crying, although it is not apparent until after the second month. There was a gradual increase in crying during the procedures of examination until it occurred among 10 per cent of the infants at 6 months and among 25 per cent during its peak at 10 months. This minority is of some interest since stranger anxiety is increasing at this age. Studies of crying in young infants have also been made by students of language. These are described in the chapter on language development in this volume. The four studies by Aldrich et al. on decrease in amount of crying in relation to increasing infant care are also reported in that chapter.

Stimulation. A number of studies (e.g., Irwin & Weiss, 1934; Weiss, 1934) are in agreement that newborns cry less when exposed to continuous sound. Salk (1960, 1961, 1962) reported 60 per cent more crying in the newborn nursery during a no-sound condition than during the continuous presentation of a recorded human heartbeat at 85 db over a four-day period. Crying was also one of several dependent variables in the study by Brackbill, Adams, Crowell, and Gray (1966) in which 24 newborns were individually exposed to a 45-minute sequence of three different auditory stimuli continuously presented at 85 db. In this study there was significantly more crying under no sound than during any type of auditory stimulation.

Tears. Marked individual differences in onset of crying with tears have been demonstrated by Penbharkkul and Karelitz (1962). Among a group of newborn infants, 13 per cent cried with tears within five days after birth, while 25 per cent had not shed a tear after thirty days. Wolff (1959) noted that tears were shed on the second day by two of the four newborns observed in detail during five days in the nursery. Botelho (1964), a physiologist, suggested that onset of psychogenic crying is a function of the maturity of the central nervous system. For this reason appearance of tears in the infant has been of interest to many scientists and even to philosophers including Aristotle.

Age Changes. There is considerable agreement among accounts of changes in the incidence of crying during the first year (Bühler, 1930; Bayley, 1932; Bridges, 1932; Kelting, 1934; Blatz & Millichamp, 1935).

Crying and Frustration. The well-known theory and research by Dollard (1939) on the relationship between frustration and aggression stimulated several studies with infants. Sears and Sears (1940) studied frustration under different strengths of the hunger drive by withdrawing the bottle after different amounts of milk had been consumed. The study was conducted with one infant of twenty-three weeks. It was found that the latency of the crying response following withdrawal varied directly with the amount of milk consumed. The strength of frustration, as measured by amount of crying, varied directly with the strength of instigation to the frustrated goal-response.

Marquis (1943) measured frustration by general body activity, mouth activity, and crying. Seven newborn infants were studied by interrupting two feedings per day for ten days. Each of these feedings was interrupted six times during one bottle feeding. The results were comparable to those of Sears and Sears (1940). It was noted that blocking of feeding activity evokes immediate frustration responses which are expressed in goal-directed mouth activity as well as general activity. Individual differences were noted in general activity and quality of responses. There was a high correlation between general activity and birth weight.

SMILING IN THE NEONATE

Smiling in the infant varies in form and in susceptibility to specific stimuli with age changes. Smiling development in the infant is best considered in terms of three stages during the first year. In all three stages the response is notably discrete and specific, although the form changes. A survey of smiling studies quite strikingly demonstrates the value of a variety of orientations.

Morphology. The morphology of smiling in the newborn (Wolff, 1963) includes both spontaneous and elicited smilelike movements of the mouth. These smiles, although quite discrete, are nevertheless quite different from the well-developed smile. Only the corners of the mouth are drawn back (Darwin, 1898; Koehler, 1954; Wolff, 1963). The muscles around the eye are not used during the first week. Wolff (1963) observed preparatory movements before the smile that include movements of the ears. These seem to be well-integrated movements rather than a passive spreading of the mouth. The smile itself is quite brief and often involves a myoclonic type of twitch.

Nonelicited Smiling. Wolff (1963) classified this smile with certain types of newborn behavior that occur spontaneously and often with regularity at certain levels of arousal, e.g., startles, penile erections, and rhythmic mouthing. Wolff regarded this smile as a "physiological mechanism," reserving the term "behavior pattern" for the more developed social smile.

State, or level of arousal, is an important variable in newborn research, since response patterns are likely to vary from one level to another (Bell, 1960, 1963; Escalona, 1962). This situation may be somewhat obscure since EEG studies indicate that distinctions in arousal patterns of cortical discharge during waking and sleeping are not as clear in the newborn as in older infants and children (Scheibel & Scheibel, 1964). Wolff (1963), however, has observed smiling in relation to several different states: regular or deep sleep, irregular or light sleep, drowsiness, alert inactivity, waking activity, waking alertness, and crying.

Because the neonatal smile has a sharp onset and almost immediately wanes, Freedman (1964, 1965) described the neonatal smile as "reflexive." Gewirtz (1965a, 1965b), however, pointed out that neonatal smiling does not conform to one of the properties of a true reflex in that it may be evoked by a wide variety of stimuli. In commenting on this phenomenon, Freedman (1964) noted that although the smile occurs in the absence of normal eliciting stimuli in the neonate, contemporary observers agree that the process is something other than the older notion of escaping gas. Freedman compared it to what the ethologist, Lorenz (1937), described as "vacuum behavior." In animals this is behavior for which the normal stimulus is not present. Spitz and Wolf (1946) have made a similar analogy, using another ethological term for this type of behavior: "overflow reaction." There are individual differences in this type of smiling; it is never seen in some infants.

Elicited Smiling. Auditory stimuli, particularly high-pitched voices, appear to be effective in eliciting smiling during the neonatal period (Wolff, 1963). Wolff has presented data on latency of smiling response to auditory stimuli, as well as on subsequent refractory periods, during irregular sleep in the first week of life. A single experiment consisted of five separate presentations of a particular sound at standard intervals. Unfortunately, the duration of presentations and of interstimulus intervals is not clear. It is of interest that there was regularity in the latency of response. If there was a smile to this auditory stimulation it occurred only on one or two of the five occasions, whereas the interval from beginning of stimulation to the smile was almost always *seven seconds*. For other responses the latency varied systematically as it did also with smiling in different states of arousal. Refractory time following response was also lengthy. It was not possible to elicit another smile for five minutes according to this study. Inasmuch as conduction of auditory stimulation from the cochlea to cortical auditory centers in older children and adults is very fast, the question remains as to why and how afferent and efferent processes in this situation are so extended in time.

There are reports of other stimuli capable of eliciting neonatal smiles. Blanton (1917) reported smiling at thirteen days to bright lights; while Watson (1919), Pratt (1930), and Dennis (1935) reported smiling within the first ten days to tickling and other tactile stimuli. Dennis also elicited the smile with olfactory stimulation.

Wolff (1963) and Freedman (1964, 1965) regard the neonatal smile as an unlearned, biologically based response. Although this behavior is not strictly a reflex, these observers agree that it differs from the social smile. Wolff prefers to regard the neonatal response as a mechanism rather than as a behavior pattern. This distinction may perhaps be compared to that made by Botelho (1964) between newborn crying and later psychogenic crying.

SOCIAL SMILING, NONSELECTIVE

There are a number of observations of what is assumed to be social smiling between two and eight weeks (Jones, 1926; Shirley, 1933; Gesell & Thompson, 1934; Söderling, 1959; Wolff, 1963; Gewirtz, 1965a, 1965b). The smile in this phase is characteristically elicited by visual stimuli which are chiefly social in origin. There is a progression during the course of this stage that is associated with the interval between two and six months. The peak of maximal nonselective smiling is reached sometime from three to six months, with variations between home and institution babies (Spitz & Wolf, 1946; Ambrose, 1961; Gewirtz, 1965a, 1965b). Gewirtz found onset of social smiling at four weeks in three groups of infants: residential institution infants, infants in the Kibbutzim in Israel, and family infants. Institution infants in this study reached a peak of smiling at twenty weeks, a month later than the other two groups (see Fig. 8.1).

Morphology. The various components of full facial smiling become increasingly well integrated during this stage, although Gewirtz (1965a, 1965b) found the integration of all elements of smiling is not complete until the peak of social smiling, around six months. The muscles around the eyes as well as those of the mouth and the cheeks are used. In comparison to the discrete movement of the mouth in neonatal smiling, the social smiling that follows takes on more massive, total body activity. This trend is in direct opposition to the views expressed by Irwin (1930) and Pratt (1930). During this period the limbs move vigorously as the social smile is prolonged and increases in strength.

There is now a fairly extensive literature on effective stimuli for eliciting nonselective social smiling. These are visual stimuli, both stationary and in movement, auditory, and somesthetic stimuli used separately or together with visual stimuli.

Visual Stimuli. Jones (1926) made one of the earliest systematic studies of infant facial smiling in a cross-sectional study. Family infants were observed in a public health clinic. With the examiner's face 12 in.

from that of the infant, the examiner smiled and made clucking noises. The youngest child to respond with a smile was thirty-nine days old, and by ninety days 100 per cent of the infants smiled. Smiling, together with sound, was considered adequate stimulation for eliciting smiles during this period. Several subsequent studies are all in agreement that a nodding, full face, together with sound of a human voice, has been preferred to the unmoving face among family and institution infants (Spitz & Wolf, 1946; Ahrens, 1954; L'Allier, 1961; Laroch & Tcheng, 1963).

Kaila (1932), working in the Charlotte Bühler nursery, was the

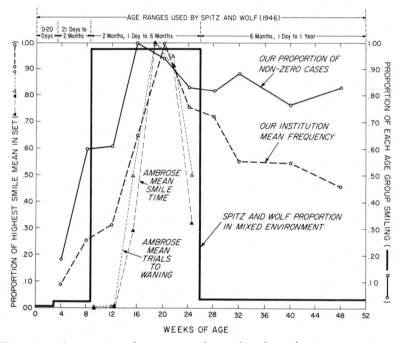

Figure 8.1. *Comparison of age curves for smiling from three investigations.*

(1) The Spitz & Wolf (1946) study of an heterogeneous sample using as their measure the proportion of Ss who smiled in an age range; (2) Ambrose's (1961) study of institution infants using the measures, mean smiling time per run and mean number of presentations to waning; and (3) Gerwirtz study's age curves in the first forty-eight weeks (twelve lunar months) for institution infants using the measures "mean frequency of smiles" and "proportion of each age group smiling." To make comparable the quantitative metrics of the Gerwirtz study and that of Ambrose, group means are transformed into the proportions they constitute of the highest mean in their set; that highest mean is assigned the value 1.00 (left axis). The four age ranges covering the first year of life for Spitz and Wolf are defined at the very top of this chart. Their proportion values (right axis) are plotted as heavy horizontal lines through each age range; these are joined by vertical lines at range limits. (From Gewirtz, 1965.)

first to explore the possibilities of variations in facial schemata for eliciting smiles. Kaila noted that infants in this period of development not only smile, but stare at faces with much fascination. Tests were made to determine the elements of the face which elicit such a strong response; these included masks, a real face, the top half of a face, and the schematic use of light or dark eyes alone on a black paper. The full front view of the face was preferred to profile. This was interpreted in Gestalt terms. Kaila and Wolff (1963) both point to the importance of the eye-to-eye contact during the development of social smiling. Wolff reports smiling only after the infant soberly inspected all features of the observer's face, one by one, then finally focused on the eyes of the observer.

A recent Russian study (Kistjakovskaya, 1965) described the onset of positive emotional expression in infants. The first evidence of positive expression appeared when the infant fixated on the face of an adult who spoke at the same time he moved forward and backward. All three factors were regarded as important aspects of the stimulus. The relation between smiling and visual fixation was emphasized, however, and was interpreted as evidence of a "drive in the activity of the visual analyzer" rather than a response to facial configuration.

The emphasis in Kistjakovskaya's study on what we might describe as a curiosity or exploratory drive introduces another variable into the growing complex of factors associated with infant smiling to visual stimuli. Following the pioneer studies of infants' visual preference for complex patterns by Berlyne (1958) and Fantz (1963), there is now an expanding literature on infant attention to complex visual schemata. However, this phenomenon has been studied in relation to smiling in only a few instances (Kagan, Henker, Hen-Tov, Levine, & Lewis, 1965; Lewis, 1965). Fantz was able to demonstrate longer fixation time in the four-day-old newborn to the configuration of a face than to other patterns. The human face remains a compelling stimulus throughout infancy.

Spitz and Wolf (1946) made an extensive study of smiling to a facial configuration. Subjects in this well-known study included 251 infants of various races and environments. They found that a grimacing mouth is preferred equally to a smile in the front-view face. Since the grimacing involved movement, this may be the basis of the preference. Stimulus conditions included presentations of a full-front face with and without a mask, two- and three-dimensional masks, part of a face, and profile of the face.

One of the objects of this study was to investigate Kaila's hypothesis of smiling as an innate response to a Gestalt configuration. These investigators differentiate between the smile to a face and the innate smiling response in the neonate which they describe as an inborn motor pattern or Anlage manifested without environmental stimulus. They conclude, however, that by three months this motor pattern, the smile, has been integrated into the pattern of emotional needs at a social level. Therefore, they do not regard the elicitation of smile by the face as an innate response to a Gestalt sign.

Although Spitz and Wolf agree that the configuration of eye-nose-forehead has a Gestalt quality which signals the smiling, they interpret this as a function of learned expectations of pleasure associated with the face. They also cite instances of infants who cried at the approach of a face at this early age. These infants had histories that indicated that unpleasant associations with the face might have been established. This finding was presented in support of the theory that response to a face by the age of three months is one that has been learned. Further evidence was presented in the differential response of three-month infants to the eyes-nose-forehead stimulus and inanimate objects and toys. There was no smiling to the latter. The human face alone is interpreted as the signal for a response as a function of emotionally cathected experience.

Further speculations about the social smiling were introduced by Spitz and Wolf (1946). They suggested that the smile and the eye-to-eye contact are products of an evolutionary process. With the development of upright posture face-to-face interaction is possible, and with the development of the human hand, face-to-face contact between mother and infant can take place.

Székely (1954) interprets the Gestalt configuration—eyes-nose-forehead, described by Spitz and Wolf (1946)—in terms of the concept of a releaser or key stimulus that acts as a signal for the onset of specific unlearned behavior. Székely referred to the sign stimuli or releasers which have been identified by ethologists as eliciting automatic instinctual response in animals (von Uexküll, J., 1921; Bruckner, 1933; Tinbergen & Kuenen, 1939). The process by which a releaser functions has been hypothesized as an "Innate Releaser Mechanism" or IRM by Lorenz (1950), Tinbergen (1951), and others. Székely has applied this set of ethological concepts and hypotheses to the human infants' smiling response to a face as Spitz and Wolf (1946) described it. Spitz (1955) made it clear that he did not intend to find an analogue between this form of human behavior and that of phylogenetically differently organized species. However, in the 1955 paper, Spitz reformulated his hypothesis about the smiling response. He described the eyes-nose-forehead configuration as ". . . a social releaser key stimulus in the intra-species relations; the behavior which it releases belongs to the feeding-nursing situation" (1955, p. 163).

In a study of institution infants by Polak, Emde, and Spitz (1964) subjects failed to discriminate between the three-dimensional face of a live human being and a life-size photograph of the same individual until almost three months of age. Between two and three months bright illumination on the face was required in order to elicit a smile. There was an increase in latency, degree, and duration of smiling to the three-dimensional live face between three and five months. During this period another response to the living face was noted, an intermittent turning away. This turning away response also differentiated between photograph and the real face. After five months there was a decrease in differentiation between the two stimuli. These investigators also reported a rhythmic quality of the smile which involved mouth, tongue, and lips.

It became stronger with the approach of the face and weakened with retreat. This reaction was compared to that observed with the approach of the bottle.

In a study of infant responses to the configuration of eyes, Ahrens (1954) compared reactions to two eyes or dots alone on an oval card with response to six such dots on a card. Six dots were preferred to two at the age of two months. Subjects were institutionalized infants. Ahrens finds an analogue in early preferential smiling to six dots with the gaping of herring gull chicks to a supernormal sign-stimulus, as reported by Baerends (1957, 1959). Ahrens refers to the ethological concept that intensity of a reaction may sometimes depend not only on what sign stimuli are present, but how many are present. This concept is supported by a number of animal studies; it was defined initially by Seitz (1940).

Salzen (1963) suggests that smiling may be elicited by visual stimuli in an infant under twelve weeks by changes in brightness of the visual field. A flashing light and a face with contrasting black and white marks on an oval were both presented to infants. The flashing light produced smiling more effectively at first, particularly when it was oscillated or rotated. After twelve weeks, however, the face became the more effective stimulus. Although Salzen used only one infant for this exploratory study, more extensive and systematic investigation should be worthwhile.

There are recent reports in which several responses to faces are measured concurrently. Kagan *et al.* (1965) and Lewis (1965) reported several studies conducted with the objective of clarifying the ambiguous variable, fixation time. This is the variable which Berlyne (1958), Fantz (1963), and others have interpreted as an indication of preference. Fixation time in the Kagan studies was one of several response measures that included heart rate as well as smiling.

Kagan *et al.* (1965) presented four three-dimensional heads to four-month-old infants. These heads formed a series of faces which varied along a continuum from a familiar type of realistic face to a novel stimulus in the form of a faceless head. Between the two extremes there were two faces varying in degrees of violation of realism. In one, the nose and mouth emerged; in the other all the features were present but in distorted arrangement. Fixation time was the same for both familiar and unfamiliar stimuli. Smiling appeared to be more differentiating than fixation time, occurring more frequently to the familiar than to the moderate violations of familiar schemata. Change in heart rate differentiated between stimuli in a response pattern which also contrasted with that of fixation time. The Kagan and Lewis studies are the first to provide an opportunity to compare data on autonomic response and smiling response to the same stimuli.

The history of research in early emotional development lacks any substantial empirical literature covering the relationship between arousal responses and behavioral indices of emotion. Nevertheless, theorists have made a close association between emotion and arousal since Lindsley (1951) first presented EEG data demonstrating the relationship and developing the theory. There is a growing literature on sensory stimulation and arousal in the infant, but the emotional significance of the behavioral indices used in these studies has been considered by only a very few investigators. Lipton, Richmond, Weinberger, and Hersher (1958), Richmond and Lipton (1959), and Lipton, Steinschneider, and Richmond (1960, 1961a, 1961b, 1966) are among the few students of autonomic functions of the infant who have made such studies.

Brackbill (1958) demonstrated the interaction of two complex processes in four-month-old infants in her operant conditioning study of smiling using intensive interpersonal interaction as the reinforcer. This interaction included visual, auditory, and tactual stimulation. In this study the examiner initially presented a rigidly sober face to the infant, but when the infant voluntarily smiled it was immediately rewarded by reciprocal smiling from the examiner who then picked up the infant, talked to it, and bounced it about. This study reported an inverse relation between amount of smiling and crying during both conditioning and extinction. This is one of the very few smiling studies providing evidence of behavior which can be interpreted in terms of affective states or emotion.

There is a recurrent tendency among some students of the smiling response in infants to find analogues in this response to animal behavior patterns that have been described by ethologists as purely automatic, instinctual behavior occurring in response to certain specific sensory stimuli (Tinbergen, 1958; Hess, 1962). The terms Innate Releaser Mechanism or IRM and supernormal sign-stimulus refer to ethological concepts about the processes underlying patterns of instinctual behavior in animals. Comparisons between these concepts and the behavior of young infants require cautious treatment. Ethologists are considering some very specific forms of behavior which function in animals to achieve specific purposes. Our knowledge of the smiling behavior of infants is still far from complete so that any such comparisons may be quite premature. The ethological concept of instinctual behavior usually refers to a series of responses that are quite automatic. Although it is true that Wolff (1963) and Freedman (1964) have both noted a reflexive early smile in the neonate, the later social smile that occurs following prolonged study of the features of the face can never be regarded as purely automatic, instinctual behavior.

Auditory and Somesthetic Stimuli. Freedman (1964) emphasized the significance of smiling to stimuli other than visual in his data on smiling in blind infants. Extensive studies conducted by Hetzer and Tudor-Hart of auditory stimuli and smiling in 126 normal infants were reported by Bühler (1933). Although the human voice elicited smiling more effectively than other auditory stimuli among infants from one day to five months of age, Bühler reported that during this age range there was the same nonselective smiling to voices as to faces. Freedman also provided details of the auditory and tactual stimuli used by L'Allier (1961) with 120 institutionalized infants and by Laroch and Tcheng (1963) with 88 family infants. These studies made comparisons between frequency of smiling to voices and to faces. The latter was always the more compelling of the two stimuli for children with normal vision.

Thompson (1941) and Freedman (1964) studied smiling in congenitally blind infants. Thompson compared the morphological changes with age in the smiling of 26 babies, including one blind baby, with Washburn's (1929) descriptions of normal infants' smiling. The sequence appeared to be the same for both groups, and it was therefore assumed that smiling is a biological and maturational phenomenon.

Freedman (1964) reported a follow-up of four blind infants to whom the Bayley Infant Mental and Motor Tests were given. In the early months, test items designed to elicit smiling responses from normal infants through visual, tactile, and auditory stimulation successfully produced fleeting smiles similar to the reflexive smile of the normal neonate. The course of smiling developed among these infants a few months behind the normal. At two months there was still a reflexive smile which appeared in a rapid series. More prolonged social smiling developed in the third and fourth months along with head turning toward the vocal source of stimulation. A physiological nystagmus characteristic of these infants ceased during this prolonged smiling.

Smiling in blind infants has been interpreted to strengthen the existing evidence of a biological basis for development of smiling and also the association of smiling with interpersonal interaction. The studies comparing smiling in fraternal and identical twins reported by Freedman (1961a, 1963, 1965) and by Freedman and Keller (1963) provide another kind of evidence that smiling has a biological component and is under genetic control. These investigators reported significantly greater similarity in developmental patterns of both smiling and fear of strangers among identical twins under twelve months in comparison with fraternal twins of the same age.

In Washburn's short-term longitudinal study (1929), 15 family children were followed from eight to fifty-two weeks. The infants were observed during developmental testing and special "games" in a laboratory situation. There was emphasis on interpersonal situations for eliciting smiles in almost all the games, although there was also a surprise situation as well as tactile and kinesthetic stimulation. Interpersonal situations included appearance and disappearance of the examiner, as well as a peek-a-boo game. All infants responded to these situations with smiling by twenty to twenty-four weeks. In contrast to the increase in frequency and the change in quality of smiling that began during this period, laughing occurred about two months later and remained more stereotyped and less expressive even though it was stimulated by the same events that elicited smiling.

Wolff (1963) was able to elicit smiling to surprise in family infants studied in their homes. This occurred beginning at age three and one-half weeks when an object was suddenly brought into the field of vision. The first social smiling appeared at the same age in the family infants in Wolff's sample. Wolff also found that nonsocial kinesthetic and tactile stimuli were the most efficient elicitors of smiling from twenty-four days of age until the end of his observations at ninety days. Procedure for this involved pat-a-cake under conditions in which the examiner held the infant's hands and moved them in pat-a-cake motions yet was himself screened from the infant's view. Smiling to this stimulation could never be habituated. This is notable because it is often maintained that smiling in infancy is most readily elicited by the stimulus of a human face. Yet, here is a nonsocial situation invariably eliciting what is described as an exceptionally strong smiling response.

SELECTIVE SMILING

Sometime after five or six months of age, infants begin to smile chiefly to familiar faces, usually those of the mother and family, more readily than to strangers. Strangers may be soberly examined by infants. If the stranger approaches too close or too fast there may be crying. During this stage, movement of the limbs while smiling is largely inhibited (Gewirtz, 1965a, 1965b).

Washburn (1929) and Spitz and Wolf (1946) reported absence of any smiling after twenty-four weeks. However, this view has subsequently been challenged. In Washburn's study smiling reappeared at forty weeks. This temporary disappearance may have been due to an increased reaction to the strange situation of the laboratory in which the study was made. Spitz and Wolf (1946) and Ambrose (1961) reported that the change in effectiveness of the face as a stimulus starts at about six months among institutional infants until all smiling of any kind disappears.

Gewirtz (1965a, 1965b) reported a temporary moderate decline in frequency of smiling among 91 family infants between four to twelve months. In this study the stimulus for smiling at all ages from one to eighteen months was a two-minute presentation of a female experimenter's face two ft. from the subject's face. The experimenter did not smile during the presentation, and the only eye-to-eye contacts that were disrupted were made in order to check a timer. For a few minutes each infant had opportunity to see the observer at a distance before the trial period. Gewirtz also studied 226 institution infants in the same manner. Among the children in this group, smiling to the stimulus continued after six months, although at a steadily decreasing rate to the end of the study at eighteen months. There was a similar decrease among 105 infants in day care centers. Still another pattern was found among the 236 infants reared in the Kibbutzim. These showed two peaks of maximal smiling, at four and six months. Following a slight decline in frequency to eight months, the rate of smiling remained stationary to twelve months. All infants showed a gradual decrease in smiling from twelve and fourteen months to sixteen and eighteen months.

The period of selective social smiling coincides with that of increasing fear of strangers and separation from mothers. Therefore, smiling studies at this age provide data relative to the development of both smiling and of fear and anxiety. By using a strange face, Gewirtz's study contributes to both areas of inquiry. This is true also of the work by Laroch and Tcheng (1963), who exposed family children to both familiar and unfamiliar male and female faces. The smiling response to the unfamiliar female face for these subjects was much the same in both studies. There was a peak at four months and another at twelve months, following a temporary decline. For the unfamiliar male face there was a peak at nine months falling off by twelve months. Among all subjects in the Laroch and Tcheng study there was more smiling to all stimuli, visual or auditory, between four and six months.

FEAR AND ANXIETY

Although the distinction between fear and anxiety is a cloudy one by any definition, it is generally held that fear is the more specific emotion resulting from identifiable stimuli, whereas anxiety is the more diffuse emotional state—less clearly perceived and less readily referrable to antecedent conditions.

Freud (1926) expressed the view that anxiety may first occur during the trauma of birth, an event which is presumably experienced by the infant as one of intense stimulation. Subsequently, a number of personality theorists have associated anxiety with infancy and events of early childhood. Among these are Rank (1929), Adler (1930), Horney (1937, 1939, 1945), and Sullivan (1965). Benjamin (1959, 1961, 1963) proposed that anxiety may appear in the first two to four weeks of life, although he does not regard this as a universal phenomenon. At this time there is apparently very rapid neurophysiological maturation which is believed to provide both for increased sensitivity to external or internal excitation and capacity for positive and negative response.

Benjamin (1963) indicated that two mechanisms may account for observed peaks of irritability among some infants during the later neonatal period. Either the mother tends to overstimulate the infant at this time of increased sensitivity, or she is unsuccessful in quieting him and reducing tension. He suggested that a major problem for young infants occurs in adjusting to varying degrees of stimulation. Too much or too little stimulation may cause stress. Benjamin referred to Freud's speculations (1900, 1920, 1926) about a passive mechanism in the very young infant, "a stimulus barrier," by which it is protected from overstimulation. In the older infant there is theoretically a shift to a more active involvement in self-protection under conditions of overstimulation. The latter stage would seem to correspond with the appearance of stranger and separation anxiety. There is frequent reference to stranger anxiety in early studies of infant behavior: Bühler (1930), Bayley (1932), Bridges (1932), Shirley (1933), Gesell and Thompson (1934). Gesell and Thompson (1934) reported that 56 per cent of the infants studied responded with "sobering" to strangers by four months, but that there was a peak of withdrawal from strangers from eight to eleven months. Morgan and Ricciuti (in press) provide one of the more extensive recent studies of stranger anxiety, but refrain from interpreting sober examination of strangers as a necessary sign of fear. (Such differences in interpretation lead to disagreement both as to the incidence and age of onset of stranger anxiety.)

Other topics of research that have appeared recently include attachment to the mother and anxiety in relation to attachment; these have been influenced chiefly by psychoanalytic concepts of fear of object loss. Spitz (1950) and Bowlby (1958, 1960) have developed this theme. Another issue of investigation has been the effect of strangeness and of intensity of stimulation on emotion (Hebb, 1946, 1955). Freedman (1961a, 1961b, 1964, 1965) has introduced evolutionary and ethological concepts to the study of anxiety.

The lines between theoretical orientations are often crossed when formulating hypotheses for research in this area. Benjamin (1963) postulated that stranger anxiety may involve both fear of loss of object as well as fear of strangeness. This suggestion was made after observing apparent fear reactions to the strange in infants as young as three months, an age when it is assumed that cognitive capacity for concern over object loss has not yet developed.

Observations of many infants led Benjamin to conclude that there must be a very clear distinction between stranger anxiety and separation anxiety. Criteria for stranger anxiety used in the Tennes and Lampl (1964) study, which was designed to test Benjamin's hypotheses, were: ". . . sobering, turning away, visual avoidance, freezing, fussing, crying and the like" (1964, p. 249). Criteria for separation anxiety were: ". . . subtle behavior changes such as reduced activity in mother's absence, extremes of affect, e.g., overwhelming sadness or furious anger, as well as the range from mild, fussy protest to extremely hard crying . . ." (1964, p. 249). These criteria were judged on a six-point rating scale. On the basis of ratings by two judges, it was possible to differentiate among age of onset, peak intensities, and termination of the two forms of infant anxiety defined above. Ratings were made from records of regular contacts with mother and child in the home and laboratory. Interjudge reliability was .94 to .98 under these conditions.

Tennes and Lampl's results showed that stranger anxiety reaches a peak at seven to nine months. (This is in accord with Spitz's [1950] concept of an eight-month anxiety.) Separation anxiety is just beginning to become apparent at eight months and reaches a peak period lasting from thirteen to eighteen months. There were no sex differences for stranger anxiety, but boys showed significantly more separation anxiety. There were individual differences in the frequency with which both forms appeared in the same child: in some instances there seemed to be a high correlation between susceptibility to stranger anxiety and to separation anxiety, although in other children there appeared to be none whatever.

Schaffer and Callender (1959) studied 76 infants from three to fifty-one weeks of age upon their entering and leaving a hospital. Two different posthospital syndromes were postulated. The first, associated with infants under twenty-eight weeks, was characterized by an apathetic expression, searching motions, and a relatively brief period of indiscriminate response to all social stimulation. Such behavior was in marked contrast to the behavior problems that frequently occurred among older infants upon returning home. Schaffer attributed the difference between the two behavior patterns to the fact that the child over twenty-eight months responds to events in the environment increasingly in terms of a developing capacity for differentiation of persons and objects.

Although infants under seven months seem less responsive to strangeness in the Schaffer and Callender study, this should not be taken to indicate that young infants are incapable of sober regard of strange objects. Kagan *et al.* (1965) and Lewis (1965) found prolonged fixation time in response to unfamiliar stimuli among infants as young as three and four months. In these infants smiling occurred in response to the realistic or familiar type of face, while sober regard occurred to less familiar stimuli. It seems possible that the sober regard in place of smiling around seven or eight months has been too readily interpreted as fear when in fact it may be a response to increasing awareness of newly emerging differentiations.

Morgan and Ricciuti (in press) studied overt forms of negative behavior, including both stranger and separation anxiety, in infants in a cross-sectional study of five age groups averaging approximately four and one half, six and one half, eight and one half, ten and one half, and twelve and one half months. These investigators specifically ruled out sober regard as an index of fear. Morgan and Ricciuti noted that one of several possible sources of variance in the fear and smiling studies may be found in the different techniques used in the contact between stranger and infant. In some studies the silent, solemn, occasionally nodding face of a stranger was presented (Spitz & Wolf, 1946; Ambrose, 1961; Polak *et al.*, 1964; Tennes & Lampl, 1964; Gewirtz, 1965a, 1965b). In others, there was a fairly vivacious interaction (Jones, 1926; Rheingold, 1956, 1961). Therefore, an effort was made in this study to vary the responsiveness of two "strangers," male and female, by using a series of standardized procedures in which the stranger gradually approached the infant, speaking and smiling at specific times, until he finally reached the infant and touched his hand. The infant, meanwhile, experienced this treatment in one of two situations, either on his mother's lap or seated in a Baby Tenda, 4 ft. from the mother.

Under the conditions of this study overt, negative behavior in response to the stranger was not clearly predominant until twelve and one half months. There was no evidence of it at four and one half months or at six and one half months, while from eight and one half to ten and one half months there was only a slightly less positive reaction than at earlier ages. At twelve and one half months there was a negative response in both situations, but a more marked negative response when the infant was in the Baby Tenda. The investigators suggest that their own behavior had probably been quite similar to what the young infants were accustomed to experiencing, so that there was no occasion for the infants to react to the unexpected. The older the infant the more probable, they reasoned, that he had developed his own idiosyncratic expectations about appropriate behavior—expectations that strangers were correspondingly less likely to fulfill.

The fear of the older infants was interpreted to be in accord not only with Hebb's views (1946, 1955), but with those of Bowlby (1960). Bowlby postulated that by the end of the first year the infant has developed foresight and can anticipate potential separation even when strangers are observed from the haven of the mother's lap. This theory suggests also that coping with strangers without the immediate presence of the mother is unquestionably difficult at this age. In contrast, the younger infant lacks either forethought or specific attachments and therefore reacts to new people by generalization from experiences learned up to that time.

Ainsworth (1964a, 1964b), Schaffer (1964), and Schaffer and Emerson (1964) provide data to support the theory of a concurrent increase in attachment with increase in stranger anxiety. Attachment in the Ainsworth study was defined as behavior that implies affection and discrimination. It is a specific, active process by which the infant elicits a response from the object and participates in a two-way process of social interaction. Ainsworth's data came from a short-term, longitudinal study of patterns of attachment among the Baganda of Africa. Her 28 infant subjects, who ranged in age from two to fifteen months at the beginning of the study, were observed during interaction with their mothers and with other adults in the family and community. They were visited by the investigator in their homes at intervals of approximately two weeks, so that phases of attachment could be observed in progress.

For the first twelve months of life, four phases of attachment behavior were identified—phases that were not always mutually exclusive.

Phase 1. Nonselective responding.

Phase 2. Discrimination of the mother, indicated by differential crying, smiling, and vocalizing. Smiling to other individuals was not precluded in this stage. This development started at eight weeks. By fifteen weeks, separation from the mother evoked crying and attempts to follow.

Phase 3. Greeting responses occurred on approach to the mother. Mother became "home base" for clinging while surveying the rest of the environment.

Phase 4. An extension of or an accentuation of phase 3. Distinctions among persons became sharper. Preferences as well as fear of strangers were intense. These preferences led to attachments as well as rejections of others.

Ainsworth (in press) recently reported another study of attachment to mothers in relation to infant exploratory behavior and to stranger anxiety. This investigation is one facet of a longitudinal study of attachment during the first year of life. The procedures for the investigation were conducted in a laboratory setting in the United States. Fourteen infants, 7 boys and 7 girls, with a median age of fifty-one weeks, were observed by a stranger; the mother was either present or absent. There were eight experimental situations.

Infants in this study accepted the stranger remarkably well, and this acceptance seemed to bear very little relation to the degree of attachment to the mother, contrary to indications in some of the earlier studies. The degree of separation anxiety, moreover, did not give a clear indication of degree of attachment. This is of interest since Shaffer and Emerson (1964) studied separation anxiety as a measure of degree of attachment to the mother. Ainsworth concludes that the competence of infants in exploring a strange environment and in dealing with separation is a function of important interactional variables between mother and infant during the first year.

Age Changes in Specific Fears. Jersild and Holmes (1936) provide maturational data on infants' fears from surveys based on parents' observations and on interviews with the parents. Their infant subjects ranged in age from birth through eighteen months. The parental reports were compared with experimental studies on children over eighteen months. Noise was reported to be the most frequent cause of fear until about two and one half years, when fear of animals became predominant. Of those infants in whom fear was reported during the first year, 75 per cent reacted fearfully to sound, 50 per cent to strangers, 37 per cent to falling, and 25 per cent to animals. During the second year, fear of strangers decreased slightly whereas fear of animals sharply increased.

Although Watson (1925b) maintained that all fears are the result of conditioning in infancy, Valentine (1930) and Jersild and Holmes (1935) have questioned the conclusion that all fears are learned, noting the sudden appearance and sometimes unpredictable nature of certain fears in both the infant and the young child.

Jersild and Holmes (1935) found that partially strange stimuli such as unusual changes in the appearance of a familiar person induced fear and possibly conflict. Jersild (1954) noted the similarity between "irrational" fears of this kind and certain aspects of fearlike behavior to "uncanny" stimuli in primates which were observed by Hebb and Riesen (1943) and Hebb (1946). Hebb made the point that:

> Fear is not "innate" but depends on some sort of cognitive or cortical conflict of learned response. This is clearest when the baby chimpanzee, who knows and welcomes attendant A and attendant B, is terrified when he sees A wearing B's coat. The role of learning is inescapable in such a case (1955, p. 252).

Several studies (Bühler, 1928; Ellesor, 1933) indicate age changes from unresponsiveness to curiosity in the young infant from two to eight months, as well as changes during the course of repeated presentation of novel stimuli. Two-year-olds have been found to progress from apprehension on initial presentation to interest, exploration, and, finally, smiling and laughter. Infants apparently need time to adjust to novel stimuli. The question of approach and conflict in connection with novelty has been considered by Glanzer (1958) and Berlyne (1960); Frenkel-Brunswick (1949) examined the factors of perception of ambiguity in relation to emotion.

The element of fear, expressed overtly in avoidance and withdrawal, may arise when the newly stimulating experience becomes too intense or involves too great a discrepancy with an already operative schema. Hebb (1955) considered this issue in relation to stranger anxiety in infants, explaining it in terms of arousal or activation theory. This theory of emotion has developed since the discovery of the reticular activating system (RAS) by Moruzzi and Magoun (1949). The RAS has several functions, not all of which are as yet understood; however, one major function is to produce a state of cortical arousal that serves to energize and to create a state of vigilance so that the organism is better able to utilize sensory cues, including those of lower than average intensity. Pleasant affective states are believed to be associated with lower levels of arousal, whereas unpleasant emotion is associated with intense activation.

Hebb (1955) suggested that mild stimuli may attract the infant "by prolonging the pattern of response that leads to this stimulation." However, strong doses of the same stimuli may repel, "facilitating conflicting and alternating responses." An example is the "positive attraction of risk taking or mild fear" (1955).

Genetic Control of Fear. Results of a study of identical and fraternal twins from birth through the first year (Freedman, 1964, 1965) suggest that fear occurs in all infants, but with variation in age of onset, duration, and form of response. The patterns of development of the smiling and fear responses are significantly more similar in identical twins than in fraternals, leading to the conclusion that both processes are under a certain amount of genetic control. In an earlier paper (1961b) Freedman suggested that fear in the infant may be a homologue of the apparently innate flight response that is found in a great majority of animal species.

Both behavior genetics and ethology emphasize the point that when a form of behavior occurs with such regularity as to be regarded as "innate" this occurs because the behavior functions to preserve the well-being or survival of the organism. It is this functional point of view that Freedman regards as a fruitful concept shared by both disciplines. However, he suggests (1966) that the whole question of what is and is not "instinctual" in human behavior can be meaningfully considered only when viewed as "evolved behavior" and that there is potential significance for study of infant emotional development in an evolutionary orientation to the field since the neurophysiological structures which control and organize emotion are believed to be phylogenetically very old.

SECOND AND THIRD YEARS OF LIFE

CRYING, SMILING, AND LAUGHING

Studies on the incidence and causes of crying in older infants have been made by Brackett (1934), Ricketts (1934) and Landreth (1941). Brackett studied crying in relation to laughing among children from seventeen to thirty-nine months. Crying and laughing, which were inversely related, were both found to be influenced by the social experiences of the nursery school; e.g., physical contact was closely related to crying; friends cried less when playing together. Blatz, Allen, and Millichamp (1936) also noted that crying decreased as laughter increased.

Landreth (1941) reported on a variety of environmental conditions influencing crying in 33 children, age two through five years. Conflict with peers was the source of 75 per cent of the crying in nursery school. After this came, in descending rank order of frequency: accidents, frustration in manipulating inanimate objects, conflicts with adults, and insecurity at leaving parents. In the home, crying was more a function of contact with adults and of pressure for conformity to routines.

Ricketts (1934) found that crying occurred more often as an expression of anger in the home than in the school. Sex differences in crying were reported; girls cried most during conflicts with other children, particularly when conflicts were induced by boys, whereas boys cried most from frustration due to difficulties in manipulating materials. Conflicts with adults as well as fears were the other important causes of crying in boys.

Brackett (1933) has given an account of smiling and laughter in a cross-sectional study of 17 children from eighteen to thirty-nine months of age. Social interaction was the occasion for 84.5 per cent of all laughter. Laughter proved to be highly consistent in frequency for any individual; furthermore, children who laughed frequently tended to play together, and those who talked a great deal were among those who also laughed often.

There is agreement among a number of studies that laughing occurs most frequently among two-year-olds when they are engaged in motor activity. While these children laugh more at their own motor activity, this occurs largely in the presence of other children (Enders, 1927; Gregg, Miller, & Linton, 1929; Kenderdine, 1931; Arrington, 1932; Ding & Jersild, 1932; Ames, 1949).

Ames (1949) noted a transition in smiling with respect to interpersonal situations. From observations of spontaneous smiling and laughter in a nursery school, Ames found that at eighteen months children smiled most frequently at their own activity—largely motor activity—and next most frequently as they were approaching their teacher for the purpose of social interaction. At twenty-one months this social situation took precedence over gross motor activity in eliciting smiles. At twenty-four months verbal participation in the social situation occurred. By thirty months the social setting switched to peers and continued to be the primary cause of smiling. Generally, smiling occurred more frequently than laughing during the preschool years.

Bridges (1931) and Kenderdine (1931) found that next to motor activity, the most frequent causes of laughter among two-year-olds were socially unacceptable situations and incongruities. There was no evidence of any other forms of humor at this age. Kenderdine also reported some indication of a positive relationship between laughing and intelligence. Among 24 children, ages two, three, and four years, there was almost twice as much laughter among the 10 children with a mean IQ of 130 as among the 14 children with a mean IQ of 118. Goodenough (1930), however, found no relationship between laughter and intelligence. (Goodenough [1930] also found that nursery school children who neither laughed excessively nor minimally were less likely to be regarded as behavior problems and that there was some indication of a positive relationship between laughter and leadership.)

In a large group of children which included only a few under three years of age, Blatz and Millichamp (1936) noted that laughter frequently occurred after completion of an event and to some extent in anticipation of a forthcoming event. This finding led to their suggestion that smiling may be considered a "socially acceptable tic" which serves as a "compensatory motor mechanism accompanying the resolution of conflicts."

In his review of theories of laughter, Piddington (1963) suggested that laughter serves the child in play and in socially conflicting situations as a resolution of conflict and of social need. Ambrose (1963) defined laughter as a means of both maintaining and terminating stimulation. In infants, laughter first appears at four months in situations in which both fear and anger or enjoyment and relaxation are experienced. Ambrose suggests that laughter as an expression of ambivalence cannot occur until the capacity for perceiving simultaneous stimulation is developed.

FEAR AND ANXIETY

In their study of the incidence of fear Jersild and Holmes (1935) exposed 104 children, from twenty-four to twenty-seven months of age, to several experimental situations: being left alone, walking on a falling board, going into a dark room, meeting a strange person, walking on high boards, hearing a sudden loud sound, and being exposed to a snake and to a large dog. Fear of loud sounds accounted for less than one fourth of the experimentally induced fear reactions that appeared in two- to three-year-old children. This is about 50 per cent less for this age than the incidence reported by parents and teachers. Fear of the two animals, in agreement with parents' reports, was the predominant source of experimentally produced fear at this age. Among two-year-olds there was twice as much fear of a dog as of a snake, but this discrepancy disappeared by age three. That fear of animals increases with age during the preschool years has also been supported by Hagman (1932) as well as by Jones and Jones (1928). Fear of the dark in the experimental situation was four times more frequent than its incidence in parents' reports.

Hagman (1932) studied 70 children from 1–11 to six years. Interviews with parents suggested that incidence of specific fears was influenced by such factors as lack of preparation, strangeness, pain, and restraint. There seemed to be some correspondence between the fears of the child and those of the mother. However, there was a peak in number of fears and in overt expression of fear at two years. Hagman presented some evidence that brighter children are more easily aroused to fear. (Jersild and Holmes [1935] reported greater susceptibility to fear at an earlier age in more intelligent children.)

There are a number of studies of fear and anxiety in preschool children in strange situations, particularly in mental testing situations. Shirley (1942) and Heathers (1954) studied the relationship of age and personality adjustment to adaptability in strange situations. Age was found to be more important than personality or home adjustment in mediating successful introductions to strange persons and situations: two- and five-year-olds made better adjustments to the first encounter with a strange environment than did three- and four-year-olds. Moreover, the character of the initial adjustment was consistently maintained through future encounters with the same situations at six-month intervals over a two-year period.

The patterns of adaptation to strange situations employed by young children were also studied by Arsenian (1943) among 24 children from eleven to thirty months of age. Experimental situations were set up in which the child was either alone with a strange person, with the child's own mother in a strange room, or alone in a strange room. All children showed evidence of initial insecurity in these circumstances, and at least ten patterns of adaptive behavior were noted. Ratings of security were made on the basis of latency before the appearance of adaptive behavior and on the pattern of adaptation (in terms of motor activity, social interaction, and goal-directed behavior).

Children's responses to experimentally induced fear and anxiety were related to motivation in a study by Johnson (1936). Three fear-inducing conditions were used while the child performed novel but difficult sensory motor tasks. Following errors and unskillful performance on the first series of trials, electric shock was administered together with a loud bell. On the second series, obtaining a desired object entailed experiencing a loud and presumably frightening sound. On the final series the child was alone in a shock inflicting although highly motivating, goal-directed task. Response to fear was moderated by level of motivation as well as assertiveness. Children who directed their attention toward recognized goals showed reduced awareness of unpleasant aspects of the situation. Individual differences in response to fear varied in relation to different modes of attack in performing the tasks.

A number of studies have been made of fear, anxiety, negativism, resistance, and response to failure in the mental testing situation (Levy & Tulchin, 1923, 1925; Levy, 1925; Reynolds, 1928; Goodenough, 1929; Nelson, 1931; Rust, 1931; Stutsman, 1931, 1934; Caille, 1933; Mayer, 1935; Dwyer, 1937; Leitch & Escalona, 1949; Moriarty, 1961). An analysis was made by Moriarty (1961) of stress-inducing factors in the testing situation. In addition, children's patterns of adapting to or coping with stress were studied in relation to personality adjustment. Girls found new tasks easier to accept, whereas boys responded more quickly and with increased integrative effort to more difficult tasks. For children from 2–9 to 6–4 performance items were less difficult than verbal items, and verbal items were less difficult than cognitive problems. Difficult tasks were often met with an increase in body adjustment that resulted in awkwardness, muscular strain, and restlessness. This mode of coping produced more precision in 19 per cent of the children, but was often not functional. Those who did not resort to this type of adjustment were either very skilled or very poor in motor skill. It was concluded that effective coping primarily depends on positive feelings of adequacy.

RESISTANCE AND NEGATIVISM

Resistance and negativism are generally to be expected in the young child from about fifteen to thirty months. This stage of development usually means that there are many refusals to comply (Bühler, 1928; Bathurst, 1933; Stolz, 1933; Jenkins, 1935; Hattwick, 1938; Benjamin, 1942; Gesell & Ilg, 1946; Pulver, 1959). Reynolds (1928) studied resistance expressed as refusals to cooperate in experimental situations similar to mental testing conditions. Negative responses were found to be transitory and variable from one situation to another, although children consistently resisted imitation more frequently than any other situation. The anxiety evoked by the test, together with demands to meet specific requirements, invite negativism at this age.

Levy and Tulchin (1923, 1925) were among the first to study anxiety and resistance during mental testing. Their work is largely descriptive, but it has been supported by subsequent studies. They found change in resistance to the situation during the acquisition of emotional control from eighteen to thirty-six months. For girls the peak of resistance occurs any time around eighteen months, whereas for boys it occurs fairly uniformly at thirty months. Girls tend to be more resistant than boys although the period of resistance is shorter.

Goodenough (1925, 1928, 1929) conducted a series of studies of emotional reactions of 990 children during mental tests. Behavior was classified on the basis of a series of descriptive categories, the most reliable of which were shyness, negativism, and distractability. Behavior was found to be influenced by age, sex, socioeconomic background, and ordinal position in the family.

ANGER AND AGGRESSION

Ricketts (1934) gathered data on the expression of anger at home and in school. Mothers supplied home reports on 27 children, and trained observers gathered data on 21 children in a nursery school. A high percentage of agreement in the observations was found between the examiner and an assistant. There seemed to be some evidence that there is more crying in the home and more pushing and pulling in the school.

Goodenough (1931) made an extensive survey through parents' daily records of anger among 45 children whose age ranged from under twelve months through four years. A not unexpected trend appeared in the direction of more primitive, explosive, nonadaptive behavior in younger children and increasing capacity with age for channeling of energy toward a goal. Anger progressed from attack to calculated direct and indirect retaliation. These reports are supported by those from Hall's early survey (1899) as well as by the systematic observations of quarrels and conflicts in nursery school made by Dawe (1934). The survey also indicated that there were more primitive explosions among boys under twelve months than among girls. Girls reached a higher peak in frequency of angry outburst at eighteen months, but showed a rapid decrease. At thirty-six months boys manifested twice as many outbursts as did girls. Boys and girls were reported to get angry at different situations. Anger occurred in boys more frequently when they were occupied and playing alone or when required to do small tasks. Both sexes had trouble with routines, although they were not always the same ones. These trends in sex differences are in general supported by Hattwick's extensive study (1937) of a wide variety of sex differences, as well as by studies of anger and aggression by Jersild and Markey (1936), Muste and Sharpe (1947), and Walters, Pearce, and Dalms (1957).

Reports on children's conflicts and quarrels fall into a variety of patterns. Dawe's study (1934) indicates that although younger children start more quarrels, older children become more aggressive during the quarrels. Findings of Jersild and Markey (1935) and Walters *et al.* (1957) support this position. Appel (1942) found that quarrels and aggressive episodes during free play in the nursery school occur for different reasons at different ages. These changes were somewhat influenced by socioeconomic factors, but the trends were consistent in nursery schools for privileged and underprivileged groups. Among two-year-old children aggressive behavior was evoked by desire for possessions, whereas among the older children such interaction involved differences of opinion and cross purposes in planning elaborate play activities.

Outbursts of anger as well as conflicts tend to be brief and transitory at all ages. Jersild and Markey (1935) noted that duration of the children's interest and attention on various activities was far greater than duration of quarrels. Quarrels tended to last no longer than 30 seconds. Walters *et al.* (1957) found that at all ages children are more affectionate than aggressive. Baruch's (1941) study of aggression in doll play suggested that aggression is expressed more readily in this situation than in nursery school at all ages. Baruch as well as Ammons and Ammons (1953) studied aggression in normal children from two through four and five years with the doll play technique. Age changes in form of aggression were noted in both studies. Direct counteraggression was high at all ages.

Jersild and Markey (1935), Murphy (1937), and Muste and Sharpe (1947) have found sex differences in the nature and quality of conflict behavior. Among 54 children, of whom 17 were under three years, Jersild and Markey noted that boys not only engage in more conflicts, but do so in a very different manner from that observed among girls.

Moreover, boys fight each other differently than they fight girls. Muste and Sharpe pointed out that boys use more physical contact and girls are more verbal during conflicts. In response to aggressive attacks, boys will counter with physical resistance, while girls are either submissive or use verbal retaliation. Murphy found that boys are more active than girls in defending another child who is being attacked.

Evidence from several studies suggests that aggression is one of several fairly stable traits. Jersild and Markey (1935) noted consistency of both aggressive and passive behavior of individual children. McKinnon (1942) conducted a five-year study during which teachers rated children from 2–10 to 4–8 on withdrawal, invasiveness, and conformity. Passive withdrawal was least responsive to change with age. Kagan and Moss (1960), from records in the Fels' longitudinal study, presented further evidence of stability in traits such as withdrawal and aggression, dependence and independence. Muste and Sharpe (1947) found that patterns of aggression or resistance have different meaning for different children.

Walker (1962) found significant sex differences in aggressiveness in relation to body build in children; Sheldon's categories (1940) were used as an index of body build. Each of the three types of build—endomorphic, mesomorphic, and ectomorphic—was found to correlate significantly with certain behavior ratings. Two of these included ratings of aggression or hostility. Endomorphism in boys was significantly correlated with aggression ratings and mesomorphism in boys, with hostility.

Barker, Dembo, and Lewin (1941) studied the effects of frustration in 30 children, age twenty-eight to sixty-one months. Levels of constructive use of play materials were used as a measure of aggression. The results varied among individual children, but showed a trend toward less creative and constructive use of old toys when new and more interesting ones were suddenly removed to a position where they could be seen but not obtained. The results were interpreted in terms of regression rather than aggression as the consequence of frustration.

Block and Martin (1955) replicated the Barker *et al.* (1941) study, adding personality measures in an effort to account for certain inconsistencies of response in the original study. Measures of ego control were made prior to frustration. Children found to be overcontrollers played constructively in the face of frustration, while the undercontrollers gave predominantly aggressive respon.·e during frustration.

Fredericksen (1942) studied aggressive and negative response to frustration under restrictive supervision in the nursery school. Subjects experienced two nursery school settings. In one setting there was a permissive environment which allowed freedom from interference during free play. In the other setting children experienced authoritarian directiveness. Experimental situations similar to mental testing conditions were used to provide measures of aggression and negative behavior. These tests were made both before and after each of the school experiences.

Following the noninterference free-play experience there was a significant decrease in submissiveness toward adults and a significant increase in verbal forms of negativism toward peers. Following the authoritarian or frustration experience there was a significant increase in submissiveness and a nonsignificant increase in verbal expressions of negativism toward peers. There was no difference in physical aggression between groups. The results of this study are supported by the findings of Dwyer (1937), Muste and Sharpe (1947), and Baldwin (1949). The relationship between submissiveness toward adults as a function of frustration conditions contradicts the theory of Dollard, Doob, Miller, Mowrer, and Sears (1939), which would lead one to expect that frustration defined in terms of interference leads consistently to aggression.

SUMMARY

Several current trends of inquiry pertinent to emotional behavior have rarely been extended to children under three years. It has been noted in the context of this discussion that the current interest in arousal and autonomic response in relation to affect and motivation has only rarely been considered in relation to infants. This area of inquiry should lead to increased understanding of the development of both transient and stable patterns of emotional behavior in relation to the type of stimulation used in various methods of infant care and child rearing. Inquiry into the rewarding or punishing effects of varying amounts and intensities of stimulation in relation to affective states, arousal, and autonomic response needs to be expanded.

Although the several areas of inquiry outlined from Darwin's pioneer work with infant emotion remain of vital significance, the sophisticated technological resources at our command are only beginning to be utilized in infant research. Investigations of innate bases of emotion or of the physiological structures and functions relative to emotional behavior in infancy are just starting to benefit from knowledge, skills, and tools of a variety of scientific disciplines.

There are as yet only a few studies of the course of emotional development in infancy as it is affected by those neural centers which control, organize, and modulate emotional expression. A start has been made in the study of individual differences, of developmental trends in arousal levels, and of sleeping and waking patterns of EEG in relation to variations of intensity of stimuli; but this inquiry has not yet been extended specifically to affective states. The genetic bases of emotional behavior or the evolutionary significance of the functional value of emotional behavior has only recently been studied in relation to infancy.

Smiling as a distinctive human form of behavior has currently received more attention from students of infancy than the other areas recommended by Darwin, yet much of this research has not yet demonstrated the emotional significance of this behavior. Increasing literature in the use of comparative animal and human studies has often been a fruitful source of theory and hypothesis, but we are still learning where to apply caution and restraint to generalizations across species.

Another current trend is an interest in the processes by which anxiety and aggression develop and perpetuate in children. The extensive body of literature on these aspects of emotional behavior rarely extends to children below three, four, or five years. There is wide recognition that the first years of life are critical in the development of personality and that certain emotional behavior patterns or traits which develop at this time may be fairly stable and consistent in later years. However, sophisticated methods of research in this aspect of infant behavior are limited indeed. Although interest in infancy has expanded over the last decade, relatively few questions are being asked about affective states in infancy or about the gradual organization of complex emotions and their expressive, autonomic, and cognitive components.

Personality Development

PSYCHOANALYTIC THEORIES

Psychoanalytic theory, as originated by Freud and elaborated and modified by some of his followers, has been a rich and influential source of ideas concerning development. In this section we shall review some of the major aspects of psychoanalytic theory as it applies to developmental issues, examine some of the points of difference between Freud's formulations and those of later theorists who have been especially impressed by the role of social and cultural forces in personality, and consider the contribution of psychoanalytic ego psychology to developmental issues.

The developmental aspects of psychoanalytic theory did not start from observations of infants and children. Instead, they arose as an attempt to understand and explain the feelings, thoughts, and behavior of troubled adults in psychotherapy as, at least in part, stemming from "the infant and the child" that still lived in the adult. The data, then, were immature behavior, either perpetuated in the life of the patient or which reappeared during stress, and the recollections of childhood which came to the mind of the patient in the course of psychotherapy. The fact that such recollections may serve purposes in the immediate relationship to the therapist and that they are notoriously subject to distortion and disguise was recognized in the concepts of defense and transference in psychotherapy. However, compensating for this loss in objectivity was the increased likelihood that the data which did concern childhood would center around those aspects of growing up that would play a persistent and significant role in emotional growth and personality formation.

The problem is somewhat like that of the historian. In turning toward the past, what he selects as being significant will reflect his own biases, and he may search the past in an attempt to shed light on current problems. Nonetheless, he is likely to focus on those things that did make a difference, and important themes are likely to emerge that would be obscured by a historian who reported all events, the large and the trivial, with equal emphasis and total recall. The ambiguity of the data upon which psychoanalytic theory grew allows for somewhat different readings of the nature of childhood experience, and we shall examine some of these differences in this chapter.

On one thing the different analytic theorists agree: childhood experience is of major importance in the development of an individual's personality. If for no other reason, psychoanalytic theory is important for students of emotional and personality development in that it has consistently taken the position that to understand the individual one must understand something of that individual's history, especially his early development, and that one's childhood, although it may be lost from conscious memory, persists as a significant determinant of the person's life. The importance of developmental considerations has been formally expressed by Gill and Rappaport (1959) by including the genetic with the dynamic, economic, adaptive, and structural points of view as basic to psychoanalytic metapsychology.

It is generally agreed that psychoanalytic theory has emphasized the importance of the first six years of life—from birth to the resolution of the Oedipus complex. It is on development during this time that we shall concentrate.

FREUDIAN DEVELOPMENTAL THEORY

Freud's theory of development is to a large extent a theory of the development of drives. When Freud discovered that his patients' recollections of their childhood could not be taken as historical fact, he did not discard them as meaningless. Instead, he came to view these recollections as an index of what the child had wished for and, as a result, Freudian theory has continued to attend more to inner strivings and fantasies than to external circumstances.

When patient after patient expressed similar childhood wishes during therapy, and as the exposure of these wishes to the patient's adult ego lead to symptom removal and better emotional health, Freud became convinced that the fate of these wishes was of great significance to personality formation. Freud's theory of psychosexual development was an attempt to organize the evolution of these wishes and to understand the lasting importance of these early stages of development.

Fundamental to the psychoanalytic theory is the view that all psychological activity results from the dynamic interaction between two sources of excitation: the instincts and their derivatives on the one hand and the forces of external stimulation on the other hand. The psychosexual theory traces the growth of the instinctual forces, forces that Freud described as a "measure of the demand made upon the mind in consequence of its connection with the body," as indicated by the changing dominance of different erogenous zones (the oral, anal, and phallic zones) as the chief source of libidinal excitation and pleasure.

There is not, however, a smooth and automatic progression through these psychosexual stages. Anna Freud (1965) comments that the analogy between the development that we can observe in the body and that of the mind is useful only to a certain point; in both there is a progressive movement from immaturity to maturity. However, she states, "While on the physical side, normally, progressive development is the only inner force in operation, on the mental side we invariably have to count with a second, additional set of influences which work in opposite directions, namely with fixation and regression" (pp. 93–94).

Fixation at a particular stage of development or a retreat to an earlier stage can have a determining influence on both adjustment and character structures and are the conceptual tools that help to account for the lasting importance of childhood in personality function. Regressions are most likely to reactivate those attachments and sources of satisfaction on which there has been some fixation, and fixation can result from a traumatic experience or from either excessive frustration or gratification at a particular psychosexual stage. In healthy progression, the individual can sustain a level of frustration that enables him to relinquish past sources of gratification and move toward more mature satisfactions.

We can only sketch the main points of the psychosexual stages. Excellent and detailed expositions can be found in Fenichel (1945), Blum (1953), Brenner (1955), Monroe (1955), and Freud (1965).

The Oral Stage. The first stage of the libidinal development takes its name from the special erogenous sensitivity of the mouth that makes the oral zone the source of greatest excitement and pleasure for the infant. The psychoanalytic emphasis on libidinal strivings calls attention to that quality of sensual enjoyment from oral activity that extends beyond the pleasure from satisfaction of hunger and can be seen in such activities as thumb sucking.

The oral stage is subdivided into the early oral phase and the later oral sadistic phase. During the early oral phase the infant passively receives and takes in the supplies from outside. Because the infant has yet to differentiate himself from those around him, he enjoys a primitive unity with the mother, one that in a sense replaces that existing before birth. This has been referred to as the primary identification of the self with the mother. The dependence on the mother, the comforting and the gratifying sense of unity with the mother, and the erogenous satisfactions that attend this union make the child particularly vulnerable to anxiety when separated from the mother. Without the mother's presence, the child may feel at the mercy of overwhelming stimulation, deserted and helpless. This separation anxiety is particularly prominent from approximately six months to two years of age.

The balance of gratification or frustration at the oral stage may lend a persistent tone either of optimism or pessimism that may characterize a person's attitude toward his whole existence. The indiscriminate elation or despair characteristic of manic-depressive psychosis can be viewed as a regressive reactivation of the infantile feeling that "the world is my oyster" on the one hand and total inner and outer emptiness on the other hand. When oral problems are regressively reactivated, the individual may experience the total helplessness, vulnerability, and emptiness of the infant who feels deserted. The highly dependent person, persistently anxious about receiving unqualified good will and affection from others, and who is not differentiated from others in his ego boundaries, may be considered to be manifesting characteristics that were appropriate for the infant but not for an adult.

During the second or oral sadistic phase the emphasis is still on incorporating and taking within what initially is without; now, however, the quality of an active, grasping incorporation replaces that of a passive sucking in. This phase is thought to coincide with the eruption of teeth, and the child's wishes and fantasies at this stage have been inferred from cannibalistic fantasies and fantasies of biting or being eaten that appear in certain children and regressed adults.

The Anal-sadistic Stage. During the anal-sadistic stage, which begins during the second year of life, the anus and the erogenous zones associated with elimination become the chief source of libidinal excitation. The pleasurable sensations of excretion assume a special importance for the child, and he discovers that he can heighten his pleasure by holding back the fecal mass. In addition to the sensuous enjoyment, the child comes to value the products of elimination. These have a peculiar psychological status: being something the body has produced, they can be regarded as a part of the self and yet they are external to the self. The mother, through her praise for the production of feces, may also contribute to the child's high evaluation of the products of elimination. Opposing this high evaluation, the practice of discarding or destroying products of elimination may bewilder the child. These experiences are seen as laying the groundwork for conflicting and ambivalent feelings about possessions, between holding onto and hoarding "valuables" or casting them away, and between a personal and a more general evaluation of objects.

The child is expected, during this stage, to learn to inhibit, to control, and to produce the contents of his bowels at appropriate times. A clash between the inner promptings and the external expectations may be acutely felt by the child as an irreconcilable conflict of wills, a lasting opposition between his inner demands and external requirements. For some, the outcome may be stubborn rebellion against external coercion; for others, an anxious compliance and fear of external force. A constructive solution can occur when the child identifies with the mother in a joint effort at socially acceptable regulation and achieves satisfaction from the mastery of his own inner promptings. All too often, however, the child feels that his own autonomy must be sacrificed by giving in to others or must be protected by an unyielding recalcitrance. The neurotic symptoms of obsessions and compulsions and the compulsive character traits of excessive frugality, obstinacy, and orderliness are seen as a persistence or reactivation of the conflicts of the anal stage.

The sadistic component aspect of this stage comes both from an enjoyment in getting rid of the feces, in a sense expelling and destroying them, and in the pleasure of defeating, often by passive aggression and withholding, those who are felt to oppose the individual's wishes to make demands upon him.

The Phallic Stage. During the phallic stage, which extends from approximately the fourth to the sixth year, the genitals become the source of greatest libidinal excitement. The penis of the boy and the clitoris of the girl are the sources of intense erogenous pleasure, and the genital organs take on a new importance and fascination to the child. This is the era of sexual curiosity, exhibitionism, voyeurism, and of children's constructing their own theories of sex differences, sexual intercourse, and of birth.

The Oedipus complex, a particular constellation of desires and fears, develops during this period. The boy, whose sexual longings are directed toward his mother, the first object of his love, comes into a direct rivalry with his father for the mother's affection. The desire for the mother and the wish to displace the father become the core of the Oedipal conflict. The intensely competitive and hostile feelings toward the father are frequently projected and ascribed to the father so the boy is exceedingly fearful and resentful of the father. Conflicting with these wishes, the boy does have positive feelings toward his father, wants his approval, needs his support and affection. These feelings often create an intensely ambivalent feeling toward the father.

This early phallic development is brought to a close by castration fear, thought to be experienced by every small boy during the Oedipal phase. This is the fear that his genital organs will be damaged as a punishment for his sexual desires toward the mother. Whether this fear is fostered by threats from adults of punishment for masturbatory activities or whether it stems from primitive thinking that the offending organ will be destroyed, the possibility of castration is confirmed in the boy's mind by the sight of female genitalia which are taken as evidence that castration can occur. In fact, it has been said that at this age children may divide people into the castrated and noncastrated rather than into male and female. In any event, the boy's wishes for his mother, his sexual longings toward her, his rivalry with his father and his fear of castration can be solved by identifying himself with his father. He can thus inhibit his dangerous desires and, through his identification with his father, vicariously possess his mother. By incorporating his view of the parental attitudes, especially those of his father, as his own, the child comes to possess a fairly organized system of attitudes and values, referred to as the superego. In this sense the superego can be considered the heir of the Oedipus complex. The superego is not just the inside source of threats and punishment; it can be the source of protection and the provider of reassuring love.

The frequently observed severity of superego functioning in some people cannot necessarily be read as the incorporation of a parent who in actuality was harsh and severe. It is frequently the incorporation of a parent who is distorted by the child's fantasies, by projected anger, and by guilt about his sexual desires.

Although a castration threat is seen as ending the Oedipal phase for the boy, it is said to drive the girl into the Oedipal phase. At the beginning of the phallic stage, the little girl is still very much like the little boy and her libidinal concerns are focused on the clitoris. The girl has the problems of shifting to the more passive organ of feminine excitement, the vagina, and she must change her sexual desires from the mother to the father. This shift is said to occur when she realizes that she does not possess a penis like boys and she gives up the mother as the object of her love, feeling that the mother is somehow responsible for this newly discovered and special deprivation. Her wish to have a penis for herself is renounced and is changed to the wish to have a penis via the male, and, in childhood, this means via the father. This brings the girl into conflict with the mother for the possession of the father. The girl can resolve the Oedipal situation, just as the boy does, by identifying with the parent of the same sex.

Psychic Structures. The theory of emergence of different psychic structures—the ego, the id and the superego—is another major contribution of psychoanalysis to developmental psychology. The course of these "institutions of the mind," like that of psychosexual development, not only follows developmental principles but can exhibit forms of fixation and regression. Unlike the course of psychosexual development through more or less distinguishable stages, the growth of psychic structures is seen more as a matter of long-range trends and shifting dominance of different organizing principles in psychological activity.

The ego is seen as differentiating out of the id through the infant's contact with the external world. The id is the reservoir of instinctual needs, the major source of drive energy, and is basically somatic in origin. These energies press for immediate fulfillment. The ego becomes the integrator and executor of the personality because numerous encounters with the external world indicate that hallucinatory wish fulfillment and magical thinking do not determine the course of events and that immediate gratification is often impossible and frequently dangerous. Satisfactions are achieved through contact with the real world, and reality testing becomes an important function of the ego. The ego's ability to find satisfaction by means of the detour activity implied by reality testing rests on the ability of the ego to delay impulse discharge. This shift in psychological functioning is also described as the progressive dominance of the reality principle over the pleasure principle in the organization of psychological activity.

This process of increasing dominance of the ego and attachment to reality was also conceptualized by Freud in terms of the distinction between the primary and secondary process of thought. "So far as we know, a psychic apparatus possessing only the primary process does not exist, and is to that extent a theoretical fiction; but this at least is a fact: that the primary processes are present in the apparatus from the beginning, while the secondary processes only take shape gradually, during the course of life, inhibiting and overlapping the primary . . ." (Freud, 1938, p. 536). The primary process is seen as being the dominant mode of thought of the infant, in psychotic thinking, in neurotic symptom formation, in the dreams and the fantasy activity of normal people. Primary process thinking is characterized by the disregard of reality considerations such as time, space, and causality, and by condensations, displacements, symbolizations, and the absence of negation. Here the wish is not only father to the thought—it directs its course, outcome, and mode of expression.

Secondary process involves rational thought, the delay of discharge, and the use of smaller amounts of energy in thought to perform a vicarious trial and error. Reality rather than wish determines the conclusions reached, and words replace visualization in the thought process.

The formation of the superego, by which the child has an internal representation of the *do's* and *don't's*, the taboos and values of the important people around him, provides a guide for conduct and an internal control of impulses. The normal ego, the end result of good development, is able to balance and integrate the often conflicting demands of reality, moral considerations, libidinal and aggressive drives.

This structural point of view provides a conceptualization of what can be seen as the major tasks of the personality and a framework in which development of cognitive structures, impulse control, defenses, and interpersonal relationships can be represented and their modes of interaction examined.

THE NEO-FREUDIAN SCHOOL

Although they are still closely related to the psychoanalytic framework, a number of influential personality theorists have rejected some aspects of Freudian theory and placed special emphasis on certain forces in development that they feel have been either underestimated or neglected in Freudian theory. This group of thinkers, variously called the neo-Freudian or the nonlibido school, has included such writers as Sullivan, Horney, and Fromm. Although they disagree on many points, they share common dissatisfaction with Freudian libido theory and Freud's biological emphasis. The de-emphasis of biological factors as central to the explanation of personality development is shown by their giving up the concept of libidinal development and assigning less importance to instinctual forces in general. Social and cultural factors, especially family interactions, are seen as what matters most in personality growth. Consistent with this point of view, personality conflicts are seen as occurring in the interpersonal rather than in the intrapsychic sphere; there is less attention to the ego's defensive and controlling activities in relation to the impulse life and more attention to the modes of interaction between the individual and others. The evolution of the self in relation to others replaces the progression of instinctual development. Rather than examining the balance of satisfaction and frustrations of oral, anal, and phallic wishes, attention is paid to the atmosphere of security or hostility that surrounds the child in his early years, the effect of overprotective or neglectful parents, and the way in which the developing child learns coping and adaptive styles.

The Theory of Harry Stack Sullivan. Sullivan's theory, which has been influential in its own right, is particularly useful in highlighting the differences between the neo-Freudian and Freudian positions. The role played by the concepts of libido and instinctual energy in Freudian theory is filled by the concept of "dynamism" for Sullivan. This he defines as "a relatively enduring configuration of energy which manifests itself in characterizable processes in interpersonal relations" (Sullivan, 1938), stressing that it is not some "fantastic substantial energy" and does not belong to or inhere in the organism. While he frees dynamism from any somatic anchorage, he does acknowledge that the body demands certain "satisfactions." These, however, play a continuous, but undifferentiated, part in personality development. What especially concerns Sullivan is the *self dynamism,* a product of social interaction, because it is made up of *reflected appraisals.* The self dynamism governs behavior by promoting behavior that gives a feeling of security, a feeling rooted in receiving approval and avoiding disapproval from *significant others.*

Within the interpersonal context Sullivan does distinguish different levels of development. The first, *infancy,* extends to the "maturation of the capacity for language behavior" (Mullahy, 1948). The infant pursues bodily satisfactions which reduce tension and result in a feeling of euphoria, a state similar to dreamless sleep. With the infant's helplessness and his dependency on others for his survival he is highly attuned to the mood of the person caring for him. Through "empathy" he knows the other's mood, and his feelings can swing from euphoria to deep distress, depending on his sensing approval or disapproval. The first glimmers of ideas about himself and others emerge and center around an image of a "good mother" and a "bad mother" which parallel a "good me" and a "bad me." The "good mother" and the "good me" are associated with feelings of euphoria while the "bad mother" and "bad me" are associated with feelings of distress. Empathy is particularly important from approximately the sixth month through the twenty-sixth month and plays the guiding role in establishing the self which acts to preserve feelings of security.

The next stage in Sullivan's scheme is *childhood* which extends from approximately the second to the sixth year when "the maturation for the capacity of living with compeers" (Mullahy, 1948) is established. The child learns to talk, to go about freely, and is viewed by others as an object of training, education, and socialization. Language becomes an increasingly useful tool for communication, and the child directs his actions in more culturally approved directions.

Next comes the *juvenile era* which extends until the individual has the "capacity for isophilic intimacy" (Mullahy, 1948). During this stage the person begins to experience his compeers as like himself, and he can define himself apart from his family. He develops the capacity to be a critical observer of his own behavior, as if he were standing outside himself.

Sullivan's stages of development proceed through the stages of preadolescence, early adolescence, and late adolescence, but we will limit ourselves to these early stages. Sullivan develops a picture of the child turned outward, seeking approval, fearing disapproval, whose self is molded by the attitudes taken within him from without. If the Freudian position can be characterized as the story of libidinal development and the child's personality as being marked and molded by these inner forces, Sullivan's can be characterized as a story of the personality being shaped by influences largely external to the individual. If, for Freud, the object attachments of the individual seem to be only secondary to and in the service of libidinal satisfaction, for Sullivan interpersonal attachments overshadow inner forces.

Consistent in his emphasis on interpersonal phenomena, Sullivan does not develop a conceptualization of psychic structure to account for intrapsychic conflicts and processes. He does, however, propose three different modes of experience, *prototaxis*, *parataxis*, and *syntaxis*, which overlap at points with the psychoanalytic conception of primary and secondary processes.

Prototaxis is the mode of experience characterized by a nonexistent or feeble distinction between self and outer world, undifferentiated states of feeling that give a "cosmic" quality to the experience and absence of serial organization of experience. This is the mode of experiencing in which the infant feels high euphoria or deep distress and forms the dichotomous concepts of "good mother" and "bad mother" and "good me" and "bad me."

The *parataxic* mode next develops. Here a distinction is made between the self and the world, and a recognition of others, especially the mother, as separate is established. Experience becomes more differentiated, and language assumes more importance. Words begin to acquire a consensual validation, and beginning, though often incorrect, causal and serial connections are made. Consensual validation is far from total, however, and personalized meanings are still the rule.

The highest stage, *syntaxis*, is the stage in which consensual validation is dominant, and symbols and thought processes follow socialized, logical, and empirical rules. Although these stages seem to form a clear hierarchy in terms of socialization, Sullivan, no more than Freud, clearly specifies the ages at which they occur; they seem to represent more an acknowledgment of the importance of cognitive development than an explanation of its sequence. For Sullivan these modes of experience are important in that they describe the cognitive capacities with which the child can enter the acculturation process, the form in which the child can perceive and attempt to comprehend the interpersonal relationships. Here Sullivan's stress is different from Freud's, whose concepts of primary and secondary processes concern the extent to which cognitive activity is dominated by either drive forces or external reality and by the compromises reached between these forces.

PSYCHOANALYTIC EGO PSYCHOLOGY

The stress on the drive determination of behavior in classic Freudian theory has appeared, at times, to imply its absolute autonomy from the environment (Rappaport, 1959). While such social conceptions as the infant's dependence on those who care for him and the highly interpersonal nature of the Oedipus complex were early emphasized by Freud they ". . . were not generalized into an explicit psychoanalytic social psychology . . ." (Rappaport, 1959).

On the other hand, the neo-Freudian's stress on environmental demands has appeared, at times, to amount to a neglect of instinctual drives and to imply an absolute autonomy from inner forces. Such a characterization of either position is somewhat extreme, but at least information about drive states and inner motives are more readily accommodated by Freudian theory; observation of social and cultural factors is more easily fitted into the neo-Freudian position. Faced with a choice between these two positions, the psychologist's decision is dictated more by ideology and temperament than by rational considerations. Making the ego and its activities the center of attention offers a promising solution to this dilemma.

One of the first systematic statements of the psychoanalytic ego psychological position was Hartmann's *Ego Psychology and the Problem of Adaptation* (Hartmann, 1958). Hartmann retained a keen awareness of the instinctual demands of the growing infant and child but recognized the interaction between the infant's prolonged helplessness and dependency, his inborn and acquired adaptive means and the social institutions that foster and channel these capacities.

Erikson's Contribution. Erikson's psychosocial conception of personality development has provided a convincing integration of social factors such as economic conditions, family structure group, tradition, and social role considerations with the psychosexual development of the growing individual and the stages of ego development. He describes a mutual regulation within a unitary conception of the individual and society by which the individual does not have to "fit in" to society and society does not totally mold the individual.

One of Erikson's most original contributions is his conception of critical steps in ego development corresponding to psychosexual development. He assumes, in proposing his chart of critical steps:

> . . . (1) that the human personality in principle develops according to steps predetermined in the growing person's readiness to be driven toward, to be aware of, and to interact with, a widening social radius; and (2) that society, in principle, tends to be so constituted as to meet and invite this succession of potentialities for interaction and attempts to safeguard and to encourage the proper rate and proper sequence of their unfolding. This is the "maintenance of the human world" (Erikson, 1963, p. 270).

He calls the steps *critical* in that they are "turning points . . . moments of decision between progress and regression, integration and retardation" (Erikson, 1963, pp. 270–271).

The critical step in ego development that corresponds to the oral stage of psychosexual development is the formation of "basic trust versus mistrust." This means that the infant "not only has learned to rely on the sameness and continuity of outer providers, but also that one may trust oneself and the capacity of one's own organs to cope with urges" (Erikson, 1963, p. 248). Favorable experiences at this stage will promote a core of "drive and hope" in the individual.

Corresponding to the anal stage, the critical step is "autonomy versus shame, doubt." Here the infant may develop lasting feelings of independence and pride in mastering his impulses, in making a choice, and in "standing on his own feet." He may also have feelings of "having exposed himself prematurely and foolishly, which we call shame, or that secondary mistrust, that looking back which we call doubt" (Erikson, 1963, p. 85). "Self-control and willpower" are the strengths that can rise out of healthy growth at this stage.

The step in ego growth that accompanies the Oedipal era is concerned with "initiative versus guilt." Here the child's dreams of glory and surge of energy may lead to a vigorous attack on tasks, but the rivalrous and competitive conflicts at this stage may lead to a guilty renunciation of such strivings. A quality of "direction and purpose" will characterize the person who has successfully grown by his experiences at this time.

Although Erikson extends his conception of steps through the adult years, we cannot follow them here, nor can we indicate the sensitivity of both his clinical observations and his awareness of social and cultural forces in forming the growing person. What we do want to stress is that his psychosocial conception of ego development can fit congenially with both libidinal development and social variables.

White's Concept of "Competence." White (1963) has critically examined the psychoanalytic theory of energy and has proposed a reformulation in terms of *independent ego energies.* He believes the classic view of the ego deriving its energy from the id through neutralization of libidinal and aggressive drives does not convincingly account for much behavior nor does it square with certain developmental observations. In particular, animal experimentation on the exploratory drive and the observations of children's explorations, manipulation, and play are difficult to explain as derivatives of instinctual drives, although they are highly motivated and important activities.

White (1963) suggests that the ego apparatus itself has independent energies from the outset, not derived from instinctual energy. This energy is called *effectance;* it is accompanied by an affect, the *feeling of efficacy;* and it has the biological significance of developing *competence.*

White's conceptualization provides a theoretical basis for a closer integration between psychoanalytic theory and the interests of academic child psychology, such as language, the practice of motor skills, and the growth of cognition. He also has reinterpreted such concepts as identification, reality testing, self-esteem, anxiety, and the clinical problem of deviation in ego development from the point of view of independent ego energies.

Rappaport's Analysis. Perhaps the most systematic study of ego psychology has been made by Rappaport (1951; 1958; 1959); his analysis of ego autonomy offers a particularly valuable approach to developmental issues. The ego may, under certain conditions, be dominated by instinctual forces just as it may, under other conditions, be directed almost totally by external pressures. The normal ego, however, is able to maintain a degree of autonomy from both drive domination and stimulus bondage, and Rappaport argues that this autonomy rests on the interaction between these two main forces, inner and outer stimulation.

From its beginning the ego is turned toward external stimulation by the ego apparatus of perception and motility. These are apparatuses of primary autonomy but additional and secondarily autonomous ego structures, such as adaptive and defensive means, arise during development through the mastery of conflict.

Just as the ties to external reality can insure a freedom from drive domination, the ego's responsiveness to inner drive and affect states protect it from enslavement to the external stimulation. The balance between these two forces can be upset either by excessive drive pressure or by extremely demanding external forces. Also, a blindness to internal promptings can result in the ego's being easily victimized by environmental pressures and a diminished regard for access to external reality, as from defenses such as denial or from externally imposed stimulus impoverishment, may leave the ego at the mercy of inner drives.

The growth of those psychological processes which attune the individual to the outer world—such as perception, motility and higher thought processes, as well as the growing awareness of inner states and wishes—are seen as vital to the formation of personality.

This suggests that the student of development would handicap himself by choosing to attend exclusively to either the inner or to the outer, to drive states or to social expectations as determinants of personality formation. The answer is not simply that both are important. It is because the developing personality *must* contend with both forces, and its satisfactions, frustrations, and growth depend on the necessary interaction and integration of these inescapable influences.

A BIOLOGICAL APPROACH TO PERSONALITY DEVELOPMENT

Modern personality theory with its emphasis on individual differences in interpersonal relations stems almost entirely from the developmental system devised by Freud. Using a metaphorical biology, Freud created a system which grew in internal complexity but remained independent of the changing scientific scene in genetics and evolutionary systematics. Although at first glance there now seem to be no visible bridges between psychoanalytic theory and modern biology, the general theory of evolution provides so wide an apron as to readily enfold the facts of an interpersonal psychology. Not only that, but since modern biological thinking acknowledges the equally great importance of environment and genotype in the basic formula "phenotype = genotype × environment," and since genotype implies phylogeny, it provides a basis for a wider range of thought than any existing psychological theory.

The field of personality will be viewed here as concerned primarily with the development of human attachments, but certainly not exclusively so. Social attachment will be considered an adaptive, evolved characteristic of many species, and the formation of human mutuality is seen as attained by way of many evolved mechanisms that are mutually reinforcing and that assure social interaction.

For the present thesis, then, personality is defined as a Gestalt array of species traits, usually related to interpersonal behavior, which vary uniquely for each individual because the genotype is unique, the individual experience is unique, and the interaction between genotype and experience is unique. The fresh aspect of this definition is that it brings the species concept to the fore and thereby provides a structure in which all hominids may be compared on the basis of their unique variation on the basic hominid theme.

This emphasis on evolved behavior is not meant to deny that familial and cultural institutions do indeed differentially influence behavior and personality. We will, rather, emphasize that such institutions only support or shape man's behavior and do not create it, as it were, out of the blue.

INDIVIDUAL DIFFERENCES

We acknowledge today two major sources of individual differences in personality—biological structure and familial-cultural milieu. The emphasis in the social sciences has been overwhelmingly on the environmental sources of variance; cultural anthropology and neo-Freudianism have joined in demonstrating to the world that people are differentially shaped by different milieu.

This concept may be termed the "modern" view to distinguish it from older views, which were definitely slanted in a biological direction. Hippocrates, for example, wrote of what today would be called biochemical or hormonal predispositions to temperament—predominance of blood, black bile, yellow bile, or phlegm yielded, respectively, sanguine, melancholic, choleric, and phlegmatic temperaments (Allport, 1937).

Many forms of typology have since been proposed, culminating in the recent systems of Jung (extroversion-introversion), Kretschmer (cyclothymic-schizothymic), and Sheldon (endomorphy-mesomorphy-ectomorphy). Each of these typologies is "dynamic" in that there is an apposition of opposing behavioral tendencies so that they generate a spectrum of possible combinations. It is perhaps because of the simplicity of these dynamic systems that they have been more influential than the complex factoring approaches, from Franz Joseph Gall's in 1835 to those of Spearman and R. Cattell, or the complex taxonomic systems from Fourier's (1851) to Murray's (MacKinnon, 1944).

Summarizing the typological approach MacKinnon writes,

> All typologies are based upon the assumption that personality is characterized by a more or less enduring structure. Typologists may disagree as to the nature of this underlying structure; some conceive of it in psychological terms, others conceptualize it physiologically, and yet others think of it in terms of neural structure. It is not by chance that most typologists have been biologically oriented. Typologists may emphasize different traits and characteristics as most fundamentally differentiating the basic types of personality but on one point they agree, namely, that there are intrinsic traits of personality (1944, pp. 24–25).

Psychoanalysis has also produced a typology, but it is unique in that it simultaneously divides mental structure into dynamically related layers or segments: the typological system, conscious vs. unconscious, or the structural system involving the dynamic balance of ego, id, and superego (Fenichel, 1945). At the same time psychoanalysis offers a theory of how character types *develop*. Psychoanalysis, in fact, appears to be the first truly developmental psychological system.

In the early days of psychoanalysis, when libido theory was predominant, libidinal fixations about the mouth, anus, phallus (or clitoris) were considered the basic ingredients of a typology, and libidinal fixation at any stage theoretically gave the developing human characteriological uniqueness in his subsequent relationships; but oral, anal, phallic, and genital characters are spoken of with decreasing frequency, except as shorthand descriptions, since their usefulness has been in serious question for many years (Orlansky, 1949). Similarly, in the early days of cultural anthropology, the influence of the psychoanalytic typology led to descriptions of oral, anal, and phallic cultures (Gorer, 1941). Although the tendency lingers on, Mead, for example, long a devotee of psychoanalytic characterology (e.g., Mead, 1949), has changed her thinking in the direction of "ego psychology" (Mead, 1955). The concept of typology clearly needs help to direct it into more viable ways.

> *What's wrong with typologies?* The philosophical basis in much of early science was typological, going back to the *eidos* of Plato. This implies that the "typical" aspects of the phenomenon can be described, and that all variation is due to imperfect replicas of the type, all variants being, in the terms of Plato's allegory, "shadows on a cave wall." Such typological thinking is still prevalent in most branches of physics and chemistry and to a considerable extent in functional biology, where the emphasis is on the performance of a single individual. The typological concept has been completely displaced in evolutionary biology by the population concept. The basis of this concept is the fact that in sexually reproducing species no two individuals are genetically alike, and that every population is therefore to be characterized only by statistical parameters such as means, variances, and frequencies. . . . Genetic variability is universal, a fact which is significant not only for the student of morphology but also for the student of behavior. It is not only wrong

to speak of *the* monkey but even of *the* rhesus monkey. The variability of behavior is evident in the study not only of such a genetically plastic species as man but even of forms with very rigid, stereotyped behaviors such as the hunting wasps. . . . The time has come to stress the existence of genetic differences in behavior, in view of the enormous amount of material the students of various forms of learning have accumulated on nongenetic variation in behavior (Mayr, 1958, p. 351).

The point is that all diploid populations (those with two sets of chromosomes, one set paternal and one set maternal) show a wide range of genetic variation and that no two genotypes are precisely alike (save in identical multiple births). This gives a population greater viability as well as increasing the possibilities for ultimate speciation. The exceedingly slim chances in man, for example, of the same mother and father producing two identical offspring can be seen from the fact that each may produce 2^{23} kinds of gametes (8,388,608). As if this were not sufficient variation, if one additionally assumed only two per cent of the genes were heterozygous, a single cross-over between each pair of strands would raise the figure to 8,388,608 followed by 23 zeros, a very conservative figure at that (Stern, 1960).

It is not surprising, then, that the search for a stable typology of personality, if indeed personality has biological roots, is a doomed project before it starts. Let us consider, for example, the genetics that most probably underlie correlations between body build and personality such as those found by Sheldon (1942). This is best illustrated by animal experimentation in which controlled matings are possible. Nevertheless, as far as we know, the logic holds for all living forms.

Stockard (1931), in his work on temperament and behavior in breeds of dogs, was able to genetically dissociate behavioral traits from body build by crossing experiments; dissociation always occurred in the F_2 and back-cross generations, as one would expect from Mendelian models. For example, he was able to take the lethargic and low-slung Basset hound and, via the proper matings, produce Basset-like dogs with high-strung behavioral characteristics. It can therefore be deduced that the lethargic low-slung Basset hound was simultaneously bred for lethargy and body build since the two are genetically independent.

In all probability there is an analogous history to the correlations found between human temperament and body build. In the history of human groups there may well have been selective packaging of genes so that today certain body builds go with certain temperaments more often than by chance; but we must assume that such correlations can be broken and that all combinations of temperament and body build are possible. Sheldon's own data bear this out in the fact that he found no pure "types." In light of modern biological thinking, then, it is safest to assume the potential for continuous variation of behavior rather than a "piling-up" into discontinuous categories or types.

The relationship between human personality and genetic variability is clearly illustrated by the following two studies comparing identical and fraternal twins. In the first investigation, a group of twins was studied on a weekly basis over their first four months of life and in the second, a group was studied on a monthly basis over the first year (Freedman & Keller, 1963; Freedman, 1965). Usually, twin studies are open to the criticism that mutual imitation or special parental treatment has caused the greater concordance in identicals, but these criticisms were effectively ruled out in these studies. Parents were unaware of zygosity and their treatment of the twins was carefully watched and assessed; also, since mutual imitation does not start until after one year of age, it could be ruled out as affecting behavior in the first year.

In the group seen weekly through four months, the focus was on the development of social attachments, with specific emphasis on eyes-closed smiling (first month and after), the time at which the infant's eyes start to fix on the adult face, the subsequent onset of social smiling and its frequency and ease of elicitation, the intensity and extent of cooing, and the timing and ease of eliciting laughter. It was found that fraternal pairs were substantially different on these measures and that identical pairs were substantially alike. Identicals often differed in the onset of these behaviors (so that what A was doing one week, B was doing the next), but the overall patterns were far more alike than in the fraternals, where both timing *and* patterning were substantially unlike.

The same general findings characterized the second study as well. In this study, monthly motion pictures were taken over the first year during which each twin of a pair was filmed separately in the same situation. At the end of the study the films of one twin were rated on a behavior scale by a group of four professionals who had worked with infants, and the films of the other twin were rated by a second comparable group. Again intrapair differences among fraternal twins were significantly larger than intrapair differences among identical twins. Two of the items that proved significantly more concordant in identicals were intensity of *social orientation* and degree of *fear of strangers*.

Given these results, there seems no reasonable alternate to the explanation that heredity plays a role in the development of the social behaviors investigated. It also follows that the behavioral phenotypes will vary from generation to generation as the genes follow general Mendelian laws, no matter whether the behavior is monogenetically or polygenetically instituted, for it is not at all likely that pertinent environmental conditions will co-vary so as to continuously compensate for genetic rearrangements. As noted in the introduction, a phenotype is always the result of a complex interaction between genotype and environment. Studies of twins reared apart, such as that of Newman, Freeman, and Holzinger (1937), have been somewhat misleading in this respect. When separate rearing leads to different performance in identicals, as was found in this study, the explanation is that $G \times E$ interaction has been different, and it is of course not proof that the behavior in question is independent of heredity. Inasmuch as biological determinism is often incorrectly equated with fixity, it is worth stressing that the tie between personality and genetics is evidence for the continuous variation of personality and evidence against typological systems. Science has been described as the making of discontinuities from continuities and continuities from discontinuities. At this stage in personality theory it seems advantageous to promulgate the latter.

CONTINUITY VS. NONCONTINUITY IN PERSONALITY

One of the earliest reports in this area is that of Neilon (1948) who contacted in late adolescence the individuals Mary Shirley had studied over their first two years of life (Shirley, 1933). General personality descriptions were made of these young men and women which were in turn blindly matched to Mary Shirley's descriptions of them as two-year-olds. Matching was well above chance and the conclusion was drawn that there is considerable continuity in personality structure.

On the other hand, studies that have tried to be more specific by using trait checklists or rating scales (Kagan & Moss, 1962; Thomas, Chess, Birch, Hertzig, & Korn, 1963; Bayley, 1964) or those that have tried to predict behavior (Fries & Woolf, 1953; Benjamin, 1959; Escalona & Heider, 1959) have been much less successful. Macfarlane (1964), for example, is more impressed by the changes than by the continuities in the thirty-five years her growth study has been active, and it is her view that the most interesting aspects of personality are those that are essentially not predictable, e.g., how someone may deal with an emergency. This is borne out by the work of MacKinnon (1948) and his O.S.S. colleagues during World War II, in which on the basis of extensive personality assessment they unsuccessfully tried to predict what people would do in various emergency situations.

In this same regard, in the study reported by Murphy (1964) in which more than sixty children were studied from infancy through prepuberty, "over half the children changed markedly in one or another aspect of functioning . . . children showing most continuity had greater developmental balance and less vulnerability in infancy, and were growing up in environments which were relatively homogeneous, stable, free from traumatizing vicissitudes, and congenial to the child's natural style of development" (p. 113). Murphy was impressed with the individual styles of coping which, whether continuous or discontinuous over the years, tend to be unique for each person.

The attempt to assess continuities by way of preset categories of rating scales has been only minimally successful, for the "meaty" individualized aspects of personality descriptions have been lost. Recent reports by Kagan and Moss (1962) and Schaeffer and Bayley (1963) on separate longitudinal studies of about thirty years' duration are to the point. Bayley and Schaeffer's report found the most stable dimensions over the years were "active, extroverted vs. inactive, introverted" behaviors, while Kagan and Moss found consistency from the preschool years to adulthood in the aggressive behavior of males and in the passivity and dependence of females. The latter finding is borne out by Honzik and Macfarlane (1964) who found greater consistency in females over the years on the independence-dependence dimension, and also by the Schaeffer and Bayley (1963) study in which relative stability among females in an active-passive dimension was found. Even though these findings are interesting, particularly from the point of view of evolved sexual dimorphism, they are rather sparse representatives of what we usually think of as personality.

Is there a contradiction in the very attempt to use prearranged categories in trying to assess personality? The author believes so and offers here an evolutionary definition of personality by way of explanation. It derives in part from the longitudinal study of twins discussed earlier (Freedman, 1965), some of whom have been followed from birth through five years.

In the course of this study there was no difficulty in describing in subtle detail the personality of fraternal individuals, but it was not possible to describe identicals with the same richness. This went beyond the investigator's own inadequacy, for even within their own families, instead of becoming a "someone," identicals often become merged as "the twins" (see Leonard, 1961). It became clear that what is called *personality* amounts to an individual's unique variation on the basic hominid theme. To put it in a different way, personality is a Gestalt of species traits, varying uniquely for each genotype. Individuals are unique because the genotype is unique, the individual's experience has been unique, and the interaction between genotype and experience has been unique. The fact that Mr. A. does most things in his own way is what makes him someone and, at the same time, since he retains basic hominid traits, we can compare him with everyone else we have known. There is, in addition to this description from "without," that aspect of personality that can only be described from "within": "The ego only persists by becoming ever more itself, in the measure in which it makes everything else itself. So man becomes a person in and through personalization" (de Chardin, 1961, p. 172). This activating and self-making ego, however, works within the constraints of one's genetic and biological parameters.

In the same vein, the Gestalt array of behavior which we are calling personality may retain the same or similar total quality, although individual traits are or are not apparent from time to time. For this reason we may find individual items on a rating scale showing little reliability over long periods of time, as Bayley (1964) found; yet as Neilon has shown, the personality retains its unique flavor. This is not a surprising conclusion since it is obvious that the various processes continue to mature up through and past the burgeoning of adolescence, and each stage is usually negotiated by the organism in terms of the total situation (Goldstein, 1939), including a phylogenetically worked-out adaptation to that point in ontogeny, e.g., toddlerhood, adolescence, and parenthood necessarily involve considerably different sets of evolved adaptations.

In our view, then, the two major nonartifactual reasons for discontinuity are (1) the fact that flexibility of behavior is a built-in characteristic of hominids; (2) different stages in ontogeny are characterized by (phylogenetically) evolved behavior adaptive to that stage.

Since all conditioned reactions require some unconditioned behavior at the outset, logically speaking, there is no behavior that does not at some level of analysis involve a heredity × environment interaction. Thus, if identical twins are raised in different linguistic environments, to take an extreme example, their speaking different languages is not independent of some genetically based ability to acquire language. However, the question of the *extent* to which a behavioral trait is inherited vs. the extent to which it is acquired is basically an unsolved problem. This is usually dealt with by calculating a "heritability" score based on within-pair differences of identical vs. same-sexed fraternal twins. Unfortunately, this method is more often than not misleading.

As for illustrations of constitutional × environmental interactions over time, the best examples come from various animal studies with inbred groups. To take but one study, Freedman (1958) reared puppies of four dog breeds in either a very permissive fashion or under a strict regimen of training and found: (1) Each breed (genotype) reacted to the same mode of rearing in a unique way. (2) The breed × environment interactions varied kaleidoscopically, depending on the test or task imposed. (3) The same behavior in one breed might be due primarily to constitution and in another primarily to conditions of rearing (termed a "phenocopy" by geneticists). (4) In the follow-up period which lasted over a year, three breeds showed a straight-line continuity in their social reactions to humans modeled on behavior learned during early rearing. (5) In one breed the permissively reared animals changed markedly over time, whereas the disciplined group continued to show the same fawning behavior developed in puppyhood. (6) Some breeds were more deeply affected by the early modes of rearing than others.

It should be made clear that this study is presented as an illustration of a few well worked-out genetic × environmental permutations, and in actual fact the number of G × E interactions must have been far more numerous. In addition, if other breeds or other methods of rearing had been used, the interactions would have probably been considerably different. In work with humans, of course, such G × E interactions cannot be dealt with in an accurate or repeatable way, but there is every reason to believe that this study offers a reasonable, general paradigm for analogous interactions that must occur in hominid growth.

CULTURE AND INBREEDING

Cultural anthropology has changed popular thought as few sciences have done in the past. We know, as did no earlier age, that the typicality shown by various nations and tribes is due largely to a lifetime of learning and social interaction within given milieus. One can see on film the Balinese boy, Karba, growing from a universal infancy into a withholding, muted, graceful, suspicious child, typical of the Balinese (Bateson & Mead, 1942).

But was it a universal infancy? This is a reference to the very real possibility that the Balinese gene pool is unique in the world as a result of its specialized genetical history, and that Balinese are somewhat differently constituted than, say, a similarly isolated New Guinean tribe. This somewhat touchy subject has received little attention in the past because of the specter of racism but, hopefully, that period is passing.

Let us first consider the genetics of the situation. In the evolutionary sense all people are related considering that at some remote stage in their history they had common ancestors, and the Adam and Eve story is allegorically correct. Thus Harrison (1964) writes

> So far as some particular population is concerned, its past size, if all individuals were unrelated, would have to have been far greater than it actually could have been, since every individual has two parents, four grandparents, eight great-grandparents, and 2^n ancestors n generations ago. Assuming that on average there have been four generations per hundred years, an individual would have 2^{40} or approximately a million million ancestors a thousand years ago, if there had been no consanguinity. It seems probable that the total population of the world in the tenth century did not exceed 200 million and it was very much smaller in yet earlier times! (p. 158).

This reasoning that renders all men relatives also makes it clear that in the history of any closed cultural group there has been considerable inbreeding. This, together with the "founder" principle, that is, the dependency of the gene pool on the founding generation, leads to the irrefutable conclusion that the gene pool is to some extent unique for each such population. In light of our previous discussion, it should be clear that this may as readily produce distinct behavioral phenotypes significant for personality as it does significant physical variations. In addition, there is the fact that different cultures may emphasize different mating tracks so that, as in the development of domestic breeds, unique cultural selective processes may lead to uniquely organized genotypes (Ginsburg & Laughlin, 1966).

There are few data in this area, but it is now well known that African babies in several sections of Africa are born with greater skeletal maturity and more developed motor abilities than comparable groups of European infants (Geber, 1956). They retain this relative precocity until the third year, when the tests become highly verbal, and when gross motor items are no longer used (e.g., how well a child plays ball, leaps, jumps rope, and so on). The Caucasian children subsequently do better with verbal abstractions. The same pattern is seen in Negro-white comparisons in the United States (Bayley, 1965; Lesser *et al.*, 1965). The usual interpretation of the switchover at age three is that there is less chance for Negro children to apply verbal abstraction in their milieus (e.g., Geber, 1956). On the other hand, there is little choice but to acknowledge the genetic aspects of the racial differences found in the first years.

There is no other carefully controlled work along these lines, but there are many possibilities. In Hawaii, for example, clear-cut differences have been observed between Japanese and Polynesian babies in their reactions to the first inoculations at three months. Polynesian babies rarely cry and, if they do, they recover quickly. Japanese babies usually have an intense reaction, remain fearful for a considerable period, and in some cases continue to cry on subsequent visits to the doctor (Marshall, 1965). Although this reaction may be indirectly due to differential tension between the mothers, it would be possible to study such group variations with the proper controls. In a recent factor analytic study of personality in twins, Loehlin (1965) found that the same factors that have a high hereditary loading also have a high environmental loading. There is the clear implication in these data that cultural institutions have developed in support of man's biological nature.

SEXUAL DIMORPHISM

Boy-girl differences are reported from time to time on many different behavioral continua (Ausubel, 1958; Mussen, 1963). For the most part these differences are explained in terms of cultural and familial influences. Bandura and Walters (1963), for example, explain the repeated findings that boys are more aggressive than girls as follows: "This finding is not surprising for children brought up in a society in which aggression is much more tolerated in boys and in which the socially approved physically aggressive models, e.g., sports and film idols, are males" (p. 378).

It is a frequent finding that females are more passive and dependent than comparable groups of males (Ausubel, 1958). Kagan and Moss (1960), on finding that females are more *consistently* passive and dependent than males from birth through adolescence, interpret their data as follows: "It was suggested that environmental disapproval and punishment of dependent behavior in young males led to inhibition of and conflict over dependency in the growing boy. The social acceptance of passive and dependent behavior in females would be expected to result in greater stability for this class of responses for women than for men" (p. 446).

Ausubel writes of children between eighteen and forty-two months as follows: "Girls apparently manifest less negativism at this age than do boys for two reasons: first, because they see themselves as more accepted and intrinsically valued by parents and have a more available like-sexed person with whom to identify, they can acquire more derived status. Second, they are able to obtain more subsidiary primary status than boys can by participating in female household tasks" (Ausubel, 1958, p. 293).

Margaret Mead noted that a difference between boys and girls which holds in all cultures is the greater investigativeness and intrusiveness of boys as evidenced, for example, in their tendency to wander farther from home. At the time (1949), she gave this finding a psychoanalytic interpretation, relating such behavior to the acquisition of the "phallic mode." It was not clear, however, whether Mead viewed the phallic mode as universally learned or as primarily the result of maturation.

To summarize these examples, young males have been found to be more negativistic, more aggressive, more investigative, and less passive and dependent than females, and in each case, with the possible exception of Mead, it was assumed that social pressures caused these sexual differences. Interestingly enough, these very traits typify male-female differences among many primate species and we must suppose, following the above, that human culture or, according to Mead's argument, human libidinal development, has patterned itself on biological differences at the subhuman level. Once again, an evolutionary perspective will help us evaluate these data. In a subsequent publication Kagan and Moss (1962) discuss the possible constitutional bases for the boy-girl differences found in their studies. It is slowly becoming clear to many workers that "social role" and "constitutional type" are facets of the same self-actualizing process, i.e., the cultural and the biological are in fact inseparable.

First, what is the function of sex? The evolutionary answer is that it provides a population with tremendous variability unobtainable in asexual reproduction, and such variability usually makes possible the continuing survival of at least some members of this population under conditions that are lethal to most. Once introduced into the course of evolution, sexual differences themselves became exploited, so to speak, via secondary sex characteristics. Etkin's discussion of differences in aggressive potential is to the point:

> A secondary sex characteristic, which may be designated as aggressive potential, is the difference between male and female with regard to capacity for fighting. This type is common among vertebrates. Most prominent among these dimorphisms are differences in size and strength. One of the extreme examples is seen in the seals and related marine carnivores. Elephant-seal males are as much as two and a half, and fur-seal males ten times as large as their females. Though this is extreme, a difference of 50 per cent or so is not at all rare among mammals. In a majority of mammals, the male tends to be bigger and heavier than the female. Only exceptionally, as in the European rabbit, is the female the larger.
>
> Aggressive potential in favor of the male often takes the form of weapons. Horns and antlers are in many instances differentiated between sexes. We are familiar with them in many species of deer. Teeth as weapons are also frequent secondary sex characteristics of mammalian males. We see this in the enlarged canine teeth in male baboons and, in extreme form, in the single large tooth of the narwal. In birds, examples of dimorphism in weapons are fewer, but the spurs of the rooster provide a good one (Etkin, 1963, p. 110).

There are many other considerations in sexual dimorphism, such as the display coloration in males of many species usually associated with territorial defense and mating. Less dimorphic animals tend to share more tasks, including nest-building, care of young, hunting, and so on.

Although it has long been recognized that there are male-forming and female-forming hormones in vertebrate embryos (Willier *et al.*, 1955), we are only now learning something about the behavioral correlates of embryonic hormonal activity. Young and his co-workers (1965), for example, injected pregnant rhesus monkeys with testosterone propionate, and thereby made male pseudohermaphrodites of the female fetuses, i.e., at birth these were virilized, genetically female monkeys. Tests of early development revealed typical male rhesus behavior with regard to social encounters—facial threats, invitations to play, and rough and tumble play were distinctly male-like. Similar injections after birth did not have comparable effects, although in rats analogous behavioral effects occurred with testosterone injections up through five days after birth. In both these studies it appeared that testosterone propionate affected the developing central nervous system in some complex way to produce the male phenotype, and recent evidence with human male pseudohermaphrodites indicates that human sexual differentiation occurs in the same way (Landau, 1966).

Despite these data, the opinion that humans are born "sexually neutral" is frequently heard. This is largely due to publications by Money and Hampson on sexual reassignment of constitutionally anomalous individuals; the clear implication has been that in humans the sexual role is predominantly a learned affair. This extreme position has become somewhat more balanced (e.g., Money, 1965), and a recent critique of the Money and Hampson view by Diamond (1965) makes a good case for returning to a more classical biological view of sexuality—not very surprising in light of the foregoing.

In summary, there can be little doubt that human dimorphism follows the general mammalian trend and that it shares similar functions. Thus when we find little boys less passive, more negativistic, more aggressive, more rivalrous, or more investigative than little girls, we probably have our mammalian-primate ancestry to thank and not some proposed libidinal stage nor some makeshift social force. This is not to deny, of course, that cultural institutions do indeed support and differentially shape such biological trends.

An evolutionary analysis of human dimorphism has never been seriously undertaken, but would probably go a long way in making sense of the numerous but scattered findings on male-female differences. It is of substantial evolutionary interest, for instance, that human females mature more quickly than males in such diverse areas as bone age, teeth eruption, language development, and later in sexual readiness (Ausubel, 1958). It seems that this is an evolved trend with a major adaptive function of extending the female reproductive years relative to the male; a "sensible" arrangement considering her limited and his relatively unlimited reproductive possibilities. There are undoubtedly other functional aspects to the relatively precocious maturation of females. Any designated evolutionary trend is inextricably involved with numerous other trends.

ATTACHMENTS

"Critical Periods" in Development of Attachments. Varying rates of growth in ontogenetic maturation are well known. So are the embryological findings that normal growth is interfered with depending on *when* an experimental transplant or teratogenic agent is introduced (Willier *et al.*, 1956). Furthermore, there are numerous findings that in postnatal life interference with normal sensory input can cause tissue degeneration and/or the dropping-out of normal responsivity. Here, again, timing is important (Riesen, 1961).

These findings have been of interest to developmental psychologists as models for viewing behavior, and hence the notion that the absence of certain experiences during some hypothetically critical time will yield a behavioral defect. In the sphere of social behavior Spitz (1945, 1965), Bowlby (1952), and Goldfarb (1955) have all stressed the importance of infants forming attachments sometime in the first year if subsequent behavior is not to be abnormal (described below). Experimental work with isolated monkeys, dogs, and other lower animals has supported this contention by demonstrating that early social deprivation, if sufficiently prolonged, can cause social animals to become permanently maimed in their social interactions (Freedman, 1961; Mason, 1965).

The postulate that there is a critical period for the formation of human attachments was first elaborated by Spitz (1945) when he presented evidence from a South American orphanage in which progressive deterioration occurred in infants after their mothers left when the infants were three months of age. According to Spitz, the care given in the foundling home—including food, hygiene, medical care and medication, and so on—was adequate in every bodily respect.

At the end of the second year about 40 per cent of these children had died, and the remainder had developmental quotients at the level of severe defectives. This information was first published in 1945, and as of his most recent publication Spitz (1965) still insists this wasting away, called *marasmus,* was due entirely to lack of "mothering." The fact is that the foundling home was located in a severe protein-deficiency belt and that marasmus was and is a major public health problem there, even among home-reared babies (Scrimshaw & Behar, 1961); it is therefore small wonder that no temperate-zone worker has ever found such lethal results from lack of mothering.

Facts such as these as well as Spitz's poor reporting (Pinneau, 1955) have cast doubt on the entire notion of the first year as a critical period in the formation of attachments, but there is nevertheless ample evidence that Spitz's pioneering work was in the right direction. Bowlby's famous monograph of 1952, *Maternal Care and Mental Health,* has withstood the test of criticism and time; in a recent re-evaluation of it Ainsworth (1962) gave the following excellent summary of the results of affective deprivation:

(1) Recovery from a single, brief, depriving separation experience seems fairly prompt and complete with respect to overt behaviour under ordinary conditions; there is evidence, however,

of vulnerability to future threats of separation—i.e., there is at least one "hidden" impairment that prevents the reversibility from being described as complete.

(2) Relief from deprivation after even fairly prolonged deprivation experiences in early infancy can result in rapid and dramatic improvement in overt behaviour and in generalized intellectual functioning; vocalization, however, may be retarded, even though the relief occurs before twelve months of age, and effects on other specific aspects of intellectual and personality functioning cannot be ruled out until these aspects have been explored in research.

(3) Prolonged and severe deprivation beginning early in the first year of life and continuing for as long as three years usually leads to severely adverse effects on both intellectual and personality functioning that do resist reversal.

(4) Prolonged and severe deprivation beginning in the second year of life leads to some grave effects on personality that do resist reversal, although the effects on general intelligence seem to be fairly completely reversible; specific impairment of intellectual functions has not yet been studied.

(5) The effects of age at the onset and relief of the deprivation experience are undoubtedly important factors in influencing reversibility, but these are not understood in enough detail to set precise limits for a "sensitive phase" of development of special processes.

(6) In general, in the first year of life, the younger the infant when deprivation is relieved (and hence the less prolonged the deprivation experience), the more normal is the subsequent development; yet after the first year of life has passed, the older the child at the onset of deprivation the more readily and completely reversible seem to be the effects of a deprivation of a given duration.

(7) Certain impairments seem to be less readily and less completely reversible than others—impairments in language, in abstraction and in the capacity for strong and lasting interpersonal attachments.

(8) Especially if undertaken when the child is still very young, intensive therapeutic efforts may result in marked improvement of some very severe effects that resist reversal through ordinary relief from deprivation.

(9) Subsequent experiences of insufficiency, distortion or discontinuity in interpersonal interaction may be important in reinforcing impairments that otherwise might have been reversed more or less completely (pp. 153–154).

Casler (1961) has emphasized the shortcomings of research in this area and suggests that perceptual deprivation rather than affective deprivation is the basis for these findings. Actually, no such sharp distinction is possible, for cognition, perception, and affective behavior all work in concert and represent our own somewhat artificial abstractions. In addition, as Ainsworth (1962) points out, in the early months of life perceptual deprivation is equivalent to social deprivation since it is primarily the caretaker who provides the infant with perceptual stimulation.

It is difficult to pinpoint the rising fear of strangers in infants as a natural end to the period in which primary attachments are formed, as Gray (1958) has proposed; but it is also a safe guess, on the basis of the data reviewed by Ainsworth, that for most infants, attachments by seven months are essential. In evolutionary terms, it is highly adaptive that attachments between the human infant and its caretaker form by this age so that subsequent development of autonomy, in the newly motile child, may take place relatively unfettered by recurring dependency. The evolutionary point, so to speak, is to form the attachment and get on with the next stage. Also, it is apparent that precise decisions about a critical period for attachment in humans is not possible in contrast, say, to imprinting in precocial ground-nesting birds. Evolutionarily speaking, the latter must be on their feet soon after hatching or they would be open to severe predation. The situation is the same in precocial mammals, such as the wild forms of sheep, goats, and cattle, all naturally preyed-upon animals, in which attachments are made within hours after birth after which the flight response to strangers develops (Freedman, 1961). In animals not under direct predator pressure, such as man, the time period in which primary attachments occur is always longer and more variable. Additionally we have in man the factor of extensive infantilization, i.e., the prolongation of dependency over the longest period of time of any mammal. Thus, attachments have a long time to form and, as we shall see in a later section, there are numerous alternate (or complementary) mechanisms through which this may be accomplished.

Erikson's (1950) surmise that a basic sense of trust or mistrust is established in the first year is a complementary way of dealing with the same set of events. Erikson (1950) has further proposed that the major theme of the second and third years is the development of autonomy. Few observers would deny that the demand for and insistence on autonomy forms a major aspect of the lives of two- and three-year-olds, nor is there much difficulty in surmising the evolutionary importance of such self-propelling investigation of the environment at this age. That parental thwarting of autonomy will result in shame, as Erikson holds, has much less to recommend it. The feeling of shame is a common Japanese emotion, for example, yet autonomy in boys is greatly encouraged and considered desirable in that culture (Haring, 1956).

As for individual differences in relation to critical periods, experimental work with animals provides a helpful paradigm. Ginsburg (1965) has demonstrated that the handling of some strains of mice during a preweaning period will exaggerate adult aggressiveness whereas handling another strain will result in unusually pacific animals. In addition, the amount of handling also makes a difference in later aggression depending on the strain of mice used. Since each strain is essentially a single sample of the species' possibilities, it is clear that tremendous variability exists in responsivity to early stress. Breeds of dogs yield similar information (Freedman, 1958), and there is no reason to suspect the same is not true of humans. Experiences critical for one child may well have entirely different effects in another, and variability rather than uniformity of response is to be expected within the broad framework of the species pattern, providing the experiences or deprivations are not completely antagonistic to the nature of the species. With regard to this last point, Murphy (1964) has pointed out that individual differences are maximal in the relatively healthy, and the extreme deprivation discussed by Ainsworth amounts to a species-wide debilitation during which individual differences become submerged by the shocking nature of the general symptomatology.

An Evolutionary View of Early Attachments. We are using the term *evolved* in order to avoid the ambiguous dichotomy of innate vs. acquired. Evolution has been termed opportunistic (Simpson, 1964), so that in a species in which learning can become well developed any major genetic innovation in behavior will be completely interdependent with learning. Imprinting, for example, obviously involves both innate and acquired elements. Rather than becoming lost in a make believe partitioning of these elements, it is preferable to speak of imprinting as "evolved behavior." This latter term has the further advantage over "innate" of having clear phylogenetic reference without any implications regarding neurophysiological processes.

In 1958 Bowlby wrote, "Psychoanalysts are at one in recognizing the child's first object relations as the foundation stone of his personality: yet there is no agreement on the nature and dynamics of this relationship" (p. 350). He then went on to make the first fresh analysis of the nature of the child's emotional tie to the mother since Freud's "Three Contributions to the Theory of Sex" (1918). Bowlby described sucking, clinging, following, crying, smiling, and possibly cooing and babbling, as evolved responses (in the Darwinian sense), all in the service of assuring an attachment between infant and adult in their earliest manifestations. Each, to be sure, was seen as serving a variety of other purposes as well and were part of other maturational trends which, transmuted to varying degrees, carry through the life span. Bowlby's major critique was that "psychoanalytic theory has become fixated on orality," and it was his avowed purpose to free psychoanalysis for broader development.

The following is intended as an extension of Bowlby's insights, and the ways he proposes that a child achieves attachments will be considered in a somewhat extended evolutionary context.

As a first step it is appropriate to consider the characteristics of modern evolutionary thinking. For one thing, evolutionary thought is often seen as circular. Something is said to have adaptive value for a species, and the proof offered for this contention is that the species has survived, e.g., imprinting or the rapid formation of primary attachments is an adaptation of ground-nesting precocial birds to intense predator pressure, and the proof is said to be that these birds have survived predator pressure.

The point is, however, that evolutionary thinking depends on a nexus of relationships in which each datum, although weak by itself, grows in strength when considered in the context of other evidence. Evolutionary theory is primarily oriented toward the understanding of an event with regard to its adaptive function rather than, say, the biochemical process underlying it. The latter form of research is sometimes called the "atomistic approach" (Waddington, 1966, p. 781) and ideally the two approaches are coupled in mutually supporting theory and discovery.

In this regard, it is assumed that all the genes within an organism act in concert and that, for example, the XX chromosomally constituted female and the XY male are not dimorphic as *direct* action of the different chromosomes and genes involved; rather the XX or XY takes the entire genome in the direction of maleness or femaleness via complex interactions, which have in turn come about phylogenetically by a series of "mechanistic" processes. In other words, evolution has yielded organization, and it is up to the scientist to discover the mechanisms involved, always having in mind total functioning.

The same holistic logic holds for the analysis of behavior, i.e., any item of behavior takes on meaning only when examined in light of the total species' adaptation (von Uexküll, 1957). Thus, an item of infant behavior, e.g., the smile or cry, must be considered in terms of total hominid adaptation, including the total life span.

From this point of view, the equation of development with ontogeny is erroneous and can lead to false conclusions; it is no more logical to start with the baby in a description of the life-span than with any other stage of life, for species survival and the evolution of adaptations involve all phases of the life-span. This is in distinction to psychological systems that assume a strict causal chain between earlier and later events.

Formation of Attachments. Before considering infant behavior a few words about biological aspects of the family system are in order. We know that the infant will generally be born into a family since the family system is universal in man (Malinowski, 1956). Why men and women form families in every culture has never been adequately analyzed, but clearly there have evolved a number of assurances that men and women will mate, and further that they will tend to stay together.

We will now go on to a consideration of the formation of attachments in the baby. The very first behavior exhibited by the newborn is the cry, a common mammalian occurrence. Detailed analyses of the behavior around human crying are only now being made (Wolfe, 1966), but crying seems to share the common mammalian function of exciting the parent to caretaking activities. In dogs, for example, a puppy removed from the nest immediately starts to cry and continues until exhausted. The bitch will usually become extremely excited, seek the source of the cry until the puppy is found, and then fetch it back. What we have here, clearly, are two complementary evolved mechanisms, and neither has to be learned.

It is a general mammalian and avian characteristic that the very young, when left alone or when lost, yelp, cry, or chirp. When these noises are heard by the parent, various forms of retrieval behavior occur. Even though such vocalization expose the young to predation, they would die in any event without parental aid; so that, like many evolutionary mechanisms, a compromise is reached between two opposing possibilities. Few mechanisms do not to some extent compromise the chances of survival, and this occurs with such frequency that compromise can be termed a general rule of evolution. Bright coloration and complex song in male songbirds aid territoriality, nonspecific dispersal, as well as mating, but marks the male's whereabouts and leaves him vulnerable to predation. Similarly, the fact that black-headed gulls remove the glistening eggshells soon after hatching probably serves to lower visibility of nest sites to predators, but while the parents are gone with the shells predators may attack the defenseless chicks (Tinbergen, 1965).

In the human, similarly, it can be demonstrated that within hours after birth most crying infants will quiet when they are held and carried. Consider how this cessation of crying coordinates beautifully with the intense anxiety felt by the parent until the infant is quieted. Aside from caretaking and feeding, body contact is the inevitable result of crying, and the human baby does as well as the macaque in getting next to the parent without the ability to cling. There seems little doubt that such contact is normally a mutually reinforcing experience, and affectionate or appeasing tactual contacts of one form or another remain an important means of relating throughout the life-span. This does not imply, as does psychoanalytic logic, that if a type of behavior occurs earlier in time it is necessarily causal to related behavior appearing later in time. Within evolutionary logic, for example, attachments between adults of a social species are as "primary" as are attachments between infant and adult.

Smiling is also quite clearly an evolved mechanism (Ambrose, 1960; Freedman, 1964). It is universally present in man and it has the same or similar interpersonal function everywhere, that of a positive greeting or of appeasement. Smiling is first seen in reflexive form in newborns, including prematures, when they are dozing with eyes closed, usually after a feeding. Even at these early ages, however, smiles can also be elicited by a voice or by rocking the infant and, since it occurs in infants whose gestational age is as low as seven months, there seems little doubt that smiling can also occur *in utero*. Visually elicited smiles occur somewhat later than auditorally elicited smiles, though they are occasionally seen within the first week of life. These are called social smiles since they occur most readily when the eyes of infant and adult meet. In the auditory mode the preference for a voice over other sounds also marks such smiles as "social" (Wolfe, 1963).

The major function of smiling, then, from a very early age is responsivity to another. As Bowlby pointed out, it provides an important means of attachment between adult and infant, and in later life it lends ease and promotes attachment in a wide variety of social encounters. It is also widely displayed between adults as a gesture of appeasement in that it is a major means of either overcoming or precluding dissension and angry feeling.

The importance of the auditory and visual receptors in the young human infant seems directly related to its general motoric immaturity. Thus the eyes begin to search for form and movement in the environment soon after birth (Fantz, 1963; Greenman, 1963), and by two weeks of age over fifty per cent of all infants will follow a moving person (Bayley, 1961).

At about two months the infant's searching for the adult face can be very impressive. If held at the shoulder an infant may hold its unsteady head back to get a view of the holder's face, craning its neck like an inquisitive goose. One is left with the ineluctable feeling that searching out the *en face* position is itself an evolved mechanism. Supporting this contention are the large numbers of experimental studies that find the face a preferred stimulus for most infants, including newborns and the fact that the adult feels "looked-at" for the first time just preceding the onset of social smiling.

The human orientation toward the face of another is undoubtedly bound up with many aspects of evolutionary adaptation, including the upright stance, relative hairlessness, and rich musculature of the face; thus, there are the myriads of obvious and subtle nonverbal communications in which hominids engage. The culture-boundness vs. culture-independence of many of these expression are under current investigation (Eibl-Eibesfeldt, 1965).

A few weeks after *en face* smiling starts, the infant begins to coo at the beholding adult who in turn feels the irresistible urge to respond, and as a result much time may be spent in such happy "conversation." Feedings and sleep have by then decreased and normally more and more time is spent in direct social interactions.

A somewhat more robust order of interaction is initiated by laughter, usually at four months, when the baby and caretaker begin to engage in mutual play. The joy the adult feels in this engagement is probably no less an evolved mechanism than is the laughter of the baby, and doubtless such mutually reinforcing emotion ends up as attachment. The factor of time spent together is also a solidifier of attachment (St. Exupéry, 1943) and this is served, of course, by all the aforementioned mechanisms.

As the infant becomes embedded in the lives of those about him, another common phenomenon emerges, the fear of strangers. As early as three months of age in some infants, a definite preference for a parent or caretaker may be seen. This may be manifested at first by preferential smiling and cooing and following with the eyes. The infant may then cry when confronted by a stranger, especially if the place is also novel, such as a doctor's office.

The possible phylogenetic origins of this response have been discussed by Freedman (1961, 1965) who points out that many mammals and birds show similar fear responses to strangers and strange places after they have formed their initial attachments. In carnivores the fear response starts as they begin to travel farther and farther from the nest (about five weeks of age in dogs). In preyed-upon herd animals the young are on their feet within minutes after birth, attachment is quickly formed to the mother, and the fear response can be seen soon thereafter. Closely related is the advent of fear of heights which follows soon after the beginnings of motility in animals and humans and without prior experience of falling (Gibson & Walk, 1960). With motility, all animals become exposed to many new dangers as their investigative drives take them from the nest, and self-protective counter drives are necessary to assure survival.

Although motility and fear of strangers are related mechanisms in lower mammals, when a human infant develops its fear of strangers— usually between six and nine months—it simply does not have the motor ability to escape a predator. It therefore seems a reasonable hypothesis that in human infants the fear of strangers serves mainly to prevent dilution of primary relationships and, in addition, serves to intensify the bonds between the infant and those already close to him. In this regard the experimental work of Kovach and Hess (1963) with chicks indicates the reaction of fright makes primary bonds even stronger, so that this function is already served in lower forms.

There have been a number of alternative explanations of the fear of strangers, and Mieli (1957) has postulated that the fear is caused by an inability to assimilate the perceptual input. One trouble with such cognitive interpretations, however, is that they never ask the prior question: why this particular response and not another?

Spitz (1950) has made a cognitive-psychoanalytic interpretation by attributing the fear reaction to the infant's insight that other people are "not mother," so that the fear reaction for Spitz is a sort of anticipatory separation anxiety. A simple experiment by Jacobson (1966) has served to eliminate this overly sophisticated interpretation, for she found that babies are simply more fearful of an adult stranger than of a child stranger who is dressed the same and rehearsed to behave just like the adult. There seems little doubt that it is the stranger *qua* stranger that is feared, and that size adds to the fright.

SUMMARY

Social attachment is an adaptive, evolved characteristic of hominids and the formation of human mutuality is attained by way of many evolved mechanisms which are mutually reinforcing and which assure social interactions. Some examples are the desire for physical proximity, the appearance of mutual watching, mutual smiling, mutual cooing, mutual laughter and play; protection of the young when they cry or become fearful may also be viewed as means by which attachment is increased as may the very act of spending time together. By the time imitation and the first use of words start, late in the first year, social bonds are normally very strong and the child is an integral part of the lives of those about him.

Imitation is clearly a magnificent means for the acquisition of all forms of behavior and it becomes an effective force toward the end of the first year. As in sucking, craning the neck to see the face, reaching, turning over, sitting and standing, the drive to emulate is extremely strong. Only in the human is it carried to such persistent extremes, and it is a comment on psychoanalytic theory that it should be concerned with "anal" play in the second year while imitation, which is flowering, has been largely undiscussed. What better way to work into eventual autonomy than to practice directly an experienced partner's methods of coping with the world?

What is the relationship between style of attachment and personality? Let us go back to Bowlby's (1958) statement that there is agreement ". . . in recognizing the child's first object relations as the foundation stone of his personality." We are in a position now to question the implicit logic of this statement, i.e., that early attachments "cause" personality. The point is that early attachments *are* personality and that we are persons, or personalities, from the very start. To speak of these early attachments as causing personality is to commit the logical fallacy of the *tabula rasa* mind, i.e., where there was nothing, something eventually appears. Though it is true that one is always becoming, one is also always *being,* and the style in which these early interactions occur is itself personality. Each infant negotiates these behaviors in a unique way, that is, in his very own variation on the basic species theme.

Regarding this latter point, as we have seen, the process of forming attachments involves the constant actualization of phylogenetically derived capacities, and a theoretical model which neglects this fact is bound to develop illogicalities to account for the appearance of these behaviors. By *actualization* we have in mind Goldstein's (1939) meaning: there is only one drive which is invariant and characteristic of all living organisms, the drive to actualize their inborn capacities. All other so-called drives are variable and subsidiary to this one.

As acknowledged by Bowlby, the tendency has been to consider infantile experience the source of later behavior, and as a consequence there has been a considerable increase in interest and in actual work with infants in the hope of getting at causes. If the author reads these trends correctly, the next step will involve attributing the origins of infant behavior to uterine life, and then to the genome and DNA. In point of fact this is a regression to "homunculus" theory; since selection can and did occur in terms of developments at all ontogenetic points, the entire life-span is a product of evolutionary adaptation, and a psychologist interested in causes of behavior must simultaneously consider phylogeny and ontogeny, difficult as it may seem.

Although this has been a far from complete analysis of how attachments and personality form, our main purpose has been to illustrate the logic of the evolutionary approach and the fact that hypotheses derived from evolutionary thinking are open to experimental work. In terms of its scope, power, and intellectual appeal evolutionary theory has no equal and is simply waiting for interested psychologists to put it to work. To repeat the words of Herman Muller (1959), "One hundred years without Darwinism are enough."

References

Adler, A. *Problems of neurosis.* P. Mairet (Ed.), New York: Cosmopolitan Book Corp., 1930.

Ahrens, R. Beitrag zur Entwicklung des Physiognomie- und Mimikerkenness. (Contribution on the development of physiognomy and mimicry recognition.) Z. *exp. angew. Psychol.*, 1954, 2, 412–454, 599–633.

Ainsworth, M. D. The effects of maternal deprivation: A review of findings and controversy in the context of research strategy. In *Public Health Papers*, 1962, 14. Geneva: World Hlth. Org.

———. Patterns of attachment behavior shown by the infant in interaction with his mother. *Merrill-Palmer Quart.*, 1964, 10, 51–58. (a) Reprinted in Y. Brackbill & G. G. Thompson (Eds.), *Behavior in infancy and early childhood: A book of readings.* New York: Free Press, 1967.

———. The development of infant-mother interaction among the Ganda. In B. M. Foss (Ed.), *Determinants of infant behavior II.* New York: Wiley, 1964. (b)

Ainsworth, M. D., & Wittig, B. A. Attachment and exploratory behavior of one-year-olds in a strange situation. In B. M. Foss (Ed.), *Determinants of infant behavior IV.* New York: Wiley, in press.

Allport, G. *Personality: A psychological interpretation.* New York: Holt, 1937.

Ambrose, J. A. The smiling and related responses in early human infancy: An experimental and theoretical study of their course and significance. Unpublished doctoral dissertation, Univer. London, 1960.

———. The development of the smiling response in early infancy. In B. M. Foss (Ed.), *Determinants of infant behavior I.* New York: Wiley, 1961.

Ames, L. B. Development of interpersonal smiling responses in the preschool years. *J. genet. Psychol.*, 1949, 74, 273–291.

Andrus, R. A tentative inventory of the habits of children from two to four years of age. *Teach. Coll. Contr. Educ.*, 1924, No. 160.

Andrus, R., & Horowitz, E. L. The effect of nursery school training: Insecure feelings. *Child Develpm.*, 1938, 9, 169–174.

Appel, M. H. Aggressive behavior of nursery school children and adult procedures in dealing with such behavior. *J. exp. Educ.*, 1942, 11, 185–199.

Appell, G., & Aubry, J. Maternal deprivation in young children. Film: 16 mm; 22 min; sound. Distributors: New York Univer. Film Library; Tavistock Child Develpm. Res. Unit, London; United Nations, Geneva, 1951.

Arrington, R. E. *Interrelations in the behavior of young children.* New York: Teachers Coll., 1932.

Arsenian, J. M. Young children in an insecure situation. *J. abnorm. soc. Psychol.*, 1943, 38, 225–249.

Ausubel, D. P. *Theory and problems of child development.* New York: Grune & Stratton, 1958.

Baerends, G. P. The ethological concept 'releasing mechanism' illustrated by a study of the stimuli eliciting egg-retrieving in the herring gull. *Anat. Record.*, 1957, 128, 518–519.

———. The ethological analysis of incubation behaviour. *Ibis*, 1959, 101, 357–368.

Baldwin, A. L. The effect of home environment on nursery school behavior. *Child Develpm.*, 1949, 20, 49–61.

Bandura, A., & Walters, R. H. Aggression. In H. W. Stevenson, J. Kagan, & C. Spiker (Eds.), *Child psychology.* Chicago: Univer. Chicago Press, 1963.

Barker, R. G., Dembo, T., & Lewin, K. Frustration and regression. *Univer. Iowa Stud. Child Welf.,* 1941, 18, No. 1.

Baruch, D. W. Aggression during doll play in a preschool. *Amer. J. Orthopsychiat.,* 1941, 11, 252–259.

Bateson, G., & Mead, M. Karba's first years. Film, 2 reels, sound. Distributors: New York Univer. Film Library, 1942.

Bathurst, J. E. A study in sympathy and resistance (negativism) among children. *Psychol. Bull.,* 1933, 30, 625.

Bayley, N. A study of crying in infants during mental and physical tests. *J. genet. Psychol.,* 1932, 40, 306–329.

Bayley, N. Personal communication, 1961.

———. Consistency of maternal and child behaviors in the Berkeley growth study. *Vita Humana,* 1964, 7, 73–95.

———. Comparisons of mental and motor test scores for ages 1–15 months by sex, birth order, race, geographical location, and education of parents. *Child Develpm.,* 1965, 36, 379–411.

Beach, F. A. Evolutionary aspects of psychoendocrinology. In A. Roe & G. G. Simpson (Eds.), *Behaviour and evolution.* New Haven: Yale Univer. Press, 1958.

Bell, R. Q. Relations between behavior manifestations in the human neonate. *Child Develpm.,* 1960, 31, 463–477.

———. Some factors to be controlled in studies of the behavior of newborns. *Biol. Neonat.,* 1963, 5, 200–214.

Benjamin, E. The period of resistance in early childhood. *Amer. J. dis. Child.,* 1942, 63, 1019–1079.

Benjamin, J. D. Prediction and psychopathologic theory. In L. Jessner & E. Pavenstadt (Eds.), *Dynamic psychopathology in childhood.* New York: Grune & Stratton, 1959.

———. Some developmental observations relating to the theory of anxiety. *J. Amer. Psychoanal. Ass.,* 1961, 9, 652–668.

———. Further comments on some developmental aspects of anxiety. In H. Gaskill (Ed.), *Counterpoint.* New York: Int. Univer. Press, 1963, 121–153.

Berlyne, D. E. The influence of the albedo and complexity of stimuli on visual fixation in the human infant. *Brit. J. Psychol.,* 1958, 49, 315–318.

———. *Conflict, arousal and curiosity.* New York: McGraw-Hill, 1960.

Blanton, M. G. The behavior of the human infant during the first thirty days of life. *Psychol. Rev.,* 1917, 24, 456–483.

Blatz, W. E., Allin, K. D., & Millichamp, D. A. A study of laughter in the nursery school child. *Univer. Toronto Stud. Child Develpm.,* 1936, No. 7.

Blatz, W. E., & Millichamp, D. A. The development of emotion in the infant. *Univer. Toronto Stud. Child Develpm.,* 1935, No. 4.

Block, J., & Martin, E. Predicting the behavior of children under frustration. *J. abnorm. soc. Psychol.,* 1955, 51, 281–285.

Blum, G. F. *Psychoanalytic theories of personality.* New York: McGraw-Hill, 1953.

Botelho, S. Y. Tears and the lacrimal gland. *Sci. Amer.,* 1964, 211, 78–86.

Bowlby, J. *Maternal care and mental health.* Geneva: World Hlth. Org. Monogr. Ser. No. 2, 1952.

———. The nature of the child's tie to his mother. *Int. J. Psychoanal.,* 1958, 39, 350–373.

———. Separation anxiety. *Int. J. Psychoanal.,* 1960, 41, 89–113. (a)

———. Symposium on psychoanalysis and the development of object relations. *Int. J. Psychoanal.,* 1960, 41, 313. (b)

Brackbill, Y. Extinction of the smiling response in infants as a function of reinforcement schedule. *Child Develpm.,* 1958, 29, 115–124. Reprinted in Y. Brackbill & G. G. Thompson (Eds.), *Behavior in infancy and early childhood: A book of readings.* New York: Free Press, 1967.

Brackbill, Y., Adams, G., Crowell, D. H., & Gray, M. L. Arousal level in neonates and preschool children under continuous auditory stimulation. *J. exp. child Psychol.*, 1966, 4, No. 2, 178–188. Reprinted in Y. Brackbill & G. G. Thompson (Eds.), *Behavior in infancy and early childhood: A book of readings.* New York: Free Press, 1967.

Brackett, C. S. Laughing and crying of preschool children. *J. exp. Educ.*, 1933, 2, 119–126.

Brenner, C. *An elementary textbook of psychoanalysis.* New York: Int. Univer. Press, 1955.

Bridger, W. H., Birns, B. M., & Blank, M. A comparison of behavioral ratings and heart rate measurements in human neonates. *Psychosom. Med.*, 1965, 27, 123–134.

Bridges, K. M. B. *The social and emotional development of the pre-school child.* London: Routledge, 1931.

———. Emotional development in early infancy. *Child Develpm.*, 1932, 3, 324–341.

Brückner, G. H. Untersuchungen zur Tiersoziologie, insbesondere der Auflösung der Familie. *Z. Psychol.*, 1933, 128, 1–110.

Bühler, C. *The first year of life.* (Translated by P. Greenberg & R. Ripin from the following three German publications: Bühler, C., & Hetzer, H. Inventar der Verhaltungsweisen des ersten Lebensjahres. *Quell. Stud. Jegendk.*, No. 5, Jena: Fischer, 1927, 125–250; Hetzer, H., & Wolf, K. Babytests. *Z. Psychol.*, 1928, 107, 62–104; Hetzer, H., & Koller, L. Vier Testreihen für das zweite Lebensjahr. *Z. Psychol.*, 1930, 117, 258–306.) New York: John Day, 1930.

———. The social behavior of children. In C. A. Murchison (Ed.), *Handbook of child psychology.* (2nd ed. rev.) Worcester: Clark Univer. Press, 1933, 347–417.

Bühler, C., & Hetzer, H. Das erste Verständnis für Ausdruck im ersten Lebensjahr. (The first understanding of expression in the first year of life.) *Z. Psychol.*, 1928, 107, 50–61.

———. Individual differences among children in the first two years of life. *Child Study*, 1929, 7, 11–13.

Bühler, C., Hetzer, H., & Mable, F. Die Affektwirksamkeit von Fremdheitseindrücken im ersten Lebensjahr. (The effectiveness of affect involving unfamiliar impressions during the first year of life.) *Z. Psychol. Physiol. der Sinnesorgane*, 1928, 107, 30–49.

Caille, R. K. *Resistant behavior of preschool children.* New York: Teachers Coll., 1933.

Casler, L. Maternal deprivation: A critical review of the literature. *Monogr. Soc. Res. Child Develpm.*, 26, 2, 1961.

Cassirer, E. *An essay on man.* New York: Yale Univer. Press, 1944.

Coghill, G. E. The early development of behavior in Amblystoma and in man. *Arch. Neurol. Psychiat.*, 1929, 21, 989–1009.

Conel, J. L. *Postnatal development of the human cerebral cortex.* Cambridge, Mass.: Harvard Univer. Press, 1939–1963.

Darwin, C. A biographical sketch of an infant. *Mind*, 1877, No. 7, 285–294.

———. *The expression of the emotions in man and animals.* New York: Appleton, 1898.

Dawe, H. C. An analysis of two hundred quarrels of preschool children. *Child Develpm.*, 1934, 5, 139–157.

de Chardin, P. *The phenomenon of man.* New York: Harper, 1965.

Dennis, W. An experimental test of two theories of social smiling in infants. *J. soc. Psychol.*, 1935, 6, 214–223.

———. Infant development under conditions of restricted practice and minimum social stimulation. *Genet. Psychol. Monogr.*, 1941, 23, 143–189.

Diamond, M. A critical evaluation of the ontogeny of human sexual behavior. *Quart. Rev. Biol.*, 1965, 40, 2, 147–175.

Ding, G. F., & Jersild, A. T. A study of the laughing and smiling of preschool children. *J. genet. Psychol.*, 1932, 40, 452–472.

Dobzhansky, T. Heredity and the nature of man. New York: Harcourt, Brace & World, 1964.

Dollard, J., Doob, L. W., Miller, N. E., Mowrer, O. H., & Sears, R. R. *Frustration and aggression.* New Haven: Yale Univer. Press, 1939.

Duffy, E. An explanation of emotional phenomena without the use of the concept "emotion." *J. genet. Psychol.*, 1941, 25, 285–293.

Dwyer, F. M. A note on resistance and rapport in psychological tests of young children. *J. genet. Psychol.*, 1937, 51, 451–454.

Eibl-Eibesfeldt, I. Personal communication, 1965.

Ellesor, N. V. Children's reactions to novel visual stimuli. *Child Develpm.*, 1933, 4, 95–105.

Enders, A. C. A study of the laughter of the preschool child in the Merrill-Palmer Nursery School. *Papers, Mich. Acad. Sci., Arts & Letters*, 1927, 8, 341–356.

English, H. B. Three cases of conditioned fear response. *J. abnorm. soc. Psychol.*, 1929, 47, 221–229.

Erikson, E. H. *Childhood and society.* New York: W. W. Norton, 1950; 2nd ed., 1963.

Escalona, S. K. The study of individual differences and the problem of state. *J. Amer. Acad. Child Psychiat.*, 1962, 1, 11–37.

Escalona, S. K., & Heider, G. M. *Prediction and outcome.* New York: Basic Books, 1959.

Escalona, S. K., & Leitch, M. Early phases of personality development: A non-normative study of infant behavior. *Monogr. Soc. Res. Child Develpm.*, 1952, 17, Ser. No. 54, No. 1.

Etkin, W. Types of social organization in birds and mammals. In W. Etkin (Ed.), *Social behavior and organization among vertebrates.* Chicago: Univer. Chicago Pr., 1964.

Ettsins, W. Types of social organization in birds and mammals. In A. Ettsins (Ed.), *Social behavior and organization among vertebrates.* Chicago: Univer. Chicago Press, 1964.

Fantz, R. L. Pattern vision in newborn infants, *Science*, 1963, 140, 296–297.

Fenichel, O. *Psychoanalytic theory of neurosis.* New York: Norton, 1945.

Fredericksen, N. The effects of frustration on negativistic behavior of young children. *J. genet. Psychol.*, 1942, 61, 203–226.

Freedman, D. G. Constitutional and environmental interactions in rearing of four breeds of dogs. *Science*, 1958, 127, 585–586.

——. The infant's fear of strangers and the flight response. *J. child Psychol. Psychiat.*, 1961, 4, 242–248. (a)

——. The differentiation of identical and fraternal twins on the basis of filmed behavior. *Proc. 2nd Int. Congr. Human Genet.* Rome: Inst. G. Mendel, 1961, Vol. 1, 259–262. (b)

——. 16 mm sound film: Development of the smile and fear of strangers. PCR-2140, Penna. Psychol. Cinema Reg., University Park, Penna., 1963.

——. Smiling in blind infants and the issue of innate vs. acquired. *J. child Psychol. Psychiat.*, 1964, 171–184.

——. An ethological approach to the genetic study of human behavior. In S. Vandenberg (Ed.), *Methods and goals in human behavior genetics.* New York: Academic Press, 1965.

——. Personal communication, 1966.

Freedman, D. G., & Keller, B. Inheritance of behavior in infants. *Science*, 1963, 140, 196–198. Reprinted in Y. Brackbill & G. G. Thompson (Eds.), *Behavior in infancy and early childhood: A book of readings.* New York: Free Press, 1967.

Freedman, D. G., King, J. A., & Elliot, O. Critical period in the social development of dogs. *Science*, 1961, 133, 1016–1017.

Frenkel-Brunswick, E. Intolerance of ambiguity as an emotional and perceptual variable. *J. Pers.*, 1949, 18, 108–143.

Freud, A. The concept of developmental lines. *Psychoanalyt. Stud. Child,* 1963, 18, 245–265.

———. *Normality and pathology in childhood.* New York: Int. Univer. Press, 1965.

Freud, S. Three contributions to the theory of sex. *Nerv. ment. Dis. Monogr.,* 1918, 7.

———. (1900) The interpretation of dreams. *Standard Edition.* 4 & 5. London: Hogarth Press, 1953.

———. (1920) Beyond the pleasure principle. *Standard Edition.* 18:7–64. London: Hogarth Press, 1955.

———. (1926) Inhibition, symptoms and anxiety. *Standard Edition.* 20:87–172. London: Hogarth Press, 1959.

———. *The problem of anxiety.* Translated by H. A. Bunker. New York: Norton, 1936.

———. The interpretation of dreams. In *The basic writings of Sigmund Freud.* New York: Random House, Modern Library, 1938.

Freyd, M. Introverts and extroverts. *Psychol. Rev.*, 1924, 31, 74–87.

Fries, M., & Woolf, D. Some hypotheses on the role of the congenital activity type in development. *Psychoanalyt. Stud. Child,* 1953, 8, 48.

Geber, M. Problémes posé par le développement du jeune enfant Africain en fonction de son milieu social. (Problems in the development of the young African child.) *Le Travail Humain,* 1956, 6, 17–29.

Gesell, A., & Ilg, F. L. *Infant and child in the culture of today: The guidance of development in home and nursery school.* New York: Harper, 1943.

Gesell, A., & Thompson, H. *Infant behavior: Its genesis and growth.* New York: McGraw-Hill, 1934.

Gewirtz, J. L. The course of infant smiling in four child-rearing environments in Israel. In B. M. Foss (Ed.), *Determinants of infant behaviour III.* London: Methuen, 1965. (a)

———. The course of smiling by groups of Israeli infants in the first eighteen months of life. *Scripta Hierosolymitana,* Vol. XIV. *Studies in psychology.* Jerusalem: Magnes Press, Hebrew Univer., 1965. (b)

Gibson, E. R., & Walk, R. D. The visual cliff. *Sci. Amer.*, 1960, 202, 2–9.

Gill, M. M., & Rappaport, D. The points of view of assumptions of metapsychology. *Int. J. Psychoanal.*, 1959, 40, 153–162.

Ginsburg, B. E. Genetic parameters in behaviour research. In J. Hirsch (Ed.), *Behavior genetic analysis.* New York: McGraw-Hill, 1967.

Ginsburg, B. E., & Laughlin, W. S. The multiple bases of human adaptability and achievement: A species point of view. *Eugenics Quart.*, in press.

Glanzer, M. Curiosity, exploratory drive, and stimulus satiation. *Psychol. Bull.*, 1953, 55, 302–315.

Goldfarb, W. Emotional and intellectual consequences of psychologic deprivation in infancy: A reevaluation. In P. Hoch & J. Zubin (Eds.), *Psychopathology of childhood.* New York: Grune & Stratton, 1955.

Goldstein, K. *The organism.* New York: American Book Co., 1939.

Goodenough, F. L. The emotional behavior of young children during mental tests. *J. juv. Res.*, 1929, 13, 204–219.

———. Interrelationships in the behavior of young children. *Child Develpm.,* 1930, 1, 29–47.

———. *Anger in young children.* Minneapolis: Univer. Minn. Press, 1931. (a)

———. The expression of emotions in infancy. *Child Develpm.*, 1931, 2, 96–101. (b)

———. Expression of the emotions in a blind-deaf child. *J. abnorm. soc. Psychol.*, 1932, 47, 328–333.

Gorer, G. Theoretical approach: 1941. In M. Mead & M. Wolfenstein (Eds.), *Childhood in contemporary cultures.* Chicago: Univer. Chicago Press, 1955.

Gray, P. H. Theory and evidence of imprinting in human infants. *J. Psychol.*, 1958, 46, 155–166.

Greenman, G. W. Visual behavior of newborn infants. In A. J. Solnit & S. A. Provence (Eds.), *Modern perspectives in child development.* New York: Int. Univer. Press, 1963.

Gregg, A., Miller, N., & Linton, E. Laughter situations as an indication of social responsiveness in young children. In D. S. Thomas (Ed.), *Some new techniques for studying social behavior.* New York: Teachers Coll., 1929.

Hagman, E. R. A study of fears of children of pre-school age. *J. exp. Educ.*, 1932, 1, 110–130.

Hall, G. S. A study of anger. *Amer. J. Psychol.*, 1899, 10, 516–591.

Hall, K. R. L., & DeVore, I. Baboon social behavior. In I. DeVore (Ed.), *Primate behavior.* New York: Holt, Rinehart, & Winston, 1965.

Haring, D. G. Comment on Japanese personal character: Pre-war. In D. G. Haring (Ed.), *Personal character and cultural milieu.* New York: Syracuse Univer. Press, 1956.

Harlow, H. G., & Zimmerman, R. R. Affectional responses in the infant monkey. *Science*, 1959, 130, 421–432.

Harrison, G. A. Human genetics. In G. A. Harrison, J. S. Weiner, J. M. Tanner, & N. A. Barnicott (Eds.), *Human biology—An introduction to human evolution, variation and growth.* New York: Oxford Univer. Press, 1964.

Hartmann, H. Psychoanalysis and developmental psychology. *Psychoanalyt. Stud. Child*, 1950, 5–12.

———. *Ego psychology and problems of adaptation.* New York: Int. Univer. Press, 1958.

Hattwick, L. Sex differences in behavior of nursery school children. *Child Develpm.*, 1937, 8, 343–355.

Hattwick, L., & Sanders, M. K. Age differences in behavior at the nursery school level. *Child Develpm.*, 1938, 9, 27–47.

Heathers, G. The adjustment of two-year-olds in a novel social situation. *Child Develpm.*, 1954, 25, 147–158.

Hebb, D. O. On the nature of fear. *Psychol. Rev.*, 1946, 53, 259–276.

———. Heredity and environment in mammalian behavior. *Brit. J. animal Behav.*, 1953, 1, 2, 43–47.

———. Drives and the C.N.S. (conceptual nervous system). *Psychol. Rev.*, 1955, 62, 243–254.

Hebb, D. O., & Riesen, A. H. The genesis of emotional fears. *Bull. Canad. Psychol. Ass.*, 1943, 3, 49–50.

Hess, E. Ethology: An approach toward the complete analysis of behavior. In R. Brown, E. Galanter, E. Hess, & G. Mandler (Eds.), *New directions in psychology.* New York: Holt, Rinehart & Winston, 1962.

Honzik, M. P. Personality consistency and change: Some comments on papers by Bayley, Macfarlane, Moss, Kagan, & Murphy. *Vita Humana*, 1964, 7, 67–72.

Horney, K. *The neurotic personality of our time.* New York: Norton, 1937.

———. *New ways in psychoanalysis.* New York: Norton, 1939.

———. *Our inner conflicts: A constructive theory of neurosis.* New York: Norton, 1945.

Irwin, O. C. The amount and nature of activities of new-born infants under constant external stimulating conditions during the first ten days of life. *Genet. Psychol. Monogr.*, 1930, 8, 1–92.

———. Infant responses to vertical movements. *Child Develpm.*, 1932, 3, 104–107.

Irwin, O. C., & Weiss, LaB. A note on mass activity in newborn infants. *Ped. Sem.*, 1930, 38, 20–30.

———. The effect of darkness on the activity of newborn infants. *Univer. Iowa Stud. Child Welf.*, 1934, 9, No. 4.

Irwin, O. C., Weiss, LaB., & Stubbs, E. M. Studies in infant behavior. I. *Univer. Iowa Stud. Child Welf.*, 1934, 9, No. 4.

Jacobson, J. Unpublished data. Univer. Chicago, 1966.

Jenkins, R. L. The management of negativism in young children. *Med. Rec.*, 1935, 142, 507–510.

Jersild, A. T. Emotional development. In L. Carmichael (Ed.), *Manual of child psychology.* New York: Wiley, 1954. Pp. 833–917.

Jersild, A. T., & Holmes, F. B. *Children's fears.* New York: Teachers Coll., 1935.

Jersild, A. T., & Markey, F. V. *Conflicts between preschool children.* New York: Bureau of Publications, Teachers Coll., 1935.

Johnson, B. Variations in emotional responses of children. *Child Develpm.*, 1936, 7, 85–94.

Jones, H. E. The conditioning of overt emotional responses. *J. educ. Psychol.*, 1931, 22, 127–130.

Jones, H. E., & Jones, M. C. A study of fear. *Childh. Educ.*, 1928, 21, 136–143.

Jones, M. C. A laboratory study of fear: The case of Peter. *Ped. Sem.*, 1924, 31, 308–316. (a)

——. Elimination of children's fears. *J. exp. Psychol.*, 1924, 7, 383–390. (b)

——. The development of early behavior patterns in young children. *J. genet. Psychol.*, 1926, 33, 537–585.

Kagan, J., Henker, B. A., Hen-Tov, A., Levine, J., & Lewis, M. Infants' differential reactions to familiar and distorted faces. Paper read at Amer. Psychol. Ass., Chicago, 1965.

Kagan, J., & Moss, H. A. Stability of passive and dependent behavior from childhood through adulthood. *Child Develpm.*, 1960, 31, 577–591.

——. *Birth to maturity: A study in psychological development.* New York: Wiley, 1962.

Kaila, E. Die Reaktion des Säugling auf das menschliche Gesicht. (The reaction of the infant to the human face.) *Annales Universitatis Aboensis,* Series B., 1932, 17, 1–114.

Kelting, L. S. An investigation of the feeding, sleeping, crying, and social behavior of infants. *J. exp. Educ.*, 1934, 3, 97–106.

Kenderdine, M. Laughter in the pre-school child. *Child Develpm.*, 1931, 2, 228–230.

Kistjakovskaya, M. J. Stimuli evoking positive emotions in infants. *Voprosy Psikhologii,* 1965, 2, 129–140.

Klein, M. *Envy and gratitude: A study of unconscious sources.* New York: Basic Books, 1957.

Koehler, O. Das Lachen als angeborene Ausdrucksbewegung. *A. For. Menschliche Vererbung und Konstitutionslehre,* 1954, 32, 390–398.

Kovach, J. K., & Hess, E. H. Imprinting effects of painful stimulation upon the following response. *J. comp. physiol. Psych.*, 1963, 56, 461–464.

L'Allier, L. Smiling as a result of aural stimuli. Ph.D. Thesis, Univer. of Montreal. Reported in J. L. Laroche & F. Tcheng. *Le sourire du Nourisson.* Publ. Univer., Louvain, 1961.

Landau, R. L. Personal communication.

Landreth, C. Factors associated with crying in young children in the nursery school and the home. *Child Develpm.*, 1941, 12, 81–97.

Laroche, J. E., & Tcheng, P. *Le sourire du Nourisson.* (Smiling of the infant.) Louvain: Publications Univer., 1963.

Leitch, M., & Escalona, S. The reaction of infants to stress. *Psychoanalyt. Stud. Child,* 1949, 3, 121–140.

Leonard, M. R. Problems in identification and ego development in twins. *Psychoanalyt. Stud. Child,* 1961, 16, 300–318.

Lesser, G. S., Fifer, G., & Clark, D. H. Mental abilities of children from different social-class and cultural groups. *Monogr. Soc. Res. Child Develpm.*, 1965, 102, 30, No. 4.

Levy, D. M. Resistant behavior of children. *Amer. J. Psychiat.*, 1925, 4, 503–507.

——. On the problem of movement restraint: Tics, stereotyped movements, hyperactivity. *Am. J. Orthopsychiat.*, 1944, 14, 644–671.

Levy, D. M., & Tulchin, S. H. The resistance of infants and children during mental tests. *J. exp. Psychol.*, 1923, 6, 304–322.

——. The resistant behavior of infants and children. II. *J. exp. Psychol.*, 1925, 8, 209–224.

Lewis, M. Exploratory studies in the development of a face schema. Paper read at Amer. Psychol. Ass., Chicago, 1965.

Lindsley, D. B. Emotion. In S. S. Stevens (Ed.), *Handbook of experimental psychology.* New York: Wiley, 1951. Pp. 473–516.

Lipton, E. L., Richmond, J. B., Weinberger, H. L., & Hersher, L. An approach to the evaluation of neonate autonomic responses. *Psychosom. Med.*, 1958, 20, 409.

Lipton, E. L., Steinschneider, A., & Richmond, J. B. Autonomic function in the neonate: II. Psychologic effects of motor restraint. *Psychosom. Med.*, 1960, 22, 57–65.

——. Autonomic function in the neonate: III. Methodological considerations. *Psychosom. Med.*, 1961, 23, 461–471. (a)

——. Autonomic function in the neonate: IV. Individual differences in cardiac reactivity. *Psychosom. Med.*, 1961, 23, 472–484. (b)

——. Autonomic function in the neonate: VII. Maturational changes in cardiac control. *Child Develpm.*, 1966, 37, 1–16.

Lochlin, J. C. An hereditary-environment analysis of personality inventory data. In S. G. Vandenberg (Ed.), *Methods and goals in human behavior genetics.* New York: Academic Press, 1965.

Lorenz, K. Über den Begriff der Instinkthandlung. (On the concept of instinctive response.) *Folia Biotheoretica*, 1937, 2, 17–50.

——. The comparative method in studying innate behaviour patterns. *Symp. soc. exp. Biol.*, 1950, 4, 221–268.

——. Companionship in bird life. In C. H. Schiller (Ed.), *Instinctive behaviour.* London: Methuen, 1957.

——. *On aggression.* New York: Harcourt Brace, 1966.

Macfarlane, J. W. Perspectives on personality consistency and change from the guidance study. *Vita Humana*, 1964, 7, 115–126.

MacKinnon, D. W. The structure of personality. In J. McV. Hunt (Ed.), *Personality and the behavior disorders*, Vol. 1. New York: Ronald Press, 1944.

——. (Ed.), *Selection of personnel for the office of strategic services: Assessment of men.* New York: Rinehart, 1948.

McKinnon, M. *Consistency and change in behavior manifestations as observed in a group of sixteen children during a five-year period.* New York: Teachers Coll., 1942.

Malinowski, B., & Briffault, R. *Marriage: Past and present.* Boston: Porter Sargent, 1956.

Marquis, P. A study of frustration in newborn infants. *J. exp. Psychol.*, 1943, 32, 123–138.

Marshall, D. Personal communication, 1965.

Mason, W. A. The effects of social restriction on the behavior of Rhesus monkeys: I. Free social behavior. In T. E. McGill (Ed.), *Readings in animal behavior.* New York: Holt, Rinehart & Winston, 1965.

Mayer, B. A. Negativistic reactions of preschool children on the new revision of the Stanford-Binet. *J. genet. Psychol.*, 1935, 46, 311–334.

Mayr, E. Behavior and systematics. In Ann Roe & G. G. Simpson (Eds.), *Behavior and evolution.* New Haven: Yale Univer. Press, 1958.

——. *Animal species and evolution.* Cambridge, Mass.: Belknap Press, Harvard Univer. Press, 1963.

Mead, M. *Male and female.* New York: William Morrow, 1949.

———. Theoretical setting. In M. Mead & M. Wolfenstein (Eds.), *Childhood in contemporary cultures.* Chicago: Univer. Chicago Press, 1955.

Meili, R. *Anfänge der Charakterentwicklung. (Beginnings of character development.)* Bern: Verlag Hans Huber, 1957.

Money, J. Psychosexual differentiation. In J. Money (Ed.), *Sex research: New developments.* New York: Holt, Rinehart, & Winston, 1965.

Monroe, R. L. *Schools of psychoanalytic thought.* New York: Dryden Press, 1955.

Morgan, G. A., & Ricciuti, H. N. Infants' responses to strangers during the first year. In B. M. Foss (Ed.), *Determinants of infant behavior IV,* New York: Wiley, in press.

Moriarty, A. Coping patterns of preschool children in response to intelligence test demands. *Genet. Psychol. Monogr.,* 1961, 64, 3–127.

Moruzzi, G., & Magoun, H. W. Brain stem reticular formation and activation of the EEG. *Clin. Neurophysiol.,* 1949, 1, 455–473.

Mowrer, O. H. A stimulus-response analysis of anxiety and its role as a reinforcing agent. *Psychol. Rev.,* 1939, 46, 553–566.

Mullahy, P. *Oedipus—myth and complex.* New York: Hermitage Press, 1948.

Muller, H. J. One hundred years without Darwinism are enough. *School Sci. Math.,* 1959, 59, 304–316.

Murphy, G. *Personality.* New York: Harper, 1947.

Murphy, L. B. *Social behavior and child personality: an exploratory study of some roots of sympathy.* New York: Columbia Univer. Press, 1937.

———. Factors in continuity and change in the development of adaptational style in children. *Vita Humana,* 1964, 7, 96–114.

Mussen, P. H., Conger, J. J., & Kagan, J. *Child development and personality.* (2nd ed.) New York: Harper & Row, 1963.

Muste, M. J., & Sharpe, D. F. Some influential factors in the determination of aggressive behavior in preschool children. *Child Develpm.,* 1947, 18, 11–28.

Neilon, P. Shirley's babies after fifteen years: A personality study. *J. genet. Psychol.,* 1948, 73, 175–186.

Nelson, F. *Personality and intelligence: A study of some responses other than intellectual noted in a simple mental test situation.* New York: Teachers Coll., 1931.

Newman, H. H., Freeman, F. N., & Holzinger, K. J. *Twins: A study of heredity and environment.* Chicago: Univer. Chicago Press, 1937.

Nichols, R. Paper read at 2nd Conf. in Human Behavior Genetics, Louisville, May, 1966.

Orlansky, H. Infant care and personality. *Psychol. Bull.,* 1949, 46, 1–48.

Penbharkkul, S., & Karelitz, S. Lacrimation in the neonatal and early infancy period of premature and full-term infants. *J. Pediatr.,* 1962, 61, 859.

Pepper, S. C. *World hypotheses.* Berkeley: Univer. Calif. Press, 1961.

Piaget, J. *The origins of intelligence in children.* New York: Int. Univer. Press, 1952.

Piddington, R. *The psychology of laughter: A study of social adaptation.* New York: Gamut Press, 1963.

Pinneau, S. R. The infantile disorders of hospitalism and anaclitic depression. *Psychol. Bull.,* 1955, 52, 429.

Polak, P. R., Emde, R. N., & Spitz, R. A. The smiling response, II: Visual discrimination and the onset of depth perception. *J. nerv. ment. Dis.,* 1964, 139, 407–415.

Pratt, K. C. The neonate. In L. Carmichael (Ed.), *Manual of child psychology.* New York: Wiley, 1954. Pp. 215–291.

Pratt, K. C., Nelson, A. K., & Sun, K. H. The behavior of the newborn infant. *Ohio State Univer. Stud. Contrib. Psychol.,* 1930, No. 10.

Pulver, Wm. Spannungen und Störungen im Verhalten des Säuglings. (Tensions and disturbances in the behavior of the infant.) *Beiträge genet. Charakterol.*, 1959, No. 2, 5–123.

Rank, O. *The trauma of birth.* New York: Harcourt Brace, 1929.

Rappaport, D. The autonomy of the ego. *Bull. Menninger Clinic*, 1951, 15, 113–123.

———. The theory of ego autonomy: A generalization. *Bull. Menninger Clinic*, 1958, 22, 13–35.

———. The structure of psychoanalytic theory: A systematizing attempt. In S. Koch (Ed.), *A study of a science.* New York: McGraw-Hill, 1959, 3, 55–183.

Reynolds, M. M. *Negativism of pre-school children: An observational experimental study.* New York: Teachers Coll., *Contr. Educ.*, 1928, No. 288.

Rheingold, H. L. The modification of social responsiveness in institutional babies. *Monogr. Soc. Res. Child Develpm.*, 1956, 21, No. 2.

———. The effect of environmental stimulation upon social and exploratory behaviour in the human infant. In B. M. Foss (Ed.), *Determinants of infant behavior. I.* New York, Wiley, 1961.

Rheingold, H. L., Stanley, W. C., & Cooley, J. A. Method for studying exploratory behavior in infants. *Science*, 1962, 136, 1054–1055.

Richmond, J. B., & Lipton, E. L. Some aspects of the neurophysiology of the newborn and their implications for child development. In L. Jessner & E. Pavenstedt (Eds.), *Dynamic psychopathology in childhood.* New York: Grune & Stratton, 1959.

Ricketts, A. F. A study of the behavior of young children in anger. *Univer. Iowa Stud. Child Welf.*, 1934, 9, No. 5.

Riesen, A. H. Stimulation as a requirement for growth and function in behavioral development. In D. W. Fiske, & S. Maddi (Eds.), *Functions of varied experience.* Homewood: Dorsey Press, 1961.

Rust, M. M. *The effect of resistance on intelligence test scores of young children.* New York: Teachers Coll., 1931.

Salk, L. The effects of the normal heartbeat sound on the behavior of the newborn infant: Implications for mental health. *World Ment. Hlth.*, 1960, 12, 168–175.

———. The importance of the heartbeat rhythm to human nature: Theoretical, clinical, and experimental observations. *Proc. Third World Congr. Psychiat.* Montreal: McGill Univer. Press, 1961, 1, 740–746.

———. Mothers' heartbeat as an imprinting stimulus. *Trans. New York Acad. Sci.*, 1962, 24, 753–763.

Salzen, E. A. Visual stimuli eliciting the smiling response in the human infant. *J. genet. Psychol.*, 1963, 102, 51–54.

Schaeffer, E. S., & Bayley, N. Maternal behavior, child behavior, and their intercorrelations from infancy through adolescence. *Monogr. Soc. Res. Child Develpm.*, 1963, 28, Ser. No. 87, No. 3.

Schaffer, H. R. Objective observations of personality development in early infancy. *Brit. J. med. Psychol.*, 1958, 31, 174–183. Reprinted in Y. Brackbill & G. G. Thompson (Eds.), *Behavior in infancy and early childhood: A book of readings.* New York: Free Press, 1967.

———. Some issues of research in the study of attachment behaviour. In B. M. Foss (Ed.), *Determinants of infant behaviour. II.* New York: Wiley, 1964, 179–196.

Schaffer, H. R., & Callender, W. M. Psychological effects of hospitalization in infancy. *Pediatrics*, 1959, 24, 528–539.

Schaffer, H. R., & Emerson, P. E. The development of social attachments in infancy. *Monogr. Soc. Res. Child Develpm.*, 1964, 29, No. 3.

Scheibel, M. E., & Scheibel, A. B. Some neural substrates of postnatal development. In M. L. Hoffman & L. W. Hoffman (Eds.), *Review of child development research.* New York: Russell Sage Foundation, 1964. Pp. 481–514.

Schneirla, T. C. An evolutionary and developmental theory of biphasic proc-
esses underlying approach and withdrawal. In M. R. Jones (Ed.), *Nebraska
symposium on motivation.* Lincoln, Neb.: Univer. Nebraska, 1959. Pp.
1–41.
——. Instinctive behavior, maturation-experience and development. In B.
Kaplan & S. Wapner (Eds.), *Perspectives in psychological theory.* New
York: Int. Univer. Press, 1960.
Schramm, D. G. J. Direction of movements of children in emotional responses. *Child Develpm.,* 1935, 6, 26–51.
Schur, M. Discussion of Dr. John Bowlby's paper. *Psychoanalyt. Stud. Child,*
1960, 15, 63.
Scott, J. P. Critical periods in behavioral development. *Science,* 1962, 138,
949–958.
Scrimshaw, N. S., & Behar, M. Protein malnutrition in young children. *Sci-
ence,* 1961, 133, 2039–2047.
Sears, R. R., & Sears, P. S. Minor studies of aggression: V. Strength of frus-
tration-reaction as a function of strength of drive. *J. Psychol.,* 1940, 9, 297–
300.
Seitz, A. Die Paarbildung bei einigen Cichliden. I. Die Paarbildung bei
Astatotilapia strigigena (Pfeffer). (The formation of couples in some
Cichlides. I. The formation of couples in *Astatotilapia strigigena.*) *Zeit._f.
Tierpsychol.,* 1940, 4, 40–84.
Sheldon, W. H., & Stevens, S. S. *The varieties of temperament.* New York:
Harper, 1942.
Sheldon, W. H., Stevens, S. S., & Tucher, W. B. *The varieties of human
physique.* New York: Harper, 1940.
Sherman, M. The differentiation of emotional responses in infants. I. Judg-
ments of emotional responses from motion picture views and from actual
observation. *J. comp. Psychol.,* 1927, 7, 265–284. (a)
——. The differentiation of emotional responses in infants: II. The ability
of observers to judge the emotional characteristics of the crying of infants,
and the voice of an adult. *J. comp. Psychol.,* 1927, 7, 335–351. (b)
Sherman, M., & Sherman, I. C. Sensori-motor responses in infants. *J. comp.
Psychol.,* 1925, 5, 53–68.
Sherman, M., Sherman, I. C., & Flory, C. D. Infant behavior. *Comp. Psychol.
Monogr.,* 1936, 12, 1–107.
Shirley, M. M. *The first two years: A study of twenty-five babies.* Vol. III
Intellectual development. Minneapolis: Univer. Minn. Press, 1933.
——. Children's adjustments to a strange situation. *J. abnorm. soc. Psychol.,*
1942, 37, 201–217.
Simpson, G. G. *The meaning of evolution.* New Haven: Yale Univer. Press,
1964.
Skawren, P. Furcht und Angst im frühen Kindesalter und ihre Abhängigkeit
von "Grundumstellungen." (Fear and anxiety in early childhood and their
dependence upon "fundamental attitudes.") *Arch. ges., Psychol.,* 1930, 77,
109–128.
Söderling, B. The first smile: A developmental study. *Acta. Paediat.,* 1959,
48, Suppl. 117, 78–82.
Spitz, R. A. Hospitalism. *Psychoanalyt. Stud. Child,* 1945, 1, 53.
——. Hospitalism: A follow-up report. *Psychoanalyt. Stud. Child,* 1946, 2,
113.
——. Anxiety in infancy: A study of its manifestations in the first year of
life. *Int. J. Psychoanal.,* 1950, 31, 132–143.
——. A note on the extrapolation of ethological findings. *Int. J. Psychoanal.,*
1955, 36, 162–165.
——. Discussion of Dr. Bowlby's paper. *Psychoanalyt. Stud. Child,* 1960, 15,
85.
——. *The first year of life.* New York: Int. Univer. Press, 1965.

Spitz, R. A., & Wolf, K. W. The smiling response: A contribution to the ontogenesis of social relations. *Genet. Psychol. Monogr.*, 1946, 34, 57–125.

Stern, K. *Principles of human genetics.* (2nd ed.) San Francisco: W. H. Freeman, 1960.

St. Exupéry, A. de *The little prince.* New York: Harcourt Brace, 1943.

Stirnimann, F. Les réactions du nouveau-né contre l'enchainement. (Reactions of the newborn against fettering.) *Rev. Franc. Pediatr.*, 1937, 13, 496–502.

Stockard, C. R. *The physical basis of personality.* New York: Norton, 1931.

Stoeffels, M. J. La réaction dite de colère chez les nouveau-nés. (The reaction of so-called anger in the neonate.) *J. Psychol. norm. path.*, 1940–41, 37–38, 92–148.

Stolz, H. R. Resistance to eating among preschool children. *Calif. & West. Med.*, 1934, 40, 159.

Stutsman, R. *Mental measurement of preschool children: With a guide for the administration of the Merrill-Palmer scale of mental tests.* Yonkers-on-Hudson, N. Y.: World Book, 1931.

———. Factors to be considered in measuring the reliability of a mental test, with special reference to the Merrill-Palmer scale. *J. educ. Psychol.*, 1934, 25, 630–633.

Sullivan, H. S. Introduction to the study of interpersonal relations. *Psychiat.*, Vol. 1, 1938.

———. *Collected works.* New York: Norton, 1965.

Székely, L. Biological remarks on fears originating in early childhood. *Int. J. Psychoanal.*, 1954, 35, 57–67.

Taylor, J. H. Innate emotional responses in infants. *Ohio State Univer. Stud.*, 1934, 12, 82–93.

Tennes, K. H., & Lampl, E. E. Stranger and separation anxiety in infancy. *J. nerv. ment. Dis.*, 1964, 139, 247–254.

Thomas, A., Chess, S., Birch, H. G., Hertzig, M. E., & Korn, S. *Behavioral individuality in early childhood.* New York: N. Y. Univer. Press, 1963.

Tinbergen, N. Social releasers and the experimental method required for their study. *Wilson Ornith. Bull.*, 1948, 60, 6–51.

———. *The study of instinct.* London: Oxford Univer. Press, 1951.

———. The shell menace. In T. E. McGill (Ed.), *Readings in animal behavior.* New York: Holt, Rinehart & Winston, 1965.

Tinbergen, N., & Kuenen, D. J. Über die Auslösenden und Richtungsgebenden Reizsituationen der Sperrbewegung von jungen Drosseln (*Turdus m. merula* und *T. e. ericetorum* Turton). (On the releasing and orienting stimulus-situations for spreading movements in young thrushes.) *Zeit. f. Tierpsychol.*, 1939, 3, 37–60.

Thompson, J. Development of facial expression of emotion in blind and seeing children. *Arch. Psychol.*, 1941, No. 264.

Valentine, C. W. The innate basis of fear. *J. genet. Psychol.*, 1930, 37, 394–419.

von Uexküll, J. *Umwelt und Innenwelt der Tiere.* (*Outer and inner world of animals.*) (2nd ed.) Berlin, 1921.

———. A stroll through the world of animals and men. In C. H. Schiller (Ed.), *Instinctive behavior.* New York: Int. Univer. Press, 1957.

Waddington, C. H. *The ethical animal.* New York: Atheneum, 1960.

———. *The nature of life.* New York: Harper Torchbook, 1966.

Walker, R. N. Body build and behavior in young children: I. Body build and nursery school teachers' ratings. *Soc. Res. Child Develpm. Monogr.*, 1962, 27, No. 3.

Walters, J., Pearce, D., & Dalms, L. Affectional and aggressive behavior of preschool children. *Child Develpm.*, 1957, 28, 15–26.

Walters, R. H., & Parke, R. D. The role of the distance receptors in the development of social responsiveness. In L. P. Lipsitt & C. C. Spiker (Eds.),

Advances in child development and behavior. II. New York: Academic Press, 1965.

Washburn, R. W. A study of the smiling and laughing of infants in the first year of life. *Genet. Psychol. Monogr.,* 1929, 6, 397–535.

Watson, J. B. *Psychology from the standpoint of behaviorist.* Philadelphia: Lippincott, 1919.

———. What the nursery has to say about instincts. *Ped. Sem.,* 1925, 32, 293–327. (a)

———. Experimental studies on the growth of the emotions. *Ped. Sem.,* 1925, 32, 328–348. (b)

Watson, J. B., & Morgan, J. J. B. Emotional reactions and psychological experimentation. *Amer. J. Psychol.,* 1917, 28, 163–174.

Watson, J. B., & Rayner, R. Conditioned emotional reactions. *J. exp. Psychol.,* 1920, 3, 1–14.

Weiss, L. A. Differential variations in the amount of activity of newborn infants under continuous light and sound stimulation. *Univer. Iowa Stud. Child Welf.,* 1934, 9, No. 4.

White, L. A. *The evolution of culture.* New York: McGraw-Hill, 1959.

White, R. W. Ego and reality in psychoanalytic theory: A proposal regarding independent ego energies. *Psychol. Issues,* Vol. 3. New York: Int. Univer. Press, 1963.

Willier, B. H., Weiss, P. A., & Hamburger, V. (Eds.) *Analysis of development.* Philadelphia: W. B. Saunders, 1955.

Wolff, P. H. Observations on newborn infants. *Psychosom. Med.,* 1959, 21, 110–118.

———. Observations on the early development of smiling. In B. M. Foss (Ed.), *Determinants of infant behavior II.* New York: Wiley, 1963. Pp. 113–133. (a)

———. Natural history of crying. In B. M. Foss (Ed.), *Determinants of infant behaviour IV.* London: Methuen & Co., Ltd., in press.

Woodworth, R. S. How emotions are identified and classified. In M. L. Reymert (Ed.), *Feelings and emotions: The Wittenberg Symposium.* Worcester: Clark Univer. Press, 1928. Pp. 222–227.

Yarrow, L. J. Maternal deprivation: Toward an empirical and conceptual reevaluation. *Psychol. Bull.,* 1961, 58, 6, 459–490.

Young, W. C. The organization of sexual behavior by hormonal action during the prenatal and larval periods in vertebrates. In F. Beach (Ed.), *Sex and behavior.* New York: Wiley, 1965.

Young, W. C., Goy, R. W., & Phoenix, C. H. Hormones and sexual behavior. In J. Money (Ed.), *Sex research: New developments.* New York: Holt, Rinehart, & Winston, 1965.

INDEXES

Name Index

505

Furfey, P. H., 185, 195
Furth, H. G., 325, 357

Gagné, R. M., 372, 392
Gale, H., 332, 348
Gale, M. C., 332, 348
Gall, F. J., 470
Garfield, S. L., 35, 44
Gatewood, M. C., 139, 195, 336, 348
Geber, M., 152, 166, 195, 477, 494
Geldard, F. A., 65, 102, 106, 116
Gellermann, L. W., 77, 116, 261, 262, 263, 279
Gellis, S. S., 66, 116, 219, 279
Gentry, E. F., 144, 170, 183, 195
Gesell, A. L., 83, 97, 116, 125, 126, 127, 128, 129, 130, 131, 132, 146, 151, 152, 168, 169, 174, 176, 190, 196, 257, 274, 275, 276, 279, 296, 332, 333, 339, 348, 373, 437, 445, 454, 494
Gewirtz, J. L., 84, 119, 251, 268, 296, 354, 436, 437, 438, 447, 494
Gheorgov, J. A., 332, 348
Gibson, E. R., 28, 41, 51, 81, 116, 121, 488, 494
Gidoll, S. H., 90, 116
Giesecke, M., 175, 196
Gill, M. M., 459
Giltay, M., 383, 392
Ginsburg, B. E., 477, 483, 494
Glanzer, M., 449, 494
Glaser, G. H., 23, 43
Glasscock, R. E., 58, 115
Goddard, K. E., 172, 198
Goldfarb, W., 335, 349, 365, 392, 481, 494
Goldstein, K., 475, 489, 494
Goldstein, R., 13, 19, 31, 43, 47, 90, 116, 222, 279
Gollin, E. E., 325, 349
Gonzales, R. C., 326, 349
Goodenough, F. L., 73, 114, 160, 162, 196, 316, 330, 332, 349, 362, 369, 392, 402, 404, 416, 423, 452, 453, 454, 494
Goodman, W. S., 13, 43
Goodwin, R. S., 13, 14, 18, 20, 21, 41
Gordon, E. W., 170, 171, 202
Gordon, K., 176, 196
Gordon, M. B., 181, 196
Gordon, N. S., 140, 141, 196
Gorer, G., 471, 494
Gorman, J. J., 66, 67, 116, 219, 279
Goss, A. E., 322, 327, 346, 349, 355
Gough, D., 196
Goy, R. W., 502
Graham, F. K., 7, 28, 43, 44, 78, 116, 164, 179, 186, 196, 263, 273, 279
Gray, G. B., 166, 194
Gray, M. L., 26, 42, 98, 114, 140, 434, 492
Gray, P. H., 483, 495
Green, E. H., 403, 404, 406, 408, 416, 423
Greenberg, N. H., 25, 26, 38, 43
Greenberg, P. J., 404, 416, 423

Greene, W. A., 98, 121
Greenman, G. W., 487, 495
Greenman, M., 186, 196
Gregg, A., 451, 495
Grigsby, O. J., 316, 349
Grings, W. W., 11, 32, 43, 222, 278
Grossman, H. J., 25, 26, 38, 43, 87, 89, 119, 144, 201
Guernsey, M., 60, 63, 116
Guilford, J. P., 188, 196
Guillaume, P., 303, 349
Guillet, C., 273, 279
Gullickson, G. R., 107, 108, 116, 179, 196
Gupta, J. M., 14, 43
Guy-Arnaud, 111, 113

Haggard, E. A., 9, 43
Haggerty, L. C. G., 349
Hagman, E. P., 407, 423
Hagman, E. R., 452, 495
Haig, C., 61, 118
Hall, G. S., 455, 495
Hall, K. R. L., 455, 495
Hall, W. S., 304, 349
Halle, M., 307, 349, 350
Haller, M., 89, 92, 93, 95, 116
Hallpike, C. S., 89, 115, 223, 278
Halverson, H. M., 106, 116, 131, 167, 168, 169, 172, 175, 196
Hamburger, V., 502
Hamilton, G. V. N., 375, 376, 393
Hampson, 480
Hanes, R. M., 52, 115
Hardy, J. B., 87, 89, 117, 182, 196
Hardy, M., 173, 197
Hardy, W. G., 31, 42, 44, 87, 89, 90, 91, 114, 117, 196, 222, 223, 278, 279
Haring, D. G., 483, 495
Harlow, H. F., 262, 279, 370, 393, 495
Harnish, D., 298, 351
Harper, P. A., 190, 191, 192, 197, 198, 369, 393
Harrison, G. A., 477, 495
Harter, G. L., 375, 380, 393
Hartmann, A. F., 186, 196
Hartmann, H., 467, 495
Hartup, W. W., 420, 423
Hasselmeyer, E. G., 109, 117
Hattwick, L. A., 341, 349, 454, 455, 495
Havighurst, R. J., 184, 194
Haynes, H., 58, 117
Hazlitt, V., 374, 375, 393
Heath, H. A., 15, 16, 45
Heathers, G., 400, 402, 407, 423, 453, 495
Hebb, D. O., 350, 446, 448, 449, 450, 495
Heck, J., 59, 62, 117
Heck, W. E., 111, 117
Heidbreder, E. F., 271, 279
Heider, G. M., 474, 493
Heiney, A. B., 163, 198
Heinlein, J. H., 176, 197
Heinstein, M. I., 367, 393
Held, R., 58, 117, 160, 169, 203, 394

Subject Index

Acquired distinctiveness of cues, 326–327

Acquired equivalence of cues, 327–328

Adaptation; *see also* Habituation
auditory, 20–21
to pain, 108

Age differences, and aggression, 455
and crying, 435
and fear, 449, 450
and group conflict, 404

Aggression, and age differences, 455
and body build, 456
and frustration, 456–457
and sex differences, 455–456

Anger, 454–455

Anxiety, and amount of stimulation, 445–446
and attachment to mother, 448–449
definition of, 445
in strange situations, 453–454
and strangers, 445–446, 447–449

Arousal, and audition, 90
and continuous stimulation, 60–62, 98–99

Articulation, baby biographies, 304
effects of training, 308–310
psycholinguistics, 307–308
tests, 304–306

Ascendancy, and integrative behavior, 412–413
and self-confidence, 411–412

Attachments, formation in family, 485–486
and laughter, 487
and smiling, 486–487

Attention, defense, 28
habituation, 30
and heart rate, 29–30
and motor activity, 28–29
orientation, 28

Audition, absolute thresholds, 91–92
anatomy of the ear, 86–87
auro-palpebral reflex, 88
diagnosis by conditioning, 222–223
and EEG, 19–20
and general activity, 88–89
habituation, 92–94
and heart rate, 18–20
neonates, 87–88
physiological responses, 90
pitch discrimination, 95–96
and respiration, 19–20
somatic responses, 88–89
sound, 85–86
sound localization, 96–97

Autonomic Lability Score, 17

Babbling, imitation, 303
in deaf infants, 301–302
phonemic contraction, 302
repetition, 302
transition to words, 302

Babinski reflex, 182

Babkin reflex, 174

Bilingualism, and intelligence test performance, 338
and language development, 337–338

Brain damage, and crying, 177–178, 299

Cardiac Response: *see* Heart

"Competence" (White), 468

Concept formation, and awareness, 383–384
causality, 388–390
definition, 381
extension, definition, 381
geometric, 382–383
intension, definition, 381
number, 382–383
object, 384–385
objective space, 386